Open-Source Property: A Free Casebook

(Bell Build, January 2026)

www.opensourceproperty.org

Stephen Clowney
James Grimmelmann
Michael Grynberg
Jeremy Sheff
Rebecca Tushnet

Build Author: Abraham Bell

Build Date: January 2026

Volume I (of III)

Copyright and Authorship Information

Table of Contents

1. Allocation

It is perhaps the most basic question that must be answered by a system of property rights: which things are owned by whom. A system of property rights must be able to distinguish between things that are owned and unowned, and tell us how ownership can be acquired (or lost). And if the property system is to respect the rights of owners to transfer their ownership (in whole or in part) to others, then once something is legitimately owned by someone, that person can transfer rightful ownership to someone else. (We will study how such transfers can come about later in this book—indeed we will find that some transfers can confer the rights of ownership on a transferee even where the transferor's rights are not so clear-cut. We will also see that there are ways for things owned by one person to become owned by another person *other than* by voluntary transfer.)

But even assuming a current owner could trace their rights of ownership back through a series of successive voluntary transfers from rightful owners—a *chain of title*, as we will come to call it—the first link in that chain *must* be something other than a transfer from a prior rightful owner. What could this something be? How do things go from being unowned to being owned? Why might we recognize some rules for such initial allocations of resources over the available alternatives?

In this chapter, we will examine the means by which potential owners acquire title, with particular attention to the most common justification for protecting someone's rights of ownership: *possession*. In most cases, the common law holds that initial ownership of a heretofore unowned thing goes to the *first to possess* that thing—that first in time is first in right. But as we will see, this rule is not as straightforward as it may seem. To begin with, reasonable people may differ as to what constitutes "possession," or what it means to be "first." Our first few cases illustrating this problem deal with first possession of *chattels* (sometimes called "personal property" or "personality"—basically any ownable thing that isn't land or attached to land).

A. Initial Allocation of Chattels

Source: R.S. SURTEES, HAWBUCK GRANGE 197 (1885), British Library, https://flic.kr/p/i38jT2

Pierson v. Post
3 Cai. R. 175 (N.Y. Sup. Ct. 1805)

THIS was an action of trespass on the case commenced in a justice's court, by the present defendant against the now plaintiff.

The declaration stated that *Post,* being in possession of certain dogs and hounds under his command, did, "upon a certain wild and uninhabited, unpossessed and waste land, called the beach, find and start one of those noxious beasts called a fox," and whilst there hunting, chasing and pursuing the same with his dogs and hounds, and when in view thereof, *Pierson,* well knowing the fox was so hunted and pursued, did, in the sight of *Post,* to prevent his catching the same, kill and carry it off. A verdict having been rendered for the plaintiff below, the defendant there sued out a *certiorari,* and now assigned for error, that the declaration and the matters therein contained were not sufficient in law to maintain an action….

TOMPKINS, J. delivered the opinion of the court.
This cause comes before us on a return to a *certiorari* directed to one of the justices of *Queens* county.

The question submitted by the counsel in this cause for our determination is, whether *Lodowick Post,* by the pursuit with his hounds in the manner alleged in his declaration, acquired such a right to, or property in, the fox, as will sustain an action against *Pierson* for killing and taking him away?

The cause was argued with much ability by the counsel on both sides, and presents for our decision a novel and nice question. It is admitted that a fox is an animal *feræ naturæ,* and that property in such animals is acquired by occupancy only. These admissions narrow the discussion to the simple question of what acts amount to occupancy, applied to acquiring right to wild animals?

If we have recourse to the ancient writers upon general principles of law, the judgment below is obviously erroneous. *Justinian's Institutes,* lib. 2. tit. 1. s. 13. and *Fleta,* lib. 3. c. 2. p. 175. adopt the principle, that pursuit alone vests no property or right in the huntsman; and that even pursuit, accompanied with wounding, is equally ineffectual for that purpose, unless the animal be actually taken. The same principle is recognised by *Bracton,* lib. 2. c. 1. p. 8.

Puffendorf, lib. 4. c. 6. s. 2. and 10. defines occupancy of beasts *feræ naturæ,* to be the actual corporal possession of them, and *Bynkershoek* is cited as coinciding in this definition. It is indeed with hesitation that *Puffendorf* affirms that a wild beast mortally wounded, or greatly maimed, cannot be fairly intercepted by another, whilst the pursuit of the person inflicting the wound continues. The foregoing authorities are decisive to show that mere pursuit gave *Post* no legal right to the fox, but that he became the property of *Pierson,* who intercepted and killed him.

It therefore only remains to inquire whether there are any contrary principles, or authorities, to be found in other books, which ought to induce a different decision. Most of the cases which have occurred in *England,* relating to property in wild animals, have either been discussed and decided upon the principles of their positive statute regulations, or have arisen between the huntsman and the owner of the land upon which beasts *feræ naturæ* have been apprehended; the former claiming them by title of occupancy, and the latter *ratione soli.* Little satisfactory aid can, therefore, be derived from the *English* reporters.

Barbeyrac, in his notes on *Puffendorf,* does not accede to the definition of occupancy by the latter, but, on the contrary, affirms, that actual bodily seizure is not, in all cases, necessary to constitute possession of wild animals. He does not, however, *describe* the acts which, according to his ideas, will amount to an appropriation of such animals to private use, so as to exclude the claims of all other persons, by title of occupancy, to the same animals; and he is far from averring that pursuit alone is sufficient for that purpose. To a certain extent, and as far as *Barbeyrac* appears to me to go, his objections to *Puffendorf's* definition of occupancy are reasonable and correct.

That is to say, that actual bodily seizure is not indispensable to acquire right to, or possession of, wild beasts; but that, on the contrary, the mortal wounding of such beasts, by one not abandoning his pursuit, may, with the utmost propriety, be deemed possession of him; since, thereby, the pursuer manifests an unequivocal intention of appropriating the animal to his individual use, has deprived him of his natural liberty, and brought him within his certain control. So also, encompassing and securing such animals with nets and toils, or otherwise intercepting them in such a manner as to deprive them of their natural liberty, and render escape impossible, may justly be deemed to give possession of them to those persons who, by their industry and labour, have used such means of apprehending them. *Barbeyrac* seems to have adopted, and had in view in his notes, the more accurate opinion of *Grotius,* with respect to occupancy. That celebrated author, lib. 2. c. 8. s. 3. p. 309. speaking of occupancy, proceeds thus: "*Requiritur autem corporalis quædam possessio ad dominium adipiscendum; atque ideo, vulnerasse non sufficit.*"[1] But in the following section he explains and qualifies this definition of occupancy: "*Sed possessio illa potest non solis manibus, sed instrumentis, ut decipulis, retibus, laqueis dum duo adsint: primum ut ipsa instrumenta sint in nostra potestate, deinde ut fera, ita inclusa sit, ut exire inde nequeat.*"[2] This qualification embraces the full extent of *Barbeyrac's* objection to *Puffendorf's* definition, and allows as great a latitude to acquiring property by occupancy, as can reasonably be inferred from the words or ideas expressed by *Barbeyrac* in his notes. The case now under consideration is one of mere pursuit, and presents no circumstances or acts which can bring it within the definition of occupancy by *Puffendorf,* or *Grotius,* or the ideas of *Barbeyrac* upon that subject.

The case cited from 11 *Mod.* 74--130.[3] I think clearly distinguishable from the present; inasmuch as there the action was for maliciously hindering and disturbing the plaintiff in the exercise and enjoyment of a private franchise; and in the report of the same case, 3 *Salk.* 9. *Holt,* Ch. J. states, that the ducks were in the plaintiff's decoy pond, and *so in his possession,* from which it is obvious the court laid much stress in their opinion upon the plaintiff's possession of the ducks, *ratione soli.*[4]

---

[1] [Translation: "Some bodily possession is required for acquiring ownership; for that reason, wounding is not enough." —*eds.*]

[2] [Translation: "But that possession can be not only by hand, but by instruments, such as traps, nets, and snares, where two things are present: first that this instrument itself be in our control, and then that the wild thing, being enclosed, cannot exit therefrom."—*eds.*]

[3] [This citation, and the following citation to *Salk.*, both refer to the case of *Keeble v. Hickeringill,* which we will come to later in this Chapter.—*eds.*]

[4] [Translation: "by reason of the soil"—*eds.*]

We are the more readily inclined to confine possession or occupancy of beasts *feræ naturæ,* within the limits prescribed by the learned authors above cited, for the sake of certainty, and preserving peace and order in society. If the first seeing, starting, or pursuing such animals, without having so wounded, circumvented or ensnared them, so as to deprive them of their natural liberty, and subject them to the control of their pursuer, should afford the basis of actions against others for intercepting and killing them, it would prove a fertile source of quarrels and litigation. However uncourteous or unkind the conduct of *Pierson* towards *Post,* in this instance, may have been, yet his act was productive of no injury or damage for which a legal remedy can be applied. We are of opinion the judgment below was erroneous, and ought to be reversed.

LIVINGSTON, J.

My opinion differs from that of the court.

Of six exceptions, taken to the proceedings below, all are abandoned except the third, which reduces the controversy to a single question.

Whether a person who, with his own hounds, starts and hunts a fox on waste and uninhabited ground, and is on the point of seizing his prey, acquires such an interest in the animal, as to have a right of action against another, who in view of the huntsman and his dogs in full pursuit, and with knowledge of the chase, shall kill and carry him away?

This is a knotty point, and should have been submitted to the arbitration of sportsmen, without poring over *Justinian, Fleta, Bracton, Puffendorf, Locke, Barbeyrac,* or *Blackstone,* all of whom have been cited; they would have had no difficulty in coming to a prompt and correct conclusion. In a court thus constituted, the skin and carcass of poor *reynard*[5] would have been properly disposed of, and a precedent set, interfering with no usage or custom which the experience of ages has sanctioned, and which must be so well known to every votary of *Diana.* But the parties have referred the question to our judgment, and we must dispose of it as well as we can, from the partial lights we possess, leaving to a higher tribunal, the correction of any mistake which we may be so unfortunate as to make. By the pleadings it is admitted that a fox is a "wild and noxious beast." Both parties have regarded him, as the law of nations does a pirate, "*hostem humani generis,*"[6] and although "*de mortuis nil nisi bonum,*"[7] be a maxim of our profession, the

---

[5] [Reynard was a clever (and often duplicitous) fox character who featured in several well-known medieval European folk tales and literary works. The character's popularity gave rise to the modern French word for "fox": *renard.* — *eds.*]
[6] [Translation: "enemy of the human race." — *eds.*]
[7] [Translation: "Of the dead say nothing but good." — *eds.*]

memory of the deceased has not been spared. His depredations on farmers and on barn yards, have not been forgotten; and to put him to death wherever found, is allowed to be meritorious, and of public benefit. Hence it follows, that our decision should have in view the greatest possible encouragement to the destruction of an animal, so cunning and ruthless in his career. But who would keep a pack of hounds; or what gentleman, at the sound of the horn, and at peep of day, would mount his steed, and for hours together, "*sub jove frigido,*"[8] or a vertical sun, pursue the windings of this wily quadruped, if, just as night came on, and his stratagems and strength were nearly exhausted, a saucy intruder, who had not shared in the honours or labours of the chase, were permitted to come in at the death, and bear away in triumph the object of pursuit? Whatever *Justinian* may have thought of the matter, it must be recollected that his code was compiled many hundred years ago, and it would be very hard indeed, at the distance of so many centuries, not to have a right to establish a rule for ourselves. In his day, we read of no order of men who made it a business, in the language of the declaration in this cause, "with hounds and dogs to find, start, pursue, hunt, and chase," these animals, and that, too, without any other motive than the preservation of *Roman* poultry; if this diversion had been then in fashion, the lawyers who composed his institutes, would have taken care not to pass it by, without suitable encouragement. If any thing, therefore, in the digests or pandects shall appear to militate against the defendant in error, who, on this occasion, was the foxhunter, we have only to say *tempora mutantur;*[9] and if men themselves change with the times, why should not laws also undergo an alteration?

It may be expected, however, by the learned counsel, that more particular notice be taken of their authorities. I have examined them all, and feel great difficulty in determining, whether to acquire dominion over a thing, before in common, it be sufficient that we barely see it, or know where it is, or wish for it, or make a declaration of our will respecting it; or whether, in the case of wild beasts, setting a trap, or lying in wait, or starting, or pursuing, be enough; or if an actual wounding, or killing, or bodily tact and occupation be necessary. Writers on general law, who have favoured us with their speculations on these points, differ on them all; but, great as is the diversity of sentiment among them, some conclusion must be adopted on the question immediately before us. After mature deliberation, I embrace that of *Barbeyrac,* as the most rational, and least liable to objection. If at liberty, we might imitate the courtesy of a certain emperor, who, to avoid giving offence to the advocates of any of these different doctrines, adopted a middle course, and by ingenious distinctions, rendered it difficult to say (as often

---

[8] [Translation: "Under frigid Jove" (*i.e.*, under a cold sky). — *eds.*]

[9] [Translation: "times change." Part of a well-known Latin aphorism, *tempora mutantur, nos et mutamur in illis*: "times change, and we change with them." — *eds.*]

happens after a fierce and angry contest) to whom the palm of victory belonged. He ordained, that if a beast be followed with *large dogs and hounds,* he shall belong to the hunter, not to the chance occupant; and in like manner, if he be killed or wounded with a lance or sword; but if chased with *beagles only,* then he passed to the captor, not to the first pursuer. If slain with a dart, a sling, or a bow, he fell to the hunter, if still in chase, and not to him who might afterwards find and seize him.

Now, as we are without any municipal regulations of our own, and the pursuit here, for aught that appears on the case, being with dogs and hounds of *imperial stature,* we are at liberty to adopt one of the provisions just cited, which comports also with the learned conclusion of *Barbeyrac,* that property in animals *feræ naturæ* may be acquired without bodily touch or manucaption, provided the pursuer be within reach, or have a *reasonable* prospect (which certainly existed here) of taking, what he has *thus* discovered an intention of converting to his own use.

When we reflect also that the interest of our husbandmen, the most useful of men in any community, will be advanced by the destruction of a beast so pernicious and incorrigible, we cannot greatly err, in saying, that a pursuit like the present, through waste and unoccupied lands, and which must inevitably and speedily have terminated in corporal possession, or bodily *seisin,* confers such a right to the object of it, as to make any one a wrongdoer, who shall interfere and shoulder the spoil. The *justice's* judgment ought, therefore, in my opinion, to be affirmed.

Judgment of reversal.

Notes and Questions

1. **Justifying Allocations.** Does awarding ownership of a previously unowned chattel to the first possessor of that chattel strike you as a good rule? Consider some arguments that might be raised for or against it:

    - Incentives: Does the rule encourage the conversion of idle resources to productive use? Does it discourage excessive or wasteful efforts to exploit resources? Does it discourage disputes or violence among rival claimants? Does it discourage claimants expend excessive resources on protecting themselves *against other* would-be claimants? When weighing these incentives in the aggregate, is the rule *efficient*? That is, does it produce the greatest net social benefit (realizing the greatest possible value from available resources net of costs)?
    - Administrability: Is the rule easy to apply? Does it give clear and ready answers? Does it make judges' and litigants' jobs easier or harder? Does it minimize the cost and time involved in resolving disputes? Can it be applied without resort to ambiguous or hard-to-obtain evidence?

- Fairness: Does the rule comport with well-considered notions of fairness? Does it treat similarly situated people similarly? Does it avoid favoring claimants based on criteria that are irrelevant or arbitrary? Does the rule reward moral behavior and punish—or at least refrain from rewarding—immoral behavior? (This assumes of course that we have a standard for moral and immoral behavior.)
- Reliance: Does the rule respect the reasonable expectations of those with an interest in contested resources? Does it avoid wasting time, money, or effort they invested in reliance on such expectations? Does it comport with tradition?
- Pragmatism: Does the rule roughly comport with the social intuitions of those who are subject to it? Do we expect the rule to be obeyed? Does it properly reflect social conventions (assuming such social conventions ought to be reflected)?
- Ecology: Is the rule consistent with responsible stewardship of resources? Does it ensure that an exhaustible resource will remain available for the benefit of future generations?

Which of these arguments strikes you as more or less important to the justification of a legal rule—particularly a rule of property law? Which of them were invoked by Justices Tompkins and Livingston in *Pierson*?

Even if we agree as to which of these arguments matter in disposing of a particular dispute, are we sure to agree whether a particular type of argument favors a particular party? For example, is Justice Livingston correct in claiming that the decision in Pierson's favor will provide insufficient incentive for hunters to capture foxes? Is Justice Tompkins correct in claiming that a decision in Post's favor would lead to increased disputes over the trophies of the chase? Does either opinion clearly establish which outcome would be the most fair? How could we know the answer to these questions?

2. **Alternatives to First Possession.** Is the rule of first possession the best available rule for allocating unowned resources? Consider some possible alternative allocation principles:

- Perhaps initial allocation should go to the first *claimant*—the first to explicitly assert a right of ownership (or manifest the intent to assert such a right, as by pursuit).
- Perhaps initial allocation should go to the *last* possessor—the person who gains and maintains possession against the efforts of all competitors.
- Perhaps possession is irrelevant: perhaps initial allocation should go to all interested claimants in equal shares.
- Perhaps the resource should be owned as a *commons*: it belongs to everybody jointly; everybody has an equal right to it and nobody has a superior right to anyone else.

- Perhaps the resources ought to be assigned to a single owner by virtue of social position, or by random selection, with the assumption that the single owner will sell to others what they want and need.
- Perhaps the government ought to own everything and simply provide rights of possession and use by means of bureaucratic and political mechanisms.
- Perhaps ownership should be determined by lot, at random.

How would each of these rules compare to the rule of first possession in terms of each of the justifications we have just reviewed for and against that rule? What do you think would be the *practical* result of choosing one of these alternative allocation regimes—i.e., how would people likely shape their behavior in response to these allocation rules?

3. Recall the second type of justification we discussed in Note 1 above: administrability. Do you think it will always be obvious that one claimant of a chattel has achieved possession and another has not? Consider the following case.

Source: "Fast to a whale, shooting the bomb lance." New Bedford Free Public Library. *Digital Commonwealth*, http://ark.digitalcommonwealth.org/ark:/50959/sb398z14j

Ghen v. Rich

8 F. 159 (D. Mass. 1881)

NELSON, D.J.

This is a libel to recover the value of a fin-back whale. The libellant lives in Provincetown and the respondent in Wellfleet. The facts, as they appeared at the hearing, are as follows:

In the early spring months the easterly part of Massachusetts Bay is frequented by the species of whale known as the fin-back whale. Fishermen from Provincetown pursue them in open boats from the shore, and shoot them with bomb-lances fired from guns made expressly for the purpose. When killed they sink at once to the bottom, but in the course of from one to three days they rise and float on the surface. Some of them are picked up by vessels and towed into Provincetown. Some float ashore at high water and are left stranded on the beach as the tide recedes. Others float out to sea and are never recovered. The person who happens to find them on the beach usually sends word to Provincetown, and the owner comes to the spot and removes the blubber. The finder usually receives a small salvage for his services. Try-works are established in Provincetown for trying out the oil. The business is of considerable extent, but, since it requires skill and experience, as well as some outlay of capital, and is attended with great exposure and hardship, few persons engage in it. The average yield of oil is about 20 barrels to a whale. It swims with great swiftness, and for that reason cannot be taken by the harpoon and line. Each boat's crew engaged in the business has its peculiar mark or device on its lances, and in this way it is known by whom a whale is killed.

The usage on Cape Cod, for many years, has been that the person who kills a whale in the manner and under the circumstances described, owns it, and this right has never been disputed until this case. The libellant has been engaged in this business for ten years past. On the morning of April 9, 1880, in Massachusetts Bay, near the end of Cape Cod, he shot and instantly killed with a bomb-lance the whale in question. It sunk immediately, and on the morning of the 12th was found stranded on the beach in Brewster, within the ebb and flow of the tide, by one Ellis, 17 miles from the spot where it was killed. Instead of sending word to Provincetown, as is customary, Ellis advertised the whale for sale at auction, and sold it to the respondent, who shipped off the blubber and tried out the oil. The libellant heard of the finding of the whale on the morning of the 15th, and immediately sent one of his boat's crew to the place and claimed it. Neither the respondent nor Ellis knew the whale had been killed by the libellant, but they knew or might have known, if they had wished, that it had been shot and killed with a bomb-lance, by some person engaged in this species of business.

The libellant claims title to the whale under this usage. The respondent insists that this usage is invalid. It was decided by Judge Sprague, in Taber v. Jenny, 1 Sprague, 315, that when a whale has been killed, and is anchored and left with marks of appropriation, it is the property of the captors; and if it is afterwards found, still anchored, by another ship, there is no usage or principle of law by which the property of the original captors is diverted, even though the whale may have dragged from its anchorage. The learned judge says:

> 'When the whale had been killed and taken possession of by the boat of the Hillman, (the first taker,) it became the property of the owners of that ship, and all was done which was then practicable in order to secure it. They left it anchored, with unequivocal marks of appropriation.'

In Bartlett v. Budd, 1 Low. 223, the facts were these: The first officer of the libellant's ship killed a whale in the Okhotsk sea, anchored it, attached a waif* to the body, and then left it and went ashore at some distance for the night. The next morning the boats of the respondent's ship found the whale adrift, the anchor not holding, the cable coiled round the body, and no

* [*Eds.* – "The waif is a pennoned pole, two or three of which are carried by every boat; and which, when additional game is at hand, are inserted upright into the floating body of a dead whale, both to mark its place on the sea, and also as token of prior possession, should the boats of any other ship draw near." HERMAN MELVILLE, MOBY-DICK 368 (1922) [1892].]

waif or irons attached to it. Judge Lowell held that, as the libellants had killed and taken actual possession of the whale, the ownership vested in them. In his opinion the learned judge says:

> 'A whale, being *ferae naturae*, does not become property until a firm possession has been established by the taker. But when such possession has become firm and complete, the right of property is clear, and has all the characteristics of property.'

He doubted whether a usage set up but not proved by the respondents, that a whale found adrift in the ocean is the property of the finder, unless the first taker should appear and claim it before it is cut in, would be valid, and remarked that 'there would be great difficulty in upholding a custom that should take the property of A. and give it to B., under so very short and uncertain a substitute for the statute of limitations, and one so open to fraud and deceit.' Both the cases cited were decided without reference to usage, upon the ground that the property had been acquired by the first taker by actual possession and appropriation.

In Swift v. Gifford, 2 Low, 110, Judge Lowell decided that a custom among whalemen in the Arctic seas, that the iron holds the whale was reasonable and valid. In that case a boat's crew from the respondent's ship pursued and struck a whale in the Arctic Ocean, and the harpoon and the line attached to it remained in the whale, but did not remain fast to the boat. A boat's crew from the libellant's ship continued the pursuit and captured the whale, and the master of the respondent's ship claimed it on the spot. It was held by the learned judge that the whale belonged to the respondents. It was said by Judge Sprague, in Bourne v. Ashley, an unprinted case referred to by Judge Lowell in Swift v. Gifford, that the usage for the first iron, whether attached to the boat or not, to hold the whale was fully established; and he added that, although local usages of a particular port ought not to be allowed to set aside the general maritime law, this objection did not apply to a custom which embraced an entire business, and had been concurred in for a long time by every one engaged in the trade.

In Swift v. Gifford, Judge Lowell also said:

> 'The rule of law invoked in this case is one of very limited application. The whale fishery is the only branch of industry of any importance in which it is likely to be much used, and if a usage is found to prevail generally in that business, it will not be open to the objection that it is likely to disturb the general understanding of mankind by the interposition of an arbitrary exception.'

I see no reason why the usage proved in this case is not as reasonable as that sustained in the cases cited. Its application must necessarily be extremely limited, and can affect but a few persons. It has been recognized and acquiesced in for many years. It requires in the first taker the only act of appropriation that is possible in the nature of the case. Unless it is sustained, this branch of industry must necessarily cease, for no person would engage in it if the fruits of his labor could be appropriated by any chance finder. It gives reasonable salvage for securing or reporting the property. That the rule works well in practice is shown by the extent of the industry which has grown up under it, and the general acquiescence of a whole community interested to dispute it. It is by no means clear that without regard to usage the common law would not reach the same result. That seems to be the effect of the decisions in Taber v. Jenny and Bartlett v. Budd. If the fisherman does all that is possible to do to make the animal his own, that would seem to be sufficient. Such a rule might well be applied in the interest of trade, there being no usage or custom to the contrary. Holmes, Com. Law, 217. But be that as it may, I hold the usage to be valid, and that the property in the whale was in the libelant.

The rule of damages is the market value of the oil obtained from the whale, less the cost of trying it out and preparing it for the market, with interest on the amount so ascertained from the date of conversion. As the question is new and important, and the suit is contested on both sides, more for the purpose of having it settled than for the amount involved, I shall give no costs.

Decree for libellant for $71.05, without costs.

Notes and Questions

1. **Primary and Secondary Rules.** Is the rule of *Ghen v. Rich* different from the rule of *Pierson v. Post*? If so, how? Are the justifications for the rule, or for the outcome, the same in each case? If not, how do they differ?

   One possible approach to answering this question might draw on a distinction between what leading legal philosopher H.L.A. Hart called *primary rules* and *secondary rules*. In Hart's account, *primary rules* are those that prescribe standards of conduct, and set forth consequences for failure to act accordingly. Statutes defining and setting forth punishments for crimes provide a straightforward example. *Secondary rules* are basically everything else, but in particular they include rules that give actors within the legal system the power to create, alter, or abolish their own primary rules. For example, contract law is largely a body of secondary rules: parties to a contract acting within those rules have the power to create legal rights and obligations that will bind them; the contract itself embodies the applicable primary rules. (For more on this distinction—and more of Hart's monumental contributions to jurisprudence—see H.L.A. HART, THE CONCEPT OF LAW.)

   Based on this admittedly limited introduction to the concept, was the determinative legal rule in *Ghen v. Rich* a primary or a secondary rule? What about in *Pierson v. Post*?

2. **Whose Custom?** In *Aberdeen Arctic Co. v. Sutter*, 4 McQ. H.L. 355 (1862), the House of Lords heard the appeal of a case involving a hired Eskimo harpooner aboard an English whaling vessel in Cumberland Inlet, a traditional native fishing ground in what is now Canada. The harpooner, one Bullygar, struck a whale with a harpoon and line, at the end of which was attached an inflated sealskin, or "drog," which the native fishermen had a custom of using to tire the harpooned animal and to make it easier to track while it swims below the surface. The whale dove immediately, so deep that Bullygar was forced to release his line, and it did not surface again until it had traveled several miles. Before Bullygar and his ship could retrieve it, another ship—the *Alibi*—came upon the wounded whale, killed it, and took it. Bullygar's captain (Sutter) sued the owners of the *Alibi* for "compensation and damages" in the amount of £1,200.

   The Law Lords found for the owners of the *Alibi*, recognizing a custom of English whalers in the shallower waters around Greenland. This custom was known as "fast and loose" (which does not—or did not—mean what you think it means). According to the "fast and loose" rule, the first ship to harpoon a whale has a right to the animal so long as the ship holds "fast" to its line, even if other ships participate in the ultimate killing and capture of the whale. But if the whale should break free—even if mortally wounded—or if the line should be intentionally cut or released—even for reasons of safety or necessity—the whale becomes "loose" and will become the property of the first ship to actually secure it. (*See* HERMAN MELVILLE, MOBY-DICK 372-75 (1922) [1892] ("Fast-Fish and Loose-Fish").)

   Sutter argued that Cumberland Inlet had long been governed by the custom of the Eskimo—which conferred ownership on the first person whose harpoon struck and remained in the animal with the drog attached—and that the English "fast and loose" rule should not apply. Lord Chancellor Westbury rejected the argument. He opined that Sutter had the burden of proving that English whaling ships entering this new fishing ground had agreed *not* to bring the "fast and loose" custom with them. Indeed, he openly doubted whether the drog fishing methods of the Eskimo—which they used primarily in seal hunting—were even capable of capturing a whale. Moreover, he suggested that even if the case were to be decided by the law of "occupancy" rather than the custom of English whalers, the result would be the same.

   Is the rule of *Ghen v. Rich* the same as the rule of *Aberdeen Arctic Co. v. Sutter*? If different, which rule is better and why?

3. Imagine you are counsel to either Pierson or Rich, and your adversary makes you an offer of settlement: to sell the contested chattel and split the proceeds evenly. What would you advise your client to do? Consider the following case.

Source: *Up For Grabs* (Crooked Hook Productions 2004)

Popov v. Hayashi

2002 WL 31833731 (Cal. Sup. Ct. San Francisco Cty. Dec. 18, 2002)

MCCARTHY, J.

FACTS

In 1927, Babe Ruth hit sixty home runs. That record stood for thirty four years until Roger Maris broke it in 1961 with sixty one home runs. Mark McGwire hit seventy in 1998. On October 7, 2001, at PacBell Park in San Francisco, Barry Bonds hit number seventy three. That accomplishment set a record which, in all probability, will remain unbroken for years into the future.

The event was widely anticipated and received a great deal of attention.

The ball that found itself at the receiving end of Mr. Bond's bat garnered some of that attention. Baseball fans in general, and especially people at the game, understood the importance of the ball. It was worth a great deal of money[10] and whoever caught it would bask, for a brief period of time, in the reflected fame of Mr. Bonds.

---

[10] It has been suggested that the ball might sell for something in excess of $1,000,000.

With that in mind, many people who attended the game came prepared for the possibility that a record setting ball would be hit in their direction. Among this group were plaintiff Alex Popov and defendant Patrick Hayashi. They were unacquainted at the time. Both men brought baseball gloves, which they anticipated using if the ball came within their reach.

… When the seventy-third home run ball went into the arcade, it landed in the upper portion of the webbing of a softball glove worn by Alex Popov. While the glove stopped the trajectory of the ball, it is not at all clear that the ball was secure. Popov had to reach for the ball and in doing so, may have lost his balance.

Even as the ball was going into his glove, a crowd of people began to engulf Mr. Popov. He was tackled and thrown to the ground while still in the process of attempting to complete the catch. Some people intentionally descended on him for the purpose of taking the ball away, while others were involuntarily forced to the ground by the momentum of the crowd.

Eventually, Mr. Popov was buried face down on the ground under several layers of people. At one point he had trouble breathing. Mr. Popov was grabbed, hit and kicked. People reached underneath him in the area of his glove. [The evidence is insufficient] to establish which individual members of the crowd were responsible for the assaults on Mr. Popov.

Mr. Popov intended at all times to establish and maintain possession of the ball. At some point the ball left his glove and ended up on the ground. It is impossible to establish the exact point in time that this occurred or what caused it to occur.

Mr. Hayashi was standing near Mr. Popov when the ball came into the stands. He, like Mr. Popov, was involuntarily forced to the ground. He committed no wrongful act. While on the ground he saw the loose ball. He picked it up, rose to his feet and put it in his pocket.

... It is important to point out what the evidence did not and could not show. Neither the camera [of a local news team fortuitously recording the incident] nor the percipient witnesses were able to establish whether Mr. Popov retained control of the ball as he descended into the crowd. Mr. Popov's testimony on this question is inconsistent on several important points, ambiguous on others and, on the whole, unconvincing. We do not know when or how Mr. Popov lost the ball.

Perhaps the most critical factual finding of all is one that cannot be made. We will never know if Mr. Popov would have been able to retain control of the ball had the crowd not interfered with his efforts to do so. Resolution of that question is the work of a psychic, not a judge.

LEGAL ANALYSIS

Plaintiff has pled causes of actions for conversion, trespass to chattel, injunctive relief and constructive trust.

Conversion is the wrongful exercise of dominion over the personal property of another. … If a person entitled to possession of personal property demands its return, the unjustified refusal to give the property back is conversion.

… Conversion does not exist, however, unless the baseball rightfully belongs to Mr. Popov. One who has neither title nor possession, nor any right to possession, cannot sue for conversion. The deciding question in this case then, is whether Mr. Popov achieved possession or the right to possession as he attempted to catch and hold on to the ball.

The parties have agreed to a starting point for the legal analysis. Prior to the time the ball was hit, it was possessed and owned by Major League Baseball. At the time it was hit it became intentionally abandoned property. The first person who came in possession of the ball became its new owner.

… Although the term possession appears repeatedly throughout the law, its definition varies depending on the context in which it is used. Various courts have condemned the term as vague and meaningless.

This level of criticism is probably unwarranted.

While there is a degree of ambiguity built into the term possession, that ambiguity exists for a purpose. Courts are often called upon to resolve conflicting claims of possession in the context of commercial disputes. A stable economic environment requires rules of conduct which are understandable and consistent with the fundamental customs and practices of the industry they regulate. Without that, rules will be difficult to enforce and economic instability will result. Because each industry has different customs and practices, a single definition of possession cannot be applied to different industries without creating havoc.

This does not mean that there are no central principles governing the law of possession. It is possible to identify certain fundamental concepts that are common to every definition of possession.

…We start with the observation that possession is a process which culminates in an event. The event is the moment in time that possession is achieved. The process includes the acts and thoughts of the would be possessor which lead up to the moment of possession.

The focus of the analysis in this case is not on the thoughts or intent of the actor. Mr. Popov has clearly evidenced an intent to possess the baseball and has communicated that intent to the world.[23] The question is whether he did enough to reduce the ball to his exclusive dominion and control. Were his acts sufficient to create a legally cognizable interest in the ball?

Mr. Hayashi argues that possession does not occur until the fan has complete control of the ball. Professor Brian Gray, suggests the following definition[:] "A person who catches a baseball that enters the stands is its owner. A ball is caught if the person has achieved complete control of the ball at the point in time that the momentum of the ball and the momentum of the fan while attempting to catch the ball ceases. A baseball, which is dislodged by incidental contact with an inanimate object or another person, before momentum has ceased, is not possessed. Incidental contact with another person is contact that is not intended by the other person. The first person to pick up a loose ball and secure it becomes its possessor."[24]

Mr. Popov argues that this definition requires that a person seeking to establish possession must show unequivocal dominion and control, a standard rejected by several leading cases.[25] Instead, he offers the perspectives of Professor Bernhardt and Professor Paul Finkelman who suggest that possession occurs when an individual intends to take control of a ball and manifests that intent by stopping the forward momentum of the ball whether or not complete control is achieved.

Professors Finkelman and Bernhardt have correctly pointed out that some cases recognize possession even before absolute dominion and control is achieved. Those cases require the actor to be actively and ably engaged in efforts to establish complete control.[27] Moreover, such efforts must be significant and they must be reasonably calculated to result in unequivocal dominion and control at some point in the near future.

---

[23] Literally.

[24] This definition is hereinafter referred to as Gray's Rule.

[25] *Pierson v. Post*, 3 Caines R. (N.Y.1805).

[27] The degree of control necessary to establish possession varies from circumstance to circumstance. "The law ... does not always require that one who discovers lost or abandoned property must actually have it in hand before he is vested with a legally protected interest. The law protects not only the title acquired by one who finds lost or abandoned property but also the right of the person who discovers such property, and is actively and ably engaged in reducing it to possession, to complete this process without interference from another. The courts have recognized that in order to acquire a legally cognizable interest in lost or abandoned property a finder need not always have manual possession of the thing. Rather, a finder may be protected by taking such constructive possession of the property as its nature and situation permit." *Treasure Salvors Inc. v. The Unidentified Wrecked and Abandoned Sailing Vessel* 640 F.2d 560, 571 (1981).

This rule is applied in cases involving the hunting or fishing of wild animals[29] or the salvage of sunken vessels. The hunting and fishing cases recognize that a mortally wounded animal may run for a distance before falling. The hunter acquires possession upon the act of wounding the animal not the eventual capture. Similarly, whalers acquire possession by landing a harpoon, not by subduing the animal.

In the salvage cases, an individual may take possession of a wreck by exerting as much control "as its nature and situation permit". Inadequate efforts, however, will not support a claim of possession. Thus, a "sailor cannot assert a claim merely by boarding a vessel and publishing a notice, unless such acts are coupled with a then present intention of conducting salvage operations, and he immediately thereafter proceeds with activity in the form of constructive steps to aid the distressed party."

These rules are contextual in nature. They are crafted in response to the unique nature of the conduct they seek to regulate. Moreover, they are influenced by the custom and practice of each industry. The reason that absolute dominion and control is not required to establish possession in the cases cited by Mr. Popov is that such a rule would be unworkable and unreasonable. The "nature and situation" of the property at issue does not immediately lend itself to unequivocal dominion and control. It is impossible to wrap one's arms around a whale, a fleeing fox or a sunken ship.

The opposite is true of a baseball hit into the stands of a stadium. Not only is it physically possible for a person to acquire unequivocal dominion and control of an abandoned baseball, but fans generally expect a claimant to have accomplished as much. The custom and practice of the stands creates a reasonable expectation that a person will achieve full control of a ball before claiming possession. There is no reason for the legal rule to be inconsistent with that expectation. Therefore Gray's Rule is adopted as the definition of possession in this case.

The central [tenet] of Gray's Rule is that the actor must retain control of the ball after incidental contact with people and things. Mr. Popov has not established by a preponderance of the evidence that he would have retained control of the ball after all momentum ceased and after any incidental contact with people or objects. Consequently, he did not achieve full possession.

That finding, however, does not resolve the case. The reason we do not know whether Mr. Popov would have retained control of the ball is not because of incidental contact. It is because

---

[29] ...*Ghen v. Rich* 8 F. 159 (D.Mass.1881); *Pierson v. Post* 3 Caines R. (N.Y.1805)....

he was attacked. His efforts to establish possession were interrupted by the collective assault of a band of wrongdoers.[34]

A decision which ignored that fact would endorse the actions of the crowd by not repudiating them. Judicial rulings, particularly in cases that receive media attention, affect the way people conduct themselves. This case demands vindication of an important principle. We are a nation governed by law, not by brute force.

As a matter of fundamental fairness, Mr. Popov should have had the opportunity to try to complete his catch unimpeded by unlawful activity. To hold otherwise would be to allow the result in this case to be dictated by violence. That will not happen.

...The legal question presented at this point is whether an action for conversion can proceed where the plaintiff has failed to establish possession or title. It can[.] An action for conversion may be brought where the plaintiff has title, possession or the right to possession.

... Consistent with this principle, the court adopts the following rule. Where an actor undertakes significant but incomplete steps to achieve possession of a piece of abandoned personal property and the effort is interrupted by the unlawful acts of others, the actor has a legally cognizable pre-possessory interest in the property. That pre-possessory interest constitutes a qualified right to possession which can support a cause of action for conversion.

... Recognition of a legally protected pre-possessory interest, vests Mr. Popov with a qualified right to possession and enables him to advance a legitimate claim to the baseball based on a conversion theory. Moreover it addresses the harm done by the unlawful actions of the crowd.

It does not, however, address the interests of Mr. Hayashi. The court is required to balance the interests of all parties.

Mr. Hayashi was not a wrongdoer. He was a victim of the same bandits that attacked Mr. Popov. ... Mr. Hayashi appears on the surface to have done everything necessary to claim full possession of the ball, [but] the ball itself is encumbered by the qualified pre-possessory interest

---

[34] Professor Gray has suggested that the way to deal with this problem is to demand that Mr. Popov sue the people who assaulted him. This suggestion is unworkable for a number of reasons. First, it was an attack by a large group of people. It is impossible to separate out the people who were acting unlawfully from the people who were involuntarily pulled into the mix. Second, in order to prove damages related to the loss of the ball, Mr. Popov would have to prove that but for the actions of the crowd he would have achieved possession of the ball. As noted earlier, this is impossible.

of Mr. Popov. At the time Mr. Hayashi came into possession of the ball, it had, in effect, a cloud on its title.

An award of the ball to Mr. Popov would be unfair to Mr. Hayashi. It would be premised on the assumption that Mr. Popov would have caught the ball. That assumption is not supported by the facts. An award of the ball to Mr. Hayashi would unfairly penalize Mr. Popov. It would be based on the assumption that Mr. Popov would have dropped the ball. That conclusion is also unsupported by the facts.

Both men have a superior claim to the ball as against all the world. Each man has a claim of equal dignity as to the other. We are, therefore, left with something of a dilemma.

Thankfully, there is a middle ground.

...The concept of equitable division has its roots in ancient Roman law. As Helmholz points out, it is useful in that it "provides an equitable way to resolve competing claims which are equally strong." Moreover, "[i]t comports with what one instinctively feels to be fair".

...The principle at work here is that where more than one party has a valid claim to a single piece of property, the court will recognize an undivided interest in the property in proportion to the strength of the claim.

...Mr. Hayashi's claim is compromised by Mr. Popov's pre-possessory interest. Mr. Popov cannot demonstrate full control. ... Their legal claims are of equal quality and they are equally entitled to the ball.

...The court therefore declares that both plaintiff and defendant have an equal and undivided interest in the ball. Plaintiff's cause of action for conversion is sustained only as to his equal and undivided interest. In order to effectuate this ruling, the ball must be sold and the proceeds divided equally between the parties....

Notes and Questions

Source: Raphael, Judgment of Solomon. Vatican Museums.

1. **Splitting the Baby.** Judge McCarthy's ruling in *Popov v. Hayashi* might be described as a classic example of "splitting the baby." In the Biblical story from which the idiom is derived, King Solomon did not "split the baby." He used an order of "splitting the baby" to suss out the true facts of the case he was called on to decide—that is, to identify the true mother of a disputed child. He relied on the assumption that no rational mother would ever agree to splitting the baby. (1 KINGS 3:16-28.). Why might a judge in a modern court of law issue a ruling that makes nobody happy? Why do you think Judge McCarthy did so in *Popov*?

   The solution adopted by Judge McCarthy is exceedingly rare. The law often views property disputes in zero-sum terms. If one person acquires ownership of the chattel, the other claimant necessarily walks away empty handed.

   Why is McCarthy's ruling so unusual? Why don't we resolve *all* disputes over initial ownership of chattels this way? Should Pierson and Post have split the value of the fox pelt? Should Ghen and Rich (or perhaps Ellis) have shared the value of the whale oil? Are there good reasons *not* to compel competing claimants of a resource to *share*? What would your kindergarten teacher say?

   Your casebook authors would never dare contradict your kindergarten teacher, but we might venture a few questions: How would you expect competing claimants to a single, indivisible resource to behave under a rule that requires them to share that resource? How do adults who share a household usually share the resources of that household?

Does it matter if the people sharing like or respect each other? How would you expect courts to resolve their disputes under a rule requiring sharing? What do you expect the reactions to such resolutions would be? What would be the effect on the value and productive use of such resources?

Finally, which of the justifications for allocation rules discussed in Note 1 after *Pierson v. Post* are implicated by these questions?

2. **Precedent.** In common-law systems, courts rely on *precedent*—earlier decided cases presenting similar facts and legal issues—to guide their decisions. Precedent may be either *binding authority*—if it issues from a court with direct appellate jurisdiction over the court deciding an identical issue—or *persuasive authority*—if it issues from a different court in an opinion the deciding court finds well-reasoned and analogous.

   In *Popov* Judge McCarthy cited and relied on our two earlier chattels cases, *Pierson v. Post* and *Ghen v. Rich*, to justify his ruling. Do you agree with Judge McCarthy's interpretation of these precedents? Do you think he applied them correctly to the facts of the case before him? Do you think he should have relied on these two decisions as persuasive authority in the *Popov* case?

   Professors Gideon Parchomovsky, Peter Siegelman and Steve Thel called for more courts to embrace sharing remedies. While acknowledging that "common law jurisprudence is predicated on a winner-take-all principle," making *Popov v. Hayashi* a "striking legal anomaly," Parchomovsky, Siegelman and Thel nevertheless argued that sharing remedies would be far more appropriate for cases involving a windfall. *Of Equal Wrongs and Half Rights*, 82 NYU L. REV. 738 (2007). Nonetheless, two decades after the case, *Popov v. Hayashi* remains a striking legal anomaly.

3. **Escape and Return.** The common law developed particular rules to deal with a captured wild animal that later escaped. In general, once such an animal is free of the control of its captor, that captor loses her property right in the animal—it becomes once again *ferae naturae*, and a new captor can become its owner by killing or capturing it, free of any claim by the original captor. If, however, the animal in question has *animus revertendi*—a natural tendency to return to its place of captivity (like, say, homing pigeons, hived bees, trained hawks or domesticated cats)—its temporary departure from the possession of the original owner does not diminish that owner's property right. *See* 2 WILLIAM BLACKSTONE, COMMENTARIES *392-93.

Might the rule of escape have any application to *Popov v. Hayashi*? Or are there other factors at work in the case that make the rule unhelpful?

4. **Postscript.** Recall Question 3 following *Ghen v. Rich*, above. Patrick Hayashi claims that before this case went to trial, he made a settlement offer to Alex Popov whereby the two men would essentially do what the court ended up ordering them to do—selling the ball and dividing the proceeds. Popov, confident in his right to sole ownership, allegedly countered with a lowball offer of $5,000 in exchange for return of the ball.[11] This turned out to be…ill advised.

   Despite speculation that Barry Bonds's record-setting home-run ball might sell for a million dollars or more, the controversy over its ownership appears to have negatively affected its market value. At auction, the ball sold for $450,000.[12] Split according to the court's order, that came out to $225,000 for each party—not a bad haul. But don't forget: this case was bitterly litigated for over a year—including a trial that proceeded over several weeks—and that ain't cheap.

   Patrick Hayashi's attorneys ultimately agreed to waive most of their fee following the resolution of the case, leaving him enough from the proceeds of the sale to cover the cost of his graduate education. He left San Francisco and began a happy new life and career in San Diego.[13]

   Alex Popov was not so lucky. The day after the ball went under the auction hammer, Popov's attorney, Martin Triano, obtained a temporary restraining order freezing Popov's share of the proceeds.[14] Mr. Triano claimed that Popov still owed him attorney's fees in the amount of $473,500.[15] Alex Popov eventually filed for bankruptcy,[16] but not

---

[11] Jay Posner, *Possessing 73rd HR ball first made his life a hassle, then movie*, SAN DIEGO UNION-TRIBUNE (June 14, 2005), *available at* http://www.utsandiego.com/uniontrib/20050614/news_1s14bondball.html.

[12] Ira Berkow, *73rd Home Run Ball Sells for $450,000*, N.Y. TIMES (June 26, 2003), *available at* http://www.nytimes.com/2003/06/26/sports/baseball-73rd-home-run-ball-sells-for-450000.html

[13] Gwen Knapp, *Finally, in Bonds ball case, someone shows some class*, S.F. CHRON. (Dec. 30, 2003) at A1, *available at* http://www.sfgate.com/sports/article/Finally-in-Bonds-ball-case-someone-shows-some-2507738.php.

[14] In re Martin Triano, Case No. CPF 03 503194, Temporary Restraining Order, June 26, 2003 (Cal. Super. Ct. San. Francisco Cty.).

[15] *Id.*, Petition filed by Martin F. Triano (June 20, 2003); *see also* David Kravets, Attorney sues fan over Bonds ball case, USA Today (July 8, 2003), *available at* http://usatoday30.usatoday.com/sports/baseball/nl/giants/2003-07-08-bonds-ball-legal-fees_x.htm.

[16] Bankruptcy Petition #: 05-32929 (N.D. Cal. Sept. 6, 2005).

before suing his attorney for malpractice and fraud.[17] The litigation between Messrs. Popov and Triano was last before a judge in September 2011, nearly 10 years after Popov had his fateful brush with a piece of sports (and legal) history. At that appearance, Mr. Popov was ordered to pay Mr. Triano an additional $22,241 in legal fees arising from their decade of litigation against one another[18]—though one suspects Mr. Triano may have some difficulty collecting the award. (There is a lesson here for lawyers, not just litigants.)

To learn more about the saga of *Popov v. Hayashi*, and to see video of the infamous home run itself, we highly recommend the 2004 feature-length documentary *Up for Grabs*.

5. **Review and Application.** On September 21, 2008, José Molina hit what would be the last home run at the old Yankee Stadium (which was demolished following the end of the season to make way for a new, glitzier facility). The ball sailed into the left-field stands, and was stopped by a net hung over the seating area specifically for the purpose of protecting fans from incoming fly balls. Several fans attempted to reach through the net to grab the ball, and one—Steve Harshman—managed to get his hand around it. But the net was still between him and the ball. Harshman told reporters he had intended to rip the ball through the net, but was interrupted by staff at the stadium, who instructed him to release it while giving assurances that they would return it to him. Harshman followed the staff's instructions, and the ball rolled down the net and into an adjacent seating area, where Bronx schoolteacher Paul Russo caught it. Yankee Stadium staff immediately confronted Russo and instructed him to turn over the ball. Russo complied, he claimed, because he thought the staff was offering to secure the ball on his behalf. Instead, to Mr. Russo's surprise and chagrin, they delivered the ball to Mr. Harshman.[19]

   Imagine Mr. Russo sues Mr. Harshman for return of the last home-run ball hit at the House that Ruth Built. What result? Would it matter if Yankee Stadium had a long-established policy of having its staff deliver game-play balls to fans who grasp them through protective netting on condition that the fan release the ball when instructed? Would it matter *why* the organization implemented such a policy?

---

[17] Popov v. Triano, Case No. CGC 04 427956, Complaint, Jan. 12, 2004 (Cal. Super. Ct. San. Francisco Cty.).
[18] In re Martin Triano, Case No. CPF 03 503194, Minute Entry, Sept. 16, 2011 (Cal. Super. Ct. San. Francisco Cty.) (granting in part Triano's motion for attorney's fees, in the amount of $22,241).
[19] James Barron, *At the Stadium, Possession Is Some Tenths of the Law*, N.Y. TIMES (Sept. 24, 2008) at B3, *available at* http://www.nytimes.com/2008/09/24/nyregion/24ball.html.

6. **Bargaining in the Shadow of the Law.** On September 19, 2024, Los Angeles Dodgers pitcher/designated hitter Shohei Ohtani hit his 50th home run of the season, becoming the first (and, so far, only) player in the history of Major League Baseball to hit 50 home runs and steal 50 bases in the same season. Roughly one year later, Goldin Auctions sold the ball for a record $4.39 million despite ongoing litigation over ownership. Goldin pocketed a $792,000 commission, while the other $3.6 million awaits resolution of the dispute among three claimants of ownership—Christian Zacek, who left the stadium with the ball, and Max Matus and Joseph Davidov, who both claimed to have taken first possession of the ball, only to be forcibly disposed by physical assaults. It was Zacek who consigned the ball with Goldin for the auction; Matus and Davidov both initially acted to block the auction. However, Goldin convinced all the claimants to go along with a "clean auction."

> "I said to them (the two parties fighting for a claim of the ball), 'Do either of you want to keep this ball or do you want to own it so you can make the most money possible?' And luckily, they said that they want to make the most money possible by selling the ball," said Goldin. "I told the story about the Barry Bonds lawsuit years ago for one of his home run balls (his record-setting 73rd in 2001) when it was tied up in court and went for much less than it would have," Goldin added. "I said you guys might be splitting $500,000, maybe $1 million each if it went three ways or whatever the court decides. Would you rather get 50 percent more like $2 million or would you rather get a 100% of $250,000 to $500,000 (if the ball is sold after the ownership dispute is settled in court)? Because if this thing goes to courts and two years from now this ball goes up for auction. Who the hell knows what it's going to get? Because it's hot now." [20]

Is Goldin right that the removal of potential clouds on ownership increases the value of the ball? If so, isn't the bargained-for resolution superior to Judge McCarthy's ruling? In this case, all the claimants will enjoy their day in court to try to get their share, but the asset itself enjoys its highest value. What doctrine would best encourage

[20] Larry Holder, *How the Shohei Ohtani 50/50 ball sold for record amount, as litigation continues a year later*, N.Y. TIMES (Dec. 23, 2025), *available at* https://www.nytimes.com/athletic/6912748/2025/12/23/shohei-ohtani-50-50-ball-lawsuits/.

this superior result? Is it *Popov v. Hayashi*'s split remedy? Would the superior result be more likely if there were a clean and clear rule of ownership?

7. **First Possession? Really?** We have now examined three different cases that purport to resolve a property dispute between an earlier pursuer and a later captor by reference to the rule of first possession. But each of them appears to come out a different way. *Pierson* awards the chattel (or its value) to the captor; *Ghen* to the pursuer; *Popov* to both in equal shares. Are these three cases really applying the same rule? If so, what nuances should we add to the maxims "first in time is first in right" or "title goes to the first possessor" in order to explain the outcomes of these three cases and help us to resolve factually similar cases we may encounter in the future? And if not, what are the *multiple* rules or considerations that govern the initial allocation of rights in chattels? Either way, how should we justify our rule(s)?

B. Allocation of Land

William Blackstone, *Commentaries on the Laws of England*
Vol. 2, p. 59 (1765).

[A]ll the land in the kingdom is supposed to be holden, mediately or immediately, of the king; who is stiled the lord paramount, or above all.

Source: Bayeux Tapestry. Left: Harold the King Is Slain. Right: William the Conqueror seated, center.

. . .

Unlike foxes, whales, and baseballs, *real property*—that is, land and structures and other improvements attached to land—isn't subject to the physical control of an individual in the same way chattels are. So what might be the legal basis for allocating private rights in real property?

Property

Claims to ownership of land in England trace back as much as a thousand years. In 1066, William, Duke of Normandy, invaded England and defeated the Anglo-Saxon King Harold at the battle of Hastings—as immortalized in the Bayeux Tapestry. William—now William the Conqueror—promptly set about parceling out rights to possess land in his new kingdom. William allocated these rights according to his political and military needs: affirming the rights of Anglo-Saxon landholders who supported him, while expropriating the land of his opponents and reallocating it to his loyal Norman nobles. These nobles received their rights of *tenure* (from the Latin word *tenere* and Norman French word *tenir*, "to hold") under obligations of *fealty* (from the Norman French *fedelité* or *fealté*, meaning fidelity or loyalty); the land each nobleman held was referred to as his *fé,* (variations: *fief*, *fee*, *feud*). Hence the name historians have applied to the resulting social system: *feudalism*. Feudal obligations typically included payment of taxes in cash or kind and rendering of services (primarily military services) to the *tenant's* (holder's) lord and king. This system of feudal grants of possessory and usufructary rights from the crown evolved over the centuries into the modern system of land ownership—a historical process we will revisit later in our chapter on Estates in Land.

Can there be any justification for the allocation of rights in land beyond the whims of a long-dead warlord and his cronies? In early modern England this was not merely an academic question. Huge changes in the legal regime governing rights to land were underway: lands in England long held as "commons" were being progressively "enclosed" (i.e., appropriated) by noble families for their private use, the personal loyalty relationships underlying feudal land tenure were being supplanted by a more self-consciously economic approach to land rights, and the colonization of the Americas brought European settlers into contact—and often conflict—with native Americans. In this period of rapid change, Britain's leading thinkers turned to the problem of justifying private property rights in land.

Thomas Hobbes, *Leviathan*

pp. 188-190 (Oxford 1909) [1651]

The NUTRITION of a Common-wealth consisteth, in the *Plenty*, and *Distribution* of *Materials* conducing to Life: In *Concoction*, or *Preparation*; and (when concocted) in the *Conveyance* of it, by convenient conduits, to the Publique use.

...The Distribution of the Materials of this Nourishment, is the constitution of *Mine*, and *Thine*, and *His*, that is to say, in one word *Propriety*; and belongeth in all kinds of Common-wealth to the Soveraign Power. For where there is no Common-wealth, there is, (as hath been already shewn) a perpetuall warre of every man against his neighbour; And therefore every thing is his that getteth it, and keepeth it by force; which is neither *Propriety* nor *Community*; but *Uncertainty*. ... Seeing therefore the Introduction of *Propriety* is an effect of Common-wealth; which can do nothing but by the Person that Represents it, it is the act onely of the Soveraign; and consisteth in the Lawes, which none can make that have not the Soveraign Power. And this they well knew of old, who called that *Νόμος*, (that is to say, *Distribution,*) which we call Law; and defined Justice, by *distributing* to every man *his own.*

... In this Distribution, the First Law, is for Division of the Land it selfe: wherein the Soveraign assigneth to every man a portion, according as he, and not according as any Subject, or any number of them, shall judge agreeable to Equity, and the Common Good. ... And though a People comming into possession of a land by warre, do not alwaies exterminate the antient Inhabitants ... but leave to many, or most, or all of them their Estates; yet it is manifest they hold them afterwards, as of the Victors distribution; as the people of *England* held all theirs of *William the Conquerour.*

William Blackstone, Commentaries on the Laws of England

vol. 2, p. 2 (1765)

There is nothing which so generally strikes the imagination, and engages the affections of mankind, as the right of property; or that sole and despotic dominion which one man claims and exercises over the external things of the world, in total exclusion of the right of any other individual in the universe. And yet there are very few, that will give themselves the trouble to consider the original and foundation of this right. Pleased as we are with the possession, we seem afraid to look back to the means by which it was acquired, as if fearful of some defect in our title; or at best we rest satisfied with the decision of the laws in our favour, without examining the reason or authority upon which those laws have been built. We think it enough that our title is derived by the grant of the former proprietor, by descent from our ancestors, or by the last will and testament of the dying owner; not caring to reflect that (accurately and strictly speaking) there is no foundation in nature or in natural law, why a set of words upon parchment should convey the dominion of land; why the son should have a right to exclude his fellow creatures from a determinate spot of ground, because his father had done so before him; or why the occupier of a particular field or of a jewel, when lying on his death-bed and no longer able to maintain possession, should be entitled to tell the rest of the world which of them should enjoy it after him. These enquiries, it must be owned, would be useless and even troublesome in common life. It is well if the mass of mankind will obey the laws when made, without scrutinizing too nicely into the reasons of making them.

John Locke, *Second Treatise of Civil Government*

Ch. 5 (1690)

Though the earth, and all inferior creatures, be common to all men, yet every man has a property in his own person: this no body has any right to but himself. The labour of his body, and the work of his hands, we may say, are properly his. Whatsoever then he removes out of the state that nature hath provided, and left it in, he hath mixed his labour with, and joined to it something that is his own, and thereby makes it his property. It being by him removed from the common state nature hath placed it in, it hath by this labour something annexed to it, that excludes the common right of other men: for this labour being the unquestionable property of the labourer, no man but he can have a right to what that is once joined to, at least where there is enough, and as good, left in common for others.

He that is nourished by the acorns he picked up under an oak, or the apples he gathered from the trees in the wood, has certainly appropriated them to himself. No body can deny but the nourishment is his. I ask then, when did they begin to be his? when he digested? or when he eat? or when he boiled? or when he brought them home? or when he picked them up? and it is plain, if the first gathering made them not his, nothing else could. That labour put a distinction between them and common: that added something to them more than nature, the common mother of all, had done; and so they became his private right. And will any one say, he had no right to those acorns or apples, he thus appropriated, because he had not the consent of all mankind to make them his? Was it a robbery thus to assume to himself what belonged to all in common? If such a consent as that was necessary, man had starved, notwithstanding the plenty God had given him....

But the chief matter of property being now not the fruits of the earth, and the beasts that subsist on it, but the earth itself; as that which takes in and carries with it all the rest; I think it is plain, that property in that too is acquired as the former. As much land as a man tills, plants, improves, cultivates, and can use the product of, so much is his property. He by his labour does, as it were, inclose it from the common. Nor will it invalidate his right, to say every body else has an equal title to it; and therefore he cannot appropriate, he cannot inclose, without the consent of all his fellow-commoners, all mankind. God, when he gave the world in common to all mankind, commanded man also to labour, and the penury of his condition required it of him. God and his reason commanded him to subdue the earth, i.e. improve it for the benefit of life, and therein lay out something upon it that was his own, his labour. He that in obedience to this command of God, subdued, tilled and sowed any part of it, thereby annexed to it something that was his property, which another had no title to, nor could without injury take from him.

Nor was this appropriation of any parcel of land, by improving it, any prejudice to any other man, since there was still enough, and as good left; and more than the yet unprovided could use....

God gave the world to men in common; but since he gave it them for their benefit, and the greatest conveniencies of life they were capable to draw from it, it cannot be supposed he meant it should always remain common and uncultivated. He gave it to the use of the industrious and rational, (and labour was to be his title to it;) not to the fancy or covetousness of the quarrelsome and contentious. He that had as good left for his improvement, as was already taken up, needed not complain, ought not to meddle with what was already improved by another's labour: if he did, it is plain he desired the benefit of another's pains, which he had no right to, and not the ground which God had given him in common with others to labour on, and whereof there was as good left, as that already possessed, and more than he knew what to do with, or his industry could reach to.

... To which let me add, that he who appropriates land to himself by his labour, does not lessen, but increase the common stock of mankind: for the provisions serving to the support of human life, produced by one acre of inclosed and cultivated land, are (to speak much within compass) ten times more than those which are yielded by an acre of land of an equal richness lying waste in common. And therefore he that incloses land, and has a greater plenty of the conveniencies of life from ten acres, than he could have from an hundred left to nature, may truly be said to give ninety acres to mankind: for his labour now supplies him with provisions out of ten acres, which were but the product of an hundred lying in common. I have here rated the improved land very low, in making its product but as ten to one, when it is much nearer an hundred to one: for I ask, whether in the wild woods and uncultivated waste of America, left to nature, without any improvement, tillage or husbandry, a thousand acres yield the needy and wretched inhabitants as many conveniencies of life, as ten acres of equally fertile land do in Devonshire, where they are well cultivated?

...Thus labour, in the beginning, gave a right of property, wherever any one was pleased to employ it upon what was common, which remained a long while the far greater part, and is yet more than mankind makes use of. Men, at first, for the most part, contented themselves with what unassisted nature offered to their necessities: and though afterwards, in some parts of the world, (where the increase of people and stock, with the use of money, had made land scarce, and so of some value) the several communities settled the bounds of their distinct territories, and by laws within themselves regulated the properties of the private men of their society, and so, by compact and agreement, settled the property which labour and industry began; and the leagues that have been made between several states and kingdoms, either expresly or tacitly disowning all claim and right to the land in the others possession, have, by common consent, given up their pretences to their natural common right, which originally they had to those countries, and so have, by positive agreement, settled a property amongst themselves, in distinct parts and parcels of the earth...

... Thus in the beginning all the world was America....

Herman Melville, *Moby-Dick*

p. 375 (1922) [1892]

What was America in 1492 but a Loose-Fish, in which Columbus struck the Spanish standard by way of waifing it for his royal master and mistress? What was Poland to the Czar? What Greece to the Turk? What India to England? What at last will Mexico be to the United States? All Loose-Fish.

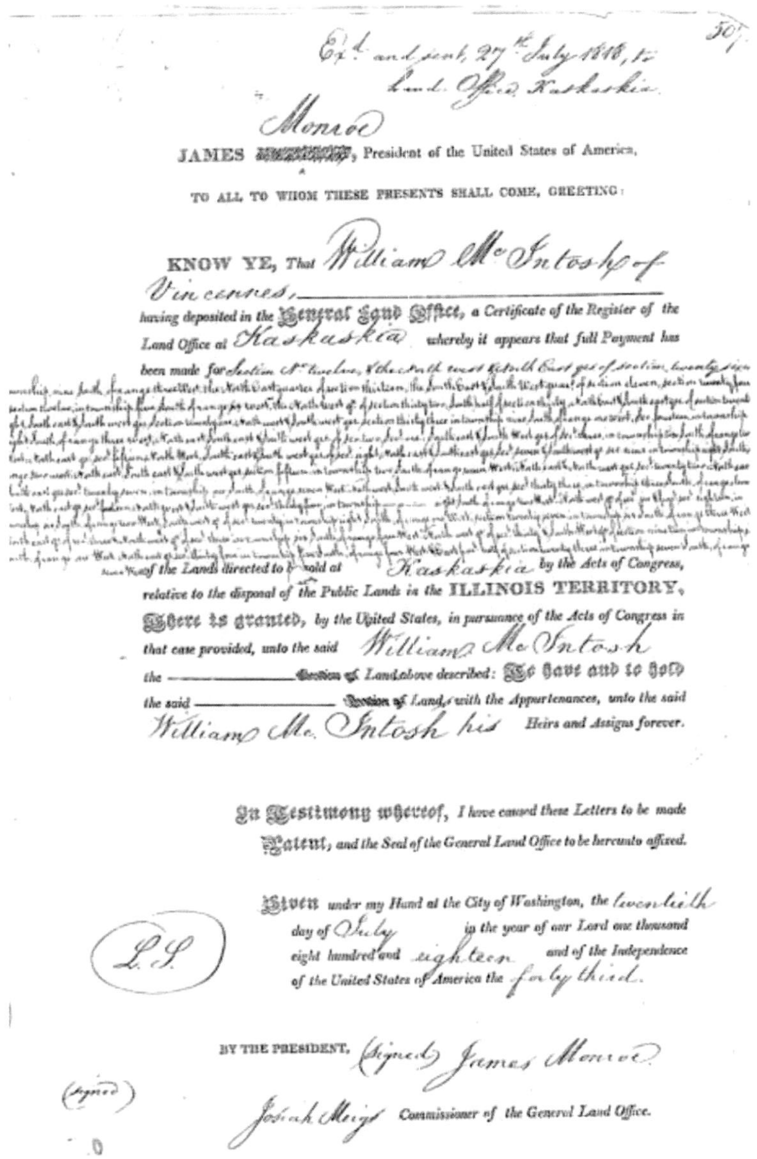

Ex.d and sent, 27th July 1818, to Land Office Kaskaskia.

Monroe

JAMES [redacted], President of the United States of America,

TO ALL TO WHOM THESE PRESENTS SHALL COME, GREETING:

KNOW YE, That William McIntosh of Vincennes, having deposited in the General Land Office, a Certificate of the Register of the Land Office at Kaskaskia whereby it appears that full Payment has been made for [illegible] of the Lands directed to be sold at Kaskaskia by the Acts of Congress, relative to the disposal of the Public Lands in the ILLINOIS TERRITORY,

There is granted, by the United States, in pursuance of the Acts of Congress in that case provided, unto the said William McIntosh the ——— Section of Land above described: To have and to hold the said ——— Section of Land, with the Appurtenances, unto the said William McIntosh his Heirs and Assigns forever.

In Testimony whereof, I have caused these Letters to be made Patent, and the Seal of the General Land Office to be hereunto affixed.

Given under my Hand at the City of Washington, the twentieth day of July in the year of our Lord one thousand eight hundred and eighteen and of the Independence of the United States of America the forty third.

L.S.

BY THE PRESIDENT, (Signed) James Monroe

(Signed) Josiah Meigs Commissioner of the General Land Office.

Johnson v. M'Intosh

21 U.S. 543 (1823)

ERROR to the District Court of Illinois. This was an action of ejectment for lands in the State and District of Illinois, claimed by the plaintiffs [Johnson and Graham's lessee] under a purchase and conveyance from the Piankeshaw Indians, and by the defendant [William McIntosh], under a grant from the United States [dated July 20, 1818]. . . . The case stated set out the following facts: . . .

1st. That on the 23d of May, 1609, James I. king of England, by his letters patent of that date, under the great seal of England, did erect, form, and establish Robert, Earl of Salisbury, and others, his associates, in the letters patent named, and their successors, into a body corporate and politic, by the name and style of 'The Treasurer and Company of Adventurers and Planters of the City of London, for the first Colony in Virginia,' . . . and did give, grant, and confirm unto this company, and their successors, under certain reservations and limitations in the letters patent expressed, 'All the lands, countries, and territories, situate, lying, and being in that part of North America called Virginia . . .

2d. That . . . immediately after the granting of the letters patent, the corporation proceeded, under and by virtue of them, to take possession of parts of the territory which they describe, and to form settlements, plant a colony, and exercise the powers of government therein; which colony was called and known by the name of the colony of Virginia.

3d. That at the time of granting these letters patent, and of the discovery of the continent of North America by the Europeans, and during the whole intermediate time, the whole of the territory, in the letters patent described ... was held, occupied, and possessed, in full sovereignty, by various independent tribes or nations of Indians, who were the sovereigns of their respective portions of the territory, and the absolute owners and proprietors of the soil; and who neither acknowledged nor owed any allegiance or obedience to any European sovereign or state whatever: and that in making settlements within this territory, and in all the other parts of North America, where settlements were made, under the authority of the English government, or by its subjects, the right of soil was previously obtained by purchase or conquest, from the particular Indian tribe or nation by which the soil was claimed and held; or the consent of such tribe or nation was secured.

4th. That in the year 1624, this corporation was dissolved . . . and all its powers, together with its rights of soil and jurisdiction . . . were revested in the crown of England . . .

5th. That some time previous to the year 1756, the French government, laying a claim to the country west of the Alleghany or Appalachian mountains, on the Ohio and Mississippi rivers, and their branches, took possession of certain parts of it, with the consent of the several tribes or nations of Indians possessing and owning them; and, with the like consent, established several military posts and settlements therein … within the limits of the colony of Virginia, as described and established in and by the letters patent of May 23d, 1609: and that the government of Great Britain, after complaining of these establishments as encroachments, and remonstrating against them, at length, in the year 1756, took up arms to resist and repel them; which produced a war between those two nations, wherein the Indian tribes inhabiting and holding the countries northwest of the Ohio, and on the Mississippi above the mouth of the Ohio, were the allies of France, and the Indians known by the name of the Six Nations, or the Iroquois, and their tributaries and allies, were the allies of Great Britain; and that on the 10th of February, 1763, this war was terminated by a definitive treaty of peace between Great Britain and France, and their allies, by which it was stipulated and agreed, that the river Mississippi, … should for ever after form the boundary between the dominions of Great Britain and those of France, in that part of North America, and between their respective allies there.

6th. That the government of Virginia, at and before the commencement of this war, and at all times after it became a royal government, claimed and exercised jurisdiction, with the knowledge and assent of the government of Great Britain, in and over the country northwest of the river Ohio, and east of the Mississippi, as being included within the bounds and limits described and established for that colony, by the letters patent of May 23d, 1609; and that in the year 1749, a grant of six hundred thousand acres of land, within the country northwest of the Ohio, and as part of Virginia, was made by the government of Great Britain to some of its subjects, by the name and style of the Ohio Company.

7th. That at and before the commencement of the war in 1756, and during its whole continuance, and at the time of the treaty of February 10th, 1763, the Indian tribes or nations, inhabiting the country north and northwest of the Ohio, and east of the Mississippi, as far east as the river falling into the Ohio called the Great Miami, were called and known by the name of the Western Confederacy of Indians, and were the allies of France in the war, but not her subjects, never having been in any manner conquered by her, and held the country in absolute sovereignty, as independent nations, both as to the right of jurisdiction and sovereignty, and the right of soil, except a few military posts, and a small territory around each, which they had ceded to France, and she held under them … and that these Indians, after the treaty, became the allies of Great Britain, living under her protection as they had before lived under that of France, but were free and independent, owing no allegiance to any foreign power whatever, and holding their lands in absolute property; the territories of the respective tribes being separated from each other, and distinguished by certain natural marks and boundaries to the Indians well known; and each tribe claiming and exercising separate and absolute ownership, in and over its own territory, both as to the right of sovereignty and jurisdiction, and the right of soil.

8th. That among the tribes of Indians, thus holding and inhabiting the territory north and northwest of the Ohio, east of the Mississippi, and west of the Great Miami, within the limits of Virginia, as described in the letters patent of May 23d, 1609, were certain independent tribes or nations, called the Illinois or Kaskaskias, and the Piankeshaw or Wabash Indians; the first of which consisted of three several tribes united into one, and called the Kaskasias, the Pewarias, and the Cahoquias; that the Illinois owned, held, and inhabited, as their absolute and separate property, a large tract of country within the last mentioned limits ...; and the Piankeshaws, another large tract of country within the same limits, and as their absolute and separate property, ...; and that these Indians remained in the sole and absolute ownership and possession of the country in question, until the sales made by them, in the manner herein after set forth.

9th. That on the termination of the war between Great Britain and France, the Illinois Indians, by the name of the Kaskaskias tribes of Indians, as fully representing all the Illinois tribes then remaining, made a treaty of peace with Great Britain, and a treaty of peace, limits, and amity, under her mediation, with the Six Nations, or Iroquois, and their allies, then known and distinguished by the name of the Northern Confederacy of Indians; the Illinois being a part of the confederacy then known and distinguished by the name of the Southern Confederacy, and sometimes by that of the Western Confederacy.

10th. That on the 7th of October, 1763, the King of Great Britain made and published a proclamation, for the better regulation of the countries ceded to Great Britain by that treaty, which proclamation is referred to, and made part of the case.

11th. That from time immemorial, and always up to the present time, all the Indian tribes, or nations of North America, and especially the Illinois and Piankeshaws, and other tribes holding, possessing, and inhabiting the said countries north and northeast of the Ohio, east of the Mississippi, and west of the Great Miami, held their respective lands and territories each in common, the individuals of each tribe or nation holding the lands and territories of such tribe in common with each other, and there being among them no separate property in the soil; and that their sole method of selling, granting, and conveying their lands, whether to governments or individuals, always has been, from time immemorial, and now is, for certain chiefs of the tribe selling, to represent the whole tribe in every part of the transaction; to make the contract, and execute the deed, on behalf of the whole tribe; to receive for it the consideration, whether in money or commodities, or both; and, finally, to divide such consideration among the individuals of the tribe: and that the authority of the chiefs, so acting for the whole tribe, is attested by the presence and assent of the individuals composing the tribe, or some of them, and by the receipt by the individuals composing the tribe, of their respective shares of the price, and in no other manner.

12th. That on the 5th of July, 1773, certain chiefs of the Illinois Indians, then jointly representing, acting for, and being duly authorized by that tribe, in the manner explained above, did, by their deed poll, duly executed and delivered, and bearing date on that day, at the post of Kaskaskias, then being a British military post, and at a public council there held by them, for and on behalf of the said Illinois nation of Indians, with William Murray, of the Illinois country, merchant, acting for himself and for [others]; and for a good and valuable consideration in the said deed stated, grant, bargain, sell, alien, lease, enfeoff, and confirm, to the said William Murray, [et al], their heirs and assigns for ever, in severalty, or to George the Third, then King of Great Britain and Ireland, his heirs and successors, for the use, benefit, and behoof of the grantees, their heirs and assigns, in severalty, by whichever of those tenures they might most legally hold, all those two several tracts or parcels of land, situated, lying, and being within the limits of Virginia, on the east of the Mississippi, northwest of the Ohio, and west of the Great Miami, and thus butted and bounded: [certain geographical boundaries]: To have and to hold the said two tracts of land, with all and singular their appurtenances, to the grantees, their heirs and assigns, for ever, in severalty, or to the king, his heirs and successors, to and for the use, benefit, or behoof of the grantees, their heirs and assigns, for ever, in severalty: as will more fully appear by the said deed poll, duly executed under the hands and seals of the grantors, and duly recorded at Kaskaskias, on the 2d of September, 1773, in the office of Vicerault Lemerance, a notary public, duly appointed and authorized. This deed, with the several certificates annexed to or endorsed on it, was set out at length in the case.

13th. That the consideration in this deed expressed, was of the value of 24,000 dollars, current money of the United States, and upwards, and was paid and delivered, at the time of the execution of the deed, by William Murray, one of the grantees, in behalf of himself and the other grantees, to the Illinois Indians, who freely accepted it, and divided it among themselves: that the conferences in which the sale of these lands was agreed on and made, and in which it was agreed that the deed should be executed, were publicly held, for the space of a month, at the post of Kaskaskias, and were attended by many individuals of all the tribes of Illinois Indians, besides the chiefs, named as grantors in the deed; that the whole transaction was open, public, and fair, and the deed fully explained to the grantors and other Indians, by the sworn interpreters of the government, and fully understood by the grantors and other Indians, before it was executed; that the several witnesses to the deed, and the grantees named in it, were such persons, and of such quality and stations, respectively, as they are described to be in the deed, the attestation, and the other endorsements on it; that the grantees did duly authorize William Murray to act for and represent them, in the purchase of the lands, and the acceptance of the deed; and that the two tracts or parcels of land which it describes, and purports to grant, were then part of the lands held, possessed, and inhabited by the Illinois Indians, from time immemorial, in the manner already stated.

14th. That all the persons named as grantees in this deed, were, at the time of its execution, and long before, subjects of the crown of Great Britain, and residents of the several places named in the deed as their places of residence; and that they entered into the land, under and by virtue of the deed, and became seised as the law requires.

15th. That on the 18th of October, 1775, Tabac, and certain other Indians, all being chiefs of the Piankeshaws, and jointly representing, acting for, and duly authorized by that nation, in the manner stated above, did, by their deed poll, duly executed, and bearing date on the day last mentioned, at the post of Vincennes, otherwise called post St. Vincent, then being a British military post, and at a public council there held by them, for and on behalf of the Piankeshaw Indians, with Louis Viviat, of the Illinois country, acting for himself, and for ... [others including] William Murray and Daniel Murray, of the Illinois country, ... and for good and valuable consideration, in the deed poll mentioned and enumerated, grant, bargain, sell, alien, enfeoff, release, ratify, and confirm to the said Louis Viviat, and the other persons last mentioned, their heirs and assigns, equally to be divided, or to George III. then king of Great Britain and Ireland, his heirs and successors, for the use, benefit, and behoof of all the above mentioned grantees, their heirs and assigns, in severalty, by which ever of those tenures they might most legally hold, all those two several tracts of land, in the deed particularly described, situate, lying, and being ... [within certain geographical boundaries]; with all the rights, liberties, privileges, hereditaments, and appurtenances, to the said tract belonging; to have and to hold to the grantees, their heirs and assigns, for ever, in severalty, or to the king, his heirs and successors, for the use, benefit, and behoof of the grantees, their heirs and assigns, as will more fully appear by the deed itself, duly executed under the hands and seals of the grantors, and duly recorded at Kaskaskias, on the 5th of December, 1775, in the office of Louis Bomer, a notary public, duly appointed and authorized. This deed, with the several certificates annexed to or endorsed on it, was set out at length.

16th. That the consideration in this deed expressed, was of the value of 31,000 dollars, current money of the United States, and upwards, and was paid and delivered at the time of the execution of the deed, by the grantee, Lewis Viviat, in behalf of himself and the other grantees, to the Piankeshaw Indians, who freely accepted it, and divided it among themselves; that the conferences in which the sale of these two tracts of land was agreed on and made, and in which it was agreed, that the deed should be executed, were publicly held for the space of a month, at the post of Vincennes, or post St. Vincent, and were attended by many individuals of the Piankeshaw nation of Indians, besides the chiefs named as grantors in the deed; that the whole transaction was open, public, and fair, and the deed fully explained to the grantors and other Indians, by skilful interpreters, and fully understood by them before it was executed; that it was executed in the presence of the several witnesses by whom it purports to have been attested, and was attested by them; that the grantees were all subjects of the crown of Great Britain, and were of such quality, station, and residence, respectively, as they are described in the deed to be; that the grantees did duly authorize Lewis Viviat to act for, and represent them, in the purchase of these two tracts of land, and in the acceptance of the deed; that these tracts of land were then part of the lands held, possessed, and inhabited by the Piankeshaw Indians, from time immemorial, as is stated above; and that the several grantees under this deed entered into the land which it purports to grant, and became seized as the law requires.

17th. That on the 6th of May, 1776, the colony of Virginia threw off its dependence on the crown and government of Great Britain, and declared itself an independent State and government, with the limits prescribed and established by the letters patent of May 23d, 1609, as curtailed and restricted by the letters patent establishing the colonies of Pennsylvania, Maryland, and Carolina, and by the treaty of February 10th, 1763, between Great Britain and France; which limits, so curtailed and restricted, the State of Virginia, by its constitution and form of government, declared should be and remain the limits of the State, and should bound its western and northwestern extent.

18th. That on the 5th of October, 1778, the General Assembly of Virginia, having taken by arms the posts of Kaskaskias and Vincennes, or St. Vincent, from the British forces, by whom they were then held, and driven those forces from the country northwest of the Ohio, east of the Mississippi, and west of the Great Miami, did, by an act of Assembly of that date, entitled, 'An act for establishing the county of Illinois, and for the more effectual protection and defence thereof,' erect that country, with certain other portions of territory within the limits of the State, and northwest of the Ohio, into a county, by the name of the county of Illinois.

19th. That on the 20th of December, 1783, the State of Virginia, by an act of Assembly of that date, authorized their Delegates in the Congress of the United States, or such of them, to the number of three at least, as should be assembled in Congress, on behalf of the State, and by proper deeds or instruments in writing under their hands and seals, to convey, transfer, assign, and make over to the United States, in Congress assembled, for the benefit of the said States, all right, title, and claim, as well of soil as jurisdiction, which Virginia had to the territory or tract of country within her limits, as defined and prescribed by the letters patent of May 23d, 1609, and lying to the northwest of the Ohio; subject to certain limitations and conditions in the act prescribed and specified; and that on the 1st of March, 1784, Thomas Jefferson, Samuel Hardy, Arthur Lee, and James Monroe, then being four of the Delegates of Virginia to the Congress of the United States, did, by their deed poll, under their hands and seals, in pursuance and execution of the authority to them given by this act of Assembly, convey, transfer, assign, and make over to the United States, in Congress assembled, for the benefit of the said States, all right, title, and claim, as well of soil as jurisdiction, which that State had to the territory northwest of the Ohio, with the reservations, limitations, and conditions, in the act of Assembly prescribed; which cession the United States accepted.

20th. That on the twentieth day of July, in the year of our Lord one thousand eight hundred and eighteen, the United States, by their officers duly authorized for that purpose, did sell, grant, and convey to the defendant in this action, William M'Intosh, all those several tracts or parcels of land, containing 11,560 acres, and butted, bounded, and described, as will fully appear in and by the patent for the said lands, duly executed, which was set out at length.

21st. That the lands described and granted in and by this patent, are situated within the State of Illinois, and are contained within the lines of the last, or second of the two tracts, described and purporting to be granted and conveyed to Louis Viviat and others, by the deed of October 18th, 1775; and that William M'Intosh, the defendant, entered upon these lands under, and by virtue of his patent, and became possessed thereof before the institution of this suit.

22d. That Thomas Johnson, one of the grantees, in and under the deed of October 18th, 1775, departed this life on or about the 1st day of October, 1819, seised of all his undivided part or share of, and in the two several tracts of land, described and purporting to be granted and conveyed to him and others by that deed, having first duly made and published his last will and testament in writing, attested by three credible witnesses, which he left in full force, and by which he devised all his undivided share and part of those two tracts of land, to his son, Joshua Johnson, and his heirs, and his grandson, Thomas J. Graham, and his heirs, the lessors of the plaintiff in this action, as tenants in common.

23d. That Joshua Johnson, and Thomas J. Graham, the devisees, entered into the two tracts of land last above mentioned, under and by virtue of the will, and became thereof seised as the law requires. That Thomas Johnson, the grantee and devisor, during his whole life, and at the time of his death, was an inhabitant and citizen of the State of Maryland; that Joshua Johnson, and Thomas J. Graham, the lessors of the plaintiff, now are, and always have been, citizens of the same State; that the defendant, William M'Intosh, now is, and at and before the time of bringing this action was, a citizen of the State of Illinois; and that the matter in dispute in this action is of the value of 2000 dollars, current money of the United States, and upwards.

24th. And that neither William Murray, nor any other of the grantees under the deed of July the 5th, 1773, nor Louis Viviat, nor any other of the grantees under the deed of October the 8th, 1775, nor any person for them, or any of them, ever obtained, or had the actual possession, under and by virtue of those deeds, or either of them, of any part of the lands in them, or either of them, described and purporting to be granted; but were prevented by the war of the American revolution, which soon after commenced, and by the disputes and troubles which preceded it, from obtaining such possession; and that since the termination of the war, and before it, they have repeatedly, and at various times, from the year 1781, till the year 1816, petitioned the Congress of the United States to acknowledge and confirm their title to those lands, under the purchases and deeds in question, but without success.

Mr. Chief Justice MARSHALL delivered the opinion of the Court.

The plaintiffs in this cause claim the land, in their declaration mentioned, under two grants, purporting to be made, the first in 1773, and the last in 1775, by the chiefs of certain Indian tribes, constituting the Illinois and the Piankeshaw nations; and the question is, whether this title can be recognised in the Courts of the United States?

The facts, as stated in the case agreed, show the authority of the chiefs who executed this conveyance, so far as it could be given by their own people; and likewise show, that the particular tribes for whom these chiefs acted were in rightful possession of the land they sold. The inquiry, therefore, is, in a great measure, confined to the power of Indians to give, and of private individuals to receive, a title which can be sustained in the Courts of this country.

As the right of society, to prescribe those rules by which property may be acquired and preserved is not, and cannot be drawn into question; as the title to lands, especially, is and must be admitted to depend entirely on the law of the nation in which they lie; it will be necessary, in pursuing this inquiry, to examine, not singly those principles of abstract justice, which the Creator of all things has impressed on the mind of his creature man, and which are admitted to regulate, in a great degree, the rights of civilized nations, whose perfect independence is acknowledged; but those principles also which our own government has adopted in the particular case, and given us as the rule for our decision.

On the discovery of this immense continent, the great nations of Europe were eager to appropriate to themselves so much of it as they could respectively acquire. Its vast extent offered an ample field to the ambition and enterprise of all; and the character and religion of its inhabitants afforded an apology for considering them as a people over whom the superior genius of Europe might claim an ascendency. The potentates of the old world found no difficulty in convincing themselves that they made ample compensation to the inhabitants of the new, by bestowing on them civilization and Christianity, in exchange for unlimited independence. But, as they were all in pursuit of nearly the same object, it was necessary, in order to avoid conflicting settlements, and consequent war with each other, to establish a principle, which all should acknowledge as the law by which the right of acquisition, which they all asserted, should be regulated as between themselves. This principle was, that discovery gave title to the government by whose subjects, or by whose authority, it was made, against all other European governments, which title might be consummated by possession.

The exclusion of all other Europeans, necessarily gave to the nation making the discovery the sole right of acquiring the soil from the natives, and establishing settlements upon it. It was a right with which no Europeans could interfere. It was a right which all asserted for themselves, and to the assertion of which, by others, all assented.

Those relations which were to exist between the discoverer and the natives, were to be regulated by themselves. The rights thus acquired being exclusive, no other power could interpose between them.

In the establishment of these relations, the rights of the original inhabitants were, in no instance, entirely disregarded; but were necessarily, to a considerable extent, impaired. They were admitted to be the rightful occupants of the soil, with a legal as well as just claim to retain possession of it, and to use it according to their own discretion; but their rights to complete sovereignty, as independent nations, were necessarily diminished, and their power to dispose of the soil at their own will, to whomsoever they pleased, was denied by the original fundamental principle, that discovery gave exclusive title to those who made it.

While the different nations of Europe respected the right of the natives, as occupants, they asserted the ultimate dominion to be in themselves; and claimed and exercised, as a consequence of this ultimate dominion, a power to grant the soil, while yet in possession of the natives. These grants have been understood by all, to convey a title to the grantees, subject only to the Indian right of occupancy.

... No one of the powers of Europe gave its full assent to this principle, more unequivocally than England. The documents upon this subject are ample and complete. ... Thus has our whole country been granted by the crown while in the occupation of the Indians. These [royal] grants purport to convey the soil as well as the right of dominion to the grantees. ... In all of them, the soil, at the time the grants were made, was occupied by the Indians. Yet almost every title within those governments is dependent on these grants. ... It has never been objected to this, or to any other similar grant, that the title as well as possession was in the Indians when it was made, and that it passed nothing on that account.

These various patents cannot be considered as nullities; nor can they be limited to a mere grant of the powers of government. A charter intended to convey political power only, would never contain words expressly granting the land, the soil, and the waters. Some of them purport to convey the soil alone; and in those cases in which the powers of government, as well as the soil, are conveyed to individuals, the crown has always acknowledged itself to be bound by the grant. Though the power to dismember regal governments was asserted and exercised, the power to dismember proprietary governments was not claimed; and, in some instances, even after the powers of government were revested in the crown, the title of the proprietors to the soil was respected.

...Thus, all the nations of Europe, who have acquired territory on this continent, have asserted in themselves, and have recognised in others, the exclusive right of the discoverer to appropriate the lands occupied by the Indians. Have the American States rejected or adopted this principle?

By the treaty which concluded the war of our revolution, Great Britain relinquished all claim, not only to the government, but to the 'propriety and territorial rights of the United States,' whose boundaries were fixed in the second article. By this treaty, the powers of government, and the right to soil, which had previously been in Great Britain, passed definitively to these States. We had before taken possession of them, by declaring independence; but neither the declaration of independence, nor the treaty confirming it, could give us more than that which we before possessed, or to which Great Britain was before entitled. It has never been doubted, that either the United States, or the several States, had a clear title to all the lands within the boundary lines described in the treaty, subject only to the Indian right of occupancy, and that the exclusive power to extinguish that right, was vested in that government which might constitutionally exercise it.

Virginia, particularly, within whose chartered limits the land in controversy lay, passed an act, in the year 1779, declaring her 'exclusive right of pre-emption from the Indians, of all the lands within the limits of her own chartered territory, and that no person or persons whatsoever, have, or ever had, a right to purchase any lands within the same, from any Indian nation, except only persons duly authorized to make such purchase; formerly for the use and benefit of the colony, and lately for the Commonwealth.' The act then proceeds to annul all deeds made by Indians to individuals, for the private use of the purchasers.

...In pursuance of the same idea, Virginia proceeded, at the same session, to open her land office, for the sale of that country which now constitutes Kentucky, a country, every acre of which was then claimed and possessed by Indians, who maintained their title with as much persevering courage as was ever manifested by any people.

The States, having within their chartered limits different portions of territory covered by Indians, ceded that territory, generally, to the United States, on conditions expressed in their deeds of cession, which demonstrate the opinion, that they ceded the soil as well as jurisdiction, and that in doing so, they granted a productive fund to the government of the Union. The lands in controversy lay within the chartered limits of Virginia, and were ceded with the whole country northwest of the river Ohio. This grant contained reservations and stipulations, which could only be made by the owners of the soil; and concluded with a stipulation, that 'all the lands in the ceded territory, not reserved, should be considered as a common fund, for the use and benefit of such of the United States as have become, or shall become, members of the confederation,' &c. 'according to their usual respective proportions in the general charge and expenditure, and shall be faithfully and *bona fide* disposed of for that purpose, and for no other use or purpose whatsoever.'

The ceded territory was occupied by numerous and warlike tribes of Indians; but the exclusive right of the United States to extinguish their title, and to grant the soil, has never, we believe, been doubted.

...The United States, then, have unequivocally acceded to that great and broad rule by which its civilized inhabitants now hold this country. They hold, and assert in themselves, the title by which it was acquired. They maintain, as all others have maintained, that discovery gave an exclusive right to extinguish the Indian title of occupancy, either by purchase or by conquest; and gave also a right to such a degree of sovereignty, as the circumstances of the people would allow them to exercise.

The power now possessed by the government of the United States to grant lands, resided, while we were colonies, in the crown, or its grantees. The validity of the titles given by either has never been questioned in our Courts. It has been exercised uniformly over territory in possession of the Indians. The existence of this power must negative the existence of any right which may conflict with, and control it. An absolute title to lands cannot exist, at the same time, in different persons, or in different governments. An absolute, must be an exclusive title, or at least a title which excludes all others not compatible with it. All our institutions recognise the absolute title of the crown, subject only to the Indian right of occupancy, and recognise the absolute title of the crown to extinguish that right. This is incompatible with an absolute and complete title in the Indians.

...Although we do not mean to engage in the defence of those principles which Europeans have applied to Indian title, they may, we think, find some excuse, if not justification, in the character and habits of the people whose rights have been wrested from them.

The title by conquest is acquired and maintained by force. The conqueror prescribes its limits. Humanity, however, acting on public opinion, has established, as a general rule, that the conquered shall not be wantonly oppressed, and that their condition shall remain as eligible as is compatible with the objects of the conquest. Most usually, they are incorporated with the victorious nation, and become subjects or citizens of the government with which they are connected. The new and old members of the society mingle with each other; the distinction between them is gradually lost, and they make one people. Where this incorporation is practicable, humanity demands, and a wise policy requires, that the rights of the conquered to property should remain unimpaired; that the new subjects should be governed as equitably as the old, and that confidence in their security should gradually banish the painful sense of being separated from their ancient connexions, and united by force to strangers.

When the conquest is complete, and the conquered inhabitants can be blended with the conquerors, or safely governed as a distinct people, public opinion, which not even the conqueror can disregard, imposes these restraints upon him; and he cannot neglect them without injury to his fame, and hazard to his power.

But the tribes of Indians inhabiting this country were fierce savages, whose occupation was war, and whose subsistence was drawn chiefly from the forest. To leave them in possession of their country, was to leave the country a wilderness; to govern them as a distinct people, was impossible, because they were as brave and as high spirited as they were fierce, and were ready to repel by arms every attempt on their independence.

What was the inevitable consequence of this state of things? The Europeans were under the necessity either of abandoning the country, and relinquishing their pompous claims to it, or of enforcing those claims by the sword, and by the adoption of principles adapted to the condition of a people with whom it was impossible to mix, and who could not be governed as a distinct society, or of remaining in their neighbourhood, and exposing themselves and their families to the perpetual hazard of being massacred.

Frequent and bloody wars, in which the whites were not always the aggressors, unavoidably ensued. European policy, numbers, and skill, prevailed. As the white population advanced, that of the Indians necessarily receded. The country in the immediate neighbourhood of agriculturists became unfit for them. The game fled into thicker and more unbroken forests, and the Indians followed. The soil, to which the crown originally claimed title, being no longer occupied by its ancient inhabitants, was parcelled out according to the will of the sovereign power, and taken possession of by persons who claimed immediately from the crown, or mediately, through its grantees or deputies.

That law which regulates, and ought to regulate in general, the relations between the conqueror and conquered, was incapable of application to a people under such circumstances. The resort to some new and different rule, better adapted to the actual state of things, was unavoidable. Every rule which can be suggested will be found to be attended with great difficulty.

However extravagant the pretension of converting the discovery of an inhabited country into conquest may appear; if the principle has been asserted in the first instance, and afterwards sustained; if a country has been acquired and held under it; if the property of the great mass of the community originates in it, it becomes the law of the land, and cannot be questioned. So, too, with respect to the concomitant principle, that the Indian inhabitants are to be considered merely as occupants, to be protected, indeed, while in peace, in the possession of their lands, but to be deemed incapable of transferring the absolute title to others. However this restriction may be opposed to natural right, and to the usages of civilized nations, yet, if it be indispensable to that system under which the country has been settled, and be adapted to the actual condition of the two people, it may, perhaps, be supported by reason, and certainly cannot be rejected by Courts of justice.

... After bestowing on this subject a degree of attention which was more required by the magnitude of the interest in litigation, and the able and elaborate arguments of the bar, than by its intrinsic difficulty, the Court is decidedly of opinion, that the plaintiffs do not exhibit a title which can be sustained in the Courts of the United States; and that there is no error in the judgment which was rendered against them in the District Court of Illinois.

Judgment affirmed, with costs.

Notes and Questions

1. The Court offers two separate concepts to describe why it has reached its result: **discovery** and **conquest**. What is the relationship between these concepts? Which of the concepts is more important for the resulting property ownership? Does your answer have anything to do with a distinction made in the decision between "soil" and "jurisdiction"?

2. **Wrong + Time = Right?** A rule of law founded on conquest strikes many as problematic. The case you read seems to reflect this discomfort. Does this discomfort play a role in shaping the outcome of the case? Or does it follow Blackstone's advice to "obey the laws when made, without scrutinizing too nicely into the reasons of making them"?

   Chief Justice Marshall seems almost embarrassed to confirm the "extravagant…pretension" that European discovery and conquest is not only a legitimate source of land titles in the United States, but the *only* legitimate source of such titles. But he does so anyway. Why?

   Can we think of a better justification for allocating ownership of land than the one endorsed by Marshall? What allocation rule would result from such a better justification? If we could come up with a better justified principle for allocating initial ownership of land, could we simply implement a system based on that principle tomorrow? Would that new rule apply only to unowned land or should it wipe out all old titles and reallocate ownership based on the new principle?

Does it make a difference that centuries have passed since the violent dispossession described in *Johnson v. M'Intosh*? Does the fact that a thousand years have passed since William the Conqueror make his expropriation of land from the Anglo-Saxons any less unjust? What about the five hundred years since European discovery of the Americas? The two hundred years since the British colonization of Australia? If the United States invaded an inhabited island in the Pacific Ocean tomorrow, and purported to sell to an American corporation legal title to land in that country that was in possession of natives claiming ownership under the laws of the conquered nation, would you expect the dispossessed natives to have a legal remedy? In what court?

Should the identity of the conquerers and the disposed alter our analysis? Do we look at title by conquest differently if it stems from conquests by the Ottoman Empire? Or Chinese or Indian empires?

Should we judge the legality of the actions using prevailing moral standards of the time, or those of today? And whose moral standards should prevail—those of the conquerors or those of the vanquished? Or should we interest ourselves only in the legal standards of the time? Should we respect today the legal consequences of long-ago acts that were lawful at the time, and are today viewed as manifestly immoral?

3. **Historical Injustices and Reparations.** Should there be a modern legal remedy for injuries to persons long dead, inflicted by persons long dead? Are the descendants of the wronged individuals the proper recipients of such a remedy? Should the descendants of the wrongdoers of the injury be held liable? What should happen when the lines of descent are attenuated or even cross one another?

In the United States, these are recurring issues that arise in discussions of the dispossession of Native Americans and the enslavement of kidnapped Africans and their descendants. *See, e.g.,* Ta-Nehisi Coates, *The Case for Reparations*, THE ATLANTIC (June 2014), (citing early American examples of reparations of former slaves, claiming that African-Americans continue to be injured by the discrimination they face in American society today, and arguing for a present-day comprehensive reparations program). Reparations are also the subject of philosophical, political, and legal discussion. Consider the following excerpt from Carol Rose, *The Moral Subject of Property*, 48 WM. & MARY L. REV. 1897, 1906-07 (2006) (footnotes omitted):

Property, as an institution, requires stability in people's expectations about their own and other people's claims. This is why property law has several claims-clearing devices that substitute Owner #2 for Owner #1 when the claims of Owner #1 have not been sufficiently publicized, and when most people think that Owner #2 is the true owner even though she is not. Adverse possession is a classic example of this sort of claims-clearing device.* Unfortunately, Owner #2's claims may have arisen in dubious circumstances or even through force or fraud, and that fact can undermine confidence in the entire institution. [Consider newly capitalist states] where [some of the newly wealthy] are widely regarded as the beneficiaries of insider favoritism and horrifically shady practices. Should their great wealth be recognized, simply for the sake of getting on with things and letting a modern economy unroll? Or would some kind of redistribution actually lead to greater stability?

Historic injustices create another source of unease: ... [for instance, for] numerous indigenous groups vis-à-vis the settler societies that displaced them, [or] descendants of slaves vis-à-vis the descendants of slave-owners. Settling all those scores could be hugely disruptive, and the passage of time itself makes proposed settlements morally ambiguous, because the original victims and perpetrators often are no longer on the scene. Why charge A in favor of B, when neither A nor B were personally involved in the past injustice? Moreover, settlements could leave open the origins of the displaced persons' own prior claims, as in the case of former aristocrats' plantations in East Germany. Just whom did their ancestors displace, far back in the Middle Ages? And so on back in time.

The age-old acquisition problem is not very salient to most property regimes, however, even though it bubbles hotly at the center in some locales. Issues of this kind usually become peripheral because we basically follow Blackstone's advice: we forget about the questionable origins of title. ... By forgetting about origins we can keep on acquiring, investing, trading, and generally making ourselves wealthier. The larger public good of stable claims normally outweighs the private lapses that were entailed in some of those claims. But not surprisingly, on occasion the situation is reversed: unjust acquisitions may seem so gross as to

* [*Eds.*—We will discuss adverse possession in a subsequent chapter.]

> eat away even the middle ground morality that makes property regimes possible. If you think that all those who succeed are thieves, why not be a thief yourself? That rhetorical question turns tit-for-tat practitioners into larcenists. Under such circumstances, public morality—even in quest of stability for property—could require some kind of restitutionary gesture, or at least some acknowledgment of past injustice.

For further philosophical treatments of reparations and responsibility for ancient wrongs, see George Sher, *Transgenerational Compensation*, 33 PHILOS. & PUB. AFF. 181 (2005) (attempting to justify reparations); Christopher W. Morris, *Existential Limits to the Rectification of Past Wrongs*, 21 AM. PHILOS. Q. 175 (1984) (casting doubt on the moral argument for reparations); Eric A. Posner & Adrian Vermeule, *Reparations for Slavery and Other Historical Injustices*, 103 COLUM. L. REV. 689 (2003) (addressing both philosophical and legal issues in reparations programs).

4. Is the United States' dispossession of Native Americans really an injustice that has faded into history? Professor Joseph Singer argues that American legal system continues to mistreat Native Americans by recognizing title with the poisoned roots of dispossession:

> [T]itle to land in the United States rests on the forced taking of land from first possessors – the very opposite of respect for first possession. Conquest is a mode of original acquisition that we cannot sweep under the rug by pretending that it accords with any recognizable principle of justice. And conquest, unfortunately, is where American history starts – as does the title to almost every parcel of land in the United States. This is a highly inconvenient (not to say stunningly demoralizing) fact, not least of all to the Indian nations that continue to inhabit the North American continent....
>
> Many of us protect ourselves from having to think too deeply about conquest by distancing ourselves from it. … If we can relegate conquest to the distant past, we can concentrate instead on the fact that the United States was founded on respect for property rights. We do not acquire property by conquest today.
>
> This comforting story is misleading at best and false at worst. We cannot comfort ourselves with the idea that conquest became a thing of the past with the American Revolution, independence from Great Britain, and the adoption of the U.S. Constitution.

Joseph William Singer, *Original Acquisition of Property: From Conquest & Possession to Democracy & Equal Opportunity*, 86 IND. L.J. 763, 766-67 (2011) (reproduced with permission of the author). Professor Singer adds, *id.* at 767-68, that most of the federal government's dispossession of Native American land occurred during the 19th century. During the early 20th century—while the Supreme Court was gaining a reputation for striking down state economic legislation in the name of protecting freedom of contract and private property (the so-called "*Lochner* era"[21])—the United States government forcibly took two-thirds of the remaining lands of the Indian nations. The Supreme Court held in 1955 that Alaska natives possessed merely a license to live on the land—revocable permission from the state to occupy Alaskan territory. As recently as 2009, the Supreme Court held that the Navajo Nation had no right to sue the federal government for damages where the Secretary of the Interior was alleged to have colluded with a mining company to undercompensate the tribe for mining rights on lands held under "joint title" between the Navajo and the United States (by law, the Secretary must approve any leases of tribal land for mining purposes). *United States v. Navajo Nation*, 556 U.S. 287 (2009).

Mabo v. Queensland (No. 2) ["Mabo's Case"]

High Court of Australia, (1992) 175 C.L.R. 1

BRENNAN J.

The Murray Islands lie in the Torres Strait, at about 10 degrees S. Latitude and 144 degrees E. Longitude. They are the easternmost of the Eastern Islands of the Strait. Their total land area is of the order of 9 square kilometres. The biggest is Mer (known also as Murray Island), oval in shape about 2.79 kms long and about 1.65 kms across. … The people who were in occupation of these Islands before first European contact and who have continued to occupy those Islands to the present day are known as the Meriam people. … The Meriam people of today retain a strong sense of affiliation with their forbears and with the society and culture of earlier times. They have a strong sense of identity with their Islands. The plaintiffs are members of the Meriam people. In this case, the legal rights of the members of the Meriam people to the land of the Murray Islands are in question.

… It may be assumed that on 1 August 1879 the Meriam people knew nothing of the events in Westminster and in Brisbane that effected the annexation of the Murray Islands and their

---

[21] Lochner v. New York, 198 U.S. 45 (1905).

incorporation into Queensland and that, had the Meriam people been told of the Proclamation [of annexation] made in Brisbane on 21 July 1879, they would not have appreciated its significance. The legal consequences of these events are in issue in this case. Oversimplified, the chief question in this case is whether these transactions had the effect on 1 August 1879 of vesting in the Crown absolute ownership of, legal possession of and exclusive power to confer title to, all land in the Murray Islands. The defendant submits that that was the legal consequence of the Letters Patent and of the events which brought them into effect. If that submission be right, the Queen took the land occupied by Meriam people on 1 August 1879 without their knowing of the expropriation; they were no longer entitled without the consent of the Crown to continue to occupy the land they had occupied for centuries past.

...In discharging its duty to declare the common law of Australia, this Court is not free to adopt rules that accord with contemporary notions of justice and human rights if their adoption would fracture the skeleton of principle which gives the body of our law its shape and internal consistency. Australian law is not only the historical successor of, but is an organic development from, the law of England. Although our law is the prisoner of its history, it is not now bound by decisions of courts in the hierarchy of an Empire then concerned with the development of its colonies.... It is not possible, a priori, to distinguish between cases that express a skeletal principle and those which do not, but no case can command unquestioning adherence if the rule it expresses seriously offends the values of justice and human rights (especially equality before the law) which are aspirations of the contemporary Australian legal system. If a postulated rule of the common law expressed in earlier cases seriously offends those contemporary values, the question arises whether the rule should be maintained and applied. Whenever such a question arises, it is necessary to assess whether the particular rule is an essential doctrine of our legal system and whether, if the rule were to be overturned, the disturbance to be apprehended would be disproportionate to the benefit flowing from the overturning.

... International law [at the time of colonization of Australia by Britain] recognized conquest, cession, and occupation of territory that was *terra nullius* as three of the effective ways of acquiring sovereignty.... Various justifications for the acquisition of sovereignty over the territory of "backward peoples" were advanced. The benefits of Christianity and European civilization had been seen as a sufficient justification from mediaeval times. Another justification for the application of the theory of *terra nullius* to inhabited territory—a justification first advanced by Vattel at the end of the 18th century—was that new territories could be claimed by occupation if the land were uncultivated, for Europeans had a right to bring lands into production if they were left uncultivated by the indigenous inhabitants.

... The fiction by which the rights and interests of indigenous inhabitants in land were treated as non-existent was justified by a policy which has no place in the contemporary law of this country.... Whatever the justification advanced in earlier days for refusing to recognize the rights and interests in land of the indigenous inhabitants of settled colonies, an unjust and discriminatory doctrine of that kind can no longer be accepted.... It is contrary both to international standards and to the fundamental values of our common law to entrench a discriminatory rule which, because of the supposed position on the scale of social organization of the indigenous inhabitants of a settled colony, denies them a right to occupy their traditional lands. It was such a rule which evoked from Deane J.[, in] Gerhardy v. Brown (1985) 159 CLR 70, at p. 149[,] the criticism that—

"the common law of this land has still not reached the stage of retreat from injustice which the law of Illinois and Virginia had reached in 1823 when Marshall C.J., in Johnson v. McIntosh, accepted that, subject to the assertion of ultimate dominion (including the power to convey title by grant) by the State, the 'original inhabitants' should be recognized as having 'a legal as well as just claim' to retain the occupancy of their traditional lands".

However, recognition by our common law of the rights and interests in land of the indigenous inhabitants of a settled colony would be precluded if the recognition were to fracture a skeletal principle of our legal system....

The land law of England is based on the doctrine of tenure. In English legal theory, every parcel of land in England is held either mediately or immediately of the King who is the Lord Paramount; the term "tenure" is used to signify the relationship between tenant and lord, not the relationship between tenant and land.... When the Crown acquired territory outside England which was to be subject to the common law, there was a natural assumption that the doctrine of tenure should be the basis of the land law. Perhaps the assumption did not have to be made....

By attributing to the Crown a radical title* to all land within a territory over which the Crown has assumed sovereignty, the common law enabled the Crown, in exercise of its sovereign power, to grant an interest in land to be held of the Crown or to acquire land for the Crown's

* [Eds.—"Radical title" is a subtle and unsettled concept; it may refer here to the common-law principle that the government—i.e., the crown—is the ultimate source of property rights in land within the territory subject to its jurisdiction.]

demesne. ... But it is not a corollary of the Crown's acquisition of a radical title to land in an occupied territory that the Crown acquired absolute beneficial ownership of that land to the exclusion of the indigenous inhabitants.... Nor is it necessary to the structure of our legal system to refuse recognition to the rights and interests in land of the indigenous inhabitants....

Recognition of the radical title of the Crown is quite consistent with recognition of native title to land, for the radical title, without more, is merely a logical postulate required to support the doctrine of tenure (when the Crown has exercised its sovereign power to grant an interest in land) and to support the plenary title of the Crown (when the Crown has exercised its sovereign power to appropriate to itself ownership of parcels of land within the Crown's territory). Unless the sovereign power is exercised in one or other of those ways, there is no reason why land within the Crown's territory should not continue to be subject to native title. It is only the fallacy of equating sovereignty and beneficial ownership of land that gives rise to the notion that native title is extinguished by the acquisition of sovereignty.

.... The ownership of land within a territory in the exclusive occupation of a people must be vested in that people: land is susceptible of ownership, and there are no other owners.... Of course, since European settlement of Australia, many clans or groups of indigenous people have been physically separated from their traditional land and have lost their connexion with it. But that is not the universal position. It is clearly not the position of the Meriam people. Where a clan or group has continued to acknowledge the laws and (so far as practicable) to observe the customs based on the traditions of that clan or group, whereby their traditional connexion with the land has been substantially maintained, the traditional community title of that clan or group can be said to remain in existence. The common law can, by reference to the traditional laws and customs of an indigenous people, identify and protect the native rights and interests to which they give rise. However, when the tide of history has washed away any real acknowledgment of traditional law and any real observance of traditional customs, the foundation of native title has disappeared. A native title which has ceased with the abandoning of laws and customs based on tradition cannot be revived for contemporary recognition. ... Once traditional native title expires, the Crown's radical title expands to a full beneficial title, for then there is no other proprietor than the Crown.

It follows that a right or interest possessed as a native title cannot be acquired from an indigenous people by one who, not being a member of the indigenous people, does not acknowledge their laws and observe their customs; nor can such a right or interest be acquired by a clan, group or member of the indigenous people unless the acquisition is consistent with the laws and customs of that people. Such a right or interest can be acquired outside those laws and customs only by the Crown.

... Sovereignty carries the power to create and to extinguish private rights and interests in land within the Sovereign's territory. It follows that, on a change of sovereignty, rights and interests in land that may have been indefeasible under the old regime become liable to extinction by exercise of the new sovereign power. The sovereign power may or may not be exercised with solicitude for the welfare of indigenous inhabitants but, in the case of common law countries, the courts cannot review the merits, as distinct from the legality, of the exercise of sovereign power. ... However, the exercise of a power to extinguish native title must reveal a clear and plain intention to do so, whether the action be taken by the Legislature or by the Executive.... A Crown grant which vests in the grantee an interest in land which is inconsistent with the continued right to enjoy a native title in respect of the same land necessarily extinguishes the native title.... Where the Crown grants land in trust or reserves and dedicates land for a public purpose, the question whether the Crown has revealed a clear and plain intention to extinguish native title will sometimes be a question of fact, sometimes a question of law and sometimes a mixed question of fact and law. Thus, if a reservation is made for a public purpose other than for the benefit of the indigenous inhabitants, a right to continued enjoyment of native title may be consistent with the specified purpose - at least for a time - and native title will not be extinguished. But if the land is used and occupied for the public purpose and the manner of occupation is inconsistent with the continued enjoyment of native title, native title will be extinguished. ... [W]here the Crown has not granted interests in land or reserved and dedicated land inconsistently with the right to continued enjoyment of native title by the indigenous inhabitants, native title survives and is legally enforceable.

[The Court declared that the Murray Islands are not crown lands, that the Meriam people were entitled to "possession, occupation, use and enjoyment" of the island of Mer (excluding certain parcels leased or physically used by the Australian, provincial, or local governments), and that the Meriam people's right to Mer is subject to the power of the Queensland government to extinguish it by law.]

MASON C.J. and McHUGH J.

We agree with the reasons for judgment of Brennan J. and with the declaration which he proposes.

In the result, six [out of seven] members of the Court (Dawson J. dissenting) are in agreement that the common law of this country recognizes a form of native title which, in the cases where it has not been extinguished, reflects the entitlement of the indigenous inhabitants, in accordance with their laws or customs, to their traditional lands and that, subject to the effect of some particular Crown leases, the land entitlement of the Murray Islanders in accordance with their laws or customs is preserved, as native title, under the law of Queensland. The main difference between those members of the Court who constitute the majority is that, … neither of us nor Brennan J. agrees with the conclusion to be drawn from the judgments of Deane, Toohey and Gaudron JJ. that, at least in the absence of clear and unambiguous statutory provision to the contrary, extinguishment of native title by the Crown by inconsistent grant is wrongful and gives rise to a claim for compensatory damages. We note that the judgment of Dawson J. supports the conclusion of Brennan J. and ourselves on that aspect of the case since his Honour considers that native title, where it exists, is a form of permissive occupancy at the will of the Crown.

We are authorized to say that the other members of the Court agree with what is said in the preceding paragraph about the outcome of the case.

[Opinions of Toohey and Gaudron JJ. and Dawson J. omitted.]

Notes and Questions

1. A system of land ownership founded on violent conquest strikes us as arbitrary and unjustifiable today. Both cases you read seem to reflect this view in their rhetoric. But do they implement such a view in their dispositions of the claims before them? Or do they follow Blackstone's advice to "obey the laws when made, without scrutinizing too nicely into the reasons of making them"?

2. Chief Justice Marshall reluctantly confirms the "extravagant…pretension" that European discovery and conquest is not only a legitimate source of land titles in the United States, but the *only* legitimate source of such titles.

   Justice Brennan is even more forceful, finding the European doctrine of acquisition by discovery "an unjust and discriminatory doctrine of that kind can no longer be accepted." But is the rule he announces any different than the rule of *Johnson v. M'Intosh*? If so, how?

   Note that the major split between the Justices in *Mabo* was not over the *existence* of native title, but on its scope. Three (of seven) Justices would have held that "If common law native title is wrongfully extinguished by the Crown, … compensatory damages can be recovered provided the proceedings for recovery are instituted within the period allowed by applicable limitations provisions," and that extinguishment by inconsistent grant in the absence of an Act of Parliament is wrongful. Opinion of Toohey and Gaudron JJ., ¶ 64-65. We will consider how the passage of time can affect an owner's ability to assert their rights in our units on Found and Stolen Property and on Adverse Possession.

C. *Ratione Soli* and Fugitive Resources: Chattels and Land

1. Wild Animals on Owned Land

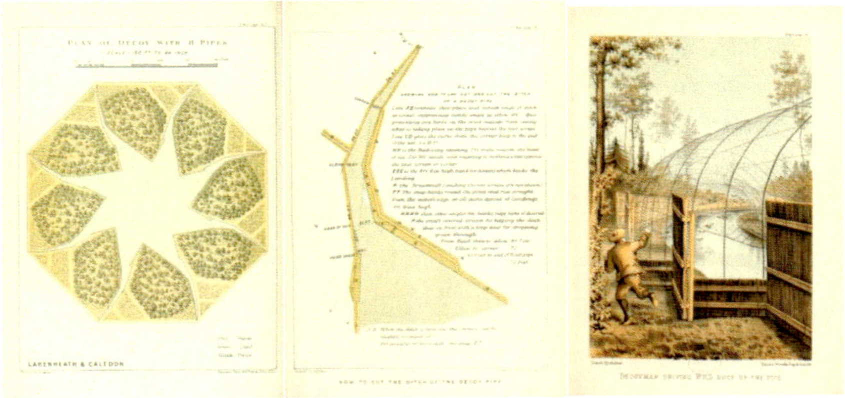

Source: RALPH PAYNE-GALLWEY, THE BOOK OF DUCK DECOYS 34, 36, 166 (1886), *available at* *https://archive.org/details/bookofduckdecoysx00payn*

Keeble v. Hickeringill
(1707) 103 Eng. Rep. 1127, 11 East 574 (Q.B.)

Action upon the case. Plaintiff declares that he was, 8th November in the second year of the Queen, lawfully possessed of a close of land called Minott's Meadow, [where he maintained] a decoy pond, to which divers wildfowl used to resort and come: and the plaintiff had at his own costs and charges prepared and procured divers decoy ducks, nets, machines and other engines for the decoying and taking of the wildfowl, and enjoyed the benefit in taking them: the defendant, knowing which, and intending to damnify the plaintiff in his vivary, and to fright and drive away the wildfowl used to resort thither, and deprive him of his profit, did, on the 8th of November, resort to the head of the said pond and vivary, and did discharge six guns laden with gunpowder, and with the noise and stink of the gunpowder did drive away the wildfowl then being in the pond: and on the 11th and 12th days of November the defendant, with design to damnify the plaintiff, and fright away the wildfowl, did place himself with a gun near the vivary, and there did discharge the said gun several times that was then charged with the gunpowder against the said decoy pond, whereby the wildfowl were frighted away, and did forsake the said pond. Upon not guilty pleaded, a verdict was found for the plaintiff and 20*l*. damages.

HOLT C.J.

I am of opinion that this action doth lie. It seems to be new in its instance, but is not new in the reason or principle of it. For, 1st, this using or making a decoy is lawful. 2dly, this employment of his ground to that use is profitable to the plaintiff, as is the skill and management of that employment. As to the first, every man that hath a property may employ it for his pleasure and profit, as for alluring and procuring decoy ducks to come to his pond. … Then when a man useth his art or his skill to take them, to sell and dispose of for his profit; this is his trade; and he that hinders another in his trade or livelihood is liable to an action for so hindering him….

[W]here a violent or malicious act is done to a man's occupation, profession, or way of getting a livelihood; there an action lies in all cases. But if a man doth him damage by using the same employment; as if Mr. Hickeringill had set up another decoy on his own ground near the plaintiff's, and that had spoiled the custom of the plaintiff, no action would lie, because he had as much liberty to make and use a decoy as the plaintiff. This is like the case of 11 H. 4, 47. One schoolmaster sets up a new school to the damage of an antient school, and thereby the scholars are allured from the old school to come to his new. (The action was held there not to lie.) But suppose Mr. Hickeringill should lie in the way with his guns, and fright the boys from going to school, and their parents would not let them go thither; sure that schoolmaster might have an action for the loss of his scholars. ...

There was an objection that did occur to me, though I do not remember it to be made at the Bar; which is, that it is not mentioned in the declaration what number or nature of wildfowl were frighted away by the defendant's shooting. … Where a man brings trespass for taking his goods, he must declare of the quantity, because he, by having had the possession, may know what he had, and therefore must know what he lost. … The plaintiff in this case brings his action for the apparent injury done him in the use of that employment of his freehold, his art, and skill, that he uses thereby. … And when we do know that of long time in the kingdom these artificial contrivances of decoy ponds and decoy ducks have been used for enticing into those ponds wildfowl, in order to be taken for the profit of the owner of the pond, who is at the expence of servants, engines, and other management, whereby the markets of the nation may be furnished; there is great reason to give encouragement thereunto; that the people who are so instrumental by their skill and industry so to furnish the markets should reap the benefit and have their action. But, in short, that which is the true reason is that this action is not brought to recover damage for the loss of the fowl, but for the disturbance.

Notes and Questions

1. What was Keeble suing Hickeringill for, and why did he prevail? Was his claim a property claim? (A related question: what is an "[a]ction on the case"? Did you look it up?) If a

property claim, what was the *res*—the thing that Keeble claimed as his property? If not a property claim, what might this case be doing in your Property casebook?

2. Whether *Keeble* is a property case or not, where did the 20£ damages measure come from?

3. You may recall that *Keeble* was discussed by Justice Tompkins in *Pierson v. Post*, though not by name. Justice Tompkins referred to different **reports** of the case than the one you read. The existence of multiple, sometimes conflicting, reports is fairly common for earlier English cases and even for some early American cases. In earlier days, judges would announce their opinions from the bench, and **reporters**—usually entrepreneurial lawyers—would take notes of these opinions (often along with the arguments of counsel), collect them, and publish them as a reference for the bar. These days judges issue written opinions, which are collected and published in "official" reporters as written. But for earlier cases, the content of a precedential authority depended on the transcription of the reporter, and reporters could be unreliable. The Modern King's Bench ("Mod.") and Salkeld ("Salk.") reports cited by Justice Tompkins are today believed to be less reliable than the East report you just read, which the reporter claimed to have based on a copy of Lord Chief Justice Holt's own manuscript. Unfortunately for Justice Tompkins, the East report of *Keeble* was not published until 1815 (ten years after *Pierson*). Had this report been available to the New York Supreme Court in 1805, do you think *Pierson* would have come out differently?

Fisher v. Steward
1 Smith 60 (New Hampshire, 1804)

Trover for a swarm of bees. There was a second count for two hundred pounds of honey in the comb.

The case was, the plaintiffs found a swarm of bees in a tree on the (defendant's) land in Claremont, marked the tree, and notified the defendant, who cut down the tree, September, 1803, and converted the honey to his own use. …

At the trial there was some dispute whether the plaintiffs or one of the defendant's family first discovered the bees, and whether the plaintiffs gave notice of the finding and marking the tree. The other parts of the case were proved.

The Court summed up, and observed that two questions had been made on the trial: first, whether the plaintiffs first discovered the bees; and, secondly, supposing they did, whether the property in the honey was in them.

The first is a question of evidence proper for the consideration of the jury.

The second is a question of law, and one about which the Court entertained no doubt.

The plaintiffs do not pretend to have any property in the land or in the tree, nor had they any property in the bees. How then came they by a property in the honey? It must have been by occupancy. But how did they occupy, or appropriate the honey to themselves? They saw the bees enter the tree, they heard them make a noise near the tree, and they marked the tree. The two first gave no right; they do not amount to occupancy. The marking of the tree was a trespass, and consequently can avail the plaintiffs nothing. The doctrine contended for by plaintiffs is injurious to the rights of property. Till the bees occupied the tree in question, it is not pretended that plaintiffs had any right in it. What gave them a right? Having seen a swarm of bees, in which they had no property, occupying it? This circumstance, whether the effect of accident, or the result of labor and skill, cannot lessen the rights of the owner of the soil. Will it be pretended that plaintiffs thereby acquired a right to the tree? If they acquired a title to the honey, they must necessarily have a right to take it away, to cut down the tree, to pass over the defendant's land for the purpose, & c. Admitting the plaintiffs could acquire property in a swarm of bees, or in the honey, by finding, in some cases, they could not do so in the present case, because such right or property interferes with the rights and property clearly vested in defendant; it is inconsistent with it; it lessens its value at least. It is much more consonant to our ideas of property to say, that the bees and honey in the defendant's trees belong to him in the same manner and for the same reasons as all mines and minerals belong to the owner of the soil.

Will it be pretended by the plaintiffs that they could have put, without defendant's permission, a swarm of bees into defendant's tree, and there kept them till they had made honey; and then, in case he cut down the tree, maintained trespass for the cutting, or trover for the honey?

One would suppose the present case was not stronger than that; here they had no right to the bees.

It has been said, that, by the usage of this part of the State, the person who finds bees acquires a property in them wherever found. We recognize no such usage. We have no local customs or usages which are binding in one part of the State and not in another. If this be the law here, it must be so in every other part of the State.

Verdict for defendant.

A Note on Ratione Soli

Lord Holt, who decided *Keeble*, is also a key—if perhaps slightly confusing—expositor of the related and peculiarly English doctrine of *ratione soli* (Latin for "by reason of the soil"), also referred to in *Pierson*. *Ratione soli* is the principle that the exclusive right to take possession of wild animals belongs to the owner of the land where the animal may be found; thus title to any animals captured or killed on owned land automatically vests in the landowner. The English rule is in stark opposition to the civil (i.e., Roman) law rule, reflected in the Institutes of Justinian,[22] which is that the captor of a wild animal acquires property rights in the animal wherever captured, though he may be liable in trespass to the owner of the real property on which the animal was pursued or taken. This distinction affects not only the right to possession of the animal itself, but also the measure of damages, because the damages from the trespass may be less than the value of the animal.

A strong principle of *ratione soli* was consolidated in mid-19th century England as part of the class wars between the landed gentry—who passionately defended game hunting as an exclusive sport for the aristocracy—and the upwardly-mobile merchant classes and more desperate farmers and poachers—who saw game as a token of luxury and a means of sustenance, respectively. *See generally* Chester Kirby, *The English Game Law System*, 38 AM. HIST. REV. 240 (1933). The aristocrats won a decisive victory in a suit by a game merchant against certain servants of the Marquis of Exeter, who had forcibly seized several dozen rabbits purchased by the merchant for resale, on grounds that they had been poached from the Marquis's lands. Blades v. Higgs, (1865) 11 Eng. Rep. 1474, 11 H.L.Cas. 621. The Law Lords ruled that wild animals are the property of the owner of the land on which they are taken, and that the Marquis's servants were therefore within their rights in repossessing the rabbits.

Ratione soli was initially rejected by the newly independent American states, in favor of a rule of "free taking." This made some sense in the America of John Locke's imagination: a vast, naturally bountiful, largely undeveloped, and sparsely populated continent. Moreover, "[i]n the

[22] J. INST. 2.1.12. The *Institutes* are a portion of the massive codification of Roman law under Byzantine (Roman) Emperor Justinian I: the *Corpus Iuris Civilis*. The *Corpus*, in turn, is an important predecessor of most modern civil law systems, which prevail in Continental European nations and many of their former colonies. Unlike common-law systems, which prevail in England and most of its former colonies (including the United States, with the exception of Louisiana), legal authority in civil law systems derives not from caselaw, but from comprehensive statutory codes. A primary distinction between common law and civil law systems is the sharply diminished role of precedent in civil law adjudication. (Recall note 2 on page 94, *supra*.)

New World, game was no sporting matter, but rather a source of food and clothing." Thomas A. Lund, *Early American Wildlife Law*, 51 N.Y.U. L. REV. 703 (1976). Thus, for the first century of the new Republic's life, landowners for the most part enjoyed no special privileges to wild animals on their otherwise idle land; hunters were presumed to be free to enter or cross unenclosed and undeveloped land in pursuit of game, even where that land was privately owned. Landowners could defeat this presumption by posting notices of their intent to exclude hunters at the boundaries of their property, but in practice posting was uncommon and generally ineffective for large holdings in the wilds of the frontier. *Id.* at 712-14.

Eventually, a small number of American cases adopted *ratione soli* (*see, e.g.*, Rexroth v. Coon, 23 A. 37 (R.I. 1885) (bees); Schulte v. Warren, 75 N.E. 783 (Ill. 1905) (fish)), but most American jurisdictions rejected the English rule of *ratione soli*. Additionally, a majority of states still allow licensed hunters to take or pursue game on unenclosed private land unless the landowner has posted against hunting or trespassing. Mark R. Sigman, Note, *Hunting and Posting on Private Land in America*, 54 DUKE L. J. 549, 558-68 (2004). (Today, wild animals are subject to a variety of state and federal regulations that fairly comprehensively govern whether, when, and under what circumstances they may be hunted or captured. *See generally* Michael C. Blumm & Lucus Ritchie, *The Pioneer Spirit and the Public Trust: The American Rule of Capture and State Ownership of Wildlife*, 35 ENVIRON. L. 673 (2005).)

One possible virtue of the doctrine of *ratione soli* is the same as the virtue of the punitive damages awards (discussed later): it may marginally discourage trespasses on land by those who would trespass for the purpose of capturing wild animals. But at what cost? And do we really need *ratione soli* when punitive damages are already available against trespassers? Or when, as *Keeble* makes clear, there are other legal remedies available against those who interfere with landowners' efforts to exploit wild animals on their land? Is there any other principled justification for either *ratione soli* or free taking, or are the rules merely sops to particular political interests? In light of all this history, what do you think *ought* to be the legal rights of landowners with respect to wild animals that happen to be on their land? Why? Is there any reason landowners should have a superior claim to anyone else?

2. Other Fugitive Resources: Oil, and Gas

We have studied a fair number of cases about property rights in wild animals. By now you may be asking yourself: who cares? This is, after all, an area of legal doctrine that you will almost certainly never encounter in your future career as a lawyer. Are we wasting your time?

Obviously we don't think so. We would offer two related reasons for studying this area of law:

First: The study of these cases has introduced you to some accessible illustrations of how we might *justify* rules for allocating control over scarce resources among competing claimants. We have already seen several justifications for the rules we have studied—moral reasons, economic reasons, reasons grounded in administrability and in other pragmatic concerns. (See Section A, Note 1, *supra.*) These are the types of justifications that move courts and policymakers, and they are the kinds of justifications that lawyers must invoke in crafting legal arguments and explaining legal rules to their clients.

Second: It is sometimes said that "the law is a seamless web." One influential interpretation of this principle, offered by legal philosopher Ronald Dworkin, is that common-law judges must attempt to decide cases by reference to "a scheme of abstract and concrete principles that provides a coherent justification for all common law precedent." Ronald Dworkin, *Hard Cases*, 88 HARV. L. REV. 1057, 1094 (1975). That is to say that a legal system's rules should not only be *justified* according to discernable principles, they should be *coherent:* the principles that justify an outcome in one area of law should apply consistently to other areas of law to the extent possible. Thus, when deciding novel cases, common-law judges will have to infer what principles are consistent with—or *fit*—the entire corpus of cases that have been decided before, decide which among those principles best *justifies* the cases, and use that principle as a guide in deciding the novel case.

At a more practical level, lawyers typically reason about novel cases by *analogy* to past cases in the same general doctrinal field. The common-law treatment of precedent is a special case of this more general principle. Thus, even though we don't see many cases involving disputes over wild animals anymore, past judicial resolutions of those disputes will inform how we decide disputes over other resources that are similar in some way. We have seen this type of reasoning by analogy already, in *Popov v. Hayashi:* a baseball is not a wild animal, but Judge McCarthy thought cases about wild animals provided instruction for the dispute before him. (Query: Why might he have thought so?) With respect to the intersection of land and chattels, we can similarly see *Keeble* and the doctrines of *ratione soli* and free taking as reflecting principles applicable to *fugitive resources:* chattels that can move of their own accord from place to place, sometimes taking them onto owned land. There are plenty of valuable resources that share this quality, and many of them are the subject of heated legal disputes even today. We will focus here on two: water and oil, beginning with oil.

Consider the following summary of how the law responded to demand for this scarce resource when it suddenly became economically important.

Briggs v. Southwestern Energy Production Company
224 A.3d 334 (Pa. 2020)

CHIEF JUSTICE SAYLOR

In this appeal by allowance, we consider whether the rule of capture immunizes an energy developer from liability in trespass, where the developer uses hydraulic fracturing on the property it owns or leases, and such activities allow it to obtain oil or gas that migrates from beneath the surface of another person's land.

I. BACKGROUND

A. The rule of capture

Oil and gas are minerals, and while in place they are considered part of the land. They differ from coal and other substances with a fixed situs in that they are fugacious in nature – meaning they tend to seep or flow across property lines beneath the surface of the earth. Such underground movement is known as "drainage." Drainage stems from a physical property of fluids in that they naturally move across a pressure gradient from high to low pressure. Indeed, the extraction of oil or gas by drilling is based, at least in part, on creating a low-pressure pathway from the mineral's subterranean location to the earth's surface.

Oil and gas have thus been described as having a "fugitive and wandering existence," *Brown v. Vandergrift*, 80 Pa. 142, 147 (Pa. 1875), and have been compared to wild animals which move about from one property to another. *See Westmoreland & Cambria Nat. Gas Co. v. DeWitt*, 130 Pa. 235, 249, 18 A. 724, 725 (1889) ("In common with animals, and unlike other minerals, [oil, gas, and water] have the power and the tendency to escape without the volition of the owner."). Accordingly, such minerals are subject to the rule of capture, which is

> [a] fundamental principle of oil-and-gas law holding that there is no liability for drainage of oil and gas from under the lands of another so long as there has been no trespass ....

BLACK'S LAW DICTIONARY 1358 (8th ed. 2004)); *accord Brown v. Spilman*, 155 U.S. 665, 669-70, 15 S. Ct. 245, 247, 39 L.Ed. 304 (1895).[1] A corollary to this rule is that an aggrieved property owner's remedy for the loss, through drainage, of subsurface oil or gas has traditionally been to offset the effects of the developer's well by drilling his or her own well, often termed an "offset well." *See Barnard v. Monongahela Gas Co.*, 216 Pa. 362, 365, 65 A. 801, 803 (1907) ("What then can the neighbor do? Nothing; only go and do likewise.").

The reference to "the lands of another" in the above quote does not suggest a developer may invade the subsurface area of a neighboring property by drilling at an angle rather than vertically (referred to as slant drilling or slant wells), or by drilling horizontally beneath the surface. This is because the title holder of a parcel of land generally owns everything directly beneath the surface. Rather, and as suggested by the "no trespass" predicate, it refers to the potential for oil and gas to migrate from the plaintiff's property to the developer's land when extracted from a common pool or reservoir spanning both parcels.

B. Hydraulic fracturing

One of the central questions in this matter involves how these principles apply where hydraulic fracturing is used to extract oil or gas from subsurface geological formations. According to the federal government, hydraulic fracturing is used in "unconventional" gas production. "Unconventional" reservoirs can cost-effectively produce gas only by using a special stimulation technique, like hydraulic fracturing .... This is often because the gas is highly dispersed in the rock, rather than occurring in a concentrated underground location. United States Environmental Protection Agency (the "EPA"), *The Process of Unconventional Natural Gas Production*, https://www.epa.gov/uog/process-unconventional-natural-gas-production (viewed Oct. 22, 2019). In terms of how the technique works, the EPA continues:

> Fractures are created by pumping large quantities of fluids at high pressure down a wellbore and into the target rock formation. Hydraulic fracturing fluid commonly consists of water, proppant and chemical additives that open and enlarge fractures within the rock formation. These fractures can extend several hundred feet away from the wellbore. The proppants – sand, ceramic pellets or other small incompressible particles – hold open the newly created fractures.

Id.

---

[1] The term "capture" is also drawn from an analogy to wild animals. At common law, a person could acquire title to such an animal by reducing it to possession.

After injection, fluid is withdrawn from the well while leaving the proppants in place to hold the fissures open. This enhances the drainage of oil or gas into the wellbore where it can be captured.

C. Factual and procedural history of this case

(i) Introduction

The parties presently favor essentially the same rule of law: they both, in substance, argue that the traditional rule of capture should apply, subject to the common-law standard for trespass of real property based on physical intrusion onto another's land. Each party, moreover, depicts the other as erroneously suggesting that an exception to this framework should pertain where hydraulic fracturing is used to obtain oil or natural gas. In particular, the plaintiffs suggest that Southwestern wishes to convert the rule of capture into a precept whereby energy developers may physically invade the property of others to capture natural gas so long as they are using hydraulic fracturing. For its part, Southwestern portrays the plaintiffs and the Superior Court decision from which it appeals as positing that the rule of capture simply does not apply when hydraulic fracturing is used for energy development on one's own land.

(ii) Undisputed facts

Adam, Paula, Joshua, and Sarah Briggs ("Plaintiffs") own a parcel of real estate consisting of approximately eleven acres in Harford Township, Susquehanna County. During all relevant times, Plaintiffs have not leased their property to any entity for natural gas production. Plaintiffs' property is adjacent to a tract of land leased by Appellant Southwestern Energy Production Company for natural gas extraction (the "Production Parcel"). Southwestern maintains wellbores on the Production Parcel and has used hydraulic fracturing to boost natural gas extraction from the Marcellus Shale formation through those wellbores.

(iii) Proceedings before the Court of Common Pleas

In November 2015, Plaintiffs commenced an action against Southwestern in which they stated two causes of action, trespass and conversion. In Count I (the trespass claim), Plaintiffs averred that Southwestern's actions constituted a trespass which deprived Plaintiffs of the value of the "natural gas extracted from under their land[.]"In Count II (the conversion claim), Plaintiffs alleged that, through its drilling activities, Southwestern had deprived Plaintiffs of their possession and use of the natural gas and converted it to Southwestern's use. Notably, Plaintiffs did not expressly allege that Southwestern's activities had caused a physical intrusion into Plaintiffs' property.

Southwestern filed a responsive pleading denying it had extracted gas from Plaintiffs' land and denying it had trespassed upon Plaintiffs' property or converted their natural gas. Southwestern specifically denied it had drilled underneath Plaintiffs' property and stated, further, that it had "only drilled for oil, gas or minerals from under properties for which [Southwestern] has leases."

After the parties engaged in discovery, Southwestern filed a motion for summary judgment and a supporting brief in which it argued that it did not physically invade Plaintiffs' property and, to the extent that it had recovered any gas through drainage from that property to the Production Parcel, again, it was entitled to judgment as a matter of law under the rule of capture. Plaintiffs ... filed their own motion for partial summary judgment as to liability, asserting that courts should not apply the rule of capture in circumstances where gas has been captured through the use of hydraulic fracturing.

By order and opinion, the common pleas court granted Southwestern's motion for summary judgment, and denied Plaintiffs' motion for partial summary judgment.... Plaintiffs filed a notice of appeal, ... in which they raised a single issue: whether the trial court erred in determining that the rule of capture precluded liability under theories of trespass and conversion, where Southwestern had used hydraulic fracturing to obtain natural gas which originated under Plaintiffs' land.

(iv) Proceedings before the Superior Court

A two-judge panel of the Superior Court reversed in a published decision....The court noted, however, that the record did not indicate whether Southwestern's operations had resulted in a subsurface intrusion into Plaintiffs' property, going so far as to express that "[t]here does not appear to be *any evidence, or even an estimate*, as to how far the subsurface fractures extend from each of the wellbore [sic] on Southwestern's lease." ... Accordingly, the panel reversed the trial court's order and remanded for additional factual development.

...[T]he Superior Court panel's analysis can reasonably be viewed as embodying two distinct, but interrelated, holdings: first, that whenever "artificial means," such as hydraulic fracturing, are used to stimulate the flow of underground resources, the rule of capture does not apply because drainage does not occur through the operation of "natural agencies," and second, that in this particular case summary judgment was premature in light of certain unspecified allegations relating to cross-boundary intrusions into Plaintiffs' land.

II. PRELIMINARY DISCUSSION

A. Trespass

In Pennsylvania, a trespass occurs when a person who is not privileged to do so intrudes upon land in possession of another, whether willfully or by mistake. This conception of trespass is not disputed by the parties. Nevertheless, meaningful appellate review at this stage is not straightforward for multiple reasons.

B. Pleading deficiencies, decisional irregularities, and issue limitation

… Plaintiffs did not assert … in their pleadings … that Southwestern had effectuated a physical intrusion onto (or into) their property. The Superior Court panel recognized this aspect of Plaintiffs' litigation position, but raised and resolved, *sua sponte*, an issue based on the opposite premise, that Plaintiffs *had* alleged a physical intrusion. Then, stating that there was no record evidence that such an intrusion had taken place, and without referencing any specific aspect of the pleadings, the panel indicated that the Complaint's allegations were alone sufficient to raise a genuine issue of fact so as to preclude summary judgment.

This is in some tension with the governing summary-judgment standard which generally centers on whether the adverse party has produced enough evidence to raise a question of material fact as to each element of the claim.

… [M]oreover, Southwestern articulated the issue for this Court's consideration in terms of whether the rule of capture should be applied in the same manner it has always been applied: to allow for the capture of oil and gas which merely drains from an adjacent property after the completion of a well using hydraulic fracturing *solely within the developer's property*. This is an issue, again, on which the parties do not presently diverge: they both answer in the affirmative. Their disagreement is limited to whether any physical intrusion has taken place – a question that is not fairly subsumed within the issue framed for our review.

III. ANALYSIS

The issue as stated by Southwestern should nonetheless be resolved for purposes of this dispute – and to provide guidance to the bench and bar – because at least part of the Superior Court's opinion can reasonably be construed as setting forth a *per se* rule foreclosing application of the rule of capture in hydraulic fracturing scenarios, and that rule rests on faulty assumptions. In particular, and most saliently, the panel appears to have indicated that one litmus for whether the rule of capture applies is whether the defendant's gas extraction methodology relies only on the natural drainage of oil or gas within a conventional pool or reservoir, or whether instead those methods utilize some means of artificial stimulation to induce drainage.

The Superior Court's position in this respect logically rests on one of two grounds: (a) the act of artificially stimulating the cross-boundary flow through the use of hydraulic fracturing solely on the developer's property in and of itself renders the rule of capture inapplicable; or (b) as Plaintiffs argue, any time natural gas migrates across property lines resulting, directly or indirectly, from hydraulic fracturing, a physical intrusion into the plaintiff's property must necessarily have taken place.

As to the first proposition, all drilling for subsurface fugacious minerals involves the artificial stimulation of the flow of that substance. The mere act of drilling interferes with nature and stimulates the flow of the minerals toward artificially-created low pressure areas, most notably, the wellbore. This Court has held that the rule of capture applies although the driller uses further artificial means, such as a pump, to enhance production from a source common to it and the plaintiff – so long as no physical invasion of the plaintiff's land occurs. *See Jones*, 194 Pa. at 384, 44 A. at 1075 (indicating that, absent physical intrusion, a developer may use "all the skill and invention of which a man is capable" to appropriate resources from under his own property). There is no reason why this precept should apply any differently to hydraulic fracturing conducted solely within the driller's property.

… Accordingly, we reject as a matter of law the concept that the rule of capture is inapplicable to drilling and hydraulic fracturing that occurs entirely within the developer's property solely because drainage of natural resources takes place as the direct or indirect result of hydraulic fracturing, or that such drainage stems from less "natural" means than conventional drainage.

The second predicate – that drainage from under a plaintiff's parcel can only occur if the driller first physically invades that property – does not lend itself to a purely legal resolution.… By design, hydraulic fracturing creates fissures in rock strata which store hydrocarbons within their porous structure. On the state of the present record, this alone does not establish that a physical intrusion into a neighboring property is necessary for such action to result in drainage from that property. We cannot rule out, for example, that a fissure created through the injection of hydraulic fluid entirely within the developer's property may create a sufficient pressure gradient to induce the drainage of hydrocarbons from the relevant stratum of rock underneath an adjacent parcel even absent physical intrusion. Nor can we discount the possibility that a fissure created within the developer's property may communicate with other, pre-existing fissures that reach across property lines. Whether these, or any other non-invasive means of drainage occasioned by hydraulic fracturing, are physically possible in a given case is a factual question to be established through expert evidence.

The Superior Court panel appears to have assumed, if implicitly, that such occurrences were impossible – but, again, there is no basis in the record for such an assumption. In all events, a plaintiff asserting a cause of action "must be able to prove all the elements of his case by proper evidentiary standards." *Papieves v. Lawrence*, 437 Pa. 373, 379, 263 A.2d 118, 121 (1970). Thus, to the extent this lawsuit goes forward on Plaintiffs' new, physical-intrusion theory, Plaintiffs will bear the burden of demonstrating that such an intrusion took place.

We have not overlooked Southwestern's argument that trespass should not be viewed as occurring miles beneath the surface of the earth. As Southwestern observes, in some jurisdictions traditional concepts of physical trespass have been relaxed where activities take place miles below the surface and the plaintiff is not deprived of the use and enjoyment of the land. Southwestern posits that this is analogous to the principle that trespass does not arise high above the surface. *See Causby*, 328 U.S. at 260-61, 66 S. Ct. at 1065. It emphasizes that other socially useful endeavors – such as carbon sequestration projects, energy storage wells, and waste disposal sites – could be jeopardized if the rule against trespass were to be enforced in an unduly stringent manner where deep subsurface activities are concerned.

Without speaking to the merit of such a claim, we note that this Court is limited to the issue as it was framed in the petition for allowance of appeal, and Southwestern has not articulated any reason an exception should be made in the present dispute. Thus, to the extent Southwestern argues it should be permitted to escape liability even if it is ultimately found to have effectuated a physical intrusion into Plaintiff's subsurface property, its claim in this regard has not been preserved for review by this Court.

This brings us to the question of whether the lawsuit can, indeed, progress on a theory of trespass by physical intrusion, and by extension, to the question of the appropriate mandate from this Court. Ordinarily, and for the reasons explained, we would deem any such contention to be absent from the litigation, as it does not appear to have been mentioned in Plaintiffs' pleadings or argued as a basis to deny Southwestern's motion for summary judgment. The Superior Court, however, evidently believed there was some legitimate basis to dispose of the appeal on the presupposition that Southwestern was alleged to have physically invaded Plaintiffs' subsurface property with hydraulic fracturing liquid and proppants; and, as noted, Southwestern has not challenged the intermediate court's action in this respect.

That being the case, … we find that the appropriate action at this juncture is to vacate the Superior Court's order and remand for reconsideration in light of the guidance provided in this opinion, and the certified record on appeal….

JUSTICE DOUGHERTY[, concurring in part and dissenting in part:]

I join the majority's holding that the rule of capture remains effective in Pennsylvania to protect a developer from trespass liability where there has been no physical invasion of another's property. In so holding, the majority correctly recognizes that if there **is** such a physical invasion the rule of capture will **not** insulate a developer engaged in hydraulic fracturing from trespass liability. As I agree with both propositions, I also agree the matter should be remanded for further proceedings involving a specific inquiry into a physical invasion. I respectfully dissent, however, from the notion that this question must be determined by the Superior Court on the present record.... Given the state of the record, which was apparently not complete at the time the trial court erroneously entered summary judgment, I would remand the matter to that court for further proceedings, including the completion of discovery on the factual question of physical invasion, and trial thereon as necessary.

Notes and Questions

1. **Questions of Fact; Questions of Law.** Do Chief Justice Saylor and Justice Dougherty disagree on the content of the legal rules in Pennsylvania regarding the ownership of oil and gas? Do they disagree on the law of trespass as it applies to mineral extraction? If the answer to both these questions is no, what is their disagreement about?

   In considering these questions, ask yourself what *actually happened* to the Briggses and their land in this case. Are you confident you can answer that question? If not, it may be difficult to say whether they should prevail on their trespass or conversion claims. This is not because the legal rule is unclear; rather it is because it may be unclear whether the rule is satisfied *given the facts in the record.* This distinction between *legal* issues and *factual* issues is central to the practice of law, and you will surely learn more about it in your civil procedure class. How does the court's resolution of the *legal* issues in the case affect the *factual questions* that the parties must answer in litigation? How should they go about answering those questions? What is likely to happen to the Briggses' claim on remand, and what would have happened if Justice Dougherty's opinion had instead carried a majority of the court? (Hint: The answer to this last question has less to do with the law of property and more to do with the law of civil procedure.)

2. **I Drink Your Milkshake.**[23] *Briggs* reaffirms a principle of long standing in oil and gas law. Imagine Alice and Bob are neighboring landowners in an oil-rich region. Alice drills an oil well at an angle, such that the wellhead is on Alice's land, but the bottom of the wellbore, from which the pipe draws oil, is under Bob's land. Bob sues Alice to enjoin

---

[23] THERE WILL BE BLOOD (Paramount Vantage/Miramax Films 2007).

the continued operation of the well and to recover the value of the oil already extracted. Under the rule of capture and the definition of trespass as discussed in *Briggs*, what result and why? *See* 1 SUMMERS OIL AND GAS § 2:3 (3d ed.) ("[I]f a well deviates from the vertical and produces oil or gas from under the surface of another landowner, that is a trespass for which the adjacent owner is entitled to damages, an accounting and injunction."). Why might it be acceptable to use a well on your land to draw the oil from under your neighbor's land, but not to drill the bottom of your well under the surface owned by your neighbor to extract the very same oil? Does the distinction have any practical effect? Does the advent of fracking technology change your answer?

3. Non-fugacious resources

Edwards v. Sims

24 S.W.2d 619 (Ky. Ct. App. 1929)

STANLEY, Commis.

Denying writ of prohibition.

This case presents a novel question.

[In a subsequent ruling, the underlying facts were presented as follows: "About twenty years ago L.P. Edwards discovered a cave under land belonging to him and his wife, Sally Edwards. The entrance to the cave is on the Edwards land. Edwards named it the "Great Onyx Cave," no doubt because of the rock crystal formations within it which are known as onyx. This cave is located in the cavernous area of Kentucky, and is only about three miles distant from the world-famous Mammoth Cave. Its proximity to Mammoth Cave, which for many years has had an international reputation as an underground wonder, as well as its beautiful formations, led Edwards to embark upon a program of advertising and exploitation for the purpose of bringing visitors to his cave. Circulars were printed and distributed, signs were erected along the roads, persons were employed and stationed along the highways to solicit the patronage of passing travelers, and thus the fame of the Great Onyx Cave spread from year to year, until eventually, and before the beginning of the present litigation, it was a well-known and well-patronized cave. Edwards built a hotel near the mouth of the cave to care for travelers. He improved and widened the footpaths and avenues in the cave, and ultimately secured a stream of tourists who paid entrance fees sufficient not only to cover the cost of operation, but also to yield a substantial revenue in addition thereto. The authorities in charge of the development of the Mammoth Cave area as a national park undertook to secure the Great Onyx Cave through condemnation proceedings, and in that suit the value of the cave was fixed by a jury at $396,000. In April, 1928, F.P. Lee, an adjoining landowner, filed this suit against Edwards and the heirs of Sally Edwards, claiming that a portion of the cave was under his land, and praying for damages, for an accounting of the profits which resulted from the operation of the cave, and for an injunction prohibiting Edwards and his associates from further trespassing upon or exhibiting any part of the cave under Lee's land. At the inception of this litigation, Lee undertook to procure a survey of the cave in order that it might be determined what portion of it was on his land. The chancellor ordered that a survey be made, and Edwards prosecuted an appeal from that order ..."]

[The procedural posture of the case is unusual. This is not an ordinary appeal.] In the recent case of Edwards v. Lee, 230 Ky. 375,19 S.W.2d 992, an appeal was dismissed which sought a review and reversal of an order of the Edmonson circuit court directing surveyors to enter upon and under the lands of Edwards and others and survey the Great Onyx Cave for the purpose of securing evidence on an issue as to whether or not a part of the cave being exploited and shown by the appellants runs under the ground of Lee. The nature of the litigation is stated in the opinion and the order set forth in full. It was held that the order was interlocutory and consequently one from which no appeal would lie.

*Passage in Great Onyx Cave**

* Photograph by Dave Bunnell, licensing (CC-BY-SA-4.0) information available at https://commons.wikimedia.org/wiki/File:Great_onyx_cave_KY.jpg

Following that decision, this original proceeding was filed in this court by appellants in that case (who were defendants below) against Hon. N.P. Sims, judge of the Edmonson circuit court, seeking a writ of prohibition to prevent him enforcing the order and punishing the petitioners for contempt for any disobedience of it. It is alleged by the petitioners that the lower court was without jurisdiction or authority to make the order, and that their cave property and their right of possession and privacy will be wrongfully and illegally invaded, and that they will be greatly and irreparably injured and damaged without having an adequate remedy, since the damage will have been suffered before there can be an adjudication of their rights on a final appeal. …

1. There is no question as to the jurisdiction of the parties and the subject-matter. It is only whether the court is proceeding erroneously within its jurisdiction in entering and enforcing the order directing the survey of the subterranean premises of the petitioners. There is but little authority of particular and special application to caves and cave rights. In few places, if any, can be found similar works of nature of such grandeur and of such unique and marvelous character as to give to caves a commercial value sufficient to cause litigation as those peculiar to Edmonson and other counties in Kentucky. The reader will find of interest the address on "The Legal Story of Mammoth Cave" by Hon. John B. Rodes, of Bowling Green, before the 1929 Session of the Kentucky State Bar Association, published in its proceedings. In Cox v. Colossal Cavern Co.,210 Ky. 612, 276 S.W. 540, the subject of cave rights was considered, and this court held there may be a severance of the estate in the property, that is, that one may own the surface and another the cave rights, the conditions being quite similar to but not exactly like those of mineral lands. But there is no such severance involved in this case, as it appears that the defendants are the owners of the land and have in it an absolute right.

Cujus est solum, ejus est usque ad coelum ad infernos (to whomsoever the soil belongs, he owns also to the sky and to the depths), is an old maxim and rule. It is that the owner of realty, unless there has been a division of the estate, is entitled to the free and unfettered control of his own land above, upon and beneath the surface. So whatever is in a direct line between the surface of the land and the center of the earth belongs to the owner of the surface. Ordinarily that ownership cannot be interfered with or infringed by third persons. 17 C. J. 391; 22 Rawle C. L. 56; Langhorne v. Turman, 141 Ky. 809,133 S.W. 1008, 34 L.R.A. (N.S.) 211. There are, however, certain limitations on the right of enjoyment of possession of all property, such as its use to the detriment or interference with a neighbor and burdens which it must bear in common with property of a like kind. 22 Rawle C. L. 77.

With this doctrine of ownership in mind, we approach the question as to whether a court of equity has a transcendent power to invade that right through its agents for the purpose of ascertaining the truth of a matter before it, which fact thus disclosed will determine certainly whether or not the owner is trespassing upon his neighbor's property. Our attention has not been called to any domestic case, nor have we found one, in which the question was determined either directly or by analogy. It seems to the court, however, that there can be little differentiation, so far as the matter now before us is concerned, between caves and mines. And as declared in 40 C. J. 947:

"A court of equity, however, has the inherent power, independent of statute, to compel a mine owner to permit an inspection of his works at the suit of a party who can show reasonable ground for suspicion that his lands are being trespassed upon through them, and may issue an injunction to permit such inspection."

There is some limitation upon this inherent power, such as that the person applying for such an inspection must show a bona fide claim and allege facts showing a necessity for the inspection and examination of the adverse party's property; and, of course, the party whose property is to be inspected must have had an opportunity to be heard in relation thereto. In the instant case it appears that these conditions were met. …

We can see no difference in principle between the invasion of a mine on adjoining property to ascertain whether or not the minerals are being extracted from under the applicant's property and an inspection of this respondent's property through his cave to ascertain whether or not he is trespassing under this applicant's property.

It appears that before making this order the court had before him surveys of the surface of both properties and the conflicting opinions of witnesses as to whether or not the Great Onyx Cave extended under the surface of the plaintiff's land. This opinion evidence was of comparatively little value, and as the chancellor (now respondent) suggested, the controversy can be quickly and accurately settled by surveying the cave; and "if defendants are correct in their contention this survey will establish it beyond all doubt and their title to this cave will be forever quieted. If the survey shows the Great Onyx Cave extends under the lands of plaintiffs, defendants should be glad to know this fact and should be just as glad to cease trespassing upon plaintiff's lands, if they are in fact doing so." The peculiar nature of these conditions, it seems to us, makes it imperative and necessary in the adminstration of justice that the survey should have been ordered and should be made.

It appearing that the circuit court is not exceeding its jurisdiction or proceeding erroneously, the claim of irreparable injury need not be given consideration. It is only when the inferior court is acting erroneously, and great or irreparable damage will result, and there is no adequate remedy by appeal, that a writ of prohibition will issue restraining the other tribunal, as held by authorities cited above.

The writ of prohibition is therefore denied.

Whole court sitting.

LOGAN, J., dissenting

The majority opinion allows that to be done which will prove of incalculable injury to Edwards without benefiting Lee, who is asking that this injury be done. I must dissent from the majority opinion, confessing that I may not be able to show, by any legal precedent, that the opinion is wrong, yet having an abiding faith in my own judgment that it is wrong.

It deprives Edwards of rights which are valuable, and perhaps destroys the value of his property, upon the motion of one who may have no interest in that which it takes away, and who could not subject it to his dominion or make any use of it, if he should establish that which he seeks to establish in the suit wherein the survey is sought.

It sounds well in the majority opinion to tritely say that he who owns the surface of real estate, without reservation, owns from the center of the earth to the outmost sentinel of the solar system. The age-old statement, adhered to in the majority opinion as the law, in truth and fact, is not true now and never has been. I can subscribe to no doctrine which makes the owner of the surface also the owner of the atmosphere filling illimitable space. Neither can I subscribe to the doctrine that he who owns the surface is also the owner of the vacant spaces in the bowels of the earth.

The rule should be that he who owns the surface is the owner of everything that may be taken from the earth and used for his profit or happiness. Anything which he may take is thereby subjected to his dominion, and it may be well said that it belongs to him. I concede the soundness of that rule, which is supported by the cases cited in the majority opinion; but they have no application to the question before the court in this case. They relate mainly to mining rights; that is, to substances under the surface which the owner may subject to his dominion. But no man can bring up from the depths of the earth the Stygian darkness and make it serve his purposes; neither can he subject to his dominion the bottom of the ways in the caves on which visitors tread, and for these reasons the owner of the surface has no right in such a cave which the law should, or can, protect because he has nothing of value therein, unless, perchance, he owns an entrance into it and has subjected the subterranean passages to his dominion.

A cave or cavern should belong absolutely to him who owns its entrance, and this ownership should extend even to its utmost reaches if he has explored and connected these reaches with the entrance. When the surface owner has discovered a cave and prepared it for purposes of exhibition, no one ought to be allowed to disturb him in his dominion over that which he has conquered and subjected to his uses.

It is well enough to hang to our theories and ideas, but when there is an effort to apply old principles to present-day conditions, and they will not fit, then it becomes necessary for a readjustment, and principles and facts as they exist in this age must be made conformable. For these reasons the old sophistry that the owner of the surface of land is the owner of everything from zenith to nadir must be reformed, and the reason why a reformation is necessary is because the theory was never true in the past, but no occasion arose that required the testing of it. Man had no dominion over the air until recently, and, prior to his conquering the air, no one had any occasion to question the claim of the surface owner that the air above him was subject to his dominion. Naturally the air above him should be subject to his dominion in so far as the use of the space is necessary for his proper enjoyment of the surface, but further than that he has no right in it separate from that of the public at large. The true principle should be announced to the effect that a man who owns the surface, without reservation, owns not only the land itself, but everything upon, above, or under it which he may use for his profit or pleasure, and which he may subject to his dominion and control. But further than this his ownership cannot extend. It should not be held that he owns that which he cannot use and which is of no benefit to him, and which may be of benefit to others.

Shall a man be allowed to stop airplanes flying above his land because he owns the surface? He cannot subject the atmosphere through which they fly to his profit or pleasure; therefore, so long as airplanes do not injure him or interfere with the use of his property, he should be helpless to prevent their flying above his dominion. Should the waves that transmit intelligible sound through the atmosphere be allowed to pass over the lands of surface-owners? If they take nothing from him and in no way interfere with his profit or pleasure, he should be powerless to prevent their passage?

If it be a trespass to enter on the premises of the landowner, ownership meaning what the majority opinion holds that it means, the aviator who flies over the land of one who owns the surface, without his consent, is guilty of trespass as defined by the common law and is subject to fine or imprisonment, or both, in the discretion of a jury.

If he who owns the surface does not own and control the atmosphere above him, he does not own and control vacuity beneath the surface. He owns everything beneath the surface that he can subject to his profit or pleasure, but he owns nothing more. Therefore, let it be written that a man who owns land does, in truth and in fact, own everything from zenith to nadir, but only for the use that he can make of it for his profit or pleasure. He owns nothing which he cannot subject to his dominion.

In the light of these unannounced principles which ought to be the law in this modern age, let us give thought to the petitioner Edwards, his rights and his predicament, if that is done to him which the circuit judge has directed to be done. Edwards owns this cave through right of discovery, exploration, development, advertising, exhibition, and conquest. Men fought their way through the eternal darkness, into the mysterious and abysmal depths of the bowels of a groaning world to discover the theretofore unseen splendors of unknown natural scenic wonders. They were conquerors of fear, although now and then one of them, as did Floyd Collins, paid with his life, for his hardihood in adventuring into the regions where Charon with his boat had never before seen any but the spirits of the departed. They let themselves down by flimsy ropes into pits that seemed bottomless; they clung to scanty handholds as they skirted the brinks of precipices while the flickering flare of their flaming flambeaux disclosed no bottom to the yawning gulf beneath them; they waded through rushing torrents, not knowing what awaited them on the farther side; they climbed slippery steeps to find other levels; they wounded their bodies on stalagmites and stalactites and other curious and weird formations; they found chambers, star-studded and filled with scintillating light reflected by a phantasmagoria revealing fancied phantoms, and tapestry woven by the toiling gods in the dominion of Erebus; hunger and thirst, danger and deprivation could not stop them. Through days, weeks, months, and years — ever linking chamber with chamber, disclosing an underground land of enchantment, they continued their explorations; through the years they toiled connecting these wonders with the outside world through the entrance on the land of Edwards which he had discovered; through the years they toiled finding safe ways for those who might come to view what they had found and placed their seal upon. They knew nothing, and cared less, of who owned the surface above; they were in another world where no law forbade their footsteps. They created an underground kingdom where Gulliver's people may have lived or where Ayesha may have found the revolving column of fire in which to bathe meant eternal youth.

When the wonders were unfolded and the ways were made safe, then Edwards patiently, and again through the years, commenced the advertisement of his cave. First came one to see, then another, then two together, then small groups, then small crowds, then large crowds, and then the multitude. Edwards had seen his faith justified. The cave was his because he had made it what it was, and without what he had done it was nothing of value. The value is not in the black vacuum that the uninitiated call a cave. That which Edwards owns is something intangible and indefinable. It is his vision translated into a reality.

Then came the horse leach's daughters crying: "Give me," "give me." Then came the "surface men" crying, "I think this cave may run under my lands." They do not know they only "guess," but they seek to discover the secrets of Edwards so that they may harass him and take from him that which he has made his own. They have come to a court of equity and have asked that Edwards be forced to open his doors and his ways to them so that they may go in and despoil him; that they may lay his secrets bare so that others may follow their example and dig into the wonders which Edwards has made his own. What may be the result if they stop his ways? They destroy the cave, because those who visit it are they who give it value, and none will visit it when the ways are barred so that it may not be exhibited as a whole.

It may be that the law is as stated in the majority opinion of the court, but equity, according to my judgment, should not destroy that which belongs to one man when he at whose behest the destruction is visited, although with some legal right, is not benefited thereby. Any ruling by a court which brings great and irreparable injury to a party is erroneous.

For these reasons I dissent from the majority opinion.

Hinman v. Pacific Air Transport
84 F.2d 755 (9th Cir. 1936)

HANEY, Circuit Judge.

Appellants allege… that they are the owners and in possession of 72 1/2 acres of real property in the city of Burbank, Los Angeles county, Cal., "together with a stratum of air-space superjacent to and overlying said tract * * * and extending upwards * * * to such an altitude as plaintiffs * * * may reasonably expect now or hereafter to utilize, use or occupy said airspace. Without limiting said altitude or defining the upward extent of said stratum of airspace or of plaintiff's ownership, utilization and possession thereof, plaintiffs allege that they * * * may reasonably expect now and hereafter to utilize, use and occupy said airspace and each and every portion thereof to an altitude of not less than 150 feet above the surface of the land * * * " ….

It is then alleged that defendants are engaged in the business of operating a commercial air line, and that at all times "after the month of May, 1929, defendants daily, repeatedly and upon numerous occasions have disturbed, invaded and trespassed upon the ownership and possession of plaintiffs' tract"; that at said times defendants have operated aircraft in, across, and through said airspace at altitudes less than 100 feet above the surface; that plaintiffs notified defendants to desist from trespassing on said airspace; and that defendants have disregarded said notice, unlawfully and against the will of plaintiffs, and continue and threaten to continue such trespasses…. The prayer asks an injunction restraining the operation of the aircraft through the airspace over plaintiffs' property and for [damages].

Appellees contend that it is settled law in California that the owner of land has no property rights in superjacent airspace, either by code enactments or by judicial decrees and that the ad coelum doctrine does not apply in California. We have examined the statutes of California, …but we find nothing therein to negative the ad coelum formula….If we could accept and literally construe the ad coelum doctrine, it would simplify the solution of this case; however, we reject that doctrine. We think it is not the law, and that it never was the law.

This formula "from the center of the earth to the sky" was invented at some remote time in the past when the use of space above land actual or conceivable was confined to narrow limits, and simply meant that the owner of the land could use the overlying space to such an extent as he was able, and that no one could ever interfere with that use.

This formula was never taken literally, but was a figurative phrase to express the full and complete ownership of land and the right to whatever superjacent airspace was necessary or convenient to the enjoyment of the land.

In applying a rule of law, or construing a statute or constitutional provision, we cannot shut our eyes to common knowledge, the progress of civilization, or the experience of mankind. A literal construction of this formula will bring about an absurdity. The sky has no definite location. It is that which presents itself to the eye when looking upward; as we approach it, it recedes. There can be no ownership of infinity, nor can equity prevent a supposed violation of an abstract conception.

The appellants' case, then, rests upon the assumption that as owners of the soil they have an absolute and present title to all the space above the earth's surface, owned by them, to such a height as is, or may become, useful to the enjoyment of their land. This height, the appellants assert in the bill, is of indefinite distance, but not less than 150 feet.

If the appellants are correct in this premise, it would seem that they would have such a title to the airspace claimed, as an incident to their ownership of the land, that they could protect such a title as if it were an ordinary interest in real property. Let us then examine the appellants' premise. They do not seek to maintain that the ownership of the land actually extends by absolute and exclusive title upward to the sky and downward to the center of the earth. They recognize that the space claimed must have some use, either present or contemplated, and connected with the enjoyment of the land itself.

Title to the airspace unconnected with the use of land is inconceivable. Such a right has never been asserted. It is a thing not known to the law.

Since, therefore, appellants must confine their claim to 150 feet of the airspace above the land, to the use of the space as related to the enjoyment of their land, to what extent, then, is this use necessary to perfect their title to the airspace? Must the use be actual, as when the owner claims the space above the earth occupied by a building constructed thereon; or does it suffice if appellants establish merely that they may reasonably expect to use the airspace now or at some indefinite future time?

This, then, is appellants' premise, and upon this proposition they rest their case. Such an inquiry was never pursued in the history of jurisprudence until the occasion is furnished by the common use of vehicles of the air.

We believe, and hold, that appellants' premise is unsound. The question presented is applied to a new status and little aid can be found in actual precedent. The solution is found in the application of elementary legal principles. The first and foremost of these principles is that the very essence and origin of the legal right of property is dominion over it. Property must have been reclaimed from the general mass of the earth, and it must be capable by its nature of exclusive possession. Without possession, no right in it can be maintained.

The air, like the sea, is by its nature incapable of private ownership, except in so far as one may actually use it. This principle was announced long ago by Justinian. It is in fact the basis upon which practically all of our so-called water codes are based.

We own so much of the space above the ground as we can occupy or make use of, in connection with the enjoyment of our land. This right is not fixed. It varies with our varying needs and is coextensive with them. The owner of land owns as much of the space above him as he uses, but only so long as he uses it. All that lies beyond belongs to the world. … Any use of such air or space by others which is injurious to his land, or which constitutes an actual interference with his possession or his beneficial use thereof, would be a trespass for which he would have remedy. But any claim of the landowner beyond this cannot find a precedent in law, nor support in reason.

…We cannot shut our eyes to the practical result of legal recognition of the asserted claims of appellants herein, for it leads to a legal implication to the effect that any use of airspace above the surface owner of land, without his consent would be a trespass either by the operator of an airplane or a radio operator. We will not foist any such chimerical concept of property rights upon the jurisprudence of this country….

Appellants are not entitled to injunctive relief upon the bill filed here, because no facts are alleged with respect to circumstances of appellants' use of the premises which will enable this court to infer that any actual or substantial damage will accrue from the acts of the appellees complained of.

The case differs from the usual case of enjoining a trespass. Ordinarily, if a trespass is committed upon land, the plaintiff is entitled to at least nominal damages without proving or alleging any actual damage. In the instant case, traversing the airspace above appellants' land is not, of itself, a trespass at all, but it is a lawful act unless it is done under circumstances which will cause injury to appellants' possession.

Appellants do not, therefore, in their bill state a case of trespass, unless they allege a case of actual and substantial damage. The bill fails to do this. It merely draws a naked conclusion as to damages without facts or circumstances to support it. It follows that the complaint does not state a case for injunctive relief....

Notes and Questions

1. Did the court in *Hinman* "find" the law of property as it applies to the airspace above land? Did it "change" the law in this regard? Or did it—as Felix Cohen argued—"create and distribute a new source of economic wealth or power"?

2. Does the court say that Hinman will never be able to obtain the relief sought? Are there any circumstances in which an injunction to restrict overflights to an altitude of over 150 feet (or any altitude) could be awarded under the court's analysis?

3. The court justified its ruling in *Hinman*, at least in part, by reference to the "practical result" that would follow a finding in the landowner's favor. What would that "practical result" be, and why did the court feel the need to avoid it? Is avoiding such undesirable "practical results" an acceptable basis for making a determination as to whether something is a person's "property"

4. **Drones.** The increasing availability of personal aerial robots ("drones") is threatening to bring *Hinman* back into the spotlight. In November of 2014, a hobbyist was flying a custom-built "hexacopter" over his parents' farm in California, when a neighbor's son shot it out of the sky with a shotgun. The neighbor claimed the drone had been flying over his land, though the drone owner disputed this. In any event, the drone owner demanded compensation for damage to the drone, and the neighbor refused. They ended up in small claims court where the neighbor was held liable for $850 in damages and court costs, on grounds that he "acted unreasonably in having his son shoot the drone down regardless of whether it was over his property or not." Jason Koebler, *The Sky's Not Your Lawn: Man Wins Lawsuit After Neighbor Shotgunned His Drone*, MOTHERBOARD (June 28, 2015), http://motherboard.vice.com/read/the-skys-not-your-lawn-man-wins-lawsuit-after-neighbor-shotgunned-his-drone.

   Imagine that instead of (or in addition to) having his son use the drone for target practice, the farmer had called the police to make a complaint of criminal trespass, or sued the drone owner for trespass. What result? Would it matter how high the drone was flying? Would it matter whether the drone was equipped with a camera? (Recall that the right to exclude is not the only right of owners; trespass may not be our farmer's only recourse. We will consider some analogous factual scenarios in our unit on Nuisance.)

5. Would the "practical result" of a finding for the landowner in *Hinman* necessarily be the same as the "practical result" of a finding in favor of a landowner suing the operator of a drone in the airspace over her land? Again, would it matter how high the drone was flying, or whether it was equipped with a camera?

D. Water

Water is essential to life, but it can also be put to a variety of other practical uses: irrigating farmland, extracting minerals from mines and oil or gas from wells, powering dams and mills, cooling industrial equipment, and as an input to manufacturing, for example. Fresh water from rainfall and snowmelt may flow over the surface of land, either free-flowing (particularly during heavy rains or spring thaws) or in defined channels as streams and lakes. Rain and snowmelt can also seep down and be absorbed by the earth as subsurface groundwater or deep aquifers. In either case, water has a fundamental physical connection to land, but it also moves freely over, under, and across land. (Sound familiar?)

Both surface and subsurface waters are renewable; they are replenished by precipitation. But they're still scarce. This scarcity comes in two basic forms, which map to the economic categories of **stocks** and **flows**. Depletion of a groundwater source at a rate exceeding its natural replenishment will eventually exhaust the **stock**—or finite total *amount*—of water at that source. A stream **flows** at a particular (though perhaps variable) *rate*, but that rate is primarily determined by ecological rather than human processes, so adding more users or more intense uses may not threaten *future* flows but does reduce the share of the flow available to each at any given time. Given these forms of scarcity, competition over water resources is inevitable, and property law may be called on to regulate that competition.

Complicating the matter, the rate of renewal of water stocks and the magnitude of water flows vary from time to time and place to place: Hawaii gets a lot more rain than Nevada, and California got a lot more rain in 1983 than it did in 2013. Reflecting this natural diversity, the American states have devised two broad categories of common-law responses to the challenge of managing conflicts over access to water, epitomized by the two cases below. The first response, **riparian rights**, dominates in the wetter, eastern states, and was firmly established by our first case, *Tyler v. Wilkinson*. The second response, **prior appropriation**, prevails in the more arid western states, and is sometimes referred to as the "Colorado Rule" given its historic association with our second case, *Coffin v. Left Hand Ditch Co.* Both cases deal with rights to flows, in particular the flow of a river. As you read these cases, try to understand how the two systems differ, and what might explain or justify the difference.

Tyler v. Wilkinson

24 F.Cas. 472, 4 Mason 397 (D. R.I. 1827)

STORY, Circuit Justice

[The Pawtucket River forms part of the boundary between Rhode Island and Massachusetts. Plaintiffs (Ebenezer Tyler and others) owned several mills on the Massachusetts side of the river. For over a century, mills on both sides of the river had been powered by the flow of the Pawtucket as directed by a dam (the "lower dam"). Defendants (Abraham Wilkinson and others) owned several mills upstream of the plaintiffs on the Rhode Island side of the river and on a man-made canal called Sergeant's Trench, which bypassed the lower dam on the western bank. Defendants erected a new dam (the "upper dam") to direct the flow of water toward their mills, interfering with the ability of plaintiffs to rely on the flow of the Pawtucket to the lower dam to power the plaintiffs' mills. Plaintiffs sued for a declaration that by "ancient usage" they had a superior claim to the waters of the Pawtucket over the defendants, whom the plaintiffs alleged were entitled only to "wastewater," or so much of the flow as was not needed by the plaintiffs. Supreme Court Justice Joseph Story, riding circuit, heard the dispute and rendered the following opinon.]

Before proceeding to an examination of these points, it may be proper to ascertain the nature and extent of the right, which riparian proprietors generally possess, to the waters of rivers flowing through their lands....

Prima facie every proprietor upon each bank of a river is entitled to the land, covered with water, in front of his bank, to the middle thread of the stream, or, as it is commonly expressed, *usque ad filum acquae*. In virtue of this ownership he has a right to the use of the water flowing over it in its natural current, without diminution or obstruction. But, strictly speaking, he has no property in the water itself; but a simple use of it, while it passes along. The consequence of this principle is, that no proprietor has a right to use the water to the prejudice of another. It is wholly immaterial, whether the party be a proprietor above or below, in the course of the river; the right being common to all the proprietors on the river, no one has a right to diminish the quantity which will, according to the natural current, flow to a proprietor below, or to throw it back upon a proprietor above. This is the necessary result of the perfect equality of right among all the proprietors of that, which is common to all. The natural stream, existing by the bounty of Providence for the benefit of the land through which it flows, is an incident annexed, by operation of law, to the land itself. When I speak of this common right, I do not mean to be understood, as holding the doctrine, that there can be no diminution whatsoever, and no obstruction or impediment whatsoever, by a riparian proprietor, in the use of the water as it flows; for that would be to deny any valuable use of it. There may be, and there must be allowed of that, which is common to all, a reasonable use. The true test of the principle and extent of the use is, whether it is to the injury of the other proprietors or not.... The maxim is applied, '*Sic utere tuo, ut non alienum laedas.*'

But of a thing, common by nature, there may be an appropriation by general consent or grant. Mere priority of appropriation of running water, without such consent or grant, confers no exclusive right. It is not like the case of mere occupancy, where the first occupant takes by force of his priority of occupancy. That supposes no ownership already existing, and no right to the use already acquired. But our law annexes to the riparian proprietors the right to the use in common, as an incident to the land; and whoever seeks to found an exclusive use, must establish a rightful appropriation in some manner known and admitted by the law. Now, this may be, either by a grant from all the proprietors, whose interest is affected by the particular appropriation, or by a long exclusive enjoyment, without interruption, which affords a just presumption of right. By our law, upon principles of public convenience, the term of twenty years of exclusive uninterrupted enjoyment has been held a conclusive presumption of a grant or right....

With these principles in view, the general rights of the plaintiffs cannot admit of much controversy. They are riparian proprietors, and, as such, are entitled to the natural flow of the river without diminution to their injury. As owners of the lower dam, and the mills connected therewith, they have no rights beyond those of any other persons, who might have appropriated that portion of the stream to the use of their mills. That is, their rights are to be measured by the extent of their actual appropriation and use of the water for a period, which the law deems a conclusive presumption in favor of rights of this nature. In their character as mill-owners, they have no title to the flow of the stream beyond the water actually and legally appropriated to the mills; but in their character as riparian proprietors, they have annexed to their lands the general flow of the river, so far as it has not been already acquired by some prior and legally operative appropriation. No doubt, then, can exist as to the right of the plaintiffs to the surplus of the natural flow of the stream not yet appropriated. Their rights, as riparian proprietors, are general; and it is incumbent on the parties, who seek to narrow these rights, to establish by competent proofs their own title to divert and use the stream.

And this leads me to the consideration of the nature and extent of the rights of the trench owners. There is no doubt, that in point of law or fact, there may be a right to water of a very limited nature, and subservient to the more general right of the riparian proprietors.... But the presumption of an absolute and controlling power over the whole flow, a continuing power of exclusive appropriation from time to time, in the riparian proprietor, as his wants or will may influence his choice, would require the most irresistible facts to support it. Men who build mills, and invest valuable capital in them, cannot be presumed, without the most conclusive evidence, to give their deliberate assent to the acceptance of such ruinous conditions. The general presumption appears to me to be that which is laid down by Mr. Justice Abbott in Saunders v.

Newman, 1 Barn. & Ald. 258: 'When a mill has been erected upon a stream for a long period of time, it gives to the owner a right, that the water shall continue to flow to and from the mill in the manner in which it has been accustomed to flow during all that time. The owner is not bound to use the water in the same precise manner, or to apply it to the same mill; if he were, that would stop all improvements in machinery. If, indeed, the alterations made from time to time prejudice the right of the lower mill (i.e. by requiring more water), the case would be different.'

In this view of the matter, the proprietors of Sergeant's trench are entitled to the use of so much of the water of the river as has been accustomed to flow through that trench to and from their mills (whether actually used or necessary for the same mills or not), during the twenty years last before the institution of this suit, subject only to such qualifications and limitations, as have been acknowledged or rightfully exercised by the plaintiffs as riparian proprietors, or as owners of the lower mill-dam, during that period. But here their right stops; they have no right farther to appropriate any surplus water not already used by the riparian proprietors, upon the notion, that such water is open to the first occupiers. That surplus is the inheritance of the riparian proprietors, and not open to occupancy.

...My opinion accordingly is, that the trench owners have an absolute right to the quantity of water which has usually flowed therein, without any adverse right on the plaintiffs to interrupt that flow in dry seasons, when there is a deficiency of water. But the trench owners have no right to increase that flow; and whatever may be the mills or uses, to which they may apply it, they are limited to the accustomed quantity, and may not exceed it.... [I]f there be a deficiency, it must be borne by all parties, as a common loss, wherever it may fall, according to existing rights ... and that the plaintiffs to this extent are entitled to have their general right established, and an injunction granted.

It is impracticable for the court to do more, in this posture of the case, than to refer it to a master to ascertain, as near as may be, and in conformity with the suggestions in the opinion of the court, the quantity to which the trench owners are entitled, and to report a suitable mode and arrangement permanently to regulate and adjust the flow of the water, so as to preserve the rights of all parties.

... The decree of the court is to be drawn up accordingly; and all further directions are reserved to the further hearing upon the master's report, &c. Decree accordingly.

Coffin v. Left Hand Ditch Co.

6 Colo. 443 (1882)

HELM, J.

Appellee, who was plaintiff below, claimed to be the owner of certain water by virtue of an appropriation thereof from the south fork of the St. Vrain creek. It appears that such water, after its diversion, is carried by means of a ditch to the James creek, and thence along the bed of the same to Left Hand creek, where it is again diverted by lateral ditches and used to irrigate lands adjacent to the last named stream. Appellants are the owners of lands lying on the margin and in the neighborhood of the St. Vrain below the mouth of said south fork thereof, and naturally irrigated therefrom.

In 1879 there was not a sufficient quantity of water in the St. Vrain to supply the ditch of appellee and also irrigate the said lands of appellant. A portion of appellee's dam was torn out, and its diversion of water thereby seriously interfered with by appellants. The action is brought for damages arising from the trespass, and for injunctive relief to prevent repetitions thereof in the future. … [T]rial was had before a jury…, and verdict and judgment given for appellee. Such recovery was confined, however, to damages for injury to the dam alone, and did not extend to those, if any there were, resulting from the loss of water.

... It is contended by counsel for appellants that the common law principles of riparian proprietorship prevailed in Colorado until 1876, and that the doctrine of priority of right to water by priority of appropriation thereof was first recognized and adopted in the constitution. But we think the latter doctrine has existed from the date of the earliest appropriations of water within the boundaries of the state. The climate is dry, and the soil, when moistened only by the usual rainfall, is arid and unproductive; except in a few favored sections, artificial irrigation for agriculture is an absolute necessity. Water in the various streams thus acquires a value unknown in moister climates. Instead of being a mere incident to the soil, it rises, when appropriated, to the dignity of a distinct usufructuary estate, or right of property. It has always been the policy of the national, as well as the territorial and state governments, to encourage the diversion and use of water in this country for agriculture; and vast expenditures of time and money have been made in reclaiming and fertilizing by irrigation portions of our unproductive territory. Houses have been built, and permanent improvements made; the soil has been cultivated, and thousands of acres have been rendered immensely valuable, with the understanding that appropriations of water would be protected. Deny the doctrine of priority or superiority of right by priority of appropriation, and a great part of the value of all this property is at once destroyed.

… We conclude, then, that the common law doctrine giving the riparian owner a right to the flow of water in its natural channel upon and over his lands, even though he makes no beneficial use thereof, is inapplicable to Colorado. Imperative necessity, unknown to the countries which gave it birth, compels the recognition of another doctrine in conflict therewith. And we hold that, in the absence of express statutes to the contrary, the first appropriator of water from a natural stream for a beneficial purpose has, with the qualifications contained in the constitution, a prior right thereto, to the extent of such appropriation.

... It is urged, however, that even if the doctrine of priority or superiority of right by priority of appropriation be conceded, appellee in this case is not benefited thereby. Appellants claim that they have a better right to the water because their lands lie along the margin and in the neighborhood of the St. Vrain. They assert that, as against them, appellee's diversion of said water to irrigate lands adjacent to Left Hand creek, though prior in time, is unlawful.

In the absence of legislation to the contrary, we think that the right to water acquired by priority of appropriation thereof is not in any way dependent upon the locus of its application to the beneficial use designed. And the disastrous consequences of our adoption of the rule contended for, forbid our giving such a construction to the statutes as will concede the same, if they will properly bear a more reasonable and equitable one.

The doctrine of priority of right by priority of appropriation for agriculture is evoked, as we have seen, by the imperative necessity for artificial irrigation of the soil. And it would be an ungenerous and inequitable rule that would deprive one of its benefit simply because he has, by large expenditure of time and money, carried the water from one stream over an intervening watershed and cultivated land in the valley of another. It might be utterly impossible, owing to the topography of the country, to get water upon his farm from the adjacent stream; or if possible, it might be impracticable on account of the distance from the point where the diversion must take place and the attendant expense; or the quantity of water in such stream might be entirely insufficient to supply his wants. It sometimes happens that the most fertile soil is found along the margin or in the neighborhood of the small rivulet, and sandy and barren land beside the larger stream. To apply the rule contended for would prevent the useful and profitable cultivation of the productive soil, and sanction the waste of water upon the more sterile lands. It would have enabled a party to locate upon a stream in 1875, and destroy the value of thousands of acres, and the improvements thereon, in adjoining valleys, possessed and cultivated for the preceding decade. Under the principle contended for, a party owning land ten miles from the stream, but in the valley thereof, might deprive a prior appropriator of the water diverted therefrom whose lands are within a thousand yards, but just beyond an intervening divide.

...The judgment of the court below will be affirmed.

Notes and Questions

1. **Different Strokes for Different Folks.** Why is the rule for control and use of surface waters different in the Eastern United States than it is in the West? Why is it different for water in New England than it is for wild animals in (old) England? Is the "priority of appropriation" rule in Colorado the same as the "free taking" rule for game in the early American frontier? If not, how and why does it differ?

   One of the important skills of lawyers (and legal scholars) is to identify *distinctions* among seemingly analogous fact patterns that could account for courts' selection of the rules they apply to those facts. So: can we identify some distinctions in the facts of these two cases that might account for the difference between, say, the eastern (riparian) rule and the western (priority of appropriation) rule for water? (Did Justice Helm identify any such distinctions in *Coffin*?)

   We might examine at least three different grounds for distinguishing these types of cases from one another. First, the characteristics of the *resource itself* may be different. That may be a relevant basis for distinguishing wild animals from water; as we have seen, it may also be a basis for distinguishing both of those resources from oil and gas. Second, the characteristics of the *society* in which the resource is being exploited may be different. As we have already noted, the interior of the American continent in the 18th century was a very different place than the English countryside—in terms of its population density and in terms of the level of development and exploitation of existing natural resources. And as the *Coffin* court noted, the quality and distribution of arable soil in the mountain west makes irrigation an "imperative necessity" to agriculture in a way "unknown to" the riparian east. Third, the particular uses of the resource may differ from one social context to another. For example, in New England, where surface water is plentiful, streams were mainly used *non-consumptively* to power industrial plants in the 19th century; in Colorado, where water is scarce, streams were used primarily for consumptive purposes—mining, farming, and drinking. *See* Carol M. Rose, *Energy And Efficiency in the Realignment of Common-Law Water Rights*, 19 J. LEG. STUD. 261, 290-93 (1990). Any of these types of distinctions could justify a change in legal rules from one case to another. Which—if any—do you think best explain the difference between *Tyler* and *Coffin*?

2. **Stock Resources.** *Tyler* and *Coffin* deal with allocation of the right to a share of the flow of a natural watercourse. But much water use depends not on surface waters, but on groundwater, extracted by means of wells and pumps. Such groundwater can behave more like a stock resource than a flow resource; excessive extraction by any one claimant *today* threatens the availability of the resource for *all* claimants *in the future*. Indeed, extraction of groundwater—and even collection of precipitation—can alter the flows of

surface channels, threatening the rights of remote riparians or prior appropriators. For this reason, some states—particularly in the more arid Western United States—have enacted comprehensive statutory codes and administrative regulations allocating water rights. California's system is among the most complex, layering early common-law riparian rights with later common-law prior appropriation rights and a subsequent statutory code administered by a powerful administrative agency with significant discretion to alter and limit water uses to respond to changing conditions. The state's regulatory reach is profound; in May of 2015 the Water Board responded to serious drought conditions by adopting emergency regulations requiring residents to refrain from most outdoor uses of water and requiring businesses to reduce their potable water usage by 25%, all on pain of a fine of $500 per day. State Water Resources Control Bd. Res. No. 2015-0032: To Adopt an Emergency Regulation for Statewide Water Conservation (May 5, 2015), available at http://www.waterboards.ca.gov/waterrights/water_issues/programs/drought/docs/emergency_regulations/rs2015_0032_with_adopted_regs.pdf.

3. **Non-Renewable Fugitive Resources.** For our other category of fugitive resource—oil and gas—stock depletion is the standard state of affairs, exacerbated by the fact that oil stocks do not replenish themselves the way water stocks do. Should this make a difference?

4. **Managing the Commons.** Some of the most groundbreaking work in economics in the past half-century—such as the Nobel Prize-winning work of Dr. Elinor Ostrom—has gone towards showing how commons-based resource management can actually work surprisingly well in contexts as diverse as Swiss mountain farms, Filipino irrigation canals, and Turkish fisheries. *See generally* ELINOR OSTROM, GOVERNING THE COMMONS (1990). Perhaps the tragedy of the commons can be resolved not by allocation of private property rights, but, rather, by developing better mechanisms for common management.

   Are the doctrines we have studied regarding allocation of fugitive resources property-based or commons-based? Take, for example, the riparian doctrine of reasonable use: can riparian owners take as much of the waters flowing past their land as they want, whenever they wish? Is there any middle ground between the "sole and despotic dominion" of Blackstone's private property and the tragic spiraling waste of Hardin's common pasture? If so, how does the law decide who gets what?

   What about the prior appropriation rule governing water rights in western states? Is it an instance of law stepping in to prevent a tragedy of the commons? That is certainly one conventional interpretation of the rule. But Professor David Schorr recently argued that early settlers in Colorado had informally worked out relatively egalitarian water allocation arrangements, which the *Coffin* court was merely protecting against destabilizing intrusions by new arrivals and powerful corporate interests. *See generally* DAVID SCHORR, THE COLORADO DOCTRINE (2012). Which makes more sense to you: that the *Coffin* court was setting economic policy to avoid overuse of scarce water, or that it was protecting the past investments and future expectations of the state's most established citizens? If you were a newly arrived farmer in Colorado when *Coffin* was announced, how would you react to the opinion?

2. Intangible Property

This section considers forms of property that cannot be seen with the eye or held in the hand. Such property raises significant conceptual issues, but, simply put, it is too significant for the legal system to ignore. You have already seen a few examples: corporate shares, for example, are a mixture of voting rights and claims to the income the corporation produces; they give a measure of control over tangible corporate assets, but they are very much distinct from those assets. And contract rights – particularly through the alchemy of assignability and negotiability – come to seem like property rights, too: companies regularly pledge their accounts receivable as security for loans, and no one bats an eye at the intangibility of the account receivable (or of the creditor's rights under the loan, for that matter). You have also now seen how people frequently hold intangible *interests* even in tangible property: a nonpossessory lien is such an interest, and you will meet many more in the study of real property. As you read the cases in this section, consider not just whether the things they describe are "property," but also whether they are "things" in the first place. To create a system of property rights, a legal system needs to be able to identify the things that are the subject of those rights, to decide who owns those things, and to be able to say when an owner's rights have been violated. Are these tasks systematically harder for intangibles, and if so, why?

Kremen v. Cohen

337 F. 3d 1024 (9th Cir. 2003)

KOZINSKI, Circuit Judge.[24]

We decide whether Network Solutions may be liable for giving away a registrant's domain name on the basis of a forged letter.

BACKGROUND

"Sex on the Internet?," they all said. "That'll never make any money." But computer-geek-turned-entrepreneur Gary Kremen knew an opportunity when he saw it. The year was 1994;

[24] [In 2009, Judge Kozinski was admonished by a judicial disciplinary panel for maintaining a publicly accessible server that included sexually explicit material. In 2017, he abruptly resigned after being accused of sexual misconduct by numerous women, including former law clerks. –*Eds.*]

domain names were free for the asking, and it would be several years yet before Henry Blodget and hordes of eager NASDAQ day traders would turn the Internet into the Dutch tulip craze of our times. With a quick e-mail to the domain name registrar Network Solutions, Kremen became the proud owner of sex.com. He registered the name to his business, Online Classifieds, and listed himself as the contact.

Con man Stephen Cohen, meanwhile, was doing time for impersonating a bankruptcy lawyer. He, too, saw the potential of the domain name. Kremen had gotten it first, but that was only a minor impediment for a man of Cohen's boundless resource and bounded integrity. Once out of prison, he sent Network Solutions what purported to be a letter he had received from Online Classifieds. It claimed the company had been "forced to dismiss Mr. Kremen," but "never got around to changing our administrative contact with the internet registration [sic] and now our Board of directors has decided to abandon the domain name sex.com." Why was this unusual letter being sent via Cohen rather than to Network Solutions directly? It explained:

> Because we do not have a direct connection to the internet, we request that you notify the internet registration on our behalf, to delete our domain name sex.com. Further, we have no objections to your use of the domain name sex.com and this letter shall serve as our authorization to the internet registration to transfer sex.com to your corporation.[2]

Despite the letter's transparent claim that a company called "Online Classifieds" had no Internet connection, Network Solutions made no effort to contact Kremen. Instead, it accepted the letter at face value and transferred the domain name to Cohen. When Kremen contacted Network Solutions some time later, he was told it was too late to undo the transfer. Cohen went on to turn sex.com into a lucrative online porn empire.

And so began Kremen's quest to recover the domain name that was rightfully his. He sued Cohen and several affiliated companies in federal court, seeking return of the domain name and disgorgement of Cohen's profits. The district court found that the letter was indeed a forgery and ordered the domain name returned to Kremen. It also told Cohen to hand over his profits, invoking the constructive trust doctrine and California's "unfair competition" statute, Cal. Bus. & Prof.Code § 17200 et seq. It awarded $40 million in compensatory damages and another $25 million in punitive damages.

---

[2] The letter was signed "Sharon Dimmick," purported president of Online Classifieds. Dimmick was actually Kremen's housemate at the time; Cohen later claimed she sold him the domain name for $1000. This story might have worked a little better if Cohen hadn't misspelled her signature.

Kremen, unfortunately, has not had much luck collecting his judgment. The district court froze Cohen's assets, but Cohen ignored the order and wired large sums of money to offshore accounts. His real estate property, under the protection of a federal receiver, was stripped of all its fixtures – even cabinet doors and toilets – in violation of another order. The court commanded Cohen to appear and show cause why he shouldn't be held in contempt, but he ignored that order, too. The district judge finally took off the gloves – he declared Cohen a fugitive from justice, signed an arrest warrant and sent the U.S. Marshals after him.

Then things started getting really bizarre. Kremen put up a "wanted" poster on the sex.com site with a mug shot of Cohen, offering a $50,000 reward to anyone who brought him to justice. Cohen's lawyers responded with a motion to vacate the arrest warrant. They reported that Cohen was under house arrest in Mexico and that gunfights between Mexican authorities and would-be bounty hunters seeking Kremen's reward money posed a threat to human life. The district court rejected this story as "implausible" and denied the motion. Cohen, so far as the record shows, remains at large.

Given his limited success with the bounty hunter approach, it should come as no surprise that Kremen seeks to hold someone else responsible for his losses. That someone is Network Solutions, the exclusive domain name registrar at the time of Cohen's antics. Kremen sued it for mishandling his domain name, invoking four theories at issue here. He argues that he had an implied contract with Network Solutions, which it breached by giving the domain name to Cohen. He also claims the transfer violated Network Solutions's cooperative agreement with the National Science Foundation – the government contract that made Network Solutions the .com registrar. His third theory is that he has a property right in the domain name sex.com, and Network Solutions committed the tort of conversion by giving it away to Cohen. Finally, he argues that Network Solutions was a "bailee" of his domain name and seeks to hold it liable for "conversion by bailee."

The district court granted summary judgment in favor of Network Solutions on all claims. [Kremen appealed. His contract claim failed on appeal because he was not a paying customer and Network Solutions made no promises to him. He was not an intended third-party beneficiary of Network Solutions' contract with the NSF. And "conversion by bailee" was not an independent tort from conversion under California law. That left his conversion claim.]

CONVERSION

Kremen's conversion claim is another matter. To establish that tort, a plaintiff must show "ownership or right to possession of property, wrongful disposition of the property right and damages." *G.S. Rasmussen & Assocs., Inc. v. Kalitta Flying Serv., Inc.*, 958 F.2d 896, 906 (9th Cir. 1992). The preliminary question, then, is whether registrants have property rights in their domain names. Network Solutions all but concedes that they do. This is no surprise, given its positions in prior litigation. *See Network Solutions, Inc. v. Umbro Int'l, Inc.*, 529 S.E.2d 80, 86 (2000) ("[Network Solutions] acknowledged during oral argument before this Court that the right to use a domain name is a form of intangible personal property.").[5] The district court agreed with the parties on this issue, as do we.

Property is a broad concept that includes "every intangible benefit and prerogative susceptible of possession or disposition." *Downing v. Mun. Court*, 198 P.2d 923 (1948). We apply a three-part test to determine whether a property right exists: "First, there must be an interest capable of precise definition; second, it must be capable of exclusive possession or control; and third, the putative owner must have established a legitimate claim to exclusivity." *G.S. Rasmussen*, 958 F.2d at 903. Domain names satisfy each criterion. Like a share of corporate stock or a plot of land, a domain name is a well-defined interest. Someone who registers a domain name decides where on the Internet those who invoke that particular name – whether by typing it into their web browsers, by following a hyperlink, or by other means – are sent. Ownership is exclusive in that the registrant alone makes that decision. Moreover, like other forms of property, domain names are valued, bought and sold, often for millions of dollars, and they are now even subject to in rem jurisdiction, see 15 U.S.C. § 1125(d)(2).

Finally, registrants have a legitimate claim to exclusivity. Registering a domain name is like staking a claim to a plot of land at the title office. It informs others that the domain name is the registrant's and no one else's. Many registrants also invest substantial time and money to develop and promote websites that depend on their domain names. Ensuring that they reap the benefits of their investments reduces uncertainty and thus encourages investment in the first place, promoting the growth of the Internet overall.

Kremen therefore had an intangible property right in his domain name, and a jury could find that Network Solutions wrongfully disposed of that right to his detriment by handing the domain name over to Cohen. The district court nevertheless rejected Kremen's conversion claim. It held that domain names, although a form of property, are intangibles not subject to conversion. This rationale derives from a distinction tort law once drew between tangible and intangible property: Conversion was originally a remedy for the wrongful taking of another's lost goods, so it applied only to tangible property. See Prosser and Keeton on the Law of Torts

---

[5] Network Solutions … stresses that Kremen didn't develop the sex.com site before Cohen stole it. But this focus on the particular domain name at issue is misguided. The question is not whether Kremen's domain name in isolation is property, but whether domain names as a class are a species of property.

§ 15, at 89, 91 (W. Page Keeton ed., 5th ed.1984). Virtually every jurisdiction, however, has discarded this rigid limitation to some degree. Many courts ignore or expressly reject it. See *Kremen*, 325 F.3d at 1045-46 n. 5 (Kozinski, J., dissenting) (citing cases); *Astroworks, Inc. v. Astroexhibit, Inc.*, 257 F.Supp.2d 609, 618 (S.D.N.Y.2003) (holding that the plaintiff could maintain a claim for conversion of his website); Val D. Ricks, *The Conversion of Intangible Property: Bursting the Ancient Trover Bottle with New Wine*, 1991 B.Y.U. L. Rev. 1681, 1682. Others reject it for some intangibles but not others. The Restatement, for example, recommends the following test:

> (1) Where there is conversion of a document in which intangible rights are merged, the damages include the value of such rights.
>
> (2) One who effectively prevents the exercise of intangible rights of the kind customarily *merged in a document* is subject to a liability similar to that for conversion, even though the document is not itself converted.

Restatement (Second) of Torts § 242 (1965) (emphasis added). An intangible is "merged" in a document when, "by the appropriate rule of law, the right to the immediate possession of a chattel and the power to acquire such possession is *represented by* [the] document," or when "an intangible obligation [is] represented by [the] document, which is regarded as equivalent to the obligation." *Id.* cmt. a (emphasis added).[6] The district court applied this test and found no evidence that Kremen's domain name was merged in a document. …

We conclude that California does not follow the Restatement's strict merger requirement. Indeed, the leading California Supreme Court case rejects the tangibility requirement altogether. In *Payne v. Elliot*, 54 Cal. 339, 1880 WL 1907 (1880), the Court considered whether shares in a corporation (as opposed to the share certificates themselves) could be converted. It held that they could, reasoning: "[T]he action no longer exists as it did at common law, but has been developed into a remedy for the conversion of every species of personal property." *Id.* at 341 (emphasis added). While Payne's outcome might be reconcilable with the Restatement, its rationale certainly is not: It recognized conversion of shares, not because they are customarily

---

[6] The Restatement does note that conversion "has been applied by some courts in cases where the converted document is not in itself a symbol of the rights in question, but is merely essential to their protection and enforcement, as in the case of account books and receipts." *Id.* cmt. b.

represented by share certificates, but because they are a species of personal property and, perforce, protected.[7]

Notwithstanding Payne's seemingly clear holding, the California Court of Appeal held in *Olschewski v. Hudson*, 87 Cal.App. 282, 262 P. 43 (1927), that a laundry route was not subject to conversion. It explained that Payne's rationale was "too broad a statement as to the application of the doctrine of conversion." *Id.* at 288, 262 P. 43. Rather than follow binding California Supreme Court precedent, the court retheorized Payne and held that corporate stock could be converted only because it was "represented by" a tangible document. *Id.*; see also *Adkins v. Model Laundry Co.*, 268 P. 939 (1928) (relying on *Olschewski* and holding that no property right inhered in "the intangible interest of an exclusive privilege to collect laundry").

Were *Olschewski* the only relevant case on the books, there might be a plausible argument that California follows the Restatement. But in *Palm Springs-La Quinta Development Co. v. Kieberk Corp.*, 115 P.2d 548 (1941), the court of appeal allowed a conversion claim for intangible information in a customer list when some of the index cards on which the information was recorded were destroyed. The court allowed damages not just for the value of the cards, but for the value of the intangible information lost. Section 242(1) of the Restatement, however, allows recovery for intangibles only if they are merged in the converted document. Customer information is not merged in a document in any meaningful sense. A Rolodex is not like a stock certificate that actually represents a property interest; it is only a means of recording information.

Palm Springs and *Olschewski* are reconcilable on their facts – the former involved conversion of the document itself while the latter did not. But this distinction can't be squared with the Restatement. The plaintiff in *Palm Springs* recovered damages for the value of his intangibles. But if those intangibles were merged in the index cards for purposes of section 242(1), the plaintiffs in *Olschewski* and *Adkins* should have recovered under section 242(2) – laundry routes surely are customarily written down somewhere. "Merged" can't mean one thing in one section and something else in the other.

California courts ignored the Restatement again in *A & M Records, Inc. v. Heilman*, 75 Cal.App.3d 554 (1977), which applied the tort to a defendant who sold bootlegged copies of musical recordings. The court held broadly that "such misappropriation and sale of the intangible

---

[7] Intangible interests in real property, on the other hand, remain unprotected by conversion, presumably because trespass is an adequate remedy. See *Goldschmidt v. Maier*, 73 P. 984, 985 (Cal.1903) (per curiam) ("[A] leasehold of real estate is not the subject of an action of trover."); *Vuich v. Smith*, 35 P.2d 365 (1934) (same). Some California cases also preserve the traditional exception for indefinite sums of money. See 5 Witkin *Torts* § 614.

property of another without authority from the owner is conversion." *Id.* at 570. It gave no hint that its holding depended on whether the owner's intellectual property rights were merged in some document. One might imagine physical things with which the intangible was associated – for example, the medium on which the song was recorded. But an intangible intellectual property right in a song is not merged in a phonograph record in the sense that the record represents the composer's intellectual property right. The record is not like a certificate of ownership; it is only a medium for one instantiation of the artistic work.

Federal cases applying California law take an equally broad view. We have applied *A & M Records* to intellectual property rights in an audio broadcast, see *Lone Ranger Television, Inc. v. Program Radio Corp.*, 740 F.2d 718, 725 (9th Cir. 1984), and to a regulatory filing, *see G.S. Rasmussen*, 958 F.2d at 906-07. Like *A & M Records*, both decisions defy the Restatement's "merged in a document" test. An audio broadcast may be recorded on a tape and a regulatory submission may be typed on a piece of paper, but neither document represents the owner's intangible interest.

The Seventh Circuit interpreted California law in *FMC Corp. v. Capital Cities/ABC, Inc.*, 915 F.2d 300 (7th Cir. 1990). Observing that "'[t]here is perhaps no very valid and essential reason why there might not be conversion' of intangible property," id. at 305 (quoting Prosser & Keeton, supra, § 15, at 92), it held that a defendant could be liable merely for depriving the plaintiff of the use of his confidential information. In rejecting the tangibility requirement, *FMC* echoes *Payne*'s holding that personal property of any species may be converted. And it flouts the Restatement because the intangible property right in confidential information is not represented by the documents on which the information happens to be recorded. …

In short, California does not follow the Restatement's strict requirement that some document must actually represent the owner's intangible property right. On the contrary, courts routinely apply the tort to intangibles without inquiring whether they are merged in a document and, while it's often possible to dream up some document the intangible is connected to in some fashion, it's seldom one that represents the owner's property interest. To the extent *Olschewski* endorses the strict merger rule, it is against the weight of authority. That rule cannot be squared with a jurisprudence that recognizes conversion of music recordings, radio shows, customer lists, regulatory filings, confidential information and even domain names.

Were it necessary to settle the issue once and for all, we would toe the line of *Payne* and hold that conversion is "a remedy for the conversion of every species of personal property." 54 Cal. at 341. But we need not do so to resolve this case. Assuming arguendo that California retains some vestigial merger requirement, it is clearly minimal, and at most requires only some connection to a document or tangible object – not representation of the owner's intangible interest in the strict Restatement sense.

Kremen's domain name falls easily within this class of property. He argues that the relevant document is the Domain Name System, or "DNS" – the distributed electronic database that associates domain names like sex.com with particular computers connected to the Internet. We agree that the DNS is a document (or perhaps more accurately a collection of documents). That it is stored in electronic form rather than on ink and paper is immaterial. It would be a curious jurisprudence that turned on the existence of a paper document rather than an electronic one. Torching a company's file room would then be conversion while hacking into its mainframe and deleting its data would not. That is not the law, at least not in California.[11]

The DNS also bears some relation to Kremen's domain name. We need not delve too far into the mechanics of the Internet to resolve this case. It is sufficient to observe that information correlating Kremen's domain name with a particular computer on the Internet must exist somewhere in some form in the DNS; if it did not, the database would not serve its intended purpose. Change the information in the DNS, and you change the website people see when they type "www.sex.com."

Network Solutions quibbles about the mechanics of the DNS. It points out that the data corresponding to Kremen's domain name is not stored in a single record, but is found in several different places: The components of the domain name ("sex" and "com") are stored in two different places, and each is copied and stored on several machines to create redundancy and speed up response times. Network Solutions's theory seems to be that intangibles are not subject to conversion unless they are associated only with a single document.

Even if Network Solutions were correct that there is no single record in the DNS architecture with which Kremen's intangible property right is associated, that is no impediment under California law. A share of stock, for example, may be evidenced by more than one document. *See Payne*, 54 Cal. at 342 ("[T]he certificate is only evidence of the property; and it is not the only evidence, for a transfer on the books of the corporation, without the issuance of a certificate, vests title in the shareholder: the certificate is, therefore, but additional evidence of title...."). A customer list is protected, even if it's recorded on index cards rather than a single piece of paper.

---

[11] The Restatement requires intangibles to be merged only in a "document," not a tangible document. Restatement (Second) of Torts § 242. Our holding therefore does not depend on whether electronic records are tangible. *Compare eBay, Inc. v. Bidder's Edge, Inc.*, 100 F. Supp. 2d 1058, 1069 (N.D. Cal. 2000) ("[I]t appears likely that the electronic signals sent by [Bidder's Edge] to retrieve information from eBay's computer system are ... sufficiently tangible to support a trespass cause of action."), *with Intel Corp. v. Hamidi,* 71 P.3d 296, (2003) (implying that electronic signals are intangible).

Audio recordings may be duplicated, and confidential information and regulatory filings may be photocopied. Network Solutions's "single document" theory is unsupported.

Network Solutions also argues that the DNS is not a document because it is refreshed every twelve hours when updated domain name information is broadcast across the Internet. This theory is even less persuasive. A document doesn't cease being a document merely because it is often updated. If that were the case, a share registry would fail whenever shareholders were periodically added or dropped, as would an address file whenever business cards were added or removed. Whether a document is updated by inserting and deleting particular records or by replacing an old file with an entirely new one is a technical detail with no legal significance.

Kremen's domain name is protected by California conversion law, even on the grudging reading we have given it. Exposing Network Solutions to liability when it gives away a registrant's domain name on the basis of a forged letter is no different from holding a corporation liable when it gives away someone's shares under the same circumstances. We have not "creat[ed] new tort duties" in reaching this result. *Cf. Moore v. Regents of the Univ. of Cal.*, 793 P.2d 479 (1990). We have only applied settled principles of conversion law to what the parties and the district court all agree is a species of property.

The district court supported its contrary holding with several policy rationales, but none is sufficient grounds to depart from the common law rule. The court was reluctant to apply the tort of conversion because of its strict liability nature. This concern rings somewhat hollow in this case because the district court effectively exempted Network Solutions from liability to Kremen altogether, whether or not it was negligent. Network Solutions made no effort to contact Kremen before giving away his domain name, despite receiving a facially suspect letter from a third party. A jury would be justified in finding it was unreasonably careless.

We must, of course, take the broader view, but there is nothing unfair about holding a company responsible for giving away someone else's property even if it was not at fault. Cohen is obviously the guilty party here, and the one who should in all fairness pay for his theft. But he's skipped the country, and his money is stashed in some offshore bank account. Unless Kremen's luck with his bounty hunters improves, Cohen is out of the picture. The question becomes whether Network Solutions should be open to liability for its decision to hand over Kremen's domain name. Negligent or not, it was Network Solutions that gave away Kremen's property. Kremen never did anything. It would not be unfair to hold Network Solutions responsible and force it to try to recoup its losses by chasing down Cohen. This, at any rate, is the logic of the common law, and we do not lightly discard it.

The district court was worried that "the threat of litigation threatens to stifle the registration system by requiring further regulations by [Network Solutions] and potential increases in fees."

Given that Network Solutions's "regulations" evidently allowed it to hand over a registrant's domain name on the basis of a facially suspect letter without even contacting him, "further regulations" don't seem like such a bad idea. And the prospect of higher fees presents no issue here that it doesn't in any other context. A bank could lower its ATM fees if it didn't have to pay security guards, but we doubt most depositors would think that was a good idea.

The district court thought there were "methods better suited to regulate the vagaries of domain names" and left it "to the legislature to fashion an appropriate statutory scheme." Id. The legislature, of course, is always free (within constitutional bounds) to refashion the system that courts come up with. But that doesn't mean we should throw up our hands and let private relations degenerate into a free-for-all in the meantime. We apply the common law until the legislature tells us otherwise. And the common law does not stand idle while people give away the property of others.

The evidence supported a claim for conversion, and the district court should not have rejected it.

Notes and Questions

1. Is your name your property? What is it about a domain name that makes it "work" as property?

2. Does *Kremen*'s three-part test for the existence of "property" work on the variety of property forms you have encountered so far? Under it, is a car property? A dog? A house? A right of publicity? Proper alignment of one's psychic aura?

3. There are thriving markets for domain names. People buy and sell them all the time, companies use them as collateral for loans, and Stephen Cohen considered sex.com valuable enough to steal. But do these economic considerations make them "property?" Recall Felix Cohen's argument against basing property rights on economic value. Does *Kremen* commit precisely the fallacy the other Cohen warned about?

4. Is tangibility the key to the case or a giant red herring? Does the court's argument in footnote 11 that under the Restatement an intangible must be merged in a document but the document need not itself be tangible suggest that there is something wrong with the Restatement's test or with the court's reading of the Restatement.

5. The Internet Corporation for Assigned Names and Numbers (ICANN) has promulgated a system of mandatory arbitration for domain-name registrants, the Uniform Domain

Name Dispute Resolution Policy (UDRP). Under the UDRP, a trademark owner can bring an expedited proceeding against anyone who has registered a domain name that is "identical or confusingly similar" to their trademark if the domain name "has been registered and is being used in bad faith." If the arbitrator finds a violation, the remedy is transfer of the domain name to the trademark owner. What does this system of protection for trademark owners' property in their trademarks do to the security of domain-name registrants' property in their domain names? Both are systems of property in names, but can they coexist?

Tribune Co. v. Oak Leaves Broadcasting Station

68 Cong. Rec. 218 (Cook Cty. Cir. Ct. Ill. Nov. 17, 1926)

DECISION OF JUDGE WILSON ON DEFENDANTS' MOTION TO DISSOLVE TEMPORARY INJUNCTION

… The bill very briefly charges that the complainant is and has been for some time a corporation organized under the laws of the State of Illinois. with its principal place of business in the city of Chicago, and is engaged in the publication of a newspaper known as the Chicago Daily Tribune. and that it has an average daily paid circulation of several hundred thousand subscribers.

It further charges that since March 29, 1924, it has been engaged in broadcasting by radio of daily programs of information, amusement, and entertainment to the general public, and particularly to that part of the general public residing in and in the vicinity of the city of Chicago, and for that purpose the complainant· operates an apparatus generally known as a broadcasting station located on the Drake Hotel and another such broadcasting station operated near the city of Elgin.

The bill further charges that it has been the custom for several years for persons engaged in broadcasting to designate their certain stations by certain combinations of letters known as call letters, and that these call letters serve to enable persons using radio receiving sets to identify the particular station. and in this instance the complainant has been using the letters WGN, which stand for the abbreviation of the World's Greatest Newspaper which appears to have been adopted by the complainant as a sort of trade name indicating the Chicago Daily Tribune.

It is further charged in the hill that it is the custom for such newspapers; owning and operating broadcasting stations to make announcements of their programs in the daily editions of the paper, and that the complainant has, since March 29, 1924, used the designation WGN, and further charges that its program is of a high-class character, and that by reason of its broadcasting it has built up a good will with the public, which is of great value to the complainant, in that it has enhanced the value of the newspaper and increased the profits.

Further charges, on information and belief, that the number of persons who listen to the said broadcasting of the complainant is in excess of 500,000 and that these persons are educated to listen in or tune in on the wave length of the complainant for the purpose of hearing and enjoying the programs so broadcasted.

The bill further charges that, when two stations are broadcasting on the same or nearly the same wave length, the result will be that the users of the radio will either hear one of the stations to the exclusion of the other or hear both of the stations at the same time, which will cause confusion to the listener, or will hear one to the exclusion of the other but accompanied by a series of noises, such as whistles and roars, which render the program practically useless.

The bill further charges that for several years the broadcasting in the United States and Canada has been done on sending wave lengths varying from 201 meters to 550 meters, inclusive, the United States Government. by an enactment of Congress, having forbidden to private and commercial broadcasters the use of wave lengths from 601 meters to 1.000 meters, and the use of wave lengths under 200 meters because of the impracticability of the use of said wave lengths under 200 meters by reason of natural causes and because of the fact that the field is open to amateurs and used by a large number of the same.

Furthermore. that most of the radio receiving sets are so constructed it to be adapted to the receiving of broadcasting within this band of wave lengths included above the 200 meters and under 500 meters.

The bill further charges that the sending waves used by broadcasting stations are also classified by the number of kilocycles denoting the frequency of vibration per second characteristic of each wave. The higher the wave length the less is the number of kilocycles, and a definite number of kilocycles is characteristic of each wave.[25]

Further charges that the radio receiving sets in general use in the United States and Canada are scaled and marked with numerical divisions and that by means of dials or indicators persons

---

[25] [Ed: The formula is $f = c/\lambda$, where λ is the wavelength in meters, f is the frequency in cycles per second, and c is the speed of light (approximately 299,792,458 meters per second). So, for example, to use WGN's numbers, 299,792,458 / 990 = 302,820 cycles per second, or 302.8 kilocycles per second.]

receiving over radio can set such dials or indicators at particular points and hear the particular broadcasting station over the particular sate length that they desire.

Further charges that the users of radios have become familiar with the different wave lengths and broadcasting stations designated by the particular letters employed and that this fact is of value to the broadcaster because the public has been educated to their particular wave length and their particular designation.

The bill also charges that knowledge of this particular wave length by a broadcaster is of great value to the broadcaster because the person receiving through the radio has been educated to know when to place his dials or indicators in order to receive a particular station and that the public generally in the locality of the complainant line become familiar with the wave length of the complainant and that its loss by interference would work great damage to the complainant. The complainant further charges that on the 14th of December, 1925, it did, and ever since then has, broadcast on a sending wave length of 302.8 meters (the kilocycles characteristic of such wave length being 990) and that it broadcasts from both the Drake Hotel and from its Elgin broadcasting station and that, at that time, no other broadcasting station in the city of Chicago or in the entire State of Illinois was using said wave length or any wave length sufficiently near to interfere with complainant's broadcasting and that this fact was generally known to the public and that the public had access by reason thereof to the programs of the complainant as broadcast over the same wave length from the two broadcasting stations and which programs were announced at different periods of time by arrangement of the complainant.

Further charges that the complainant has expended large slims of money during said period of time in the building up and betterment of said broadcasting stations and in the furnishing of high-class talent for its programs and in the payment of salaries and expenses in its business of broadcasting. …

That the defendants, the Oak Leaves Broadcasting Station (Inc.), and the Coyne Electrical School (Inc.) are corporations existing under and by virtue of the laws of Illinois, and that the defendant, Guyon, is a resident of Chicago, Ill., engaged in business in said city under the name of Guyon's Paradise Ball Room, and operates a dance hall in the city of Chicago.

The bill further charges that the broadcasting station, heretofore used and operated by the defendants, Oak Leaves Broadcasting Station (Inc.), and Coyne Electrical School (Inc.), which had been operated from Oak Park, a suburb of the city of Chicago, was moved to 124 North Crawford Avenue, where Guyon's Paradise Ball Room is located, and is being now operated from that point, and charges that the said defendant, Guyon, became the owner and operator of said broadcasting station and that the other defendants have some interest in saint station which is unknown to the complainant, but which is charged to be true on information and belief.

The bill further charges that said station of the defendants had originally used a wave length of 220 meters (1,350 kilocycles) … and that, later, it changed its wave length to 249.9 meters (1,200 kilocycles), which it continued to use until on or about September 7, 1926, and further charges that the defendants had never enjoyed any considerable degree of the good will of the public, nor was it popular with the users of radio receiving sets, but was comparatively unknown in Chicago or its vicinity.

That on or about September 7, 1926, the said Guyon's Paradise Broadcasting Station, used and operated by the defendants, changed its sending wave length to a wave length either the same as that of tee complainant (i.e. 302.8) or one having a frequency of considerably less than 50 kilocycles different than that of the complainant, and that it is now using said wave length and has from that time until the date of the filing of the bill herein … .

The bill further charges that the defendants have, since September 7, 1926, used the said new wave length during the hours of the day when complainant is broadcasting, and that by reason thereof said broadcasting by the said defendants has interfered with and destroyed complainant's broadcasting to the public in the city of Chicago and throughout the region where complainant's newspaper circulates, and that by reason thereof radio receivers have been unable to hear the programs of the complainant, and that if it is allowed to continue it will work incalculable damage and injury to the good will of the complainant's broadcasting, and consequently will injure the circulation of the complainant so far as its newspaper is concerned and deprive it of great profits.

Further charges that there are other wave lengths which are usable by the defendants and that this wave length can be changed with practically no expense and within a short period of time.

The bill prays for an order restraining the defendants from broadcasting from said station in such a manner as to interfere with the broadcasting of the complainant, and more particularly from using any wave length within 100 miles of the city of Chicago having a frequency of less than 1,040 kilocycles per second, or more than 940 kilocycles per second. charging, in effect, that any wave length within that designated number of kilocycles would necessarily cause an interference with the broadcasting of the complainant.

The answer … admits that where a broadcasting station is operating on a wave length the frequency of which is within 50 kilocycles per second of the number of kilocycles per second characteristic of the wave length of the first station, that some interference will result but that such interference is natural where stations are operating in close proximity one to the other, but that where two broadcasting stations in the same locality are properly constructed and operated and the wave length employed sharply defined and the power of sold stations substantially equal there will be no appreciable interference by the stations if they are separated by 40 kilocycles. . . .

The answer admits that on September 7, 1926, the said defendants' station changed its wave length, but denies that they are broadcasting over the same wave length as that of the complainant, but state that they are sending over a wave length which is removed 40 kilocycles from the wave length used by the complainant, and that said wave being used is 315.6 meters with a frequency of 950 kilocycles.

The answer further admits that the defendant … has since about September, 1926, used and operated the broadcasting station described in the bill of complaint Guyon's Paradise Broadcasting Station, but denies that they are drowning out the hearers of WGN, and state that, if such is the fact, it is because said complainant's broadcasting station is improperly constructed and operated.

The answer further admits that on or about September 7, 1926, there was available to them a wave length of 249.9 metres with a frequency of 1,200 kilocycles, but state that said wave length is not desirable for the purpose of broadcasting and that its use would render WGES of little or no value as a broadcasting station.

And further sets forth that there are other wave lengths which would be usable by the defendants, but states that their use would cause greater interference to other broadcasters than the interference now caused to WGN by the use of the present wave length now employed by them.

The defendants further charge that they have invested large sums of money in and about their plant and will suffer damage in the event the temporary injunction heretofore issued should not be dissolved.

The facts in this case, as charged by the bill and admitted by the answer, together with the additional facts set out in the bill as matters of defense, disclose a situation new and novel in a court of equity and a consideration of the law applicable to the facts requires an understanding of the present conditions for the purpose of ascertaining whether or not the old adage of "Old laws should be adapted to new facts" should be applied and for that reason a short statement of general existing conditions is not out of order at this time before considering the legal and equitable aspects of the cause.

It is a matter of general knowledge that in the last few years there has grown up in the United States, as well as abroad, a well recognized calling or business known as broadcasting which consists in sending from a central station, electrically equipped, programs of music and amusement. speeches by men of prominence, news of the day and items of interest taking plaice in the world, and that these various programs are received by the public over radio receiving sets which have been installed in homes, hotels, and various other places, and that a large industry has grown up and developed in the milking and manufacturing of radio sets, so that in the United States, at this time, there are millions of dollars invested by the public at large, which has made the investment for the purpose of and with the knowledge that they could receive these programs, speeches, and items of interest from various broadcasting stations located in various parts of the United States and in other countries.

It might also be stated that, so far as broadcasting stations are concerned, there has almost grown up a custom which recognizes the rights of the various broadcasters, particularly in that certain broadcasters use certain hours of the day, while the other broadcasters remain silent during that particular period of time. Again, in this particular locality, a certain night is set aside as silent night, when all local broadcasters cease broadcasting in order that the radio receivers may be able to tune in on outside distant stations.

Wave lengths have been bought and sold and broadcasting stations have changed hands for a consideration. Broadcasting stations have contracted with each other so as to broadcast without conflicting and in this manner be able to present their different programs to the waiting public. The public itself has become educated to the use or its receiving sets so as to be able to obtain certain particular items of news, speeches. or programs over its own particular sets.

The theory of the bill in this case is based upon the proposition that by usage of a particular wave length for a considerable length of time and by reason of the expenditure of a considerable amount of money in developing its broadcasting station and by usage of a particular wave length educating the public to know that that particular wave length is the wave length of the complainant: and by furnishing programs which have been attractive and thereby cause a great number of people to listen in to their particular programs that the said complainant has created and carved out for itself a particular right or easement in and to the use of said wave length which should he recognized in a court of equity and that outsiders should not be allowed thereafter, except for good cause shown, to deprive them of that right and to make use of a field which had been built up by the complainant at a considerable cost in money and a considerable time in pioneering. …

The defendants further insist that a wave length can not be made the subject of private control and, further and lastly, that as a matter of fact they are not interfering with the complainant by the use of the present wave length employed by them from their broadcasting station. …

[The court discussed the 1912 federal statute which required a license to broadcast by radio and restricted the wavelengths available, as discussed above. It concluded that the statute did not displace state law.]

In the first place, it is argued that there are no rights in the air and that the law has no right or authority to restrict the using of wave lengths or to exclude others from their use. In answer to this it might be said that Congress has already attempted to regulate the use of the air in its enactment of August 13, 1912, by providing that only certain strata of the air or ether may be used for broadcasting purposes and, further, requiring persons to take out a license before they are permitted to exercise the use of the air or ether. Moreover, it appears to this court that the situation is such from the past development of the industry of broadcasting and radio receiving and from the apparent future, as indicated by the past, that, unless some regulatory measures are provided for by Congress or rights recognized by State courts, the situation will result in chaos and a great detriment to the advancement of an industry which is only in its infancy.

While it is true that the case in question is novel in its newness, the situation is not devoid, however, of legal equitable support. The serve answer might be made, as was made in the beginning; that there was no property right, or could be, in a name or sign, but there has developed a long line of cases, both in the Federal and State courts, which has recognized, under the law known as the law of unfair competition, the right to obtain a property right in a name or word or collection of names or words [Ed: i.e., a trademark] which gives the person who first made use of the same a property right therein, provided that by reason of their use, he has succeeded in building up a business and created a good will which has become known to the public and to the trade and which has served as a designation of some particular output so that it has become generally recognized as the property of such person. The courts have held that persons who attempt to imitate or to make use of such trade name or names or words evidently do so for the purpose of enriching themselves through the efforts of some other person who by the investment of money and time has created something of value. Equity has invariably protected the rights of such persons in the use of said names.

It is also true that the courts have recognized, particularly in the west, the right to the use of running water for the purposes of mining and other uses. (*Atchison v. Peterson*, 20 Wall. 507; *Cache La Poudre Reservoir v. Water Supply & Storage Co.*, 25 Colo. 161.)

Some of the States have also recognized the rights of telephone and telegraph companies in the operation of their lines free from interference by lines of other companies placed in such close proximity as to create confusion by reason of electrical interference. (*Western Union Telegraph Co. v. Los Angeles Electric Co.*, 70 Fed. 178; *Northwestern Telephone Exchange Co. v. Twin City Telephone Co.*, 89 Minn, 4115; and other cases.)

It us argued that the electrical cases generally involve a franchise and thereby a property right. but the cases on electrical interference are cited more particularly for the purpose of their analogy to the case at bar and not as authorities on the question.

In regard to the water cases, counsel for the defendants call our attention to the rule in this State, as set forth in the case of *Druley v. Adam* (102 Ill. 177), where the court says in its opinion, page 193, "The law has been long settled in this State that there can be no property merely in the water of a running stream. The owner of laud over which a stream of water flows has, as incident to his ownership of the land, a property right in the flow of the water at that place for all the beneficial uses that may result from it, whether for motive power in propelling machinery or in imparting fertility to the adjacent soil, etc. ; in other words, he has a usufruct in the water while it passes; but all other riparian proprietors have precisely the same rights in regard to it and, apart from the right of consumption fur supplying natural wants, neither can, to the injury of the other, abstract the water or divert or arrest its flow."

The same court, however, in its opinion, on page 201, while holding that the western water cases are not applicable, recognized the law as laid down in those cases and distinguished them on the ground that it is apparent that the law necessarily arose in those eases by reason of the peculiar circumstances and necessities existing in those countries at the time.

It is the opinion of the court that, under the circumstances as now exist, there is a peculiar necessity existing and that there are such unusual and peculiar circumstances surrounding the question at issue tat a court of equity is compelled to recognize rights which have been acquired by reason of the outlay and expenditure of money and the investment of time and that the circumstances and necessities are such, under the circumstances of this case, as will justify a court of equity in taking jurisdiction of the cause. Such being the case, it becomes the duly of the court to consider the last question, namely, whether or not there is such an interference by the defendants with the broadcasting station of complainant that the temporary injunction heretofore granted should be kept in force until a final hearing of the cause.

[W]e believe that the equities of the situation are in favor of the complainant on the facts as heretofore shown, particularly in that the complainant has been using said wave length for a considerable length of time and has built up a large clientage, whereas the defendants are but newly in the field and will not suffer as a result of in injunction in proportion to the damage that would be sustained by the complainant after having spent a much greater length of time in the education of the general radio-receiving public to the wave length in question.

We are of the opinion further that, under the circumstances in this case, priority of time creates a superiority in right, and the fact of priority having been conceded by the answer it would seem to this court that it would lie only just that the situation should be preserved in the status in which it was prior to the time that the defendants undertook to operate over or near the wave length of the complainant. …

It is difficult to determine at this time how a radio station should be properly run, but it is, also, true that the science of broadcasting and receiving is being subject every day to change and it is possible that within it short time this may be accomplished, although it is the opinion of the court from an examination of the affidavits and exhibits in the cause that 40 kilocycles is not at this time recognized as a safe limitation for the prevention of interference between stations located in the same locality. It is true that stations sufficiently removed from each other can broadcast even over the same wave length, but it necessarily follows that they must be so far apart that the wave lengths do not reach or come in contact with each other to the extent of creating interference.

In the case at bar the contestants are so located with reference to each other that the court does not feel that 40 kilocycles is sufficient. The court is of the opinion, however, that until there has been a final hearing of this cause no order prohibiting the defendants from the use of any particular wave length should be entered and to that extent the order heretofore entered will be modified so that it will read that the defendants are restrained and enjoined from broadcasting over a wave length sufficiently near to the one used by the complainant so as to cause any material interference with the programs or announcements of the complainant over and from its broadcasting station to the radio public within a radius of 100 miles, and in order that the defendants may be apprised of the feeling of the court in this regard, while the order is not expressly one of exact limitation, nevertheless the court feels that a distance removed 50 kilocycles front the wave length of the complainant would be a safe distance and that if the defendants use a wave length in closer proximity than the one stated it must be at the risk of the defendants in this cause.

Notes and Questions

1. *Oak Leaves* is a road not taken. This report of the case comes from the *Congressional Record.* Senator Clarence Dill (D-WA) had it read into the record on December 10, 1926 (i.e. the month after it was decided) because of its bearing on a radio regulation bill he co-sponsored.[26] That bill became the Radio Act of 1927, which established the licensing

---

[2626] Being read into the record is not necessarily a sign of importance. Five pages later, Senator Byron Harrison (D-MS) had one of Aesop's fables read into the record to make a point about Republican political maneuvering.

system whose essentials are still in force today. Broadcasters require a license from the Federal Communications Commission; those licenses specify, in some detail, the frequency on which they can broadcast, the locations of their transmitters, and the power they can use. The licenses started out being heavily regulated to ensure that each broadcaster's programs served the public interest, but over time the licensing process has become far more ministerial. Subject to some concentrated-ownership restrictions and a few miscellaneous content rules (e.g. compliance with the Emergency Broadcasting System and some rules on children's programming), a broadcaster is free to transmit whatever programming it wants as long as it complies with the FCC's technical requirements. The result is a system that divides the airwaves into geographic and frequency blocks, and gives each of these blocks an exclusive licensee. Anyone else broadcasting on these frequencies in these places is violating the law. Similar systems hand out the right to use other frequencies for other purposes (e.g. mobile phone towers, police radios, satellite communications, etc.). In effect, any unauthorized use of someone else's assigned spectrum is illegal.

Compare this system with the common-law process illustrated by *Oak Leaves*. One obvious difference how one acquires rights in a frequency: prior use versus governmental assignment. Which of the two seems more likely to lead to an efficient allocation of resources to those best able to make good use of them? Which is fairer to participants? Which is more likely to serve the interests of the listening public? Another evident different is the different tests for violation of another's rights. Is it fair to say that the FCC exclusive licensing are protected by a kind of right against trespass, while *Oak Leaves* more closely resembles the test for nuisance? Are there any other relevant differences?

The change in the FCC's policies over time is interesting, too. If broadcasting is to be based on licenses, how ought those licenses be given out? And should the FCC care what a licensee does with a license after that? There was a time when listeners' groups routinely filed lawsuits to keep radio stations from changing their formats. *See, e.g.*, *Citizens Committee to Keep Progressive Rock v. FCC*, 478 F. 2d 926 (D.C. Cir. 1973) (remanding to FCC for hearing on whether to allow WGLN to change from "progressive rock" to "middle of the road"). Would that be a better system? Or should the FCC get even further out of the business and not care how licensees use their assigned spectrum at all – e.g., if a licensee wants to stop transmitting FM radio and use the spectrum for mobile phone calls, why should the FCC care? Does calling broadcasting licenses "property" do anything to answer these questions?

Here's another alternative: no licenses at all, and let anyone use the spectrum however they see fit. Before you scoff at this "commons" approach to spectrum allocation, consider that this is how WiFi works. You don't need an FCC license to plug in a home wireless router. The frequency range from 2.4 gigahertz (i.e. 2.4 billion cycles per second) to 2.5 gigahertz is "unlicensed"; the FCC regulates the maximum power that a device can emit, but otherwise, anyone is basically free to use any device they want however they want. How well does your WiFi connection typically work? What about the chaos of interference *Oak Leaves* feared? Would this approach work on a wider scale?

2. *Oak Leaves* presents its holding as an almost inevitable consequence of the nature of spectrum. But what is spectrum? Radio broadcasting works by running an electric current through the right kind of circuit, which results in electromagnetic radiation spreading in certain ways that people with the right kinds of devices can detect. Why isn't the relevant "property" here the transmitter and the receiver (both tangible personal property), or the land over which the radiation passes (real property)? So why not handle broadcasting cases using personal property torts ("You damaged my radio tower by interfering with its transmissions") or real property torts ("You trespassed by sending electromagnetic radiation over my land")? Consider this passage from Ronald Coase, *The Federal Communications Commission*, 2 J. L. Econ. 1 (1959):

   What does not seem to have been understood is that what is being allocated by the Federal Communications Commission, or, if there were a market, what would be sold, is the right to use a piece of equipment to transmit signals in a particular way. Once the question is looked at in this way, it is unnecessary to think in terms of ownership of frequencies or the ether. Earlier we discussed a case in which it had to be decided whether a confectioner had the right to use machinery which caused noise and vibrations in a neighboring house. It would not have facilitated our analysis of the case if it had been discussed in terms of who owned sound waves or vibrations or the medium (whatever it is) through which sound waves or vibrations travel. Yet this is essentially what is done in the radio industry. The reason why this way of thinking has become so dominant in discussions of radio law is that it seemed to have developed by using the analogy of the law of airspace. In fact, the law of radio and television has been commonly treated as part of the law of the air. It is not suggested that this approach need lead to the wrong answers, but it tends to obscure the question that is being decided. Thus, whether we have the right to shoot over another man's land has been thought of as depending on who owns the airspace over the land. It would be simpler to discuss what we should be allowed to do with a gun. … The problem confronting the radio industry is that signals transmitted by one person may interfere with those transmitted by another. It can be solved by delimiting the rights which various persons possess.

   Is this any more helpful than *Oak Leaves*'s analogies to trademarks and water rights?

A related argument is that "spectrum" is the wrong abstraction for regulating multiple people's simultaneous broadcasting. It is true that given the amplitude-modulating radio technology of 1926, WGN's and WGES's broadcasts on nearby frequencies from nearby locations were likely to cause frustrating interference for listeners. But technology changes, and more broadcast technologies don't depend on exclusive assignments of slices of spectrum. One approach is "spread-spectrum," in which a device transmits at a given frequency only for a very short burst and then "hops" to a different frequency for the next bit of its transmission, and so on. This is basically how modern cell phones communicate with towers; the system allows many devices to "share" the same nominal slice of spectrum. Another emerging technology is "ultra-wideband," in which a device transmits on an immensely wide range of frequencies but with very low power – so low that it interferes only minimally with other spectrum users. There are also techniques that involve shaping the geometry of a transmission so it travels only in desired directions. What would *Oak Leaves* have to say about these new technologies? Is it more or less accommodating of them than the FCC's regulatory system?

3. What do you make of the defendant's argument that WGN's station was "improperly constructed and operated?" If WGES is causing interference to WGN's signal, should it matter that WGN could avoid the problem by fixing its equipment? Should it matter how much the changes would cost? On how well-established the appropriate technical standards are?

   For that matter, what about better receivers? If more modern radios would allow people in the Chicago area to tune in to WGN at 990 kilohertz without hearing interference from WGES at 950 kilohertz (and vice versa), should WGN really be able to push WGES off the airwaves just because some listeners have antiquated radios? (To borrow the court's analogy to trademarks, what if some people are just confused all the time about everything?)

   These can be high-stakes fights. The company LightSquared wanted to build a nationwide wireless network using a mixture of cell towers and satellites. It had FCC permission to use frequencies between 1525 and 1559 megahertz, but the next spectrum band up, from 1559 to 1610 megahertz, was allocated to "radionavigation satellite services" – i.e., GPS. Technical reports agreed with the arguments of GPS makers that LightSquared's proposed transmissions would cause many GPS units, including some on airplanes, to stop working. LightSquared argued that this was not because it would be improperly transmitting outside its assigned band, but because GPS units would be improperly *listening* to transmissions outside of their assigned band. According to

LightSquared, inexpensive filters in GPS units would have fixed the problem – but there are millions of GPS units already out there in the world without those filters. In the end, the FCC scrapped LightSquared's plan. Would you have? LightSquared spent three years in bankruptcy following the FCC's decision, and racked up nearly $2 billion in losses. Could a better system of property rights in spectrum have avoided the conflict entirely?

4. Does *Oak Leaves* give legal recognition to property that already exists or create property where none existed before? Or is "property" the wrong way to refer to WGN's rights here?

United States v. Turoff

701 F. Supp. 981 (E.D.N.Y. 1988)

GLASSER, District Judge:

Defendants have moved to dismiss the indictment in this case on the ground that … it fails to allege a violation of the mail fraud statute, 18 U.S.C. § 1341.

For the reasons stated below, defendants' motion is denied.

FACTS …

According to the indictment, in late 1978, the TLC, which regulates the City's medallion taxicabs, authorized the issuance of 100 temporary taxi medallions to a corporation ("Research Cab Corporation") to be formed by defendant Donald Sherman. The purpose of the temporary medallions was to test the feasibility of diesel engines in New York City taxicabs.

The indictment alleges that in late 1980, the TLC's chairman, defendant Turoff, caused an additional 23 unauthorized medallions to be diverted to his codefendants and placed on gasoline- and diesel-powered taxicabs registered to Research Cab and to Tulip Cab Corporation. These taxicabs allegedly operated in the City from late 1980 to early 1985. Defendants Donald and Ronald Sherman allegedly deposited the proceeds from those taxicabs, which exceeded $500,000, in the bank account of a shell corporation ("Exdie Cab Corporation").

Allegedly, defendants never paid the TLC the annual license renewal fees for the unauthorized medallions. In connection with the conspiracy, the defendant Turoff allegedly gave false and misleading information to the TLC Commissioners and the Mayor's office, and destroyed TLC records on the Tulip Cab Corporation and all the defendants allegedly gave false and misleading information to the New York State Commission of Investigation. The indictment alleges fourteen instances in which the mails were used to effectuate the scheme.

DISCUSSION

I.

The mail fraud statute under which defendants have been indicted was first enacted in 1872. In its present form, it now reads:

> Whoever, having devised or intending to devise any scheme or artifice to defraud, or for obtaining money or property by means of false or fraudulent pretenses, representations, or promises, or to sell, dispose of, loan, exchange, alter, give away, distribute, supply, or furnish or procure for unlawful use any counterfeit or spurious coin, obligation, security, or other article, or anything represented to be or intimated or held out to be such counterfeit or spurious article, for the purpose of executing such scheme or artifice or attempting to do so, places in any post office or authorized depository for mail matter, any matter or thing whatever to be sent or delivered by the Postal Service, or takes or receives therefrom, any such matter or thing, or knowingly causes to be delivered by mail according to the direction thereon, or at the place at which it is directed to be delivered by the person to whom it is addressed, any such matter or thing, shall be fined not more than $1,000 or imprisoned not more than five years, or both.

Defendants move to dismiss the indictment on the ground that it does not state a cognizable violation of the mail fraud statute as interpreted in *McNally v. United States*, 483 U.S. 350 (1987). In *McNally*, the Supreme Court reversed the mail fraud convictions of Charles J. McNally and James E. Gray on the ground that the mail fraud statute does not reach schemes which violate "the intangible right of the citizenry to good government." The case involved a scheme devised by Gray, who held two top government posts in the Kentucky state government, and Howard P. "Sonny" Hunt, a state Democratic party chairman who had been given de facto power by the governor to select the insurance agencies from which the state would buy its policies. Hunt selected a certain agency as the state's agent for securing a workmen's compensation policy, on the condition that that agency would share any resulting commissions in excess of $50,000 a year with twenty-one other insurance agencies specified by Hunt. Among the designated agencies was one controlled by Hunt and Gray (who had formed it for the exclusive purpose of obtaining the excess commissions). McNally served as the agency's front man. …

[McNally and Gray were convicted of mail fraud.]

The jury convicted defendants, and the Court of Appeals affirmed the convictions, relying on many prior decisions holding that "the mail fraud statute proscribes schemes to defraud citizens of their intangible rights to honest and impartial government."

The Supreme Court reversed, holding that "[t]he mail fraud statute clearly protects property rights, but does not refer to the intangible right of the citizenry to good government." The Court framed the issue in the case narrowly:

> The issue is thus whether a state officer violates the mail fraud statute if he chooses an insurance agent to provide insurance for the State but specifies that the agent must share its commissions with other named insurance agencies, in one of which the officer has an ownership interest and hence profits when his agency receives part of the commissions. We note that as the action comes to us, there was no charge and the jury was not required to find that the Commonwealth itself was defrauded of any money or property. It was not charged that in the absence of the alleged scheme the Commonwealth would have paid a lower premium or secured better insurance. Hunt and Gray received part of the commissions but those commissions were not the Commonwealth's money. Nor was the jury charged that to convict it must find that the Commonwealth was deprived of control over how its money was spent. Indeed, the premium for insurance would have been paid to some agency, and what Hunt and Gray did was to assert control that the Commonwealth might not otherwise have made over the commissions paid by the insurance company to its agent.... We hold, therefore, that the jury instruction on the substantive mail fraud count permitted a conviction for conduct not within the reach of § 1341[2] …

Most significantly for this case, the Court in *McNally* held that, because the mail fraud statute "had its origin in the desire to protect individual property rights, ... any benefit which the Government derives from the [mail fraud] statute must be limited to the Government's interest as property-holder." Accordingly, in the present case, the government's failure to demonstrate the City's interest "as property-holder" in the medallions would be fatal to that charge in the indictment that is based upon the fraudulent procurement of the medallions.

---

[2] The narrowness of *McNally*'s holding was underscored in *Carpenter v. United States*, 484 U.S. 19, (1987), which held that a newspaper had a property right under § 1341 in the exclusive pre-publication use of confidential business information, and noted that "McNally did not limit the scope of § 1341 to tangible as distinguished from intangible property rights."

However, even if the court accepted this argument, the indictment would still stand insofar as it is based on the scheme to avoid payment of license renewal fees. Money is the most concrete and tangible of property. In *Reiter v. Sonotone Corp.*, 442 U.S. 330 (1979), the Court stated: "In its dictionary definitions and in common usage 'property' comprehends anything of material value owned or possessed... . Money, of course, is a form of property." On this basis alone, defendant's motion to dismiss the indictment must be denied.

As regards the medallions, the court concludes that the fraudulent misappropriation of them deprived the City of a property interest cognizable under the mail fraud statute.

Defendants cite *United States v. Evans*, 844 F.2d 36 (2d Cir. 1988) for the proposition that the City's interest in the medallions "is ancillary to a regulation, not to property." *Id.*, 844 F.2d at 42. Evans concerned a scheme to transfer arms regulated by the federal government from various foreign nations to Iran. The scheme required defendants to deceive the government about the true identity of the purchasing country in order to obtain the necessary approval for the transaction. The government's right to regulate such transfers arose either from a statutorily-required clause in the contract between the United States and the original foreign buyer, or by regulation.

The Second Circuit, affirming the district court's dismissal of the mail and wire fraud counts against defendants, held that the government had not shown that it had some property interest in the arms. Furthermore, the court rejected the government's contention that "the right of the United States Government to prevent the resale or retransfer of U.S. military weaponry from foreign nations to other, unacceptable foreign powers" constituted "an interest in, and a right to exercise control over, property" for purposes of the mail fraud statute. *Id.*, 844 F.2d at 40.

In addressing the latter argument, the court rejected the government's analogies to common law property rights. The court reasoned that, while a right to control the future alienation and use of a thing can be a traditional property right (e.g., the fee simple determinable, the fee simple subject to a condition subsequent, the possibility of reverter, and the power of termination), that does not mean that every such right is cognizable under the mail and wire fraud statutes.[4]

---

[4] I note that the possessory and future interests named are not intrinsically "devices through which a nonpossessor controls land" or "control[s] alienation." 844 F.2d at 41. The estates in land described are expressions of the extent of one's present interest in property measured in terms of time. The owner of a fee simple determinable has a present, possessory interest in property which will continue "until" or "so long as" a specified event does or does not occur. The possibility of reverter is the present interest one has in the future use and enjoyment of the property when the fee simple determinable ends. The owner of a fee simple subject to a condition subsequent has a present possessory interest in property "upon condition that"

Specifically, the court noted that the government's right to control arms transfers between foreign powers would never permit the United States to possess the weapons in question, and had no effect on the purchaser's title to the arms or the seller's right to profits from the sale. Rather, the regulatory scheme governing such transfers "substitutes for the traditional property remedies of replevin, damages or specific performance, a substitution that is further proof that the right is not property." *Id.*, 844 F.2d at 41. Moreover, the court expressed its reluctance to apply common law property rules in the fundamentally different context of weapons transfers, which are governed by foreign policy and human rights considerations in addition to the usual economic laws of supply and demand.

The court summed up by finding that the government's interest in the weapons was essentially regulatory:

> All of these distinctions suggest to us that the government's interest here is ancillary to a regulation, not to property. A law prohibiting a particular use of a commodity that the government does not use or possess ordinarily does not create a property right. If it did, many government regulations would create property rights. For example, laws preventing the sale of heroin or the dumping of toxic waste would create government property rights in the drugs or chemicals. Admittedly, the line between regulation and property is difficult to draw with scientific precision ... and we do not mean to imply that the government never has a property interest in the limits it imposes on property use.

Id., 844 F.2d at 42 (citation omitted).

Evans is distinguishable. As discussed above, in *Evans* the United States had no possessory interest in the weapons, nor did the deception practiced by the defendants affect the purchaser's title to the weapons or the seller's right to profit from the sale of the weapons. Here, defendants are accused of taking 23 items of tangible personal property from the City's possession. Title to those medallions in the hands of third persons would be affected. Citation of authority is not required for the principle that a thief cannot transfer title even to a bona fide purchaser for value. While the government in Evans had no possessory interest in the weapons, the TLC in

---

or "provided that" a specified event does or does not occur. The power of termination is the present interest one has in the future use and enjoyment of that property upon the exercise of his power to terminate the possessory estate. All the estates described are present property interests in the sense that they are all descendible, devisable and alienable. N.Y.Est.Powers & Trusts Law § 6–5.1 (McKinney 1967). That a person who acquired either of those estates in property by or through a scheme or artifice to defraud would acquire a present interest in property is beyond cavil.

this case did have a possessory interest in the medallions. It maintained them under lock and key at its offices. It had title to them. An action for conversion of those medallions would lie and either replevin or damages would be an available and appropriate remedy. … Given the impetus to return to the arcane learning of the law of property prompted by McNally, a quotation from Book III of Blackstone's Commentaries on the Laws of England (Lewis' Ed.1902) seems appropriate. At pages 145–46 that venerable author wrote:

> The wrongful taking of goods being thus most clearly an injury, the next consideration is, what remedy the Law of England has given for it. And this is, in the first place, the restitution of the goods themselves so wrongfully taken, with damages for the loss sustained by such unjust invasion; which is effected by action of replevin; ...

That the medallions themselves are a valuable, marketable commodity was adverted to years ago by Professor Charles A. Reich in his seminal article entitled *The New Property*, 73 Yale L.J. 733 (1964). He wrote, at page 735:

> A New York City taxi medallion, which costs very little when originally obtained from the city, can be sold for over twenty thousand dollars.

In a footnote at that point, the author observed:

> 7. A New York Taxi Medallion is a piece of tin worth 300 times its weight in gold. No new transferable medallions have been issued since 1937. Their value in 1961 was estimated at $21,000 to $23,000; banks will lend up to $13,000 on one. The cabbie pays the City only $200 a year for his medallion. There is a brisk trade in them: out of 11,800, about 600 changed hands in 1961. One company, National Transportation Co., sold 100 medallions at $21,000 each, a transaction totaling $2,100,000. A non-transferable license, of which there are a few, has no market value. *N.Y. Times*, Dec. 5, 1961, p. 46, col. 3.

The government also contends that the medallion is, in essence, the equivalent of an easement to use the city streets. At the risk of dwelling too long on the esoterica of property, the medallions could not properly be equated with easements. An easement is generally appurtenant, which is to say that it is a right which the owner of one parcel of land (the dominant tenement) may exercise in or over the land of another (the servient tenement) for the benefit of the former. An easement in gross is a right created in a person to use the land of another, which the owner of that easement may enjoy even though he does not own or possess a dominant estate. Although the concept of an easement in gross has been recognized, such an easement is rare. The government's contention would have been more technically correct had it characterized the medallion as a "special franchise" which confers a right to do something in the public highway which, except for the grant, would be a trespass.

A franchise is property. It is assignable, taxable and transmissible. *Hatfield v. Straus*, 82 N.E. 172 (1907). A mere license, on the other hand, is nothing more than a personal, revocable privilege. See, e.g., *Brooklyn Heights R.R. Co. v. Steers*, 106 N.E. 919 (1914). It would not be seriously disputed that a taxicab "license" is, accurately speaking, a special franchise which is not revocable at will and may not be taken away except by due process. *Hecht v. Monaghan*, 121 N.E.2d 421 (1954). *See also*, *Wignall v. Fletcher*, 303 N.Y. 435 (1952). The resolution of this motion will not be dependent, however, upon the technically correct characterization of the matter in issue as being either a franchise, license, or easement.

The government also contends that the physical medallions themselves are "property" for purposes of the mail fraud statute. The defendants ridicule that contention by deprecatingly referring to the medallions as nothing more than "23 pieces of tin". Thus, the defendants impliedly, but never explicitly, assert a de minimis qualification to the tort of conversion or the crime of larceny. No authority is cited to support that oblique assertion, nor is the court aware of any. In his dissenting opinion in *McNally*, Justice Stevens was prescient when he expressed doubt about the gravity of the ramifications of the Court's decision and said that "Congress can, of course, negate it by amending the statute." As has already been noted, Congress did exactly that. Justice Stevens went on, however, to observe that:

> Even without Congressional action, prosecutions of corrupt officials who use the mails to further their schemes may continue since it will frequently be possible to prove *some* loss of money or property.

Id. (emphasis added). In this respect Justice Stevens was also prescient. The medallion is a tangible, physical object. The Administrative Code of the City of New York § 19–502(h) provides as follows:

> "Medallion" means the metal plate issued by the commission for displaying the license number of a licensed taxicab on the outside of the vehicle.

By charging the defendants with obtaining by false and fraudulent representations and promises 23 unauthorized taxi medallions, the government is seeking to prosecute these defendants by attempting to prove they caused some loss of property as alleged.

In *Evans*, upon which the defendants so heavily rely, the defendants were charged with making false statements to United States agencies to obtain approval to export arms. Here, the defendants are accused of taking 23 items of tangible personal property (the metal plates) from the City of New York in which the City did have a possessory interest. This is not a case where it is alleged that the citizenry is merely deprived of the honest services of a public official. This is a case where the public official is accused of conspiring with others to misappropriate tangible personal property. To view this case otherwise would be to hold, in effect, that a City cashier who embezzled money merely deprived the City of her honest and faithful services to which the embezzled money is an inconsequential appurtenance. …

Whether the medallions are tangible property or not to support a charge of mail fraud may also be discerned by asking whether the wrongful taking of the medallions from the offices of the TLC would be larceny. Defendants advise that a state prosecution has been commenced on that ground. See N.Y. Penal Law § 155.00(1) (McKinney 1988), defining property for purpose of state larceny statute as "any article, substance or thing of value". Thus, the reluctance of the *McNally* Court to read the mail fraud statute as criminalizing conduct on the part of a state official which is not otherwise prohibited by state law need not deter here. …

Mindful that "an overspeaking judge is no well-tuned cymbal," I nevertheless make several additional observations.

The rule announced in *McNally* was that the mail fraud statute is applicable only to "frauds involving money or property" and not to schemes relating to good government. It logically followed, said the Court in *Evans*, 844 F.2d at 39, "that the deceived party must lose some money or property." *Carpenter* explained that McNally did not limit the scope of the mail fraud statute "to tangible as distinguished from intangible property rights." From those pronouncements, the view has been expressed that obtaining from a sovereign by means of a fraudulent scheme utilizing the mails, a license to engage in a business, profession or occupation is not a violation of the mail fraud statute because the license, although property in the hands of the licensee is not property in the hands of the licensor. Upon reflection, the view is that A has nothing which, when he gives it to B, becomes something. This brings to mind L. Carroll, Through the Looking Glass, Ch. V (Modern Library Ed. at p. 200):

> ... the Queen remarked ... "I'm just one hundred and one, five months and a day."
>
> "I can't believe *that*" said Alice.
>
> "Can't you?" the Queens said in a pitying tone. "Try again; draw a long breath and shut your eyes."
>
> Alice laughed. "There's no use trying," she said: "one *ca'n't* believe impossible things."
>
> "I daresay you haven't had much practice," said the Queens. "When I was your age, I always did it for half-an-hour a day, why, sometimes I've believed as many as six impossible things before breakfast."

To view the sovereign's power to grant licenses, or franchises, or easements as being something other than money or property is to equate, erroneously in my view, the sovereign with an individual or corporation. What the latter sells, buys, creates or manufactures and the proceeds derived from those activities is money or property in the traditional sense. The sovereign can buy and sell and manufacture and derive proceeds from those activities only by virtue of the power it possesses as sovereign – namely its police power, its power to tax, etc. It is only through the exercise of those powers that the sovereign obtains the revenues which enable it to function at all and acquire, if it chooses, "property" in the traditional sense. To rob the sovereign of the due exercise of that power by schemes or artifices to defraud, is to rob it of "property" as surely as the goods or chattels or money obtained from a private person by similar schemes or artifices.

The view of cases that licenses are only property in the hands of the licensee, but never in the hands of the government represents an inversion of historical fact. In the seminal article to which reference has already been made, which urged that various important government benefits (including licenses) be accorded a status akin to "property," Professor Charles Reich noted that traditionally, just the opposite was true – licenses, and all other forms of government largess were considered government property long before the property rights of the licensee or recipient were accorded legal recognition:

The chief obstacle to the creation of private rights in [government] largess [e.g., licenses, welfare benefits, services, contracts and franchises] has been the fact that *it is originally public property, comes from the state, and may be withheld completely.* But this need not be an obstacle. *Traditional property also comes from the state, and in much the same way.* Land, for example, traces back to grants from the sovereign. In the United States, some was the gift of the King of England, some that of the King of Spain. The sovereign extinguished Indian title by conquest, became the new owner, and then granted title to a private individual or group. Some land was the gift of the sovereign under laws such as the Homestead and Preemption Acts. Many other natural resources – water, minerals and timber, passed into private ownership under similar grants. In America, land and resources all were originally government largess. In a less obvious sense, personal property also stems from government. Personal property is created by law; it owes its origin and continuance to laws supported by the people as a whole. These laws "give" the property to one who performs certain actions. Even the man who catches a wild animal "owns" the animal only as a gift from the sovereign, having fulfilled the terms of an offer to transfer ownership.

Reich, *The New Property,* 73 Yale L.J. 733, 778 (1964) (footnotes omitted; emphasis added).

The salutary fact that, in modern times, courts have recognized the property rights of licensees[5] need not blind us to the equally compelling fact that licenses, like other forms of public largess, originate in the state and are "public property," in the first instance. …

Notes and Questions

1. Reich's article is closely linked with *Goldberg v. Kelly*, 397 U.S. 254 (1970), which held that welfare benefits could not be terminated without notice and a hearing. In a footnote, the Court quoted *The New Property* and added, "It may be realistic today to regard welfare entitlements as more like 'property' than a 'gratuity.' Much of the existing wealth in this country takes the form of rights that do not fall within traditional common-law concepts of property." *Id.* at 262 n.8. Two years later, in *Board of Regents of State Colleges v. Roth*, 408 U.S. 564 (1972), the Court held that a state college professor on a renewable one-year contract did not have a "property" interest in continued employment, so he had no Fourteenth Amendment right to a statement of reasons for the nonrenewal of his contract.[27] The court had this to say about the nature of "property":

> To have a property interest in a benefit, a person clearly must have more than an abstract need or desire for it. He must have more than a unilateral expectation of it. He must, instead, have a legitimate claim of entitlement to it. It is a purpose of the ancient institution of property to protect those claims upon which people rely in their daily lives, reliance that must not be arbitrarily undermined. It is a purpose of the constitutional right to a hearing to provide an opportunity for a person to vindicate those claims.
>
> Property interests, of course, are not created by the Constitution. Rather, they are created and their dimensions are defined by existing rules or understandings that

---

[5] *See, e.g.*, *Bell v. Burson*, 402 U.S. 535 (1971) (driver's license); *Dixon v. Love*, 431 U.S. 105 (1977) (same); *Mackey v. Montrym*, 443 U.S. 1 (1979) (same); *Gibson v. Berryhill*, 411 U.S. 564 (1973) (license to practice optometry); *Willner v. Committee on Character and Fitness*, 373 U.S. 96 (1963) (license to practice law); *Barry v. Barchi*, 443 U.S. 55 (1979) (horse trainers' harness racing license).

[27] The court had previously held that written contracts or state tenure law could create the necessary interest to trigger due process protections, *see Slochower v. Board of Higher Ed. of New York City*, 350 U.S. 551 (1956), and a companion case to *Roth* held that a professor might be entitled to due process protections when he alleged the existence of an implicit understanding that professors who had been employed for seven years would be dismissed only for cause. *Perry v. Sindermann*, 408 U.S. 593, 601–03 (1972),

> stem from an independent source such as state law –rules or understandings that secure certain benefits and that support claims of entitlement to those benefits.

Id. at 577. Is this an improvement on *Kremen*'s formulation? Does it work for all property, all intangible property, or just for government benefits? What do you make of its thoughts about where property comes from?

2. Money is property because it is "concrete and tangible," says the court in *Turoff*. Really? What if medallion owners pay their license renewal fees by check? By credit card? Is it more or less tangible than the "piece of tin" that is a taxicab medallion, the public's right to honest services, or the franchise of operating a taxicab?

3. The Springfield Athletic Commission regulates boxing in the sense that boxing for money or charging admission to a boxing match within the state of Springfield is prohibited unless the match takes place under regulations promulgated by the Commission. Some of the Commission's rules establish a system of weight classes and determine who is the "World" champion within each of those classes. Vinnie Watson is the current World Heavyweight Boxing Champion, as determined by the Commission, whose rules allow it to revoke his title unless he "defends his title against a suitable challenger" at least once per year. Watson was been challenged to a match by Drederick Tatum, but declined the challenge. The Commission then voted to revoke Watson title and award it to Tatum instead; Watson has sued the Commission, claiming that Tatum's poor won-loss record makes him not a "suitable" challenger. Do alleging that the Commission's actions deny him "property, without due process of law" within the meaning of the Fourteenth Amendment. Is his title property? Does it matter whether the Commission has demanded that he return the ceremonial belt that new champions hold over their heads?

4. Taxicab medallions typically can be sold on the open market. Liquor licenses typically require a hearing before a local alcoholic beverages commission before they can be transferred. A license to practice law is personal and cannot be transferred at all. Does this mean that liquor licenses and law licenses are not "property?"

5. Is a franchise excludable? If someone steals the medallion from off your taxicab, can you sue for replevin or conversion? What are the damages? Does possession of the medallion give them the right to operate a taxicab on the streets of New York? What are you to do in the meantime – in fact, what if you never find the thief? Is your franchise gone? Now suppose that instead of stealing your medallion, a fraudster forges one, using your

medallion number. Presumably this is an offense under state law, but does it invade your property rights in your franchise? What if the fraudster forges a medallion using an unassigned number?

6. If Uber starts operating in your city without the approval of the TLC, does that violate your property rights in your franchise? If the TLC doesn't take action, can you sue the city for failing to enforce its franchise laws? Does it matter whether you have an exclusive franchise – e.g., to be the only operator of shuttle van service at an airport – or a nonexclusive franchise – e.g., to be one of a number of operators of shuttle van service at the airport? Or, from the other side, can the *denial* of a franchise invade property rights? Is there a "property" interest in being allowed to operate a taxicab for hire, such that a city government triggers the Fourteenth Amendment when it refuses to allow Uber-dispatched cars to pick up passengers within city limits?

3. Intellectual Property

A. Overview

This section takes up intellectual property: rights governing the ownership of information. There is no one distinctive set of doctrines governing all intellectual property in the same way that the law of finders applies to all (well, most) personal property or the law of trespass applies to all (well, most) real property. Instead, the name "intellectual property" is a catch-all used to group several related sets of legal rights, each of which gives the rightsholder an exclusive right to use certain information in certain ways. A defendant who uses that information in that way without the rightsholder permission is said to be an *infringer*.

It is common, and in some respects accurate, to describe the rightsholder as the "owner" of the information, but keep in mind that only certain specified uses count as infringement. There is no body of intellectual property law that prohibits possessing or thinking about information, for example. Instead, different bodies of intellectual property law restrict different kinds of uses. In each case, the scope of the owner's rights is closely tied to what kinds of information that body of law protects and to the rules governing when someone becomes a rightsholder. The latter is a familiar question: just as first possession gives initial title to personal property, and discovery is at the root of title to real property, creation can provide intellectual property rights. But the former is a new kind of question; we have taken it largely for granted that land is proper subject matter for real property and other tangible things are proper subject matter for personal property. Intellectual property is different, because not every kind of information qualifies. In copyright, for example, processes are not proper subject matter: as a consequence, the list of ingredients in a recipe and the steps for combining them are not copyrightable – even if they meet all of copyright law's other requirements.

Learning a body of intellectual property law, therefore, requires learning its subject matter, its rules of initial ownership, and its rules of infringement. In this section, we will study three such bodies from the federal level: copyrights, patents, and trademarks. We will study copyright in more detail as an example, and then examine patents and trademarks to see how they are both similar to and different from copyright's model But there are other systems of intellectual property law as well. Here are a few of the most important ones:

- Federal **copyright law** protects "original works of authorship," like novels, biographies, songs, screenplays, paintings, blueprints, and sculptures. Copyright law has a very low threshold for protection: a work must merely display a "modicum of creativity" and have been written down ("fixed in a tangible medium of expression"). The copyright so obtained is valid during its author's lifetime, and for the next seventy years after that. It gives copyright owners the exclusive right to reproduce their works, to make adaptations of them, to distribute them to the public, and to perform or display them publicly – but this right only applies against people who copy from the owner. Someone who independently and coincidentally comes up with similar expression is an author in her own right, not an infringer. Below, for example, are two photographs of the same iceberg, taken by different photographers from nearby locations at almost exactly the same time. Neither infringes on the other.

Left: Sarah Scurr. Right: Marisol Ortiz Elfeldt

- Federal **patent law** protects "any new and useful process, machine, manufacture, or composition of matter." Examples include mechanical devices like tractor plows and can openers, chemical processes used to refine oil, pharmaceutical products like anti-HIV drugs, and, a little infamously, a "Method and apparatus for automatically exercising a curious animal" by encouraging it to chase a laser pointer. *See* U.S. Pat. No. 6,701,872. To obtain a patent, an inventor must go through a detailed and expensive application process, which involves convincing the U.S. Patent and Trademark Office (USPTO) that her invention is genuinely new ("novel"), that it represents a sufficient advance on previous inventions (that it be "nonobvious"), and that it has some practical use in the world, however slight ("utility"). She must also disclose to the public, in detail, how her invention works and how best to use it. Once the USPTO issues a patent, it gives the owner the exclusive right for twenty years (from the date she filed her application with the USPTO) to make, use, offer to sell, or sell the invention. (This means that anyone is free to copy or to study the *patent* on a new kind of steering wheel, but they cannot make, use, or sell *steering wheels* as described in the patent.)

- **Trademark law**, which is a hybrid of state and federal rights. Its basis for protection is a little different. A trademark is a word or symbol, like NIKE or the "swoosh" logo that distinguishes goods or services in the marketplace. One gains trademark rights by using a mark on goods so that consumers associate the mark with a particular source – i.e., they know that NIKE shoes come from one company (Nike) and not another (Adidas or Reebok). These associations are called "goodwill" and it is common to say that what a trademark owner owns is the goodwill (even though it exists only in consumers' minds). These rights exist under state common law as soon as the goodwill exists; trademark owners can also register their marks with the USPTO, which gives nationwide and not just local rights. Trademark law gives a trademark owner the right to prevent uses of the mark that cause "consumer confusion" about the source of goods: a consumer who sees non-Nike shoes falsely labeled NIKE and who mistakenly believes they come from Nike has been confused about the origin of the goods, and Nike can sue the company slapping its trademark on ersatz shoes.

- **Trade secret law** was previously almost entirely a matter of common law, but now almost all states have adopted a version of the Uniform Trade Secrets Act, and the federal Defend Trade Secrets Act of 2016 substantially incorporates the UTSA's definitions. To be protected as a trade secret, information must be valuable because it is secret. Canonical examples of trade secrets include chain restaurants' secret sauces, customer lists, business plans, manufacturing designs, information on the location of valuable resources like shipwrecks and oil fields, and inventions in the development stage before they are ready to be patented. (Because obtaining a patent involves extensive disclosure, it is impossible to have a patent and a trade secret on exactly the same information; one of the major strategic decisions inventors must make when they apply for a patent is how much to include in the application to obtain a stronger or broader patent, and how much to try to hold back as a trade secret.) In general, a defendant is liable only for obtaining a trade secret through "improper means." Breach of a duty of confidentiality is far and away the most common such means – such as when employees take company documents stamped "CONFIDENTIAL" with them to their new jobs at a competitor. More colorfully, industrial espionage, such as breaking into labs or hacking into computers, is also improper means. Note that trade secret law, like copyright law, protects only against infringers who obtain the secret information, directly or indirectly, from the owner: independent rediscovery of the same information is a complete defense. So is reverse engineering, in which a defendant takes publicly available information (including legally obtained copies of the owner's goods containing or made using with the trade secret) and studies it to understand how the secret works.

- State-created **rights of publicity**, discussed in more detail in the section on property in people, protect against the commercial use of one's name, picture, voice, or other indicia of identity without permission. For example, photoshopping a celebrity's face onto a model wearing one of your company's sweaters and using the photograph in an ad for those sweaters is likely to trigger the right of publicity. Some states require that one's identity have "commercial value" to bring a right of publicity suit, others do not. (How would one build up commercial value in one's identity? It is something one can do deliberately, or does it just happen to some people and not others?) The federal trademark law, the Lanham Act, provides a closely related cause of action for false claims about endorsement: quoting a person as saying "I always shop at Acme Hardware" is actionable if the person didn't say it and you don't have their permission to quote them as saying it.

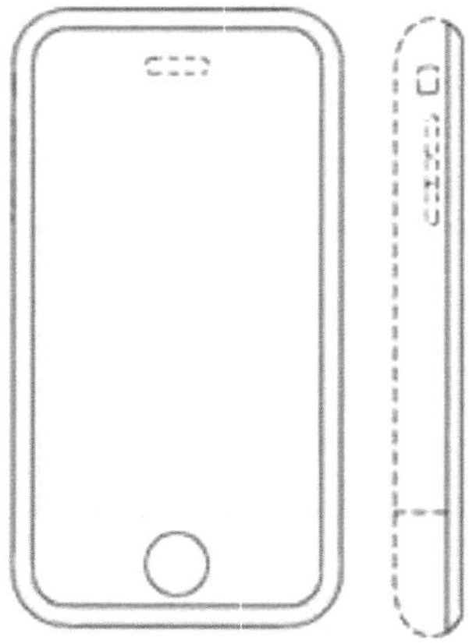

- In addition to the patents discussed above (technically, "utility patents"), the federal government also issues **design patents** on "any new, original, and ornamental design for an article of manufacture" and **plant patents** for "any distinct and new variety of plant." Design patents have become big business, particularly in the technology world where the shape of a device and its user interface are crucial aspects in selling it to consumers. Apple, for example, has sued Samsung for infringing several design patents on elements of the iPhone design; the saga of this litigation is ongoing, but as of now, Apple is defending a $400 million damage award on appeal.

Despite the name, it is highly controversial whether intellectual property should be considered a species of "property" at all. As you read the cases in this section, consider why advocates might want to embrace or deny that label, and what if anything is at stake. Also, pay close attention to the distinction between the intellectual property rights in an object and property rights in the object itself. (In copyright terms, this is the distinction between a "work" and a "copy" of the work.) These rights can overlap or conflict, and some of the most important doctrines of intellectual property law are devoted to sorting out these issues. Finally, consider the extent to which the fact that intellectual property rights deal with information raises distinctive free expression concerns.

B. Copyright

Feist Publications, Inc. v. Rural Telephone Service Co.
499 U.S. 340 (1991)

JUSTICE O'CONNOR delivered the opinion of the Court.

This case requires us to clarify the extent of copyright protection available to telephone directory white pages.

I

Rural Telephone Service Company, Inc., is a certified public utility that provides telephone service to several communities in northwest Kansas. It is subject to a state regulation that requires all telephone companies operating in Kansas to issue annually an updated telephone directory. Accordingly, as a condition of its monopoly franchise, Rural publishes a typical telephone directory, consisting of white pages and yellow pages. The white pages list in alphabetical order the names of Rural's subscribers, together with their towns and telephone numbers. The yellow pages list Rural's business subscribers alphabetically by category and feature classified advertisements of various sizes. Rural distributes its directory free of charge to its subscribers, but earns revenue by selling yellow pages advertisements.

[Feist published a telephone directory, containing both white and yellow pages, covering a much larger geographic area. It contained 46,878 white-pages listings. Feist requested a license to Rural's listings; Rural refused.]

Unable to license Rural's white pages listings, Feist used them without Rural's consent. Feist began by removing several thousand listings that fell outside the geographic range of its area-wide directory, then hired personnel to investigate the 4,935 that remained. These employees verified the data reported by Rural and sought to obtain additional information. As a result, a typical Feist listing includes the individual's street address; most of Rural's listings do not. Notwithstanding these additions, however, 1,309 of the 46,878 listings in Feist's 1983 directory were identical to listings in Rural's 1982-1983 white pages. Four of these were fictitious listings that Rural had inserted into its directory to detect copying.

Rural sued for copyright infringement in the District Court for the District of Kansas taking the position that Feist, in compiling its own directory, could not use the information contained in Rural's white pages. Rural asserted that Feist's employees were obliged to travel door-to-door or conduct a telephone survey to discover the same information for themselves. Feist responded that such efforts were economically impractical and, in any event, unnecessary because the information copied was beyond the scope of copyright protection. The District Court granted summary judgment to Rural .... In an unpublished opinion, the Court of Appeals for the Tenth Circuit affirmed .... .

II

A

This case concerns the interaction of two well-established propositions. The first is that facts are not copyrightable; the other, that compilations of facts generally are. Each of these propositions possesses an impeccable pedigree. ...

The key to resolving the tension lies in understanding why facts are not copyrightable. The *sine qua non* of copyright is originality. To qualify for copyright protection, a work must be original to the author. Original, as the term is used in copyright, means only that the work was independently created by the author (as opposed to copied from other works), and that it possesses at least some minimal degree of creativity. 1 M. Nimmer & D. Nimmer, Copyright §§ 2.01[A], [B] (1990) (hereinafter Nimmer). To be sure, the requisite level of creativity is extremely low; even a slight amount will suffice. The vast majority of works make the grade quite easily, as they possess some creative spark, "no matter how crude, humble or obvious" it might be. Id., § 1.08[C][1]. Originality does not signify novelty; a work may be original even though it closely resembles other works so long as the similarity is fortuitous, not the result of copying. To illustrate, assume that two poets, each ignorant of the other, compose identical poems. Neither work is novel, yet both are original and, hence, copyrightable. ...

Originality is a constitutional requirement. The source of Congress' power to enact copyright laws is Article I, § 8, cl. 8, of the Constitution, which authorizes Congress to "secur[e] for limited Times to Authors . . . the exclusive Right to their respective Writings." In two decisions from the late 19th century—*The Trade-Mark Cases*, 100 U. S. 82 (1879); and *Burrow-Giles Lithographic Co. v. Sarony*, 111 U. S. 53 (1884)—this Court defined the crucial terms "authors" and "writings." In so doing, the Court made it unmistakably clear that these terms presuppose a degree of originality. ...

It is this bedrock principle of copyright that mandates the law's seemingly disparate treatment of facts and factual compilations. "No one may claim originality as to facts." Nimmer, § 2.11[A], p. 2-157. This is because facts do not owe their origin to an act of authorship. The distinction is one between creation and discovery: The first person to find and report a particular fact has not created the fact; he or she has merely discovered its existence. ...

Factual compilations, on the other hand, may possess the requisite originality. The compilation author typically chooses which facts to include, in what order to place them, and how to arrange the collected data so that they may be used effectively by readers. These choices as to selection and arrangement, so long as they are made independently by the compiler and entail a minimal

degree of creativity, are sufficiently original that Congress may protect such compilations through the copyright laws. …

This inevitably means that the copyright in a factual compilation is thin. Notwithstanding a valid copyright, a subsequent compiler remains free to use the facts contained in another's publication to aid in preparing a competing work, so long as the competing work does not feature the same selection and arrangement. …

B

As we have explained, originality is a constitutionally mandated prerequisite for copyright protection. The Court's decisions announcing this rule predate the Copyright Act of 1909, but ambiguous language in the 1909 Act caused some lower courts temporarily to lose sight of this requirement. …

Making matters worse, these courts developed a new theory to justify the protection of factual compilations. Known alternatively as "sweat of the brow" or "industrious collection," the underlying notion was that copyright was a reward for the hard work that went into compiling facts. The classic formulation of the doctrine appeared in *Jeweler's Circular Publishing Co.*, 281 F., at 88:

> "The right to copyright a book upon which one has expended labor in its preparation does not depend upon whether the materials which he has collected consist or not of matters which are publici juris, or whether such materials show literary skill *or originality*, either in thought or in language, or anything more than industrious collection. The man who goes through the streets of a town and puts down the names of each of the inhabitants, with their occupations and their street number, acquires material of which he is the author" (emphasis added).

… Without a doubt, the "sweat of the brow" doctrine flouted basic copyright principles. Throughout history, copyright law has "recognize[d] a greater need to disseminate factual works than works of fiction or fantasy." *Harper & Row*, 471 U. S., at 563. But "sweat of the brow" courts took a contrary view; they handed out proprietary interests in facts and declared that authors are absolutely precluded from saving time and effort by relying upon the facts contained in prior works. …

C

… In enacting the Copyright Act of 1976, Congress dropped the reference to "all the writings of an author" and replaced it with the phrase "original works of authorship." 17 U. S. C. § 102(a). …

As discussed earlier, however, the originality requirement [for compilations] is not particularly stringent. A compiler may settle upon a selection or arrangement that others have used; novelty is not required. Originality requires only that the author make the selection or arrangement independently (i. e., without copying that selection or arrangement from another work), and that it display some minimal level of creativity. Presumably, the vast majority of compilations will pass this test, but not all will. There remains a narrow category of works in which the creative spark is utterly lacking or so trivial as to be virtually nonexistent. Such works are incapable of sustaining a valid copyright. …

In summary, the 1976 revisions to the Copyright Act leave no doubt that originality, not "sweat of the brow," is the touchstone of copyright protection in directories and other fact-based works. … The revisions explain with painstaking clarity that copyright requires originality, § 102(a); that facts are never original, § 102(b); that the copyright in a compilation does not extend to the facts it contains, § 103(b); and that a compilation is copyrightable only to the extent that it features an original selection, coordination, or arrangement, § 101. …

III …

The selection, coordination, and arrangement of Rural's white pages do not satisfy the minimum constitutional standards for copyright protection. As mentioned at the outset, Rural's white pages are entirely typical. Persons desiring' telephone service in Rural's service area fill out an application and Rural issues them a telephone number. In preparing its white pages, Rural simply takes the data provided by its subscribers and lists it alphabetically by surname. The end product is a garden-variety white pages directory, devoid of even the slightest trace of creativity.

Rural's selection of listings could not be more obvious: It publishes the most basic information—name, town, and telephone number—about each person who applies to it for telephone service. This is "selection" of a sort, but it lacks the modicum of creativity necessary to transform mere selection into copyrightable expression. Rural expended sufficient effort to make the white pages directory useful, but insufficient creativity to make it original.

We note in passing that the selection featured in Rural's white pages may also fail the originality requirement for another reason. Feist points out that Rural did not truly "select" to publish the names and telephone numbers of its subscribers; rather, it was required to do so by the Kansas Corporation Commission as part of its monopoly franchise. Accordingly, one could plausibly conclude that this selection was dictated by state law, not by Rural.

Nor can Rural claim originality in its coordination and arrangement of facts. The white pages do nothing more than list Rural's subscribers in alphabetical order. This arrangement may, technically speaking, owe its origin to Rural; no one disputes that Rural undertook the task of alphabetizing the names itself. But there is nothing remotely creative about arranging names alphabetically in a white pages directory. It is an age-old practice, firmly rooted in tradition and so commonplace that it has come to be expected as a matter of course. It is not only unoriginal, it is practically inevitable. This time-honored tradition does not possess the minimal creative spark required by the Copyright Act and the Constitution. …

Because Rural's white pages lack the requisite originality, Feist's use of the listings cannot constitute infringement. This decision should not be construed as demeaning Rural's efforts in compiling its directory, but rather as making clear that copyright rewards originality, not effort. As this Court noted more than a century ago, "`great praise may be due to the plaintiffs for their industry and enterprise in publishing this paper, yet the law does not contemplate their being rewarded in this way.'" *Baker v. Selden*, 101 U. S., at 105.

Notes and Questions

7. Even on a sweat-of-the-brow theory, there is a decent argument that Rural didn't have to sweat very much. But if originality rather than investment of labor is the basis for copyright protection, then some who labor will not be rewarded with a copyright. Take *Jeweler's Circular Publishing Co.*, quoted in *Feist*. The plaintiff published a 326-page directory of jewelers, *Trade-Marks of the Jewelry and Kindred Trades*. It obtained the information in the directory at great effort, by writing to a large number of jewelers. The defendant – according to the court, at least – skipped this work by copying from the plaintiff's book rather than by doing its own research. Presumably, after *Feist*, there is no copyright in books like *Trade-Marks of the Jewelry and Kindred Trades*. Does this result make sense? Without copyright, will telephone books and jewelers' directories cease to exist because no one will invest in creating them?

Castle Rock Entertainment v. Carol Publishing Group
150 F.3d 132 (2d Cir. 1998)

JOHN M. WALKER, Jr., Circuit Judge:

This case presents two interesting and somewhat novel issues of copyright law. The first is whether The Seinfeld Aptitude Test, a trivia quiz book devoted exclusively to testing its readers' recollection of scenes and events from the fictional television series Seinfeld, takes sufficient protected expression from the original, as evidenced by the book's substantial similarity to the television series, such that, in the absence of any defenses, the book would infringe the copyright in Seinfeld. The second is whether The Seinfeld Aptitude Test (also referred to as The SAT) constitutes fair use of the Seinfeld television series. …

We conclude that The SAT unlawfully copies from Seinfeld and that its copying does not constitute fair use and thus is an actionable infringement. Accordingly, we affirm the judgment in favor of Castle Rock.

Background

The material facts in this case are undisputed. Plaintiff Castle Rock is the producer and copyright owner of each episode of the Seinfeld television series. The series revolves around the petty tribulations in the lives of four single, adult friends in New York: Jerry Seinfeld, George Costanza, Elaine Benes, and Cosmo Kramer. Defendants are Beth Golub, the author, and Carol Publishing Group, Inc., the publisher, of The SAT, a 132-page book containing 643 trivia questions and answers about the events and characters depicted in Seinfeld. These include 211 multiple choice questions, in which only one out of three to five answers is correct; 93 matching questions; and a number of short-answer questions. The questions are divided into five levels of difficulty, labeled (in increasing order of difficulty) "Wuss Questions," "This, That, and the Other Questions," "Tough Monkey Questions," "Atomic Wedgie Questions," and "Master of Your Domain Questions." Selected examples from level 1 are indicative of the questions throughout The SAT:

> 1. To impress a woman, George passes himself off as
> a) a gynecologist
> b) a geologist
> c) a marine biologist
> d) a meteorologist
>
> 11. What candy does Kramer snack on while observing a surgical procedure from an operating-room balcony?
>
> 12. Who said, "I don't go for those nonrefundable deals ... I can't commit to a woman ... I'm not committing to an airline."?
> a) Jerry
> b) George
> c) Kramer

The book draws from 84 of the 86 Seinfeld episodes that had been broadcast as of the time The SAT was published. Although Golub created the incorrect answers to the multiple choice questions, every question and correct answer has as its source a fictional moment in a Seinfeld episode. Forty-one questions and/or answers contain dialogue from Seinfeld. The single episode most drawn upon by The SAT, "The Cigar Store Indian," is the source of 20 questions that directly quote between 3.6% and 5.6% of that episode (defendants' and plaintiffs calculations, respectively).

The name "Seinfeld" appears prominently on the front and back covers of The SAT, and pictures of the principal actors in Seinfeld appear on the cover and on several pages of the book. On the back cover, a disclaimer states that "This book has not been approved or licensed by any entity involved in creating or producing Seinfeld." The front cover bears the title "The Seinfeld Aptitude Test" and describes the book as containing "[h]undreds of spectacular questions of minute details from TV's greatest show about absolutely nothing." The back cover asks:

> Just how well do you command the buzz-words, peccadilloes, petty annoyances, and triflingly complex escapades of Jerry Seinfeld, Elaine Benes, George Costanza, and Kramer — the fabulously neurotic foursome that makes the offbeat hit TV series Seinfeld tick?
>
> ....
>
> If you think you know the answers — and really keep track of *Seinfeld* minutiae — challenge yourself and your friends with these 550 trivia questions and 10 extra matching quizzes. No, *The Seinfeld Aptitude Test* can't tell you whether you're Master of Your Domain, but it will certify your status as King or Queen of *Seinfeld* trivia. So twist open a Snapple, double-dip a chip, and open this book to satisfy your between-episode cravings.

Golub has described The SAT as a "natural outgrowth" of Seinfeld which, "like the Seinfeld show, is devoted to the trifling, picayune and petty annoyances encountered by the show's characters on a daily basis." According to Golub, she created The SAT by taking notes from Seinfeld programs at the time they were aired on television and subsequently reviewing videotapes of several of the episodes, as recorded by her or various friends.

The SAT's publication did not immediately provoke a challenge. The National Broadcasting Corporation, which broadcasted Seinfeld, requested free copies of The SAT from defendants and distributed them together with promotions for the program. Seinfeld's executive producer characterized The SAT as "a fun little book." There is no evidence that The SAT's publication diminished Seinfeld's profitability, and in fact Seinfeld's audience grew after The SAT was first published.

Castle Rock has nevertheless been highly selective in marketing products associated with Seinfeld, rejecting numerous proposals from publishers seeking approval for a variety of projects related to the show. Castle Rock licensed one Seinfeld book, The Entertainment Weekly Seinfeld Companion, and has licensed the production of a CD-ROM product that includes discussions of Seinfeld episodes; the CD-ROM allegedly might ultimately include a trivia bank. Castle Rock claims in this litigation that it plans to pursue a more aggressive marketing strategy for Seinfeld-related products, including "publication of books relating to Seinfeld."

In November 1994, Castle Rock notified defendants of its copyright and trademark infringement claims. In February 1995, after defendants continued to distribute The SAT, Castle Rock filed this action alleging federal copyright and trademark infringement and state law unfair competition. Subsequently, both parties moved, pursuant to Fed.R.Civ.P. 56, for summary judgment on both the copyright and unfair competition claims.

The district court granted summary judgment to Castle Rock on the copyright claim. It held that defendants had violated plaintiff's copyrights in Seinfeld and that such copying did not constitute fair use. … The parties then stipulated to damages and attorneys' fees on the copyright infringement claim and, presumably to facilitate the appeal, to the dismissal without prejudice of all remaining claims. … The district court entered final judgment on the copyright infringement claim, awarded Castle Rock $403,000 with interest, permanently enjoined defendants from publishing or distributing The SAT, and ordered defendants to destroy all copies of The SAT in their custody or control. Defendants now appeal.

II. Copyright Infringement

The Copyright Act of 1976 ("Copyright Act"), 17 U.S.C. §§ 101-803, grants copyright owners a bundle of exclusive rights, including the rights to "reproduce the copyrighted work in copies" and "to prepare derivative works based upon the copyrighted work." *Id.* § 106. "Copyright infringement is established when the owner of a valid copyright demonstrates unauthorized copying." *Repp v. Webber,* 132 F.3d 882, 889 (2d Cir.1997); *see Feist Publications, Inc. v. Rural Tel. Serv. Co.,* 499 U.S. 340, 361, 111 S.Ct. 1282, 113 L.Ed.2d 358 (1991). There are two main components of this *prima facie* case of infringement: "a plaintiff must first show that his work was actually copied .... [and] then must show that the copying amounts to an improper or unlawful appropriation." *Laureyssens v. Idea Group, Inc.,* 964 F.2d 131, 139-40 (2d Cir.1992) (quotation marks and citations omitted). Actual copying may be established "either by direct evidence of copying or by indirect evidence, including access to the copyrighted work, similarities that are probative of copying between the works, and expert testimony." *Id.* at 140. … "It is only after actual copying is established that one claiming infringement" then proceeds to demonstrate that the copying was improper or unlawful by showing that the second work bears "substantial similarity" to protected expression in the earlier work. *Webber,* 132 F.3d at 889; *Laureyssens,* 964 F.2d at 140.

In the instant case, no one disputes that Castle Rock owns valid copyrights in the Seinfeld television programs and that defendants actually copied from those programs in creating The

SAT. Golub freely admitted that she created The SAT by taking notes from Seinfeld programs at the time they were aired on television and subsequently reviewing videotapes of several of the episodes that she or her friends recorded. Since the fact of copying is acknowledged and undisputed, the critical question for decision is whether the copying was unlawful or improper in that it took a sufficient amount of protected expression from Seinfeld as evidenced by its substantial similarity to such expression.

A. "Substantial Similarity"

We have stated that "substantial similarity"

> requires that the copying [be] quantitatively *and* qualitatively sufficient to support the legal conclusion that infringement (*actionable* copying) has occurred. The qualitative component concerns the copying of expression, rather than ideas [, facts, works in the public domain, or any other non-protectable elements].... The quantitative component generally concerns the amount of the copyrighted work that is copied,

which must be more than "de minimis." Ringgold v. Black Entertainment Television, Inc., 126 F.3d 70, 75 (2d Cir.1997) (emphasis added).

As to the quantitative element, we conclude that The SAT has crossed the de minimis threshold. At the outset, we observe that the fact that the copying appears in question and answer form is by itself without particular consequence: the trivia quiz copies fragments of Seinfeld in the same way that a collection of Seinfeld jokes or trivia would copy fragments of the series. ... Had The SAT copied a few fragments from each of 84 unrelated television programs (perhaps comprising the entire line-up on broadcast television), defendants would have a stronger case under the de minimis doctrine. By copying not a few but 643 fragments from the Seinfeld television series, however, The SAT has plainly crossed the quantitative copying threshold under Ringgold.

As to Ringgold's qualitative component, each SAT trivia question is based directly upon original, protectable expression in Seinfeld. As noted by the district court, The SAT did not copy from Seinfeld unprotected facts, but, rather, creative expression. Cf. Feist, 499 U.S. at 364, 111 S.Ct. 1282 (finding no infringement where defendant produced a multi-county phone directory, in part, by obtaining names and phone numbers from plaintiffs' single-county directory). Unlike the facts in a phone book, which "do not owe their origin to an act of authorship," id. at 347, 111 S.Ct. 1282, each "fact" tested by The SAT is in reality fictitious expression created by Seinfeld's authors. The SAT does not quiz such true facts as the identity of the actors in Seinfeld, the number of days it takes to shoot an episode, the biographies of the actors, the location of the Seinfeld set, etc. Rather, The SAT tests whether the reader knows that the character Jerry places a Pez dispenser on Elaine's leg during a piano recital, that Kramer enjoys going to the airport because he's hypnotized by the baggage carousels, and that Jerry, opining on how to identify a virgin, said "It's not like spotting a toupee." Because these characters and events spring from the imagination of Seinfeld's authors, The SAT plainly copies copyrightable, creative expression.

We find support for this conclusion in a previous case in which we held that a series of still photographs of a ballet may in some cases infringe the copyright in an original choreographic work. See Horgan v. Macmillan, Inc., 789 F.2d 157, 163 (2d Cir.1986). The defendants in Horgan claimed that still photographs could not "capture the flow of movement, which is the essence of dance," that "the staged performance could not be recreated from the photographs," and thus, that the photographs were not substantially similar to the choreographic work. Id. at 161-62 (quotation marks omitted). Although noting that the issue "was not a simple one," this court rejected that argument, holding that "the standard for determining copyright infringement is not whether the original could be recreated from the allegedly infringing copy, but whether the latter is substantially similar to the former." Id. at 162 (quotation marks omitted). That observation applies with equal force to the trivia quiz fragments in this case. Although Seinfeld could not be "recreated" from The SAT, Castle Rock has nevertheless established both the quantitative and qualitative components of the substantial similarity test, establishing a prima facie case of copyright infringement.

B. Other Tests

As defendants note, substantial similarity usually "arises out of a claim of infringement as between comparable works .... [where] because of the equivalent nature of the competing works, the question of similarity can be tested conventionally by comparing comparable elements of the two works." Because in the instant case the original and secondary works are of different genres and to a lesser extent because they are in different media, tests for substantial similarity other than the quantitative/qualitative approach are not particularly helpful to our analysis.

Under the "ordinary observer" test, for example, "[t]wo works are substantially similar where `the ordinary observer, unless he set out to detect the disparities, would be disposed to overlook them, and regard [the] aesthetic appeal [of the two works] as the same.'" Arica Inst., Inc. v. Palmer, 970 F.2d 1067, 1072 (2d Cir.1992) (quoting Peter Pan Fabrics, Inc. v. Martin Weiner Corp., 274 F.2d 487, 489 (2d Cir.1960) (L.Hand, J.) (comparing dress designs)) (alterations in original). Undoubtedly, Judge Hand did not have in mind a comparison of aesthetic appeal as between a television series and a trivia quiz and, in the usual case, we might question whether any "ordinary observer" would "regard [the] aesthetic appeal" in a situation-comedy television program as being identical to that of any book, let alone a trivia quiz book, about that program. Cf. Laureyssens, 964 F.2d at 132, 141 (applying "ordinary observer" test to compare two sets of foam rubber puzzles). We note here, however, that plaintiff has a plausible claim that there is a common aesthetic appeal between the two works based on The SAT's plain copying of Seinfeld and Golub's statement on the back cover that the book was designed to complement the aesthetic appeal of the television series. See The SAT ("So twist open a Snapple, double-dip a chip, and open this book to satisfy your between episode cravings.").

Under the "total concept and feel" test, urged by defendants, we analyze "the similarities in such aspects as the total concept and feel, theme, characters, plot, sequence, pace, and setting" of the original and the allegedly infringing works. Williams v. Crichton, 84 F.3d 581, 588 (2d Cir.1996) (comparing children's books with novel and movie); Reyher v. Children's Television Workshop, 533 F.2d 87, 91 (2d Cir.1976) (comparing children's book with story in Sesame Street Magazine). Defendants contend that The SAT and the Seinfeld programs are incomparable in conventional terms such as plot, sequence, themes, pace, and setting. For example, The SAT has no plot; "[t]he notion of pace ... cannot be said even to exist in the book"; The SAT's "sequence has no relationship to the sequences of any of the Seinfeld episodes, since it is a totally random and scattered collection of questions relating to events that occurred in the shows"; and The SAT's only theme "is how much a Seinfeld fan can remember of 84 different programs." The total concept and feel test, however, is simply not helpful in analyzing works that, because of their different genres and media, must necessarily have a different concept and feel. Indeed, many "derivative" works of different genres, in which copyright owners have exclusive rights, see 17 U.S.C. § 106, may have a different total concept and feel from the original work. …

The SAT easily passes the threshold of substantial similarity between the contents of the secondary work and the protected expression in the original.

III. Fair Use

Defendants claim that, even if The SAT's copying of Seinfeld constitutes prima facie infringement, The SAT is nevertheless a fair use of Seinfeld. "From the infancy of copyright protection," the fair use doctrine "has been thought necessary to fulfill copyright's very purpose, `[t]o promote the Progress of Science and useful Arts.'" Campbell v. Acuff-Rose Music, Inc., 510 U.S. 569, 575, 114 S.Ct. 1164, 127 L.Ed.2d 500 (1994) (quoting U.S. Const., art. I, § 8, cl. 8). As noted in Campbell, "in truth, in literature, in science and in art, there are, and can be, few, if any, things, which in an abstract sense, are strictly new and original throughout. Every book in literature, science and art, borrows, and must necessarily borrow, and use much which was well known and used before." Id. (quotation marks omitted). Until the 1976 Copyright Act, the doctrine of fair use grew exclusively out of the common law. See id. at 576, 114 S.Ct. 1164; Folsom v. Marsh, 9 F.Cas. 342, 348 (C.D.Mass.1900) (CCD Mass. 1841) (Story, J.) (stating fair use test); Pierre N. Leval, Toward a Fair Use Standard, 103 Harv. L.Rev. 1105, 1105 (1990) ("Leval").

[Court analyzes and denies fair use.]

F. Aggregate Assessment
Considering all of the factors discussed above, we conclude that the copyright law's objective "[t]o promote the Progress of Science and useful Arts" would be undermined by permitting The SAT's copying of Seinfeld, see Arica, 970 F.2d at 1077, and we therefore reject defendants' fair use defense. …

Notes and Questions

1. *Castle Rock* illustrates two essential copyright doctrines: the substantial similarity test for infringement and the fair use defense. Compare them with the tests used in real- and personal-property torts like trespass, nuisance, and conversion. Which of them are more definite and which are more open-ended? What might account for the difference? Land has definite boundaries; what are the "boundaries" of a copyrighted work?

2. Fair use comes in many forms. Examples of uses protected as fair uses include 2 Live Crew's filthy cover rap version of the Roy Orbison song "Oh, Pretty Woman," Campbell v. Acuff-Rose Music, Inc., 510 U.S. 569 (1994), a retelling of Gone With the Wind from the slaves' point of view, Suntrust Bank v. Houghton Mifflin Co., 268 F.3d 1257 (11th Cir. 2001), using a VCR to record live over-the-air TV shows to watch them later, Sony Corp. of America v. Universal City Studios, Inc., 464 U. S. 417, 451 (1984), making digital copies of physical books to create a search engine, Authors Guild v. Google, Inc., 804 F.3d 202 (2d Cir. 2015), quoting from an author's works as part of a critical biography, New Era Publications Intl. v. Carol Pub. Group, 904 F.2d 152 (2d. Cir. 1990), reproducing Grateful Dead concert posters as part of a timeline in a coffee-table book about the band's history, Bill Graham Archives v. Dorling Kindersley Ltd., 448 F.3d 605 (2d. Cir. 2006), and making copies of a work to be used as evidence in a lawsuit, Jartech, Inc. v. Clancy, 666 F.2d 403 (9th Cir. 1982). Is there any unifying principle tying together such disparate uses?

UMG Recordings, Inc. v. Augusto
628 F. 3d 1175 (9th Cir. 2011)

CANBY, Circuit Judge:

The material facts of the case are undisputed. UMG is among the world's largest music companies. One of its core businesses is the creation, manufacture, and sale of recorded music, or phonorecords, the copyrights of which are owned by UMG. These phonorecords generally take the form of compact discs ("CDs").

Like many music companies, UMG ships specially-produced promotional CDs to a large group of individuals ("recipients"), such as music critics and radio programmers, that it has selected.

There is no prior agreement or request by the recipients to receive the CDs. UMG does not seek or receive payment for the CDs, the content and design of which often differs from that of their commercial counterparts. UMG ships the promotional CDs by means of the United States Postal Service and United Parcel Service. Relatively few of the recipients refuse delivery of the CDs or return them to UMG, and UMG destroys those that are returned.

Most of the promotional CDs in issue in this case bore a statement (the "promotional statement") similar to the following:

> This CD is the property of the record company and is licensed to the intended recipient for personal use only. Acceptance of this CD shall constitute an agreement to comply with the terms of the license. Resale or transfer of possession is not allowed and may be punishable under federal and state laws.

Some of the CDs bore a more succinct statement, such as "Promotional Use Only—Not for Sale."

Augusto was not among the select group of individuals slated to receive the promotional CDs. He nevertheless managed to acquire numerous such CDs, many of which he sold through online auctions at eBay.com. Augusto regularly advertised the CDs as "rare ... industry editions" and referred to them as "Promo CDs."

After several unsuccessful attempts at halting the auctions through eBay's dispute resolution program, UMG filed a complaint against Augusto in the United States District Court for the Central District of California, alleging that Augusto had infringed UMG's copyrights in eight promotional CDs for which it retained the "exclusive right to distribute." The district court granted summary judgment in favor of Augusto, and UMG appealed. . . ..

Although UMG, as the owner of the copyright, has exclusive rights in the promotional CDs, "[e]xemptions, compulsory licenses, and defenses found in the Copyright Act narrow [those] rights." *Wall Data Inc. v. Los Angeles Cnty. Sheriff's Dept.*, 447 F.3d 769, 777 (9th Cir. 2006). Augusto invokes the "first sale" doctrine embodied in § 109(a) of the Act. 17 U.S.C. § 109(a). He argues that the circumstances attending UMG's distribution of the discs effected a "sale" (transfer of ownership) of the discs to the original recipients and that, under the "first sale" doctrine, the recipients and subsequent owners of those particular copies were permitted to sell or otherwise dispose of those copies without authorization by the copyright holder. ...

UMG, on the other hand, contends that the promotional statement effected a license with the recipients and, because the recipients were not owners but licensees of the CDs, neither they nor Augusto were entitled to sell or otherwise transfer the CDs.

The first sale doctrine provides that "the owner of a particular copy or phonorecord lawfully made under [the Act], or any person authorized by such owner, is entitled, without the authority of the copyright owner, to sell or otherwise dispose of the possession of that copy or phonorecord." 17 U.S.C. § 109(a). Notwithstanding its distinctive name, the doctrine applies not only when a copy is first sold, but when a copy is given away or title is otherwise transferred without the accouterments of a sale. The seminal illustration of the principle is found in *Bobbs-Merrill Co. v. Straus*, 210 U.S. 339 (1908), where a copyright owner unsuccessfully attempted to restrain the resale of a copyrighted book by including in it the following notice: "The price of this book at retail is $1 net. No dealer is licensed to sell it at a less price, and a sale at less price will be treated as an infringement of the copyright." The Court noted that the statutory grant to a copyright owner of the "sole right of vending" the work did not continue after the first sale of a given copy.. "The purchaser of a book, once sold by authority of the owner of the copyright, may sell it again, although he could not publish a new edition of it." The attempt to limit resale below a certain price was therefore held invalid.

The rule of *Bobbs-Merrill* remains in full force, enshrined as it is in § 109(a) of the Act: a copyright owner who transfers title in a particular copy to a purchaser or donee cannot prevent resale of that particular copy. We have recognized, however, that not every transfer of possession of a copy transfers title. Particularly with regard to computer software, we have recognized that copyright owners may create licensing arrangements so that users acquire only a license to use the particular copy of software and do not acquire title that permits further transfer or sale of that copy without the permission of the copyright owner. …

The same question is presented here. Did UMG succeed in creating a license in recipients of its promotional CDs, or did it convey title despite the restrictive labeling on the CDs? We conclude that, under all the circumstances of the CDs' distribution, the recipients were entitled to use or dispose of them in any manner they saw fit, and UMG did not enter a license agreement for the CDs with the recipients. Accordingly, UMG transferred title to the particular copies of its promotional CDs and cannot maintain an infringement action against Augusto for his subsequent sale of those copies.

Our conclusion that the recipients acquired ownership of the CDs is based largely on the nature of UMG's distribution. First, the promotional CDs are dispatched to the recipients without any prior arrangement as to those particular copies. The CDs are not numbered, and no attempt is made to keep track of where particular copies are or what use is made of them. As explained in greater detail below, although UMG places written restrictions in the labels of the CDs, it has not established that the restrictions on the CDs create a license agreement.

We also hold that, because the CDs were unordered merchandise, the recipients were free to dispose of them as they saw fit under the Unordered Merchandise Statute, 39 U.S.C. § 3009, which provides in pertinent part that,

> (a) [e]xcept for ... free samples clearly and conspicuously marked as such,... the mailing of unordered merchandise... constitutes an unfair method of competition and an unfair trade practice....
>
> (b) Any merchandise mailed in violation of subsection (a) of this section ... may be treated as a gift by the recipient, who shall have the right to retain, use, discard, or dispose of it in any manner he sees fit without any obligation whatsoever to the sender. ...

Id. § 3009(a), (b) (emphasis added). The statute defines "unordered merchandise" as "merchandise mailed without the prior expressed request or consent of the recipient" but leaves "merchandise" itself undefined. Id. § 3009(d). Although the statute applies in terms to "mailed" merchandise, the Federal Trade Commission has applied its prohibitions to other types of shipment, as violations of § 5 of the Federal Trade Commission Act, 15 U.S.C. § 45. See 43 Fed.Reg. 4113 (Jan. 31, 1978). …

There are additional reasons for concluding that UMG's distribution of the CDs did not involve a consensual licensing operation. Some of the statements on the CDs and UMG's purported method of securing agreement to licenses militate against a conclusion that any licenses were created. The sparest promotional statement, "Promotional Use Only—Not for Sale," does not even purport to create a license. But even the more detailed statement is flawed in the manner in which it purports to secure agreement from the recipient. The more detailed statement provides:

> This CD is the property of the record company and is licensed to the intended recipient for personal use only. Acceptance of this CD shall constitute an agreement to comply with the terms of the license. Resale or transfer of possession is not allowed and may be punishable under federal and state laws.

It is one thing to say, as the statement does, that "acceptance" of the CD constitutes an agreement to a license and its restrictions, but it is quite another to maintain that "acceptance" may be assumed when the recipient makes no response at all. This record reflects no responses. Even when the evidence is viewed in the light most favorable to UMG, it does not show that any recipients agreed to enter into a license agreement with UMG when they received the CDs.

Because the record here is devoid of any indication that the recipients agreed to a license, there is no evidence to support a conclusion that licenses were established under the terms of the promotional statement. Accordingly, we conclude that UMG's transfer of possession to the recipients, without meaningful control or even knowledge of the status of the CDs after shipment, accomplished a transfer of title. …

Because we conclude that UMG's method of distribution transferred the ownership of the copies to the recipients, we have no need to parse the remaining provisions in UMG's purported licensing statement; UMG dispatched the CDs in a manner that permitted their receipt and retention by the recipients without the recipients accepting the terms of the promotional statements. UMG's transfer of unlimited possession in the circumstances present here effected a gift or sale within the meaning of the first sale doctrine, as the district court held. …

Notes and Questions

1. The first sale doctrine draws a sharp distinction between ownership of a *work* (which remains in UMG) and ownership of a *copy* of that work (which passes to the recipients, thence to Augusto, thence to his eBay buyers). Every major body of intellectual property law has a similar doctrine: the intellectual property rights holder's rights over a particular item end when it gives up its personal property rights in the item. Because of this, it depends heavily on the law of personal property to define who is an "owner" of that item.

2. Do you see why libraries would be impossible without first sale? The market for used books, records, and DVDs depends on it. Publishers, for their part, can be more ambivalent about it. In the summer of 2014, the law school casebook publisher WoltersKluwer anounced a program called "Connected Casebook" under which students would buy discounted access to online versions of their casebooks. Participating students would receive a paper copy of the casebook for use in the class, but would be required to return the book at the end of the semester. What effects would this have on the used-book market? On students' first sale rights?

C. Patents

Innovention Toys, LLC v. MGA Entertainment, Inc.

637 F. 3d 1314 (Fed. Cir. 2011)

LOURIE, Circuit Judge.

MGA Entertainment, Inc.; Wal-Mart Stores, Inc.; and Toys "R" Us, Inc. (collectively, "MGA") appeal from the summary judgment decision of the United States District Court for the Eastern District of Louisiana that the asserted claims of U.S. Patent 7,264,242 ("the '242 patent") were infringed and were not invalid for obviousness. Innovention Toys, LLC v. MGA Entm't, Inc.,

665 F.Supp.2d 636 (E.D.La. 2009). Because the district court correctly found no genuine issues of material fact regarding infringement based on its construction of the claim term "movable," we affirm the court's grant of summary judgment of literal infringement. The district court, however, erred in several of its factual findings underlying its nonobviousness determination. We therefore vacate the court's grant of summary judgment of nonobviousness and remand.

BACKGROUND

I.

Innovention Toys, LLC ("Innovention") brought suit against MGA for infringement of the '242 patent, which claims a chess-like, light-reflecting board game and methods of playing the same. The disclosed game includes a chess-styled playing surface, laser sources positioned to project light beams over the playing surface when "fired," mirrored and non-mirrored playing pieces used to direct the lasers' beams, and non-mirrored "key playing pieces" equivalent to the king pieces in chess. See '242 patent col.2 l.64-col.3 l.35. To play the game, players take turns either moving a playing piece to an unoccupied, adjacent square or rotating (reorienting) a piece within a square. Id. col.3 ll.21-24; col.8 l.49-col.9 l.12. After moving or rotating a piece, a player then fires his laser, and if the laser's beam strikes the non-mirrored surface of a playing piece, that piece is eliminated from the game. Id. col.3 ll.26-30; col.9 ll.13-17. To win the game, a player must direct his laser beam to strike, or illuminate, his opponent's non-mirrored key playing piece, ending the game. Id. col.3 ll.17-20; col.6 ll.44-47.

All the asserted claims, claims 31-33, 39-41, 43-44, 48-50, and 53-54, include a "key playing pieces" limitation in which the key pieces are "movable." Claim 31 is representative:

> A board game for two opposing players or teams of players comprising:
> a game board, movable playing pieces having at least one mirrored surface, *movable* key playing pieces having no mirrored surfaces, and a laser source,
> wherein alternate turns are taken to move playing pieces for the purpose of deflecting laser beams, so as to illuminate the key playing piece of the opponent.

Id. claim 31 (emphasis added).

MGA counterclaimed, denying infringement and alleging, inter alia, that the '242 patent was invalid under 35 U.S.C. § 103. In making its obviousness argument, MGA relied on the combination of (1) two articles describing computer-based, chess-like strategy games, Laser Chess and Advanced Laser Chess (collectively, "the Laser Chess references"); and (2) U.S. Patent 5,145,182 ("the Swift patent") describing a physical, chess-like, laser-based strategy game.

The Laser Chess game is described in an article entitled "Laser Chess™ First Prize $5,000.00 Winner Atari ST Programming Contest," published in the April 1987 edition of Compute!. J.A.

1775-78. Advanced Laser Chess is described in an article published in the Summer 1989 edition of Compute!'s Amiga Resource. J.A. 1784-87. Both articles disclose chess-like computer games with virtual lasers and mirrored and non-mirrored pieces, which are moved or rotated by players during alternating turns on a virtual, chess-like playing board. The goal of each game is to manipulate one's laser beam using the various game pieces to eliminate the other player's non-mirrored king piece by striking it with the laser beam. In Laser Chess, a player's king piece may move squares during game play: "[The king] can capture any opposing piece by moving onto its square." J.A. 1776. Similarly, in Advanced Laser Chess "Kings possess the ability to capture other pieces [by moving on top of them]." J.A.1784.

The Swift patent discloses a physical (rather than electronic) strategy game in which players take turns placing mirrored game pieces onto squares of a chess-styled game board. The players position the pieces so as to direct their laser's beam towards the opposing player's scoring module and away from their own. A player scores when his laser beam, having been deflected around the game board, strikes his opponent's scoring module. The scoring modules are mounted to the frame of the game board, see Swift patent col.2 ll.51-56, and thus are not physically capable of movement on the game board.

MGA's accused game, Laser Battle, is a physical board game for playing a chess-like strategy game. Players take turns moving or rotating mirrored playing pieces so as to direct a laser beam to strike the opposing player's non-mirrored Tower playing piece to win the game. According to the rules of Laser Battle, in "Classic Game Play," the Tower pieces are placed on the board at the beginning of the game at one of various standard positions. J.A. 1986. Although the Towers are physically capable of movement on the game board, the rules provide that they "should always remain in their original positions on the board." J.A.1985. However, the standard starting configuration illustrated in the rules show that the Tower pieces can be placed at different locations on the board, and the rules state that during "Advanced Game Play," the Towers need not remain in their standard positions. J.A.1986.

II.

On October 14, 2009, the district court ruled on the parties' cross-motions for summary judgment of infringement and invalidity. *Innovention Toys,* 665 F.Supp.2d 636. The district court granted Innovention's motion for summary judgment of literal infringement. *Id.* at 647. The court first construed the claim term "movable" in light of the term's plain meaning as "capable of movement as called for by the rules of the game or game strategy." *Id.* at 644-45. In so holding, the court rejected MGA's more "cramped" construction that the movement must be "from space to space or by rotation within a single space." *Id.* at 643-45; *see also id.* at 644 n. 15. The district court also rejected Innovention's broader construction of "movable" to mean "able to be moved, or possible to move," without any tie to the rules or strategy of the game. *Id.* at 642-43.

Based on its construction, the district court then found that the accused Laser Battle game's Tower pieces met the "movable" claim limitation, the only disputed limitation. The court found that those key pieces were "moveable" when the players selected and "set up the game pieces in various start formations and layouts." Id. at 647 n. 18. The court reasoned that even if "the instructions to Laser Battle suggest that its key pieces, the Towers, are not supposed to be moved during game play," they "are capable of movement . . . in that they fit into the recessed spaces on the board like the other pieces, and are capable of rotation within whatever recessed space a player may choose to place the Tower in for the start of game play." Id. at 646-47. The court also observed that although the instructions to Laser Battle note that "[t]he Towers should always remain in their original positions on the board," id. at 647 n. 18, they also explain that "[e]xcept for Advanced Game Play, the Target Tower and the Laser Guns will remain in their standard positions in all formations," see id. at 647 n. 18 & 19; J.A.1986. This instruction suggests that the Tower pieces could be moved in Advanced Game Play because they fit in and are rotatable in the recessed spaces on the board.

The district court also granted Innovention's motion for summary judgment of nonobviousness. Id. at 655. The court first found that the Laser Chess references were non-analogous art because they described electronic, rather than real-world, laser games. Id. at 653. The district court then held that, because MGA had provided no evidence to support a finding as to the level of ordinary skill in the art, MGA's obviousness argument could be pursued only on the basis of what would have been obvious to a layperson. Id. at 654. The court then decided that because MGA had not provided any evidence that a layperson would have known of the Laser Chess articles or would have had any reason to modify the teachings of the Laser Chess references, MGA had failed to state a prima facie case of obviousness. Id.

Finally, the court found that Innovention had demonstrated several secondary considerations of nonobviousness. These included (1) commercial success based on the sale of 140,000 games by Innovention, a small company with minimal marketing capabilities, and evidence that fans had started clubs and tournaments around the world; (2) long-felt need based on the game's sudden success and media praise; and (3) industry praise based on, inter alia, the game's nomination for Outstanding Technology of the Year by the International Academy of Science and its being one of five finalists for the Toy Industry Association's 2007 Game of the Year award. Id. at 654-55. In light of its summary judgment rulings, the district court granted Innovention's motion for a permanent injunction on January 13, 2010.

MGA appealed. We have jurisdiction pursuant to 28 U.S.C. § 1295(a)(1).

DISCUSSION

This court reviews a district court's decision on summary judgment *de novo,* reapplying the same standard applied by the district court. *Iovate Health Scis., Inc. v. Bio-Engineered Supplements & Nutrition, Inc.,* 586 F.3d 1376, 1380 (Fed. Cir.2009). Summary judgment is appropriate "if the movant shows that there is no genuine dispute as to any material fact and the movant is entitled to judgment as a matter of law." Fed.R.Civ.P. 56(a).

I. Infringement

A determination of infringement involves two steps: First, the court determines the scope and meaning of the asserted patent claims. The court then compares the properly construed claims to the allegedly infringing device to determine whether all of the claim limitations are present, either literally or by a substantial equivalent. Cybor Corp. v. FAS Techs., Inc., 138 F.3d 1448, 1454 (Fed.Cir.1998) (en banc). …

On appeal, MGA does not argue that the district court erred in construing "movable" to mean "capable of movement as called for by the rules of the game or game strategy." Rather, MGA argues that the court improperly broadened its construction during the second step of the infringement analysis by adding capable of movement "during game set up," and thus erred in finding that Laser Battle's Tower pieces meet the "movable" limitation. Under the court's original construction, MGA asserts, Laser Battle's instructions definitively show that the Tower pieces are not to be moved, either from space to space or by rotation within a space, as part of the game's rules or strategy. Rather, MGA urges, the only way that the Tower pieces can be "movable" during game play or strategy is if the players ignore the game's rules and cheat. Moreover, according to MGA, because all the pieces must be moved onto the game board at some point, the district court's altered construction renders everything "movable" and the "movable" limitation superfluous.

Innovention responds that Laser Battle's Tower pieces are clearly "capable of movement"; each Tower piece is a separate component that can be placed at any space on the game board and afterwards rotated within that space or moved to another space. In other words, Innovention argues, the Towers are "movable" since they are not permanently mounted to the game board as are the key playing pieces (scoring modules) disclosed in the Swift patent. Furthermore, according to Innovention, Laser Battle's instructions do not require the Tower pieces to remain stationary during all game play; the rules invite players to create "more intricate games" and tell players that the Towers "remain in their standard positions in all formations" except during "Advanced Game Play." J.A.1986-87.

We agree in main with the district court's infringement analysis, and we affirm the district court's decision holding that MGA's Laser Battle game literally infringes the asserted claims of the '242 patent. During claim construction, the district court rejected MGA's narrower construction of "movable" in which "movable" was limited to the movements explicitly permitted by the rules of the game during game play, i.e., movable from space to space or by rotation within a single space. Innovention Toys, 665 F.Supp.2d at 642-43. Rather, the court embraced a definition that distinguished "movable" from "mounted" by contrasting the "movable key playing pieces" of the '242 patent with the fixed scoring modules of Swift. In particular, the district court stated that while the "key pieces disclosed in the Swift reference are permanently fixed to the game board and, therefore, cannot be moved prior to or during game play," the key pieces of the '242 patent "may be positioned in different spaces at the beginning of each game and can also be moved during game play." Id. at 644; see also id. at 644 n. 15. Thus, the court's construction of "movable" includes the capability of being positioned in different spaces during set up (i.e., at the beginning of each game) and the capability of being moved during Advanced Game Play. In other words, the Tower pieces "are capable of movement as called for by the rules of the game or game strategy."

Accordingly, MGA is incorrect when it argues that the district court expanded its construction of "movable" during the second step of the infringement analysis. The court's construction, not just its application, encompasses movement during game set up. Moreover, such a construction does not render "movable" superfluous, as MGA asserts, since it distinguishes the '242 patent's key pieces from the mounted scoring modules disclosed in Swift. Laser Battle's Tower pieces thus meet the "movable" limitation under the district court's consistent construction based on the pieces' undisputed ability to be physically positioned in different squares on the game board. No reasonable jury could find otherwise. …

II. Obviousness

Under the Patent Act, "[a] patent may not be obtained . . . if the differences between the subject matter sought to be patented and the prior art are such that the subject matter as a whole would have been obvious at the time the invention was made to a person having ordinary skill in the art to which said subject matter pertains." 35 U.S.C. § 103(a). Although the ultimate determination of obviousness under § 103 is a question of law, it is based on several underlying factual findings, including (1) the scope and content of the prior art; (2) the level of ordinary skill in the pertinent art; (3) the differences between the claimed invention and the prior art; and (4) evidence of secondary factors, such as commercial success, long-felt need, and the failure of others. Graham v. John Deere Co., 383 U.S. 1, 17-18, 86 S.Ct. 684, 15 L.Ed.2d 545 (1966). A patent is presumed valid, 35 U.S.C. § 282, and this presumption can be overcome only by clear and convincing evidence to the contrary. Bristol-Myers Squibb Co. v. Ben Venue Labs., Inc., 246 F.3d 1368, 1374 (Fed.Cir.2001).

MGA argues that, rather than being nonobvious, the asserted claims would have been obvious based on the combination of the Laser Chess references, which teach the claimed game in electronic form, and the Swift patent, which teaches a physical laser-based game. According to MGA, the district court erred both (1) in concluding that because the '242 patent relates to a physical game, the Laser Chess articles were non-analogous art; and (2) in assuming that a person of skill in the art was a layperson rather than, as put forth by Innovention, a mechanical engineer with knowledge of optics. Finally, MGA argues, Innovention's unsupported and conclusory assertions of secondary considerations fail to overcome MGA's prima facie case of obviousness. …

We conclude that the district court clearly erred in several of the factual findings underlying its obviousness analysis. The district court erred in finding that the Laser Chess references fail to qualify as analogous art. The court also erred in concluding that the level of skill in the art is that of a layperson. We address each in turn.

A. Analogous Art

A reference qualifies as prior art for a determination under § 103 when it is analogous to the claimed invention. In re Clay, 966 F.2d 656, 658 (Fed.Cir.1992). "Two separate tests define the scope of analogous art: (1) whether the art is from the same field of endeavor, regardless of the problem addressed, and (2) if the reference is not within the field of the inventor's endeavor, whether the reference still is reasonably pertinent to the particular problem with which the inventor is involved." In re Bigio, 381 F.3d 1320, 1325 (Fed.Cir.2004). …

Innovention argues that the Laser Chess articles are non-analogous art because the '242 patent's inventors were concerned with making a non-virtual, three-dimensional, laser-based board game, a project that involves mechanical engineering and optics, not computer programming. The district court appears to have agreed, finding that the Laser Chess references were non-analogous art since each discloses "an electronic version of the '242 patent." Innovention Toys, 665 F.Supp.2d at 653. The court, however, failed to consider whether a reference disclosing an electronic, laser-based strategy game, even if not in the same field of endeavor, would nonetheless have been reasonably pertinent to the problem facing an inventor of a new, physical, laser-based strategy game. In this case, the district court clearly erred in not finding the Laser Chess references to be analogous art based on this test as a matter of law. See Wyers v. Master Lock Co., 616 F.3d 1231, 1238 (Fed.Cir.2010) (holding as a matter of law that prior art padlock seals were analogous since directed to the same problem of preventing the ingress of contaminants into the locking mechanism).

The '242 patent and the Laser Chess references are directed to the same purpose: detailing the specific game elements comprising a chess-like, laser-based strategy game. Specifically, the '242 patent describes (1) the game's components, including the game board, '242 patent col.4 ll.45-56, and various types of playing pieces, id. col.6 l.48-col.7 l.24; (2) the game's specific rules, including how the pieces may move on the game board during a player's turn, id. col.3 ll.21-28, col.8 l.49-col.9 l.17; and (3) the game's ultimate objective, namely, illuminating an opponent's key playing piece with a laser beam, id. col.6 ll.45-47. The specification even distinguishes prior art patents based on these game elements, stating that U.S. Patent 3,516,671 lacks "the unique elements and rules of the ['242 patent's] invention," id. col.1 ll.47-50, and U.S. Patent 6,702,286 contemplates a game in which the objective is not to "illuminate playing pieces," but rather "to maneuver one's pieces to flank (or surround) those of the opposing player," id. col.2 ll.16-21.

The Laser Chess references likewise describe specific playing pieces, rules, and objectives to create a chess-like, laser-based strategy game. Both Laser Chess and Advanced Laser Chess disclose, for example, (1) various game pieces, each with unique capabilities, J.A. 1775-77, 1784-85; (2) rules for each player's turn, J.A. 1777-78, 1785-86; and (3) an ultimate objective of eliminating an opponent's king piece, J.A. 1775, 1784.

Accordingly, the '242 patent and the Laser Chess references relate to the same goal: designing a winnable yet entertaining strategy game. The '242 patent's specification confirms that game design was one objective facing its inventors. In particular, the specification states that "[s]trategy games may differ in a variety of ways," such as in board layout, the number and types of playing pieces, and the manner in which each piece moves on the game board, and that "[e]ach of these variations affects the strategy of the play and the degree of skill required to play the game." '242 patent col.2 ll.19-46. The specification thus admonishes that if the game elements "are overly simplistic, the game is too easy, will usually end in a draw or a predictable manner, and quickly become uninteresting for the average player." Id. col.2 ll.49-54. Conversely, according to the specification, if the game elements "are overly complicated, the game takes too long to learn [and] is frustrating and uninteresting for the average player." Id. col.2 ll.57-60.

The specific combination of game elements disclosed and claimed in the '242 patent thus deals with the problem of game design, and game elements from any strategy game, regardless how implemented, "logically would have commended itself to an inventor's attention in considering [this] problem." Clay, 966 F.2d at 659. Basic game elements remain the same regardless of the medium in which they are implemented: whether molded in plastic by a mechanical engineer or coded in software by a computer scientist. And, as MGA's evidence shows, inventors of numerous prior art patents contemplated the implementation of their strategy games in both physical and electronic formats. Innovention Toys, 665 F.Supp.2d at 650 n. 23. For example, the Swift patent states that "[a]lthough the preferred embodiment is played by two players, obvious modifications of the game allow for . . . a single player playing against a computer." Swift col.2 ll.47-51. Thus, because no reasonable jury could find that the Laser Chess references do not qualify as analogous prior art, and the district court erred in not so concluding as a matter of law.

Because of its error, the district court failed to properly consider the scope and content of the relevant prior art as well as the differences between that art and the claimed invention, including whether one of ordinary skill in the art would have been motivated to combine the teachings of the Laser Chess references with the Swift patent in light of the standard articulated in KSR International Co. v. Teleflex, Inc., 550 U.S. 398, 127 S.Ct. 1727, 167 L.Ed.2d 705 (2007). We therefore remand these factual determinations to the district court to consider in the first instance. Furthermore, should the district court conclude that MGA has made out a prima facie case of obviousness based on the Laser Chess articles and the Swift patent, the court must then determine whether Innovention's secondary considerations overcome MGA's prima facie case. …

III. Permanent Injunction

The district court, based on its grant of summary judgment of infringement and nonobviousness, granted a permanent injunction to Innovention. Because we vacate and remand the district court's decision of summary judgment of nonobviousness, we also vacate the district court's permanent injunction. …

Notes and Questions

1. Copyright law requires only independent creation, a modicum of creativity, and fixation in a tangible medium of expression. These are all easy thresholds to meet: scribble on a napkin and you're done. But patent law has much more rigorous screening doctrines.

> *Novelty*. An invention must be *novel* in an absolute sense. A patent will not be granted if "the claimed invention was patented, described in a printed publication, or in public use, on sale, or otherwise available to the public." 35 U.S.C. § 102.
>
> *Nonobviousness*. An invention must not be "obvious … to a person having ordinary skill in the art to which the claimed invention pertains." *Id.* § 103. This means that only significant improvements on the prior art are patentable, and not minor advances. As Justice Kennedy explained for the Supreme Court in *KSR Intern. Co. v. Teleflex, Inc.*, 127 S. Ct. 1727, 1746 (2007):
>
>> We build and create by bringing to the tangible and palpable reality around us new works based on instinct, simple logic, ordinary inferences, extraordinary ideas, and sometimes even genius. These advances, once part of our shared knowledge, define a new threshold from which innovation starts once more. And as progress beginning from higher levels of achievement is expected in the normal course, the results of ordinary innovation are not the subject of exclusive rights under the

patent laws. Were it otherwise patents might stifle, rather than promote, the progress of useful arts.

Reduction to Practice and Enablement. It is not enough to have the idea for an invention ("conceive" of it) or even to write it down. An inventor must also "reduce the invention to practice" by establishing that it works for its intended purpose. What is more, in her patent application – which will be published if and when she is issued a patent (or sooner, under some circumstances) – she must "enable" the invention by providing "a written description of the invention, and of the manner and process of making and using it, in such full, clear, concise, and exact terms as to enable any person skilled in the art to which it pertains, or with which it is most nearly connected, to make and use the same." 35 U.S.C. § 112(a). (Notice the "person skilled in the art" is back for a return appearance; she is the hypothetical reasonable person of patent law.)

2. Until 2011, the United States patent law worked on a "first to invent" basis. If more than one applicant came to the USPTO with an application for the same invention, the patent would be awarded to the one who could prove the earliest date of conception for the invention (provided that she was reasonably diligent about reducing it to practice and had not abandoned it), regardless of who filed first. But in 2011, to bring the U.S. closer to patent systems in the rest of the world, the Leahy-Smith America Invents Act, Pub. L. No. 112-29, 125 Stat. 284 (2011) ("AIA") switched to a "first to file" basis. Now (subject to some exceptions) the patent will be issued to the inventor whose application was filed first, regardless of who was first to conceive of the invention or reduce it to practice. Which of these systems strikes you as fairer? Which will be better at promoting invention and encouraging inventors to disclose their inventions to the public? Which is easier to administer? Which is more consistent with the principles of first possession you studied in the context of personal property?

3. The test for patent infringement is whether every limitation in a claim is present in the defendant's product or process. So if a patent claim includes an axle and a wheel, a product containing both an axle and a wheel will infringe, but a product containing only an axle but not a wheel will not. The hard part, however, is that a court will need to interpret the words of a claim to determine what kinds of things it does and does not describe. (In *Innovention Toys*, the crucial term is "movable.") How is this test different from the substantial-similarity and fair-use tests in copyright law?

   The claims of a patent, it is sometimes said, establish the "metes and bounds" of the owner's rights in the same way that a description of real property does ("… thence 30 feet 6 inches north, thence 74 feet 1 inch west …"). Is this an accurate metaphor? Which provides clearer notice to potential defendants of what they can and cannot do?

4. The patent equivalent to first sale is the doctrine of *exhaustion*: the owner of an item covered by a patent may legally sell or use it without the patent owner's permission. She just can't make more. For example, in *Bowman v. Monsanto Co.*, 133 S. Ct. 1761 (2013), Monsanto owned a patent on a pesticide-resistant strain of soybeans and charged farmers a premium price for these "Roundup Ready" beans. Bowman, who liked the beans but not the price, bought Roundup Ready soybeans not from Monsanto, but from other other farmers' harvests. The Supreme Court unanmiously held that Bowman was an infringer. When he planted the beans he "made" more patented beans without Monsanto's permission. Bowman argued that there should be an exception for technologies that automatically replicate themselves, but the Court rejected this "blame-the-bean defense."

5. Patent remedies are broadly similar to copyright remedies. But there are a few notable differences. For one thing, there are no statutory damages. Instead, courts are authorized to award the plaintiff up to treble damages in cases of "willful" infringement. For another, instead of copyright's restitutionary damage measure, patent law specifies that the patentee is entitled to "damages adequate to compensate for the infringement, but in no event less than a reasonable royalty for the use made of the invention by the infringer." 35 U.S.C. § 284.

6. Patent rights are broader than copyright rights in an important way. While copyright has an independent creation defense, patent does not. Even if you have never heard of the plaintiff or her patent, if you make, use, or sell the invention it describes, you are an infringer. Recent years have seen a boom in litigation by so-called "non-practicing entitles" – or, less charitably, patent "trolls," so called because they allegedly lurk in the shadows like trolls in fairy tails and then spring out to demand tolls from unsuspecting travelers who have unknowingly wandered onto their bridges. We will return with some regularity to the problem of notice in property law; would you expect notice problems more or less severe in intellectual property than for real and tangible personal property?.

D. Trademarks

Dixi-Cola Laboratories v. Coca-Cola Co.
117 F. 2d 352 (4th Cir. 1941)

SOPER, Circuit Judge: …

The plaintiff is the owner of the trademark "Coca-Cola" for a syrup to be used with carbonated water as a beverage. The defendants make and sell a concentrate and a syrup to be used in the production of a similar beverage under the names, MarBert the Distinctive Cola and Dixi-Cola. The defendants do not use the word "coca"; but they claim the right to use the word "cola" in the combinations mentioned. The evidence shows that they have also used other terms, such as Apola Cola and Lola-Kola, but as to them they now make no defense. The plaintiff concedes that the names Dixi-Cola and MarBert the Distinctive Cola are not so similar to the name Coca-Cola, that a purchaser of the beverage known as Dixi-Cola or MarBert the Distinctive Cola would be led to believe that he was buying the beverage Coca-Cola, but the plaintiff nevertheless charges infringement on the ground that the use of the word "cola" in defendants' trade-marks or trade-names leads the public to believe that their products originate with the plaintiff. …

The broad claim of the plaintiff to the exclusive use of the word "cola" in a trade-mark or trade-name is based upon the contention that Coca-Cola is a technical common-law trade-mark, adopted as a fanciful and arbitrary word by the first producer of the beverage in 1886. The plaintiff also relies on five registrations of the mark in the United States Patent Office, one under the Act of March 3, 1881, 21 Stat. 502, and four under the Act of February 20, 1905, 33 Stat. 724, 15 U.S.C.A. § 81 et seq. …

It is certainly beyond dispute that the word "Coca-Cola" is the exclusive property of the Coca-Cola Company. The evidence in the pending case shows that what was said of the name in *Coca-Cola Co. v. Koke Co.*, 254 U.S. 143 [(1920)], and *Coca-Cola Co. v. Old Dominion Beverage Corp.*, [271 F. 600 (4th Cir. 1921)], is equally true today. There has been no let-up in the popular demand for the drink or in the extent of its advertising. On the contrary, both have greatly increased. In 1920 the gallons of syrup sold were 18,656,445 and the advertising expense $2,330,710.40, while in 1938 the gallons sold were 48,508,414, and the advertising expense $7,122,863.31. No one else can lawfully use the word "Coca-Cola" for a trade-mark, even though it originally may have been a descriptive name.

The plaintiff, however, is not content with this measure of protection. It insists in addition that no one shall use the word "cola" in a trade-mark, even in connection with a prefix that prevents all confusion with the name Coca-Cola. The reason given is that the word is so closely associated with Coca-Cola in the public mind that any drink, bearing the word as part of its name, will be thought to proceed from the same source. Forty-one witnesses from Baltimore, Springfield and

Birmingham testified that when they saw goods labeled by a name containing the suffix "cola," they were led to believe, not that the goods were Coca-Cola, but that they originated with the Coca-Cola Company. Hence, it is said, the defendants have appropriated the result of the plaintiff's efforts and expenditures, and imperiled the reputation of the Coca-Cola Company and its product.

Confusion of origin, as well as confusion of goods, from the use of the same trade-mark, may constitute infringement, especially when the name has a fanciful and arbitrary character. We must, therefore, consider the defense now set up to this phase of the plaintiff's case that the word "cola" is a descriptive and generic term, open to all the world, which may be lawfully used as part of a trademark by competitors so long as the whole trade-mark is not confusingly similar to Coca-Cola.

There are many cases which hold that it is not infringement for a trader to use as part of his trade-name to designate his product a descriptive or generic word which has already been adopted by another, provided that the competing marks, taken as a whole, are clearly distinguishable. Thus "Sal-Vet" was held not infringed by "Sal Tone", since the word "Sal", meaning salt, was descriptive of the principal ingredient of both products, and no ordinary purchaser would confuse one of the complete names with the other. *S. R. Feil Co. v. John E. Robins Co.* [220 F .650 (7th Cir. 1915)].

In the light of these decisions, it is important to inquire whether or not the word "cola" has a descriptive significance apart from its use in the trade-mark Coca-Cola, and has become a generic term, generally used to indicate a class of beverage. The answer is to be found, we believe, in scientific and popular literature, in the discussions of Coca-Cola cases by the courts, and the attitude of the Coca-Cola Company itself in the conduct of its business. The beverage was devised and the name Coca-Cola was adopted by John S. Pemberton in Atlanta in 1886. The product was sold under a label registered in the Patent Office, which advertised Coca-Cola syrup as an extract for carbonated beverages possessing a peculiar flavor and the tonic and nerve stimulant qualities of the coca plant and cola nuts. Both of these substances were well known at that time. The word "cola" was recognized as the name of a tree native to Africa, which bears the small brown "cola nut" that was introduced in England in 1865 and later in the United States. Prior to 1886 the stimulant qualities of the cola nut were frequently referred to in pharmaceutical and scientific publications and periodicals, and it was suggested that it could be used to make a beverage that would successfully compete with tea and coffee as a refreshing and invigorating drink.

These facts led to the contention in the court below that at best the word Coca-Cola, taken as a whole, is a descriptive name, entitled to protection only because it has acquired a secondary significance. But the contention was rejected. It was said that while relatively small amounts of coca and cola extracts are found in the drink, the basic ingredients are sugar, phosphoric acid and a small amount of caffeine; and also that the words comprising the mark were so little known to the general public when adopted that they did not suggest at that time that the beverage was made from coca leaves or cola nuts. Hence it was decided that the name is not clearly descriptive of the product, but should be considered a coined word with all the characteristics of a technical trade mark. Other courts have reached the same conclusion. [citing cases]. …

The decision of the Supreme Court in *Coca-Cola Co. v. Koke Co.* has already been mentioned. The court rejected the charge that the right to protection against infringement because of misrepresentations implied by the name that the product contained cocaine, which had formerly been used in small amounts, but had been eliminated after the passage of the Food and Drug Act. The court said, "We are dealing here with a popular drink not with a medicine, and although what has been said might suggest that its attraction lay in producing the expectation of a toxic effect the facts point to a different conclusion. Since 1900 the sales have increased at a very great rate corresponding to a like increase in advertising. The name now characterizes a beverage to be had at almost any soda fountain. It means a single thing coming from a single source, and well known to the community. It hardly would be too much to say that the drink characterizes the name as much as the name the drink. In other words 'Coca-Cola' probably means to most persons the plaintiff's familiar product to be had everywhere rather than a compound of particular substances. … The coca leaves and whatever of cola nut is employed may be used to justify the continuance of the name or they may affect the flavor as the plaintiff contends, but before this suit was brought the plaintiff had advertised to the public that it must not expect and would not find cocaine, and had eliminated every thing tending to suggest cocaine effects except the name and the picture of the leaves and nuts, which probably conveyed little or nothing to most who saw it. It appears to us that it would be going too far to deny the plaintiff relief against a palpable fraud because possibly here and there an ignorant person might call for the drink with the hope for incipient cocaine intoxication. The plaintiff's position must be judged by the facts as they were when the suit was begun, not by the facts of a different condition and an earlier time." …

It must be concluded, we think, from this history that the word "Coca-Cola," taken as a whole, is in some sense descriptive of the drink which it designates. It is true that the name identifies the goods of the plaintiff, but it has also come to characterize them. This process has been hastened by the fact that the combination of extract of coca leaves and extract of cola nuts employed by Pemberton was new, and it gave to the product a new and distinctive flavor for which there was no other name than that which he employed. Hence the drink came to be known to the public by this name in much the same fashion as other soft drinks are named for a small quantity of flavoring ingredient rather than the large quantities of sugar and water that mainly compose them. The process was further stimulated by the great public response to the drink and the activities of numerous competitors who speedily entered the field and were enabled lawfully to make the same or a similar beverage, since Coca-Cola was not covered by a patent.

The record is replete with references to the number of competing drinks in this class. The District Judge in his opinion said that "since Coca-Cola appeared, there has been a veritable flood of drinks of this type, as evidenced by the fact that there have been no less than 143 registrations in the United States Patent Office of names embodying the word 'cola' as a suffix." In 1907 the Supreme Court of Mississippi, in the case of *Coca-Cola Co. v. Skillman*, 91 Miss. 677, 44 So. 985, discussed a statute imposing a privilege tax on Coca-Cola, Celery-Cola, Afri-Cola, Hecks Cola, Cola-Beta, Colavin, Nervola, and Nervocola, or any similar or proprietary drinks. Some cola drinks have had a long and continuous history. Thus the record shows that Lime-Cola has been made for more than twenty years in the United States and that Pepsi-Cola has been in existence as a beverage for more than thirty-five years.

The adoption of the word "cola" to characterize a class of drinks thus came about very naturally, to some extent with the consent of the Coca-Cola Company, as we shall see, and to a greater extent because in the course of events it could not be prevented. It was attended by a vast increase after 1886 in the literature relating to the cola nut and its uses. Publications of various types recognized the fact that it could be used as an ingredient of a soft drink. Numerous references to the cola nut and to cola syrup and extract and their use in beverages, called cola drinks, appeared throughout the following years in dictionaries, encyclopedias, pharmaceutical magazines, trade journals and government publications. During the same period the word was adopted as part of the trade name of a large number of competing beverages. The result is that today the phrase "cola drinks" indicates to the general public beverages which in taste and appearance resemble Coca-Cola. …

It must not be supposed that the Coca-Cola Company has not fought vigorously to protect its valuable right from invasion. Suits against competitors have averaged one a week during the last thirty years. Many of these competitors have been guilty of fraud and unfair competition, and all of them, it is safe to say, have sought to participate in the profits which experience had shown could be derived from making a drink like Coca-Cola. …

None of these reported decisions goes further than the decision of this court in *Coca-Cola Co. v. Old Dominion Beverage Corp.*, involving the use of the name "Taka Cola," and the unreported decision of the present writer in *Coca-Cola Co. v. Philips Bros.* in the District Court of Maryland, involving the word "Champion-Cola." In both cases the names were regarded as so close to the name "Coca-Cola" as to be likely to result in the confusion of the goods. In both there was unfair competition in the simulation of the color scheme, of the script of the Coca-Cola Company, or in the confusing display of the competing name. …

No reported case has come to our attention which distinctly holds that the word "cola" cannot be used as part of a name of a beverage provided that the whole name is not confusingly similar to Coca-Cola. It is urged, however, that we should make such a decision in this case for the reasons, which found favor in the District Court, that no such thing as a cola beverage in the present sense of the term, was known or spoken of prior to the advent of Coca-Cola in 1886, and that the Coca-Cola Company has always asserted its claim to the exclusive use of the term. In our opinion, these considerations, even if sustained by the evidence, are not controlling in the face of the fact that the word "cola" does not today indicate the plaintiff's product but a class of drinks to which the goods of the defendants and many other competitors belong. The applicable rule, supported by authority, is thus stated in the Restatement of Torts: "§ 735. (1) A designation which is initially a trade-mark or trade name ceases to be such when it comes to be generally understood as a generic or descriptive designation for the type of goods, services or business in connection with which it is used." Comment (a) to the foregoing sub-section (1) reads as follows: "Significance of change in meaning. When one has a monopoly of the initial distribution of a specific article over a period of time, and especially if the descriptive name for the article is one difficult to pronounce or remember, there is a likelihood that the designation which he adopts as his trade-mark for the article will be incorporated into the language as the usual generic designation for an article of that type. When that happens, the designation becomes merely descriptive of the goods and no longer identifies a particular brand or performs any of the functions of a trade-mark or trade name. Moreover, the designation must then be used by others if there is to be any effective competition in the sale of the goods. It is immaterial that the person first adopting the designation made every reasonable effort to avoid this result or that the designation was coined by him and derived meaning only from his use. The designation may be used by others, subject to the limitations of Sub-Section (2) and of Sec. 712 relating to fraudulent marketing."

We are, however, in accord with the conclusion of the District Court that the conduct of the defendants has been such as to justify a decree restricting their business activities in the future along certain lines. The evidence amply justifies the finding that distributors of their products in New England, New York and St. Louis, and to a less extent in Baltimore, have attempted to sell and have sold their syrup to customers, engaged in the fountain trade, with the understanding that the drink made therefrom should be sold as and for Coca-Cola. The officers of the defendant corporation had knowledge of these activities and participated therein. The sale of syrup to the fountain trade constituted about ten per cent of the total business of the defendant.

The evidence also justifies the finding that the bottled beverage made by bottlers from defendant's concentrate was passed off as Coca-Cola in various bars and taverns. It is difficult to ascertain how wide-spread this practice has been, but there is some evidence that an officer of the corporation encouraged the practice. The defendants were also fully aware of the use of the infringing word "Lola-Kola" by bottlers, and indeed agreed to place this word on all packages of its concentrate sold to Lola Bottlers, Inc. Under these circumstances, it is a reasonable conclusion that the defendants have conspired with their customers to palm off their goods for those of the Coca-Cola Company whenever it was safe to do so.

The remedy for these illegal acts, which appears in the decree, is the issuance of an injunction against the defendants enjoining them from committing any acts calculated to cause any product other than the plaintiff's to be known or sold as "Coca-Cola" or "Koke," or any colorable imitation thereof. The defendants are also enjoined "(f) From giving to any part of their merchandise not sold by defendants, their agents or distributors, in bottles to consumers, a color imitating or resembling the color of plaintiff's product, if or when defendants know, or in the exercise of reasonable care should know, that the purchaser thereof intends to dispense such merchandise to the consumer other than in bottles, or intends to bottle the beverage made from such product and to use on the bottles, labels or caps some extrinsic, deceiving element that in conjunction with the color imitating plaintiff's color enables such purchaser to pass off his, her or their product for plaintiff's product." …

Notes and Questions

1. Both copyright and patent award rights to people who create information. Trademark law is different. After Defense Secretary Donald Rumsfeld used the phrase "shock and awe" to describe the initial bombing campaign of the Iraq War, the USPTO received dozens of trademark applications for the phrase SHOCK AND AWE, for goods ranging from video games to fireworks to eyewear. *See* Sabra Chartrand, *Trademarking 'Shock and Awe'*, N.Y. TIMES, Apr. 21, 2003, http://www.nytimes.com/2003/04/21/technology/21PATE.html. None of these applicants created the phrase. What they hoped to create – and what trademark law protects – is the goodwill in consumers' minds associating the phrase with their particular goods. Any user of a mark who succeeds in creating those associations obtains trademark rights against confusing uses of the mark. So trademark rights flow from use, and they endure as long as the use continues. Compare and contrast this basis of protection with the other bases we have studied – and keep it in mind. Rights based on use will be important in our discussion of natural resources.

2. The basic species of trademark infringement is confusion about source: the consumer buys the defendant's product rather than the plaintiff's in the mistaken belief that it *is*

the plaintiff's product. This form of confusion, known as *passing off*, is actionable even when the defendant scrupulously avoids using the plaintiff's trademark but still manages to trick consumers about what they are buying. (Scene: Restaurant, interior, day. Patron: "I'll have a Coke, please." Waiter: "Here you go." *Waiter serves Patron a glass of MarBert the Distinctive Cola.*) There is a close kinship between this theory of liability and the hypothetical, discussed in *Keeble v. Hickeringill*, of the schoolmaster who scares of his competitor's students by shooting a gun in the air. Both are forms of *unfair competition*: stealing customers from a competitor with dishonest or dangerous business practices.

But trademark law today is not limited to passing off. Another species of trademark liability is *dilution*, in which the defendant allegedly harms the trademark itself.

> First, there is concern that consumer search costs will rise if a trademark becomes associated with a variety of unrelated products. Suppose an upscale restaurant calls itself "Tiffany." There is little danger that the consuming public will think it's dealing with a branch of the Tiffany jewelry store if it patronizes this restaurant. But when consumers next see the name "Tiffany" they may think about both the restaurant and the jewelry store, and if so the efficacy of the name as an identifier of the store will be diminished. Consumers will have to think harder — incur as it were a higher imagination cost — to recognize the name as the name of the store. So "blurring" is one form of dilution.
>
> Now suppose that the "restaurant" that adopts the name "Tiffany" is actually a striptease joint. Again, and indeed even more certainly than in the previous case, consumers will not think the striptease joint under common ownership with the jewelry store. But because of the inveterate tendency of the human mind to proceed by association, every time they think of the word "Tiffany" their image of the fancy jewelry store will be tarnished by the association of the word with the strip joint. So "tarnishment" is a second form of dilution. Analytically it is a subset of blurring, since it reduces the distinctness of the trademark as a signifier of the trademarked product or service.

Ty, Inc. v. Perryman, 306 F.3d 509, 511 (7th Cir. 2002). Is these forms of harm against which trademark law ought to guard? Or are they the result of taking the metaphor of a trademark as "property" too seriously?

3. Trademark law has a strong consumer-protection flavor. This gives it a close connection to false advertising law, but note that trademark law targets a particular species of misleading statements: those that involve misleading uses of trademarks. Unsurprisingly, then, trademark law has defenses for people who use trademarks in basically truthful

ways. Comparative advertising, for example, allows a defendant to use the plaintiff's trademark rather than circumlocutions like "the other leading brand" in statements like "Four out of five taste-testers preferred Pepsi to Coke." And nominative fair use (not to be confused with the completely different defense of fair use in copyright) lets defendants describe their products in terms of the plaintiff's, as in "The best Toyota repair shop in the Tri-State Area." It also affects trademark law's exhaustion doctrine, because secondhand items bearing a trademark may well be meaningfully different than new items precisely because they are used. Would you buy a used golf ball? A used car? A used textbook? Used underwear? It is legal to sell such items with the original trademarks – provided their used status and their current condition are accurately disclosed.

4. It is common for different kinds of intellectual property to apply to different aspects of the same thing. Take an iPhone. Apple has utility patents covering numerous aspects of how it works, such the slide-to-unlock feature and shatterproof glass coatings. It has copyrights in the iOS software and icon designs. It has trademarks on IPHONE and the Apple logo. It has design patents in aspects of the iPhone's shape. Just as intellectual property rights can overlap or interfere with other property rights, different kinds of intellectual property rights can overlap or interfere. And just as first sale/exhaustion polices some of these boundaries, other doctrines help keep intellectual property systems from stepping on each other's toes. For example, "functional" material cannot be protected as a trademark. In *TrafFix Devices, Inc. v. Marketing Displays, Inc.*, 532 U.S. 23 (2001), MDI obtained a patent on a "dual-spring" design for road signs that helped keep

them from tipping over on windy days. After the patent expired, a competitor, TrafFix, introduced its own dual-spring road signs. MDI sued for *trademark* infringement, claiming that the dual-spring design was a source-indicating feature, i.e., that consumers recognized that the dual springs indicated they were buying a MDI sign. No dice, said the Supreme Court. Even if consumers did associate the dual springs with MDI, giving it trademark rights in the design would improperly extend its patent rights past the end of their proper term. Competitors like TrafFix need to be free to copy any feature of the design that is "essential to the use or purpose of the article" or that "affects the cost or quality of the article." A similar doctrine excludes functional material from copyright protection. *See* 17 U.S.C. § 102(b) ("In no case does copyright protection for an original work of authorship extend to any idea, procedure, process, system, method of operation, concept, principle, or discovery … .").

E. Other Kinds of Intellectual Property

Cheney Bros. v. Doris Silk Co.
35 F.2d 279 (2nd Cir. 1929)

L. HAND, Circuit Judge:

The plaintiff, a corporation is a manufacturer of silks, which puts out each season many new patterns, designed to attract purchasers by their novelty and beauty. Most of these fail in that purpose, so that not much more than a fifth catch the public fancy. Moreover, they have only a short life, for the most part no more than a single season of eight or nine months. It is in practice impossible, and it would be very onerous if it were not, to secure design patents upon all of these; it would also be impossible to know in advance which would sell well, and patent only those. Besides, it is probable that for the most part they have no such originality as would support a design patent. Again, it is impossible to copyright them under the Copyright Act (17 USCA § 1 et seq.), or at least so the authorities of the Copyright Office hold. So it is easy for any one to copy such as prove successful, and the plaintiff, which is put to much ingenuity and expense in fabricating them, finds itself without protection of any sort for its pains.

Taking advantage of this situation, the defendant copied one of the popular designs in the season beginning in October, 1928, and undercut the plaintiff's price. This is the injury of which it complains. The defendant, though it duplicated the design in question, denies that it knew it to be the plaintiff's, and there thus arises an issue which might be an answer to the motion. However, the parties wish a decision upon the equity of the bill, and, since it is within our power to dismiss it, we shall accept its allegation, and charge the defendant with knowledge.

The plaintiff asks for protection only during the season, and needs no more, for the designs are all ephemeral. It seeks in this way to disguise the extent of the proposed innovation, and to persuade us that, if we interfere only a little, the solecism, if there be one, may be pardonable. But the reasoning which would justify any interposition at all demands that it cover the whole extent of the injury. A man whose designs come to harvest in two years, or in five, has prima facie as good right to protection as one who deals only in annuals. Nor could we consistently stop at designs; processess, machines, and secrets have an equal claim. The upshot must be that, whenever any one has contrived any of these, others may be forbidden to copy it. That is not the law. In the absence of some recognized right at common law, or under the statutes -- and the plaintiff claims neither -- a man's property is limited to the chattels which embody his invention. Others may imitate these at their pleasure.

True, it would seem as though the plaintiff had suffered a grievance for which there should be a remedy, perhaps by an amendment of the Copyright Law, assuming that this does not already cover the case, which is not urged here. It seems a lame answer in such a case to turn the injured party out of court, but there are larger issues at stake than his redress. Judges have only a limited power to amend the law; when the subject has been confided to a Legislature, they must stand aside, even though there be an hiatus in completed justice. An omission in such cases must be taken to have been as deliberate as though it were express, certainly after long-standing action on the subject-matter. Indeed, we are not in any position to pass upon the questions involved, as Brandeis, J., observed in *International News Service v. Associated Press*. We must judge upon records prepared by litigants, which do not contain all that may be relevant to the issues, for they cannot disclose the conditions of this industry, or of the others which may be involved. Congress might see its way to create some sort of temporary right, or it might not. Its decision would certainly be preceded by some examination of the result upon the other interests affected. Whether these would prove paramount we have no means of saying; it is not for us to decide. Our vision is inevitably contracted, and the whole horizon may contain much which will compose a very different picture.

Notes and Questions

1. Not all information is subject to intellectual property protection. As *Chaney Bros.* illustrates, court will not simply fashion a remedy for the victim of copying by looking to a general right against imitation. Instead, they will give recovery when the victim can point to some specific and well-established body of intellectual property law giving rights over a particular kind of information. One consequence of this attitude, illustrated here, is that fashion designs are protected neither by federal statutory law or copyright law nor by state common law. And yet the fashion industry exists, and regularly produces new designs – and lots of them. Does this mean that intellectual property laws are unnecessary in general?

2. Indeed, part of the point of the case is the existence of federal copyright law provides a reason for state law *not* to apply. How would the goals of the copyright laws be undermined if states were to supply protection here? (The Copyright Act of 1976 is even more unequivocal on this point; it explicitly preempts "all legal or equitable rights that are equivalent to any of the exclusive rights within the general scope of copyright … in works of authorship that are fixed in a tangible medium of expression and come within the subject matter of copyright." 17 U.S.C. § 301(a).)

3. In recent years, Congress has considered a number of bills that would extend copyright-like protections (albeit with shorter terms) to fashion designs. Would these bills be good or bad for the fashion industry? For clothing buyers?

Property

4. Found and Stolen Property

Finders keepers, losers weepers?

Armory v. Delamirie

(1722) 1 Strange 505, 93 Eng. Rep. 664 (K.B.)

The plaintiff being a chimney sweeper's boy found a jewel and carried it to the defendant's shop (who was a goldsmith) to know what it was, and delivered it into the hands of the apprentice, who under pretence of weighing it, took out the stones, and calling to the master to let him know it came to three halfpence, the master offered the boy the money, who refused to take it, and insisted to have the thing again; whereupon the apprentice delivered him back the socket without the stones. And now in trover against the master these points were ruled:

1. That the finder of a jewel, though he does not by such finding acquire an absolute property or ownership, yet he has such a property as will enable him to keep it against all but the rightful owner, and consequently may maintain trover.

2. That the action well lay against the master, who gives a credit to his apprentice, and is answerable for his neglect.

3. As to the value of the jewel several of the trade were examined to prove what a jewel of the finest water that would fit the socket would be worth; and the Chief Justice directed the jury, that unless the defendant did produce the jewel, and shew it not to be of the finest water, they should presume the strongest against him, and make the value of the best jewels the measure of their damages: which they accordingly did.

Questions

1. One way of describing the holding of *Armory* is that it sets out the rights of finders. Suppose that the "rightful owner" of the jewel, Lord Hobnob, had shown up in the shop while the chimney-sweep and the apprentice were arguing over the jewel. Who would have been entitled to the jewel? If the chimney-sweep is not the "rightful owner," why does he still win the case? What kind of interest does he have in the jewel?

2. A second way of describing of describing the holding of *Armory* is that it illustrates "relativity of title." As between the plaintiff and the defendant, the party with the relatively better claim to title wins, even if their title is in some sense defective in an absolute sense. Relativity of title is intimately connected to the idea of "chains of title":

competing claimants to a piece of property each do their best to trace their claims back to a rightful source. What is the source of the chimney-sweep's claim to the jewel? And the jeweler's? Does this explain the outcome of the case? What result if the jeweler had proven that he had signed a contract to purchase the jewel from Lord Hobnob but that Lord Hobnob had lost the jewel before delivering it?

3. A third way of describing the holding of *Armory* is that it rejects the jeweler's attempt to assert a *jus tertii* (Latin for "right of a third party") defense. The defendant cannot defeat the plaintiff's otherwise-valid claim to the jewel by arguing that a third party – Lord Hobnob – has an even better claim. Put differently, we might say that "as against a wrongdoer, possession is title." *Jeffries v. Great W. Ry. Co.*, (1856) 119 Eng. Rep. 680, 681 (Q.B.). Does this narrowing of focus to the parties before the court make sense?

   Here is one way to think about it. Suppose that Lord Hobnob shows up in court while *Armory* is being argued and explains that the jewel slipped from his finger while he was strolling in Lincoln's Inn Fields. Who is entitled to the jewel? What if Lord Hobnob shows up and explains that he tossed the jewel aside in the mud, saying "I have become tired of this bauble; it bores me and I no longer wish to have it." What if he explains that he handed it to the chimney-sweep, saying "I wish you to have this jewel; may it serve you better than it has me." But recall that in the actual case, Lord Hobnob was nowhere to be found; no one even knew his identity. Does it matter to the outcome of *Armory v. Delamirie* how the jewel passed from Lord Hobnob's hands to the chimney-sweep's?

   If you are still not convinced, consider this. If the jeweler could set up Lord Hobnob's title to show that the chimney-sweep's title was defective, would the chimney-sweep be entitled to present evidence that Lord Hobnob's title was defective, say because Lord Hobnob stole the jewel from a visiting Frenchman in 1693? Cutting off inquiry into third parties' claims also helps cut off inquiry into old claims. Can you see why this might be an appealing choice for a system of property law?

4. We are not quite done with Lord Hobnob. Consider the remedy the plaintiff obtains: an award of the value of the jewel, rather than the jewel itself. This is in effect a forced sale of the jewel, which the defendant can keep after paying the plaintiff's damage award. *Now* who owns the jewel? What if Lord Hobnob shows up now? Can he also bring trover, and if so, will the jeweler be forced to pay out a second time? In fact, why is Paul de Lamerie, the goldsmith whose name the court mangles, on the hook for his apprentice's wrongdoing? What if the apprentice pocketed the jewel and never turned it over to the master?

5. About that damage award. Why is the jury instructed to presume that the jewel was "of the finest water?" (i.e. highest quality)?

Other Variations on *Armory*

Just how far does the holding of *Armory v. Delamirie* ("That the finder of [property], though he does not by such finding acquire an absolute property or ownership, yet he has such a property as will enable him to keep it against all but the rightful owner") go? Consider three nineteenth-century cases about lost lumber. Are they required by *Armory*? Consistent with *Armory*? Consistent with each other? Which is most persuasive?

In *Clark v. Maloney*, 3 Del. 68 (1840), the plaintiff found ten logs floating in a bay after a storm. He tied them up in the mouth of a creek, but they (apparently) got free again and the defendants (apparently) found them floating up the creek. *Held*, the plaintiffs were entitled to the logs:

> Possession is certainly prima facie evidence of property. It is called *prima facie* evidence because it may be rebutted by evidence of better title, but in the absence of better title it is as effective a support of title as the most conclusive evidence could be. It is for this reason, that *the finder of a chattel, though he does not acquire an absolute property in it, yet has such a property, as will enable him to keep it against all but the rightful owner*. The defence consists, not in showing that the defendants are the rightful owners, or claim under the rightful owner; but that the logs were found by them adrift in Mispillion creek, having been loosened from their fastening either by accident or design, and they insist that their title is as good as that of the plaintiff. But it is a well settled rule of law that the loss of a chattel does not change the right of property; and for the same reason that the original loss of these logs by the rightful owner, did not change his absolute property in them, but he might have maintained trover against the plaintiff upon refusal to deliver them, so the subsequent loss did not divest the *special* property of the plaintiff. It follows, therefore, that as the plaintiff has shown a special property in these logs, which he never abandoned, and which enabled him to keep them against all the world but the rightful owner, he is entitled to a verdict.

In *Anderson v. Gouldberg*, 53 N.W. 636 (Minn. 1892), the defendants took ninety-three logs from the plaintiff's mill. The defendants claimed that the plaintiff had cut the logs on their land, but the plaintiff replied (and a jury agreed) that he had actually cut the logs by trespassing on the land of a third party. *Held*: the plaintiff was entitled to the logs:

> Therefore the only question is whether bare possession of property, though wrongfully obtained, is sufficient title to enable the party enjoying it to maintain replevin against a

> mere stranger, who takes it from him. We had supposed that this was settled in the affirmative as long ago, at least, as the early case of *Armory v. Delamirie*, so often cited on that point. When it is said that to maintain replevin the plaintiff's possession must have been lawful, it means merely that it must have been lawful as against the person who deprived him of it; and possession is good title against all the world except those having a better title. Counsel says that possession only raises a presumption of title, which, however, may be rebutted. Rightly understood, this is correct; but counsel misapplies it. One who takes property from the possession of another can only rebut this presumption by showing a superior title in himself, or in some way connecting himself with one who has. One who has acquired the possession of property, whether by finding, bailment, or by mere tort, has a right to retain that possession as against a mere wrongdoer who is a stranger to the property. Any other rule would lead to an endless series of unlawful seizures and reprisals in every case where property had once passed out of the possession of the rightful owner.

Anderson states what is overwhelmingly the majority rule. Seven years after *Anderson*, North Carolina took the opposite course. In *Russell v. Hill*, 34 S.E. 640 (N.C. 1899), two different people held what appeared to be state grants to the same tract of land, and the plaintiff cut timber on the land with the wrong one's permission. While the logs were floating in a river, the defendants – unconnected with either of the purported landowners – took them away and sold them. *Held*: the defendants were entitled to the logs (internal quotation marks omitted):

> In some of the English books, and in some of the Reports of our sister states, cases might be found to the contrary, but that those cases were all founded upon a misapprehension of the principle laid down in the case of *Armory v. Delamirie*. There a chimney sweep found a lost jewel. He took it into his possession, as he had a right to do, and was the owner, because of having it in possession, unless the true owner should become known. That owner was not known, and it was properly decided that trover would lie in favor of the finder against the defendant, to whom he had handed it for inspection, and who refused to restore it. But the court said the case would have been very different if the owner had been known.

Is this an accurate reading of *Armory*? The court also expressed concern about the defendant's potential liability to the true owner:

> It is true that, as possession is the strongest evidence of the ownership, property may be presumed from possession. … But if it appears on the trial that the plaintiff, although in possession, is not in fact the owner, the presumption of title inferred from the possession is rebutted, and it would be manifestly wrong to allow the plaintiff to recover the value of the property; for the real owner may forthwith bring trover against the defendant, and

> force him to pay the value the second time, and the fact that he paid it in a former suit would be no defense. Consequently trover can never be maintained unless a satisfaction of the judgment will have the effect of vesting a good title in the defendant.

Is the fear of double liability sufficient reason to allow the defendant to escape liability entirely? Based on a review of the court records in the case, John V. Orth writes that the true owner in *Russell v. Hill* was "no bodiless abstraction but had in fact a name and identity: [Fabius Haywood] Busbee, one of the state's leading lawyers, a man well known to every member of the supreme court that decided the case." John V. Orth, Russell v. Hill *(N.C. 1899): Misunderstood Lessons*, 73 N.C. L. REV. 2031, 2034 (1995). Does this help explain *Russell*?

Professor Orth, arguing for a middle ground between *Anderson* and *Russell*, argues that *Armory* should protect only prior possessors who took the property in good faith: "A technical wrongdoing, such as an innocent trespass, as the source of possession should not disable the possessor from securing judicial protection against an unauthorized taking, but a willful trespass at the root of title should. Plaintiff in *Russell,* in other words, deserved a new trial at which to show, not his title, but his *bona fides*" *Id.* at 2060. Is this a better rule?

McAvoy v. Medina

93 Mass. (11 Allen) 548 (1866)

TORT to recover a sum of money found by the plaintiff in the shop of the defendant.

[I]t appeared that the defendant was a barber, and the plaintiff, being a customer in the defendant's shop, saw and took up a pocket-book which was lying upon a table there, and said, "See what I have found." The defendant came to the table and asked where he found it. The plaintiff laid it back in the same place and said, "I found it right there." The defendant then took it and counted the money, and the plaintiff told him to keep it, and if the owner should come to give it to him; and otherwise to advertise it; which the defendant promised to do. Subsequently the plaintiff made three demands for the money, and the defendant never claimed to hold the same till the last demand. It was agreed that the pocket-book was placed upon the table by a transient customer of the defendant and accidentally left there, and was first seen and taken up by the plaintiff, and that the owner had not been found. …

DEWEY, J.

It seems to be the settled law that the finder of lost property has a valid claim to the same against all the world except the true owner, and generally that the place in which it is found creates no exception to this rule.

But this property is not, under the circumstances, to be treated as lost property in that sense in which a finder has a valid claim to hold the same until called for by the true owner. This property was voluntarily placed upon a table in the defendant's shop by a customer of his who accidentally left the same there and has never called for it. The plaintiff also came there as a customer, and first saw the same and took it up from the table. The plaintiff did not by this acquire the right to take the property from the shop, but it was rather the duty of the defendant, when the fact became thus known to him, to use reasonable care for the safe keeping of the same until the owner should call for it. In the case of *Bridges v. Hawkesworth*, 7 Eng. Law & Eq. R. 424, the property, although found in a shop, was found on the floor of the same, and had not been placed there voluntarily by the owner, and the court held that the finder was entitled to the possession of the same, except as to the owner. But the present case more resembles that of *Lawrence v. The State,* 1 Humph. (Tenn.) 228, and is indeed very similar in its facts. The court there take a distinction between the case of property thus placed by the owner and neglected to be removed, and property lost. It was there held that "to place a pocket-book upon a table and to forget to take it away is not to lose it, in the sense in which the authorities referred to speak of lost property."

We accept this as the better rule, and especially as one better adapted to secure the rights of the true owner.

In view of the facts of this case, the plaintiff acquired no original right to the property, and the defendant's subsequent acts in receiving and holding the property in the manner he did does not create any.

Questions

1. One important to term that is often used in similar cases, though not in the case of *McAvoy v. Medina* is "locus in quo." Literally, locus in quo means the place of the event (or the place in which)—in the context of lost and mislaid objects, locus in quo means the place where the object was found. *McAvoy v. Medina* concerns a dispute between the finder and the owner/possessor of the locus in quo. In *McAvoy*, the finder clearly established possession of the object before the owner of the locus in quo, but the court prefers the rights of the owner of the locus in quo. Under what circumstances does the owner of the locus in quo prevail, and against whom?

2. In *Lawrence v. State*, on which *McAvoy* relies, the customer did come back for his lost pocketbook containing $480 in bank notes, which he had left on a table while the barber went out to make change. To quote the court: "The barber left the shop to get the bill changed, and, a fight occurring in the streets, the [customer's] attention was arrested thereat and he left the shop, his pocket-book lying on the table." When he returned, the

barber "denied all knowledge of the pocket-book" but then "expended [the bank notes] in the purchase of confections, etc." A criminal prosecution for grand larceny followed, and the barber argued that the pocketbook had been lost because larceny only applies when the defendant takes property from the possession of the victim. The court held that because the pocketbook on a table was merely **mislaid**, rather than "lost," it was still within the customer's "constructive possession." First of all, is this plausible? And second, is this a good fit for the facts of *McAvoy*?

3. By way of contrast, in *Bridges v. Hawkesworth*, which *McAvoy* distinguishes, the plaintiff found a small parcel on the floor of the defendant's shop and immediately showed it to the defendant's employee. The parcel contained bank notes; the plaintiff "requested the defendant to deliver them to the owner." Three years later, with no owner having returned, the court held the plaintiff as finder was entitled to the notes. "If the notes had been accidentally kicked into the street, and then found by someone passing by, could it be contended that the defendant was entitled to them, from the mere fact of their having been dropped in his shop? … Certainly not. The notes were never in the custody of the defendant, nor within the protection of his house before they were found, as they would have had they been intentionally deposited there, and the defendant has come under no responsibility." First, what do you make of the *Bridges* court's argument that the shopkeeper's entitlement to the notes should turn on whether he would have been held responsible to the true owner for losing them? And second, is this any better a fit for the facts of *McAvoy*?

4. What do you make of the argument that awarding the pocket-book to the shopkeeper is "one better adapted to secure the rights of the true owner?"

5. In addition to lost and mislaid property, there is also abandoned property: property which the owner has voluntarily relinquished with no intent to reclaim. Since abandoned property is again unowned, the usual rules of first possession apply. (As you have seen, these rules themselves are not as simple as "first possessor wins."). How easy is it to tell the three apart? Why?

6. In *Benjamin v. Lindner Aviation*, 534 N.W.2d 400 (Iowa 1995) in which an airplane inspector found $18,000 in cash inside the wing of an airplane in 1992 while the plane was parked in his employer's hangar for maintenance. The money, which consisted primarily of $20 bills dating to the 1950s and 1960s, was in two four-inch packets wrapped in handkerchiefs and tied with string and then wrapped again in aluminum foil. The packets were inserted behind a panel on the underside of the plane's wing; the panel was secured with rusty screws that had not been removed in several years. The inspector,

the employer, and the bank that owned the plane (after repossessing it from a prior owner who had defaulted on a loan) all made claims to the money. Was it lost, mislaid, or abandoned, and who was entitled to it?

7. Another category sometimes mentioned in the found-property caselaw is treasure trove: money, gold, or silver intentionally placed underground, which is found long enough later that it is likely the owner is dead or will never return for it. At common law in England, treasure trove belonged to the King. Most American states now treat treasure trove like any other found property. Is this a sensible rejection of an archaic and pointless quirk of the common-law, or was there something to the doctrine?

8. In *Hannah v. Peel*, [1945] K.B. 509, the British government requisitioned Gwernhaylod House in 1940 for use during World War II and paid the owner, Major Hugh Edward Ethelston Peel £250 per year. The house had been conveyed to Major Peel in 1938 but it was unoccupied from then until when it was requisitioned. Duncan Hannah, a lance-corporal with the Royal Artillery, was stationed in the house and was adjusting a blackout curtain in August 1940 when he found something loose in a crevice on top of the window-frame. It turned out to be a brooch covered in cobwebs and dirt; he informed his commanding officer and then turned it over to the police. Two years later, the police gave it to Major Peel, who sold it for £66. Lance-Corporal Hannah sued and was awarded the value of the brooch. The court discussed numerous cases, including *Bridges v. Hawkesworth* and *South Staffordshire Water Co. v. Sharman*, [1896] 2 Q.B. 44, which awarded two rings found by a workman embedded in the mud at the bottom of a pool to the company that owned the land. From them, it extracted a rule that "a man possesses everything which is attached to or under his land." Since Major Peel "was never physically in possession of these premises" and hence had no "prior possession" of the brooch, Lance-Corporal Hannah was entitled to it as a finder. Is this possession-based approach a better way of analyzing found-property cases than the categorical lost-vs-mislaid American approach exemplified by *McAvoy*? Or is *Hannah* an oddball outlier driven by the court's desire to do right by a wartime serviceman "whose conduct was commendable and meritorious," especially as against an absentee landlord from the local gentry? Note that English cases have not accepted the lost-vs.-mislaid distinction.

O'Keeffe v. Snyder

416 A.2d 862 (N.J. 1980)

The opinion of the Court was delivered by POLLOCK, J.

This is an appeal from an order of the Appellate Division granting summary judgment to plaintiff, Georgia O'Keeffe, against defendant, Barry Snyder, d/b/a Princeton Gallery of Fine Art, for replevin of three small pictures painted by O'Keeffe. In her complaint, filed in March,

1976, O'Keeffe alleged she was the owner of the paintings and that they were stolen from a New York art gallery in 1946. Snyder asserted he was a purchaser for value of the paintings, he had title by adverse possession, and O'Keeffe's action was barred by the expiration of the six-year period of limitations provided by N.J.S.A. 2A:14-1 pertaining to an action in replevin. Snyder impleaded third party defendant, Ulrich A. Frank, from whom Snyder purchased the paintings in 1975 for $35,000.

The trial court granted summary judgment for Snyder on the ground that O'Keeffe's action was barred because it was not commenced within six years of the alleged theft. The Appellate Division reversed and entered judgment for O'Keeffe. A majority of that court concluded that the paintings were stolen, the defenses of expiration of the statute of limitations and title by adverse possession were identical, and Snyder had not proved the elements of adverse possession. Consequently, the majority ruled that O'Keeffe could still enforce her right to possession of the paintings.

The dissenting judge stated that the appropriate measurement of the period of limitation was not by analogy to adverse possession, but by application of the "discovery rule" pertaining to some statutes of limitation. He concluded that the six-year period of limitations commenced when O'Keeffe knew or should have known who unlawfully possessed the paintings, and that the matter should be remanded to determine if and when that event had occurred.

We granted certification …

I

The record, limited to pleadings, affidavits, answers to interrogatories, and depositions, is fraught with factual conflict. Apart from the creation of the paintings by O'Keeffe and their discovery in Snyder's gallery in 1976, the parties agree on little else.

O'Keeffe contended the paintings were stolen in 1946 from a gallery, An American Place. The gallery was operated by her late husband, the famous photographer Alfred Stieglitz.

An American Place was a cooperative undertaking of O'Keeffe and some other American artists… . In 1946, Stieglitz arranged an exhibit which included an O'Keeffe painting, identified as Cliffs. According to O'Keeffe, one day in March, 1946, she and Stieglitz discovered Cliffs was missing from the wall of the exhibit. O'Keeffe estimates the value of the painting at the time of the alleged theft to have been about $150.

About two weeks later, O'Keeffe noticed that two other paintings, Seaweed and Fragments, were missing from a storage room at An American Place. She did not tell anyone, even Stieglitz, about the missing paintings, since she did not want to upset him.

Before the date when O'Keeffe discovered the disappearance of Seaweed, she had already sold it (apparently for a string of amber beads) to a Mrs. Weiner, now deceased. Following the grant of the motion for summary judgment by the trial court in favor of Snyder, O'Keeffe submitted a release from the legatees of Mrs. Weiner purportedly assigning to O'Keeffe their interest in the sale.

O'Keeffe testified on depositions that at about the same time as the disappearance of her paintings, 12 or 13 miniature paintings by Marin also were stolen from An American Place. According to O'Keeffe, a man named Estrick took the Marin paintings and "maybe a few other things." Estrick distributed the Marin paintings to members of the theater world who, when confronted by Stieglitz, returned them. However, neither Stieglitz nor O'Keeffe confronted Estrick with the loss of any of the O'Keeffe paintings.

There was no evidence of a break and entry at An American Place on the dates when O'Keeffe discovered the disappearance of her paintings. Neither Stieglitz nor O'Keeffe reported them missing to the New York Police Department or any other law enforcement agency. Apparently the paintings were uninsured, and O'Keeffe did not seek reimbursement from an insurance company. Similarly, neither O'Keeffe nor Stieglitz advertised the loss of the paintings in Art News or any other publication. Nonetheless, they discussed it with associates in the art world and later O'Keeffe mentioned the loss to the director of the Art Institute of Chicago, but she did not ask him to do anything because "it wouldn't have been my way." O'Keeffe does not contend that Frank or Snyder had actual knowledge of the alleged theft.

Stieglitz died in the summer of 1946, and O'Keeffe explains she did not pursue her efforts to locate the paintings because she was settling his estate. In 1947, she retained the services of Doris Bry to help settle the estate. Bry urged O'Keeffe to report the loss of the paintings, but O'Keeffe declined because "they never got anything back by reporting it." Finally, in 1972, O'Keeffe authorized Bry to report the theft to the Art Dealers Association of America, Inc., which maintains for its members a registry of stolen paintings. The record does not indicate whether such a registry existed at the time the paintings disappeared.

In September, 1975, O'Keeffe learned that the paintings were in the Andrew Crispo Gallery in New York on consignment from Bernard Danenberg Galleries. On February 11, 1976, O'Keeffe discovered that Ulrich A. Frank had sold the paintings to Barry Snyder, d/b/a Princeton Gallery of Fine Art. She demanded their return and, following Snyder's refusal, instituted this action for replevin.

Frank traces his possession of the paintings to his father, Dr. Frank, who died in 1968. He claims there is a family relationship by marriage between his family and the Stieglitz family, a contention that O'Keeffe disputes. Frank does not know how his father acquired the paintings, but he recalls seeing them in his father's apartment in New Hampshire as early as 1941-1943, a period that precedes the alleged theft. Consequently, Frank's factual contentions are inconsistent with O'Keeffe's allegation of theft. Until 1965, Dr. Frank occasionally lent the paintings to Ulrich Frank. In 1965, Dr. and Mrs. Frank formally gave the paintings to Ulrich Frank, who kept them in his residences in Yardley, Pennsylvania and Princeton, New Jersey. In 1968, he exhibited anonymously Cliffs and Fragments in a one day art show in the Jewish Community Center in Trenton. All of these events precede O'Keeffe's listing of the paintings as stolen with the Art Dealers Association of America, Inc. in 1972.

Frank claims continuous possession of the paintings through his father for over thirty years and admits selling the paintings to Snyder. Snyder and Frank do not trace their provenance, or history of possession of the paintings, back to O'Keeffe.

As indicated, Snyder moved for summary judgment on the theory that O'Keeffe's action was barred by the statute of limitations and title had vested in Frank by adverse possession. For purposes of his motion, Snyder conceded that the paintings had been stolen. On her cross motion, O'Keeffe urged that the paintings were stolen, the statute of limitations had not run, and title to the paintings remained in her.

II

[The court held that there was a genuine factual dispute whether the paintings had been stolen.]

III

On the limited record before us, we cannot determine now who has title to the paintings. That determination will depend on the evidence adduced at trial. Nonetheless, we believe it may aid the trial court and the parties to resolve questions of law that may become relevant at trial.

Our decision begins with the principle that, generally speaking, if the paintings were stolen, the thief acquired no title and could not transfer good title to others regardless of their good faith and ignorance of the theft. Proof of theft would advance O'Keeffe's right to possession of the paintings absent other considerations such as expiration of the statute of limitations.

On this appeal, the critical legal question is when O'Keeffe's cause of action accrued. The fulcrum on which the outcome turns is the statute of limitations in N.J.S.A. 2A:14-1, which provides that an action for replevin of goods or chattels must be commenced within six years after the accrual of the cause of action. …

Since the alleged theft occurred in New York, a preliminary question is whether the statute of limitations of New York or New Jersey applies. The New York statute, N.Y. Civ. Prac. Law §

214 (McKinney), has been interpreted so that the statute of limitations on a cause of action for replevin does not begin to run until after refusal upon demand for the return of the goods. Here, O'Keeffe demanded return of the paintings in February, 1976. If the New York statute applied, her action would have been commenced within the period of limitations.

The traditional rule to determine which of two statutes of limitations is applicable is that the statute of the forum governs unless the limitation is a condition of the cause of action. However, this Court has discarded the mechanical rule that the statute of limitations of the forum must be employed in every suit on a foreign cause of action. *Heavner v. Uniroyal, Inc.*, 63 N.J. 130, 140-141 (1973). Heavner set out five requirements for barring an action by applying a statute of limitations other than the appropriate New Jersey statute: (1) the cause of action arose in the other state; (2) the parties are all present in and amenable to jurisdiction in the other state; (3) New Jersey has no substantial interest in the matter; (4) the substantive law of the other jurisdiction is applicable, and (5) the limitations' period of the other jurisdiction has expired at the time of the commencement of the suit in New Jersey. The Heavner rule provides a limited and special exception to the general rule that the rule of the forum determines the applicable period of limitations. In the present case, none of the parties resides in New York and the paintings are located in New Jersey. On the facts before us, it would appear that the appropriate statute of limitations is the law of the forum, N.J.S.A. 2A:14-1. On remand, the trial court may reconsider this issue if the parties present other relevant facts.

IV

On the assumption that New Jersey law will apply, we shall consider significant questions raised about the interpretation of N.J.S.A. 2A:14-1. The purpose of a statute of limitations is to stimulate to activity and punish negligence and promote repose by giving security and stability to human affairs. A statute of limitations achieves those purposes by barring a cause of action after the statutory period. In certain instances, this Court has ruled that the literal language of a statute of limitations should yield to other considerations.

To avoid harsh results from the mechanical application of the statute, the courts have developed a concept known as the discovery rule. The discovery rule provides that, in an appropriate case, a cause of action will not accrue until the injured party discovers, or by exercise of reasonable diligence and intelligence should have discovered, facts which form the basis of a cause of action. The rule is essentially a principle of equity, the purpose of which is to mitigate unjust results that otherwise might flow from strict adherence to a rule of law.

This Court first announced the discovery rule in *Fernandi*, supra, 35 N.J. at 434. In *Fernandi*, a wing nut was left in a patient's abdomen following surgery and was not discovered for three years. The majority held that fairness and justice mandated that the statute of limitations should not have commenced running until the plaintiff knew or had reason to know of the presence of the foreign object in her body. …

Similarly, we conclude that the discovery rule applies to an action for replevin of a painting under N.J.S.A. 2A:14-1. O'Keeffe's cause of action accrued when she first knew, or reasonably should have known through the exercise of due diligence, of the cause of action, including the identity of the possessor of the paintings. …

In determining whether O'Keeffe is entitled to the benefit of the discovery rule, the trial court should consider, among others, the following issues: (1) whether O'Keeffe used due diligence to recover the paintings at the time of the alleged theft and thereafter; (2) whether at the time of the alleged theft there was an effective method, other than talking to her colleagues, for O'Keeffe to alert the art world; and (3) whether registering paintings with the Art Dealers Association of America, Inc. or any other organization would put a reasonably prudent purchaser of art on constructive notice that someone other than the possessor was the true owner.

V

The acquisition of title to real and personal property by adverse possession is based on the expiration of a statute of limitations. R. Brown, The Law of Personal Property (3d ed. 1975), § 4.1 at 33 (Brown). Adverse possession does not create title by prescription apart from the statute of limitations.

To establish title by adverse possession to chattels, the rule of law has been that the possession must be hostile, actual, visible, exclusive, and continuous. …

[T]here is an inherent problem with many kinds of personal property that will raise questions whether their possession has been open, visible, and notorious. … For example, if jewelry is stolen from a municipality in one county in New Jersey, it is unlikely that the owner would learn that someone is openly wearing that jewelry in another county or even in the same municipality. Open and visible possession of personal property, such as jewelry, may not be sufficient to put the original owner on actual or constructive notice of the identity of the possessor.

The problem is even more acute with works of art. Like many kinds of personal property, works of art are readily moved and easily concealed. O'Keeffe argues that nothing short of public display should be sufficient to alert the true owner and start the statute running. Although there is merit in that contention from the perspective of the original owner, the effect is to impose a heavy burden on the purchasers of paintings who wish to enjoy the paintings in the privacy of their homes. …

The problem is serious. According to an affidavit submitted in this matter by the president of the International Foundation for Art Research, there has been an "explosion in art thefts" and there is a "worldwide phenomenon of art theft which has reached epidemic proportions".

The limited record before us provides a brief glimpse into the arcane world of sales of art, where paintings worth vast sums of money sometimes are bought without inquiry about their provenance. There does not appear to be a reasonably available method for an owner of art to record the ownership or theft of paintings. Similarly, there are no reasonable means readily available to a purchaser to ascertain the provenance of a painting. It may be time for the art world to establish a means by which a good faith purchaser may reasonably obtain the provenance of a painting. An efficient registry of original works of art might better serve the interests of artists, owners of art, and bona fide purchasers than the law of adverse possession with all of its uncertainties. Although we cannot mandate the initiation of a registration system, we can develop a rule for the commencement and running of the statute of limitations that is more responsive to the needs of the art world than the doctrine of adverse possession.

We are persuaded that the introduction of equitable considerations through the discovery rule provides a more satisfactory response than the doctrine of adverse possession. The discovery rule shifts the emphasis from the conduct of the possessor to the conduct of the owner. The focus of the inquiry will no longer be whether the possessor has met the tests of adverse possession, but whether the owner has acted with due diligence in pursuing his or her personal property.

For example, under the discovery rule, if an artist diligently seeks the recovery of a lost or stolen painting, but cannot find it or discover the identity of the possessor, the statute of limitations will not begin to run. The rule permits an artist who uses reasonable efforts to report, investigate, and recover a painting to preserve the rights of title and possession.

Properly interpreted, the discovery rule becomes a vehicle for transporting equitable considerations into the statute of limitations for replevin. In determining whether the discovery rule should apply, a court should identify, evaluate, and weigh the equitable claims of all parties. If a chattel is concealed from the true owner, fairness compels tolling the statute during the period of concealment. That conclusion is consistent with tolling the statute of limitations in a medical malpractice action where the physician is guilty of fraudulent concealment.

It is consistent also with the law of replevin as it has developed apart from the discovery rule. In an action for replevin, the period of limitations ordinarily will run against the owner of lost or stolen property from the time of the wrongful taking, absent fraud or concealment. Where the chattel is fraudulently concealed, the general rule is that the statute is tolled …

The discovery rule will fulfill the purposes of a statute of limitations and accord greater protection to the innocent owner of personal property whose goods are lost or stolen. …

By diligently pursuing their goods, owners may prevent the statute of limitations from running. The meaning of due diligence will vary with the facts of each case, including the nature and value of the personal property. For example, with respect to jewelry of moderate value, it may be sufficient if the owner reports the theft to the police. With respect to art work of greater value, it may be reasonable to expect an owner to do more. In practice, our ruling should contribute to more careful practices concerning the purchase of art.

The considerations are different with real estate, and there is no reason to disturb the application of the doctrine of adverse possession to real estate. Real estate is fixed and cannot be moved or concealed. The owner of real property knows or should know where his property is located and reasonably can be expected to be aware of open, notorious, visible, hostile, continuous acts of possession on it.

Our ruling not only changes the requirements for acquiring title to personal property after an alleged unlawful taking, but also shifts the burden of proof at trial. Under the doctrine of adverse possession, the burden is on the possessor to prove the elements of adverse possession. Under the discovery rule, the burden is on the owner as the one seeking the benefit of the rule to establish facts that would justify deferring the beginning of the period of limitations.

VI

Read literally, the effect of the expiration of the statute of limitations under N.J.S.A. 2A:14-1 is to bar an action such as replevin. The statute does not speak of divesting the original owner of title. By its terms the statute cuts off the remedy, but not the right of title. Nonetheless, the effect of the expiration of the statute of limitations, albeit on the theory of adverse possession, has been not only to bar an action for possession, but also to vest title in the possessor. There is no reason to change that result although the discovery rule has replaced adverse possession. History, reason, and common sense support the conclusion that the expiration of the statute of limitations bars the remedy to recover possession and also vests title in the possessor. …

Before the expiration of the statute, the possessor has both the chattel and the right to keep it except as against the true owner. The only imperfection in the possessor's right to retain the chattel is the original owner's right to repossess it. Once that imperfection is removed, the possessor should have good title for all purposes. Ames, *The Disseisin of Chattels*, 3 HARV. L. REV. 313, 321 (1890) (Ames). As Dean Ames wrote: "An immortal right to bring an eternally prohibited action is a metaphysical subtlety that the present writer cannot pretend to understand." *Id.* at 319.

Recognizing a metaphysical notion of title in the owner would be of little benefit to him or her and would create potential problems for the possessor and third parties. The expiration of the six-year period of N.J.S.A. 2A:14-1 should vest title as effectively under the discovery rule as under the doctrine of adverse possession. …

VII

We next consider the effect of transfers of a chattel from one possessor to another during the period of limitation under the discovery rule. Under the discovery rule, the statute of limitations on an action for replevin begins to run when the owner knows or reasonably should know of his cause of action and the identity of the possessor of the chattel. Subsequent transfers of the chattel are part of the continuous dispossession of the chattel from the original owner. The important point is not that there has been a substitution of possessors, but that there has been a continuous dispossession of the former owner.
Professor Ballantine explains:

> Where the same claim of title has been consistently asserted for the statutory period by persons in privity with each other, there is the same reason to quiet and establish the title as where one person has held. The same flag has been kept flying for the whole period. It is the same ouster and disseisin. If the statute runs, it quiets a title which has been consistently asserted and exercised as against the true owner, and the possession of the prior holder justly enures to the benefit of the last. [H. Ballantine, *Title by Adverse Possession*, 32 HARV. L. REV. 135, 158 (1919)] …

For the purpose of evaluating the due diligence of an owner, the dispossession of his chattel is a continuum not susceptible to separation into distinct acts. Nonetheless, subsequent transfers of the chattel may affect the degree of difficulty encountered by a diligent owner seeking to recover his goods. To that extent, subsequent transfers and their potential for frustrating diligence are relevant in applying the discovery rule. An owner who diligently seeks his chattel should be entitled to the benefit of the discovery rule although it may have passed through many hands. Conversely an owner who sleeps on his rights may be denied the benefit of the discovery rule although the chattel may have been possessed by only one person.

We reject the alternative of treating subsequent transfers of a chattel as separate acts of conversion that would start the statute of limitations running anew. …

Treating subsequent transfers as separate acts of conversion could lead to absurd results. As explained by Dean Ames: –

> … If a converter were to sell the chattel, five years after its conversion, to one ignorant of the seller's tort, the disposed owner's right to recover the chattel from the purchaser

> would continue five years longer than his right to recover from the converter would have lasted if there had been no sale. In other words, an innocent purchaser from a wrong-doer would be in a worse position than the wrong-doer himself, – a conclusion as shocking in point of justice as it would be anomalous in law. [Ames, *supra* at 323, footnotes omitted]

It is more sensible to recognize that on expiration of the period of limitations, title passes from the former owner by operation of the statute. Needless uncertainty would result from starting the statute running anew merely because of a subsequent transfer. …

We reverse the judgment of the Appellate Division in favor of O'Keeffe and remand the matter for trial in accordance with this opinion.

Questions

1. What did O'Keeffe do to locate the paintings? At least according to the court, what more could she have done? What more should she have done? What did the Franks and Snyder do to make their possession of the paintings clear? What more could they have done? What more should they have done? Did the court properly balance the parties' interests? Did it give the right incentives to future parties in their positions?

2. The court argues that switching from adverse possession to the discovery rule "shifts the emphasis from the conduct of the possessor to the conduct of the owner." Is this a good description of the difference between the two tests? Is the court's explanation of its reasons for the change persuasive?

3. Notice *O'Keeffe*'s discussion of the choice-of-law problem. O'Keeffe's suit was timely under the New York statute of limitations but may not have been under New Jersey's. In theory, choice of law is simple for property: the law of the property's "situs" (i.e. location) controls.[28] The rule is easy enough to apply to real property, although even there hard cases are possible.[29] But personal property can move around, generating

[28] Relatedly, courts have *in rem* jurisdiction over property located within their state's borders, and the traditional rule has been that courts have no jurisdiction at all over real property outside their state's borders. Why might these rules have developed? Do they seem likely to simplify litigation or complicate it?

[29] *See, e.g.*, *Durfee v. Duke*, 375 U.S. 106 (1963), in which the Missouri River, which forms the boundary between Nebraska and Missouri, had shifted its channel from the east of the land in question to the west of it. If the river had shifted suddenly (by "avulsion"), the boundary stayed where it was and the land was legally in Nebraska. But if the river had shifted course

contacts with multiple states. Suppose the contacts had been flipped, so that the painting was stolen in New Jersey but was currently in New York. Should New York law have applied? Another possible rule is that the law of the place where the property is now applies. What incentives would that rule create? How about a rule selecting the law of the place where the property was at the time of the relevant events? (Wait. What *are* the "relevant events" in a replevin case involving the statute of limitations?) Another layer of difficulty in choice of law comes from the characterization problem: is the validity of a mortgage securing a loan with an illegally high rate of interest a "property" issue (governed by the situs rule) or a "contract" issue (governed by the place the contract was made or the place of residence of the parties)? The characterization question puts *O'Keeffe*'s use of medical-malpractice tort principles in a replevin case in a new light, doesn't it?

The New York Mess

As noted in *O'Keeffe*, New York has a three-year statute of limitations for personal-property actions, and traditionally applied a demand-and-refusal rule to start the statute running. Two further doctrines complicate the picture. One is that the demand-and-refusal rule only applies against good-faith purchasers; the limitations period in a suit against a thief starts at the time of the theft. (Do you see how this result, illogical as it may sound, follows from the logic that the the good-faith purchaser is not considered a wrongdoer until she refuses a demand for return of the property?) The other is that an owner who unreasonably delays making a demand for the return of property, at least where she knows the identity of the possessor, may find her suit barred by the equitable doctrine of laches.

In *DeWeerth v. Baldinger*, 836 F.2d 103 (2d Cir. 1987), a landscape by Claude Monet owned by Gerda DeWeerth disappeared from a castle in Southern Germany where American soldiers were quartered during World War II. It turned up on the art market in the mid-1950s and was eventually sold by a New York gallery to Edith Baldinger, who kept it in her apartment in New York. In 1981, DeWeerth's nephew tracked the painting to the gallery's sale to Baldinger and made a demand for its return which was refused. The Second Circuit, sitting in diversity, held

---

slowly (by "accretion"), the boundary moved with the river and the land was in Missouri. Since the plaintiff claimed title under a Nebraska foreclosure proceeding and the defendant claimed title under a Missouri swamp land patent, the case turned on which state the land was in.

that New York "would impose a duty of reasonable diligence in attempting to locate stolen property," not just a duty to demand its return in a reasonable time after the property is located:

> For if demand is delayed, then so is accrual of the cause of action, and the good-faith purchaser will remain exposed to suit long after an action against a thief or even other innocent parties would be time-barred. … In this case, plaintiff's proposed exception to the rule would rob it of all of its salutary effect: The thief would be immune from suit after three years, while the good-faith purchaser would remain exposed as long as his identity did not fortuitously come to the property owner's attention. A construction of the rule requiring due diligence in making a demand to include an obligation to make a reasonable effort to locate the property will prevent unnecessary hardship to the good-faith purchaser, the party intended to be protected. … A rule requiring reasonable diligence in attempting to locate stolen property is especially appropriate with respect to stolen art. Much art is kept in private collections, unadvertised and unavailable to the public. An owner seeking to recover such property will almost never learn of its whereabouts by chance. Yet the location of stolen art may frequently be discovered through investigation.

The court concluded that DeWeerth's efforts were "minimal" before her nephew took up the case in 1981, so Baldinger kept the Monet.

That was 1987. Shortly thereafter, the same issue came up through the New York state court system. In *Guggenheim Foundation v. Lubell*, 569 N.E.2d 426 (N.Y. 1991), a painting by Marc Chagall was stolen from the Guggenheim Museum by a mailroom employee in the 1960s. The Lubells bought the painting from a reputable dealer in 1967; the museum demanded it back in 1986. The court rejected *O'Keeffe*, repudiated *DeWeerth*'s interpretation of New York law, and reaffirmed the New York demand-and-refusal rule. It specifically rejected the discovery rule with its requirement of reasonable diligence by the owner:

> Our case law already recognizes that the true owner, having discovered the location of its lost property, cannot unreasonably delay making demand upon the person in possession of that property. … Further, the facts of this case reveal how difficult it would be to specify the type of conduct that would be required for a showing of reasonable diligence. Here, the parties hotly contest whether publicizing the theft would have turned up the gouache. According to the museum, some members of the art community believe that publicizing a theft exposes gaps in security and can lead to more thefts; the museum also argues that publicity often pushes a missing painting further underground. In light of the fact that members of the art community have apparently not reached a consensus on the best way to retrieve stolen art, it would be particularly inappropriate for this Court to spell out arbitrary rules of conduct that all true owners of stolen art work would have

> to follow to the letter if they wanted to preserve their right to pursue a cause of action in replevin. All owners of stolen property should not be expected to behave in the same way and should not be held to a common standard. The value of the property stolen, the manner in which it was stolen, and the type of institution from which it was stolen will all necessarily affect the manner in which a true owner will search for missing property. We conclude that it would be difficult, if not impossible, to craft a reasonable diligence requirement that could take into account all of these variables and that would not unduly burden the true owner.
>
> Further, our decision today is in part influenced by our recognition that New York enjoys a worldwide reputation as a preeminent cultural center. To place the burden of locating stolen artwork on the true owner and to foreclose the rights of that owner to recover its property if the burden is not met would, we believe, encourage illicit trafficking in stolen art. Three years after the theft, any purchaser, good faith or not, would be able to hold onto stolen art work unless the true owner was able to establish that it had undertaken a reasonable search for the missing art. This shifting of the burden onto the wronged owner is inappropriate. In our opinion, the better rule gives the owner relatively greater protection and places the burden of investigating the provenance of a work of art on the potential purchaser.

Armed with the New York Court of Appeals's holding in *Guggenheim*, Gerda DeWeerth filed a Rule 60(b) motion for relief from judgment, arguing that the decision against her rested on a misinterpretation of New York law and that she should not have been subjected to a diligent-search requirement. The District Court agreed with her, but the Second Circuit reversed in *DeWeerth v. Baldinger,* 38 F.3d 1266 (2d Cir. 1994), emphasizing the need for finality in litigation:

> We conclude that the prior *DeWeerth* panel conscientiously satisfied its duty to predict how New York courts would decide the due diligence question, and that *Erie* and its progeny require no more than this. The fact that the New York Court of Appeals subsequently reached a contrary conclusion in *Guggenheim* does not constitute an "extraordinary circumstance" that would justify reopening this case in order to achieve a similar result.

Finally, consider *SongByrd Inc. v. Estate of Grossman*, 206 F.3d 172 (2d Cir. 2000), another diversity case under New York law. Henry Byrd, who recorded under the name "Professor Longhair," was a celebrated jazz musician. He went to Woodstock, New York for a studio recording session for Bearsville Records in the 1970s. The session was considered unsatisfactory at the time, so the tapes were never released. Instead, Arthur Davis, the record-store owner who discovered Byrd, sent the tapes to Bearsville "as demonstration tapes only, without any intent for either Albert Grossman or Bearsville Records Inc. to possess these aforementioned tapes as owner."

Byrd's attorney wrote two letters to Bearsville requesting the return of the tapes in 1975, but there was no evidence in the record that the letters were even received. Byrd died in 1980, and after Bearsville's founder died in 1985, his estate licensed the recordings to two record companies. One of the resulting albums won Byrd a (posthumous) Grammy for Best Traditional Blues Album of 1987. SongByrd, the successor-in-interest to Byrd's rights, sued in 1995. The Second Circuit held that the conversion claim was barred, because the defendant "began using the master tapes as its own when it licensed portions of them to Rounder in 1986."

> The conversion alleged by SongByrd occurred no later than that date. The demand-and-refusal rule, which functioned to delay accrual of the claim in [*Guggenheim*] … for the benefit of the true owner, normally provides some benefit to the good-faith possessor by precipitating its awareness that continued possession will be regarded as wrongful by the true owner. New York has not required a demand and refusal for the accrual of a conversion claim against a possessor who openly deals with the property as its own.

As an alternative basis for its holding, the court added that the plaintiff had unreasonably delayed making its demand.

> Even if a demand were required for accrual of SongByrd's claim, [*Guggenheim*] instructs that a plaintiff may not unreasonably delay in making a demand for property whose location is known. Byrd, either independently or through his agents, had known since the 1970s that the master tapes were in Grossman's possession, and the unanswered letters to Grossman in 1975 for return of the master tapes probably sufficed to alert him to Grossman's disregard of his ownership claim, thereby rendering any demand thereafter unreasonably delayed. In any event, his successors' delay in not making a demand in 1987, when Bearsville's licensing of the master tapes became well known in the music world as a result of the Grammy Award for Byrd's recordings, was clearly unreasonable.

After *DeWeerth*, *Guggenheim*, and *SongByrd*, does New York have a coherent approach to the statute of limitations in personal property cases? Does it depend whether the case is brought in state or federal court? Has New York done better or worse than New Jersey at balancing the competing interests at stake?

5. Adverse Possession

Few doctrines taught in the first year of law school make a worse first impression than adverse possession. Adverse possession enables a non-owner to gain title to land (or personal property, but we will focus here on land) after the expiration of the statute of limitations for the owner to recover possession. That sounds bad, and the thought of "squatters" becoming owners gets its share of bad press. But historically the doctrine has performed, and continues to serve, important functions.

The basic requirements, if not their wording and application, are common from state to state. As one treatise summarizes, an adverse possessor must prove possession that is:

> (1) hostile (perhaps under a claim of right);
>
> (2) exclusive;
>
> (3) open and notorious;
>
> (4) actual; and
>
> (5) continuous for the requisite statutory period.

16 POWELL ON REAL PROPERTY § 91.01. States routinely add to the list. California law, for example, requires that

> the claimant must prove: (1) possession under claim of right or color of title; (2) actual, open, and notorious occupation of the premises constituting reasonable notice to the true owner; (3) possession which is adverse and hostile to the true owner; (4) continuous possession for at least five years; and (5) payment of all taxes assessed against the property during the five-year period.

Main St. Plaza v. Cartwright & Main, LLC, 124 Cal. Rptr. 3d 170, 178 (Cal. App. 2011) (citations and quotations omitted).

A. Adverse Possession Rationales

But why allow adverse possession? One court summarized the doctrine's history and purposes as follows:

> … a brief history of adverse possession may be of assistance. After first using an amalgamation of Roman and Germanic doctrine, our English predecessors in common law later settled upon statutes of limitation to effect adverse possession. See Axel Teisen,

Contributions of the Comparative Law Bureau, 3 A.B.A. J. 97, 126, 127, 134 (1917). In practice, the statutes eliminated a rightful owner's ability to regain possession after the passing of a certain number of years, thereby vesting de facto title in the adverse possessor. For example, a 1623 statute of King James I restricted the right of entry to recover possession of land to a period of twenty years. Essentially, in England, the "[o]riginal policy supporting the development of adverse possession reflected society's unwillingness to take away a 'right' which an adverse possessor thought he had. Similarly, society felt the loss of an unknown right by the title owner was minimal." William G. Ackerman & Shane T. Johnson, Comment, *Outlaws of the Past: A Western Perspective on Prescription and Adverse Possession*, 31 Land & Water L. Rev. 79, 83 (1996)....

In the United States, although the 1623 statute of King James I "came some years after the settling of Jamestown (the usual date fixed as the crystalizing of the common law in America), its fiat is generally accepted as [our] common law. Hence 'adverse possession' for 20 years under the common law in this country passes title to the adverse possessor with certain stated qualifications." 10 *Thompson on Real Property* § 87.01 at 75. Today, all fifty states have some statutory form of adverse possession ....

....Courts and commentators generally ascribe to "four traditional justifications or clusters of justifications which support transferring the entitlement to the [adverse possessor] after the statute of limitations runs: the problem of lost evidence, the desirability of quieting titles, the interest in discouraging sleeping owners, and the reliance interests of [adverse possessors] and interested third persons." Thomas W. Merrill, *Property Rules, Liability Rules, and Adverse Possession*, 79 Nw. U. L. Rev. 1122, 1133 (1984). Effectively, our society has made a policy determination that "all things should be used according to their nature and purpose" and when an individual uses and preserves property "for a certain length of time, [he] has done a work beneficial to the community." Teisen, 3 A.B.A. J. at 127. For his efforts, "his reward is the conferring upon him of the title to the thing used." Id. Esteemed jurist Oliver Wendell Holmes, Jr. went a step further than Teisen, basing our society's tolerance of adverse possession on the ideal that "[a] thing which you have enjoyed and used as your own for a long time, whether property or an opinion, takes root in your being and cannot be torn away without your resenting the act and trying to defend yourself, however you came by it." O Centro Espirita Beneficente Uniao Do Vegetal v. Ashcroft, 389 F.3d 973, 1016 (10th Cir. 2004) (quoting Oliver Wendell Holmes, Jr., *The Path of the Law*, 10 Harv. L. Rev. 457, 477 (1897)).

Regardless of how deeply the doctrine is engrained in our history, however, courts have questioned "whether the concept of adverse possession is as viable as it once was, or whether the concept always squares with modern ideals in a sophisticated, congested,

> peaceful society." *Finley*, 160 Cal. Rptr. at 427. Commentators have also opined that, along with the articulated benefits of adverse possession, numerous disadvantages exist including the "infringement of a landowner's rights, a decrease in value of the servient estate, and the encouraged [over]exploitation and [over]development of land. In addition, they … [include] the generation of animosity between neighbors, a source of damages to land or loss of land ownership, and the creation of uncertainty for the landowner."* Ackerman, 31 Land & Water L. Rev. at 92. In reality, "[a]dverse possession '[i]s nothing more than a person taking someone else's private property for his own private use.' It is hard to imagine a notion more in contravention of the ideals set forth in the U.S. Constitution protecting life, liberty and property." Ackerman, 31 Land & Water L. Rev. at 94-95 (quoting 2 C.J.S. Adverse Possession § 2 (1972)).
>
> Although this Court duly recognizes its role as the judicial arm of government tasked with applying the law, rather than making law, it is not without an eyebrow raised at the ancient roots and arcane rationale of adverse possession that we apply the doctrine to this modern property dispute.

Cahill v. Morrow, 11 A.3d 82, 86-88 (R.I. 2011). Do you share the court's skepticism? Consider the rationales discussed above against the following case.

Tieu v. Morgan

265 P.3d 98 (Ore. App. 2011)

HADLOCK, J.

The parties dispute ownership of a strip of land that runs parallel to defendants' driveway. Plaintiff, who owns residential property adjoining that strip of land, filed suit seeking (1) a declaration that he owns the disputed strip and (2) an injunction prohibiting defendants from trespassing on that property. Defendants counterclaimed, asserting that they acquired the disputed strip through adverse possession, and subsequently moved for summary judgment on that counterclaim. The trial court granted defendants' motion and entered a judgment declaring that defendants had acquired the strip through adverse possession. Plaintiff appeals, and we affirm….

* [*Eds.*—The modifications to the quotation from Ackerman are ours, not the court's.]

Property

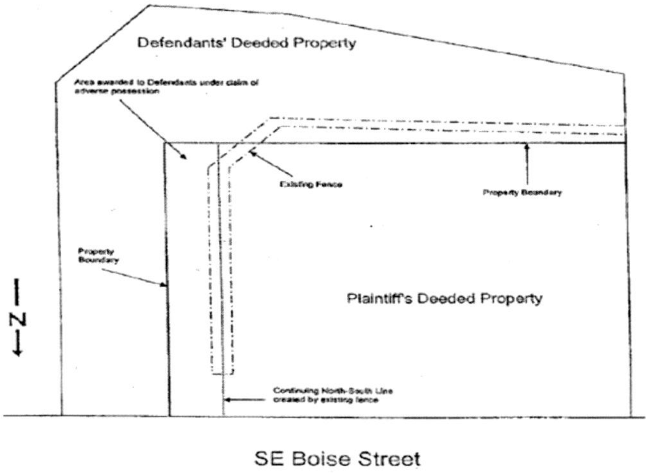

(DRAWING NOT TO SCALE)

The two parcels subject to this appeal are adjoining residential tax lots in a Portland subdivision. Tax lot 3100 is rectangular, with its north side fronting Southeast Boise Street. Tax lot 3200 is a flag lot that is situated largely south of lot 3100; its driveway (the "flagpole") runs north from the main portion of the lot (the "flag") to Southeast Boise Street, parallel to the eastern edge of lot 3100. The disputed three-foot-wide strip lies between lot 3200's driveway and lot 3100. Defendants own lot 3200. Plaintiff owns lot 3100 and also is the record owner of the disputed strip.

A north-south stretch of fence on plaintiff's property runs along the western boundary of the disputed strip, parallel to defendants' driveway. The fence starts roughly halfway down the driveway from Southeast Boise Street, running south, then turns 45 degrees to the southwest, cutting off the southeast corner of lot 3100, then makes another 45-degree turn before continuing west, roughly following the east-west boundary between lots 3100 and 3200. The diagonal portion of the fence that cuts the corner of lot 3100 includes a gate wide enough to accommodate a boat trailer. As noted, the disputed three-foot-wide strip lies between defendants' driveway and the north-south fence on lot 3100; its practical effect is to widen the "flagpole" portion of lot 3200.

The fencing that separates the two properties has existed for decades. As of 1984, the two lots were owned by Robert Stevens, who installed most of the fencing that year, including about half of the north-south stretch located west of lot 3200's driveway. In 1994, Robert Stevens sold lot 3200 to his son, James Stevens, believing that the deed he conveyed to James included all property on the east side of a north-south line defined by that portion of the fence, *i.e.*, the disputed strip. Although he never specifically discussed the issue with his father, James also believed that his purchase of the flag lot included the disputed strip along his driveway. James explained that he had "no reason to know—to think [that the fence] would be in the wrong location."

During the four years that James owned the flag lot, he granted Robert permission to occasionally use James's driveway and the disputed strip, so that Robert could drive a large vehicle and boat trailer through the diagonal gate into Robert's back yard. In 1996, James installed a sewer line in the center of the disputed strip, running all the way from Southeast Boise Street to the house on lot 3200. When James later put lot 3200 on the market, he advertised it as having a "fully fenced yard," based on his belief that his ownership included the disputed strip.

James sold lot 3200 to defendants in 1998. The lot was not surveyed in conjunction with that sale; nor did the parties to the sale discuss the lot's recorded boundaries, review paperwork or maps, or perform any investigation specifically related to that subject.

Defendants have made use of the disputed strip since they purchased lot 3200. Defendant Francine Morgan runs a daycare business from her home, and parents regularly use the disputed strip when dropping off and picking up their children. In 1999, defendants extended the fence paralleling the strip north by roughly 40 feet, choosing not to extend the fence all the way to Southeast Boise Street after Robert suggested that they leave that area unfenced to accommodate maneuvering large vehicles in and out of their driveways. Defendants have laid gravel and bark dust on the disputed strip a number of times and have maintained the fence by replacing posts and fence boards. While Robert still owned lot 3100, he specifically asked defendants' permission each time he wanted to use the disputed strip to access or move his boat, and defendants granted that permission.

Plaintiff bought lot 3100 from Robert in early 2006. Before purchasing the property, plaintiff had it surveyed and learned that the north-south fence was not located on the deeded boundary between lots 3100 and 3200. A survey pin marking the recorded boundary was placed at that time. Plaintiff claims that he told defendant Francine Morgan soon after the survey was completed that he planned to move the fence to the deeded property line within two years. According to plaintiff, Francine neither disputed plaintiff's right to move the fence nor claimed ownership of land between the survey marker and the fence. Defendants deny that such a conversation occurred.

In 2008, plaintiff attempted to remove the north-south portion of the fence. After defendants protested, plaintiff initiated this action, seeking a declaration that he owned the disputed strip. As noted, defendants asserted in a counterclaim that they had acquired the strip through adverse possession. The trial court ultimately granted summary judgment to defendants, ruling that the undisputed facts established that defendants had acquired the disputed strip through adverse possession….

ORS 105.620 codifies the common-law elements of adverse possession, requiring a claimant to prove by clear and convincing evidence that the claimant or the claimant's predecessors in interest maintained actual, open, notorious, exclusive, hostile, and continuous possession of the property for ten years. In addition to those common-law elements, the statute also requires the claimant to have had an honest belief of actual ownership when he or she entered into possession of the property.

Plaintiff makes arguments related to each of the statutory elements, first claiming that defendants did not establish actual, open, notorious, exclusive, or continuous possession of the entire disputed strip. We recently summarized what proof is required to satisfy those elements of an adverse-possession claim:

> "The element of actual use is satisfied if a claimant established a use of the land that would be made by an owner of the same type of land, taking into account the uses for which the land is suited. To establish a use that is open and notorious, plaintiffs must prove that their possession is of such a character as to afford the owner the means of knowing it, and of the claim. The exclusivity of the use also depends on how a reasonable owner would or would not share the property with others in like circumstances. A use is continuous if it is constant and not intermittent. The required constancy of use, again, is determined by the kind of use that would be expected of such land."

Stiles v. Godsey, 233 Or. App. 119, 126, 225 P.3d 81 (2009) (internal quotations and citations omitted).

Here, the land in question is a three-foot-wide strip, covered mostly with gravel or bark dust, adjacent to a narrow driveway. Defendants and their predecessor have used the strip as an extension of that driveway since 1994, both to accommodate wide vehicles and to provide additional loading room for defendant Francine Morgan's daycare clients. That use is consistent with ownership and with the land's character. Moreover, that use was "open" and "notorious," particularly when considered together with James's act of locating his sewer line on the strip and, later, defendants' maintenance of and improvements to the fence. Finally, defendants and their predecessor used the strip continuously from 1994 (when James bought the lot) to at least 2006 (when plaintiff bought lot 3100 from Robert), *i.e.*, for longer than the statutory 10-year adverse-possession period. Thus, the undisputed facts establish defendants' actual, open, notorious, exclusive, and continuous use of the property.

Plaintiff's contrary argument rests on the fact that the disputed strip is not completely separated from his residential lot by a fence; he emphasizes that the fence at issue does not extend all the way to Southeast Boise Street, but starts partway down the driveway.... Here, even though the fence does not extend to the street, it adequately defines the entire disputed strip, indicating that it is separate from the land that abuts it to the west.

Plaintiff also contends that defendants' use of the disputed strip was not "exclusive" because Robert sometimes used the property even after the fence was built. But adverse-possession claimants are allowed the freedom to allow others to occasionally use their property, in the manner that neighbors are wont to do, without thereby abandoning their claim. In this case, Robert asked permission of defendants and their predecessors each time that he used the disputed strip; that permissive use was consistent with defendants' ownership of the land and does not defeat their claim to it.

We also reject plaintiff's argument that defendants' use of the disputed strip was not "hostile" because, he claims, defendants had a conscious doubt regarding the property line. Under ORS 105.620(2)(a), a claimant "maintains 'hostile possession' of property if the possession is under claim of right or with color of title." A "claim of right" may be established through proof of an honest but mistaken belief of ownership, resulting, for example, from a mistake as to the correct location of a boundary. The mistaken belief must be a "pure" mistake, however, and not one based upon "conscious doubt" about the true boundary. Furthermore, ORS 105.620(1)(b) requires that the claimants (or their predecessors) have had an "honest belief" of actual ownership that (1) continued through the vesting period, (2) had an objective basis, and (3) was reasonable under the circumstances.

In *Mid-Valley Resources, Inc. v. Engelson*, 170 Ore App 255 (2000), we concluded that the defendants had failed to establish pure mistake about the location of a boundary line because one of the defendants had a conscious doubt on that subject. That *Mid-Valley* defendant had testified that she had not known where the property line was when she was a child, and she still did not know at the time of trial whether a particular fence was located on that boundary. That defendant's uncertainty about the property line's location defeated the defendants' adverse-possession claim.

Here, by contrast, the undisputed evidence clearly establishes that defendants and their predecessor, James, always believed that the fence marked the north-south line between lots 3200 and 3100. James assumed when he bought lot 3200 in 1994 that the fence was on the property line, and he perpetuated that belief in defendants by telling them, when they bought the property, that it was "fully fenced." Robert, then the record owner of the disputed strip, confirmed those mistaken beliefs when he did not object to installation of the sewer line, to defendants' use of the strip, or to defendants' extension of the fence. No evidence in the record supports plaintiff's assertion that defendants had a "conscious doubt" about whether the fence was actually located on the line separating their property from plaintiff's. Defendants did suggest in their depositions that they had not given much thought to the property line's location until the dispute arose with plaintiff. Read in context, however, those statements simply confirm defendants' *certainty* that the property line was the same as the fence line; the statements do not indicate that defendants had any conscious doubt as to the boundary's location.

Moreover, no evidence calls into question the reasonableness of defendants' belief that they owned the disputed strip. That strip of land is small in relation to the size of lots 3200 and 3100, it regularly has been used as an extension to the width of an existing driveway, it is well suited to that purpose, and it is partly fenced off from plaintiff's property. Under the circumstances, defendants' belief that they owned the disputed strip was reasonable.

In sum, the undisputed evidence establishes clearly and convincingly that defendants and their predecessor, James, had an "honest belief" that the disputed strip was part of lot 3200 and that they continuously maintained actual, open, notorious, exclusive, and hostile possession of that strip for well over 10 years, from 1994 at least until plaintiff bought lot 3100 in 2006.[6] We conclude that defendants' adverse-possession claim to the disputed strip vested in 2004, giving them title and extinguishing any claim that plaintiff might otherwise have had to that land.

Notes and Questions

1. Does the result in *Tieu* jibe with the rationales for adverse possession recited in the note preceding it? Which ones? *Cahill* suggests that these rationales are less relevant today than in the past. Do you agree? Should the defendants in *Tieu* have been without recourse?

2. *Tieu* involves an error in a conveyance. The parties' predecessors in interest thought they had bargained to transfer land that they didn't. This is a common source of adverse possession litigation. Other recurring fact patterns include mistaken deed descriptions, surveying errors, and accidental encroachments by neighbors. Adverse possession claims

---

[6] We reject plaintiff's argument that defendants cannot satisfy the 10-year adverse-possession period by tacking their possession to that of James. An adverse-possession claimant may tack his possessory interests to those of a predecessor "if there is evidence that the predecessor intended to transfer whatever adverse possessory rights he or she may have acquired." Fitts v. Case, 243 Ore App 543, 549, 267 P3d 160 (2011). Here, James clearly intended his transfer of lot 3200 to defendants to include the disputed strip, given his belief that the fence marked the boundary line and his advertisement of lot 3200 as "fully fenced."

may also follow the souring of relationships, perhaps between cotenants or one involving permissive land use. None of these cases necessarily involve bad faith actors; although the doctrine may indeed be applied in favor of the mere trespasser, depending on the jurisdiction's interpretation of the state of mind required to satisfy the "hostility" element. We will discuss this issue further below.

3. Title based on adverse possession is as good as any. To think through the implications of that observation, imagine the following facts. Neighbor A mistakenly builds a fence on her neighbor's land and gains title to the enclosed land by adverse possession. Neighbor B then notices the encroachment and demands that A move the fence. She agrees, but changes her mind two years later and rebuilds it. B sues for trespass. Who wins?

4. **Open and notorious possession**. Whatever its merits, adverse possession is strong medicine. The doctrine therefore provides safeguards to prevent a title owner from losing her property without adequate notice by, for example, requiring that the possession be open and notorious—it has to be the kind of act that an owner would notice.

   But even overt acts may not be obvious threats to ownership rights. A fence on someone else's property certainly seems open and notorious, but what if it is just an inch or two over the border? What about the three-foot incursion at issue in *Tieu*? What if it had been built while the plaintiff was in occupation of his lot? Do we expect owners to commission surveys anytime a neighbor builds near the property line? See *Manillo v. Gorski*, below.

5. **Adverse possession and the property owner**. State-to-state variation about whether encroachments need to be obvious may reflect a deeper question about the purpose of adverse possession. Some authorities view the doctrine as having an object of punishing inattentive owners who sleep on their rights. If so, then perhaps it makes sense to require an incursion to be sufficiently obvious that a property owner would not need to conduct a survey to determine the existence of a violation.

   But should sleeping owners be the target of the doctrine? Are property owners who fail to assert their rights also less likely to develop their property (or sell it to someone who will)? And if that is the underlying end, are there any problems with using adverse possession doctrine as a means to it?

6. **Adverse possession as reward**. The reciprocal view—that adverse possession exists to reward the possessors—has two flavors. One is externally focused. The possessor, by putting the land to productive use, "has done a work beneficial to the community." Axel Teisen, 3 A.B.A. J. 97, 127 (1917). The other is more internal:

> A thing which you have enjoyed and used as your own for a long time, whether property or an opinion, takes root in your being and cannot be torn away without your resenting the act and trying to defend yourself, however you came by it. The law can ask no better justification than the deepest instincts of man. It is only by way of reply to the suggestion that you are disappointing the former owner, that you refer to his neglect having allowed the gradual dissociation between himself and what he claims, and the gradual association of it with another.

Oliver Wendell Holmes, *The Path of the Law,* 10 HARV. L. REV. 457, 477 (1897). Do either of these views resonate? What does this rationale tell you about what the state of mind of the adverse possessor should be?

7. **Third-party interests.**

> The statute has not for its object to reward the diligent trespasser for his wrong nor yet to penalize the negligent and dormant owner for sleeping upon his rights; the great purpose is automatically to quiet all titles which are openly and consistently asserted, to provide proof of meritorious titles, and correct errors in conveyancing.

Henry W. Ballantine, *Title by Adverse Possession*, 32 HARV. L. REV. 135, 135 (1918) (footnotes omitted). By providing stability to existing property arrangements after the passage of time, adverse possession simplifies transactions by relieving purchasers and mortgagees of the risk that they are dealing with title founded on a long-ago mistake or trespass. The doctrine is a healing mechanism that realigns possession and paperwork when they've gotten too badly out of sync. The benefit extends to the legal system as well by relieving courts of the need to delve into the details of long-forgotten events.

8. **Adverse possession's information function**. Adverse possession also enables rights that exist as a matter of custom (e.g., "the Smiths always farm that strip of land") to receive legal status. A banker in a distant city may not understand (or trust) allocations based on local understandings, but that doesn't matter if the claims are translated into

recordable title.[30] The land may now serve as the object of a sale or collateral for a loan for an expanded audience, enhancing its value. Adverse possession's role in converting informal understandings into formal rights illustrates law's ability to facilitate the aggregation and dissemination of information across society. Can you think of others?

9. **Tacking**. What happens if a series of possessors occupy a property, but none of them are present long enough for the limitations period to run? *Tieu* notes in passing the concept of tacking, which enables a succession of adverse possessors to collectively satisfy the statutory period. The usual approach is to allow tacking so long as the successive possessors are in "privity": a relationship in which the prior possessor knowingly and intentionally transfers whatever interest she holds to the subsequent possessor. *See, e.g.*, Stump v. Whibco, 715 A.2d 1006 (N.J. Super. Ct. App. 1998) ("Tacking is generally permitted "unless it is shown that the claimant's predecessor in title did not intend to convey the disputed parcel.") (citations and quotation omitted). So the clock continues to run if one possessor sells or leases the occupied land, but there is no privity if one trespasser wanders onto the lot after another leaves (or worse, dispossesses the earlier trespasser by force).

   Recall the question of whether adverse possession doctrine is more properly focused on rewarding deserving possessors or punishing inattentive owners. Does the U.S. approach to tacking shed light on our answer? The English view is to allow tacking without privity. *Cf.* James Ames, LECTURES ON LEGAL HISTORY 197 (1913) ("English lawyers regard not the merit of the possessor, but the demerit of the one out of possession. The statutes of limitation provide . . . not that the adverse possessor shall acquire title, but that the one who neglects for a given time to assert his right shall thereafter not enforce it.").

10. **Adverse possession and the environment**. An underlying premise of the rationales discussed above is that land should be used. For an argument that this tilt makes adverse possession doctrine environmentally harmful, *see* John G. Sprankling, *An Environmental Critique of Adverse Possession*, 79 CORNELL L. REV. 816, 840 (1994) (arguing that

---

[30] "Quiet title" suits perform this function. They are actions that establish the claimant's title to land and foreclose the ability of others to contest it. Although quiet title suits are not necessary to gain rights under adverse possession doctrine, they are very important to adverse possessors. Do you see why? If you cannot answer the question, ask yourself whether you would ever buy property from an adverse possessor.

"American adverse possession law is fundamentally hostile to the private preservation of wild lands" and proposing exemption to doctrine for privately held wild lands) .

Manillo v. Gorski

255 A.2d 258 (N.J. 1969)

HANEMAN, J.

Plaintiffs filed a complaint in the Chancery Division seeking a mandatory and prohibitory injunction against an alleged trespass upon their lands. Defendant counterclaimed for a declaratory judgment which would adjudicate that she had gained title to the disputed premises by adverse possession under N.J.S. 2A:14-6 which provides:

> "Every person having any right or title of entry into real estate shall make such entry within 20 years next after the accrual of such right or title of entry, or be barred therefrom thereafter."

After plenary trial, judgment was entered for plaintiffs. Defendant appealed to the Appellate Division. Before argument there, this Court granted defendant's motion for certification.

The facts are as follows: In 1946, defendant and her husband entered into possession of premises in Keansburg known as Lot No. 1007 in Block 42, under an agreement to purchase. Upon compliance with the terms of said agreement, the seller conveyed said lands to them on April 16, 1952. Defendant's husband thereafter died. The property consisted of a rectangular lot with a frontage of 25 feet and a depth of 100 feet. Plaintiffs are the owners of the adjacent Lot 1008 in Block 42 of like dimensions, to which they acquired title in 1953.

In the summer of 1946 Chester Gorski, one of the defendant's sons, made certain additions and changes to the defendant's house. He extended two rooms at the rear of the structure, enclosed a screened porch on the front, and put a concrete platform with steps on the west side thereof for use in connection with a side door. These steps were built to replace existing wooden steps. In addition, a concrete walk was installed from the steps to the end of the house. In 1953, defendant raised the house. In order to compensate for the resulting added height from the ground, she modified the design of the steps by extending them toward both the front and the rear of the property. She did not change their width.

Defendant admits that the steps and concrete walk encroach upon plaintiffs' lands to the extent of 15 inches. She contends, however, that she has title to said land by adverse possession. Plaintiffs assert contrawise that defendant did not obtain title by adverse possession as her possession was not of the requisite hostile nature. They argue that to establish title by adverse possession, the entry into and continuance of possession must be accompanied by an intention to invade the rights of another in the lands, i.e., a knowing wrongful taking. They assert that, as defendant's encroachment was not accompanied by an intention to invade plaintiffs' rights in the land, but rather by the mistaken belief that she owned the land, and that therefore an essential requisite to establish title by adverse possession, i.e., an intentional tortious taking, is lacking.

The trial court concluded that defendant had clearly and convincingly proved that her possession of the 15-inch encroachment had existed for more than 20 years before the institution of this suit and that such possession was "exclusive, continuous, uninterrupted, visible, notorious and against the right and interest of the true owner." There is ample evidence to sustain this finding except as to its visible and notorious nature, of which more hereafter. However, the judge felt impelled by existing New Jersey case law, holding as argued by plaintiffs above, to deny defendant's claim and entered judgment for plaintiffs. The first issue before this Court is, therefore, whether an entry and continuance of possession under the mistaken belief that the possessor has title to the lands involved, exhibits the requisite hostile possession to sustain the obtaining of title by adverse possession.

The first detailed statement and acceptance by our then highest court, of the principle that possession as an element of title by adverse possession cannot be bottomed on mistake, is found in *Folkman v. Myers*, 93 N.J. Eq. 208 (E. & A. 1921), which embraced and followed that thesis as expressed in *Myers v. Folkman*, 89 N.J.L. 390 (Sup. Ct. 1916). It is not at all clear that this was the common law of this State prior to the latter case. An earlier opinion, *Davok v. Nealon*, 58 N.J.L. 21 (Sup. Ct. 1895), held for an adverse possessor who had entered under the mistaken belief that he had title without any discussion of his hostile intent. However, the court in *Myers v. Folkman* distinguished *Davock* from the case then under consideration by referring to the fact that "Charles R. Myers disclaims any intent to claim what did not belong to him and apparently never asserted a right to land outside the bounds of his title ..." (Emphasis supplied). The factual distinction between the two cases, according to Myers, is that in the later case there was not only an entry by mistake but also an articulated disclaimer of an intent by the entrant to claim title to lands beyond his actual boundary. Folkman, although apparently relying on Myers, eliminated the requirement of that decision that there be expressed an affirmative disclaimer, and expanded the doctrine to exclude from the category of hostile possessors those whose entry and continued possession was under a mistaken belief that the lands taken were embraced within the description of the possessor's deed. In so doing, the former Court of Errors and Appeals aligned this State with that branch of a dichotomy which traces its genesis to *Preble v. Main Cent. R. Co.*, 27 A. 149 (Sup. Jud. Ct. Me. 1893) and has become known as the Maine doctrine. In *Preble*, the court said:

> "There is every presumption that the occupancy is in subordination to the true title, and, if the possession is claimed to be adverse, the act of the wrongdoer must be strictly

> construed, and the character of the possession clearly shown. *Roberts v. Richards*, 24 A. 425, and authorities cited. `The intention of the possessor to claim adversely," says Mellen, C.J., in *Ross v. Gould*, `is an essential ingredient in disseisin.' And in *Worcester v. Lord*, the court says: `To make a disseisin in fact, there must be an intention on the part of the party assuming possession to assert title in himself.' Indeed, the authorities all agree that this intention of the occupant to claim the ownership of land not embraced in his title is a necessary element of adverse possession and in case of occupancy by mistake beyond a line capable of being ascertained this intention to claim title to the extent of the occupancy must appear to be absolute, and not conditional; otherwise the possession will not be deemed adverse to the true owner. It must be an intention to claim title to all land within a certain boundary on the face of the earth, whether it shall eventually be found to be the correct one or not. If, for instance, one in ignorance of his actual boundaries takes and holds possession by mistake up to a certain fence beyond his limits, upon the claim and in the belief that it is the true line, with the intention to claim title, and thus, if necessary, to acquire `title by possession' up to that fence, such possession, having the requisite duration and continuity, will ripen into title. *Hitchings v. Morrison*, 72 Me. 331, is a pertinent illustration of this principle. See, also, *Abbott v. Abbott*, 51 Me. 575; *Ricker v. Hibbard*, 73 Me. 105.
>
> If, on the other hand, a party through ignorance, inadvertence, or mistake occupies up to a given fence beyond his actual boundary, because he believes it to be the true line, but has no intention to claim title to that extent if it should be ascertained that the fence was on his neighbor's land, an indispensable element of adverse possession is wanting. In such a case the intent to claim title exists only upon the condition that the fence is on the true line. The intention is not absolute, but provisional, and the possession is not adverse."

This thesis, it is evident, rewards the possessor who entered with a premeditated and predesigned "hostility" — the intentional wrongdoer and disfavors an honest, mistaken entrant. …

The other branch of the dichotomy relies upon *French v. Pearce*, 8 Conn. 439 (Sup. Ct. Conn. 1831). The court said in Pearce on the question of the subjective hostility of a possessor:

> "Into the recesses of his [the adverse claimant's] mind, his motives or purposes, his guilt or innocence, no enquiry is made. …
>
> … The very nature of the act [entry and possession] is an assertion of his own title, and the denial of the title of all others. It matters not that the possessor was mistaken, and had he been better informed, would not have entered on the land."

The Maine doctrine has been the subject of much criticism in requiring a knowing wrongful taking. The criticism of the Maine and the justification of the Connecticut branch of the dichotomy is well stated in 6 Powell, Real Property (1969) ¶ 1015:

> "Do the facts of his possession, and of his conduct as if he were the owner, make immaterial his mistake, or does such a mistake prevent the existence of the prerequisite claim of right. The leading case holding the mistake to be of no importance was *French v. Pearce*, decided in Connecticut in 1831. ... This viewpoint has gained increasingly widespread acceptance. The more subjectively oriented view regards the `mistake' as necessarily preventing the existence of the required claim of right. The leading case on this position is *Preble v. Maine Central* R.R., decided in 1893. This position is still followed in a few states. It has been strongly criticized as unsound historically, inexpedient practically, and as resulting in better treatment for a ruthless wrongdoer than for the honest landowner. ... On the whole the law is simplified, in the direction of real justice, by a following of the Connecticut leadership on this point."

Again, 4 Tiffany, Real Property (3d ed. 1939) criticizes the employment of mistake as negating hostility as follows:

> "... Adopting this view, it is only in so far as the courts, which assert the possible materiality of the mistake, recognize a contrary presumption, of an intention on the part of the wrongful possessor not to claim title if he is mistaken as to the boundary, that the assertion of the materiality of mistake as to boundary becomes of substantial importance. That the presumption is properly in favor of the adverse or hostile character of the possession rather than against it has been previously argued, but whatever presumption in this regard may be recognized, the introduction of the element of mistake in the discussion of the question of adverse possession is, it is submitted, unnecessary and undesirable. In no case except in that of a mistake as to boundary has the element of mistake been regarded as having any significance, and there is no reason for attributing greater weight thereto when the mistake is as to the proper location of a boundary than when it is a mistake as to the title to all the land wrongfully possessed. And to introduce the element of mistake, and then limit its significance by an inquiry as to the intention which the possessor may have as to his course of action in case there should be a mistake, an intention which has ordinarily no existence whatsoever, is calculated only to cause confusion without, it is conceived, any compensating advantage."

Our Appellate Division in *Predham v. Holfester*, 32 N.J. Super. 419 (App. Div. 1954) although acknowledging that the Maine doctrine had been severely criticized felt obliged because of stare decisis to adhere thereto. See also *Rullis v. Jacobi*, 79 N.J. Super. 525 (Ch. Div. 1963).

We are in accord with the criticism of the Maine doctrine and favor the Connecticut doctrine for the above quoted reasons. As far as can be seen, overruling the former rule will not result in undermining any of the values which stare decisis is intended to foster. The theory of reliance, a cornerstone of stare decisis, is not here apt, as the problem is which of two mistaken parties is entitled to land. Realistically, the true owner does not rely upon entry of the possessor by mistake as a reason for not seeking to recover possession. Whether or not the entry is caused by mistake or intent, the same result eventuates — the true owner is ousted from possession. In either event his neglect to seek recovery of possession, within the requisite time, is in all probability the result of a lack of knowledge that he is being deprived of possession of lands to which he has title.

Accordingly, we discard the requirement that the entry and continued possession must be accompanied by a knowing intentional hostility and hold that any entry and possession for the required time which is exclusive, continuous, uninterrupted, visible and notorious, even though under mistaken claim of title, is sufficient to support a claim of title by adverse possession.

However, this conclusion is not dispositive of the matter sub judice. Of equal importance under the present factual complex, is the question of whether defendant's acts meet the necessary standard of "open and notorious" possession. It must not be forgotten that the foundation of so-called "title by adverse possession" is the failure of the true owner to commence an action for the recovery of the land involved, within the period designated by the statute of limitations. The justifications for the doctrine are aptly stated in 4 Tiffany, Real Property (3d ed. 1939) § 1134 as follows:

> "The desirability of fixing, by law, a definite period within which claims to land must be asserted has been generally recognized, among the practical considerations in favor of such a policy being the prevention of the making of illegal claims after the evidence necessary to defeat them has been lost, and the interest which the community as a whole has in the security, of title. The moral justification of the policy lies in the consideration that one who has reason to know that land belonging to him is in the possession of another, and neglects, for a considerable period of time, to assert his right thereto, may properly be penalized by his preclusion from thereafter asserting such right. It is, apparently, by reason of the demerit of the true owner, rather than any supposed merit in the person who has acquired wrongful possession of the land, that this possession, if continued for the statutory period, operates to debar the former owner of all right to recover the land."

See also 5 Thompson, Real Property (1957 Replacement).

In order to afford the true owner the opportunity to learn of the adverse claim and to protect his rights by legal action within the time specified by the statute, the adverse possession must be visible and notorious. In 4 Tiffany, supra (Supp. 1969), the character of possession for that purpose, is stated to be as follows:

> "... it must be public and based on physical facts, including known and visible lines and boundaries. Acts of dominion over the land must be so open and notorious as to put an ordinarily prudent person on notice that the land is in actual possession of another. Hence, title may never be acquired by mere possession, however long continued, which is surreptitious or secret or which is not such as will give unmistakable notice of the nature of the occupant's claim."

See also 5 Thompson, supra, § 2546; 6 Powell, Real Property, ¶ 1013 (1969).

Generally, where possession of the land is clear and unequivocal and to such an extent as to be immediately visible, the owner may be presumed to have knowledge of the adverse occupancy. In *Foulke v. Bond*, 41 N.J.L. 527(E. & A. 1879), the court said:

> "Notoriety of the adverse claim under which possession is held, is a necessary constituent of title by adverse possession, and therefore the occupation or possession must be of that nature that the real owner is presumed to have known that there was a possession adverse to his title, under which it was intended to make title against him." (Emphasis supplied)

However, when the encroachment of an adjoining owner is of a small area and the fact of an intrusion is not clearly and self-evidently apparent to the naked eye but requires an on-site survey for certain disclosure as in urban sections where the division line is only infrequently delineated by any monuments, natural or artificial, such a presumption is fallacious and unjustified. See concurring opinion of Judge (now Justice) Francis in *Predham v. Holfester.* The precise location of the dividing line is then ordinarily unknown to either adjacent owner and there is nothing on the land itself to show by visual observation that a hedge, fence, wall or other structure encroaches on the neighboring land to a minor extent. Therefore, to permit a presumption of notice to arise in the case of minor border encroachments not exceeding several feet would fly in the face of reality and require the true owner to be on constant alert for possible small encroachments. The only method of certain determination would be by obtaining a survey each time the adjacent owner undertook any improvement at or near the boundary, and this would place an undue and inequitable burden upon the true owner. Accordingly we hereby hold that no presumption of knowledge arises from a minor encroachment along a common boundary. In such a case, only where the true owner has actual knowledge thereof may it be said that the possession is open and notorious.

It is conceivable that the application of the foregoing rule may in some cases result in undue hardship to the adverse possessor who under an innocent and mistaken belief of title has undertaken an extensive improvement which to some extent encroaches on an adjoining property. In that event the situation falls within the category of those cases of which *Riggle v. Skill*, 9 N.J. Super. 372 (Ch. Div. 1950), affirmed 7 N.J. 268 (1951) is typical and equity may furnish relief. Then, if the innocent trespasser of a small portion of land adjoining a boundary line cannot without great expense remove or eliminate the encroachment, or such removal or elimination is impractical or could be accomplished only with great hardship, the true owner may be forced to convey the land so occupied upon payment of the fair value thereof without regard to whether the true owner had notice of the encroachment at its inception. Of course, such a result should eventuate only under appropriate circumstances and where no serious damage would be done to the remaining land as, for instance, by rendering the balance of the parcel unusable or no longer capable of being built upon by reason of zoning or other restrictions.

We remand the case for trial of the issues (1) whether the true owner had actual knowledge of the encroachment, (2) if not, whether plaintiffs should be obliged to convey the disputed tract to defendant, and (3) if the answer to the latter question is in the affirmative, what consideration should be paid for the conveyance. The remand, of course, contemplates further discovery and a new pretrial.

Remanded for trial in accordance with the foregoing.

B. "Hostility" and Intent

Adverse possession requires possession that is "hostile" and, often, "under a claim of right." Hostility is not animosity. "Hostile possession can be understood as possession that is opposed and antagonistic to all other claims, and that conveys the clear message that the possessor intends to possess the land as his or her own." 16 POWELL ON REAL PROPERTY § 91.01[2]. The requirement thus prevents permissive occupancy from ripening into ownership; a lessor need not worry that the tenant will claim title by adverse possession. *See, e.g.*, Rise v. Steckel, 652 P.2d 364, 372 (1982) ("[T]he ten-year statutory period for adverse possession did not begin to run until defendant asserted to plaintiff that he was possessing the property in his own right, rather than as a tenant at sufferance."). A "claim of right," sometimes called claim of title,[31] means that

[31] Which is not the same thing as "color of title," as discussed below.

the possessor is holding the property as an owner would. This could be seen as synonymous with the hostility requirement, but not all jurisdictions treat the concept this way. The Powell treatise states that the predominant view in the United States is that good faith is not required for adverse possession, 16 POWELL § 91.01[2], but as you may have already noticed in the *Tieu* case above, intent often matters.

Cahill v. Morrow

11 A.3d 82 (R.I. 2011)

INDEGLIA, J.

The property in dispute is located on Gooseberry Road in the Snug Harbor section of South Kingstown, Rhode Island. Identified as lot 19 on assessor's plat 88-1, the land is sandwiched between lot 20, currently owned by Cahill, and lot 18, formerly coowned by members of the Morrow family. Morrow is the record owner of the subject property, lot 19.

In 1969, Morrow's husband, George Morrow, purchased lot 19, and the same year George and his brothers jointly purchased lot 18. At the time of lot 19's purchase, it was largely undeveloped, marked only by a preexisting clothesline, grass, and trees. Since that time, the Morrows have not improved or maintained lot 19, but have paid all property taxes assessed to it. As such, instead of vacationing on their lot 19, the Morrows annually spent two weeks in the summer at the cottages on the adjacent lot 18. During these vacations, the Morrow children and their cousins played on lot 19's grassy area. Around 1985, the Morrows ceased summering on Gooseberry Road,[3] but continued to return at least once a year to view the lot. Morrow stopped visiting lot 19 in October 2002, after her husband became ill, and she did not return again until July 2006.

In 1971, two years after George Morrow purchased lot 19, Cahill's mother bought the land and house designated as lot 20 as a summer residence. Between 1971 and 1975, Cahill and her brother did some work on lot 19. They occasionally cut the grass, placed furniture, and planted trees and flowers on it.

Cahill's mother passed away in 1975, and in 1977, after purchasing her siblings' shares, Cahill became the sole record owner of the lot 20 property. Once she became lot 20's owner, Cahill began living in the house year-round. From that time through 1991, she and her boyfriend,

---

[3] In 1991, George Morrow and his joint-owner brothers sold lot 18.

James M. Cronin, testified that they continued to mow lot 19's grass on occasion. In addition, she hung clothing on the clothesline, attached flags to the clothesline pole, used the picnic table, positioned a bird bath and feeder, and planted more flowers and trees. Cahill placed Adirondack chairs on lot 19 and eventually replaced the clothesline and picnic table. In 1987, Cahill held the first annual "cousins' party" allowing her relatives free rein with respect to her property and lot 19 for playing, sitting, and car parking. She also entertained friends and family on lot 19 during other summer days. Mary Frances McGinn, Cahill's cousin, likewise recalled that lot 19 was occupied by Cahill kindred during various family functions throughout this time period. Cahill admitted that she never objected to neighborhood children using lot 19, however.

During the period of 1991 through 1997, Cahill testified that she planted more flowers and trees, in addition to cutting the grass occasionally. Cahill also stored her gas grill and yard furniture on the lot and had her brother stack lobster pots for decorative purposes. In 1991 or 1992, she began hosting the annual "Cane Berry Blossom Festival," another outdoor event that used both her lot and lot 19 as the party venue. Like the other gatherings, the festival always took place on a day during a warm-weather month. In 1997 or 1998, she installed a wooden border around the flower beds.

On July 22, 1997, Cahill wrote to George Morrow expressing an interest in obtaining title to lot 19. In the 1997 letter, Cahill stated: "I am interested in learning if your narrow strip of property is available for sale. If so, I would be interested in discussing purchasing it from you." Cahill continued: "If there is a possibility that you would like to sell it, could you please either call me or send me a note?" Cahill did not receive a response.

In the "late 1990s," though Cahill is unclear whether this occurred before or after the 1997 letter, a nearby marina sought permission to construct and elevate its property. Cahill attended the related zoning board hearings and expressed her concerns about increased flooding on lot 19 due to the marina elevation. She succeeded in having the marina developer grade part of lot 19 to alleviate flooding. Additionally, Cahill instituted her own trench and culvert drainage measures to divert water off of lot 19 and then reseeded the graded area. By Cahill's own admission, however, her trenching and reseeding work occurred in 1999 or 2000.

Subsequent to 2001, the new owners of lot 18[5] stored their boat on lot 19 and planted their own flowers and small trees on the property. In 2002, when the town (with approval from George Morrow) erected a stone wall and laid a sidewalk on the Gooseberry Road border of lot 19,

---

[5] In approximately 2001, new owners purchased lot 18 from the Morrow brothers' successor.

Cahill loamed and planted grass on that portion of the lot. Also in 2002, Cahill asked Morrow's two sisters on separate occasions whether George Morrow would be interested in selling lot 19. The Morrows gave no response to her 2002 inquiries. In 2003, George Morrow passed away.

After making her third inquiry concerning the purchase of lot 19 in 2002, Cahill testified, she continued using the property in a fashion similar to her prior practice until December 2005, when she noticed heavy-machinery tire marks and test pits on the land. Thereafter, she retained counsel and authorized her attorney to send a letter on January 10, 2006 to Morrow indicating her adverse possession claim to a "20-foot strip of land on the northerly boundary" of lot 19. According to a survey of the disputed property, however, the width of lot 19 from the northerly boundary (adjacent to Cahill's property) to lot 18 is 49.97 feet and therefore, more than double what Cahill originally claimed in this letter. Nonetheless, on April 25, 2006, Cahill instituted a civil action requesting a declaration that based on her "uninterrupted, quiet, peaceful and actual seisin and possession" "for a period greater than 10 years," she was the true owner of lot 19 in its entirety. On July 25, 2007, the trial justice agreed that Cahill had proved adverse possession under G.L. 1956 § 34-7-1 and vested in her the fee simple title to lot 19....

In Rhode Island, obtaining title by adverse possession requires actual, open, notorious, hostile, continuous, and exclusive use of property under a claim of right for at least a period of ten years.

Here, the trial justice recited the proper standard of proof for adverse possession and then found that Cahill had

> "met her burden of establishing all of the elements of an adverse possession claim to lot 19 by her and her mother's continuous and uninterrupted use of the parcel for well in excess of ten years. She maintained the property, planted and improved the property with shrubs, trees, and other plantings, sought drainage control measures, and used the property as if it were her own since 1971. She established that use not only by her own testimony, but as corroborated by other witnesses, photographs, and expert testimony relative to the interpretation of aerial photographs."

At trial, as here on appeal, Morrow argued that Cahill's offers to purchase the property invalidated her claim of right and the element of hostile possession. To dispose of that issue, the trial justice determined that "even assuming that [Cahill's] inquiry is circumstantial evidence of her knowledge that George Morrow, and subsequently Margaret [Morrow], were the legal title holders of [lot] 19, that does not destroy the viability of this adverse possession claim." The trial justice relied upon our opinion in *Tavares*, 814 A.2d at 350, to support his conclusion. Recalling that this Court stated in *Tavares* that "even when the claimants know they are nothing more than black-hearted trespassers, they can still adversely possess the property in question under a claim [of] right to do so if they use it openly, notoriously, and in a manner that is adverse to the true owner's rights for the requisite ten-year period," the trial justice found that Cahill's outward acknowledgement of Morrow's record title did not alone "negate her claim of right." He further found that "even if somehow the expression of interest in purchasing lot 19, made initially in 1997, stopped the running of the ten[-]year period under * * * § 34-7-1, the evidence was overwhelming that [Cahill] and her predecessor in title had commenced the requisite ten-year period beginning in 1971."

On appeal, Morrow challenges the trial justice's legal conclusion that Cahill's offers to purchase lot 19 did not extinguish her claim of right, hostile possession, and ultimately, the vesting of her title by adverse possession. Morrow also contends that the trial justice erred in finding that Cahill's testimonial and demonstrative evidence was sufficient to prove adverse possession under the clear and convincing burden of proof standard. We agree that as a matter of law the trial justice failed to consider the impact of Cahill's offers to purchase on the prior twenty-six years of her lot 19 use. As a result, we hold that this failure also affects his factual determinations.

1. 1997 Offer-to-Purchase Letter

In *Tavares*, this Court explained that "requir[ing] adverse possession under a claim of right is the same as requiring hostility, in that both terms simply indicate that the claimant is holding the property with an intent that is adverse to the interests of the true owner." *Tavares*, 814 A.2d at 351 (quoting 16 Powell on Real Property, § 91.05[1] at 91-28 (2000)). "Thus, [we said] a claim of right may be proven through evidence of open, visible acts or declarations, accompanied by use of the property in an objectively observable manner that is inconsistent with the rights of the record owner." Here, the first issue on appeal is how an offer to purchase has an impact on these elements....

...[I]n *Tavares*, 814 A.2d at 351, with regard to "establishing hostility and possession under a claim of right," we explained that "the pertinent inquiry centers on the claimants' *objective manifestations* of adverse use rather than on the claimants' *knowledge* that they lacked colorable legal title." (Emphases added.) Essentially, *Tavares* turned on the difference between the adverse possession claimant's "knowledge" regarding the owner's title and his "objective manifestations" thereof. In that case, the adverse-possession claimant surveyed his land and discovered "that he did not hold title to the parcels in question." After such enlightenment, however, the claimant objectively manifested his claim of ownership to the parcels by "posting no-trespass signs, constructing stone walls, improving drainage, and wood cutting." This Court explained that simply having knowledge that he was not the title owner of the parcels was not enough to destroy his claim of right given his objective, adverse manifestations otherwise. In fact, we went so far as to state that "even when claimants know that they are nothing more than black-hearted trespassers, they can still adversely possess the property in question under a claim of right to do so if they use it openly, notoriously, and in a manner that is adverse to the true owner's rights for the requisite ten-year period." This statement is legally correct considering that adverse possession does not require the claimant to make "a good faith mistake that he or she had legal title to the land." 16 Powell on Real Property § 91.05[2] at 91-23. However, to the extent that *Tavares*'s reference to "black-hearted trespassers" suggests that this Court endorses an invade-and-conquer mentality in modern property law, we dutifully excise that sentiment from our jurisprudence.

In the case before this Court, Cahill went beyond mere knowledge that she was not the record owner by sending the offer-to-purchase letter. As distinguished from the *Tavares* claimant who did not communicate his survey findings with anyone, Cahill's letter objectively declared the superiority of George Morrow's title to the record owner himself. *See also* Shanks v. Collins, 1989 OK 115, 782 P.2d 1352, 1355 (Okla. 1989) ("A recognition by an adverse possessor that legal title lies in another serves to break the essential element of continuity of possession.").

In the face of this precedent, Cahill contends that the trial justice accurately applied the law by finding that an offer to purchase does not automatically negate a claim of right in the property. While we agree that this proposition is correct with respect to offers made in an effort to make peace in an ongoing dispute, we disagree that this proposition applies in situations, as here, where no preexisting ownership dispute is evident.... Her offer was not an olive branch meant to put an end to pending litigation with the Morrows. Rather, it was a clear declaration that Cahill "wanted title to the property" from the record owner. By doing so, she necessarily acknowledged that her interest in lot 19 was subservient to George Morrow's....

Accordingly, the trial justice erred by considering any incidents of ownership exhibited by Cahill after the 1997 letter to George Morrow interrupted her claim....

2. The Impact of Cahill's Offer to Purchase on her Pre-1997 Adverse-Possession Claim

Furthermore, we also conclude that the trial justice should not have assumed that even if Cahill's "inquiry is circumstantial evidence of her knowledge that George Morrow, and subsequently [Morrow], were the legal title holders of [lot] 19, that does not destroy the viability of this adverse possession claim." We agree that an offer to purchase does not automatically invalidate a claim already vested by statute, but we nonetheless hold that the objective manifestations that another has superior title, made after the statutory period and not made to settle an ongoing dispute, are poignantly relevant to the ultimate determination of claim of right and hostile possession during the statutory period....

3. Questions of Fact Remain

Despite the significant deference afforded to the trial justice's findings of fact, such findings are not unassailable. Here, we find clear error in the trial justice's conclusion that "even if somehow the expression of interest in purchasing [lot] 19, made initially in 1997, stopped the running of the ten[-]year period * * * the evidence was overwhelming that [Cahill] and her predecessor in title had commenced the requisite ten-year period beginning in 1971." Given our opinion that some of Cahill's lot 19 activities cannot be considered because of the time frame of their occurrence, we disagree that the trial record can be classified as presenting "overwhelming" evidence of adverse possession.

.... On remand, the trial justice is directed to limit his consideration to pre-1997 events and make specific determinations whether Cahill's intermittent flower and tree planting, flag flying, clothesline replacing, lawn chair and beach-paraphernalia storing, and annual party hosting are adequate. Furthermore, given our ruling today, the trial court must evaluate the nature of Cahill's and her predecessor's twenty-six-year acts of possession in the harsh light of the fact that Cahill openly manifested the existence of George Morrow's superior title on three occasions....

FLAHERTY, J., dissenting.

.... Simply put, I do not agree that the correspondence between plaintiff and defendant in which plaintiff offers to purchase defendant's interest in lot 19 is the smoking gun the majority perceives it to be. As is clear from a fair reading of plaintiff's testimony, she believed that she owned the property as a result of her longtime use of and dominion over it. But her testimony also demonstrates that she drew a crisp distinction between whatever ownership rights she may have acquired and record title, which she recognized continued to reside in the Morrows.... Even if that letter were as significant as the majority contends, there is no doubt that it was sent after the statutory period had run. It is beyond dispute that plaintiff's correspondence could not serve to divest her of title if she had already acquired it by adverse possession.... There certainly was credible evidence for the trial justice to find that plaintiff had used the property as her own for well over twenty years before she corresponded with Mr. Morrow in 1997....

Dombkowski v. Ferland

893 A.2d 599 (Me. 2006)

DANA, J.

....Although "some courts and commentators fail to distinguish between the elements of *hostility* and *claim of right,* or simply consider *hostility* to be a subset of the *claim of right* requirement[,] *see, e.g., Johnson v. Stanley,* 96 N.C. App. 72, 384 S.E.2d 577, 579 (1989)[,] ... under Maine law, the two elements are distinct." *Striefel,* 1999 ME 111, P13 n.7, 733 A.2d at 991.

"'Hostile' simply means that the possessor does not have the true owner's permission to be on the land, and has nothing to do with demonstrating a heated controversy or a manifestation of ill will, or that the claimant was in any sense an enemy of the owner of the servient estate." *Id.* P13, 733 A.2d at 991 (quotation marks and citation omitted). "Permission negates the element of hostility, and precludes the acquisition of title by adverse possession." *Id.* "'Under a claim of right' means that the claimant is in possession as owner, with intent to claim the land as [its] own, and not in recognition of or subordination to [the] record title owner." *Id.* P14, 733 A.2d at 991 (quotation marks omitted).

Under Maine's common law, as part of the claim of right element, we have historically examined the subjective intentions of the person claiming adverse possession. *See Preble v. Maine C. R. Co.,* 85 Me. 260, 264, 27 A. 149, 150 (1893). Under this approach, which is considered the minority rule in the country, "one who by mistake occupies ... land not covered by his deed with no intention to claim title beyond his actual boundary wherever that may be, does not thereby acquire title by adverse possession to land beyond the true line." *Preble,* 85 Me. at 264, 27 A. at 150; *see also McMullen,* 483 A.2d at 700 ("[If] the occupier intend[s] to hold the property only if he were in fact legally entitled to it[, the] occupation [is] 'conditional' and [cannot] form the basis of an adverse possession claim."). The majority rule in the country is based on *French v. Pearce,* 8 Conn. 439 (1831), and recognizes that the possessor's mistaken belief does not defeat a claim of adverse possession. [The court then interpreted legislation to overrule Maine precedents and allow mistaken possession to meet the claim of right requirement.]

Notes and Questions

1. **Doctrine v. practice**. Richard Helmholz has argued that though adverse possession doctrine generally does not require the adverse possessor to plead good faith, judicial practice is to disfavor those who know they are trespassing compared to those acting out of a good faith mistake. Richard H. Helmholz, *Adverse Possession and Subjective Intent*, 61 WASH. U. L. Q. 331, 332 (1983). Is *Cahill* an example of this dynamic?

   In recent decades, state legislatures have increasingly demanded good faith on the part of the possessor (the Oregon statute in *Tieu* requiring honest belief in ownership, for example, was passed in 1989). *See* 16 POWELL ON REAL PROPERTY § 91.05 (collecting examples).

2. Should good faith be required? And if so, what is good faith? Is it an honest belief about the facts on the ground (e.g., whether the fence builder is correct that his fence is on the right side of the boundary line)? Or is it an attitude about one's potential adversary (a willingness to move the fence if wrong)? Either view creates evidentiary difficulties.

   Even when good faith is not part of the analysis as a formal matter, Helmholz argues that judges and juries often cannot help but "prefer the claims of an honest man over those of a dishonest man." Helmholz, *supra*, at 358. Might this be a satisfactory middle ground? Are there advantages to having courts officially ignore intent while applying a de facto bar to the bad faith possessor when there is evidence of dishonesty? Or is it problematic to have legal practice depart from official doctrine?

Perhaps another way to reconcile the benefits of adverse possession with the distaste for bad faith possessors would be to allow dishonest possessors to keep the land, but pay for the privilege. Thomas W. Merrill, *Property Rules, Liability Rules, and Adverse Possession*, 79 NW. U. L. REV. 1122, 1126 (1984) (suggesting "requiring indemnification only in those cases where the [true owner] can show that the [adverse possessor] acted in bad faith."). As Merrill notes, a California appellate court required such payment in a case concerning a prescriptive easement (which is similar to adverse possession except that it concerns the *right to use* someone else's land rather than its ownership), only to be overturned by the state supreme court. *Id.* (discussing Warsaw v. Chicago Metallic Ceilings, Inc., 676 P.2d 584 (Cal. 1984)). The proposal may remind you of the *Manillo* case discussed above. How does it differ?

3. A minority of states, as Dombkowski indicates, require adverse possessors to prove their subjective intent to take the land without regard to the existence of other ownership interests. This is sometimes referred to as the "aggressive trespass" standard: "I thought I did not own it [and intended to take it]." Margaret Jane Radin, *Time, Possession, and Alienation*, 64 WASH. U. L.Q. 739, 746 (1986) (brackets in the original). Is there a reason to prefer it? Lee Anne Fennell argues for a knowing trespass requirement that requires the adverse possessor to document her knowledge:

> [A] documented knowledge requirement facilitates rather than punishes efforts at consensual dealmaking. One of the most definitive ways of establishing that a possessor knew she was not the owner of the disputed land is to produce evidence of her purchase offer to the record owner. Currently, such an offer often destroys one's chance at adverse possession because it shows one is acting in bad faith if one later trespasses; one does far better to remain in ignorance (or pretend to) and never broach the matter with the record owner. Under my proposal, such offers would go from being fatal in a later adverse possession action to being practically a prerequisite. As a result, it would be much more likely that any resulting adverse possession claim will occur only where a market transaction is unavailable. A documented knowledge requirement would also reduce litigation costs and increase the certainty of land holdings. Actions or records establishing that the trespass was known at the time of entry, necessary if the possessor ever wishes to gain title under my approach, would serve to streamline trespass actions

that occur before the statute has run. Moreover, an approach that refuses to reward innocent mistakes would be expected to reduce mistake-making.

Lee Anne Fennell, *Efficient Trespass: The Case for "Bad Faith" Adverse Possession*, 100 NW. U. L. REV. 1037, 1041-44 (2006) (footnotes omitted). One's position on these matters may depend on which scenarios one believes are most common in adverse possession cases and adjust the state of mind required to include or exclude them accordingly. Should the state of mind required depend on the context? A state might, for example, require good faith for encroachments, but bad faith or color of title if the possessor seeks to own the parcel as a whole. Is this a good idea?

C. Finer Points of Adverse Possession Law

1. **Actual and Continuous Possession**. Adverse possessors are not required to live on the occupied property, what matters is acting like a true owner would. That use, however, must be continuous, not sporadic. *Compare, e.g.*, Lobdell v. Smith, 690 N.Y.S.2d 171, 173 (N.Y. App. Div. 3d Dep't 1999) (although undeveloped land "does not require the same quality of possession as residential or arable land," no adverse possession where claimant "seldom visited the parcel except to occasionally pick berries or hunt small game"), *with* Nome 2000 v. Fagerstrom, 799 P.2d 304, 310 (Alaska 1990) (claimants of a rural parcel suitable for recreational and subsistence activities "visited the property several times during the warmer season to fish, gather berries, clean the premises, and play.... That others were free to pick berries and fish is consistent with the conduct of a hospitable landowner, and undermines neither the continuity nor exclusivity of their possession."). Regular use of a summer home may constitute continuous use. *See, e.g.*, Nechow v. Brown, 120 N.W.2d 251, 252 (Mich. 1963).

2. **Color of title**. Claim of title, an intent to use land as one's own, is distinct from color of title, which describes taking possession under a defective instrument (like a deed based on a mistaken land survey). States often apply more lenient adverse possession standards to claims made under color of title. *Compare, e.g.*, Fl. St. § 95.16, *with id.* § 95.18. Why do you think that is?

   Entry under color of title may also affect the scope of the land treated as occupied by the adverse possessor. 2 C.J.S. *Adverse Possession* § 252 ("Adverse possession under color of title ordinarily extends to the whole tract described in the instrument constituting color of title."). *But see* Wentworth v. Forne, 137 So. 2d 166, 169 (Miss. 1962) ("In brief, when the land involved is, in part, occupied by the real owner, the adverse possession, even when this possessor has color of title, is confined to the area actually possessed.").

3. **Adverse possession by and against the government**. Although government agencies may acquire title by adverse possession, the general rule is that public property held for public use is not subject to the doctrine. Why do you think that is?

4. **Disabilities**. The title owner of land may be subject to a disability (e.g., status as a minor, mental incapacity) that may extend the time to bring an ejectment action against an unlawful occupant. States generally spell out such exceptions by statute.

5. **A Moving Target.** States vary their adverse possession rules to take into account a variety of factors (e.g., claim under color of title, payment of property taxes, enclosure or cultivation of land, etc.). These factors may change with the times. In the aftermath of the financial crisis, for example, reports of trespassers occupying foreclosed, vacant properties with the goal of acquiring title via adverse possession prompted renewed attention to the doctrine. Florida enacted legislation that requires those seeking adverse possession without color of title to pay all outstanding taxes on the property within one year of taking possession and disclose in writing the possessor's identity, date of possession, and a description of the property sufficient to enable the identification of the property in the public records. Local officials are then required to make efforts to contact the record owner of the property. Fl. St. § 95.18. The form created under the statute is reprinted below. Are measures like these useful? Consider the problem of "zombie foreclosures." A property may be vacant because the owners received a notice of foreclosure and left. Sometimes the lenders never complete the foreclosure process, perhaps to avoid the costs that come with ownership of the property. Title therefore remains with the out-of-possession owners, who remain responsible for taxes, association fees, and the like. What outcome should adverse possession law seek to promote in such cases?

FLORIDA DEPARTMENT OF REVENUE

RETURN OF REAL PROPERTY IN ATTEMPT TO ESTABLISH ADVERSE POSSESSION WITHOUT COLOR OF TITLE

Section 95.18, Florida Statutes

DR-452
R. 07/13
Provisional
Effective 01/14

THIS RETURN DOES NOT CREATE ANY INTEREST ENFORCEABLE BY LAW IN THE DESCRIBED PROPERTY

For residential structures, a person who occupies or attempts to occupy a residential structure solely by claim of adverse possession prior to making a return, commits trespass under s. 810.08, F.S. A person who occupies or attempts to occupy a residential structure solely by claim of adverse possession and offers the property for lease to another commits theft under s. 812.014, F.S.

COMPLETED BY ADVERSE POSSESSION CLAIMANT

The person claiming adverse possession (claimant) must file this return with the property appraiser in the county where the property is located as required in s. 95.18(1), F.S.

Name of claimant(s)			
Mailing address		Phone	
		Parcel ID, if available	
		☐ the property claimed is only a portion of this parcel ID	
Date of filing		Date claimant entered into possession of property	

Legal description of property claimed — Fields will expand online, or you may add pages.
Must be full and complete. If the property appraiser cannot identify the property from the legal description, you may be required to obtain a survey.

This property has been: (Check all that apply.)	☐ protected by substantial enclosure	☐ cultivated, maintained, or improved in a usual manner

Describe your use of the property, in detail below.

Dates of payments of any outstanding taxes or liens levied by the state, county or municipality:

Under penalty of perjury, I declare that I have read the foregoing return and that the facts stated in it are true and correct. I further acknowledge that the return does not create any interest enforceable by law in the described property.

Signature of claimant(s) ______________________

____

State of Florida
County of ______________
This instrument was sworn to and subscribed before me on __________ by ______________________,
personally known to me or who produced ______________________ as identification.

____
Signature and seal, notary public

COMPLETED BY PROPERTY APPRAISER

Received in the office of the property appraiser of ______________ County, Florida, on __________.
A signed copy of this return has been delivered to the claimant(s). A copy will be sent to the owner of record.

______________________ Signature, property appraiser or deputy __________ Date

TO THE OWNER OF RECORD

A tax payment made by the owner of record before April 1 the year after the taxes were assessed will have priority over a payment made by the claimant. An adverse possession claim will be removed if the owner of record or tax collector furnishes a receipt to the property appraiser showing payment of taxes by the owner of record during the period of the claim. (S. 95.18, F.S.)

This return is a public record and may be inspected by any person under s. 119.01, F.S.

Howard v. Kunto

477 P.2d 210 (Wash.App. 1970)

PEARSON, J.

Land surveying is an ancient art but not one free of the errors that often creep into the affairs of men. In this case, we are presented with the question of what happens when the descriptions in deeds do not fit the land the deed holders are occupying. Defendants appeal from a decree quieting title in the plaintiffs of a tract of land on the shore of Hood Canal in Mason County.

At least as long ago as 1932 the record tells us that one McCall resided in the house now occupied by the appellant-defendants, Kunto. McCall had a deed that described a 50-foot-wide parcel on the shore of Hood Canal. The error that brings this case before us is that the 50 feet described in the deed is not the same 50 feet upon which McCall's house stood. Rather, the described land is an adjacent 50-foot lot directly west of that upon which the house stood. In other words, McCall's house stood on one lot and his deed described the adjacent lot. Several property owners to the west of defendants, not parties to this action, are similarly situated.

Over the years since 1946, several conveyances occurred, using the same legal description and accompanied by a transfer of possession to the succeeding occupants. The Kuntos' immediate predecessors in interest, Millers, desired to build a dock. To this end, they had a survey performed which indicated that the deed description and the physical occupation were in conformity. Several boundary stakes were placed as a result of this survey and the dock was constructed, as well as other improvements. The house as well as the others in the area continued to be used as summer recreational retreats.

The Kuntos then took possession of the disputed property under a deed from the Millers in 1959. In 1960 the respondent-plaintiffs, Howard, who held land east of that of the Kuntos, determined to convey an undivided one-half interest in their land to the Yearlys. To this end, they undertook to have a survey of the entire area made. After expending considerable effort, the surveyor retained by the Howards discovered that according to the government survey, the deed descriptions and the land occupancy of the parties did not coincide. Between the Howards and the Kuntos lay the Moyers' property. When the Howards' survey was completed, they discovered that they were the record owners of the land occupied by the Moyers and that the Moyers held record title to the land occupied by the Kuntos. Howard approached Moyer and in return for a conveyance of the land upon which the Moyers' house stood, Moyer conveyed to the Howards record title to the land upon which the Kunto house stood. Until plaintiffs Howard obtained the conveyance from Moyer in April, 1960, neither Moyer nor any of his predecessors ever asserted any right to ownership of the property actually being possessed by Kunto and his predecessors. This action was then instituted to quiet title in the Howards and Yearlys. The Kuntos appeal from a trial court decision granting this remedy.

At the time this action was commenced on August 19, 1960, defendants had been in occupance of the disputed property less than a year. The trial court's reason for denying their claim of adverse possession is succinctly stated in its memorandum opinion: "In this instance, defendants have failed to prove, by a preponderance of the evidence, a continuity of possession or estate to permit tacking of the adverse possession of defendants to the possession of their predecessors."

Finding of fact 6, which is challenged by defendants, incorporates the above concept and additionally finds defendant's possession not to have been "continuous" because it involved only "summer occupancy."

[In its entirety, the finding states: "In the instant case the defendants' building was not simply over the line, but instead was built wholly upon the wrong piece of property, not the property of defendants, described in Paragraph Four (4) of the complaint herein, but on the property of plaintiffs, described in Paragraph Three of the complaint and herein. That the last three deeds in the chain of title, covering and embracing defendants' property, including defendants' deed, were executed in other states, specifically, California and Oregon. And there is no evidence of pointing out to the grantees in said three deeds, aforesaid, including defendants' deed, of any specific property, other than the property of defendants, described in their deed, and in Paragraph Four (4) of the complaint, and herein; nor of any immediate act of the grantees, including defendants, in said Three (3) deeds, aforesaid, of taking possession of any property, other than described in said three (3) deeds, aforesaid; and the testimony of husband, defendant, was unequivocally that he had no intention of possessing or holding anything other than what the deed called for; and, that there is no showing of any continuous possession by defendants or their immediate predecessors in interest, since the evidence indicates the property was in the nature, for us, as a summer occupancy, and such occupancy and use was for rather limited periods of time during comparatively short portions of the year, and was far from continuous."]

Two issues are presented by this appeal:

(1) Is a claim of adverse possession defeated because the physical use of the premises is restricted to summer occupancy?

(2) May a person who receives record title to tract A under the mistaken belief that he has title to tract B (immediately contiguous to tract A) and who subsequently occupies tract B, for the purpose of establishing title to tract B by adverse possession, use the periods of possession of tract B by his immediate predecessors who also had record title to tract A?

In approaching both of these questions, we point out that the evidence, largely undisputed in any material sense, established that defendant or his immediate predecessors did occupy the premises, which we have called tract B, as though it was their own for far more than the 10 years as prescribed in RCW 4.16.020.

We also point out that finding of fact 6 is not challenged for its factual determinations but for the conclusions contained therein to the effect that the continuity of possession may not be established by summer occupancy, and that a predecessor's possession may not be tacked because a legal "claim of right" did not exist under the circumstances.

We start with the oft-quoted rule that:

[T]o constitute adverse possession, there must be actual possession which is *uninterrupted,* open and notorious, hostile and exclusive, and under a *claim of right* made in good faith for the statutory period.

(Italics ours.) *Butler v. Anderson,* 71 Wash. 2d 60, 64, 426 P.2d 467 (1967). *Also see Fadden v. Purvis,* 77 W.D.2d 22, 459 P.2d 385 (1969) and cases cited therein.

We reject the conclusion that summer occupancy only of a summer beach home destroys the continuity of possession required by the statute. It has become firmly established that the requisite possession requires such possession and dominion "as ordinarily marks the conduct of owners in general, in holding, managing, and caring for property of like nature and condition." *Whalen v. Smith,* 183 Iowa 949, 953, 167 N.W. 646 (1918). *Also see Mesher v. Connolly,* 63 Wash. 2d 552, 388 P.2d 144 (1964); *Skoog v. Seymour,* 29 Wash. 2d 355, 187 P.2d 304 (1947); *Butler v. Anderson, supra; Fadden v. Purvis, supra.*

We hold that occupancy of tract B during the summer months for more than the 10-year period by defendant and his predecessors, together with the continued existence of the improvements on the land and beach area, constituted "uninterrupted" possession within this rule. To hold otherwise is to completely ignore the nature and condition of the property. *See Fadden v. Purvis, supra.*

We find such rule fully consonant with the legal writers on the subject. In F. Clark, Law of Surveying and Boundaries, § 561 (3d ed. 1959) at 565: "Continuity of possession may be established although the land is used regularly for only a certain period each year." Further, at page 566:

This rule [which permits tacking] is one of substance and not of absolute mathematical continuity, provided there is no break so as to sever two possessions. It is not necessary that the occupant should be actually upon the premises continually. If the land is occupied during the period of time during the year it is capable of use, there is sufficient continuity.

We now reach the question of tacking. The precise issue before us is novel in that none of the property occupied by defendant or his predecessors coincided with the property described in their deeds, but was contiguous.

In the typical case, which has been subject to much litigation, the party seeking to establish title by adverse possession claims *more* land than that described in the deed. In such cases it is clear that tacking is permitted.

In *Buchanan v. Cassell,* 53 Wash. 2d 611, 614, 335 P.2d 600 (1959) the Supreme Court stated:

> This state follows the rule that a purchaser may tack the adverse use of its predecessor in interest to that of his own where the land was intended to be included in the deed between them, but was mistakenly omitted from the description. *El Cerrito, Inc. v. Ryndak,* 60 Wash. 2d 847, 376 P.2d 528 (1962).

The general statement which appears in many of the cases is that tacking of adverse possession is permitted if the successive occupants are in "privity." *See Faubion v. Elder,* 49 Wash. 2d 300, 301 P.2d 153 (1956). The deed running between the parties purporting to transfer the land possessed traditionally furnishes the privity of estate which connects the possession of the successive occupants. Plaintiff contends, and the trial court ruled, that where the deed does not describe *any* of the land which was occupied, the actual transfer of possession is insufficient to establish privity.

To assess the cogency of this argument and ruling, we must turn to the historical reasons for requiring privity as a necessary prerequisite to tacking the possession of several occupants. Very few, if any, of the reasons appear in the cases, nor do the cases analyze the relationships that must exist between successive possessors for tacking to be allowed. *See* W. Stoebuck, *The Law of Adverse Possession In Washington* in 35 Wash. L. Rev. 53 (1960).

The requirement of privity had its roots in the notion that a succession of trespasses, even though there was no appreciable interval between them, should not, in equity, be allowed to defeat the record title. The "claim of right," "color of title" requirement of the statutes and cases was probably derived from the early American belief that the squatter should not be able to profit by his trespass.

However, it appears to this court that there is a substantial difference between the squatter or trespasser and the property purchaser, who along with several of his neighbors, as a result of an inaccurate survey or subdivision, occupies and improves property exactly 50 feet to the east of that which a survey some 30 years later demonstrates that they in fact own. It seems to us that there is also a strong public policy favoring early certainty as to the location of land ownership which enters into a proper interpretation of privity.

On the irregular perimeters of Puget Sound exact determination of land locations and boundaries is difficult and expensive. This difficulty is convincingly demonstrated in this case by the problems plaintiff's engineer encountered in attempting to locate the corners. It cannot be expected that every purchaser will or should engage a surveyor to ascertain that the beach home he is purchasing lies within the boundaries described in his deed. Such a practice is neither reasonable nor customary. Of course, 50-foot errors in descriptions are devastating where a group of adjacent owners each hold 50 feet of waterfront property.

The technical requirement of "privity" should not, we think, be used to upset the long periods of occupancy of those who in good faith received an erroneous deed description. Their "claim of right" is no less persuasive than the purchaser who believes he is purchasing *more* land than his deed described.

In the final analysis, however, we believe the requirement of "privity" is no more than judicial recognition of the need for some reasonable connection between successive occupants of real property so as to raise their claim of right above the status of the wrongdoer or the trespasser. We think such reasonable connection exists in this case.

Where, as here, several successive purchasers received record title to tract A under the mistaken belief that they were acquiring tract B, immediately contiguous thereto, and where possession of tract B is transferred and occupied in a continuous manner for more than 10 years by successive occupants, we hold there is sufficient privity of estate to permit tacking and thus establish adverse possession as a matter of law.

We see no reason in law or in equity for differentiating this case from *Faubion v. Elder,* 49 Wash. 2d 300, 301 P.2d 153 (1956) where the appellants were claiming *more* land than their deed described and where successive periods of occupation were allowed to be united to each other to make up the time of adverse holding. … This application of the privity requirement should particularly pertain where the holder of record title to tract B acquired the same with knowledge of the discrepancy.

Judgment is reversed with directions to dismiss plaintiffs' action and to enter a decree quieting defendants' title to the disputed tract of land in accordance with the prayer of their cross complaint.

ARMSTRONG, C.J., and PETRIE, J., concur.

Notes and Questions

1. **Tacking**. If A were to enter and possess Blackacre adversely, and then B were to enter into adverse possession of Blackacre the moment A left, would B be able to tack A's possession to her own in order to reach the required minimum time required by the adverse possession statute? English common law, unlike the U.S., does not require privity for tacking. Why is privity important? In what sense is there privity in *Howard v. Kunto*?

Note that tacking can occur on both sides of the adverse possession issue --- both for the owner and for the adverse possessor.

2. **Relation back.** According to the doctrine of "relation back," once a claimant establishes all the elements for an adverse possession, the adverse possessor is deemed to have been the owner from the very beginning of the adverse possession (that is, from the moment the adverse possessor first entered into adverse possession).

6. Good-Faith Acquirors

A chimney-sweep finds a jewel. He gives it to his friend, a jeweler, who designs and crafts a gold ring around the jewel's unique shape. Frederica van Snoot sees the ring, buys it for $10,000, and wears it around town. One day, Jeremiah Hobnob recognizes the jewel he lost last month and demands it back. As against the chimney-sweep, this is an easy case; nowhere near enough time has passed to satisfy the statute of limitations, even in a jurisdiction that imposes a stringent duty of diligent search on owners. But the jeweler and van Snoot are harder cases, because both of them have made investments. The jeweler invested gold and labor to turn the jewel into a ring. For her part, van Snoot paid out $10,000. If Hobnob is entitled to the jewel, the jeweler or van Snoot or both will end up poorer than when they started.

The general rule for transfers is straightforward. A buyer can receive no better title than the seller had to transfer. If Alice purports to sell Barbara's watch to Clara, Clara receives nothing, because Barbara had nothing to sell. The Latin name for this doctrine is *nemo dat quod non habet*—literally, one cannot give what one does not have.

The common law mitigated the harshness of this result with several doctrines. One is the rule of *accession*, which we will see shortly. One version of accession provided that someone who sufficiently improves another person's property is allowed to keep it. Importantly, the hornbook version of this rule is that accession only operates in favor of *good-faith* improvers; someone who knows the property is not hers acts at her own peril when she combines it with her own property or labor. The jeweler in the example opening this chapter is potentially protected by accession.

A more important doctrine for protecting innocent third parties granted *good faith purchasers for value* the ability to gain good title, protected from the unknown claims of third parties. Like accession, the doctrine—in some contexts known as the *market overt* rule—only protects only parties who act in good faith, i.e., those who do not know or have reason to know they are buying property with clouded title. Frederica van Snoot may be just such a purchaser.

This section presents these two doctrines. As you read, pay close attention to the preconditions that allow them to be invoked; despite their similarities, they have important differences. For example, it is hornbook law that "a thief takes no title and can give none": good-faith purchase can never cut off the claims of an owner from whom the property was stolen. But accession can, as you will see. Also, observe that while ownership of the property may be the primary question in these cases, it is often not the only issue. Once ownership is allocated, courts often require restitutionary payments to shift losses from more innocent to more culpable parties.

A. Accession

Wetherbee v. Green
22 Mich. 311 (1871)

This was an action of replevin, brought by George Green, Charles H. Camp and George Brooks, in the circuit court for the county of Bay, against George Wetherbee, for one hundred and fifty-eight thousand black ash barrel-hoops, alleged to be of the value of eight hundred dollars. …

COOLEY J.:

The defendants in error replevied of Wetherbee a quantity of hoops, which he had made from timber cut upon their land. Wetherbee defended the replevin suit on two grounds. First, he claimed to have cut the timber under a license from one Sumner, who was formerly tenant in common of the land with Green, and had been authorized by Green to give such license. [This defense failed; Sumner was not authorized to let Wetherbee cut timber on the land.]

But if the court should be against him on this branch of the case, Wetherbee claimed further that replevin could not be maintained for the hoops, because he had cut the timber in good faith, relying upon a permission which he supposed proceeded from the parties having lawful right to give it, and had, by the expenditure of his labor and money, converted the trees into chattels immensely more valuable than they were as they stood in the forest, and thereby he had made such chattels his own. And he offered to show that the standing timber was worth twenty-five dollars only, while the hoops replevied were shown by the evidence to be worth near seven hundred dollars; also [facts tending to show Wetherbee's lack of knowledge of Sumner's duplicity]. The evidence offered to establish these facts was rejected by the court, and the plaintiffs obtained judgment.

The principal question which, from this statement, appears to be presented by the record, may be stated thus: Has a party who has taken the property of another in good faith, and in reliance upon a supposed right, without intention to commit wrong, and by the expenditure of his money or labor, worked upon it so great a transformation as that which this timber underwent in being transformed from standing trees into hoops, acquired such a property therein that it cannot be followed into his hands and reclaimed by the owner of the trees in its improved condition?

The objections to allowing the owner of the trees to reclaim the property under such circumstances are, that it visits the involuntary wrong-doer too severely for his unintentional trespass, and at the same time compensates the owner beyond all reason for the injury he has sustained. In the redress of private injuries the law aims not so much to punish the wrongdoer as to compensate the sufferer for his injuries; and the cases in which it goes farther and inflicts punitory or vindictive penalties are those in which the wrong-doer has committed the wrong recklessly, willfully, or maliciously, and under circumstances presenting elements of aggravation. Where vicious motive or reckless disregard of right are not involved, to inflict upon a person who has taken the property of another, a penalty equal to twenty or thirty times its value, and to compensate the owner in a proportion equally enormous, is so opposed to all legal idea of justice and right and to the rules which regulate the recovery of damages generally, that if permitted by the law at all, it must stand out as an anomaly and must rest upon peculiar reasons.

As a general rule, one whose property has been appropriated by another without authority has a right to follow it and recover the possession from any one who may have received it; and if, in the mean time, it has been increased in value by the addition of labor or money, the owner may, nevertheless, reclaim it, provided there has been no destruction of substantial identity. So far the authorities are agreed. A man cannot generally be deprived of his property except by his own voluntary act or by operation of law; and if unauthorized parties have bestowed expense or labor upon it, that fact cannot constitute a bar to his reclaiming it, so long as identification is not impracticable. But there must, nevertheless, in reason be some limit to the right to follow and reclaim materials which have undergone a process of manufacture. Mr. Justice Blackstone lays down the rule very broadly, that if a thing is changed into a different species, as by making wine out of another's grapes, oil from his olives, or bread from his wheat, the product belongs to the new operator, who is only to make satisfaction to the former proprietor for the materials converted: 2 Bl. Com., 404. We do not understand this to be disputed as a general proposition, though there are some authorities which hold that, in the case of a willful appropriation, no extent of conversion can give to the willful trespasser a title to the property so long as the original materials can be traced in the improved article. The distinction thus made between the case of an appropriation in good faith and one based on intentional wrong, appears to have come from the civil law, which would not suffer a party to acquire a title by accession, founded on his own act, unless he had taken the materials in ignorance of the true owner, and given them a form which precluded their being restored to their original condition: 2 Kent, 363. While many cases have followed the rule as broadly stated by Blackstone, others have adopted the severe rule of the civil law where the conversion was in willful disregard of right. The New York cases of *Betts v. Lee*, 5 Johns., 348; *Curtis v. Groat*, 6 Johns., 168, and *Chandler v. Edson*, 9 Johns., 362, were all cases where the willful trespasser was held to have acquired no property by a very radical conversion, and in *Silsbury v. McCoon*, 3 N. Y., 378, 385, the whole subject is very fully examined … . [In *Silsbury*, a thief who turned the plaintiff's corn into whiskey did not thereby acquire ownership of it.] But we are not called upon in this case to express any opinion regarding the rule applicable in the case of a willful trespasser, since the authorities agree in holding that, when the wrong had been involuntary, the owner of the original materials is precluded, by the civil law and common law alike, from following and reclaiming the property after it has undergone a transformation which converts it into an article substantially different.

The cases of confusion of goods are closely analogous. It has always been held that he who, without fraud, intentional wrong, or reckless disregard of the rights of others, mingled his goods with those of another person, in such manner that they could not be distinguished, should, nevertheless, be protected in his ownership so far as the circumstances would permit. The question of motive here becomes of the highest importance; for, as Chancellor Kent says, if the commingling of property "was willfully made without mutual consent, * * the common law gave the entire property, without any account, to him whose property was originally invaded, and its distinct character destroyed: Popham's Rep. 38, Pl. 2. If A will willfully intermix his corn or hay with that of B, or casts his gold into another's crucible, so that it becomes impossible to distinguish what belonged to A from what belonged to B, the whole belongs to B. But this rule only applies to wrongful or fraudulent intermixtures. There may be an intentional intermingling, and yet no wrong intended, as where a man mixes two parcels together, supposing both to be his own; or, that he was about to mingle his with his neighbor's, by agreement, and mistakes the parcel. In such cases, which may be deemed accidental intermixtures, it would be unreasonable and unjust that he should lose his own or be obliged to take and pay for his neighbor's, as he would have been under the civil law: In many cases there will be difficulty in determining precisely how he can be protected with due regard to the rights of the other party; but it is clear that the law will not forfeit his property in consequence of the accident or inadvertence, unless a just measure of redress to the other party renders it inevitable.

The important question on this branch of the case appears to us to be, whether standing trees, when cut and manufactured into hoops, are to be regarded as so far changed in character that their identity can be said to be destroyed within the meaning of the authorities. And as we enter upon a discussion of this question, it is evident at once that it is difficult, if not impossible, to discover any invariable and satisfactory test which can be applied to all the cases which arise in such infinite variety. "If grain be taken and made into malt, or money taken and made into a cup, or timber taken and made into a house, it is held in the old English law that the property is so altered as to change the title:" 2 Kent, 363. But cloth made into garments, leather into shoes, trees hewn or sawed into timber, and iron made into bars, it is said may be reclaimed by the owner in their new and original shape: Some of the cases place the right of the former owner to take the thing in its altered condition upon the question whether its identity could be made out by the senses. But this is obviously a very unsatisfactory test, and in many cases would wholly defeat the purpose which the law has in view in recognizing a change of title in any of these cases. That purpose is not to establish any arbitrary distinctions, based upon mere physical reasons, but to adjust the redress afforded to the one party and the penalty inflicted upon the other, as near as circumstances will permit, to the rules of substantial justice[.]

It may often happen that no difficulty will be experienced in determining the identity of a piece of timber which has been taken and built into a house; but no one disputes that the right of the original owner is gone in such a case. A particular piece of wood might, perhaps, be traced without trouble into a church organ, or other equally valuable article; but no one would defend a rule of law which, because the identity could be determined by the senses, would permit the owner of the wood to appropriate a musical instrument, a hundred or a thousand times the value of his original materials, when the party who, under like circumstances, has doubled the value of another man's corn by converting it into malt, is permitted to retain it, and held liable for the original value only. Such distinctions in the law would be without reason, and could not be tolerated. When the right to the improved article is the point in issue, the question, how much the property or labor of each has contributed to make it what it is, must always be one of first importance. The owner of a beam built into the house of another loses his property in it, because the beam is insignificant in value or importance as compared to that to which it has become attached, and the musical instrument belongs to the maker rather than to the man whose timber was used in making it--not because the timber cannot be identified, but because, in bringing it to its present condition the value of the labor has swallowed up and rendered insignificant the value of the original materials. The labor, in the case of the musical instrument, is just as much the principal thing as the house is in the other case instanced; the timber appropriated is in each case comparatively unimportant.

No test which satisfies the reason of the law can be applied in the adjustment of questions of title to chattels by accession, unless it keeps in view the circumstance of relative values. When we bear in mind the fact that what the law aims at is the accomplishment of substantial equity, we shall readily perceive that the fact of the value of the materials having been increased a hundred-fold, is of more importance in the adjustment than any chemical change or mechanical transformation, which, however radical, neither is expensive to the party making it, nor adds materially to the value. There may be complete changes with so little improvement in value, that there could be no hardship in giving the owner of the original materials the improved article; but in the present case, where the defendant's labor--if he shall succeed in sustaining his offer of testimony – will appear to have given the timber in its present condition nearly all its value, all the grounds of equity exist which influence the courts in recognizing a change of title under any circumstances.

We are of opinion that the court erred in rejecting the testimony offered. The defendant, we think, had a right to show that he had manufactured the hoops in good faith, and in the belief that he had the proper authority to do so; and if he should succeed in making that showing, he was entitled to have the jury instructed that the title to the timber was changed by a substantial change of identity, and that the remedy of the plaintiff was an action to recover damages for the unintentional trespass. …

Questions

1. What factors matter most to the court's holding? Is this a case about the relative value contributed by the plaintiff and defendant, about the difficulty of identifying the plaintiff's original property, about the difficulty of separating it, or about the degree to which it has been physically altered? Consider *Atlas Assurance Co. v. Gibbs*, 183 A. 690 (Conn. 1936), which involved the engine from a damaged car (the Hibben car) that had been properly sold and the body of a car (the Sherline car) that had been stolen. The defendant's predecessor in title combined the two to make one working car. In an action for replevin by the assignee of title to the Sherline car, who should get what?

2. How important is Wetherbee's good faith? What if he had been told by Green that Sumner lacked authority, but had examined Sumner's title in some detail and concluded that Green was wrong? What if Wetherbee steals a set of paints and uses it to create a portrait that sells for $500,000?

3. Note that Green retains "an action to recover damages for the unintentional trespass." What is the measure of those damages? Given that Weatherbee owns the hoops via accession, why does he need to pay? Or, to look at it another way, why *doesn't* an adverse possessor need to pay for the value of the property he retains after the statute of limitations has run?

4. Sometimes property transforms itself. A cow from Farmer Jones's herd wanders onto Farmer Smith's land, where it is impregnated by Farmer Smith's bull. Who owns the calf? Does it matter where the cow gives birth? Felix Cohen, in *Dialogue on Private Property*, 9 RUTGERS L. REV. 357 (1954), claimed that every legal system in human history appears to have resolved these cases in the same way. Compare the case in which Farmer Smith's bull kicks Farmer Jones's cow and badly injures it. What result then?

5. Another theme in confusion cases involves the distinction between unique and fungible property. If I mistakenly pour your 55-gallon drum of water into my storage tank, you are entitled to draw 55 gallons of water from the tank, even though it is astoundingly improbable that you will get back the same water molecules you started with. Water is water. If I mistakenly mix your your bottle of 1967 Chateau de Snoot wine with my bottle of 2015 Rotgut Red, I can't give you a bottle of the resulting mixture and call it even. (What *are* you entitled to?)

   But note that uniqueness is something courts create as well as discover. At the start of the 19th century, wheat and other grains were stored and sold as though they were unique goods; each farmer's and merchant's sacks of grain were treated as distinct from each other farmer's and merchant's. Today, grains have been standardized and are sold as a commodity without regard to the particular farmer or merchant: a merchant could order 100 bushels of U.S. No. 1 Hard Red Spring Wheat without needing to specify or worry about what particular farms it came from. A key to this shift was courts' willingness to treat grain (and many other agricultural commodities) as fungible. A merchant whose sacks of wheat were dumped into a grain elevator without his consent would be entitled to the same quantity of wheat of the same standard class, not to his specific sacks or even to wheat with the same more specific characteristics. What was gained and what was lost in this shift?

Uniform Commercial Code

§ 2-312. Warranty of title …

(1) Subject to subsection (2) there is in a contract for sale a warranty by the seller that

(a) The title conveyed shall be good, and its transfer rightful; and

(b) The goods shall be delivered free from any security interest or other lien or encumbrance of which the buyer at the time of contracting has no knowledge.

(2) A warranty under subsection (1) will be excluded or modified only by specific language or by circumstances which give the buyer reason to know that the person selling does not claim title in himself or that he is purporting to sell only such right or title as he or a third person may have. …

§ 2-403. Power to transfer; good faith purchase of goods; "entrusting"

(1) A purchaser of goods acquires all title which his transferor had or had power to transfer except that a purchaser of a limited interest acquires rights only to the extent of the interest purchased. A person with voidable title has power to transfer a good title to a good faith purchaser for value. When goods have been delivered under a transaction of purchase the purchaser has such power even though

(a) The transferor was deceived as to the identity of the purchaser, or

(b) The delivery was in exchange for a check which is later dishonored, or

(c) It was agreed that the transaction was to be a "cash sale," or

(d) The delivery was procured through fraud punishable as larcenous under the criminal law.

(2) Any entrusting of possession of goods to a merchant who deals in goods of that kind gives him power to transfer all rights of the entruster to a buyer in ordinary course of business.

(3) "Entrusting" includes any delivery and any acquiescence in retention of possession regardless of any condition expressed between the parties to the delivery or acquiescence and regardless of whether the procurement of the entrusting or the possessor's disposition of the goods have been such as to be larcenous under the criminal law.

Questions

1. What do these two provisions have to do with each other? *Hint*: think about circumstances in which the warranty of § 2-312 would be violated and consider whether § 2-403 comes into play, and vice-versa.

Kotis v. Nowlin Jewelry, Inc.

844 S.W.2d 920 (1992)

DRAUGHN, Justice.

Eddie Kotis appeals from a judgment declaring appellee, Nowlin Jewelry, Inc., the sole owner of a Rolex watch, and awarding appellee attorney's fees. Kotis raises fourteen points of error. We affirm.

On June 11, 1990, Steve Sitton acquired a gold ladies Rolex watch, President model, with a diamond bezel from Nowlin Jewelry by forging a check belonging to his brother and misrepresenting to Nowlin that he had his brother's authorization for the purchase. The purchase price of the watch, and the amount of the forged check, was $9,438.50. The next day, Sitton telephoned Eddie Kotis, the owner of a used car dealership, and asked Kotis if he was interested in buying a Rolex watch. Kotis indicated interest and Sitton came to the car lot[.] Kotis purchased the watch for $3,550.00. Kotis also called Nowlin's Jewelry that same day and spoke with Cherie Nowlin.

Ms. Nowlin told Kotis that Sitton had purchased the watch the day before. Ms. Nowlin testified that Kotis would not immediately identify himself. Because she did not have the payment information available, Ms. Nowlin asked if she could call him back. Kotis then gave his name and number. Ms. Nowlin testified that she called Kotis and told him the amount of the check and that it had not yet cleared. Kotis told Ms. Nowlin that he did not have the watch and that he did not want the watch. Ms. Nowlin also testified that Kotis would not tell her how much Sitton was asking for the watch.

John Nowlin, the president of Nowlin's Jewelry, testified that, after this call from Kotis, Nowlin's bookkeeper began attempting to confirm whether the check had cleared. When they learned the check would not be honored by the bank, Nowlin called Kotis, but Kotis refused to talk to Nowlin. Kotis referred Nowlin to his attorney. On June 25, 1990, Kotis' attorney called Nowlin and suggested that Nowlin hire an attorney and allegedly indicated that Nowlin could buy the watch back from Kotis. Nowlin refused to repurchase the watch.

After Sitton was indicted for forgery and theft, the district court ordered Nowlin's Jewelry to hold the watch until there was an adjudication of the ownership of the watch. Nowlin then filed suit seeking a declaratory judgment that Nowlin was the sole owner of the watch. Kotis filed a counterclaim for a declaration that Kotis was a good faith purchaser of the watch and was entitled to possession and title of the watch. After a bench trial, the trial court rendered judgment declaring Nowlin the sole owner of the watch. The trial court also filed Findings of Fact and Conclusions of Law.

In point of error one, Kotis claims the trial court erred in concluding that Sitton did not receive the watch through a transaction of purchase with Nowlin, within the meaning of Tex.Bus. & Com.Code Ann. § 2.403(a). Where a party challenges a trial court's conclusions of law, we may sustain the judgment on any legal theory supported by the evidence. Incorrect conclusions of law will not require reversal if the controlling findings of facts will support a correct legal theory.

Kotis contends there is evidence that the watch is a "good" under the UCC, there was a voluntary transfer of the watch, and there was physical delivery of the watch. Thus, Kotis maintains that the transaction between Sitton and Nowlin was a transaction of purchase such that Sitton acquired the ability to transfer good title to a good faith purchaser under § 2.403 [which was identical in relevant part to the UCC excerpt quoted above]. …

Neither the code nor case law defines the phrase "transaction of purchase." "Purchase" is defined by the code as a "taking by sale, discount, negotiation, mortgage, pledge, lien, issue or reissue, gift or any other voluntary transaction creating an interest in property." Tex. Bus. & Com. Code Ann. § 1.201(32) (Vernon 1968). Thus, only voluntary transactions can constitute transactions of purchase.

Having found no Texas case law concerning what constitutes a transaction of purchase under § 2.403(a), we have looked to case law from other states. Based on the code definition of a purchase as a voluntary transaction, these cases reason that a thief who wrongfully takes the goods against the will of the owner is not a purchaser. *See Suburban Motors, Inc. v. State Farm Mut. Automobile Ins. Co.*, 268 Cal. Rptr. 16, 18 (Cal. Ct. App. 1990); *Charles Evans BMW, Inc. v. Williams* 395 S.E.2d 650, 651-52 (Ga. Ct. App. 1990); *Inmi-Etti v. Aluisi*, 492 A.2d 917 (Md. Ct. App. 1985). On the other hand, a swindler who fraudulently induces the victim to deliver the goods voluntarily is a purchaser under the code.

In this case, Nowlin's Jewelry voluntarily delivered the watch to Sitton in return for payment by check that was later discovered to be forged. Sitton did not obtain the watch against the will of the owner. Rather, Sitton fraudulently induced Nowlin's Jewelry to deliver the watch voluntarily. Thus, we agree with appellant that the trial court erred in concluding that Sitton did not receive the watch through a transaction of purchase under § 2.403(a). We sustain point of error one.

In point of error two, Kotis contends the trial court erred in concluding that, at the time Sitton sold the watch to Kotis, Sitton did not have at least voidable title to the watch. In point of error nine, Kotis challenges the trial court's conclusion that Nowlin's Jewelry had legal and equitable title at all times relevant to the lawsuit. The lack of Texas case law addressing such issues under the code again requires us to look to case law from other states to assist in our analysis.

In *Suburban Motors, Inc. v. State Farm Mut. Automobile Ins. Co.*, the California court noted that § 2.403 provides for the creation of voidable title where there is a voluntary transfer of goods. Section 2.403(a)(1)-(4) set forth the types of voluntary transactions that can give the purchaser voidable title. Where goods are stolen such that there is no voluntary transfer, only void title results. Subsection (4) provides that a purchaser can obtain voidable title to the goods even if "delivery was procured through fraud punishable as larcenous under the criminal law." This subsection applies to cases involving acts fraudulent to the seller such as where the seller delivers the goods in return for a forged check. Although Sitton paid Nowlin's Jewelry with a forged check, he obtained possession of the watch through a voluntary transaction of purchase and received voidable, rather than void, title to the watch. Thus, the trial court erred in concluding that Sitton received no title to the watch and in concluding that Nowlin's retained title at all relevant times. We sustain points of error two and nine.

In point of error three, Kotis claims the trial court erred in concluding that Kotis did not give sufficient value for the watch to receive protection under § 2.403, that Kotis did not take good title to the watch as a good faith purchaser, that Kotis did not receive good title to the watch, and that Kotis is not entitled to the watch under § 2.403. In points of error four through eight, Kotis challenges the trial court's findings regarding his good faith, his honesty in fact, and his actual belief, and the reasonableness of the belief, that the watch had been received unlawfully.

Under § 2.403(a), a transferor with voidable title can transfer good title to a good faith purchaser. Good faith means "honesty in fact in the conduct or transaction concerned." Tex.Bus. & Com. Code Ann. § 1.201(19) (Vernon 1968). The test for good faith is the actual belief of the party and not the reasonableness of that belief. *La Sara Grain v. First Nat'l Bank*, 673 S.W.2d 558, 563 (Tex.1984).

Kotis was a dealer in used cars and testified that he had bought several cars from Sitton in the past and had no reason not to trust Sitton. He also testified that on June 12, 1990, Sitton called and asked Kotis if he was interested in buying a Ladies Rolex. Once Kotis indicated his interest in the watch, Sitton came to Kotis's place of business. According to Kotis, Sitton said that he had received $18,000.00 upon the sale of his house and that he had used this to purchase the watch for his girlfriend several months before. Kotis paid $3,550.00 for the watch. Kotis further testified that he then spoke to a friend, Gary Neal Martin, who also knew Sitton. Martin sagely advised Kotis to contact Nowlin's to check whether Sitton had financed the watch. Kotis testified that he called Nowlin's after buying the watch.

Cherie Nowlin testified that she received a phone call from Kotis on June 12, 1990, although Kotis did not immediately identify himself. Kotis asked if Nowlin's had sold a gold President model Rolex watch with a diamond bezel about a month before. When asked, Kotis told Ms. Nowlin that Sitton had come to Kotis' car lot and was trying to sell the watch. Ms. Nowlin testified that Kotis told her he did not want the watch because he already owned a Rolex. Ms. Nowlin told Kotis that Sitton had purchased the watch the day before. Kotis asked about the method of payment. Because Ms. Nowlin did not know, she agreed to check and call Kotis back. She called Kotis back and advised him that Sitton had paid for the watch with a check that had not yet cleared. When Ms. Nowlin asked if Kotis had the watch, Kotis said no and would not tell her how much Sitton was asking for the watch. Ms. Nowlin did advise Kotis of the amount of the check.

After these calls, the owner of Nowlin's asked his bookkeeper to call the bank regarding Sitton's check. They learned on June 15, 1990 that the check would be dishonored. John Nowlin called Kotis the next day and advised him about the dishonored check. Kotis refused to talk to Nowlin and told Nowlin to contact his attorney. Nowlin also testified that a reasonable amount to pay for a Ladies President Rolex watch with a diamond bezel in mint condition was $7,000.00-$8,000.00. Nowlin maintained that $3,500.00 was an exorbitantly low price for a watch like this.

The trier of fact is the sole judge of the credibility of the witnesses and the weight to be given their testimony. Kotis testified that he lied when he spoke with Cherie Nowlin and that he had already purchased the watch before he learned that Sitton's story was false. The judge, as the trier of fact, may not have believed Kotis when he said that he had already purchased the watch. If the judge disbelieved this part of Kotis' testimony, other facts tend to show that Kotis did not believe the transaction was lawful. For example, when Kotis spoke with Nowlin's, he initially refused to identify himself, he said that he did not have the watch and that he did not want the watch, he refused to divulge Sitton's asking price, and he later refused to talk with Nowlin and advised Nowlin to contact Kotis' attorney. Thus, there is evidence supporting the trial court's finding that Kotis did not act in good faith.

There are sufficient facts to uphold the trial court's findings even if the judge had accepted as true Kotis' testimony that, despite his statements to Nowlin's, he had already purchased the watch when he called Nowlin's. The testimony indicated that Kotis was familiar with the price of Rolex watches and that $3,550.00 was an extremely low price for a mint condition watch of this type. An unreasonably low price is evidence the buyer knows the goods are stolen. Although the test is what Kotis actually believed, we agree with appellee that we need not let this standard sanction willful disregard of suspicious facts that would lead a reasonable person to believe the transaction was unlawful. Thus, we find sufficient evidence to uphold the trial court's findings regarding Kotis' lack of status as a good faith purchaser. We overrule points of error three through eight. …

We affirm the trial court's judgment.

Notes and Questions

1. As noted, the common-law baseline is *nemo dat quod non habet*: no man can give what he does not have. If I "give" you a car I don't own, you don't own it either. If I sell you a tract of land encumbered by a mortgage and an easement, you receive only as much as I owned, so you take the land subject to the mortgage and the easement. This *nemo dat* baseline is the source of the maxim that a thief cannot give good title. So if Sitton had held up Nowlin's at gunpoint, how would the case have come out, and on what reasoning?

   § 2-403(1), as applied in *Kotis*, distinguishes the thief's "void" title from merely "voidable" title: the quality of title obtained by the buyer in a transaction that is for some reason defective. If the seller in that defective transaction discovers the problem, she has a right to unwind the transaction (and get her stuff back). But until she does, the buyer has the power to convey not just his own, voidable title, but something even better. A good-faith purchaser for value receives good title, *even as against the original seller*. Her right to unwind the transaction has been cut off. This is a harsh way to treat an innocent victim of fraud or mistake. Why would property law do something like that?

2. How did the parties get into this mess? Obviously Sitton is most to blame, but is there anything Kotis or Nowlin could have done? Who is left holding the bag and why? Is there anything Kotis can do to recover his $3,550.00?

3. § 2-403 provides for two tests that the buyer must meet to be protected (in addition to the threshold question of whether his seller had voidable title): he must act in good faith and he must give "value." Which of these tripped up Kotis? And what is the reason for not protecting donees along with buyers?

Note on Negotiability

Another version of the good-faith purchaser doctrine developed in the law of intangible property called "negotiable instruments." In the centuries before the development of good national and international banking systems, merchants commonly did business by passing around various promises or instructions to pay. So, for example, Abel might buy a cartload of barrels of wine from Baker on March 1 by giving Baker a signed promise to pay £200 on June 1. Baker could in theory sit on this *promissory note* until June 1 and then demand payment from Abel. But instead, Baker was more likely to use the note to pay his own debts: he might, for example, give it to Crumleigh on April 1 to buy a gold chain. Baker would sign, or *indorse*, the note, making Crumleigh an assignee of Baker's right to collect from Abel, so that come June 1, Crumleigh could present the note to Abel and demand payment. Of course, there was no need to stop there: Crumleigh could indorse the note over to Daniels, and so on. In such a way, credit became a kind of currency, with the note (collecting indorsements as it went) functioning as a token to indicate who currently held the right to collect when the debt came due on June 1.

Another kind of signed promise, the *bill of exchange*, functioned similarly. The difference was where Abel's note was a promise by Abel to pay, a bill of exchange would be an instruction from Abel to a third party to pay. Perhaps the bill would be "drawn on" Abel's business partner Absalom, or perhaps more usefully it would be drawn on another merchant who had agreed to extend Abel credit or make payments against amounts Abel had deposited with him. If this sounds a bit like banking, it is not a coincidence; the modern check is a direct descendent of the medieval bill of exchange.

Now back to our story. Suppose that Abel discovers that the wine Baker sold him was rotten, good only as vinegar. Abel chases down Baker, only to learn that Baker has already indorsed the note over to Crumleigh, who has already done the same to Daniels. Come June 1, Daniels demands payment, but Abel refuses, pointing to the worthless vinegar. Baker didn't hold up his side of the deal; why should Abel have to do the same? In *Miller v Race*, (1758) 97 Eng. Rep. 398 (K.B.), the great commercial jurist Lord Mansfield gave an answer:

> After stating the case at large, he declared that at the trial, he had no sort of doubt, but this action was well brought, and would lie against the defendant in the present case; upon the general course of business, and from the consequences to trade and commerce: which would be much incommoded by a contrary determination. … A bank-note is constantly and universally, both at home and abroad, treated as money, as cash; and paid and received, as cash; and it is necessary, for the purposes of commerce, that their currency should be established and secured.

The point is that if Daniels needs to check the details of the Abel-Baker transaction – including inspecting the wine – to determine whether he will be paid on Abel's note, he will refuse. He doesn't know Abel; he doesn't even know Baker. The doctrine of *Miller v. Race* is a good-faith-purchaser doctrine for negotiable instruments; it lets Daniels rely on the note itself, rather than inspecting the details over the underlying transaction. That in turn lets the note circulate as money, enabling other transactions that otherwise would have frozen up for lack of financing.

The doctrine of negotiability – "negotiation" being the act of assigning the promise to pay from one recipient to another, typically by indorsing the note and/or physically handing it over – took root in the United States. Indeed, *Swift v. Tyson* – famous for being the case overruled in *Erie Railroad Co. v. Tompkins*, 304 U.S. 64, 78 (1938) ("There is no federal general common law.") – was a case about negotiability. Norton and Keith convinced Tyson to sign a bill of exchange for $540.30, made payable to Norton, who then negotiated it to Swift to pay off a preexisting debt. But when Swift demanded payment from Tyson, Tyson replied that he had given it to Norton and Keith "as part consideration for the purchase of certain lands in the state of Maine, which Norton and Keith represented themselves to be the owners of" but were not. The case turned on whether Swift was a "bona fide holder for a valuable consideration, without notice," in which case he was entitled to collect from Tyson regardless of the land fraud Norton and Keith had perpetrated on Tyson. The only issue there was whether cancellation of the preexisting debt to Swift meant that Swift had given "valuable consideration" for the note, and again Justice Story's reasoning was pragmatic:

> And we have no hesitation in saying, that a pre-existing debt does constitute a valuable consideration in the sense of the general rule already stated, as applicable to negotiable instruments. … It is for the benefit and convenience of the commercial world to give as wide an extent as practicable to the credit and circulation of negotiable paper, that it may pass not only as security for new purchases and advances, made upon the transfer thereof, but also in payment of and as security for pre-existing debts. … But establish the opposite conclusion, that negotiable paper cannot be applied in payment of or as security for pre-existing debts, without letting in all the equities between the original and antecedent parties, and the value and circulation of such securities must be essentially diminished, and the debtor driven to the embarrassment of making a sale thereof, often at a ruinous discount, to some third person, and then by circuity to apply the proceeds to the payment of his debts. … Probably more than one-half of all bank transactions in our country, as well as those of other countries, are of this nature. The doctrine would strike a fatal blow at all discounts of negotiable securities for pre-existing debts.

Today, negotiability shows up in many areas of commercial law. One good illustration comes from Article 3 of the Uniform Commercial Code. A person is a "holder in due course" of a negotiable instrument (and here, think "check" or "promissory note") if

(1) The instrument when issued or negotiated to the holder does not bear such apparent evidence of forgery or alteration or is not otherwise so irregular or incomplete as to call into question its authenticity; and

(2) The holder took the instrument (i) for value, (ii) in good faith, (iii) without notice that the instrument is overdue or has been dishonored or that there is an uncured default with respect to payment of another instrument issued as part of the same series, (iv) without notice that the instrument contains an unauthorized signature or has been altered, (v) without notice of any claim to the instrument [either to recover the instrument after a theft or to rescind the transaction in which it was transferred], and (vi) without notice that any party has a defense or claim in recoupment ...

UCC § 3-302(a). That's a long list of circumstances, but they're what you'd expect. In addition to the usual requirement that the holder in due course give value (and hence have a reliance interest in being paid), these are all issues that either affect the authenticity of the instrument itself (paragraph (1)) or go to the the holder's notice that something sketchy is afoot. But if a person qualifies as a holder in due course, she receives extensive protections:

(a) Except as stated in subsection (b), the right to enforce the obligation of a party to pay an instrument is subject to the following:

(1) A defense of the obligor based on (i) infancy of the obligor to the extent it is a defense to a simple contract, (ii) duress, lack of legal capacity, or illegality of the transaction which, under other law, nullifies the obligation of the obligor, (iii) fraud that induced the obligor to sign the instrument with neither knowledge nor reasonable opportunity to learn of its character or its essential terms, or (iv) discharge of the obligor in insolvency proceedings;

(2) A defense of the obligor stated in another section of this title or a defense of the obligor that would be available if the person entitled to enforce the instrument were enforcing a right to payment under a simple contract; and

(3) A claim in recoupment of the obligor against the original payee of the instrument ...

(b) The right of a holder in due course to enforce the obligation of a party to pay the instrument is subject to defenses of the obligor stated in subsection (a)(1), but is not subject to defenses of the obligor stated in subsection (a)(2) or claims in recoupment stated in subsection (a)(3) against a person other than the holder.

UCC § 3-305. Notice the difference between the unconditional defenses in (a)(1) and the "personal" defenses in (a)(2) and (a)(3). Only a few of the contract defenses – infancy, incapacity, fraud in the factum, and bankruptcy – are available against a holder in due course. Something like Baker's delivery of spoiled wine, even though it would give Abel a right to refuse payment against Baker, will not be effective against a holder in due course like Daniels. The effect is to turn a promise to pay into something stronger. It is freely transferrable and it is no longer subject to the individual defenses of the original promisor. In other words, assignability plus negotiability turn an *in personam* contract right into something that looks much more like an *in rem* property right. (Does this remind you at all of how the courts turned unique things into fungible commodities in note 5 after *Wetherbee*? It should.)

Negotiability is a powerful doctrine, and it can be a dangerous one. It can be hard on promisors, particularly when they are the victims of fraud that doesn't appear on the face of the negotiable instrument itself. In particular, negotiability can be highly dangerous for consumers. If the promissory notes for their debts have been sold by the initial creditor to another financial institution, that institution may be able to collect on the debt even if the initial transaction was fraudulent, unconscionable, or even criminal. For that reason, the Federal Trade Commission's Holder in Due Course Rule, 16 C.F.R. pt. 433, requires consumer credit contracts to include language specifically disclaiming negotiability. But the rule does not apply to mortgage loans, *see, e.g.*, Johnson v. Long Beach Mortg. Loan Trust 2001-4, 451 F. Supp. 2d 16, 54-55 (D.D.C. 2006). We will see some of the mischief and misdeeds that resulted from the serial negotiation of residential mortgages in the section on the mortgage crisis. For a sustained argument that the doctrine of negotiability has long outlived its original purpose and does more harm than good in an age of robust financial infrastructure, see JAMES STEVEN ROGERS: THE END OF NEGOTIABLE INSTRUMENTS: BRINGING PAYMENT SYSTEMS LAW OUT OF THE PAST (2011).

7. Gifts

Rules about transferring property are created by law. There are only certain ways people can rearrange property relations. Some rearrangements happen even if the people involved don't want them, and some don't happen even if the people involved do want them. Knowing the rules is a way to understand which transfers work and why.

There are several methods of transferring property. The key voluntary methods are gifts, sales, and transfers at death, which can be divided into transfers by will (also known as transfer by devise) and transfers by operation of law because of the decedent's intestacy (dying without a will). Although most litigated transfers involve sales, it is useful to study gifts in order to appreciate the significance of possession to ownership. Relatedly, gift law highlights that some problems in contract law arise only out of *executory* promises: completed promises involving property will often be valid as gifts, even if they lacked consideration. Gift law also provides an introduction to methods of transferring land, particularly transfers by deed and transfers by will.

In order for a valid gift to occur, three elements must be present: (1) the donor must *intend* to give the property as a gift; (2) the donor must *deliver* the property to the donee; and (3) the donee must *accept* the gift. We won't spend much time on the third element, because when the property has some value, acceptance will generally be presumed in the absence of an explicit rejection.

Unlike a sale or a contract, a gift does not require consideration. This leads to concerns that often shape judicial doctrine. First, without tangible consideration, we need to keep people from lying about what was given to them. Because gift issues often arise after the alleged donor died, courts have been concerned to protect the donor's heirs from having the donor's estate stripped by people who claim to be donees.

Second and relatedly, we desire to protect the system of written wills and to encourage its use. A standard will must be signed and witnessed. A system that easily allows pre-mortem gifts might undermine people's incentives to take the time to write a will – they might think they can always just give their property away when death approaches – and also harm the legitimate expectations of those who are named in a will. If the person who writes a will, known as the testator, identifies specific property in her will, but sells it or gives it away before she dies, the devise in the will is nullified; it's no longer her property to give away when she dies. Although people named as devisees in a will have no *legal* rights to the property before the testator dies, they might nonetheless have practically and morally compelling expectations – especially if we worry about the people surrounding a dying person exercising undue influence and extracting gifts that the dying person wouldn't give if she were thinking more clearly. Thus, by making it more difficult to give gifts, we may protect the overall system of property transfers. This concern can lead courts to find that no gift has been made even when the would-be donor very clearly wanted to give the property away. Consider as you read whether this overall structural concern is justified.

A. Intent

Although laypeople may not be aware of this distinction, there is a huge legal difference between "I will give you this car when you graduate" and "I now give you this car." (In the next section we will investigate a third variant, in which the gift is of a future interest.) "I will give you this car" is a mere promise with no legal force. No matter how serious the speaker's intent is, it is not an intent to make a present gift, and it will therefore not result in a gift.

Intent is rarely an issue in gift cases, but it can arise when it is not clear what the donor intended to give: Suppose O says to D, "I want you to have the jewelry box on my dresser and the jewelry inside," believing that she's storing costume jewelry in the box. D takes the box, but inside there are no costume jewels, only a diamond necklace. What gift has been made? What if O says "I want you to have the jewelry box and its contents," and the contents are bearer bonds worth $100,000? If O is deceased when the issue is litigated, how would you determine her intent?

B. Delivery

Simply put, the property must in some way pass out of the grantor's control in order for a gift to be valid; this is known as delivery. Professor Philip Mechem summarized the reasons for the requirement:

> (1) Delivery has psychological significance, forcing the donor to confront the loss of the property: the "wrench of delivery" protects the donor from poor choices.
>
> (2) Delivery signifies the gift to third party witnesses, settling doubts about whether what was intended was a mere promise to make a gift in the future or a present gift.
>
> (3) Delivery lets the property itself bear mute witness to the fact of the gift: possession itself has evidentiary weight.

Philip Mechem, *The Requirement of Delivery in Gifts of Chattels and of Choses in Action Evidenced by Commercial Instruments*, 21 ILL. L. REV. 341, 348-49 (1926); but see Chad A. McGowan, *Special Delivery: Does the Postman Have to Ring at All – the Current State of the Delivery Requirement for Valid Gifts*, 31 REAL PROP. PROB. & TR. J. 357 (1996) (critiquing Mechem).

Land doesn't move, at least not for these purposes, so manual delivery is impossible, and "symbolic" delivery of land has always been accepted. At early common law, the transfer of land involved a ceremony called livery of seisin, in which the transferor physically handed over a clod of dirt or a twig from the land to the transferee. Fortunately, transfer of an interest in land is now generally accomplished by a written instrument, known as a deed. At a minimum, a deed must describe the land to be transferred, contain some words indicating an intent to make a present transfer of title, and the grantor's signature (which courts construe liberally – almost any mark or symbol of the grantor's approval, including the signature of the grantor's agent, will be sufficient). These formalities will be covered in more detail in the land conveyancing section.

What about personal property? Most gifts, especially gifts of personal property, are given during life. Nonetheless, many litigated cases arise around near-death gifts. As you read, consider why the case law would diverge so much from the practice of giving.

In re Estate of Evans

356 A.2d 778 (Pa. 1976)

Appellant, Vivian Kellow, objected to the inventory, proposed schedule of distribution and final accounting of the executor of the estate of Arthur Evans. After appellant finished the presentation of her case, the lower court granted appellees' motion to dismiss appellant's objections. … The thrust of her appeal to this Court is that certain contents of a safe deposit box were the subject of an *inter vivos* gift to her from Arthur Evans, the deceased, and, consequently, should not have been included in his estate.

Appellant, the niece of Arthur Evans' deceased wife, began working for the Evans family when she was 16. For several years she took care of Mrs. Evans who for some years prior to death was an invalid. Appellant cooked meals for the Evanses, cleaned their house, did their laundry and generally cared for Mrs. Evans. She received adequate compensation for performing these needed services. When Mrs. Evans died, appellant continued to cook at least one hot meal a day for Mr. Evans, do his laundry and make sure his house was tidy. After appellant was married, she continued to perform these same services and visited Mr. Evans once a day. In May of 1971, following one of his four hospitalizations, the deceased moved into appellant's home.

Although at times Mr. Evans was confined to his bed because of water in his legs, he frequently took walks, had visits with his lawyers and made trips to his bank. On October 22, 1971, appellant's husband drove Mr. Evans and a friend of his, Mr. Turley, to town so that Mr. Evans might go to the bank. Turley testified that Mr. Evans spent about one hour going through the contents of his safe deposit box. Before leaving the bank, the deceased obtained both keys to the box.

Various witnesses presented by appellant testified to seeing the keys to the safe deposit box beneath appellant's mattress and to statements by Mr. Evans to the effect that the contents of the safe deposit box had been given to appellant. Mr. Evans entered the hospital for the last time on November 5, 1971. During this last hospital stay, Reverend Cunnings visited with him and was told that Mr. Evans was giving the Reverend's church $10,000.00 and that he had given the rest of his possessions and the keys to his safe deposit box to appellant. Mr. Evans expired on November 23, 1971.

Appellant relinquished the keys to the safe deposit box to a bank officer, but not without protesting that the contents of the box were hers. The box revealed a holographic will of Mr. Evans dated September 16, 1965, and approximately $800,000.00 in bonds, preferred and common stock and several miscellaneous items.[32]

The lower court correctly noted that the requirements for a valid *inter vivos* gift were donative intent and delivery, actual or constructive. With respect to donative intent, the court found:

> 'Turning to the facts of this case, certainly no one can reasonably argue that Arthur Evans lacked sufficient motive to make a gift to Vivian. The record clearly manifests, both by his conduct and his statements, donative intent, the first prerequisite.'

Nevertheless, the court ruled that no delivery had been made. This result was predicated upon a finding that the deceased had not divested himself of complete dominion and control over the safe deposit box. After properly noting that constructive delivery is sufficient when manual delivery is impractical or inconvenient, the court reasoned:

> The record contains no evidence of circumstances which were such that it was impractical or inconvenient to deliver the contents of this box into the actual possession or control of Vivian.

Arthur Evans, although suffering physical infirmities and apprehensive of death, was nonetheless ambulatory. On October 22, 1971, he appeared at the Nanticoke National Bank in the company of Harold Turley and Leroy Kellow and spent approximately one hour going over the contents of his safe deposit box in a cubicle provided in the bank for that purpose. He left the bank after redepositing the contents and took with him only the keys which independent testimony indicates he delivered to Vivian the next day. There was no manual delivery of the contents. The contents of the box remained undisturbed. The box, and its contents, were registered in the name of the decedent at the date of his death. The objects of the gift were not

---

[32] The will was uncontested and under its terms provided for a $1,000.00 bequest to appellant.

placed in the hands of Vivian, nor was there placed within her power the means of obtaining the contents.'…

> 'A claim of a gift *inter vivos* against the estate of the dead must be supported by clear and convincing evidence. In order to effectuate an *inter vivos* gift there must be evidence of an intention to make a gift and a delivery, actual or constructive, of a nature sufficient not only to divest the donor of all dominion over the property but also invest the donee with complete control over the subject-matter of the gift. … [Tomayko v. Carson, 368 Pa. 379, 385 (1951).

In the instant case, the controversy focuses on whether there was an adequate delivery. … :

> … 'If there remains something for the donor to do before the title of the donee is complete, the donor may decline the further performance and resume his own,' … '(i)t is not possible that a chancellor would compel an executor or administrator to complete a gift by the doing of any act which the alleged donor if living might have refused to do, and thereby revoked his purpose to give.' … 'Though every other step be taken that is essential to the validity of the gift, if there is no delivery, the gift must fail. Intention cannot supply it; words cannot supply it; actions cannot supply it. It is an indispensable requisite, without which the gift fails, regardless of consequence.' The consequence is that no matter how often or how emphatically the desire or intention of the donor to make the gift has been expressed, upon his death before delivery has been completed, the promise or purpose to give is revoked.

We have recognized that in some cases due to the form of the subject matter of the gift or due to the immobility of the donor actual, manual delivery may be dispensed with and constructive or symbolic delivery will suffice. In Ream Estate, 413 Pa. 489, 198 A.2d 556 (1964), for example, the Court found there had been a valid constructive delivery of an automobile where the donor gave the keys to the alleged donee and also gave him the title to the car after executing an assignment of it leaving the designation of the assignee blank. The assignment was executed in the presence of a justice of the peace and the evidence was overwhelming that the name of the donee was to be inserted upon the death of the decedent. …

Appellant relies heavily on Leadenham's Estate, 289 Pa. 216, 137 A. 247 (1927), and Leitch v. Diamond National Bank, 234 Pa. 557, 83 A. 416 (1912). These decisions, however, support the Court's finding that there was no delivery in the instant case. In Leadenham's Estate, supra, the donor had rented a separate safe deposit box in the name of the intended donee, put the contents of his box into the newly rented one and delivered the keys to it to the donee. On those facts we held that the constructive delivery of the keys was sufficient to sustain the *inter vivos* gift because the donor had divested himself of dominion and control and invested the donee with complete dominion and control.

In Leitch v. Diamond National Bank, supra, the donor and donee were husband and wife and had lived together harmoniously for many years. The husband had three safe deposit boxes registered in his name and the name of his wife and he designated one of them as his wife's. He gave her the keys to that box. The Court found that she had complete control over that box and that he only entered it with her permission. Since she had complete control over the access to the box the Court found there was a valid delivery of the contents of the box to her.

In both of these cases, the determinative factor was that the donee had complete dominion and control over the box and its contents. In that posture we ruled that giving the keys to the box to the donee was a valid constructive delivery. In the instant case, appellant did not have dominion and control over the box even though she was given the keys to it. The box remained registered in Mr. Evans' name and she could not have gained access to it even with the keys. Mr. Evans never terminated his control over the box, consequently he never made a delivery, constructive or otherwise.

Although appellant suggests that it was impractical and inconvenient for Mr. Evans to manually deliver the contents of his box to her because of his physical condition and the hazards of taking such a large sum of money out of the bank to her home, we need only note that the deceased was obviously a shrewd investor, familiar with banking practices, and could have made delivery in a number of simple, convenient ways. First, he was not on his deathbed. He was ambulatory and not only went to the bank on October 22, 1971, but took walks thereafter and did not enter the hospital until November 5, 1971. On the day he went to the bank he could have rented a second safe deposit box in appellant's name, delivered the contents of his box to it and then given the keys to appellant. He could have assigned the contents of his box to appellant. For that matter, he could have written a codicil to his will.

The lower court noted that the deceased was an enigmatic figure. It is not for us to guess why people perform as they do. On the record before us it is clear that regardless of Mr. Evans' intention to make a gift to appellant, he never executed that intention and we will not do it for him. On these facts, we are constrained to hold that there was not an *inter vivos* gift to appellant and that the contents of the safe deposit box were properly included in the inventory of Mr. Evans' estate….

ROBERTS, Justice (dissenting).

I dissent. The central issue in this case is whether donor made an adequate delivery of the gift to donee. The majority finds that adequate delivery was not made because the safe deposit box was leased solely in donor's name and supports this conclusion by pointing out that there were several alternative means of delivering the gift which would have been adequate. I believe that the inquiry should not be what form of delivery would have been clearly sufficient, but rather whether the delivery made by donor was adequate. I believe that it was.

In Rynier Estate, 349 Pa. 471, 32 A.2d 736 (1943), we said that delivery is determined on the facts of each case, with reference to the donor's intent.

> 'As the chief factor in the determination of the question whether a legal delivery has been effected is the intention of the donor to transfer title to the donee, as manifested by his words and actions and by the circumstances surrounding the transaction, it is evident that each case must depend largely upon its own facts.'

… The majority suggests that donor was 'obviously a shrewd investor, familiar with banking practices. . . .' From this 'familiar(ity) with banking practices,' which is nowhere shown on the record, and the absence of a joint lease for the box, it apparently concludes that donor did not intend a gift. There are two reasons why this result is not correct.

First, there is no doubt in this case that donor intended a gift. He told many people that he had given the contents of the box to appellant. In fact, there is competent testimony that donor directed donee to display the keys, hidden under her mattress, to several witnesses.

Second, it is apparent from the record that donor believed undisputed and unconditional delivery of the keys to be sufficient to complete the gift. Most of this Court's cases dealing with *inter vivos* gifts of the contents of safe deposit boxes turn on the delivery or nondelivery of the keys to the box to the donee. If the key was delivered, the gift was normally upheld; if the key was not delivered, the gift was set aside, whether or not the box was jointly leased. I have found no case which turned on the presence or absence of a joint lease. Given this line of authority, and accepting the majority's conclusion that donor was sophisticated in these matters, it must be concluded that donor believed delivery of the keys to the box completed the gift. If this were not so, why would donor cause donee to take several witnesses into her bedroom to show them that she had the keys and why would he speak in terms that indicated a completed gift—'I *gave* to Vivian . . . the keys and the contents *are* hers.' Because it is donor's intention to transfer title which is crucial to a valid delivery, and because this donor intended to transfer title, I dissent from the majority's conclusion….

Notes and Questions

1. The majority writes, "regardless of Mr. Evans' intention to make a gift to appellant, he never executed that intention and we will not do it for him." But it also quotes approvingly the lower court's statement that "[t]he record clearly manifests, both by his

conduct and his statements, [Mr. Evans'] donative intent." Has the court contradicted itself, or can these statements be squared?

2. Why does the court note that Vivian Kellow "received adequate compensation" for the services she provided to Arthur Evans? What were his motivations for the attempted gift, and why are the appellees contesting it? Does the family setting shed any light on the positions of the majority and dissent?

3. The common law required manual delivery of personal property for a valid gift unless the object was too big to move. If the object was too big to move, substitutes for physical delivery were acceptable. Keys are a classic example: handing over car keys is "constructive" or "symbolic" delivery of the car. The keys symbolize the car (symbolic delivery) and provide the means for exercising dominion and control over it (constructive delivery). Today, because all states require car owners to register the title to their cars, many states require that a gift of a car is not complete unless the donor also hands over the title documents. Why would the law require delivery of the title documents? What happens when someone who doesn't know this rule hands over only the keys, and then a year later changes her mind and demands the car back? (You should see here how a title system can both make it easier to determine who owns property and easier for legally unsophisticated people to make significant mistakes.)

   Why isn't saying "I give you this car" without delivery enough to complete the gift? The keys could be handed over later, after all. If there's a present donative intent, what further purpose does a delivery requirement serve? Most answers focus on the evidentiary role played by delivery: possession of the property by the putative donee is strong evidence that the putative donor really did make a gift. This is especially important because most gift disputes arise after the putative donor's death. Notice to third parties who deal with the property and need to know who owns it is another common rationale. But when might a putative donee's possession not be particularly probative of whether a gift had occurred? Suppose a father allows his daughter to use his second car when she moves to town, and that this continues for six months. If, after they have a falling out, the father sought to retrieve the car, how would you figure out whether this was a loan or a gift?

4. Modern courts often relax the delivery requirement to allow constructive or symbolic delivery even of smaller, more portable items, but some delivery requirement remains. Suppose the would-be donor signed a document in front of two witnesses saying "I now give my daughter $100,000," and gave the document to his daughter. But the donor didn't actually deliver the money. Should we relax the delivery requirement because we are very confident that a gift was intended? Or does delivery still serve an important purpose? See Devol v. Dye, 24 N.E. 246 (Ind. 1890) ("The intention of a donor in peril

of death, when clearly ascertained and fairly consummated within the meaning of well-established rules, is not to be thwarted by a narrow and illiberal construction of what may have been intended for and deemed by him a sufficient delivery."); Ferrell v. Stinson, 11 N.W.2d 701 (Iowa 1943) (deed made out to intended donee was kept in box in donor's house, and recorded after grantor's death; held: delivered given strong evidence of donor's intent and fact that seriously ill grantor was physically inable to access box after executing deed); *cf.* Hocks v. Jeremiah, 759 P.2d 312 (Or. App. 1988) (bonds and diamond ring placed over a period of years in a safe deposit box held jointly with putative grantee were not properly delivered). What should have happened in the *Ferrell* case if the grantor had made out the deed, put it in the box, and then a week later, still in her sickbed, made out a deed to another person and handed *that* second deed to the intended grantee?

5. The Restatement (Third) of Property: Wills and Other Donative Transfers § 6.2, Comment yy, takes the position that personal property can be validly given without delivery "if the donor's intent to make a gift is established by clear and convincing evidence." Is this the right rule? As you'll see in the next case, some states require clear and convincing evidence of the presence of each element for any gift.

Newman v. Bost

122 N.C. 524, 29 S.E. 848 (1898)

FURCHES, J.

The plaintiff, in her complaint, demands $3,000, collected by defendant, as the administrator of J. F. Van Pelt, on a life insurance policy, and now in his hands; $300, the value of a piano upon which said Van Pelt collected that amount of insurance money; $200.94, the value of household property sold by defendant as belonging to the estate of his intestate; and $45, the value of property in the plaintiff's bedroom, and sold by the defendant as a part of the property belonging to the intestate's estate. The $3,000, money collected on the life insurance policy, and the $200.94, the price for which the household property sold, plaintiff claims belonged to her by reason of a donatio causa mortis from said Van Pelt. The $45, the price for which her bedroom property sold, and the $300, insurance money on the piano, belonged to her also, by reason of gifts inter vivos. The rules of law governing all of these claims of the plaintiff are in many respects the same, and the discussion of one will be to a considerable extent a discussion of all.

To constitute a donatio causa mortis, two things are indispensably necessary—an intention to make the gift, and a delivery of the thing given. Without both of these requisites, there can be no gift causa mortis; and both these are matters of fact to be determined by the jury, where there is evidence tending to prove them. The intention to make the gift need not be announced by the donor in express terms, but may be inferred from the facts attending the delivery; that is, what the donor said and did. But it must always clearly appear that he knew what he was doing, and that he intended a gift. So far there is but little diversity of authority, if any. As to what constitutes or may constitute delivery has been the subject of discussion and adjudication in most or all the courts of the Union and of England, and they have by no means been uniform; some of them holding that a symbolical delivery-that is, some other article delivered in the name and stead of the thing intended to be given-is sufficient; others holding that a symbolical delivery is not sufficient, but that a constructive delivery is—that is, the delivery of a key to a locked house, trunk, or other receptacle is sufficient. They distinguish this from a symbolical delivery, and say that this is in substance a delivery of the thing, as it is the means of using and enjoying the thing given; while others hold that there must be an actual manual delivery to perfect a gift causa mortis. This doctrine of donatio causa mortis was borrowed from the Roman civil law by our English ancestors. There was much greater need for such a law at the time it was incorporated into the civil law and into the English law than there is now. Learning was not so general, nor the facilities for making wills so great, then as now. But the civilians, while they incorporated this doctrine into their law, did not do so without guarding it with great care. They required that a donatio causa mortis should be established by at least five witnesses to the facts constituting the gift. And why it was that our English ancestors should have adopted the doctrine, without also adopting the manner in which it should be proved, seems to be unexplained; but they did so, and only required the facts to be proved by one witness, as in this case. It seems to us that there was greater reason in England, as there is here, for requiring in to be established by five witnesses, than in Rome, after the statute of frauds and of wills, as this doctrine of causa mortis is in direct conflict with the spirit and purpose of those statutes—the prevention of fraud. It is a doctrine, in our opinion, not to be extended, but to be strictly construed, and confined within the bounds of our adjudged cases. We were at first disposed to confine it to cases of actual manual delivery, and are only prevented from doing so by our loyalty to our own adjudications. But it is apparent from the adjudications that our predecessors felt the restrictions of former adjudications, and that they were not disposed to extend the doctrine.

We will not go into the general review of the many cases cited in the well-considered briefs filed in the case on both sides. Were we to do this, it would lead us into a labyrinth of discussion without profit, as we would not feel bound by the decisions of other jurisdictions, and would put our own construction on the doctrine of donatio causa mortis, but for decisions of our own state. Many of the cases cited by the plaintiff are distinguishable from ours, if not all of them.

The case of Thomas v. Lewis (a Virginia case) was probably more relied on by the plaintiff than any other case cited, and for that reason we mention it by name. This case, in its essential facts, is distinguishable from the case under consideration. There are articles present were taken out of the bureau drawer, handed to the donor, and then delivered by him to the donee. According to all the authorities, this was a good gift causa mortis. The box and safe, the key to which the donor delivered to the donee, were not presents, but were deposited in the vault of the bank; and, so far as shown by the case, it will be presumed, from the place where they were, and the purpose for which things are usually deposited in a bank vault, that they were only valuable as a depository for such purposes, as holding and preserving money and valuable papers, bonds, stocks, and the like. This box and safe would have been of little value to the donee for any other purpose. But, more than this, the donor expressly stated that "all you find in this box and this safe is yours." There is no mistake that it was the intention of the donor to give what was contained in the box and in the safe. As my Lord Coke would say, "Note the diversity" between that case and the case at bar. There the evidences of debt contained in the bureau, which was present, were taken out, given to the donor, and by him delivered to the donee. This was an actual manual delivery, good under all the authorities. But no such thing was done in this case as to the life insurance policy. It was neither taken out of the drawer, nor mentioned by the donor, unless it is included in the testimony of Enos Houston, who at one time, in giving in his testimony, says that Van Pelt gave her the keys; saying, "What is in this house is yours;" and at another time, on cross-examination, he said to Julia, "I intend to give you this furniture in this house;" and at another time, "What property is in this house is yours." The bureau in which was found the life insurance policy, after the death of Van Pelt, was present in the room where the keys were handed to Julia; and the life insurance policy could easily have been taken out and handed to Van Pelt, and by him delivered to Julia, as was done in the case of Thomas v. Lewis, supra. But this was not done. The safe and box, in Thomas v. Lewis, were not present, so that the contents could not have been taken out and delivered to the donee by the donor. The ordinary use of a stand of bureaus is not for the purpose of holding and securing such things as a life insurance policy, though they may often be used for that purpose, while a safe and a box deposited in the vault of a bank are. A bureau is an article of household furniture, used for domestic purposes, and generally belongs to the ladies' department of the household government, while the safe and box, in Thomas v. Lewis, are not. The bureau itself, mentioned in this case, was such property as would be valuable to the plaintiff. We have very carefully compared the case of Thomas v. Lewis and this case for the purpose of nothing the distinction between them, and, as we have already said, we have taken this case, since it was pressed upon our attention in the brief of the plaintiff's counsel, as being more nearly like the case at bar than any other cited, and as it was impossible for us to give a separate consideration to all of them.

It is held that the law of delivery in this state is the same in gifts inter vivos and in donatio causa mortis. Adams v. Hayes, 24 N. C. 361. And there are expressions used by Judge Gaston in the argument that would justify us in holding that in all cases of gifts, whether inter vivos or donatio causa, there must be an absolute manual delivery, to constitute, or, probably more correctly speaking, to complete, a gift, as it takes first the intention to give, and then the delivery, as it is the inflexible rule that there can be no gift of either kind without both the intention to give and the delivery. … There must be a delivery.

The leading case in this state is Adams v. Hayes, and this cites and approves Ward v. Turner, as the leading case on the subject of gifts causa mortis, and the correct exposition of the law on that subject; and we have felt it to be our duty to follow that case, so well considered by the very able court, as constituted at that time. Following this case, founded on Ward v. Turner, we feel bound to give effect to constructive delivery, where it plainly appears that it was the intention of the donor to make the gift, and where the things intended to be given are not present, or, where present, are incapable of manual delivery from their size or weight; but where the articles are present, and are capable of manual delivery, this must be had. This is as far as we can go. It may be thought by some that this is a hard rule—that a dying man cannot dispose of his own. But we are satisfied, when properly considered, it will be found to be a just rule. But it is not a hard rule. The law provides how a man can dispose of all his property, both real and personal. To do this, it is only necessary for him to observe and conform to the requirement of these laws. It may be thought by some persons to be a hard rule that does not allow a man to dispose of his land by gift causa mortis, but such is the law. The law provides that every man may dispose of all of his property by will, when made in writing. And it is most singular how guarded the law is to protect the testator against fraud and imposition by requiring that every word of the will must be written and signed by the testator, or, if written by some one else, it must be attested by at least two subscribing witnesses, who shall sign the same in his presence and at his request, or the will is void. This is as to written wills. But the law provides for another kind of will, not written before the testator's death, called "nuncupative wills." This kind only applies to personal property, and until recently was limited to small amounts. See how much more guarded they are than gifts causa mortis. Such wills as these must be witnessed by at least two witnesses called by the testator specially for that purpose, and they must be reduced to writing within ten days, and proved and recorded within six months. In gifts causa mortis it requires but one witness, probably one servant as a witness to a gift of all the estate a man has. No publicity is to be given that the gift has been made, and no probate or registration is required. The statute of wills is a statute against fraud, considered in England and in this state to be demanded by public policy. And yet, if symbolical deliveries of gifts causa mortis are to be allowed, or if constructive deliveries be allowed to the extent claimed by the plaintiff, the statute of wills may prove to be of little value. For such considerations, we see every reason for restricting, and none for extending, the rules heretofore established, as applicable to gifts causa mortis.

It being claimed and admitted that the life insurance policy was present in the bureau drawers in the room where it is claimed the gift was made, and being capable of actual manual delivery, we are of the opinion that the title to the insurance policy did not pass to the plaintiff, but remained the property of the intestate of the defendant. But we are of the opinion that the bureau and any other article of furniture, locked and unlocked by any of the keys given to the plaintiff, did pass, and she became the owner thereof. This is upon the ground that while these articles were present, from their size and weight, they were incapable of actual manual delivery; and that the delivery of the keys was a constructive delivery of these articles, equivalent to an actual delivery if the articles had been capable of manual delivery. Still following Ward v. Turner, we are of the opinion that the other articles of household furniture (except those in the plaintiff's private bedchamber) did not pass to the plaintiff, but remained the property of the defendant's intestate.

We do not think the articles in the plaintiff's bedchamber passed by the donatio causa mortis, for the same reason that the other articles of household furniture did not pass—want of delivery, either constructive or manual. But, as to the furniture in the plaintiff's bedroom ($45), it seems to us that there was sufficient evidence of both gift and delivery to support the finding of the jury, as a gift inter vivos. The intention to give this property is shown by a number of witnesses, and contradicted by none. The only debatable ground is as to the sufficiency of the delivery. But, when we recall the express terms in which he repeatedly declared that it was hers; that he had bought it for her, and had given it to her; that it was placed in her private chamber, her bedroom, where we must suppose that she had the entire use and control of the same—it would seem that this was sufficient to constitute a delivery. There was no evidence that we remember disputing these facts, but, if there was, the jury have found for the plaintiff, upon sufficient evidence at least to go to the jury, as to this gift and its delivery.

As to the piano there was much evidence tending to show the intention of Van Pelt to give it to the plaintiff, and that he had given it to her, and we remember no evidence to the contrary. And as to this, like the bedroom furniture, the debatable ground, if there is any debatable ground, is the question of delivery. It was placed in the intestate's parlor, where it remained until it was burned. The intestate insured it as his property, collected and used the insurance money as his own, often saying that he intended to buy the plaintiff another piano, which he never did. It must be presumed that the parlor was under the dominion of the intestate, and not of his cook, housekeeper, and hired servant. And unless there is something more shown than the fact that the piano was bought by the intestate, placed in his parlor, and called by him "Miss Julia's piano," we cannot think this constituted a delivery. But as the case goes back for a new trial, if the plaintiff thinks she can show a delivery, she will have an opportunity of doing so; but she will understand that she must do so according to the rules laid down in this opinion—that she must show actual or constructive delivery, equivalent to actual manual delivery. We see no ground upon which the plaintiff can recover the insurance money if the piano was not hers.

We do not understand that there was any controversy as to the plaintiff's right to recover for her services, which the jury have estimated to be $125. The view of the case we have taken has relieved us from a discussion of the exception to evidence and as to the charge of the court.

There is no such thing in this state as "symbolical delivery" in gifts either inter vivos or donatio causa mortis in this state. There is a hint in that direction in the case of Shirley v. Whitehead, supra, and this is now overruled. There is error. New trial.

Gruen v. Gruen

496 N.E.2d 869 (N.Y. 1986)

Plaintiff commenced this action seeking a declaration that he is the rightful owner of a painting which he alleges his father, now deceased, gave to him. He concedes that he has never had possession of the painting but asserts that his father made a valid gift of the title in 1963 reserving a life estate for himself. His father retained possession of the painting until he died in 1980. Defendant, plaintiff's stepmother, has the painting now and has refused plaintiff's requests that she turn it over to him. She contends that the purported gift was testamentary in nature and invalid insofar as the formalities of a will were not met or, alternatively, that a donor may not make a valid *inter vivos* gift of a chattel and retain a life estate with a complete right of possession. Following a seven-day nonjury trial, Special Term found that plaintiff had failed to establish any of the elements of an *inter vivos* gift and that in any event an attempt by a donor to retain a present possessory life estate in a chattel invalidated a purported gift of it. The Appellate Division held that a valid gift may be made reserving a life estate and, finding the elements of a gift established in this case .... We now affirm.

The subject of the dispute is a work entitled "Schloss Kammer am Attersee II" painted by a noted Austrian modernist, Gustav Klimt. It was purchased by plaintiff's father, Victor Gruen, in 1959 for $8,000. On April 1, 1963 the elder Gruen, a successful architect with offices and residences in both New York City and Los Angeles during most of the time involved in this action, wrote a letter to plaintiff, then an undergraduate student at Harvard, stating that he was giving him the Klimt painting for his birthday but that he wished to retain the possession of it for his lifetime. This letter is not in evidence, apparently because plaintiff destroyed it on instructions from his father. Two other letters were received, however, one dated May 22, 1963 and the other April 1, 1963. Both had been dictated by Victor Gruen and sent together to plaintiff on or about May 22, 1963. The letter dated May 22, 1963 reads as follows:

> "Dear Michael:
>
> "I wrote you at the time of your birthday about the gift of the painting by Klimt.
>
> "Now my lawyer tells me that because of the existing tax laws, it was wrong to mention in that letter that I want to use the painting as long as I live. Though I still want to use it, this should not appear in the letter. I am enclosing, therefore, a new letter and I ask you to send the old one back to me so that it can be destroyed.

"I know this is all very silly, but the lawyer and our accountant insist that they must have in their possession copies of a letter which will serve the purpose of making it possible for you, once I die, to get this picture without having to pay inheritance taxes on it.

"Love,
"s/Victor".

Enclosed with this letter was a substitute gift letter, dated April 1, 1963, which stated:

"Dear Michael:

"The 21st birthday, being an important event in life, should be celebrated accordingly. I therefore wish to give you as a present the oil painting by Gustav Klimt of Schloss Kammer which now hangs in the New York living room. You know that Lazette and I bought it some 5 or 6 years ago, and you always told us how much you liked it.

"Happy birthday again.

"Love,
"s/Victor".[33]

Plaintiff never took possession of the painting nor did he seek to do so. Except for a brief period between 1964 and 1965 when it was on loan to art exhibits and when restoration work was performed on it, the painting remained in his father's possession, moving with him from New York City to Beverly Hills and finally to Vienna, Austria, where Victor Gruen died on February 14, 1980. Following Victor's death plaintiff requested possession of the Klimt painting and when defendant refused, he commenced this action.

The issues framed for appeal are whether a valid *inter vivos* gift of a chattel may be made where the donor has reserved a life estate in the chattel and the donee never has had physical possession of it before the donor's death and, if it may, which factual findings on the elements of a valid *inter vivos* gift more nearly comport with the weight of the evidence in this case, those of Special Term or those of the Appellate Division. The latter issue requires application of two general rules. First, to make a valid *inter vivos* gift there must exist the intent on the part of the

---

[33] [Ed. note: as we will discuss below, Victor Gruen evaded substantial taxes on this gift by pretending that he did not reserve a life estate.]

donor to make a present transfer; delivery of the gift, either actual or constructive to the donee; and acceptance by the donee. Second, the proponent of a gift has the burden of proving each of these elements by clear and convincing evidence.

Donative Intent

There is an important distinction between the intent with which an *inter vivos* gift is made and the intent to make a gift by will. An *inter vivos* gift requires that the donor intend to make an irrevocable present transfer of ownership; if the intention is to make a testamentary disposition effective only after death, the gift is invalid unless made by will.

Defendant contends that the trial court was correct in finding that Victor did not intend to transfer any present interest in the painting to plaintiff in 1963 but only expressed an intention that plaintiff was to get the painting upon his death. The evidence is all but conclusive, however, that Victor intended to transfer ownership of the painting to plaintiff in 1963 but to retain a life estate in it and that he did, therefore, effectively transfer a remainder interest in the painting to plaintiff at that time. Although the original letter was not in evidence, testimony of its contents was received along with the substitute gift letter and its covering letter dated May 22, 1963. The three letters should be considered together as a single instrument and when they are they unambiguously establish that Victor Gruen intended to make a present gift of title to the painting at that time. But there was other evidence for after 1963 Victor made several statements orally and in writing indicating that he had previously given plaintiff the painting and that plaintiff owned it. Victor Gruen retained possession of the property, insured it, allowed others to exhibit it and made necessary repairs to it but those acts are not inconsistent with his retention of a life estate. … Victor's failure to file a gift tax return on the transaction was partially explained by allegedly erroneous legal advice he received, and while that omission sometimes may indicate that the donor had no intention of making a present gift, it does not necessarily do so and it is not dispositive in this case.

Defendant contends that even if a present gift was intended, Victor's reservation of a lifetime interest in the painting defeated it. … Defendant recognizes that a valid *inter vivos* gift of a remainder interest can be made not only of real property but also of such intangibles as stocks and bonds. Indeed, several of the cases she cites so hold. That being so, it is difficult to perceive any legal basis for the distinction she urges which would permit gifts of remainder interests in those properties but not of remainder interests in chattels such as the Klimt painting here. The only reason suggested is that the gift of a chattel must include a present right to possession. [Permitting] a gift of the remainder in this case, however, is consistent with the distinction, well recognized in the law of gifts as well as in real property law, between ownership and possession or enjoyment. Insofar as some of our cases purport to require that the donor intend to transfer both title and possession immediately to have a valid *inter vivos* gift, they state the rule too broadly and confuse the effectiveness of a gift with the transfer of the possession of the subject of that gift. The correct test is " 'whether the maker intended the [gift] to have no effect until after the maker's death, or whether he intended it to transfer some present interest.'" As long as the evidence establishes an intent to make a present and irrevocable transfer of title or the right of ownership, there is a present transfer of some interest and the gift is effective immediately. Thus, in Speelman v. Pascal, we held valid a gift of a percentage of the future royalties to the play "My Fair Lady" before the play even existed. There, as in this case, the donee received title or the right of ownership to some property immediately upon the making of the gift but possession or enjoyment of the subject of the gift was postponed to some future time.

Defendant suggests that allowing a donor to make a present gift of a remainder with the reservation of a life estate will lead courts to effectuate otherwise invalid testamentary dispositions of property. The two have entirely different characteristics, however, which make them distinguishable. Once the gift is made it is irrevocable and the donor is limited to the rights of a life tenant not an owner. Moreover, with the gift of a remainder title vests immediately in the donee and any possession is postponed until the donor's death whereas under a will neither title nor possession vests immediately....

Delivery

In order to have a valid *inter vivos* gift, there must be a delivery of the gift, either by a physical delivery of the subject of the gift or a constructive or symbolic delivery such as by an instrument of gift, sufficient to divest the donor of dominion and control over the property. As the statement of the rule suggests, the requirement of delivery is not rigid or inflexible, but is to be applied in light of its purpose to avoid mistakes by donors and fraudulent claims by donees. Accordingly, what is sufficient to constitute delivery "must be tailored to suit the circumstances of the case." The rule requires that " '[t]he delivery necessary to consummate a gift must be as perfect as the nature of the property and the circumstances and surroundings of the parties will reasonably permit.' "

Defendant contends that when a tangible piece of personal property such as a painting is the subject of a gift, physical delivery of the painting itself is the best form of delivery and should be required. Here, of course, we have only delivery of Victor Gruen's letters which serve as instruments of gift. Defendant's statement of the rule as applied may be generally true, but it ignores the fact that what Victor Gruen gave plaintiff was not all rights to the Klimt painting, but only title to it with no right of possession until his death. Under these circumstances, it would be illogical for the law to require the donor to part with possession of the painting when that is exactly what he intends to retain.

Nor is there any reason to require a donor making a gift of a remainder interest in a chattel to physically deliver the chattel into the donee's hands only to have the donee redeliver it to the donor. As the facts of this case demonstrate, such a requirement could impose practical burdens on the parties to the gift while serving the delivery requirement poorly. Thus, in order to accomplish this type of delivery the parties would have been required to travel to New York for the symbolic transfer and redelivery of the Klimt painting which was hanging on the wall of Victor Gruen's Manhattan apartment. Defendant suggests that such a requirement would be stronger evidence of a completed gift, but in the absence of witnesses to the event or any written confirmation of the gift it would provide less protection against fraudulent claims than have the written instruments of gift delivered in this case.

Acceptance

Acceptance by the donee is essential to the validity of an *inter vivos* gift, but when a gift is of value to the donee, as it is here, the law will presume an acceptance on his part. Plaintiff did not rely on this presumption alone but also presented clear and convincing proof of his acceptance of a remainder interest in the Klimt painting by evidence that he had made several contemporaneous statements acknowledging the gift to his friends and associates, even showing some of them his father's gift letter, and that he had retained both letters for over 17 years to verify the gift after his father died. Defendant relied exclusively on affidavits filed by plaintiff in a matrimonial action with his former wife, in which plaintiff failed to list his interest in the painting as an asset. These affidavits were made over 10 years after acceptance was complete and they do not even approach the evidence in Matter of Kelly where the donee, immediately upon delivery of a diamond ring, rejected it as "too flashy". We agree with the Appellate Division that interpretation of the affidavit was too speculative to support a finding of rejection and overcome the substantial showing of acceptance by plaintiff.

Accordingly, the judgment appealed from and the order of the Appellate Division brought up for review should be affirmed, with costs.

Notes and Questions:

1. **Postscript.** Michael took possession and immediately sold the painting for $5 million. A decade later it was resold for $23 million.

2. **Future Interests.** Michael's remainder interest is a type of "future interest." It is a future interest because Michael can only take *possession* in the future. However, as a legal matter, Michael's future interest exists before his right to take possession does. Victor needed to have a present donative intent in order to make a valid gift, and he had that intent: he intended to give Michael *something* when he wrote. That something was a future interest.

Corresponding to Michael's remainder interest is Victor Gruen's "life estate," which is a present possessory interest as long as Victor Gruen lives – and thus the court holds that Victor may keep possession of the painting, despite the delivery requirement. He isn't giving Michael a present possessory interest, so requiring him to deliver the painting wouldn't serve the ordinary purpose served by delivery of uniting the property owner with physical possession of the property.

Does *Gruen*'s willingness to recognize legal future interests in personal property undermine the certainty provided by a delivery requirement? What if Victor had intended an even more complicated transfer – perhaps giving the painting to his widow for as long as she lived, then to Michael? This could have raised troubling issues of who owned what.

3. **Tax fraud.** If the donor retains a life estate in property transferred *inter vivos*, that property will be included in the donor's estate for estate tax purposes. I.R.C. §2036(a). As a result, the estate tax owed will be the same as if the property hadn't been transferred at all. This provision is designed to discourage evasion of the estate tax (which was substantially more onerous when this case was litigated). Victor did just this, but his lawyer told him to "doctor up" the transaction so that he wouldn't have to pay the resulting taxes. *Do not do this.* It is called tax fraud, and you may be disbarred, or worse. Relatedly, backdating the letter raises serious ethical problems, and it too could have serious consequences for a lawyer who advised backdating in situations where the date of the transfer matters. Should Victor's apparently successful tax evasion have factored into the court's decision on the state law question of whether the gift was valid? If so, how?

4. **Substitutes for testamentary transfers?** Consider the outcomes of the following scenarios:

    - Victor Gruen writes the same letter giving his son Michael a future interest, but simply shows it to Michael rather than mailing it.

    - Victor writes a letter granting Michael total ownership of the painting, without reserving a life estate for himself, and mails the letter to Michael, then dies before being able to deliver the painting.

    - Victor writes a will in 1963 devising the painting to Michael. Victor dies in 1980. (What interest, if any, does Michael own in the painting before Victor dies?)

    - Victor writes a letter saying "I intend for you to have the painting when I die."

As you should see, the last possibility is an attempted testamentary transfer, but it is unlikely to meet the requirements for a transfer by will. Rather than being a present transfer of a future interest, it's a statement of intent to make a transfer in the future. Is the difference between what Victor actually did and "I intend for you to have the painting when I die" big enough to explain the different results? If this rule allows legally savvy people to carry out their intent more successfully than laypeople innocent of the law, is that a good thing or a bad thing, compared to the alternatives? Some states now allow land transfers in this form – a deed that expressly says it won't take effect until the death of the grantor will be honored, but only if it's recorded before the death of the grantor. See Mo. Stat. Ann. §461.025(1). Would you support such a law?

5. **Another Variant of Symbolic or Constructive Delivery: Delivery to a Place.** Sometimes, the would-be donor does not physically hand the object or document to the donee, but instead puts it in a particular place, from which she expects the donee to retrieve it. Should this constitute delivery? Courts have disagreed about the details, but if the putative donee does not have any right to control the place and other people do, then there is no delivery. For example, a household servant does not have dominion over the whole house, so a piano placed in the living room would not be delivered to such a servant, even if there was explicit donative intent. Another rule is that, if the putative donee has exclusive dominion over the place, there is delivery. Thus, furniture placed in a live-in servant's bedroom in her employer's house would be delivered to the servant. *See* Newman v. Bost, *supra.* (In such a case, disputes might still arise over donative intent.)

   What about shared spaces? Suppose four people are living together in a house, and A tells B that she's giving him a book, which she leaves on the kitchen table for him. The kitchen is shared by all four residents. Should this be sufficient delivery? Does the fact that she could easily instead have put the book in his bedroom, which *is* under his exclusive control, make any difference? (What should we expect laypeople to know about the law of gifts?) *Cf.* Robinson v. Hoalton, 2 P.2d 34 (Cal. 1931) (personal property was validly delivered when there was an oral grant and the donor and donee lived together: "The rule as to delivery is not so strictly applied to transactions between members of a family living in the same house ….").

   Disclosure of the location of an item may also serve as delivery, at least when it is otherwise hidden or inaccessible. *See* Waite v. Grubbe, 73 P. 206 (Ore. 1903) (disclosing location of buried cash sufficed for valid gift); Teague v. Abbott, 100 N.E. 27 (Ind. Ct. App. 1912) (disclosing combination to safe sufficed for valid gift).

6. **Intermediated Delivery.** Can you identify a unifying principle behind the constructive/symbolic delivery cases? Following the logic of these cases, suppose that, while Buffy Summers is working at the fast food restaurant Doublemeat Palace, her friends leave a present for her at the door, before the restaurant opens. When the manager comes to open up, he takes the present for himself. Who should bring the claim against him, Buffy or her friends?

   Handing the property, or an appropriate symbol of the property, to a third party for delivery to the donee will also complete delivery, as long as the donor has no power to recall the third party. If the donor can still control the third party and interrupt the delivery, by contrast, then the delivery is not complete. These principles have led courts to diverge on the proper treatment of checks: because a check can be stopped by the payor at any time before it's cashed,[34] the majority of courts say there's no delivery until that time. The payor has not given up complete control until the check is cashed. *See, e.g.*, *Rosano v. United States*, 67 F. Supp. 2d 113 (E.D.N.Y. 1999); *In re Estate of Heyn*, 47 P.3d 724 (Colo. Ct. App. 2002); *Woo v. Smart*, 442 S.E.2d 690 (Va. 1994). Other courts say that, at least with respect to gifts made in anticipation of death (of which more below), when the check is *not* stopped before the donor dies, the gift is complete even before the check is cashed.

7. **Delivering Intangibles.** Given the delivery requirement, how would you accomplish the gift of an intangible right, such as a copyright or a share of stock?

C. Acceptance

As you've seen, acceptance is generally presumed for gifts of value. Given that presumption, one might question why acceptance is an element of a valid gift at all. There are, however, unusual circumstances in which a potential donee will want to reject a gift.

If the donee doesn't want to accept the gift, then the donee may "disclaim" the gift. This usually only arises in cases of attempted transfers by will.

---

[34] Be aware that the law governing checks is complicated, and stopping a check may not always succeed or may have other consequences – this note just discusses how courts in gift cases have treated checks.

D. Irrevocability of Gifts

A gift, once given, is usually *irrevocable*: once the gift is complete, the donor may not change her mind and demand the gift back. The donee may voluntarily *give* the property back, but that's a second transfer of ownership. Irrevocability makes it important to be able to figure out when the gift was complete, because before it is complete, it is revocable.

Suppose that Bobby Singer leaves his junkyard to Dean Winchester in his will. Dean moves in, then realizes after two days that he doesn't want to run a junkyard, disclaims the gift, and tells Bobby's residual heirs – Bobby's second cousins – that the property is theirs. Is it?

Suppose that, on Spencer Hastings's eighteenth birthday, her parents put the keys to a car in an envelope by her place at the table. However, before the birthday meal, the family gets into a screaming fight, and the parents snatch up the keys from the table and say they no longer think Spencer deserves the car. Who owns the car?

There are two notable footnotes to the rule that gifts are irrevocable: Gifts *causa mortis* and conditional gifts. In the materials that follow, we will explore complications relating to both. As you read, keep an eye on the ways in which courts are interpreting the various elements of a gift in order to achieve an overall result they find appropriate.

1. Gifts *causa mortis.*

The law of gifts concerns *inter vivos* gifts, that is, gifts given by living people (the Latin literally means "between the living"). It is possible for property to be transferred by the dead. However, the category of law that discusses such transfers by the dead is described as the law of inheritance and it is not part of the law of gifts at all (even though we may refer to property given by will as a testamentary "gift").

A special category of gift law exists to deal with *inter vivos* gifts that are are given because the donor fears he is soon to die. These gifts are known as gifts *causa mortis* (literally, "gifts on account [or 'because'] of death"). They are not governed by the laws of inheritance (also known as the law of wills and estates), because they are given during the donor's and donee's lifetime. However, there are special rules governing such gifts to try to accommodate the special circumstances of the donor, but at the same time to avoid giving the donor a way to avoid the formal restrictions on testamentary gifts.

The elements of a gift *causa mortis* are the same as the elements as any other *inter vivos* gift: (1) intent, (2) delivery, and (3) acceptance. However, in order for the gift to qualify as a gift *causa mortis* the donor must also (4) anticipate imminent death. A gift *causa mortis* is automatically subject to a condition subsequent: if the donor survives the peril that caused her to fear death, the gift is either revoked or revocable. In most states, the gift is revoked automatically, while in others the donor may choose to revoke the gift. In the latter states, delay may be troublesome. *See* Restatement (Second) of Property: Donative Transfers §31.3 ("A failure to revoke within a reasonable time after the donor is no longer in apprehension of imminent death eliminates the right of revocation."). In all states, if the donor dies from the anticipated cause, then the gift becomes irrevocable. Some jurisdictions extend this to situations in which the donor dies from something else within roughly the same time frame or in which the cause of death is related to the anticipated peril.

Suppose D is going into the hospital for heart surgery that might end in death. She says to her son, "I fear I will die; I want you to have the contents of my safe deposit box," and gives him the key. While the surgery is a success, she dies a week later from an infection acquired in the hospital. Is the gift valid? What if she dies six months later from the same infection? See Brind v. Int'l Trust Co., 179 P. 148 (Colo. 1919) (putative donor didn't die from the operation that caused her to fear death, but six months later from the ailment that had triggered the operation; held: no gift *causa mortis*, because putative donor was specific about the operation as the cause of the gift, and her lawyer told her that she probably needed to take further action to reaffirm the gift, but she didn't).

Courts are often suspicious of gifts *causa mortis*. For instance, courts may apply the delivery requirement more stringently than in other gift cases. Is this reluctance justified?

For example, in *Foster v. Reiss*, 112 A.2d 553 (N.J. 1955), the putative donee obtained the property at issue by taking a note written to him from the hospital bedside of his estranged wife, who was then unconscious. The note disclosed the location of money and bank books (which gave access to savings accounts) hidden in their house. The husband found out about the note from a friend who'd been directed to tell him about it. He took the note, went home, and found the cash and the bank books. She died a few days later, never having regained consciousness. Her will gave $1 to her estranged husband and the rest of her estate to her children and grandchildren, who sued to recover the cash and the bank books. The court held that there had been no gift *causa mortis*, and said the following:

> [A] gift *causa mortis* is essentially of a testamentary nature and as a practical matter the doctrine, though well established, is an invasion into the province of the statute of wills ....
>
> 'These gifts *causa mortis* are dangerous things. The law requires, before Mr. Hitt can come into this court and claim $10,000 as an ordinary testamentary gift from Mrs. Thompson, that he should produce an instrument in writing signed by Mrs. Thompson, and also

> acknowledged with peculiar solemnity by her in the presence of two witnesses, who thereupon subscribed their names as witnesses. That is what Mr. Hitt would have to prove if he claimed a testamentary gift in the ordinary form of one-third of Mrs. Thompson's estate. And yet, in cases of these gifts *causa mortis*, it is possible that a fortune of a million dollars can be taken away from the heirs, the next of kin of a deceased person, by a stranger, who simply has possession of the fortune, claims that he received it by way of gift, and brings parol testimony to sustain that claim.' Varick v. Hitt, 55 A. 139, 153 (Ch.1903), affirmed 66 N.J.Eq. 442, 57 A. 406 (E. & A.1904).
>
> Gifts *causa mortis* are not favored in the law … 'for the reason that this mode of disposition permits property without limit of value to be transferred by mere delivery, and the proof thereof to be made when death has closed the lips of the claimed donor.'…
>
> The first question confronting us is whether there has been 'actual, unequivocal, and complete delivery during the lifetime of the donor, wholly divesting him (her) of the possession, dominion, and control' of the property. …
>
> The test was this: that the transfer was such that, in conjunction with the donative intention, it completely stripped the donor of his dominion of the thing given, whether that thing was a tangible chattel or a chose in action.'
>
> Thus, under New Jersey law actual delivery of the property is still required except where 'there can be no actual delivery' or where 'the situation is incompatible with the performance of such ceremony.' In the case of a savings account, where obviously there can be no actual delivery, delivery of the passbook or other indicia of title is required.

The court found that there had been no delivery. Instead, the putative donee had merely taken possession of the property, at a time when the would-be donor was incapacitated and incapable of authorizing him to act for her. The court emphasized the separateness of the two elements of intent and delivery:

> As stated in Madison Trust Co. v. Allen, supra, 105 N.J.Eq. 230, 235, 147 A. 546, 548, 'the burden of proof is upon the alleged donee to clearly prove both delivery *and* donative intent' (emphasis supplied). This was clearly brought out by the court in Parker v. Copland, 70 N.J.Eq. 685, 64 A. 129, 130 (E. & A.1906):
>
> … [T]he crucial test is not the strenuousness of the language in which the gift is couched, but in 'the transfer,' which is something that is both different from the donative intention and yet capable of acting in conjunction with it, so that both are necessary to the creation of an enforceable gift. … [W]hen two steps are required by law to complete a transaction, the excess of one cannot supply the lack of the other ….

> Thus, an informal writing such as we have here does not satisfy the separate and distinct requirement of delivery, but rather there must be such delivery of the property that the donor stands absolutely deprived of his control over it. …
>
> We must not forget that since a gift *causa mortis* is made in contemplation of death and is subject to revocation by the donor up to the time of his death it differs from a legacy only in the requirement of delivery. Delivery is in effect the only safeguard imposed by law upon a transaction which would ordinarily fall within the statute of wills. To eliminate delivery from the requirements for a gift *causa mortis* would be to permit any writing to effectuate a testamentary transfer, even though it does not comply with the requirements of the statute of wills.

The court quoted an earlier case emphasizing the risks of false testimony in such cases: "'Around every other disposition of the property of the dead, the legislative power has thrown safeguards against fraud and perjury; around this mode the requirement of actual delivery is the only substantial protection, and the courts should not weaken it by permitting the substitution of convenient and easily proven devices.'"

A strong dissent emphasized that the donor was fully competent when she wrote her note, clearly intended to make the gift, and never revoked the gift. The dissent would have honored her clearly stated intent because "justice fairly cries out for the fulfillment of [the] wife's wishes":

> I find neither reason nor persuasive authority anywhere which compels this untoward result. See Gulliver and Tilson, Classification of Gratuitous Transfers, 51 Yale L.J. 1, 2 (1941):
>
> 'One fundamental proposition is that, under a legal system recognizing the individualistic institution of private property and granting to the owner the power to determine his successors in ownership, the general philosophy of the courts should favor giving effect to an intentional exercise of that power. This is commonplace enough but it needs constant emphasis, for it may be obscured or neglected in inordinate preoccupation with detail or dialectic. A court absorbed in purely doctrinal arguments may lose sight of the important and desirable objective of sanctioning what the transferror wanted to do, even though it is convinced that he wanted to do it.'

Concerns over fraud or uncertainty, the dissent thought, were irrelevant here, where the donor's wishes "were freely and clearly expressed in a written instrument and the donee's ensuing possession was admittedly bona fide." The dissent noted that, in contradiction to New Jersey's approach, other courts have *relaxed* the delivery requirement in cases of gifts *causa mortis*, rather than strengthening it. Such courts reason that gifts *causa mortis* generally come about as the result of some emergency that makes it impossible to write a formal will. While delivery is still important to avoid problems of figuring out what was really given, the requirements for sufficient delivery ought to be liberally interpreted to protect the donor's intent. Here, for example, the wife's authorization of the husband to take physical possession, and the fact that he did indeed take physical possession before she died, ought to have sufficed. As the dissent saw it, "[w]hen Ethel Reiss signed the note and arranged to have her husband receive it, she did everything that could reasonably have been expected of her to effectuate the gift *causa mortis*; and while her husband might conceivably have attempted to return the donated articles to her at the hospital for immediate redelivery to him, it would have been unnatural for him to do so."

Which position is more persuasive to you? Should it make a difference if the putative donee were an unrelated friend? If the heirs named in the will were unrelated friends?

As noted above, in many cases, a donee's control over the place in which the gift was left is likely to suffice for delivery. Why didn't the husband's possession of the house in which the money was hidden in *Foster* suffice for delivery?

2. Conditional gifts

Speaking more generally, while gifts must be irrevocable, there are those who argue that a gift is valid if a conditions subsequent is attached to the gift. A gift with a condition subsequent is a gift that is irrevocably granted, but will nevertheless return to the donor if a condition *subsequent* is not fulfilled—for example, a student's parents might give him a car, conditioned on his graduating law school in three years. If the student fails to graduate in that time, the car must be returned. During that period, however, the gift is otherwise irrevocable: the parents cannot change their minds in year two and demand the car back, as long as the student remains willing to fulfill the condition and remains on track to do so.

Since many gifts are given orally, how can we know which are conditional, and what those conditions are? Would you support a rule that conditions can only be imposed on gifts if the conditions are written down? *See* State ex rel. Pai v. Thom, 563 P.2d 982 (Haw. 1977) (delivery of a deed with an oral condition was irrevocable even if condition was unsatisfied); *but see* Martinez v. Martinez, 678 P.2d 1163 (N.M. 1984) (allowing grantor of deed to offer parol evidence of oral condition). *Pai* states the traditional common law rule for transfers of land – why do you think this is so? What might justify relaxing the traditional rule?

Should the law permit conditional gifts? Can conditions sometimes be implied on gifts of certain types of personal property? Consider the following case, involving an engagement ring.

Albinger v. Harris

48 P.3d 711 (Mont. 2002)

Who owns a ring given in anticipation of marriage after the engagement is broken? Michelle L. Harris (Harris) appeals the disposition of an engagement ring by the Eighth Judicial District Court, Cascade County, Montana, and Michael A. Albinger (Albinger) cross-appeals the denial of reimbursement for certain telephone charges incurred by Harris and the award of damages for a prior, unlitigated assault and battery claim. We reverse the disposition of the engagement ring, affirm the denial of reimbursement for telephone charges and affirm the award for pain, suffering and emotional distress.

We frame the issues on appeal as follows:

1. Did the District Court err in determining an engagement ring is a conditional gift that may be revoked upon termination of the engagement?...

FACTUAL AND PROCEDURAL BACKGROUND

Harris and Albinger met in June 1995, and began a troubled relationship that endured for the next three years, spiked by alcohol abuse, emotional turmoil and violence. Albinger presented Harris with a diamond ring and diamond earrings on December 14, 1995. The ring was purchased for $29,000. Days after accepting the ring, Harris returned it to Albinger and traveled to Kentucky for the holidays. Albinger immediately sent the ring back to Harris by mail. The couple set a tentative wedding date of June 27, 1997, but plans to marry were put on hold as Harris and Albinger separated and reconciled several times. The ring was returned to or reclaimed by Albinger upon each separation, and was re-presented to Harris after each reconciliation.

Albinger and Harris lived together in Albinger's home from August 1995 until April 1998. During this time, Albinger conferred upon Harris a new Ford Mustang convertible, a horse and a dog, in addition to the earrings and ring. Harris gave Albinger a Winchester hunting rifle, a necklace and a number of other small gifts. Albinger received a substantial jury award for injuries sustained in a 1991 railroad accident. He paid all household expenses and neither party was gainfully employed during their cohabitation.

On the night of February 23, 1997, during one of the couple's many separations, Albinger broke into the house where Harris was staying. He stood over Harris' bed, threatened her with a knife and shouted, "I'm going to chop your finger off, you better get that ring off." After severely beating Harris with a railroad lantern, Albinger forcibly removed the ring and departed. Harris sued for personal injuries and the county attorney charged Albinger by information with aggravated burglary, felony assault, and partner and family member assault. The next month, after another reconciliation, Harris requested the county attorney drop all criminal charges in exchange for Albinger's promise to seek anger management counseling and to pay restitution in the form of Harris' medical expenses and repair costs for damage to her friend's back door. Harris also directed her attorney to request the court dismiss the civil complaint without prejudice.

The parties separated again in late April 1998. Albinger told Harris to "take the car, the horse, the dog, and the ring and get the hell out." During their last month together, Harris ran up approximately $1,000 in telephone charges on Albinger's credit card. Harris had been free to use Albinger's telephone throughout the relationship, and Albinger paid the bills. Harris moved from Great Falls, Montana to Kentucky, where she now resides. The parties dispute who was responsible for the end of the relationship. No reconciliation followed, marriage plans evaporated and Harris refused to return the ring.

Albinger filed a complaint on August 31, 1998, seeking recovery of the ring or its monetary value and payment for $1,000 in telephone charges. Harris counterclaimed for damages resulting from the assault of February 23, 1997.

At the conclusion of the trial, both parties submitted briefs discussing how the statute barring actions for breach of promise to marry, § 27-1-602, MCA, impacts an action to recover an engagement ring. The District Court found the ring to be a gift in contemplation of marriage, and reasoned that § 27-1-602, MCA, did not bar the action because the case could be decided on common-law principles, as opposed to contract theories. The court implied the existence of a condition attached to the gift of the engagement ring. Disregarding allegations of fault for "breaking" the engagement, the court concluded that the giver is entitled to the return of the ring upon failure of the condition of marriage.

On September 2, 1999, the District Court awarded the engagement ring or its reasonable value and court costs to Albinger, and denied recovery for the telephone charges. ... From this judgment, Harris appeals the disposition of the ring and Albinger cross-appeals the denial of telephone charges ....

Did the District Court err in determining an engagement ring is a conditional gift that may be revoked upon termination of the engagement?

Albinger and Harris gave one another numerous gifts of substantial value during their engagement. The ring is the only item now in controversy....

Legal ownership of the gift of an engagement ring when marriage plans are called off is an issue of first impression in Montana. In 1963, the Legislature barred access to the courts for actions arising from breach of the promise to marry. The District Court determined that this action brought to recover an antenuptial gift is maintainable, notwithstanding § 27-1-602, MCA, which states:

> All causes of action for breach of contract to marry are hereby abolished. However, where a plaintiff has suffered actual damage due to fraud or deceit or a defendant has been unjustly enriched, the plaintiff may maintain an action for fraud or deceit or unjust enrichment and recover therein only the actual damage proved or for the benefit wrongfully obtained or restitution of property wrongfully withheld where such action otherwise is maintainable under existing law.

... Albinger argues that the engagement ring was a conditional gift that he could revoke when the implied condition of marriage failed. Hence, Harris' refusal to return the ring upon demand constituted unjust enrichment. Harris contends she deserves the ring because Albinger repeatedly beat her, forcibly took the ring back, and was the one who finally ended the engagement by ordering Harris to move out of the residence where they had been living together.

The District Court declined to undertake a determination of which party was at fault in terminating the engagement. The court cited the following three reasons: 1) judicial holdings that fault is an inappropriate concern in matters of family relations; 2) pragmatic difficulties in discerning fault when the conduct of both parties likely contributes to the failure of a relationship; and, 3) aversion to concepts of legal "rightness" and "wrongness" regarding the choice of a marriage partner. We agree, and affirm that judicial fault-finding is irrelevant and immaterial in the adjudication of matters of antenuptial gifting under existing law, absent fraud or deceit.

The District Court employed the "conditional gift" theory advanced by Albinger to determine present ownership of the disputed engagement ring. The theory holds that an implied condition of marriage attaches to the gift of a ring upon initial delivery due to the ring's symbolic association with the promise to marry and, when the condition of marriage fails, the incomplete gift may be revoked by the giver. Albinger urges this Court to affirm the District Court's conclusion that the ownership of an engagement ring remains with the one who gave the ring when plans to marry are called off.

Only in engagement ring cases does precedent from other jurisdictions weigh heavily for conditional gift theory in the absence of an expressed condition. Considering it "unduly harsh and unnecessary" to require a hopeful suitor to express any condition upon which a ring might be premised, many courts stepped in to impute the condition of marriage. In practice, courts presume the existence of the implied condition of marriage attaching to an engagement ring in the absence of an expressed intent to the contrary....

ABOLITION OF BREACH OF PROMISE ACTIONS

Historic breach of promise jurisprudence tended to view an engagement ring as either a pledge of personal property given to secure a marital promise or as consideration for the contract of marriage. When a contract to marry was abrogated, the jilted lover could seek redress in a breach of promise action that sounded in contract law, but availed the plaintiff of tort damages. "The law allows punitive or vindictive damages to be assessed by the jury; and all the circumstances attending the breach before, at the time, and after may be given in evidence in aggravation of damages." The plaintiffs were almost invariably women seeking economic relief for themselves, compensation for pregnancy and material support for children of the relationship. Whatever "heart balm" was awarded to assuage lost love, ruined reputation or foreclosed opportunities to marry well "rest[ed] in the sound discretion of the jury."

By the mid-1930's, several state legislatures questioned the efficacy of court "interference with domestic relations" and passed statutes barring actions for breach of promise to marry, alienation of affections, criminal conversation and other inappropriate conduct of the "private realm." See Rebecca Tushnet, Rules of Engagement (1998), 107 Yale Law Journal 2583, 2586-91. Commentators noted all of these actions "afforded a fertile field for blackmail and extortion by means of manufactured suits in which the threat of publicity is used to force a settlement." "There is good reason to believe that even genuine actions of this type are brought more frequently than not with purely mercenary or vindictive motives [and] that it is impossible to compensate for such damage with what has derisively been called 'heart balm.' "

In the wake of "anti-heart balm" statutes that barred breach of contract to marry actions, courts heard a plethora of legal theories designed to involve them in settling antenuptial property disputes while avoiding the language of contract law. The results were mixed. Some courts allowed actions in replevin. Others entertained claims for restitution and unjust enrichment. Out of this legal morass, conditional gift analysis emerged as a popular way to resolve acrimonious engagement ring disputes. While some states pursue a fault-based determination for awarding the ring in equity, the modern wave aligns ring disposition with no-fault divorce property disposition and follows a bright-line rule of ring return....

CONDITIONAL GIFT THEORY

According to Montana law, "a gift is a transfer of personal property made voluntarily and without consideration." ... When clear and convincing evidence demonstrates the presence of the essential elements of donative intent, voluntary delivery and acceptance, the gift is complete and this Court will not void the transfer when the giver experiences a change of heart.

Another essential element of a gift is that it is given without consideration. A purported "gift" that is part of the inducement for "an agreement to do or not to do a certain thing," becomes the consideration essential to contract formation. An exchange of promises creates a contract to marry, albeit an unenforceable one. When an engagement ring is given as consideration for the promise to marry, a contract is formed and legal action to recover the ring is barred by the abolition of the breach of promise actions.

... Albinger maintains he held a reversionary interest in the gift of the engagement ring grounded in an implied condition subsequent. Montana law recognizes the transfer of personal property subject to an express or implied condition which must be satisfied before title vests, as either a contract, or as a gift in view of death. Since actions stemming from breach of the contract to marry are barred by our "anti-heart balm" statute, Albinger urges the Court to adopt a conditional gift theory patterned on the law relevant to a gift in view of death. Under Montana law, no gift is revocable after acceptance except a gift in view of death. While some may find marriage to be the end of life as one knows it, we are reluctant to analogize gifts in contemplation of marriage with a gift in contemplation of death. This Court declines the invitation to create a new category of gifting by judicial fiat.

GENDER BIAS

... The Montana Legislature made the social policy decision to relieve courts of the duty of regulating engagements by barring actions for breach of promise. While not explicitly denying access to the courts on the basis of gender, the "anti-heart balm" statutes closed courtrooms across the nation to female plaintiffs seeking damages for antenuptial pregnancy, ruined reputation, lost love and economic insecurity. During the mid-20th Century, some courts continued to entertain suits in equity for antenuptial property transfers. The jurisprudence that rose upon the implied conditional gift theory, based upon an engagement ring's symbolic associations with marriage, preserved a right of action narrowly tailored for ring givers seeking ring return.... The proposed no-fault adjudication of a disputed engagement ring also ignores the particular circumstances of a couple's decision not to marry.

Conditional gift theory applied exclusively to engagement ring cases, carves an exception in the state's gift law for the benefit of predominately male plaintiffs....While antenuptial traditions vary by class, ethnicity, age and inclination, women often still assume the bulk of pre-wedding costs, such as non-returnable wedding gowns, moving costs, or non-refundable deposits for caterers, entertainment or reception halls. Consequently, the statutory "anti-heart balm" bar continues to have a disparate impact on women. If this Court were to fashion a special exception for engagement ring actions under gift law theories, we would perpetuate the gender bias attendant upon the Legislature's decision to remove from our courts all actions for breach of antenuptial promises.

ENGAGEMENT RING DISPOSITION

To preserve the integrity of our gift law and to avoid additional gender bias, we decline to adopt the theory that an engagement ring is a gift subject to an implied condition of marriage. We hold that the engagement ring was an unconditional, completed gift upon acceptance and remains in Harris' ownership and control....

Justice TERRY N. TRIEWEILER concurring [as to the telephone charges] and dissenting.

Gender discrimination is a bad thing. I am glad the majority is against it. However, I regret that the majority has taken this opportunity to declare their good intentions because gender equity has about as much to do with this case as banking law. ...

The simple fact is that if women are more likely to be the subject of an action to recover a conditional gift given in anticipation of a marriage which does not occur, it is because they are more frequently the recipient of the gift. Should we just prohibit gifts in anticipation of marriage altogether because men are more likely to have to pay for them?

... The District Court found in Finding No. 7 that each time, except for the last time, the couple broke up (and they broke up frequently), the ring was either returned by Michelle or taken back by Michael. These findings were fully supported by the evidence. For example, Michael testified as follows:

> Q. Now, when you gave her the engagement ring, were you contemplating that you were going to get married?
>
> A. That was the whole idea.
>
> Q. Was there any way in your mind that the engagement ring was just a ring and she could keep it whether you were married or not?
>
> A. No....

It is equally clear from the record that the engagement ring was treated differently by the couple than other gifts which had been given by Michael to Michelle while they were engaged. He testified as follows:

> Q. Okay. Now, you heard her testify, didn't you, about the other gifts you'd given her?

A. Yes, I did.

Q. The 1995 Mustang that cost about $24,000, was that in contemplation of getting married?

A. No.

Q. Have you ever made any demand that she return that to you?

A. No.

Q. How about the diamond earrings that were the Christmas gift? Have you ever made any demands that she return those because they were given in contemplation of marriage?

A. No.

Q. How about the horse?

A. No.

Q. Any gift you gave her beside the engagement ring, did you ever contend that those other gifts were made in contemplation of marriage?

A. No. They were gifts. Those are gifts.

… [A]n older line of cases limited a donor's recovery of the gift to situations where the engagement is dissolved by agreement or unjustifiably broken by the donee. However, the court concluded that the notion of one party being at blame for the termination of an engagement is archaic and outdated.

… [E]ither gender can [be] given an engagement ring. For example, in Vigil v. Haber (1994), 119 N.M. 9, 888 P.2d 455, the parties exchanged engagement rings. However, their relationship deteriorated, the couple separated, and following their separation a hearing examiner determined that the parties should return the rings they had given each other. The plaintiff immediately returned the ring he had along with other of the defendant's possessions. However, the defendant objected to returning the engagement ring that had been given to her. The New Mexico Supreme Court held that the ring was a conditional gift depend[e]nt on the parties' marriage and should be returned. What if the roles had been reversed and the woman had returned the engagement ring given to her but the man had refused to do so? According to this Court, she would not be allowed to recover the engagement ring that she had given to her fiancé, no matter how substantial the value and unfair the result because requiring the return of engagement rings is unfair to women.

The second problem with the majority's assumptions is the assumption that conditional gift law as it relates to gifts exchanged in anticipation of marriage only applies to wedding rings. It does not. For example, in Pavlicic, a case which disproves the theory that jurisprudence cannot be written in readable prose, the plaintiff was a 75-year-old man when the 26-year-old defendant asked for his hand in marriage. While he first protested on the basis of his age, she assured him that she was no longer interested in "young fellows" and prevailed upon him to make the commitment. Over the course of the next four years, she then prevailed upon him to pay the mortgage on her home, buy her two new cars, an engagement ring, a diamond for her mother's ring, remodel her house, and advance her $5000 to purchase a saloon which they could jointly operate. The problem was that after she received the money for the saloon, she disappeared. She was next seen in another town operating Ruby's bar and married to a man two years her junior.

As noted by the Pennsylvania Supreme Court:

> When George emerged from the mists and fogs of his disappointment and disillusionment he brought an action in equity praying that the satisfaction of the mortgage on Sara Jane's property be stricken from the record, that she be ordered to return the gifts which had not been consumed, and pay back the moneys [sic] which she had gotten from him under a false promise to marry.

The Pennsylvania Supreme Court held that George's action was not barred by the state's "Heart Balm Act" and that all gifts, not just the wedding ring, were conditional gifts in anticipation of marriage which must be returned or repaid. …

The point is that there is no reason to limit the law of "conditional gifts" in anticipation of marriage to engagement rings. …

Notes and Questions

1. Would the court rule the same way if a woman had given a man an engagement ring, or a man had given a man an engagement ring? Compare Lindh v. Surman, 742 A.2d 643 (Pa. 1999) (adopting the majority no-fault rule requiring return of the ring in any broken engagement).

2. Does the adoption of a no-fault rule require the mandatory return of the ring in every case? Wouldn't a no-return rule also be a no-fault rule that distributed the losses differently?

3. If the dissent is correct, could Albinger have sought the return of his other gifts?

4. The dissent argues that the anti-heartbalm laws were fully consistent with no-fault conditional gift theory, but see Tushnet, *supra*:

   > [The early post-reform cases like *Pavlicic*, holding that women had to return engagement rings when they were at fault for breaking the engagement,] subtly shifted the justification for antiheartbalm laws in a paternalistic direction. The laws were no longer understood to protect wholly innocent men who had not promised anything to mercenary women; instead, they were construed to protect men who had foolishly, but willingly, made actual promises to marry and who then gave gifts in reliance on a woman's deceitful promise. Blackmail and extortion disappeared, leaving trickery and desire-induced gullibility as the only rationales for the rule. Whereas prereform cases had presumed that women were vulnerable to a naturally dominating male influence, the emerging line of engagement gift cases were premised on the view that women could misuse their power over love-blinded men. There was a related shift in the presumed goal of a promise-breaker's deceit: Duplicitous men attempting to get sex were replaced as the targets of premarital law by duplicitous women attempting to get material goods.

   If the reason for having a unique rule for engagement rings grows out of a history of sexist views of women, does that support the majority's conclusion?

5. Cooper v. Smith, 800 N.E.2d 372 (Ohio Ct. App. 2003), concluded that the engagement ring was a conditional gift recoverable without fault, but that other premarital gifts to a then-fiancee – including a car, a computer, a tanning bed, and horses – were irrevocable *inter vivos* gifts unless they were expressly conditioned on the ocurrence of the marriage, and gifts to ex-fiancee's mother were also irrevocable:

   > The engagement ring has a special significance because it symbolizes the couple's promise to marry. As a symbol of the promise to marry, what value does the ring have for the donee once the engagement is ended?[35] Moreover, we realize that a

[35] [*Ed. note:* As a symbol of the promise to marry, what value does the ring have for the *donor* once the engagement is ended?]

> donor proposing to his or her beloved is unlikely to expressly condition the gift of the engagement ring on the occurrence of the marriage. Not only do we realize how unlikely this is, we recognize how unromantic such a requirement would be. Thus, because of the engagement ring's symbolic significance, we are willing to imply a condition to the gift of the engagement ring. Unless the parties have agreed otherwise, the donor is entitled to recover the engagement ring (or its value) if the marriage does not occur, regardless of who ended the engagement.
>
> While we are willing to imply a condition concerning the engagement ring, we are unwilling to do so for other gifts given during the engagement period. Unlike the engagement ring, the other gifts have no symbolic meaning. Rather, they are merely "token[s] of the love and affection which [the donor] bore for the [donee]."… "Many gifts are made for reasons that sour with the passage of time." Unfortunately, gift law does not allow a donor to recover/revoke an *inter vivos* gift simply because his or her reasons for giving it have "soured."
>
> … If we were to imply a condition on gifts given during the engagement period, then every gift the donor gave, no matter how small or insignificant, would be recoverable.… We believe that the best approach is to treat gifts exchanged during the engagement period (excluding the engagement ring) as absolute and irrevocable *inter vivos* gifts unless the donor has expressed an intent that the gift be conditioned on the subsequent marriage.

What's the difference between a gift being "symbolic" and a gift being a "token[]" of "love and affection" – aren't those synonyms? Why not then imply the same conditions on other premarital gifts?

Does it matter that willingness and ability to perform, and not actual performance, is the usual rule for all conditional gifts except for the engagement ring? This would roughly equate to the older fault rule in broken engagement cases. *See* Curtis v. Anderson, 106 S.W.3d 251 (Tex. Ct. App. 2003) (agreement that fiancee would return ring if marriage did not occur had to be in writing to be enforceable; applying fault rule and finding that donor, as person responsible for calling off marriage, was not entitled to return of engagement ring under conditional gift doctrine). But is it actually "fault" to break an engagement where at least one party doesn't want to get married?

6. How will this rule affect the behavior of engaged couples in Montana? (Did you know the majority no-fault rule before reading this section?)

7. Susan and Sarah announce their engagement. Numerous gifts arrive before the day of the wedding, some at a "bridal shower" and some just before the wedding. On the morning of the wedding, Susan and Sarah call off their engagement. Who owns the gifts? (If you think the gifts don't have to be returned, how should Susan and Sarah split them?) What if Sarah has a stroke and dies the day before the wedding? If Susan and Sarah marry on Sunday and divorce on Monday?

8. **Other odious conditions.** Tennessee Div. of the United Daughters of the Confederacy v. Vanderbilt Univ., 174 S.W.3d 98 (Tenn. Ct. App. 2005), involved a 1933 donation from the UDC of $50,000 to Peabody College. The gift came with the express condition that a dormitory must be maintained with the inscription "Confederate Memorial Hall." In 1979, Peabody College merged into Vanderbilt University, which in 2002 sought to change the name to repudiate the association with slavery and racial exclusion. The court of appeals found that Vanderbilt could not do so unless it returned the present value of the gift. Is that the right result? The court said that it wasn't within the court's mandate "to resolve the larger cultural and social conflicts regarding whether and how those who fought for the Confederacy should be honored or remembered." A concurring judge commented that a majority of those who fought for the Confederacy owned no slaves, and called Vanderbilt's stance a "misperception." (Query: Is the alleged misperception about what Confederate soldiers fought to preserve?)

   Was the problem merely that the court of appeals didn't find the condition odious *enough*? In fact, the agreement between the UDC and Peabody apparently called for Peabody to house young women descended from Confederate soldiers for free in the dormitory. Vanderbilt stopped the free housing, with no objection. In the litigation, Vanderbilt argued that the conditions were never properly put in place, but the court of appeals rejected its arguments. As a result, Vanderbilt changed the name on all official documents and the university's website, but kept "Confederate Memorial Hall" on the building itself. Eventually, Vanderbilt decided to repay the gift (valued at $1.2 million in 2016) and change the name of the building to "Memorial Hall." As you will see, this condition – apparently destined to persist forever – raises issues of "dead hand" control by past owners, issues we have seen before and will see again.

E. Review Problems

1. Abbie Mills lends her friend Ichabod Crane a book when Ichabod is visiting her home. A week later, she calls Ichabod and tells him to keep the book. Does he own the book? At what point did he come to own the book?

2. Walter Bishop, on his deathbed, tells Olivia Dunham, "Because I love you like a daughter and I want to ensure your financial security, I want you to have my house in Disturbia City. Continue to rent it out as I have done and you will always have an income." He hands her the deed to the house, then dies. Walter's will leaves all his property to Peter Bishop. For the last five years, the property has been rented to Astrid Farnsworth as a furnished dwelling. Peter Bishop sues Dunham for possession of the furniture in the house as well as the rare book collection stored on the bookshelves of the house. Who owns the furniture, and why? Who owns the rare book collection, and why?

3. Victoria Grayson hires Amanda Clarke as nanny to her children, Charlotte and Daniel Grayson. One day, Clarke praises one of Victoria Grayson's diamond necklaces. Grayson says, "You can have it if Charlotte and Daniel are accepted into Evernight Academy. In the meantime, you can wear it." Clarke thanks Grayson and wears the necklace thereafter. Right before the Evernight entrance results are released, Grayson fires Clarke, telling her, "I despise you and I will never do anything for you!" Clarke leaves, taking the necklace with her. A day later, Charlotte and Daniel are accepted into Evernight. A day after that, Victoria Grayson sends a letter to Clarke demanding the return of the necklace. Who owns the necklace and why?

4. Damon and Stefan Salvatore, brothers, owned their family home. They fought, and, in an attempt to placate Stefan, Damon executed a deed transferring his ownership interest in the home to Stefan. Damon went to Stefan's study and handed him the deed. Stefan dropped the deed (it landed on his desk) and yelled, "You'll never buy my forgiveness!" Then he punched Damon and left town. Damon continued to live in the house. Two years later, with Stefan still gone, Damon executed a new deed transferring his ownership interest to Elena Gilbert, who had no idea about the previous deed. Damon handed the deed to Elena, telling her, "With all my family has done to yours, this is the least I can do." She thanked him. A year later, Stefan returned. Damon's first deed was still on Stefan's desk, albeit very dusty. At that point, Stefan put the deed in his safety deposit box at the bank and thanked Damon for the gesture. Damon said, "No problem." Which gift was completed first?

5. Fox Mulder gives Dana Scully a keychain with an Apollo 11 medallion on it. But when she tries to put her keys on it, the ring doesn't work. He tells her, "Let me have that fixed for you," and she lets him have the keychain. Afterwards, he decides that he doesn't want her to have the keychain. Who owns the keychain?

8. Wills and Intestacy

Lon L. Fuller, *Consideration and Form*

41 COLUM. L. REV. 799 (1941)

§ 2. *The Evidentiary Function.* – The most obvious function of a legal formality is, to use Austin's words, that of providing "evidence of the existence and purport of the contract, in case of controversy." The need for evidentiary security may be satisfied in a variety of ways: by requiring a writing, or attestation, or the certification of a notary. It may even be satisfied, to some extent, by such a device as the Roman stipulatio, which compelled an oral spelling out of the promise in a manner sufficiently ceremonious to impress its terms on participants and possible bystanders.

§ 3. *The Cautionary Function.* – A formality may also perform a cautionary or deterrent function by acting as a check against inconsiderate action. The seal in its original form fulfilled this purpose remarkably well. The affixing and impressing of a wax wafer-symbol in the popular mind of legalism and weightiness-was an excellent device for inducing the circumspective frame of mind appropriate in one pledging his future. To a less extent any requirement of a writing, of course, serves the same purpose, as do requirements of attestation, notarization, etc.

§ 4. *The Channeling Function.* – ... That a legal formality may perform a function not yet described can be shown by the seal. The seal not only insures a satisfactory memorial of the promise and induces deliberation in the making of it. It serves also to mark or signalize the enforceable promise; it furnishes a simple and external test of enforceability. ... The thing which characterizes the law of contracts and conveyances is that in this field forms are deliberately used, and are intended to be so used, by the parties whose acts are to be judged by the law. To the business man who wishes to make his own or another's promise binding, the seal was at common law available as a device for the accomplishment of his objective. In this aspect form offers a legal framework into which the party may fit his actions, or, to change the figure, it offers channels for the legally effective expression of intention.

John H. Langbein, *Substantial Compliance with the Wills Act*

88 HARV.. L. REV. 489 (1975)

4. *The Protective Function.* – Courts have traditionally attributed to the Wills Act the object "of protecting the testator against imposition at the time of execution." The requirement that attestation be made in the presence of the testator is meant "to

prevent the substitution of a surreptitious will." Another common protective requirement is the rule that the witnesses should be disinterested, hence not motivated to coerce or deceive the testator.

Stevens v. Casdorph

203 W. Va. 450 (1988)

PER CURIAM: …

On May 28, 1996, [Patricia Eileen Casdorph and Paul Douglas Casdorph] took Mr. Homer Haskell Miller to Shawnee Bank in Dunbar, West Virginia, so that he could execute his will.[1] Once at the bank, Mr. Miller asked Debra Pauley, a bank employee and public notary, to witness the execution of his will. After Mr. Miller signed the will, Ms. Pauley took the will to two other bank employees, Judith Waldron and Reba McGinn, for the purpose of having each of them sign the will as witnesses. Both Ms. Waldron and Ms. McGinn signed the will. However, Ms. Waldron and Ms. McGinn testified during their depositions that they did not actually see Mr. Miller place his signature on the will. Further, it is undisputed that Mr. Miller did not accompany Ms. Pauley to the separate work areas of Ms. Waldron and Ms. McGinn.

Mr. Miller died on July 28, 1996. The last will and testament of Mr. Miller, which named Mr. Paul Casdorph as executor, left the bulk of his estate to the Casdorphs. The Stevenses, nieces of Mr. Miller, filed the instant action to set aside the will. …[4]

The Stevenses' contention is simple. They argue that all evidence indicates that Mr. Miller's will was not properly executed. Therefore, the will should be voided. The procedural requirements at issue are contained in W.Va. Code § 41-1-3 (1997). The statute reads:

> No will shall be valid unless it be in writing and signed by the testator, or by some other person in his presence and by his direction, in such manner as to make it manifest that the name is intended as a signature; and moreover, unless it be wholly in the handwriting of the testator, *the signature shall be made or the will acknowledged by him in the presence of at least two competent witnesses, present at the same time; and such witnesses shall subscribe the will in the presence of the testator, and of each other*, but no form of attestation shall be necessary. (Emphasis added.)

---

[4] As heirs, the Stevenses would be entitled to recover from Mr. Miller's estate under the intestate laws if his will is set aside as invalidly executed. …

The relevant requirements of the above statute calls for a testator to sign his/her will or acknowledge such will in the presence of at least two witnesses at the same time, and such witnesses must sign the will in the presence of the testator and each other. In the instant proceeding the Stevenses assert, and the evidence supports, that Ms. McGinn and Ms. Waldron did not actually witness Mr. Miller signing his will. Mr. Miller made no acknowledgment of his signature on the will to either Ms. McGinn or Ms. Waldron. Likewise, Mr. Miller did not observe Ms. McGinn and Ms. Waldron sign his will as witnesses. Additionally, neither Ms. McGinn nor Ms. Waldron acknowledged to Mr. Miller that their signatures were on the will. It is also undisputed that Ms. McGinn and Ms. Waldron did not actually witness each other sign the will, nor did they acknowledge to each other that they had signed Mr. Miller's will. ...

Our analysis begins by noting that "the law favors testacy over intestacy." However, we clearly held in syllabus point 1 of *Black v. Maxwell,* 131 W. Va. 247, 46 S.E.2d 804 (1948), that "testamentary intent and a written instrument, executed in the manner provided by [W.Va. Code § 41-1-3], existing concurrently, are essential to the creation of a valid will." *Black* establishes that mere intent by a testator to execute a written will is insufficient. The actual execution of a written will must also comply with the dictates of W.Va. Code § 41-1-3. The Casdorphs seek to have this Court establish an exception to the technical requirements of the statute. In *Wade v. Wade,* 119 W. Va. 596 (1938), this Court permitted a narrow exception to the stringent requirements of the W.Va. Code § 41-1-3. This narrow exception is embodied in syllabus point 1 of *Wade*:

> Where a testator acknowledges a will and his signature thereto in the presence of two competent witnesses, one of whom then subscribes his name, the other or first witness, having already subscribed the will in the presence of the testator but out of the presence of the second witness, may acknowledge his signature in the presence of the testator and the second witness, and such acknowledgment, if there be no indicia of fraud or misunderstanding in the proceeding, will be deemed a signing by the first witness within the requirement of Code, 41-1-3, that the witnesses must subscribe their names in the presence of the testator and of each other. ...

Wade stands for the proposition that if a witness acknowledges his/her signature on a will in the physical presence of the other subscribing witness *and the testator*, then the will is properly witnessed within the terms of W.Va. Code § 41-1-3. In this case, none of the parties signed or acknowledged their signatures in the presence of each other. This case meets neither the narrow exception of *Wade* nor the specific provisions of W.Va. Code § 41-1-3.

WORKMAN, J., dissenting:

The majority once more takes a very technocratic approach to the law, slavishly worshiping form over substance. In so doing, they not only create a harsh and inequitable result wholly contrary to the indisputable intent of Mr. Homer Haskell Miller, but also a rule of law that is against the spirit and intent of our whole body of law relating to the making of wills.

There is absolutely no claim of incapacity or fraud or undue influence, nor any allegation by any party that Mr. Miller did not consciously, intentionally, and with full legal capacity convey his property as specified in his will. The challenge to the will is based solely upon the allegation that Mr. Miller did not comply with the requirement of West Virginia Code 41-1-3 that the signature shall be made or the will acknowledged by the testator in the presence of at least two competent witnesses, present at the same time. The lower court, in its very thorough findings of fact, indicated that Mr. Miller had been transported to the bank by his nephew Mr. Casdorph and the nephew's wife. Mr. Miller, disabled and confined to a wheelchair, was a shareholder in the Shawnee Bank in Dunbar, West Virginia, with whom all those present were personally familiar. When Mr. Miller executed his will in the bank lobby, the typed will was placed on Ms. Pauley's desk, and Mr. Miller instructed Ms. Pauley that he wished to have his will signed, witnessed, and acknowledged. After Mr. Miller's signature had been placed upon the will with Ms. Pauley watching, Ms. Pauley walked the will over to the tellers' area in the same small lobby of the bank. Ms. Pauley explained that Mr. Miller wanted Ms. Waldron to sign the will as a witness. The same process was used to obtain the signature of Ms. McGinn. Sitting in his wheelchair, Mr. Miller did not move from Ms. Pauley's desk during the process of obtaining the witness signatures. The lower court concluded that the will was valid and that Ms. Waldron and Ms. McGinn signed and acknowledged the will "in the presence" of Mr. Miller. ...

The majority embraces the line of least resistance. The easy, most convenient answer is to say that the formal, technical requirements have not been met and that the will is therefore invalid. End of inquiry. Yet that result is patently absurd. That manner of statutory application is inconsistent with the underlying purposes of the statute. Where a statute is enacted to protect and sanctify the execution of a will to prevent substitution or fraud, this Court's application of that statute should further such underlying policy, not impede it. When, in our efforts to strictly apply legislative language, we abandon common sense and reason in favor of technicalities, we are the ones committing the injustice.

Questions

1. **Wills Act Formalities**. The requirements to make a valid will vary from state to state, but in general a will must be in writing, signed by the testator, and attested by two witnesses. How well do these formalities serve the various purposes identified by Fuller

and Langbein? Which of them failed in *Stevens v. Casdorph*? How? Why is the court so stringent about enforcing the formalities?

2. **Informal Wills**. Whether out of ignorance about the law, skittishness in thinking about their own death, or bad advice, people do all kinds of things that blatantly fail to qualify as wills under the traditional test. They write chatty emails to family members explaining what they want to happen to their property after their death; they scrawl marginalia on old wills, crossing out specific bequests and adding new ones; they leave behind multiple conflicting undated "last" wills. What should courts do in such cases? In one memorably tragic case, Cecil George Harris used his pocketknife to scratch the words, "In case I die in this mess, I leave all to the wife. Cecil Geo Harris." into the fender of a tractor he was fatally pinned under. It was upheld as a valid *holographic will*: a will that has been handwritten and signed by the testator. A majority of states recognize holographic wills, although their specific requirements vary and an estates attorney should never rely on the validity of one. (For example, Maryland recognizes holographic wills only by testators serving in the armed services abroad. MD. CODE ESTATES & TRUSTS § 4-103(a)).

3. **Interpretive Problems**. The general interpretive rule for wills is the "intent of the testator." Is there any reason this might be a harder problem for wills than for other types of legal instruments? Consider:

    - T's will leaves "all my property to my daughters A and B." Five years after making the will but ten years before his death, T and his wife have another child, C.
    - T's will leaves "my red Toyota to my nephew A." After making the will, T wrecks the red Toyota and buys a blue Toyota to replace it.
    - T's will leaves $10,000 to A, $10,000 to B, and his antique writing desk to C. After expenses, T's estate consists of $5,000 in cash and the writing desk.
    - T's will leaves his estate equally to his sisters A and B. A dies in the same car accident as T. She leaves behind two children, C and D. T has one child of his own, E, from whom he is estranged.

Maryland Code, Estates and Trusts

§ 3-101. Order of distribution of net intestate estate

Any part of the net estate of a decedent not effectively disposed of by his will shall be distributed by the personal representative to the heirs of the decedent in the order prescribed in this subtitle.

§ 3-102. Share of surviving spouse

(a) In general. -- The share of a surviving spouse shall be as provided in this section.

(b) Surviving minor child. -- If there is a surviving minor child, the share shall be one-half.

(c) No surviving minor child, but surviving issue. -- If there is no surviving minor child, but there is surviving issue, the share shall be the first $ 15,000 plus one-half of the residue.

(d) No surviving issue, but surviving parent. -- If there is no surviving issue but a surviving parent, the share shall be the first $ 15,000 plus one-half of the residue.

(e) No surviving issue or parent. -- If there is no surviving issue or parent, the share shall be the whole estate. …

§ 3-103. Division among surviving issue

The net estate, exclusive of the share of the surviving spouse, or the entire net estate if there is no surviving spouse, shall be divided equally among the surviving issue ……

§ 3-104. Distribution when there is no surviving issue …

(b) Parents and their issue. — … it shall be distributed to the surviving parents equally, or if only one parent survives, to the survivor; or if neither parent survives, to the issue of the parents, by representation.

(c) Grandparents and their issue. — …

(d) Great-grandparents and their issue. — …

(e) No surviving blood relative. — If there is no surviving blood relative entitled to inherit under this section, it shall be divided into as many equal shares as there are stepchildren of the decedent …

Questions

1. If you don't make a will, the state will make one for you. This portion of the Maryland Code describes the default inheritance rules for people who die domiciled in Maryland without a will. How well do you think they track people's expectations about what will happen to their property after they die? In addition to *total intestacy* – dying without a will – the intestacy statute also applies in cases of *partial intestacy* – dying with a will that fails to dispose of all of one's property. How might that happen?

9. Land Transactions

In 1250, to transfer ownership of land, the grantor and grantee would physically go to the land. The grantor would physically (or perhaps metaphysically) put the grantee in possession by handing over a clod of dirt. The grantee would swear homage to the grantor, and the grantor would swear to defend the grantee's title. This was a public ceremony, performed in front of witnesses who could later be called on to recall what had happened if necessary. In contrast, written conveyances – called "charters" – were treated with skepticism; they were considered an inferior form of evidence because of the risk of forgery.

In the seven and a half centuries since, this attitude has completely flipped. Now, land transactions are paper transactions: the Statute of Frauds almost always requires a written conveyance – now called a "deed" – to transfer an interest in real property. Transfers by operation of law (primarily through adverse possession and intestacy) are very much the exception. In addition, land transactions are influenced by the common law's attitude that land is of distinctive importance, so that parties dealing with it need especial clarity about their rights, and by the fact that land transactions are often high-stakes, with hundreds of thousands, millions, or sometimes even billions of dollars at issue. This section focuses on the written instruments at the heart of land transactions. It considers when a deed is required, when a deed is effective, how deeds are interpreted, and what they promise about the property and the interest being conveyed.

Indiana Code

§ 32-21-1-1 – Requirement of written agreement; agreements or promises covered

(a) This section does not apply to a lease for a term of not more than three (3) years.

(b) A person may not bring any of the following actions unless the promise, contract, or agreement on which the action is based, or a memorandum or note describing the promise, contract, or agreement on which the action is based, is in writing and signed by the party against whom the action is brought or by the party's authorized agent: …

(4) An action involving any contract for the sale of land.

§ 32-21-1-13 – Conveyance of land; written deed required

Except for a bona fide lease for a term not exceeding three (3) years, a conveyance of land or of any interest in land shall be made by a deed that is:

(1) written; and

(2) subscribed, sealed, and acknowledged by the grantor … or by the grantor's attorney.

Questions

1. What is the difference between these two sections? Why are both necessary?

2. Consider the following sequence of text messages:

   A: still want apt 4C @ 321 sesame st?

   B: $450,000 ok?

   A: deal. :-) -A

   B: yay! kthx bai

   Can either of the parties treat this as an enforceable contract for the sale of land?

Harding v. Ja Laur

315 A.2d 132 (Md. Ct. Spec. App. 1974)

GILBERT, Judge: ...

The bill alleged that a deed had been obtained from the appellant through fraud practiced upon her by the agent of Ja Laur Corporation. The bill further averred that the paper upon which the appellant had affixed her signature was "falsely and fraudulently attached to the first page of a deed identified as the same deed" through which the appellee, Ja Laur Corporation, and its assigns, the other appellees, claim title. ...

There is no dispute that the appellant signed some type of paper. Her claim is not that her signature was forged in the normal sense, i.e., someone copied or wrote it, but rather that the forgery is the result of an alteration. Mrs. Harding alleges that at the time that she signed a blank paper she was told that her signature was necessary in order to straighten out a boundary line. She represents that she did not know that she was conveying away her interest in and to a certain 1517 acres of land in Montgomery County.

The parcel of land that was conveyed by the allegedly forged deed is contiguous to a large tract of real estate in which Ja Laur and others had "a substantial interest." It appears from the bill that Mrs. Harding's land provided the access from the larger tract to a public road, so that its value to the appellees is obvious. Mrs. Harding excuses herself for signing the "blank paper" by averring that she did so at the instigation of an attorney, an agent of Ja Laur, who had "been a friend of her deceased husband, and ... represented her deceased husband in prior business and legal matters, and that under [the] circumstances [she] did place her complete trust and reliance in the representations made to her ..." by the attorney. The "blank paper" was signed "on or about April 2, 1970." Mrs. Harding states that she did not learn of the fraud until the "summer of 1972." At that time an audit, by the Internal Revenue Service, of her deceased husband's business revealed the deed to Ja Laur, and its subsequent conveyance to the other appellees.

In *Smith v. State*, 256 A.2d 357, 360 (1970), we said that:

> Forgery has been defined as a false making or material alteration, with intent to defraud, of any writing which, if genuine, might apparently be of legal efficacy or the foundation of a legal liability. More succinctly, forgery is the fraudulent making of a false writing having apparent legal significance. It is thus clear that one of the essential elements of forgery is a writing in such form as to be apparently of some legal efficacy and hence capable of defrauding or deceiving.

Perkins, *Criminal Law* ch. 4, § 8 (2d ed. 1969) states, at 351:

> A material alteration may be in the form of (1) an addition to the writing, (2) a substitution of something different in the place of what originally appeared, or (3) the removal of part of the original. The removal may be by erasure or in some other manner, such as by cutting off a qualifying clause appearing after the signature.

A multitude of cases hold that forgery includes the alteration of or addition to any instrument in order to defraud. That a deed may be the subject of a forgery is beyond question.

The Bill of Complaint alleges that the signature of Mrs. Harding was obtained through fraud. More important, however, to the issue is whether or not the bill alleges forgery. In our view the charge that appellant's signature was written upon a paper, which paper was thereafter unbeknown to her made a part of a deed, if true, demonstrates that there has been a material alteration and hence a forgery. ...

We turn now to the discussion of whether *vel non* the demurrers of Macro Housing, Inc. and Montgomery County, the other appellees, should have been sustained. There was no allegation in the bill that their agent had perpetrated the fraud upon Mrs. Harding. If they are to be held in the case, it must be on the basis that they are not *bona fide* purchasers without notice. The title of a *bona fide* purchaser, without notice, is not vitiated even though a fraud was perpetrated by his vendor upon a prior title holder. A deed obtained through fraud, deceit or trickery is voidable as between the parties thereto, but not as to a *bona fide* purchaser. A forged deed, on the other hand, is void *ab initio*. ...

[T]he common law rule that a forger can pass no better title than he has is in full force and effect in this State. A forger, having no title can pass none to his vendee. Consequently, there can be no *bona fide* holder of title under a forged deed. A forged deed, unlike one procured by fraud, deceit or trickery is void from its inception. The distinction between a deed obtained by fraud and one that has been forged is readily apparent. In a fraudulent deed an innocent purchaser is protected because the fraud practiced upon the signatory to such a deed is brought into play, at least in part, by some act or omission on the part of the person upon whom the fraud is perpetrated. He has helped in some degree to set into motion the very fraud about which he later complains. A forged deed, on the other hand, does not necessarily involve any action on the part of the person against whom the forgery is committed. So that if a person has two deeds presented to him, and he thinks he is signing one but in actuality, because of fraud, deceit or trickery he signs the other, a bona fide purchaser, without notice, is protected. On the other hand, if a person is presented with a deed, and he signs that deed but the deed is thereafter altered e.g. through a change in the description or affixing the signature page to another deed, that is forgery and a subsequent purchaser takes no title.

In the instant case, the Bill of Complaint, for the reasons above stated, alleged a forgery of the deed by which Ja Laur took title from Mrs. Harding. This allegation, if true, renders that deed a nullity. Ja Laur could not have passed title to the other appellees, Macro Housing, Inc. and Montgomery County. Those two appellees would therefore have no title to the land of Mrs. Harding. ...

Questions

1. What is the point of the distinction between forging a deed (sometimes called "fraud in the factum") and tricking someone into signing it ("fraud in the inducement")? As between the fraudster and the victim, is there a significant difference? What about once third parties get involved?

2. Mrs. Harding signs a blank piece of paper, which Ja Laur then staples to a deed. Forgery? What if she signs the same piece of paper *after* it is stapled to the deed? Do the policy reasons for distinguishing forgery from fraud provide a convincing reason to treat these cases differently?

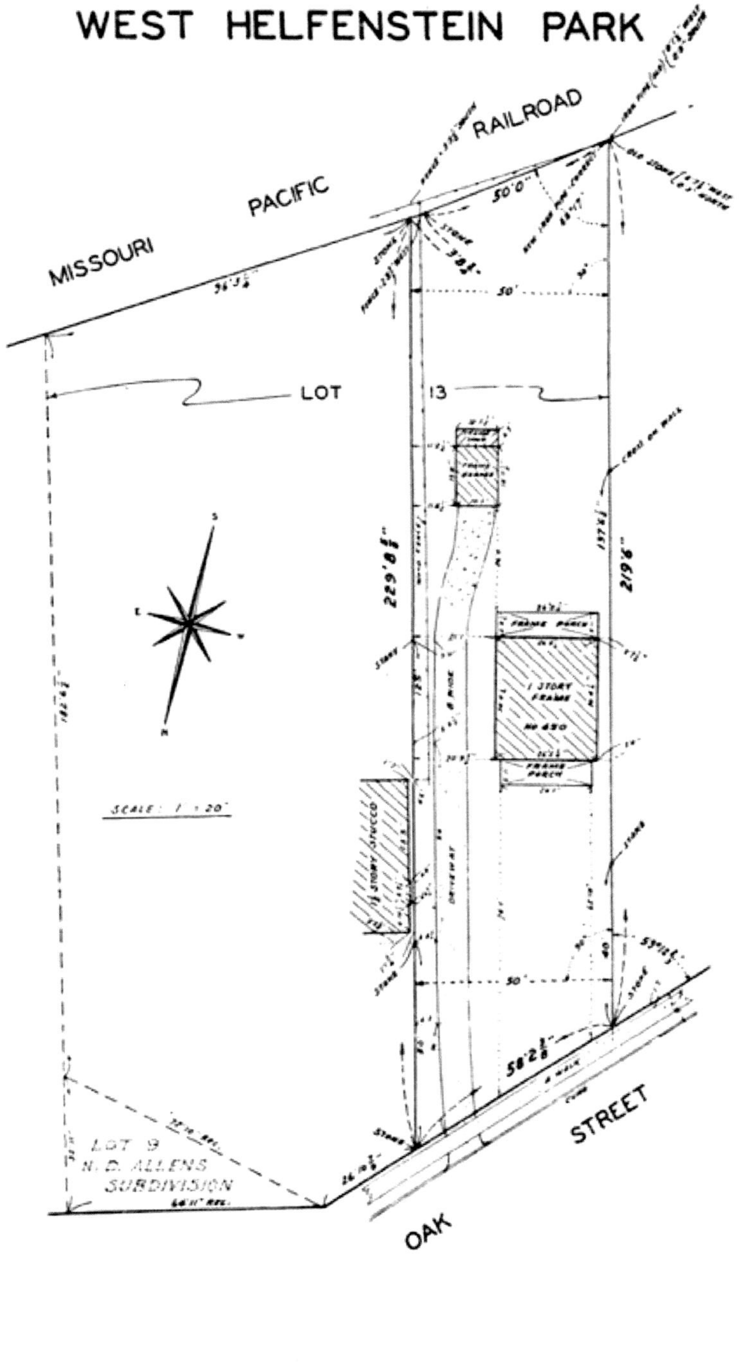

Walters v. Tucker

281 S.W.2d 843 (Sup. Ct. Mo. 1955)

This is an action to quiet title to certain real estate situate in the City of Webster Groves, St. Louis County, Missouri. Plaintiff and defendants are the owners of adjoining residential properties fronting northward on Oak Street. Plaintiff's property, known as 450 Oak Street, lies to the west of defendants' property, known as 446 Oak Street. The controversy arises over their division line. Plaintiff contends that her lot is 50 feet in width, east and west. Defendants contend that plaintiff's lot is only approximately 42 feet in width, east and west. The trial court, sitting without a jury, found the issues in favor of defendants and rendered judgment accordingly, from which plaintiff has appealed.

The common source of title is Fred F. Wolf and Rose E. Wolf, husband and wife, who in 1922 acquired the whole of Lot 13 of West Helfenstein Park, as shown by plat thereof recorded in St. Louis County. In 1924, Mr. and Mrs. Wolf conveyed to Charles Arthur Forse and wife the following described portion of said Lot 13:

> The West 50 feet of Lot 13 of West Helfenstein Park, a Sub-division in United States Survey 1953, Twp. 45, Range 8 East, St. Louis County, Missouri, … .

Plaintiff, through mesne conveyances carrying a description like that above, is the last grantee of and successor in title to the aforesaid portion of Lot 13. Defendants, through mesne conveyances, are the last grantees of and successors in title to the remaining portion of Lot 13.

At the time of the above conveyance in 1924, there was and is now situate on the tract described therein a one-story frame dwelling house (450 Oak Street), which was then and continuously since has been occupied as a dwelling by the successive owners of said tract, or their tenants. In 1925, Mr. and Mrs. Wolf built a 1 1/2-story stucco dwelling house on the portion of Lot 13 retained by them. This house (446 Oak Street) continuously since has been occupied as a dwelling by the successive owners of said portion of Lot 13, or their tenants.

Despite the apparent clarity of the description in plaintiff's deed, extrinsic evidence was heard for the purpose of enabling the trial court to interpret the true meaning of the description set forth therein. At the close of all the evidence the trial court found that the description did not clearly reveal whether the property conveyed 'was to be fifty feet along the front line facing Oak Street or fifty feet measured Eastwardly at right angles from the West line of the property …'; that the 'difference in method of ascertaining fifty feet would result in a difference to the parties of a strip the length of the lot and approximately eight feet in width'; that an ambiguity existed which justified the hearing of extrinsic evidence; and that the 'West fifty feet should be measured on the front or street line facing Oak Street.' The judgment rendered in conformity with the above finding had the effect of fixing the east-west width of plaintiff's tract at about 42 feet.

Plaintiff contends that the description in the deed is clear, definite and unambiguous, both on its face and when applied to the land; that the trial court erred in hearing and considering extrinsic evidence; and that its finding and judgment changes the clearly expressed meaning of the description and describes and substitutes a different tract from that acquired by her under her deed. Defendants do not contend that the description, on its face, is ambiguous, but do contend that when applied to the land it is subject to 'dual interpretation'; that under the evidence the trial court did not err in finding it contained a latent ambiguity and that parol evidence was admissible to ascertain and determine its true meaning; and that the finding and judgment of the trial court properly construes and adjudges the true meaning of the description set forth in said deed.

[The plaintiff and defendants introduced dueling survey plats. The one included here is the plaintiff's. North is at the bottom. Note in particular the locations of the two houses and of the driveway. It may help to mark on the plat where the defendant's proposed line would fall.]
It is seen that Lot 13 extends generally north and south. It is bounded on the north by Oak Street (except that a small triangular lot from another subdivision cuts off its frontage thereon at the northeast corner). On the south it is bounded by the Missouri Pacific Railroad right of way. Both Oak Street and the railroad right of way extend in a general northeast-southwest direction, but at differing angles. ...

Both plats show a concrete driveway 8 feet in width extending from Oak Street to plaintiff's garage in the rear of her home, which, the testimony shows, was built by one of plaintiff's predecessors in title. The east line of plaintiff's tract, as measured by the Joyce (plaintiff's) survey, lies 6 or 7 feet east of the eastern edge of this driveway. Admittedly, the driveway is upon and an appurtenance of plaintiff's property. On the Elbring (defendants') plat, the east line of plaintiff's lot, as measured by Elbring, is shown to coincide with the east side of the driveway at Oak Street and to encroach upon it 1.25 feet for a distance of 30 or more feet as it extends between the houses. Thus, the area in dispute is essentially the area between the east edge of the driveway and the line fixed by the Joyce survey as the eastern line of plaintiff's tract. ...

The description under which plaintiff claims title, to wit: 'The West 50 feet of Lot 13 ...', is on its face clear and free of ambiguity. It purports to convey a strip of land 50 feet in width off the west side of Lot 13. So clear is the meaning of the above language that defendants do not challenge it and it has been difficult to find any case wherein the meaning of a similar description has been questioned.

The law is clear that when there is no inconsistency on the face of a deed and, on application of the description to the ground, no inconsistency appears, parol evidence is not admissible to show that the parties intended to convey either more or less or different ground from that described. But where there are conflicting calls in a deed, or the description may be made to apply to two or more parcels, and there is nothing in the deed to show which is meant, then parol evidence is admissible to show the true meaning of the words used.

No ambiguity or confusion arises when the description here in question is applied to Lot 13. The description, when applied to the ground, fits the land claimed by plaintiff and cannot be made to apply to any other tract. When the deed was made, Lot 13 was vacant land except for the frame dwelling at 450 Oak Street. The stucco house (446 Oak Street) was not built until the following year. Under no conceivable theory can the fact that defendants' predecessors in title (Mr. and Mrs. Wolf) thereafter built the stucco house within a few feet of the east line of the property described in the deed be construed as competent evidence of any ambiguity in the description. ...

Whether the above testimony and other testimony in the record constitute evidence of a mistake in the deed we do not here determine. Defendants have not sought reformation, and yet that is what the decree herein rendered undertakes to do. It seems apparent that the trial court considered the testimony and came to the conclusion that the parties to the deed did not intend a conveyance of the 'West 50 feet of Lot 13', but rather a tract fronting 50 feet on Oak Street. And, the decree, on the theory of interpreting an ambiguity, undertakes to change (reform) the description so as to describe a lot approximately 42 feet in width instead of a lot 50 feet in width, as originally described. That, we are convinced, the courts cannot do.

Questions

1. Why does the court apply such a strict integration rule?

2. The boundary line as enforced by the court comes within inches of the defendants' house. This does not seem like an ideal state of affairs. (Then again, the defendant's theory would have drawn the boundary line through the plaintiffs' driveway.) Are there any doctrines that can clean up the messes that result when (by accident or otherwise) strict interpretation of deeds produces results at odds with natural features, structures, or uses of land?

3. The deed here used three different techniques to describe the land. Start at the end. "United States Survey 1953, Twp. 45, Range 8 East, St. Louis County, Missouri" is a reference to a government survey. Townships are standard 36-square-mile tracts established by federal government survey; "Twp. 45, Range 8 East" identifies a specific township in Missouri. Next, "of Lot 13 of West Helfenstein Park" is a reference to the *subdivision plat* filed by the developer who laid out the neighborhood; the plat is a survey map filed in the county recording office that shows the boundaries of individual parcels. Finally, "The West 50 feet" is a (crude attempt at) a *metes and bounds* description of the property in terms of its boundaries. Metes and bounds descriptions may refer to geospatial coordinates (e.g. latitude and longitude as measured by GPS), to natural landmarks ("Millers' Creek"), artificial markers ("the survey stake labelled G34"), and

distances and directions ("300 feet along a course at 45°). How precise are these various means of description? Which of them strike you as most prone to error?

4. Note that the boundary lines as shown on the survey map are at an angle to the north-south axis. Does this affect how the court should interpret the deed?

Loughran v. Kummer
146 A. 534 (Pa. 1929)

KEPHART, J.

Appellee, a bachelor 67 years of age, conveyed, for $1, land in Pittsburgh to Mrs. Kummer, appellant, who was one of his tenants. A bill was filed to set aside this deed; the grounds laid were confidential relationship, undue influence, and impaired mentality. Inasmuch as the facts must again be considered, we will mention only such as raise the legal question on which the case was decided; we venture no opinion on the other facts.

The court below found from the evidence that a deed absolute on its face had been executed, acknowledged, and delivered to appellant by appellee, on condition that it should not be recorded until the latter's death; that undoubtedly in his mind this meant that the deed was not to take effect until after his death; and that he, demanding the return of the deed within a very few days after the delivery, thus revoked it and with that revocation revoked the gift. Appellant deceived appellee when she stated the deed had been destroyed. The excuse given was appellee was worried and she wanted to ease his mind by making him believe that it had been destroyed. …

The question we are asked to consider is whether a deed absolute on its face, acknowledged, executed, and delivered under circumstances as here indicated, vested such title in the grantee as could be revoked for the above reasons. It amounts in substance to this, that the grantor said the deed should not be recorded until after his death, and the grantee in accepting the deed took it on that condition. The evidence on which this finding was based was all oral, and the scrivener and defendant denied any such condition was imposed when the deed was delivered. All control over the deed was relinquished when it was handed appellant. The presumption must be that at that time it was the intention to pass title. 'The general principle of law is that the formal act of signing, sealing and delivering is the consummation of the deed, and it lies with the grantor to prove clearly that appearances are not consistent with truth. The presumption stands against him, and the burden is on him to destroy it by clear and positive proof that there was no delivery and that it was so understood at the time. … Where we have, as here, a deed, absolute and complete in itself, attacked as being in fact otherwise intended, … there is a further presumption that the title is in conformity with the deed, and it should not be dislodged except by clear, precise, convincing and satisfactory evidence to the contrary.' *Cragin's Estate*, 117 A. 445 (Pa. 1922).

The gift here was executed, and that defendant was not to record it was not of the slightest consequence when viewed as against these major actions, delivery and passing of title. It was merely a promise the keeping of which lay in good faith, the breach of which entailed no legal consequences. To have effected the grantor's purpose, the intervention of a third party was absolutely essential. There are circumstances where acknowledgment, together with physical possession of the deed in the grantee, does not conclusively establish an intention to deliver, and the presumption arising from signing, sealing, and acknowledging, accompanied by manual possession of the deed by the grantee, is not irrebuttable, but this presumption can be overcome only by evidence that no delivery was in fact intended and none made. Such evidence is not present in this case. Here the grantor by his own testimony intended the grantee to get the land. The only question was when it was to take effect.

Here is one of the instances in which the law fails to give effect to the honest intention of the parties, for the reason that they have not adopted the proper legal means of accomplishing their object. Therefore the legal effect of such delivery is not altered by the fact that both parties suppose the deed will not take effect until recorded, and that it may be revoked at any time before record, or by contemporaneous agreements looking to the reconveyance of the property to the grantor or to the third party upon the happening of certain contingent events or the nonperformance of certain conditions.

The reason for these rules is obvious. It is quite possible to prove in most deliveries that some parol injunction was attached to the formal delivery of the deed; if they are to be given the effect her[e] contended, there would be no safety in accepting a deed under most circumstances. It opens the door to the fabrication of evidence that would inevitably be appalling and go far toward violating the security of written instruments. We have so held in matters of less import than the conveyance of land. The rule must not be relaxed as to realty. Such conveyances are vastly more important, as they involve instruments of title and ownership which are used as a means of extending credit. Title to land ought not to be exposed to the peril of successful attack except where the right is clear and undoubted, and whatever may be our desire to recognize circumstances argued as unfortunate, we cannot go to the extent of overthrowing principles of law governing conveyances of real estate that have stood the test of ages.

In *Cragin's Estate*, supra, the deeds were in a tin box for more than 23 years in an envelope indorsed with the words: 'To be recorded upon Mrs. Cragin's death, if before me.' The deed was in grantee's possession, and it was urged the delivery was conditional. We said that indorsement may have been placed on the envelope for other reasons than to defer the transfer of title. In the present case it was evident appellee did not want his relatives to learn of the conveyance. Recording would be necessary to pass a title examiner's inspection, but nonrecording did not prevent the title from passing. It has been quite generally held that an oral understanding on the delivery of a deed that it should not be recorded will not affect the absolute character of the conveyance if free of other conditions. An agreement to deliver a deed in escrow to the person in whose favor it is made, and who is likewise a party to it, will not make the delivery conditional. If delivered under such an agreement, it will be deemed an absolute delivery and a consummation of the execution of the deed. …

Questions

1. The old phrase is that a deed was effective when it was "signed, sealed, and delivered." But the seal is obsolete, so the principal elements are that it be a sufficient writing (discussed above), that it be signed, and that it be delivered. Delivery of deeds has much in common with delivery in the law of gifts; it too can be a subtle question. In a famous passage of his landmark 17th-century treatise, *Institutes of the Lawes of England*, Edward Coke wrote, "As a deed may be delivered to a party without words, so may a deed be delivered by words without any act of delivery." That sounds paradoxical, but Coke continued, "as if the writing sealed lies upon the table, and the [grantor] says to the [grantee], 'Go and take up that writing, it is sufficient for you;' or 'it will serve your turn;' or 'Take it as my deed;' or the like words; either is a sufficient delivery." Is that better?

2. In *Wiggill v. Cheney*, 597 P.2d 1351 (Utah 1979), Lillian Cheney executed a deed to Flora Cheney and put it in a safety deposit box in the names of Lillian Cheney and Francis E. Wiggill. Lillian told Francis that his name was on the box, that on her death he would be granted access to the box, and that "in that box is an envelope addressed to all those concerned. All you have to do is give them that envelope and that's all." On her death, he gained access to the box, took the deed, and gave it to Flora. Delivery?

3. There are at least two ways to do delivery "right." One is to sign and hand over a deed at closing, when all of the necessary parties are in the same room and can execute all of the appropriate documents effectively simultaneously. Another is to use an escrow: a third party who receives custody of the signed deed along with instructions to deliver it to the grantee when appropriate events have taken place. What if the escrow agent disregards her instructions and hands over the deed early? Can a grantor who is concerned the transaction will fall through demand the deed back from the escrow agent?

4. *Loughran* is more complicated because the parties intended a conditional gift that would take effect at Loughran's death, rather than immediately. Grantors often try to put other

kinds of conditions on transfers. In *Martinez v. Martinez*, 678 P.2d 1163 (N.M. 1984), Delfino and Eleanor Martinez gave their son Carlos and his wife Sennie a deed to a property in exchange for assuming a mortgage in it. Delfino and Eleanor instructed Carlos and Sennie to take the deed to the bank to be held in escrow until Carlos and Sennie had paid off the mortgage, but they recorded it first. Carlos and Sennie had marital difficulties and fell behind on the mortgage; eventually Delfino and Eleanor paid off the balance. Who owns the property?

5. The *Loughran* court says the parties "have not adopted the proper legal means of accomplishing their object." What does it mean? Is there anything they could have done differently that would avoided this mess?

New York Real Property Law

§ 258 – Short forms of deeds and mortgages.

The use of the following forms of instruments for the conveyance and mortgage of real property is lawful, but this section does not prevent or invalidate the use of other forms:

Statutory Form A (Individual)

DEED WITH FULL COVENANTS.

This indenture, made the ...... day of .... nineteen hundred and ......, between ....(insert residence) party of the first part, and .... (insert residence) party of the second part,

Witnesseth, that the party of the first part, in consideration of .... dollars, lawful money of the United States, paid by the party of the second part, does hereby grant and release unto the party of the second part, ... and assigns forever, all .... (description), together with the appurtenances and all the estate and rights of the party of the first part in and to said premises,

To have and to hold the premises herein granted unto the party of the second part, ... and assigns forever. And said .... covenants as follows:

First. That said .... is seized of said premises in fee simple, and has good right to convey the same;

Second. That the party of the second part shall quietly enjoy the said premises;

Third. That the said premises are free from incumbrances;

Fourth. That the party of the first part will execute or procure any further necessary assurance of the title to said premises;

Fifth. That said .... will forever warrant the title to said premises.

In witness whereof, the party of the first part has hereunto set his hand and seal the day and year first above written.

In presence of:

Statutory Form D. (Individual)

QUITCLAIM DEED.

This indenture, made the .... day of ...., nineteen hundred and ...., between ...., (insert residence), party of the first part, and ...., (insert residence), party of the second part:

Witnesseth, that the party of the first part, in consideration of .... dollars, lawful money of the United States, paid by the party of the second part, does hereby remise, release, and quitclaim unto the party of the second part, ... and assigns forever, all (description), together with the appurtenances and all the estate and rights of the party of the first part in and to said premises.

To have and to hold the premises herein granted unto the party of the second part, ... and assigns forever.

In witness whereof, the party of the first part has hereunto set his hand and seal the day and year first above written.

In presence of:

Questions

1. What is the difference between these two deed forms? Why would a grantee ever accept a quitclaim deed?

Brush Grocery Kart, Inc. v. Sure Fine Market, Inc.
47 P.3d 680 (Colo. 2002)

JUSTICE COATS delivered the opinion of the court: ...

In October 1992 Brush Grocery Kart, Inc. and Sure Fine Market, Inc. entered into a five-year "Lease with Renewal Provisions and Option to Purchase" for real property, including a building to be operated by Brush as a grocery store. Under the contract's purchase option provision, any time during the last six months of the lease, Brush could elect to purchase the property at a price equal to the average of the appraisals of an expert designated by each party.

Shortly before expiration of the lease, Brush notified Sure Fine of its desire to purchase the property and begin the process of determining a sale price. Although each party offered an appraisal, the parties were unable to agree on a final price by the time the lease expired. Brush then vacated the premises, returned all keys to Sure Fine, and advised Sure Fine that it would discontinue its casualty insurance covering the property during the lease. Brush also filed suit, alleging that Sure Fine failed to negotiate the price term in good faith and asking for the appointment of a special master to determine the purchase price. Sure Fine agreed to the appointment of a special master and counterclaimed, alleging that Brush negotiated the price term in bad faith and was therefore the breaching party.

During litigation over the price term, the property was substantially damaged during a hail storm. With neither party carrying casualty insurance, each asserted that the other was liable for the damage. The issue was added to the litigation at a stipulated amount of $60,000. ... The court then found that under the doctrine of equitable conversion, Brush was the equitable owner of the property and bore the risk of loss. It therefore declined to abate the purchase price or award damages to Brush for the loss.

Brush appealed the loss allocation, and the court of appeals affirmed on similar grounds. ...

In the absence of statutory authority, the rights, powers, duties, and liabilities arising out of a contract for the sale of land have frequently been derived by reference to the theory of equitable conversion. This theory or doctrine, which has been described as a legal fiction, is based on equitable principles that permit the vendee to be considered the equitable owner of the land and debtor for the purchase money and the vendor to be regarded as a secured creditor. The changes in rights and liabilities that occur upon the making of the contract result from the equitable right to specific performance. Even with regard to third parties, the theory has been relied on to determine, for example, the devolution, upon death, of the rights and liabilities of each party with respect to the land, and to ascertain the powers of creditors of each party to reach the land in payment of their claims.

The assignment of the risk of casualty loss in the executory period of contracts for the sale of real property varies greatly throughout the jurisdictions of this country. What appears to yet be a slim majority of states places the risk of loss on the vendee from the moment of contracting, on the rationale that once an equitable conversion takes place, the vendee must be treated as owner for all purposes. Once the vendee becomes the equitable owner, he therefore becomes responsible for the condition of the property, despite not having a present right of occupancy or control. In sharp contrast, a handful of other states reject the allocation of casualty loss risk as a consequence of the theory of equitable conversion and follow the equally rigid "Massachusetts Rule," under which the seller continues to bear the risk until actual transfer of the title, absent an express agreement to the contrary. A substantial and growing number of jurisdictions, however, base the legal consequences of no-fault casualty loss on the right to possession of the property at the time the loss occurs. This view has found expression in the Uniform Vendor and Purchaser Risk Act, and while a number of states have adopted some variation of the Uniform Act, others have arrived at a similar position through the interpretations of their courts. ...

In *Wiley v. Lininger*, 204 P.2d 1083, [(1949)] where fire destroyed improvements on land occupied by the vendee during the multi-year executory period of an installment land contract, we held, according to the generally accepted rule, that neither the buyer nor the seller, each of whom had an insurable interest in the property, had an obligation to insure the property for the benefit of the other. We also adopted a rule, which we characterized as "the majority rule," that "the vendee under a contract for the sale of land, being regarded as the equitable owner, assumes the risk of destruction of or injury to the property *where he is in possession*, and the destruction or loss is not proximately caused by the negligence of the vendor." *Id.* (emphasis added). The vendee in possession was therefore not relieved of his obligation to continue making payments according to the terms of the contract, despite material loss by fire to some of the improvements on the property. ... Those jurisdictions that indiscriminately include the risk of casualty loss among the incidents or "attributes" of equitable ownership do so largely in reliance on ancient authority or by considering it necessary for consistent application of the theory of equitable conversion. Under virtually any accepted understanding of the theory, however, equitable conversion is not viewed as entitling the purchaser to every significant right of ownership, and particularly not the right of possession. As a matter of both logic and equity, the obligation to maintain property in its physical condition follows the right to have actual possession and control rather than a legal right to force conveyance of the property through specific performance at some future date. See 17 SAMUEL WILLISTON, A TREATISE ON THE LAW OF CONTRACTS § 50:46, at 457-58 (Richard A. Lord ed., 4th ed. 1990) ("[I]t is wiser to have the party in possession of the property care for it at his peril, rather than at the peril of another.").

The equitable conversion theory is literally stood on its head by imposing on a vendee, solely because of his right to specific performance, the risk that the vendor will be unable to specifically perform when the time comes because of an accidental casualty loss. It is counterintuitive, at the very least, that merely contracting for the sale of real property should not only relieve the vendor of his responsibility to maintain the property until execution but also impose a duty on the vendee to perform despite the intervention of a material, no-fault casualty loss preventing him from ever receiving the benefit of his bargain. Such an extension of the theory of equitable conversion to casualty loss has never been recognized by this jurisdiction, and it is neither necessary nor justified solely for the sake of consistency.

By contrast, there is substantial justification, both as a matter of law and policy, for not relieving a vendee who is entitled to possession before transfer of title, like the vendee in *Wiley*, of his duty to pay the full contract price, notwithstanding an accidental loss. In addition to having control over the property and being entitled to the benefits of its use, an equitable owner who also has the right of possession has already acquired virtually all of the rights of ownership and almost invariably will have already paid at least some portion of the contract price to exercise those rights. By expressly including in the contract for sale the right of possession, which otherwise generally accompanies transfer of title, the vendor has for all practical purposes already transferred the property as promised, and the parties have in effect expressed their joint intention that the vendee pay the purchase price as promised. ...

In the absence of a right of possession, a vendee of real property that suffers a material casualty loss during the executory period of the contract, through no fault of his own, must be permitted to rescind and recover any payments he had already made. ...

Here, Brush was clearly not in possession of the property as the equitable owner. Even if the doctrine of equitable conversion applies to the option contract between Brush and Sure Fine and could be said to have converted Brush's interest to an equitable ownership of the property at the time Brush exercised its option to purchase, neither party considered the contract for sale to entitle Brush to possession. Brush was, in fact, not in possession of the property, and the record indicates that Sure Fine considered itself to hold the right of use and occupancy and gave notice that it would consider Brush a holdover tenant if it continued to occupy the premises other than by continuing to lease the property. The casualty loss was ascertainable and in fact stipulated by the parties, and neither party challenged the district court's enforcement of the contract except with regard to its allocation of the casualty loss. Both the court of appeals and the district court therefore erred in finding that the doctrine of equitable conversion required Brush to bear the loss caused by hail damage.

Questions

1. Why is the risk of loss during the executory period even a thing? Why would the parties leave time between signing a contract of sale and closing? Why not just hand over a deed on the spot?

2. If the grocery store had been damaged by hail during the five-year lease preceding the sale, who would have borne the risk of loss? Would it matter whether Brush had taken possession of the property? Who bears the risk of loss if Brush owns a grocery store subject to Sure Fine's mortgage?

10. Recording Acts

Famed con artist George C. Parker specialized in selling the Brooklyn Bridge. Parker and other con artists working in New York around the start of the 20th century would convince victims that they stood to make a fortune charging tolls. Unfortunately, the buyers obtained nothing, no matter how fancy the paperwork Parker offered them, because Parker did not own the bridge. *Nemo dat quod non habet* was the Latin motto of the common law: "No man can give what he does not have." Parker, having no title, could give none to his buyers.

Today, "I've got a bridge to sell you" is a punchline: only an incredible rube, we like to believe, could be so gullible as to think that a man in the street with a "Bridge for Sale" sign is actually its owner. But the problem arises even in less dramatic cases. Suppose Dorothy Dupe is scheduled to buy Blackacre on Wednesday from Sadie Scamalot. What if on Tuesday Scamalot sells Blackacre to Charles Clueless first? Then on Wednesday before the "sale," Scamalot is no longer the owner of Blackacre, and under *nemo dat*, Dupe owns nothing after the "sale." Sometimes, equity would intervene to protect a second buyer who lacked notice of the prior sale – but such doctrines have serious risks for Clueless, who may have no idea that Scamalot is about to turn around and "sell" Blackacre again.

The heart of the problem here is that Clueless and Dupe don't know enough about potential conflicting claims to Blackacre. Dupe can't find Clueless to confirm that she should be dealing with him rather than with Scamalot, and Clueless can't find Dupe to warn her off from buying something Scamalot no longer owns. Recording systems try to prevent some of these messes by making available better information about who owns what. If Clueless *recorded* his interest in Blackacre by making it a matter of public record, then it becomes reasonable to treat Dupe as having *constructive notice* of Clueless's claim of ownership: even if she didn't check the records, she should have. Conversely, if Clueless fails to record, there is much less Dupe can do to protect herself, so it becomes reasonable to let Dupe take title free and clear of Clueless's claim. Thus, the system gives Clueless a strong incentive to record and gives Dupe a strong incentive to check the records. As a result, there are good records of people's property claims. Clueless and Dupe never get into this mess in the first place, and Scamalot's scheme fails.

Recording systems are useful even in the absence of fraud; they create the trust and certainty needed to make land transactions common and reliable. Most home sales today happen between people who do not otherwise know each other and don't otherwise expect to transact again. How can the buyer be sure the seller is really the owner? A recording system provides the answer. Perhaps more importantly, a recording system gives *lenders* sufficient assurance that they'll be able to recover something in case of a loan default; with that security, they are willing to loan more and at lower rates.

For this and other reasons, a recording system can be a vital part of a large-scale, modern economy. According to the *New York Times*, for example, the absence of a functioning recording system in Greece "scares off foreign investors; makes it hard for the state to privatize its assets, as it has promised to do in exchange for bailout money; and makes it virtually impossible to collect property taxes." Suzanne Daley, *Who Owns This Land? In Greece, Who Knows?*, NEW YORK TIMES, May 26, 2013. Clear title is often important for access to government services and even water and electricity connections: otherwise it's not clear where the checks and bills should go.

The materials in this section work through real property recording systems from the inside out. First, an excerpt from an article by Carol Rose traces some recurring themes in the history of recording law. Second, *Belmont* considers what it means to "record" a document and under what circumstances it ought to be treated as giving notice. Third, *Hartig* examines the process of searching title records: what must a reasonable buyer do to confirm that there are no conflicting claims? *Argent* then considers the main variations on this scheme under state recording acts, many of which create additional incentives to record quickly by creating a "race" to the recording office. *Hughes* illustrates the kinds of messes that can arise even with a reasonably well-functioning recording system. The Note on Informal Title finishes by considering some of the systemic advantages that have been claimed for well-functioning recording systems, and some of the empirical evidence for and against those claims.

Carol M. Rose, *Crystals And Mud In Property Law*
40 STAN. L. REV. 577 (1988)
(excerpts reprinted by permission)

... In establishing recording systems, legislatures have lent support to private parties' efforts to sharpen the definition of their entitlements. The *raison d'etre* of such systems is to clarify and perfectly specify landed property rights for the sake of easy and smooth transfers of land.

But the Anglo-American recording system in fact has been a saga of frustrated efforts to make clear who has what in land transfers. Common law transfers of land required a certain set of formalities between the parties, but thereafter, conflicting claims were settled by the age-old principle, 'first in time, first in right.' Thus, on Tuesday I might sell my farm to you, and on Wednesday I might wrongfully purport to sell it once again to innocent Farmer Brown. Poor Farmer Brown remains landless even though he knew nothing about the prior sale to you and indeed had no way of knowing about it. This outcome was hardly satisfactory from a property rights perspective. 'First in time, first in right' may work well enough in a community where everyone knows all about everyone else's transactions, but outside that context, the doctrine does little to put people on notice of who owns what, and the opportunities for conflicting claims are endless.

But the efforts to remedy this flaw have gone through new cycles of certainty and uncertainty. Henry VIII attempted – without great success – to establish public registration of land claims through the Statute of Enrollments in 1536. Versions of the Statute resurfaced in Massachusetts' 1640 recording act and in other seventeenth and eighteenth century colonial recording acts, all of which were much more widely (though still somewhat irregularly) applied than their Henrician model had been.

Henry's Statute and its original American counterparts reflected an emphatically crystalline view of property. Their literal language suggests that they were versions of what has come to be called a 'race' statute) the first purchaser to record (the winner of the 'race' to the registry) can hold his title against all other claimants, whether or not he was in fact the first to purchase. In such a system, the official records become an unimpeachable source of information about the status of land ownership; the law counts the record owner, and only the record owner, as the true owner. The purchaser can buy in reliance on the records without fear of divestment by some unknown interloper, and without the need to make some cumbersome extra-record search for such potential interlopers.

This system was too crystalline to last. The characters to muck up this crystalline system [are] ninnies, hard-luck cases, and the occasional scoundrels who take advantage of them. What are we to do, for example, with the silly fellow who buys an interest in property but simply forgets to record? Or with the more conscientious one who does attempt to record his interest, but whose records wind up in the wrong book? Or with the lost soul whose impeccably correct filing is dropped behind the radiator by the neglectful clerk? Some courts take a hard line, perhaps concluding that the first owner was in a better position than our innocent outsider – that is, the next purchaser – to detect and correct the flaws in the records. But our sympathies for the luckless unrecorded owner put pressure on the recording system that would divest him in favor of the later-arriving outsider. – –

Our sympathies are all the greater when the outsider is not so innocent after all. What shall we do, say, when the unrecorded first buyer is snookered out of his claim by a later purchaser who knows perfectly well that the land had already been sold? Shall we allow this nasty second buyer to perfect a claim simply because he carefully follows the official recording rules? This thought was too much for the courts of equity, and too much for American legislatures as well. By the early nineteenth century, the British equity courts had imported an element of non-record 'notice' into what had initially been a 'race' system. Under these doctrines, the later purchaser could take free of the prior claims only if he did not *know* about those prior claims, either from the records or from non-record facts that should put him 'on notice.' American legislatures followed this move to such a degree that, at present, only a handful of states maintain a race system with any rigor. The other states deny the subsequent claim of the person who had or should have had notice of the earlier claim.

This development means mud: What 'should' a purchaser know about, anyway? To be sure, if someone is living on the land, perhaps the potential purchaser should make a few inquiries about the occupant's status. But what if the 'occupant's' acts are more ambiguous, consisting of, say, shovelling some manure onto the contested land? Well, said one court, a buyer should have asked about the source of all that manure – and since he didn't, and thus did not find out about the manure shoveller's prior but unrecorded claim, the later buyer did not count as an innocent; his title was a nullity.

With the emergence of this judicial outlook, the crystalline idea of the recording system has come full cycle back to mud. To be sure, the recording system can give one a fair guess about the legal status of any given property. But by the end of the last century, as a Massachusetts court put it, 'it would be seldom that a case could occur where some state of facts might not be imagined which, if it existed, would defeat a title.' Thus, the test of a title's 'marketability' became a question of whether the title was subject to 'reasonable' doubt – a matter, of course, for the discretion of the court. In the meantime, a whole title insurance industry sprang up to calm the fears of would-be purchasers who wanted to avoid questions about which doubts were reasonable and which were not. It is this industry, in a sense, that once again makes crystals out of the recording system's mud; and according to the reformers, it is this industry that now stands in the way of a more rational method of cleaning up the mess once and for all.

Yet one must wonder whether cleaning up the mess might not just repeat the cycle of mud/crystal/mud. One of the most popular suggestions for reform is the so-called 'Torrens' system, named for someone who thought that shipping registry methods could be used beneficially in real estate. In this system, all claims on a given property – sales, liens, easements, etc. – are first registered and then incorporated in a certificate. Torrens registration echoes eerily the colonial 'race' statutes: No unregistered claim counts, and the owner's certificate for a given property acts as the complete record of everything that anyone might claim.

Well, perhaps not everything: Government liens, fraudulent transactions, and, according to some courts, even simple errors or neglect in registration can produce unregistered claims that count. Hence this neo-race system provides no complete relief from the recording system's mud. Even after we look at the Torrens certificate, we still have to be on the lookout for the G-men, the forgers, and the ninnies who neglected to register their claims properly. Not a lot of mud, to be sure, but just wait. In some jurisdictions with a long history of Torrens registration, courts have in effect reestablished a 'notice' system, defeating the interest of one who registers his claim when he knows about a prior unregistered one – or merely when he *should* have known about the prior claim. This practice, of course, means that the registry and certificate no longer count as the complete source of information about a property's title status.

The most striking aspect of these developments is that first the title recording acts, and later the registration systems, represented deliberate choices to establish crystaline rules for the sake of simplicity and ease of land sales and purchases. People who failed to use the records or registries were supposed to lose their claims, no matter how innocent they might have been, and no matter how nastily their opponents might have behaved. Yet these very crystalline systems have drifted back into mud through the importation of equitable ideas of notice – only to be replaced by new crystalline systems in the form of private contract or public legislation….

Let us suppose that we have a system for the clarification of property titles. Might we have a tendency to overuse the system, so that in the end it becomes so hopelessly bogged down in detail that the purpose of clarity is defeated? Certainly our traditional land records have this quality. Some early cases permitted only fee interests to be recorded, but it was the very attractiveness of the system that created pressure to allow the recordation of other interests; liens, for example, or easements. Indeed, some claims may be in the records even though they are not legally recordable. Then too, many claims are recorded and just stay put over time, and sometimes even conflict with other recorded claims. The layers of these recorded but unextinguished claims can grow so thick that it hardly seems worth the time to go back and check them all. So, in a sense, we treat our clarifying systems – in this case the recording mechanisms – as a kind of 'commons.' The resulting system overload, in turn, creates a certain disgust with the lush proliferation of records. In fact, one of our current recording reforms would simply extinguish claims that have not been asserted during a given period.

Thus, the very attractiveness of making clear one's claims by recording them defeats the purpose of the system, that is, to clarify all claims against a given property. One sees the same pattern in the excessively long contracts that attempt to specify all possible contingencies and that no one actually reads; however comforting it might be to 'have it in writing,' it really isn't worth the effort to nail down everything, and the overly precise contract may wind up being just as opaque as – and perhaps even more arbitrary than – the one that leaves adjustments to the contingencies of future relations.

The trouble, then, is that an attractively simple legal device draws in too many users, or too complex a set of uses. And that, of course, is where the simple rule becomes a booby trap. It is this booby trap aspect of what seems to be clear, simple rules – that scenario of disproportionate loss by some party-that seems to drive us to muddy up crystal rules with the exceptions and the post hoc discretionary judgments.

Nat'l Packing Corp. v. Belmont

547 N.E.2d 373 (Ohio Ct. App. 1988)

DOAN, J.

In the instant appeal, we must determine whether to apply the venerable doctrine of *idem sonans* to the facts and circumstances set forth in the record. …

The record reveals that the plaintiff, National Packaging Corporation ("NPC"), sued Michael Bolan, d.b.a. Trade Packaging, in the Franklin County Court of Common Pleas. On November 25, 1983, NPC obtained a judgment for $3,331.76 plus interest; and, at a later time, it certified the judgment in Hamilton County, with Bolan's name incorrectly spelled "B-O-L-E-N" in the docket book. At the time the judgment was certified, Michael Bolan owned property in Hamilton County at 8107 Camargo Road and 815 Indian Hill Road.

Bolan's ex-wife, Elaine (now Elaine Belmont), brought a foreclosure action against the property located at 815 Indian Hill Road to collect overdue child-support payments. The property was sold in a sheriff's sale to L. Michael and Elaine Belmont (Bolan's ex-wife and her new husband). Because NPC's judgment was filed under an incorrect spelling of Bolan's name, NPC did not receive notice of the sheriff's sale and was unable to protect its interest in the property.

The Belmonts subsequently sold the Indian Hill Road property to Richard E. and Vera DeCamp. It was only after this second conveyance that NPC brought its own foreclosure action, asserting the certified judgment from Franklin County against both the Indian Hill Road property and the Camargo Road property.

The Belmonts moved to dismiss NPC's complaint in a filing that the trial court treated as a motion for summary judgment. The DeCamps then moved for summary judgment against NPC and the Belmonts. NPC responded with its own motion for summary judgment against the Belmonts and the DeCamps. On April 30, 1987, the trial court overruled NPC's motion for summary judgment, entered summary judgment for the DeCamps and the Belmonts against NPC and held that the DeCamps' motion for summary judgment against the Belmonts was moot. The court dismissed all other claims existing among these three parties, adding a Civ. R. 54(B) certification in a *nunc pro* [*tunc*] entry dated July 6, 1987, and this appeal followed.

In its single assignment of error, NPC asserts that the trial court erred to its prejudice by overruling its motion for summary judgment. Relying upon the doctrine of *idem sonans*,[1] it argues that the certified judgment filed under a similar sounding but incorrect spelling of the debtor Bolan's name, retaining the same initial letters as the correctly spelled name, should have been held to give rise to a valid lien for the benefit of NPC and to provide the appropriate constructive notice to title searchers.

The doctrine of *idem sonans* was adopted by the Ohio Supreme Court in *Lessee of Pillsbury* v. *Dugan's Administrator* (1839), 9 Ohio 117. There the court held that Mrs. Pillsbury was on sufficient notice that her one-eighth interest in certain real estate was being adjudicated, even though the petition for partition listed her as "Pillsby." Its reasoning was expressed in these terms:

> "In adjudicating upon transactions occurring in the early settlement of our state, we must never forget the absence of precedents and system, the different usages introduced by people emigrating from every part of the country, the want of knowledge or neglect of technical learning, and the risk of loss of evidence from the lapse of time. Hence errors of form have always been overlooked, where the acts of a court are manifest, and its jurisdiction established. …
>
> "It is not every mistake in names which will invalidate an instrument or proceeding. *This effect will follow where the person can not be identified,* or where the error is such as to describe another. But words are intended to be spoken; and where the sound is substantially preserved, bad spelling will not vitiate. * * *" (Emphasis added.) *Id.* at 119-120.

The petition in *Pillsbury* otherwise identified Mrs. Pillsbury by reference to her father, who died seized of the subject real estate, and to her apparent siblings and in-laws. Further, the petition

---

[1] The doctrine of idem sonans is defined in 70 OHIO JURISPRUDENCE 3d (1986) 21-22, *Names*, Section 18, as follows:

> "The arbitrary orthography and pronunciation given to proper names, and the variant spelling resulting from ignorance have led the courts to formulate the doctrine of `idem sonans,' which means `sounding the same.' Under this doctrine a mistake in spelling the name of a party is immaterial if both modes of spelling have the same sound. The grounds for applying the doctrine to slight variations in spelling is that of de minimis non curat lex – the principle that the law is not concerned with trifles. The general rule in Ohio seems to be that a change in the spelling of a word which does not alter its meaning, or in the spelling of a name where the idem sonans is preserved, is not a material variance. Thus, it is not every mistake in names which will invalidate an instrument or proceeding. To have this effect, the mistake must be such that a person cannot be identified, or that the error describes another. Since words are intended to be spoken, bad spelling will not vitiate their intended effect where the sound is substantially preserved."

correctly identified the real estate. Thus, she could be identified in spite of her misspelled name. . . .

The Ohio Supreme Court next mentioned the doctrine of *idem sonans* in *Buchanan* v. *Roy's Lessee* (1853), 2 Ohio St. 251, a quiet-title action initiated by Nicholas Longworth. The court, in dicta, mused that the misspelling of Sarah Roy's name as Sarah Ray, in a notice by publication, standing alone might be fatal to the action. Without squarely deciding the question, however, the court went on to note that Sarah Roy could otherwise be identified in the published notice. Thus the "otherwise identified" standard was carried forward from *Pillsbury* to *Buchanan.*

In 1869, the Ohio Supreme Court again dealt with *idem sonans,* this time in a criminal matter. In *Turpin* v. *State* (1869), 19 Ohio St. 540, a case involving an allegedly forged signature, there was a variance between the spelling of the name as it appeared on the state's exhibit ("R-e-n-n-i-c-k" or "R-u-n-i-c-k"), and the spelling of the name as it appeared in an indictment ("R-e-n-i-c-k"). The court, however, found no fatal flaw in the variance … .

NPC cites *Rauch* v. *Immel* (1936), 55 Ohio App. 71, 23 Ohio Law Abs. 629, 8 O.O. 354, 8 N.E.2d 569, and *Horton* v. *Matheny* (1943), 72 Ohio App. 187, 27 O.O. 69, 51 N.E.2d 41, as the basis for validation of its claimed error. We note, however, that in *Rauch* the doctrine was applied to a misnomer in a notice of a lawsuit, and in *Horton* it was applied to a misspelling in a deed description. In these two cases, as in *Pillsbury, Buchanan,* and *Turpin,* the error did not involve misspellings in a name index.

The case of *Gleich* v. *Earnest* (1930), 36 Ohio App. 326, 173 N.E. 212, is NPC's best authority because it is factually analogous to the instant matter. In *Gleich,* the court held that *idem sonans* validated the assertion of a mechanic's lien against the purchaser of the property at a foreclosure sale, even though the foreclosure suit did not name the lienholder. The lienholder had filed its lien against "C. C. Ernest," when in fact the property was held in the name of "Chester C. Earnest." The court's decision upholding the lienholder's position rested upon the testimony of two abstractors who testified that they would have searched the records under both "Ernest" and "Earnest."

In the matter *sub judice,* three experts have given affidavits stating that the doctrine of *idem sonans* should not be applied today as a standard for determining the marketable title of real estate on the basis of irregularities in last names or surnames, and that by custom it is not applied by abstractors in southwestern Ohio.

We hold that the doctrine of *idem sonans* is inapplicable to names that are misspelled in judgment-lien name indexes. We are not a frontier society of pioneers with little education or an absence of precedent and system. Since the Supreme Court issued its opinion in *Pillsbury* in 1839, we have experienced a tremendous growth in the population and the economy, and those developments have spawned countless real estate sales and a volume of litigation resulting in an abundance of indexed judgment liens. In modern society we cannot overlook matters of form by continuing to indulge the outmoded premises of our societal infancy. To impose rigidly the doctrine of *idem sonans* to name indexes now maintained for judgment liens would tax all land abstractors beyond reasonable limits and require them to be poets, phonetic linguists, or multilingual specialists. The additional time necessary to examine name indexes under such a stringent doctrine would make the examinations financially prohibitive.

The appellees, in their brief, demonstrate the difficulty in applying the doctrine of *idem sonans* to the range of spellings implicated in the instant case: Bolan, Bolen, Bolin, Bowlin, Bowlan, Bowlen, Bolun; the addition of double "l," "ein," and "ien" spellings does not even exhaust all conceivable spelling possibilities. The impossibility of the task created by the doctrine of *idem sonans* is further illustrated by the fact that we, as a society and state, are no longer a small homogeneous population primarily of European abstraction. Since our infancy, we have added Asian, African, South American, Oriental and Arabic surnames. The spelling, sound, and pronunciation of our population's surnames create an insurmountable burden for an abstractor to face in appreciating all the possible variations. Under all the circumstances, a strict application of the doctrine today would leave a real estate purchaser with a lingering fear that misspelled lienholders, either negligently or deliberately, might be lurking under the *idem sonans* doctrine in the judgment-debtor indexes.

We further conclude that the misspelling of Bolan as "B-o-l-e-n," does not rise to being "otherwise identifiable." Unlike many states that statutorily require land descriptions with lien filings, Ohio's indexes merely require a name.

Finally, with the exception of *Gleich,* the courts have not strictly applied *idem sonans.* We find instead a conditional application, which includes as a factor whether the individual is otherwise identified, and in only one case has the doctrine been applied to listings in a judgment-lien name index. We cannot, in sum, find any authority mandating strict application of the *idem sonans* doctrine. …

Questions

1. True or false: the result in *Belmont* follows from the principle of *nemo dat*? True or false: the result in *Belmont* follows from the principle that a good-faith purchaser for value takes free of conflicting transfers of which she had no notice? What work, if any, are these principles doing in the case?

2. What result if a deed as delivered to the clerk reads "Bolan" but the clerk enters it in the indexes under "Bolen?" Under "Nolan?" What if the clerk neglects to index it at all? What if the clerk drops the deed behind the radiator and forgets about it?

3. Elaine Bolan changed her name to Elaine Belmont when she remarried. If during her first marriage, she co-signed a mortgage with her now ex-husband Michael Bolan, will a title searcher find it in a search under "Belmont?" Whose problem is that? What if her new name is Elaine Bolan-Belmont?

4. Problems also arise in determining what a recorded deed actually gives notice of. In *Luthi v. Evans*, 576 P.2d 1064 (Kan. 1978), Grace Owens executed a deed in 1971 granting International Tours "all interest of whatsoever nature in all working interests and overriding royalty interest in all Oil and Gas Leases in Coffey County, Kansas, owned by [Owens]." The deed, which was properly recorded, listed seven leases in Coffey County, but Owens also owned an eighth, the Kufahl lease. Who owns the Kufahl lease? Four years later, Owens gave a deed to the Kufahl lease to J.R. Burris, who had no actual knowledge of the deed to International Tours. Who owns the Kufahl lease now? Would the result be the same if the deed to International Tours had referred instead to "all Oil and Gas Leases described in the attached Schedule A," and Schedule A had listed all eight leases, but the deed had been recorded without Schedule A?

5. Land records are increasingly maintained using computer databases rather than paper records. Does this cut for or against applying the doctrine of *idem sonans*? Are there ways to improve the quality of the recording system by using computers, so that mistakes like this (and others) are less likely?

6. In 2008, the *New York Daily News* "stole" the Empire State Building by recording a phony deed to it in New York City's recording system. The deed purported to transfer ownership of the building to "Nelotis Properties L.L.C."; it bore a fake notary stamp and purported to be "witnessed" by Fay Wray, the actress who starred in *King Kong*. Clerks made no attempt to verify any of the information on the deed, which was duly recorded. Should they have?

7. Tax protesters – people who challenge the authority of government to collect taxes – sometimes record multi-million-dollar "liens" against the houses of local tax officials and government lawyers. Unlike the lien in *Belmont*, which resulted from a judgment of an Ohio state court, these "liens" arise from the actions of "common law courts" established by the protesters themselves. What effect does recording one of these "liens" have? What can the victims do about it? How might a state government deal with the general problem of fraudulent recording?

Hartig v. Stratman

729 N.E.2d 237 (2000)

SHARPNACK, Chief Judge: …

Melvin and Louise Stratman are the owners of real property located at 2208 E. Walnut St. in Evansville, Indiana. The property next door, at 2210 E. Walnut St., is owned by [Timothy] Hartig. The instant dispute centers around a shared driveway that is located on both parcels of property, with the majority of the driveway being on Hartig's property.

The record of title to Hartig's property discloses that Hartig purchased the property from Sean Holmes on September 28, 1995. Holmes in turn purchased the property from John Connell on May 31, 1994. On the same day that Connell sold the property to Holmes, Connell entered into a written easement agreement with the Stratmans regarding the shared driveway. The agreement gave the Stratmans a perpetual easement over the portion of the driveway that is located upon the parcel at 2210 E. Walnut St. and gave the property owners at 2210 E. Walnut St. a perpetual easement over the portion of the driveway that is located upon the Stratman parcel. The Stratman-Connell easement agreement was recorded in the Vanderburgh County Recorder's Office on June 8, 1994, at 2:25 p.m. The deed transferring the property at 2210 E. Walnut Street from Connell to Holmes was also recorded on June 8, 1994, but it was recorded one minute earlier, at 2:24 p.m. It is undisputed that when Holmes sold the property to Hartig, he did not inform Hartig about the existence of the driveway easement agreement.

Thereafter, on February 13, 1998, the Stratmans filed a complaint alleging that Hartig was blocking the driveway and refusing to allow them to use it. [The Stratmans claimed a prescriptive easement to use the driveway; the court dismissed their complaint.] Then, on August 26, 1998, the Stratmans filed a "Second Paragraph of Amended Complaint," asserting the right to use the driveway by virtue of the Connell-Stratman easement agreement. Thereafter, Hartig filed a motion for summary judgment, which the trial court denied on June 29, 1999. …

B.

Hartig next contends that he is entitled to summary judgment because the Connell-Stratman driveway easement agreement was recorded outside his chain of title and therefore not binding on him. Indiana's recording statute provides:

> Every conveyance or mortgage of lands or of any interest therein … shall be recorded in the recorder's office … ; and every conveyance [or] mortgage … shall take priority according to the time of the filing thereof, and such conveyance [or] mortgage … shall be fraudulent and void as against any subsequent purchaser, … or mortgagee in good faith and for a valuable consideration, having his deed [or] mortgage … first recorded.

Ind. Code § 32-1-2-16. The purpose of this statute is to provide protection to subsequent purchasers and mortgagees. This protection is derived from the fact that a landowner will not be deemed to have constructive notice of adverse claims that appear outside the chain of title.

To determine the chain of title, the prospective purchaser must go to the recorder's office and search through the grantor index, beginning with the person who received the grant of land from the United States and continuing until the conveyance of the tract in question. The particular grantor's name is not searched thereafter.

Here, when Hartig conducted a title search of the property at 2210 E. Walnut St., he would have discovered the conveyance to Connell. Next, Hartig would have discovered the conveyance from Connell to Holmes that was recorded on June 8, 1994, at 2:24 p.m. Hartig would not have discovered the Connell-Stratford [Ed: presumably "Connell-Stratman"] easement agreement that was recorded one minute later, however, because Connell's name would not have been searched after the conveyance to Holmes was discovered. Therefore, the easement agreement is not within Hartig's chain of title and he cannot be deemed to have constructive notice of its existence. Accordingly, we hold that the trial court erred in denying Hartig's motion for summary judgment with respect to the issue of the driveway easement agreement.

Questions

1. Would it have been easier or harder for Hartig to have discovered the Connell-Stratman easement agreement than it would have been for the DeCamps to have discovered NPC's judgment in *Belmont*?

2. *Morse v. Curtis*, 2 N.E. 929 (Mass. 1885), explained,

   If [a title examiner] can start with an owner who is known to have a good title … he is obliged to run through the index of grantors until he finds a conveyance by the owner of the land in question. After such conveyance the former owner becomes a stranger to the title, and the examiner must follow down the name of the new owner to see if he has conveyed the land, and so on. It would be a hardship to require an examiner to follow in the index of grantors the name of every person who at any time, through, perhaps, a long chain of title, was the owner of the estate.

   Does this policy persuasively justify *Hartig*?

3. Suppose the Stratmans reason as follows: Hartig bought without notice, so we lost to him, but we can fix the notice problem going forward. We'll put up a big sign on our

front yard at 2208 E. Walnut St. reading, "We own a driveway easement across 2210 E. Walnut St." True or false: if the Stratmans do this, anyone who buys the house from Hartig takes with notice of the easement and is therefore bound by it. Would it make a difference if Hartig v. Stratman had never been litigated and reduced to judgment?

4. In Hartig, the Connell-Stratford deed was outside Hartig's chain of title because it was recorded too late: after Connell was no longer the record owner. Deeds can also be recorded too early: before the grantor is the record owner. How could that happen? Suppose that the Bluth Corporation is building a subdivision on land in Sudden Valley that it is purchasing from the federal government. Although the contract of sale with the government has been signed, the delivery of the actual deed to Bluth has been delayed for complex bureaucratic reasons. You represent the Devon Bank, which is financing the development with a loan to Bluth, which will be secured with a mortgage on the land. The bank's manager proposes that the bank go through with the loan and protect its interest by recording the mortgage immediately and ensuring that Bluth records the deed from the government as soon as it issues. Is this a good idea?

5. Who is a "purchaser … for a valuable consideration" entitled to the protection of a recording act? In Hood v. Webster, 2 N.E.2d 43 (N.Y. 1936), Florence Hood executed a deed to a farm to her brother-in-law William Hood in 1913; the deed was escrowed and was to be delivered to William at Florence's death. In 1928, Florence executed and delivered another deed to the same farm, this time to her nephew, Howard Webster. Howard's deed recited that it was given for "One Dollar and other good and valuable consideration." Florence died in 1933. Held: the "recital was not enough to put [Howard] into the position of purchaser[] for a valuable consideration." Is this right? What if the deed had recited that it was given for "Ten Billion Dollars and other good and valuable consideration?" What if Howard had testified that the farm was worth $20,000 and he had given Florence $1,000 in cash? The dissent argued that the record showed that William had reneged on a promise to pay Florence $200 a month for life, and that Howard had "come to live with [Florence] and help her on the farm" when she executed the deed to him. Do these facts affect your view of the case?

Argent Mortgage Co. v. Wachovia Bank N.A.

52. So. 3d 796 (Dist. Ct. App. 2010)

GRIFFIN, J.

Argent Mortgage Company, LLC ["Argent"] appeals the trial court's entry of judgment in favor of Wachovia Bank National Association, as Trustee Under Pooling and Servicing Agreement Dated as of November 1, 2004, Asset Backed Pass–Through Certificates Series 2004–WWF1

["Wachovia"]. Argent argues that the trial court erred by finding that the mortgage now owned by Wachovia has priority over Argent's mortgage. We reverse.

On August 31, 2004, Gene M. Burkes and Ann Burkes ["the Burkes"] as borrower/mortgagor and Olympus Mortgage Company as lender/mortgagee executed a mortgage ["the Olympus Mortgage"] on real property as security for a $90,000.00 loan. The Olympus Mortgage was recorded on January 5, 2005. Subsequently, the Olympus Mortgage was assigned to Wachovia. As a result of default, Wachovia filed a complaint to foreclose the Olympus Mortgage and to enforce lost loan documents. Wachovia joined Argent as a defendant, alleging that Argent might claim some interest in or lien upon the subject property by virtue of a recorded mortgage.

On December 10, 2004, the Burkes as borrower/mortgagor and Argent as lender/mortgagee executed a mortgage ["the Argent Mortgage"] as security for a $65,000.00 loan on the same real property that is the subject of the Olympus Mortgage. The Argent Mortgage was recorded on January 31, 2005. Subsequently, Wells Fargo Bank became the owner of the Argent Mortgage. An action to foreclose the Argent Mortgage was initiated as a result of default.

[Argent and Wachovia filed cross motions for summary judgment.] Ultimately, the trial court deemed "the Florida statutes on recordation," namely sections 695.01 and 695.11, Florida Statutes, "to be of the race-notice variety," found that the Olympus Mortgage should have priority over the Argent Mortgage, and entered a partial final judgment in favor of Wachovia.

On appeal, … Argent asserts that section 695.01, Florida Statutes, alone determines which mortgage has priority, that section 695.01 is, and, for over a century, has been recognized to be a "notice" statute, not a "race-notice" statute and that, under section 695.01, the Argent Mortgage has priority over the Olympus Mortgage.

Wachovia acknowledges that section 695.01, Florida Statutes, is a "notice" type of recording statute. However, Wachovia contends that amendments made to section 695.11, Florida Statutes, have converted Florida into a "race-notice" state.

As an initial matter, it bears explaining that recording statutes are classified into three categories: race, notice, and race-notice. These can generally be described as follows:

- Under a *race* recording statute, a subsequent mortgagee of real property will prevail against a prior mortgagee of the said real property if the subsequent mortgage is recorded before the prior mortgage.
- Under a *notice* recording statute, a subsequent mortgagee of real property for value and without notice (actual and constructive) of a prior mortgage of the said real property will prevail against the prior mortgagee.

- Under a *race-notice* recording statute, a subsequent mortgagee of real property for value and without notice (actual and constructive) of a prior mortgage of the said real property will prevail against the prior mortgagee if the subsequent mortgage is recorded before the prior mortgage.

Importantly, under either a notice or a race-notice recording statute, the subsequent mortgagee cannot be without constructive notice if the prior mortgage has been recorded as of the time of execution of the subsequent mortgage.

Application of each type of recording statute to the undisputed facts here yields the following results:

- Wachovia prevails under a race recording statute because the Olympus Mortgage was recorded before the Argent Mortgage;
- Argent prevails under a notice recording statute because it is a subsequent mortgagee for value and did not have notice of the Olympus Mortgage at the time of execution of the Argent Mortgage; and
- sisWachovia prevails under a race-notice recording statute because, although Argent is a subsequent mortgagee for value and did not have notice of the Olympus Mortgage at the time of execution of the Argent Mortgage, the Olympus Mortgage was recorded before the Argent Mortgage.

Commentators appear uniformly to categorize section 695.01 as a "notice" type of recording statute. *See* 2–26 RALPH E. BOYER, FLORIDA REAL ESTATE TRANSACTIONS § 26.02 (Matthew Bender & Co., Inc. 2010) ("Florida has a notice type recording statute, the primary function of which is to protect subsequent purchasers (which for purposes of this discussion includes mortgagees and creditors who are within the statute's protection) against claims arising from prior unrecorded instruments ....").

Florida courts over time have described and applied Florida's recording statute in a manner that is consistent with a "notice" type of recording statute. [citing cases] Florida's approach to the problem was succinctly described by the Florida Supreme Court in *Van Eepoel Real Estate Co. v. Sarasota Milk Co.*, 100 Fla. 438, 129 So. 892, 895 (1930):

> [I]t is generally held, in states having recording statutes similar to ours, that if A conveys lands to B, a bona fide purchaser for value, who does not go into possession and who failed to record his deed until after A conveys the same land to C, a second bona fide purchaser for value without notice of B's interest, and B then records his deed before C records his, the title of C shall nevertheless prevail as between C and B, because it is the

> fault of B that he did not immediately record his deed, thereby permitting C to deal with the property and part with his consideration without knowledge of B's interest. So B is estopped and the equities are with C.

Section 695.01, notwithstanding, the trial court accepted Wachovia's argument that a 1967 amendment to a different statute, section 695.11, Florida Statutes, entitled, "Instruments deemed to be recorded from time of filing" converted Florida from a "notice" to a "race-notice" jurisdiction.[36] The earliest version of section 695.11 dates back to 1885. Examination of the language of the 1906, 1920, and 1935 iterations of section 695.11, make clear that this statute was intended to provide a mechanism for determining the time at which an instrument was deemed to be recorded. Nothing in the case law suggests that section 695.11 modifies section 695.01. … [3]

Wachovia relies on an earlier opinion of this Court, *Rice v. Greene*, 941 So.2d 1230 (Fla. 5th DCA 2006), in support of its contention that Florida has a race-notice type of recording statute. In *Rice,* this Court … found:

> In other words, an unrecorded deed is not good or effectual in law or equity against creditors or subsequent purchasers for valuable consideration who are without notice of the transaction. Therefore, *because Mr. Greene had no notice* of the earlier warranty deed between Mr. Rice and Mrs. Schwartz *and paid valuable consideration* for the property, *Mr. Greene's recording of his warranty deed before Mr. Rice gives Mr. Greene priority to the property.*

Id. at 1232 (emphasis added). According to Wachovia, this language proves that priority in recording is key. Notably, however, *Rice* does not mention section 695.11 and recording was not an issue. The subsequent purchaser in *Rice* (Mr. Greene) had priority to the property under a notice type of recording statute because he paid value for the property and did not have notice

---

[36] [Ed: Section 695.11 reads, "All instruments which are authorized or required to be recorded in the office of the clerk of the circuit court of any county in the State of Florida, … and which are filed for recording on or after the effective date of this act, shall be deemed to have been officially accepted by the said officer, and officially recorded, at the time she or he affixed thereon the consecutive official register numbers … and at such time shall be notice to all persons. The sequence of such official numbers shall determine the priority of recordation. An instrument bearing the lower number in the then-current series of numbers shall have priority over any instrument bearing a higher number in the same series."]

[3] Case law confirms that the purpose of section 695.11 is to determine the time at which an instrument is deemed to be recorded and to serve as notice. [citing cases] Section 695.11 has an important purpose to determine the priority between judgment liens. [citing cases] Because a certified copy of a judgment must be recorded in order to create a lien on real property, a judgment that is recorded earlier in time, namely one that bears a lower official register number, will win priority.

(actual or constructive) of the earlier warranty deed at the time of the conveyance. The fact that Mr. Greene's deed was recorded before Mr. Rice's does not affect the outcome under a notice type of recording statute. Although a portion of the sentence in *Rice,* on which Wachovia relies, mentions recording, in that case, it was superfluous.

We conclude that Florida is, and remains, a "notice" jurisdiction, and notice controls the issue of priority. Since Argent is a subsequent mortgagee for value and did not have notice of the Olympus Mortgage at the time of execution of the Argent Mortgage, the Argent Mortgage has priority over the Olympus Mortgage. As such, the trial court erred by entering partial summary final judgment in favor of Wachovia on the issue of priority.

FLA. STAT. § 695.01

No conveyance, transfer, or mortgage of real property, or of any interest therein, nor any lease for a term of 1 year or longer, shall be good and effectual in law or equity against creditors or subsequent purchasers for a valuable consideration and without notice, unless the same be recorded according to law … .

N.C. STAT. § 47-18

No (i) conveyance of land, or (ii) contract to convey, or (iii) option to convey, or (iv) lease of land for more than three years shall be valid to pass any property interest as against lien creditors or purchasers for a valuable consideration from the donor, bargainer or lesser but from the time of registration thereof in the county where the land lies… .

ALASKA STAT. § 40.17.080

… A conveyance of real property in the state, other than a lease for a term of less than one year, is void as against a subsequent innocent purchaser in good faith for valuable consideration of the property or a part of the property whose conveyance is first recorded. …

Questions

1. What kind of recording acts are the three state statutes listed above? Explain how the categorization – race, notice, or race-notice – follows from the text of the statute.

2. Who would have won in *Argent* if Argent had recorded on January 3 instead of on January 31? What about in a race jurisdiction? In a race-notice jurisdiction?

3. Who would have won in *Argent* if the Burkes had disclosed the existence of the Olympus Mortgage to Argent on December 6? On December 16? What about in a race jurisdiction? In a race-notice jurisdiction?

Board of Education of Minneapolis v. Hughes
136 N.W. 1095 (Minn. 1912)

BUNN, J.

Action to determine adverse claims to a lot in Minneapolis. … The trial resulted in a decision in favor of plaintiff, and defendants appealed from an order denying a new trial.

The facts are not in controversy and are as follows: On May 16, 1906, Carrie B. Hoerger, a resident of Faribault, owned the lot in question, which was vacant and subject to unpaid delinquent taxes. Defendant L. A. Hughes offered to pay $25 for this lot. His offer was accepted, and he sent his check for the purchase price of this and two other lots bought at the same time to Ed. Hoerger, husband of the owner, together with a deed to be executed and returned. The name of the grantee in the deed was not inserted; the space for the same being left blank. It was executed and acknowledged by Carrie B. Hoerger and her husband on May 17, 1900 [Ed: presumably 1906], and delivered to defendant Hughes by mail. The check was retained and cashed. Hughes filled in the name of the grantee, but not until shortly prior to the date when the deed was recorded, which was December 11, 1910. On April 27, 1909, Duryea & Wilson, real estate dealers, paid Mrs. Hoerger $25 for a quitclaim deed to the lot, which was executed and delivered to them, but which was not recorded until December 21, 1910. On November 19, 1909, Duryea & Wilson executed and delivered to plaintiff a warranty deed to the lot, which deed was filed for record January 27, 1910. It thus appears that the deed to Hughes was recorded before the deed to Duryea & Wilson, though the deed from them to plaintiff was recorded before the deed to defendant.

The questions for our consideration may be thus stated: (1) Did the deed from Hoerger to Hughes ever become operative? (2) If so, is he a subsequent purchaser whose deed was first duly recorded, within the language of the recording act?

The decision of the first question involves a consideration of the effect of the delivery of a deed by the grantor to the grantee with the name of the latter omitted from the space provided for it, without express authority to the grantee to insert his own or another name in the blank space. It is settled that a deed that does not name a grantee is a nullity, and wholly inoperative as a conveyance, until the name of the grantee is legally inserted. … [T]he deed to defendant Hughes was not operative as a conveyance until his name was inserted as grantee. [But] Hughes had implied authority from the grantor to fill the blank with his own name as grantee, and … when he did so the deed became operative.

When the Hughes deed was recorded, there was of record a deed to the lot from Duryea & Wilson to plaintiff, but no record showing that Duryea & Wilson had any title to convey. The deed to them from the common grantor had not been recorded. We hold that this record of a deed from an apparent stranger to the title was not notice to Hughes of the prior unrecorded conveyance by his grantor. He was a subsequent purchaser in good faith for a valuable consideration, whose conveyance was first duly recorded; that is, Hughes' conveyance dates from the time when he filled the blank space, which was after the deed from his grantor to Duryea & Wilson. He was, therefore, a 'subsequent purchaser,' and is protected by the recording of his deed before the prior deed was recorded. The statute cannot be construed so as to give priority to a deed recorded before, which shows no conveyance from a record owner. It was necessary, not only that the deed to plaintiff should be recorded before the deed to Hughes, but also that the deed to plaintiff's grantor should be first recorded.

Our conclusion is that the learned trial court should have held on the evidence that defendant L. A. Hughes was the owner of the lot.

Questions

1. The deed from Duryea & Wilson to the plaintiff is called a "wild deed." Why? Draw a diagram of the conveyances in *Hughes*, noting which of them were recorded. What would someone searching the title to the property have found? Put another way, what went wrong here? Whose fault was it? What can or should a recording system do about it?

2. What kind of recording act does Minnesota have, according to *Hughes*? How can you tell? Would the result have been different under either of the other types of recording acts?

3. What result if Hughes had filled in his name on the blank deed when he received it from Hoerger in 1906 rather than when he recorded it in 1910?

Note on Recording Systems and Informal Title

Up to a billion people worldwide are squatters, living on land they have no legal right to occupy, usually on the outskirts of cities. They're vulnerable to eviction or at least extortion from officials who take advantage of their lack of legal rights. Moreover, the influential economist Hernando De Soto has argued that record title would help poor people enter the formal economy by giving them clear ownership of assets. Poor people are often highly entrepreneurial, but face great barriers entering the formal economy – and thus their efforts may lead to fines and jail rather than to wealth. As owners, they'd have better incentives to invest in improving their land; they could also pledge their land to lenders in order to raise capital to start legitimate businesses; and they might even be able to get insurance in case of disaster. See HERNANDO DE SOTO, THE MYSTERY OF CAPITAL: WHY CAPITALISM TRIUMPHS IN THE WEST AND FAILS EVERYWHERE ELSE (2000). In the U.S., about 70% of new business credit comes from using title to other assets, such as homes, as collateral. The likelihood of being able to recover from these identifiable assets is the foundation of much willingness to lend. De Soto argues that: "Property is much more than a body of norms. It is also a huge information system that processes raw data until it is transformed into facts that can be tested for truth, and thereby destroys the main catalysts of recessions and panics – ambiguity and opacity." Hernando de Soto, *Toxic Assets Were Hidden Assets*, WALL ST. J., Mar. 25, 2009. Legal title and a robust recording system provides reliable information.

De Soto's views have been highly influential, but also controversial. Record title might help for specific situations, but the government first has to decide to give the title to the people who are living on the land, and that generally requires formally dispossessing someone else – often someone wealthy who will fight back. De Soto favors squatters' rights, and his argument depends in many ways on the same foundation as adverse possession. However, if the "legal" owners' title was unjustly acquired – which is often the case – then squatters' rights can also be founded on theories of labor or first in time.

Does formalizing title work? The evidence is mixed. De Soto's ideas were adopted as part of land title reform in Peru. In a six-year period, more than 1.2 million households, containing 6.3 million people, received title to the properties they were living on. Using similar areas that weren't subject to reform as controls, Erica Field determined that labor force participation increased and child labor decreased. Apparently, many squatter families try to run a small business out of their house so they can safeguard the homestead at the same time; with legal title, that's no longer necessary. However, there was not much evidence of increased access to credit, contrary to de Soto's predictions. See Erica Field, *Entitled to Work: Urban Property Rights and Labor Supply in Peru*, 122 Q.J. ECON. 1561 (2007). By contrast, in Thailand, the size of loans obtained from banks by farmers with formalized property was more than 50% larger than loans to farmers without record title. Results from around the world are ambiguous; formal title sometimes seems to spur investment, and sometimes it doesn't. See CLAUDIA R. WILLIAMSON, THE TWO SIDES OF DE SOTO: PROPERTY RIGHTS, LAND TITLING, AND DEVELOPMENT, ANNUAL PROCEEDINGS OF THE WEALTH AND WELL-BEING OF NATIONS 95 (2011).

Moreover, it's important not to make the overgeneralized claim that "strong" or "clear" property rights are necessary for economic development. It should already be clear to you that Western property rights vary a lot and can be subject to lots of their own uncertainties, from the acts required to possess a previously unowned resource to the boundaries of an intellectual property right. England industrialized while its property law was highly unclear. What's needed is sufficient certainty to go forward, not perfect certainty – and that certainty can come from various sources, including but not limited to formal law.

The first Chinese law focusing specifically on property rights did not become effective until 2007. China's unprecedented real estate development during the prior two decades thus occurred without any published law of real estate; investors committed hundreds of billions of dollars without assurance of what they would own even if all went well. See GREGORY M. STEIN, MODERN CHINESE REAL ESTATE LAW (2012). In Shenzhen, an economic powerhouse of a city with over 10 million residents, half of the buildings have no legal titles. Instead, professionals have developed practices and networks, including government officials (with a bit of bribery thrown in), that facilitate transactions even among strangers. *See* Shitong Qiao, *Planting Houses in Shenzhen: A Real Estate Market without Legal Titles*, 29 CAN. J.L. & SOC. 253 (2013). Qiao quotes an official at the Shenzhen Real Estate Ownership Registration Center: "Nobody cares whether they have legal titles or not. You say they are illegal: dare you void the contracts? … There is a huge amount of transactions – you say farmers cannot sell, it is illegal [because the Chinese government owns all rural land], but they do it privately with little ado. Are you to tell them whether it is legal or illegal?" Another quote from a senior official: "[I]t is a war against the people that cannot be won." Facts on the ground matter. On the other hand, China has also repeatedly suffered from conflicts, sometimes violent, between developers who claim government sanction and squatters who assert that their actual possession should be respected.

At a minimum, record title can be useless without an overall well-functioning legal system. If corruption is a nation's problem, title won't solve that by itself. In addition, expropriation by the wealthy or well-connected is an enduring problem. Without careful implementation of a titling system, it's the already-powerful who end up with legal title – either initially, or when the formal system's property taxes start to kick in. A De Soto-type titling program in Cambodia led to fires and forced evictions of slum dwellers, followed by transfers of newly valuable inner-city land to wealthy developers. *See* John Gravois, *The de Soto Delusion*, SLATE, Jan. 29, 2005. Older programs to provide title to members of Indian tribes, supposedly to help them integrate into the broader U.S. economy, suffered from similar problems. *See* Ezra Rosser, *Anticipating de Soto: Allotment of Indian Reservations and the Dangers of Land-Titling*, in HERNANDO DE SOTO AND PROPERTY IN A MARKET ECONOMY (D. Benjamin Barros ed., 2010).

If De Soto is right, the U.S. may have turned its back on his insights by inflicting serious damage on our land recording system and investing too much in financial instruments for which no centralized records are available. Even without the mortgage crisis, in the U.S., not everyone has record title, especially in low-income communities where property often transfers by intestate inheritance. In Louisiana, for example, an estimated 15% of the homeowners who applied for federal housing assistance after Hurricane Katrina – approximately 20,000 homeowners – lacked clear record title. This problem affected many homeowners concentrated in the low-income neighborhoods of New Orleans Parish and is one reason they received smaller amounts of help than many other, better-off neighborhoods. In Texas, about one out of five low-income households applying for hurricane recovery assistance had at least one title issue impeding their ability to access assistance. See Heather Way, *Informal Homeownership in the United States and the Law*, 29 ST. L. U. PUB. L. REV. 113 (2009); see also Jane E. Larson, *Informality, Illegality, and Inequality*, 20 YALE L. & POL'Y REV. 137 (2002) (discussing large-scale squatter communities in Texas); Zoe Loftus-Farren, *Tent Cities: An Interim Solution to Homelessness and Affordable Housing Shortages in the United States*, 99 CALIF. L. REV. 1037 (2011). Should the U.S. consider schemes for titling people or communities presently without record title?

Problems

1. Peter and Nathan Petrelli are the record owners of land in Disturbia. They hold the land as joint tenants. Peter conveys his interest to Angela Petrelli, who pays fair market value for it. Angela gives her interest to her granddaughter Claire Bennet, who records. Peter and Nathan then sell the land to Matt Parkman, who doesn't know anything about Peter's earlier conveyance to Angela. Matt records. Disturbia's recording statute reads in relevant part as follows: "Every conveyance is void as against any subsequent purchaser of the same property, or any part thereof, in good faith and for a valuable consideration, whose conveyance is first duly recorded." Who owns what, and why?

2. Peter Bishop and Olivia Dunham are the record owners of Fringeacre as joint tenants with right of survivorship. Bishop and Dunham grant Bishop's father, Walter Bishop, an easement to pasture his cows on Fringeacre. Walter does not record the easement. Later, Dunham gives her interest in Fringeacre as a gift to Astrid Farnsworth, who does not know about Walter Bishop's easement, and who records. When Dunham subsequently dies, Peter Bishop sells Fringeacre to Philip Broyles, who had seen Walter's cows grazing on the property; when Broyles asked Peter about the cows, Peter said, "Yeah, I let my dad do that." Broyles records. The relevant recording statute is: "No conveyance or mortgage of an interest in land is valid against any subsequent purchaser for value without notice thereof, unless it is recorded." Who owns what, and why? How, if at all, would the answer change if the recording statute read, "Every unrecorded conveyance of an interest in land shall be void as against any subsequent purchaser in good faith and for a valuable consideration whose conveyance shall be first duly recorded"?

3. Damon Salvatore conveys Blackacre to Bonnie Bennet. Salvatore subsequently conveys Blackacre to Caroline Forbes for valuable consideration. Forbes lacks knowledge of the deed to Bennet. Bennet records, then Forbes records. Thereafter, Forbes sells the western half of Blackacre to Jeremy Gilbert, and the eastern half back to Salvatore. Who

owns Blackacre and why? Answer with respect to each of the following laws (Hint: first identify what type of statute this is):

a. "No conveyance or mortgage of an interest in land is valid against any subsequent purchaser for value without notice thereof, whose conveyance is first recorded."
b. "No conveyance or mortgage of an interest in land is valid against any subsequent purchaser for value without notice thereof, unless it is recorded."
c. "No conveyance or mortgage of an interest in land is valid against any subsequent purchaser whose conveyance is first recorded."

11. Scope of Rights

A. Encroachments

Pile v. Pedrick
31 A. 646 (Pa. 1895)

WILLIAMS, J.

The learned judge of the court below was right in holding that the wall in controversy was not a party wall. It was not intended to be. The defendants were building a factory, and, under the advice of their architect, decided to build within their own lines, in order to avoid the danger of injury to others from vibration which might result from the use of their machinery. They called upon the district surveyor to locate their line, and built within it, as so ascertained. Subsequent surveys by city surveyors have determined that the line was not accurately located at first, but was about 1 ½ inches over on the plaintiffs'. This leaves the ends of the stones used in the foundation wall projecting into the plaintiffs' lands, below the surface, 1 3/8 inches. This unintentional intrusion into the plaintiffs' close is the narrow foundation on which this bill in equity rests. The wall resting on the stone foundation is conceded to be within the defendants' line. The defendants offered, nevertheless, to make it a party wall, by agreement, and give to plaintiffs the free use of it, as such, on condition that the windows on the third and fourth floors should remain open until the plaintiffs should desire to use the wall. This offer was declined. The trespass was then to be remedied in one of two ways: It could be treated, with the plaintiffs' consent, as a permanent trespass, and compensated for in damages, or the defendants could be compelled to remove the offending ends of the stones to the other side of the line. The plaintiffs insisted upon the latter course, and the court below has, by its decree, ordered that this should be done. The defendants then sought permission to go on the plaintiffs' side of the line and chip off the projecting ends, offering to pay for all inconvenience or injury the plaintiffs or their tenants might suffer by their so doing. This they refused. Nothing remained but to take down and rebuild the entire wall from the defendants' side, and with their building resting on it. This the decree requires, but in view of the course of the litigation the learned judge divided the costs. This is the chief ground of complaint on this appeal. Costs are not of course, in equity. They may be given or withheld as equity and good conscience require. It often happens that a chancellor is constrained to enforce a legal right under circumstances that involve hardship to the defendant, and in such cases it is, as it should be, common to dispose of the costs upon a consideration of all the circumstances, and the position and conduct of the parties. The costs in this case were within the power of the chancellor. They were disposed of in the exercise of his official discretion, and we see no reason to doubt that they were disposed of properly. The decree is affirmed; the costs of this appeal to be paid by the appellants.

Pile v. Pedrick

31 A. 647 (Pa. 1895)

WILLIAMS, J.

This is an appeal from the same decree just considered in Pile v. Pedrick, 31 Atl. 646. It is not denied that the foundation wall on which the appellant has built was located under a mistake made by the district surveyor, and does in fact project slightly into the plaintiffs' land. For one inch and three-eighths, the ends of the stones in the wall are said to project beyond the division line. The defendants have no right, at law or in equity, to occupy land that does not belong to them, and we do not see how the court below could have done otherwise than recognize and act upon this principle. They must remove their wall, so that it shall be upon their land. This the court directed should be done within a reasonable time. To avoid further controversy over this subject, we will so far modify the decree as to permit such removal to be made within one year from the date of filing hereof. In all other respects the decree is affirmed; the appellants to pay all costs made by them upon this appeal.

Golden Press v. Rylands

235 P.2d 592 (Colo. 1951)

STONE, J.

Plaintiffs Rylands and Reid owned a parcel of land fronting on West Colfax Avenue, Jefferson County, upon which were located their residence and garage and some rental cottages. Defendant Golden Press, Inc., constructed a one-story brick and cinder block business building on its property which adjoined plaintiffs' property on the east. According to plaintiffs' survey here unchallenged, the west wall of defendant's building is two inches clear of the lot line at the front or south end, is exactly on the line at the north end, and is approximately 160 feet in length.

In the action here involved, plaintiffs allege that in con[s]tructing the building defendant caused its foundation and footings to extend from two to three and a half inches upon plaintiffs' land. ... Plaintiffs prayed for injunction requiring that defendant remove all footings and foundations upon their property.... Upon issue raised by general denial the case was tried to a jury as to the issue of damages alleged by trespass, the court reserving the determination of the issue of injunction. On the issue of damages the jury returned a verdict in favor of the defendant. The court then found encroachment as alleged and granted mandatory injunction requiring that defendant's projecting footings be removed from plaintiffs' property....

Defendant specifies and argues error in setting aside the verdict of the jury....

There remains for consideration the portion of the decree requiring defendant to remove the footings of its building where they encroach upon the property of the plaintiffs. Ordinarily, mandatory injunction will issue to compel removal of encroaching structures, but it is not to be issued as a matter of course. On appeal to the court for an equitable remedy, the court must consider the peculiar equities of the case. A study of many decisions discloses no specific and universally-accepted rule as to encroachments. Even in jurisdictions like Massachusetts, in which it has been declared that mandatory injunction for removal of encroachment can only be denied where estoppel or laches is shown, Beaudoin v. Sinodinos, 313 Mass. 511, there are numerous cases where injunction has been refused in the absence of those defenses. See cases cited as exceptional in Gerogosian v. Un. Realty Co., 289 Mass. 104. Generally in other jurisdictions such harsh rule is not followed. Sometimes a slight and harmless encroachment is held to be within the rule "de minimis," as in Tramonte v. Colarusso, 256 Mass. 299, and McKean v. Alliance Land Co., 200 Cal. 396, and generally the courts require that he who seeks equity should do equity and come with clean hands. Tramonte v. Colarusso, supra; Mc-Kee v. Fields, 187 Or. 323.

Where the encroachment is deliberate and constitutes a willful and intentional taking of another's land, equity may well require its restoration regardless of the expense of removal as compared with damage suffered therefrom; but where the encroachment was in good faith, we think the court should weigh the circumstances so that it shall not act oppressively. 5 Pomeroy's Equity Jurisprudence, page 852, § 508. While the mere balance of convenience is not the proper test, yet relative hardship may properly be considered and the court should not become a party to extortion. Restatement of the Law, Torts, § 941. Where defendant's encroachment is unintentional and slight, plaintiff's use not affected and his damage small and fairly compensable, while the cost of removal is so great as to cause grave hardship or otherwise make its removal unconscionable, mandatory injunction may properly be denied and plaintiff relegated to compensation in damages. Owenson v. Bradley, 50 N.D. 741; Nebel v. Guyer, 99 Cal.App.2d 30; Mary Jane Stevens Co. v. First Nat'l Bldg. Co., 89 Utah. 456.

In the case before us issue was raised in the argument as to whether or not the encroachment was intentional. There was no finding on this issue by the trial court and the decree is not necessarily predicated upon intent. In the absence of proof to the contrary there is a presumption that men act in good faith and that they intend to do what they have the right to do. Prior to the building of the wall, plaintiffs and defendant each employed a surveyor, but neither was called as a witness and the results of their surveys are not disclosed except that, as stated by plaintiff Reid, before there was any digging done plaintiffs employed Prouty to survey and defendants employed Linn to survey "and there semed to be a little difficulty in their agreeing. Mr. Prouty came out and made another survey, and Mr. Linn came out and made another survey and, of course, all this time the building was progressing." Plaintiff Rylands testified that she called Prouty to survey twice "because there was trouble between the lines. They had called their surveyor, and they weren't satisfied, and we weren't satisfied, and Mr. Prouty was called back to resurvey, to look the figures over, and the lines," during the course of construction. There is no indication from the record as to whether or not these surveyors agreed after their resurveys. Plaintiffs rely entirely as to the location of the line upon the survey by Coberly and his assistant, who were employed by plaintiffs and made their survey just prior to the trial and long after the wall was completed. Plaintiff Rylands' brother, Thomas P. Nother, upon whom plaintiffs relied to show knowledge and intent as to the line on the part of defendant's agents, testified as to Coberly's survey: "He found out their north end of their building was right on the line, and the south end of their building was a little bit inside the line, that is how I determined that they were over with their footings so far." With reference to the earlier surveys, witness Nother testified that before the concrete was poured for the foundation, he informed Mr. Ernst who was superintendent of construction that his building was about eight inches over the line and Ernst replied, "You're wrong, we have got our own surveyor. He has put us on the line"; that witness answered, "Well, I am not going to argue about it, I am warning you, you are over your line," and that thereupon the superintendent had the laborers move the forms over.

Defendant's witness Argo, who had charge of constructing the wall, testified that he had a survey line run by Linn and they dug the hole for the footings right straight down to the property line; that the lady next door had made a statement that they were on her property and they had another survey run and "the surveyor told us we better move over, as I remember, two inches, and we did." He further testified, "We weren't going to form that footing, and then the people next door made a little fuss about us being on their property, so we put a form in for that footing, so it would be on our side."

There is disclosed continued argument by plaintiffs with representatives of defendant during construction of the wall as to trespassing on their lands, but we find no evidence from the record challenging the good faith of defendant's representative in locating the footings.

Again we note that while plaintiffs were continually complaining as to trespass of the workmen on their property, they took no steps for injunction or other legal determination of the disputed line until after both the foundation and upper wall were completed.

Further, we note that the encroachment here complained of is very slight. It is conceded that the wall above the foundation does not project over the property line and that the only encroachment consists of a projection of the footings a distance of two inches at the middle, increasing to three and a half inches at the north end. The top of these footings is about seven feet below the surface of the ground and they go down to nine feet below the surface. They constitute no interference whatever with plaintiffs' present use of the property as a driveway and iris bed, and the only testimony as to future damage was to the effect that if plaintiffs wished to build to their line with a basement, they would have to detour around this slight projection of defendant's footings.

The testimony indicates that the value of plaintiffs' lands is approximately $200 per front foot, so that if defendant had taken the entire strip of three and a half inches both at and below the surface, its value would have been only about $55, and the value of the portions extending from seven to nine feet below the surface and only along the rear eighty feet of wall would appear to be very small. Plaintiffs, at the trial, refused defendant permission to enter upon their property for the purpose of chipping off the encroaching footings with a jack hammer, and demanded that they be removed from defendant's side of the land, if necessary by tearing down the wall. The expense and hardship of such removal would be so great in comparison with any advantage of plaintiffs to be gained thereby that we think it would be unconscionable to require it, and that under all the circumstances disclosed mandatory injunction should have been denied by the trial court, with permission for plaintiffs to proceed, if desired, in damages.

Accordingly, the injunctive decree is reversed and the case remanded for further proceedings, if desired, consistent herewith.

HILLIARD, J., not participating.

Notes and Questions

1. **The rule**. What is the rule in the case of encroachments? When a trespasser builds a structure on a neighbor's land, under what circumstances does the trespasser have to remove the encroachment? In a case that follows the approach of *Golden Press v. Rylands*, who ends up owning the encroaching structure (or the part that encroaches)? Is the trespass forgiven?

B. Improvers

Raab v. Casper

51 Cal.App.3d 866 (3d Dis. Cal. 1975)

FRIEDMAN, Acting P.J.

Plaintiffs and defendants own adjoining foothill tracts acquired through a common grantor. Plaintiffs' parcel, about 20 acres in size, is longitudinally shaped, with its narrow dimension at the north and south ends. Mr. and Mrs. Casper, the defendants, own two separate parcels, immediately to the west, one of three and one half acres adjoining the northern portion of plaintiffs' tract, another of four and one half acres adjoining the southern portion. Plaintiffs' amended complaint sought a mandatory injunction and damages; it alleged in effect two separate, continuing trespasses by defendants; defendants had built a 25 by 35 foot cabin entirely on plaintiffs' land, at its northwest corner near the northerly end of the common boundary; toward the southerly end of the common boundary, defendants had built a family home, approximately one third of the premises being located on plaintiffs' land.

According to the findings, the common north-south boundary had never been surveyed or marked; the true boundary had been established through a survey by Harvey Butler filed for record in April 1972;[1] commencing in January 1970, defendants started building a small house (i.e., cabin), which was actually located across the boundary, at the northwest corner of plaintiffs' land. The court also found that in September 1970 plaintiffs complained to defendants that they believed the cabin was located on plaintiffs' property; at that time Casper had completed the foundation, exterior walls, roofs and interior partitions, septic tank and leachline, but not the interior work; Casper continued with construction of the cabin and completed it; defendants did not take the cabin site by adverse possession; defendants had not acted maliciously or willfully, but believed in good faith that they were building the cabin on their own property.

As to the cabin built at the northwestern corner of plaintiffs' land, the court concluded that defendants were good faith improvers. (See Code Civ. Proc., §§ 871.1-871.7.) Its judgment realigned the northerly common boundary to give defendants the .287 acres where their cabin was situated; awarded plaintiffs $700 as compensation for the reasonable value of the land, $500 for the cost of a survey, $750 attorney's fee and $70 per year rent until entry of judgment (slightly less than three years). Plaintiffs appeal.

Much of plaintiffs' brief on appeal consists of an evidentiary attack on the findings, including that which fixed $700 as the value of the cabin site awarded defendants. This court adheres to the rule which prevents appellate inquiry into evidentiary conflicts and requires the acceptance of trial court findings which are supported by substantial evidence. … Nevertheless, the findings and judgment are characterized by several prejudicial errors of law which require reversal.

The good-faith-improver legislation (Code Civ. Proc., § 871.1 et seq.) was enacted in 1968. A "good faith improver" is defined as one who makes an improvement to land in good faith and under a mistaken belief that he is the landowner. (Code Civ. Proc., § 871.1.) Such an improver may seek judicial relief but has the burden of establishing his entitlement to relief; the "degree

---

[1] Plaintiffs had bought and paid for this survey after the dispute arose.

of [his] negligence" should be taken into account in determining his good faith and in determining what relief is consistent with substantial justice. (Code Civ. Proc., § 871.3).[2] The court may not grant relief if a setoff or right of removal would accomplish substantial justice. (Code Civ. Proc., § 871.4.) Subject to this limitation, the court may effect such adjustments in the parties' positions as are consistent with substantial justice under the circumstances; the relief shall protect the injured owner against pecuniary losses (including litigation expense) but avoid his unjust enrichment; in shaping relief, the court may consider the injured owner's future plans and his need for the land. (§ 871.5.)

We find no case law construing this legislation. It possesses decisional ancestry in the equity doctrine which grants damages but denies injunctive relief against an innocent encroachment which could be removed only at heavy cost and which does not cause irreparable damage to the injured landowner. (Brown Derby Hollywood Corp. v. Hatton, 61 Cal. 2d 855, 858; Donnell v. Bisso Brothers, 10 Cal. App. 3d 38, 45-46.) It may, on occasion, be tied to the law which permits removal of fixtures erroneously and in good faith attached to the land of another. (Civ. Code, § 1013.5.)

The 1968 law adds a synthetic, somewhat alien ingredient to the concept of good faith. In its traditional sense good faith connotes a moral quality; it is equated with honesty of purpose, freedom from fraudulent intent and faithfulness to duty or obligation. (People v. Nunn, 46 Cal. 2d 460, 468 [296 P.2d 813]; see 18A Words and Phrases (Perm. Ed. 1956), p. 83 et seq.) Code of Civil Procedure section 871.3 declares that the improver's "degree of negligence" should be taken into account in determining his good faith and in shaping the relief. Thus, in applying this particular legislation, good faith becomes an artificial attribute, calling for a measure of care as well as honesty. Lack of care as well as dishonesty may negate or diminish good faith. Moreover, section 871.3 calls for consideration of the degree of negligence. Without evoking conventional choices between ordinary and gross negligence, the statute invites consideration of varying intensities of negligence.

---

[2] We quote section 871.3 in full: "A good faith improver may bring an action in the superior court or, subject to Section 396, may file a cross-complaint in a pending action in the superior or municipal court for relief under this chapter. In every case, the burden is on the good faith improver to establish that he is entitled to relief under this chapter, and the degree of negligence of the good faith improver should be taken into account by the court in determining whether the improver acted in good faith and in determining the relief, if any, that is consistent with substantial justice to the parties under the circumstances of the particular case."

Accustomed as judges and lawyers are to equating good faith with honesty, we are not likely to consider the element of negligence unless it is specifically demanded. In a good-faith-improver suit, a set of trial court findings which omits mention of negligence becomes suspect. It supplies the reviewing court no means of ascertaining whether the trial judge really considered the improver's negligence. Failure to find on a material issue is a fundamental defect, requiring reversal. (See cases cited 4 Witkin, Cal. Procedure, § 337, p. 3139.)

Here the trial court found that defendants "did not act maliciously, intentionally or willfully in constructing the small house [cabin], but acted in the good-faith belief that they were constructing said house on their property." The lack of any reference to negligence arouses appellate suspicion that negligence may have been neglected.

The suspicion is confirmed by evidence supporting an inference of negligence on the part of Mr. Casper, who built the cabin. Some 10 years earlier he had indulged in assumptions regarding the boundary line to the south; these assumptions had led him to install part of the yard around his home, part of his driveway and utility lines on the land of plaintiffs. He admitted on the witness stand that he had never known or ascertained the location of the property corners. He had extrapolated his easterly boundary from a line between a jack pine and a manzanita tree; he based this belief on an oral statement made by the seller when he bought the land in 1959. In September 1970 plaintiffs first observed Mr. Casper's partially completed cabin and warned him that he was building on their property. Up to that point he had spent $1,956.28 on the cabin. He disregarded the warning and spent an additional $2,206.85 to complete the cabin. He did so without a survey and without offering to share in the cost of a survey. Plaintiffs spent $1,757.20 for the survey, which the trial court later accepted as the true boundary line.

There is an analogy here to the encroachment decisions which point out that continuation of the offending construction in defiance of the injured owner's opposition is inconsistent with good faith. (Brown Derby Hollywood Corp. v. Hatton, supra, 61 Cal.2d at p. 859; City of Dunsmuir v. Silva, 154 Cal. App. 2d 825, 828). The good-faith-improver legislation of 1968 was drafted and submitted by the California Law Revision Commission, which accompanied section 871.1 with a comment fully consistent with the good faith concept described in the encroachment decisions. We append the Law Revision Commission's comment in the margin.[3]

---

[3] "Under this section, a person is not a 'good faith improver' as to any improvement made after he becomes aware of facts that preclude him from acting in good faith. For example, a person who builds a house on a lot owned by another may obtain relief under this chapter if he acted in good faith under the erroneous belief, because of a mistake of law or fact, that he was the owner of the land. However, if the same person makes an additional improvement after he has discovered that

At this juncture of the case the findings declare: "That at the time of commencement of the construction of the small house, Defendant reasonably believed he was building the same on his land and had made reasonable effort to confirm that fact." The declaration is pregnant with an admission that at some later time defendants no longer possessed that reasonable belief. Whatever defendant Casper's good faith and whatever his reasonable care preceding the warning of September 1970, these elements underwent a transformation after he received that warning.

This appeal presents the precise situation described in the Law Revision Commission's comment (fn. 3, ante), that is, a project characterized by good faith at its inception (according to the trial court findings) but suffering a shift in that characteristic when a warning of possible trespass or encroachment is received before completion. In choosing to proceed with his project in the face of the owner's warning, the improver exposes the owner to injury not measurable in dollars alone. The owner may ultimately receive the reasonable value of his lost land. His injury lies not so much in financial loss as in deprivation of a choice inherent in ownership. Ownership of land includes the freedom not to dispose of it. The good-faith-improver legislation gives the improver something akin to a private power of eminent domain. (See Donnell v. Bisso Brothers, supra, 10 Cal.App.3d at p. 46.) The greater the improver's investment, the greater his potential appeal to the court's conscience. The law should not permit him to worsen the true owner's position after the latter has warned him of a possible trespass. Hence, deliberate augmentation of an initial investment after a warning of trespass is a legally significant factor, one which a trial court should not ignore.

In weighing the grant, denial or apportionment of relief, a trial court should consider any interim warning, the character and relative cost of the improvements made before and after the warning and the unitary or separable character of the improvements. As did Solomon, the law should recognize that a unitary improvement cannot be chopped in half -- one part entitled to statutory relief, the other not. Despite the comment of the Law Revision Commission, it is not practical to fasten separate findings of good and bad faith upon separate physical parts of an indivisible physical project. The court may conclude that the improver's intransigence equates with negligence rather than dishonesty. In view of the record, the trial court's failure to make a finding on negligence is reversible error.

---

he is not the owner of the land, he would not be entitled to relief under this chapter with respect to the additional improvement."

. . .

As to defendants' dwelling house to the southward, the court found that approximately 10 years before the lawsuit defendants had established part of their driveway, utility lines, yard and landscaping on plaintiffs' land. It concluded that the occupancy had been open, obvious and hostile, had lasted for more than five years, during which time defendants had paid all taxes. Accordingly, the court held that defendants had acquired by prescription an "easement" covering their driveway, utility lines and yard.

The evidence and findings do not sustain the award. There is a difference between a prescriptive use of land culminating in an easement (i.e., an incorporeal interest) and adverse possession which creates a change in title or ownership (i.e., a corporeal interest); the former deals with the use of land, the other with possession; although the elements of each are similar, the requirements of proof are materially different. (See Glatts v. Henson, 31 Cal. 2d 368, 371-372; Cleary v. Trimble, 229 Cal. App. 2d 1).

As the difference between prescriptive use and adverse possession is sometimes obscure, so is the difference between an exclusive easement and outright title. The former is a right to use property of another; every incident of ownership not inconsistent with enjoyment of the easement is reserved to the owner of the servient tenement; the latter may make use of any of the property which does not unduly interfere with the easement. (3 Witkin, Summary of Cal. Law, Real Property, §§ 340, 352, 353.) An exclusive interest labeled "easement" may be so comprehensive as to supply the equivalent of an estate, i.e., ownership. In determining whether a conveyance creates an easement or estate, it is important to observe the extent to which the conveyance limits the uses available to the grantor; an estate entitles the owner to the exclusive occupation of a portion of the earth's surface. (See Elliott v. McCombs, 17 Cal. 2d 23, 28; Yuba Inv. Co. v. Yuba Consol. G. Fields, 184 Cal. 469, 474-475; Van Slyke v. Arrowhead etc. Power Co., 155 Cal. 675, 678-679; Rest., Property, § 471.) "If a conveyance purported to transfer to A an unlimited use or enjoyment of Blackacre, it would be in effect a conveyance of ownership to A, not of an easement." (3 Powell on Real Property, § 405, p. 389, quoted in Russell v. Palos Verdes Properties, 218 Cal. App. 2d 754, 772).

In this case defendants had installed on plaintiff's side of the common boundary not only utility lines and part of the driveway to their home, but also part of their yard and landscaping. The judgment declares that defendants are entitled to an easement for roadway and utility lines "together with an easement for the maintenance of lawn, fences, shrubs, fruit trees, and landscaping around the Casper house ...." Although adroitly phrased to avoid the language of a grant of title, the last-quoted clause was undoubtedly designed to give defendants unlimited use of the yard around their home. Defendants doubtless did not intend plaintiffs, owners of the nominal servient tenement, to picnic, camp or dig a well in their yard. They doubtless did not intend to own a house on one side of the boundary with an unmarketable yard on the other. The findings and judgment were designed to exclude plaintiffs from defendants' domestic establishment, employing the nomenclature of easement but designed to create the practical equivalent of an estate.

Achievement of that objective required proof and findings of the elements of adverse possession, not prescriptive use. The required elements were exclusive possession, adverse to the true owners, color of title or claim of right, continuity for five years and payment of taxes. (Code Civ. Proc., § 325; 3 Witkin, Summary of Cal. Law, Real Property, §§ 47-61).

The findings recite no exclusivity of use. For that reason alone, they will not support a judgment of adverse possession.

The findings declare that defendants "were assessed for and did pay taxes ... on all of the improvements which were separately assessed ...." This finding is completely contradicted by the evidence. Both sides placed their county assessment notices in evidence. These notices show that the affected parcels were assessed by the assessor's parcel numbers. There is no proof whatever that defendants' domestic grounds were assessed separately to defendants, divorced from the assessor's parcel comprising plaintiffs' property.

Where only an easement by prescription is claimed, the easement is considered appurtenant to the claimant's land for tax purposes and need not be assessed separately. (Taormino v. Denny, 1 Cal. 3d 679, 686, fn. 3; Costa v. Fawcett, 202 Cal. App. 2d 695, 701-702). Where the claim is adverse possession and not mere prescriptive use, payment of taxes for the statutory period is essential. (Ernie v. Trinity Lutheran Church, 51 Cal. 2d 702, 707). As a general rule, where adjoining lots are assessed merely by numbers and without reference to a survey, the claimant cannot establish adverse possession because he cannot establish payment of taxes. (McDonald v. Drew, 97 Cal. 266, 269; Wilder v. Nicolaus, 50 Cal. App. 776, 785). Nevertheless, where one party is visibly in possession of land under a claim of right and has placed valuable improvements on the land, the natural inference is that the assessor did not base his assessment on the true boundary but valued the land and improvements visibly possessed by the claimants. (Price v. De Reyes, 161 Cal. 484, 489-490; Drew v. Mumford, 160 Cal. App. 2d 271, 276). Thus, although the finding relative to taxes is untrue, defendants are not precluded from proving payment of taxes.

Both phases of the judgment are characterized by serious error and both must be reversed. Relative to the area around defendants' dwelling house, the trial court and parties should give separate consideration to the yard and landscaping as distinguished from the easements for driveway and utility lines. To the extent that defendants are relying on adverse possession rather than prescriptive use, the burden is on defendants to show that they paid taxes assessed against the improvements. (Glatts v. Henson, supra, 31 Cal.2d at p. 372.)

Judgment reversed.

Regan, J., and Evans, J., concurred.

C. Fixtures

Strain v. Green

172 P.2d 216 (Wash. 1946)

ROBINSON, J.

On August 7, 1943, Jacob Green agreed to sell to William Strain his waterfront home on Mercer Island for thirty-five thousand dollars, "Payable as follows: Cash on delivery of sufficient Warranty Deed and evidence of clear title." It was, however, provided in the earnest money receipt that the "Greens are to have 60 days time to move out of the house." On August 20, 1943, Green and wife executed a statutory warranty deed to Strain and wife, which they duly acknowledged and delivered to the purchasers on August 27th, receiving the purchase price in full. At some time thereafter, they left the premises, taking with them, from the basement, the hot water tank and enclosed electric heater, the venetian blinds from the windows, certain lighting fixtures, and three mirrors, two of which were rather firmly attached to the walls. It was also claimed, in the ensuing lawsuit, that they unlawfully carried away a fireplace screen, a tool house, and certain chicken wire, with the posts which supported it. The total value of the articles removed was alleged to be $1,105.

On November 8, 1943, Mr. Hamley, as attorney for the Strains, demanded, in writing, that all of said property be returned to the premises. No part of the demand being complied with, this action was brought in March, 1944. The plaintiffs prayed for a judgment requiring the defendants to return the property, or, in case that that could not be done, for $1,105, and additional sums alleged to have been necessarily expended by the plaintiffs on account of the removal from the property, or which they would be required to expend to reinstall it.

It appears from the evidence that, when the defendants purchased the home, they found the hot water system inadequate and put in a large, modern insulated tank, with an automatic electric control. When they left the house, they disconnected that tank from the plumbing and electric system and reconnected the much smaller tank which was serving the house when they bought it. This the plaintiffs found wholly inadequate and supplemented it, as far as, in view of wartime scarcities, they were able to do so, by buying and hooking up two large tanks and making certain other additions.

When the plaintiffs agreed to buy the house, and up until they had completed the payment on the purchase price, there was a large and beautiful crystal chandelier in the center of the dining room ceiling, and five other matching fixtures in that room and adjoining rooms. The distinctive feature of these articles was their ornamentation by a great number of pendants of imported crystal glass. These fixtures the Greens also disconnected and took with them. Before departing, however, they bought and installed, in place of the fixtures removed, some highly inferior plastic imitations.

When the plaintiffs purchased the house, there was a large plate glass mirror on one of the dining room walls. It had been installed in the following manner: A large piece of three-eighths-inch plywood was firmly nailed to the plastered wall, and the mirror was attached to this backing by screws. The mirror itself was, of course, readily removed. The Greens removed it and left the plastered wall with the large square of plywood in the middle of it. The mirror having been removed, the plywood had no visible excuse for being there, and the Strains removed it. It still had twenty-six nails in it when introduced in evidence, and holes where there had been a dozen or so more. When the plywood was pried from the wall, each nail brought some of the plaster with it. The mirror over the living room fireplace was attached to the wall in the same manner, although fewer nails were used. This mirror the Greens also removed. The mirror in what was known as the powder room also had a plywood backing, but there is no very convincing testimony that the plywood was nailed, or attached, to the wall, and Mrs. Green's testimony was to the effect that the mirror merely rested upon a table and was held in place by a wire which ran to a hook above it, just as pictures are hung.

As for the other articles, the venetian blinds were of odd sizes, cut and built especially for the windows of the house. The so-called tool house turned out to be a child's playhouse, and there was no evidence that chicken wire was ever taken from the premises.

The trial court held that the automatic hot water tank was a fixture, and must be returned. The venetian blinds were also held to be fixtures, and ordered returned. Certain damages were awarded with respect to reinstallations. As the defendants have not cross-appealed, we are not concerned with that portion of the judgment. The court, however, held that the light fixtures and mirrors were personal property, which the defendants had a right to remove, and it is from that holding that this appeal is taken.

We will not undertake to write a treatise on the law of fixtures. Every lawyer knows that cases can be found in this field that will support any position that the facts of his particular case require him to take. As early as 1899, the court said, in Philadelphia Mtg. Trust Co. v. Miller, 20 Wn. 607, 56 P. 382, 72 Am. St. 138, 44 L.R.A. 559:

"There is a wilderness of authority on this question of fixtures . . . cases . . . are so conflicting that it would be profitless to undertake to review or harmonize them."

Throughout the trial, the trial judge repeatedly referred to that case as "the Miller case," and counsel, in his opening brief, refers to it as "the leading case in this jurisdiction." It held that four mantels, a bathtub, and a hot water heater connected with the plumbing were not fixtures. Since much reliance is placed upon that decision, we will quote rather freely from the opinion:

> "Anciently, mantels were uniformly built as a part of the house, and therefore became a fixture to the realty. . . . But advancing mechanical science and taste have evolved an altogether differently constructed mantel, and mantels such as are described by the testimony in this case are now constructed without reference to any particular house or particular fireplace. They are what are called `stock' mantels, and are sold separately and made adaptive to any kind of a house. They are, in fact, as much a separate article of merchandise as a bedstead or a table. . . . The same advancement has been made in bath tubs. The old-fashioned bath tub, that was sealed in and actually made a part of the bath room, has largely given place to the more convenient bath tub, that rests upon legs and can be attached to any heating system that happens to prevail in the house where it is used. And so with heaters or boilers. In this instance the boiler is in no way attached to the building, excepting by its plumbing connections. It could be detached without in any way injuring the realty; . . . The testimony shows that the building back of the mantels, or that portion of it which was concealed by the mantels, was plastered and kalsomined; that for about three years the mantels were not fastened to the wall in any way, but supported themselves in the position they occupied, and that, after that time, they were fastened to the wall by screws to render them more stable and keep them from toppling. The boiler and bath tub were not placed in the building for several years after the mortgage was given."

It would seem that the court could not very well have held otherwise than it did, without encroaching upon the province of the jury; for it is further said:

> "The question of whether or not the particular piece of furniture or machinery is a chattel or fixture has been held by a majority of the courts to be a mixed question of law and fact. In this case the court instructed the jury. These instructions were not excepted to and must be presumed to have correctly stated the law; and, the jury having found the facts in favor of the respondent, we would be loth to disturb their findings, unless we were compelled to say that, as a matter of law, the property sued for was a part of the realty."

Respondents also strongly rely on Hall v. Law Guarantee Trust Society, 22 Wn. 305, 60 P. 643, 79 Am. St. 935. The first headnote to this case reads as follows:

"Gas and electric light fixtures and globes, a windmill, a hot water tank, curtains, window and door screens, when attached to a house, are not fixtures as between a mortgagor and a mortgagee."

Referring to these two cases, the first of which was decided in 1899, and the second in 1900, respondents say, in their brief, that they "have never been overruled in this state and are the law today." Although they may never have been expressly overruled, they at least have been outmoded. We think it highly improbable that it would now be held, even in a case between a mortgagor and a mortgagee, that a mantel, or a bathtub, or an electric hot water heater connected with both the plumbing and the electrical system, is not a fixture. The law relating to fixtures has slowly and gradually changed as times have changed. Various household appliances, not formerly held to be fixtures, have become so in this "built-in" era. But the major changes are probably the result of an awareness of the fact that the luxuries of a given generation become the necessities of the next. It seems highly improbable that any present-day court would hold that a foreclosed mortgagor, on surrendering the premises, could lawfully disconnect, and take with him, the household bathtub.

We think the court had in mind the two cases just discussed and, perhaps, some others of like tenor, when it said, in Hall v. Dare, 142 Wn. 222, 252 P. 926, 50 A.L.R. 635, a case in which it was held that a flag pole, which could be removed without breaking any fastenings, was a fixture, that:

> "Some of the early decisions of this court, when superficially read, may seem not wholly in harmony with our conclusions here reached, but we know of no expression of views by this court made since rendering our decision in Filley v. Christopher, supra [39 Wn. 22, 80 P. 834], to be other than consistent with the conclusion we here reach, which is that the pole became, by the manner and circumstances of its erection by the owner, a fixture and part of the realty, and hence passed to the defendant by the mortgage foreclosure and the deed from Mrs. Huber."

In the instant case, the appellants state that the following questions are involved:

> "1. Do electric light equipment and chandeliers become fixtures upon being attached in the usual manner to the walls and ceiling of a dwelling by the owner in possession?
>
> "2. Do large ornamental mirrors mounted on plywood backing become fixtures upon being attached to the walls of a dwelling by the owner in possession thereof?"

The respondents' statement of the questions involved accurately indicates the theory upon which the trial court held the light fixtures and mirrors were rightfully removed. They read as follows:

> "1. Should a chandelier and sidelights that have belonged to a family for thirteen years and have been moved with the family from house to house four times become fixtures in the last house when the family had no intention of making them such?
>
> "2. Should mirrors that belonged to a family for fifteen years and had been moved from house to house become fixtures in the last of the four houses when the family had no intentions of making them such?"

As indicated by the questions propounded by the defendants, both Mr. and Mrs. Green categorically testified that they never had any intention that the chandelier, sidelights, and mirrors should ever become fixtures, and that they had removed them, as personal property, from the former houses in which they had lived. Furthermore, their testimony was in no way rebutted.

We do not wish it to be understood that we in any way question the veracity of the respondents, but we are here considering an alleged rule that may be involved in future cases; and, treating the matter wholly impersonally, if a witness testifies that, when he put a chandelier in a house, he intended to take it out if he should ever sell the house, in what possible way can his evidence be disputed? And, passing that, by what ex post facto system of mind reading could a purchaser determine the vendor's state of mind when he installed the chandelier? There is no evidence whatever in the instant case that the respondents told the appellants that they had ever had such an intention until after the appellants had bought, and paid for, the house. If it be held in this case that the secret intention of the defendants is determinative of the question whether or not the articles involved are fixtures, that holding will encourage and invite persons less honest than the respondents to attempt to remove from premises sold every at-all-movable article that can be disconnected without breakage.

It has never been the law of this jurisdiction, nor, we think, of any other, that the secret intention of the owner who affixed the disputed article, of itself, determines whether or not it was a fixture or a mere personal chattel.

Speaking of Ballard v. Alaska Theatre Co., 93 Wn. 655, 161 P. 478, the respondents say, in their brief:

> "As the case says: 'Where the intent is discovered it is generally controlling.' We agree with this; the only evidence of intent in this case is the testimony and the actions of Mr.

> and Mrs. Green and they testified that their intention was never to part with the personalty they placed there: the chandelier, sidelights and the mirrors."

We would be unwilling to characterize the opinion in that case as the leading case in this jurisdiction, but it states certain propositions which are still the law of this state, and some of them have been so almost from the beginning. We quote from the opinion:

> "The intent is not to be gathered from testimony of the actual state of the mind of the party making the annexation (Washington Nat. Bank v. Smith, 15 Wn. 160, 45 P. 736); but is to be inferred, when not determined by an express agreement, from the nature of the article affixed, the relation and situation to the freehold of the party making the annexation, the manner of the annexation, and the purpose for which it is made."

The case cited in the above quotation was decided fifty years ago, in 1896. Turning to the opinion in the case, we find the following statement on page 169:

> "That the intention with which machinery is placed upon the real estate is one of the elements to be taken into consideration in determining whether or not it remains a chattel or becomes a part of such real estate is conceded, *but it does not follow that such intention can be shown by testimony as to the actual state of the mind of the person who attached the machinery to the real estate at the time it was attached. On the contrary his intention must be gathered from circumstances surrounding the transaction and from what was said and done at the time, and cannot be affected by his state of mind retained as a secret.*" (Italics ours.)

It is also said, in Ballard v. Alaska Theatre Co., supra:

> "When the annexation is made by a tenant or licensor the presumption is that he did not intend to enrich the freehold, but intended to reserve title to the chattel annexed in himself, while from an annexation by the owner of the property, the presumption is the other way. [Citing cases.]
>
> "It therefore often happens that the same character of article annexed to the realty in the same way will be held to be a trade fixture and removable when annexed by a tenant, but real property and not removable when annexed by the owner of the property."

The opinion in Hall v. Dare, supra, by reference, approves the rule laid down in Filley v. Christopher, 39 Wn. 22, 80 P. 834, 109 Am. St. 853, in which it is said:

"The true criterion of a fixture is the united application of these requisites: (1) Actual annexation to the realty, or something appurtenant thereto; (2) application to the use or purpose to which that part of the realty with which it is connected is appropriated; and (3) the intention of the party making the annexation to make a permanent accession to the freehold."

Respondents in this case were owners when they installed the articles in question. The presumption, then, is (as held in the last of the quotations hitherto made from Ballard v. Alaska Theatre Co., supra) that it was their intention to enrich the freehold. This presumption is not overcome by evidence of secret intention, as is shown by the first of the quotations hitherto made from the same case, and then more plainly by the other quotation to the same effect from Washington Nat. Bank v. Smith, supra. Nor is the fact that the respondents successfully removed the articles from house to house of much, if any, probative value.

The chandelier and sidelights were actually annexed to the realty, and, clearly, for the use or purpose of that part of the realty (the house) with which they were connected. Their purpose, of course, was to make it livable. The fact that such articles are universally called "light fixtures" is, though not determinative, some evidence that they are fixtures. The fact that, after removing the chandelier and sidelights, the respondents replaced them with others amounts to an implied admission on their part that a house without light fixtures would not be a complete house. In our opinion, the chandelier and sidelights were fixtures in law and in fact.

The mirrors — at least two of them — present a much closer question. We are satisfied that there is no adequate proof that the powder room mirror was physically annexed to the realty, and as to that mirror, which seems to have been the most valuable of the three, we need not inquire further. It was not a fixture. The others present a unique situation. Each of them could be taken down from the respective walls by removing a few screws, but in each case that would leave on the wall a large square of plywood which could not be removed, in the one case, without damaging the plaster, and, in the other, without leaving some damage by nail holes, and a portion of the wall, of a different shade. We have arrived at the opinion that each of these mirrors and its plywood backing should be regarded as one article, and that in each case that article should be regarded as having been a portion of the house walls, and that, as such, they went with the house to the purchasers by the warranty deed, which contained no reservations whatsoever.

Except as to the powder room mirror, the judgment, in so far as appealed from, is reversed, and the cause remanded to the trial court for the entry of judgment in accordance herewith.

BEALS, C.J., BLAKE, and JEFFERS, JJ., concur.

Goddard v. Winchell

52 N.W. 1124 (Iowa 1892)

GRANGER, J.

The district court found the following facts, with some others, not important on this hearing: "First. That the plaintiff, John Goddard, is, and has been since about 1857, the owner in fee simple if the north half of section number three, in township number ninety-eight, range number twenty-five, in Winnebago county, Iowa, and was such owner at the time of the fall of the meteorite hereinafter referred to. Second. That said land was prairie land, and that the grass privilege for the year 1890 was leased to one James Elickson. Third. That on the second day of May, 1890, an aerolite [i.e., meteorite] passed over northern and northwestern Iowa, and the aerolite, or fragment of the same, in question in this action, weighing, when replevied, and when produced in court on the trial of this cause, about sixty-six pounds, fell onto the plaintiff's land, described above, and buried itself in the ground to a depth of three feet, and became imbedded therein at a point about twenty rods from the section line on the north. Fourth. That the day after the aerolite in question fell it was dug out of the ground with a spade by one Peter Hoagland, in the presence of the tenant, Elickson; that said Hoagland took it to his house, and claimed to own same, for the reason that he had found same and dug it up. Fifth. That on May 5, 1890, Hoagland sold the aerolite in suit to the defendant, H. Y. Winchell, for one hundred and five dollars, and the same was at once taken possession of by the said defendant, and that the possession was held by him until same was taken under the writ of replevin herein; that the .defendant knew at the time of his purchase that it was an aerolite, and that it fell on the prairie south of Hoagland's land. * * * Tenth. I find the value of said aerolite to be one hundred and one dollars ($101) as verbally stipulated in open court by the parties to this action ; that the same weighs about sixty-six pounds, is of a black, smoky color on the outside, showing the effects of heat, and of a lighter and darkish gray color on the inside; that it is an aerolite, and fell from the heavens on the second of May, 1890; that a member of Hoagland's family saw the aerolite fall, and directed him to it."

As conclusions of law, the district court found that the aerolite became a part of the soil on which it fell; that the plaintiff was the owner thereof; and that, the act of Hoagland in removing it was wrongful. It is insisted by the appellant that the conclusions of law are erroneous; that the enlightened demands of the time in which we live call for, if not a modification, a liberal construction, of the ancient rule, "that what-ever is affixed to the soil belongs to the soil," or, the more modern statement of the rule, that "a permanent annexation to the soil, of a thing in itself personal, makes it a part of the realty." In behalf of the appellant is invoked a rule alike ancient and of undoubted merit — that of "title by occupancy" — and we are cited to the language of Blackstone, as follows: "Occupancy is the taking possession of those things which before belonged to nobody;" and "whatever movables are found upon the surface of the earth, or in the sea, and are unclaimed by any owner, are supposed to be abandoned by the last proprietor, and as such are returned into the common stock and mass of things, and therefore they belong, as in a state of nature, to the first occupant or finder." In determining which of these rules is to govern in this case, it will be well for us to keep in mind the controlling facts giving rise to the different rules, and note wherein, if at all, the facts of this case should distinguish it. The rule sought to be avoided has alone reference to what becomes a part of the soil, and hence belongs to the owner thereof, because attached or added thereto. It has no reference whatever to an independent acquisition of title, that is, to an acquisition of property existing independent of other property. The rule invoked has reference only to property of this independent character, for it speaks of movables "found upon the surface of the earth or in the sea." The term "movables" must not be construed to mean that which can be moved, for, if so, it would include much known to be realty; but it means such things as are not naturally parts of earth or sea, but are on the one or in the other. Animals exist on the earth and in the sea, but they are not, in a proper sense, parts of either. If we look to the natural formation of the earth and sea, it is not difficult to understand what is meant by "movables," within the spirit of the rule cited. To take from the earth what nature has placed there in its formation, whether at the creation or through the natural processes of the acquisition and depletion of its particular parts, as we witness it in our daily observations, whether it be the soil proper or some natural deposit, as of mineral or vegetable matter, is to take a part of the earth, and not movables.

If, from what we have said, we have in mind the facts giving rise to the rules cited we may well look to the facts of this case to properly distinguish it. The subject of the dispute is an aerolite, of about sixty-six pounds' weight, that "fell from the heavens" on the land of the plaintiff, and was found three feet below the surface. It came to its position in the earth through natural causes. It was one of nature's deposits, with nothing in its material composition to make it foreign or unnatural to the soil. It was not a movable thing "on the earth." It was in the earth, and in a very significant sense immovable; that is, it was only movable as parts of earth are made movable by the hand of man. Except for the peculiar manner in which it came, its relation to the soil would be beyond dispute. It was in its substance, as we understand, a stone. It was not of a character to be thought of as "unclaimed by any owner," and, because unclaimed, "supposed to be abandoned by the last proprietor," as should be the case under the rule invoked by the appellant. In fact, it has none of the characteristics of the property contemplated by such a rule.

We may properly note some of the particular claims of the appellant. His argument deals with the rules of the common law for acquiring real property, as by escheat, occupancy, prescription, -forfeiture, and alienation, which it is claimed were all the methods known, barring inheritance. We need not question the correctness of the statement, assuming that it has reference to original acquisition, as distinct from acquisitions to soil already owned, by accretion or natural causes. The general rules of the law, by which the owners of riparian titles are made to lose or gain by the doctrine of accretions, are quite familiar. These rules are not, however, of exclusive application to such owners. Through the action of the elements, wind and water, the soil of one man is taken and deposited in the field of another; and thus all over the country, we may say, changes are constantly going on. By these natural causes the owners of the soil are giving and taking as the wisdom of the controlling forces, shall determine. By these operations one may' be affected with a substantial gain, and another by a similar loss. These gains are of accretion, and the deposit becomes the property of the owner of the soil on which it is made.

A scientist of note has said that from six to seven hundred of these stones fall to our earth annually. If they are, as indicated in argument, departures from other planets, and if among the planets of the solar system there is this interchange, bearing evidence of their material composition, upon what principle of reason or authority can we say that a deposit thus made shall not be of that class of property that it would be if originally of this planet and in the same situation? If "these exchanges have been going on through the countless ages of our planetary system, who shall attempt to determine what part of the rocks, and formations of especial value to the scientist, rest ing in and upon the earth, are of meteoric acquisition, and a part of that class of property designated in argument as "unowned things," to be the property of the fortunate finder instead of the owner of the soil, if the rule contended for is to obtain? It is not easy to understand why stones or balls of metallic iron, deposited as this was, should be governed by a differ ent rule than obtains from the deposit of boulders, stones, and drift upon our prairies by glacier action; and who would contend that these deposits from floating bodies of ice belong, not to the owner of the soil, but to the finder? Their origin or source may be less mysterious, but they, too, are "telltale messengers" from far-off lands, and have value for historic and scientific investigation.

It is said that the aerolite is without adaptation to the soil, and only valuable for scientific purposes. Nothing in the facts of the case will warrant us in saying that it was not as well adapted for use by the owner of the soil as any stone, or, as the appellant is pleased to denominate it, "ball of metallic iron." That it may be of greater value for scientific or other purposes may be admitted, but that fact has little weight in determining who should be its owner. We cannot say that the owner of the soil is not as interested in, and would not as readily contribute to, the great cause of scientific advancement, as the finder, by chance or otherwise, of these silent messengers. This aerolite is of the value of one hundred and one dollars, .and this fact, if no other, would remove it from uses where other and much less valuable materials would answer an equally good purpose, and place it in the sphere of its greater usefulness.

The rule is cited, with cases for its support, that the finder of lost articles, even where they are found on the property, in the building, or with the personal effects of third persons, is the owner thereof against all the world, except the true owner. The correctness of the rule may be conceded, but its application to the case at bar is very doubtful. The subject of this controversy was never lost or abandoned. Whence it came is not known, but, under the natural law of its government, it became a part of this earth, and, we think, should be treated as such. It is said by the appellant that this case is unique, that no exact precedent can be found, and that the conclusion must be based largely upon new considerations. No similar question has, to our knowledge, been determined in a court of last resort. In 15 American and English Encyclopedia of Law, page 388, is the following language: "An aerolite is the property of the owner of the fee upon which it falls. Hence a pedestrian on the highway, who is first to discover such a stone, is not the owner of it; the highway being a mere easement for travel." It cites the case of Maas v. Amana Society, 16 Alb. Law J. 76, and 13 Irish Law Times, 381, each of which periodicals contains an editorial notice of such a case having been decided in Illinois, but no reported case is to be found. Anderson's Law Dictionary states the same rule of law, with the same references, under the subject of "Accretions." In 20 Alb. Law J. 299, is a letter to the «editor from a correspondent, calling attention to a case determined in France, where an aerolite found by a peasant was held not to be the property of the "proprietor of the field," but that of the finder. These references are entitled, of course, to slight, if any, consideration, the information as to them being too meager to indicate the trend of legal thought.

Our conclusions are announced with some doubts as to their correctness, but they arise not so much from the application of known rules of law to proper facts as from the absence of defined rules for these particular- cases. The interest manifested has induced us to give the case careful thought. Our conclusions seem to us nearest analogous to the generally accepted rules of law bearing on kindred questions, and to subserve the ends of substantial justice. The question we have discussed is controlling in the case, and we need not consider others.

The judgment of the district court is affirmed.

12. Estates and Future Interests

A. Introduction

All land under the dominion of the English crown is held "mediately or immediately, of the king"—that is, the crown has "radical title" to all land under its political dominion. William the Conqueror declared that all land in England was literally the king's property; everyone else had to settle for the privilege of holding it for him—the privilege of *tenure* (from the Norman French word "tenir"—to hold). Tenurial rights were intensely personal in early feudal society: the right to hold land was a privilege granted by the crown in exchange for an oath of allegiance and a promise of military service by the tenant—the oath of homage. The word homage derives from the French word *homme*—literally "man"—precisely because the ceremony surrounding the oath created not only the right of tenure, but a political and military relationship between "lord and man."[37] In exchange for the tenant's loyal support, or *fealty*, the lord warranted the tenant's right to hold a plot of land, called a fief, or *fee*.

---

[37] The ceremony of homage, recorded by the 13th-century jurist and ecclesiastic Henry de Bracton, required the tenant to come to the lord in a public place, and there "to place both his hands between the two hands of his lord, by which there is symbolized protection, defense and warranty on the part of the lord and subjection and reverence on that of the tenant, and say these words: 'I become your man with respect to the tenement which I hold of you … and I will bear you fealty in life and limb and earthly honour … and I will bear you fealty against all men … saving the faith owed the lord king and his heirs.' And immediately after this [to] swear an oath of fealty to his lord in these words: 'Hear this, lord N., that I will bear you fealty in life and limb, in body, goods, and earthly honour, so help me God and these sacred relics.'" 2 Bracton Online 232 http://bracton.law.harvard.edu/Unframed/English/v2/232.htm. The Anglo-Saxon Chronicle contains a remarkable and much-debated passage in which William the Conqueror is said to have held court at Salisbury twenty years into his reign, and there summoned and taken direct oaths of homage and fealty from every landowner "of any account" in the whole of England. *See* H. A. Cronne, *The Salisbury Oath*, 19 HISTORY 248 (1934); J.C. Holt, *1086*, in COLONIAL ENGLAND, 1066-1215, at 31 (1997).

Homage Ceremony
Source: JAMES HENRY BREASTED & JAMES HARVEY ROBINSON, 1 OUTLINES OF EUROPEAN HISTORY 399 (1914).

Acceptance of this form of military tenure obligated the tenant to provide a certain number of knights when called on by the king, and the land held by the tenant was supposed to provide sufficient material support to enable him to meet this military obligation. Sometimes, by the process of *subinfeudation*, the King's direct tenants (or "tenants-in-chief") could spread this burden around by in turn accepting homage from other, lesser nobles and freemen, each of whom would be responsible to the tenant-in-chief for a portion of the tenant-in-chief's obligation to provide knight-service. The tenants-in-chief thereby became "mesne lords" in their own right ("mesne" being Norman French for "middle" or "intermediate"). There could be several layers of mesne lords (i.e., "land lords") in the feudal hierarchy, at the bottom of which were "tenants in demesne" ("demesne" being Norman French for "domain" or "dominion")—who actually held the land rather than subinfeudating it further. Of course, holding land did not mean one actually worked it; a tenant in demesne often left the cultivation and productive use of land to those of lower social status. These could be "villeins"—serfs legally bound to the land by birth—or "leasehold" tenants—a leasehold being a right to hold land for a term of years in exchange for payment of rent in cash or (more often) kind, and of lesser status than the "freehold" estate held by feudal tenants tracing their rights up the feudal pyramid to the crown.

Because a feudal tenant's land rights were intimately connected to this web of personal, political, and military relationships, there was no logical reason why the tenant ought to be free to transfer those rights to anyone else—and good reason for the lords to resist such alienation of the fee by their tenants. Indeed, fees could be forfeited to the lord for the tenant's breach of the homage relationship or commission of some other "felony," and on the tenant's death it was not clear that his family members had the right to inherit the fee. The king was assumed to have the right to retake the fee and re-grant it to a preferable new tenant upon his displeasure with or the death of the old tenant (it was his land, after all). Within a century, however, the dynastic ambitions of the baronage compelled King Henry I to concede (in his Coronation Charter of 1100) that a recently deceased baron's heir could redeem his fee upon payment of "a just and lawful relief"—i.e., a payment of money to the crown, as a kind of inheritance tax. Under the principle of primogeniture that took hold in England around this time, the lord's heir was his eldest son; landowners were not free to choose who would take over their tenancy after their death. Thus, subject to the payment of a relief, the fee became *descendible*—capable of being inherited from one generation to the next—and the grant of a descendible tenancy by the crown was now made not "to Lord Hobnob," but "to Lord Hobnob *and his heirs*." To this day, the latter phrase remains the classic common-law formula for creating the broadest interest in land that the law will recognize: the *fee simple absolute*.

Descendibility of the fee simple having been settled early in the history of English land law, the broader question of full alienability took several more centuries to work out. The history of medieval English land law is a history of tenants trying to secure their families' wealth and power by expanding alienability and evading tenurial obligations to their lords and the crown, while the crown and higher nobility tried to adapt the law to preserve their status and prevent such evasions. There is a dialectical quality to this history. For example: for complicated reasons subinfeudation quickly came to present a greater threat to the economic interests of the higher ranks of the feudal hierarchy than simple substitution of one tenant for another. Thus, in 1290 the Statute of Quia Emptores banned subinfeudation. But in doing so it validated substitution, and with it the practice of selling an entire fee in exchange for money during the life of the tenant. Similarly, in 1536, at the insistence of King Henry VIII, the Statute of Uses abolished many clever schemes adopted by tenants to use intermediaries to direct the disposition of real property interests after death and to put those interests outside the reach of the law courts (and of the crown's feudal authority). But in doing so, the statute validated one type of flexible property arrangement we have come to know as a *trust*. Moreover, the removal of the primary mechanism lawyers had developed to meet tenants' demand for intergenerational planning was sufficiently unpopular that Henry felt compelled to consent to the enactment of the Statute of Wills in 1540—finally permitting tenants to pass their legal estates in land by will rather than being at the whim of the rule of primogeniture. Finally, since the 16th century, primogeniture has given way to a more complex system of default inheritance rights for various relatives of the deceased who leaves no will; these rights are designed to try to approximate what legislatures think the *decedent* would have wanted, not necessarily what is best for the government. This set of default rights comprises the law of *intestate succession*, which we will discuss in a separate unit (or which you may study in a separate course on trust and estates law).

Various other statutes and common-law developments over the centuries culminated in the system of possessory estates and future interests that were imported into the North American English colonies, and thus into the independent American states (excluding Louisiana). Underlying them all is a fundamental distinction that traces back to the "radical title" asserted by William the Conqueror in 1066: **there is a conceptual difference between the ownership *of land* and the ownership of *a legal interest in that land.*** This distinction remains important to modern property law, and this unit will introduce you to the types of legal interests in land that American law will recognize. In particular, it examines how the common law divides up legal interests in land among successive owners over time.

Before delving into this material, we should warn you that the estates system has limited relevance even for the practicing real estate lawyer of today. The study of estates and future interests remains in property courses for three primary reasons: (1) the estates are still legally valid property interests, and their complexity can therefore can be a danger to lawyers who encounter them and are unfamiliar with them; (2) many of the legal estates and future interests in real property can be usefully extended to *equitable* interests in property held in trust, and the estate system is therefore still important knowledge for lawyers in the field of wills and trusts; and (3) the bar examiners are fond of testing aspirant attorneys on future interests—perhaps simply because they are fairly mechanical and therefore highly testable.

Mastering the system of estates and future interests requires considerable exercise of the lawyerly skills of close reading, logical reasoning, and breaking down a big problem into lots of smaller problems. As a matter of legal practice, contemporary lawyers should always consider alternative ways to divide up interests in property. In particular, the modern lawyer should look to the available options in the law of trusts and the various forms of business associations—such as corporations—that can own property in their capacity as fictional legal "persons." We discuss these strategies in a separate chapter on trusts and corporate property.

B. Concepts, Vocabulary, and Conventions

To begin understanding how the law divides up interests in land over time, we begin with the fundamental distinction between **possessory estates** (present interests) and **future interests**. A **possessory estate** is a legal interest that confers on its owner *the right to present possession* of some thing. A **future interest** is a legal interest *that exists in the present*, but does not entitle the owner to possession until some point *in the future*.

This may sound confusing, but you are probably already familiar with an arrangement that follows this pattern: a lease. A lease is a transaction in which the landlord gives the tenant a possessory estate (a leasehold estate), and *retains* a future interest—the right to retake possession after the lease term ends. This retained future interest—an unqualified right to future possession retained by the party who created the possessory interest that precedes it—is called a **reversion.** (Landlord-tenant relationships are obviously more complicated than this—they entail a number of contractual rights and obligations and are heavily regulated by statutory and decisional law and, in many cases, administrative codes. We cover these relationships more thoroughly in our unit on Landlord and Tenant.)

The idea that both landlord and tenant can have legal interests in the same parcel of land at the same time, even though only one of them has the right to *possess* the land at any given time, is a good introduction to the concept of future interests. If you think about it, you will probably recognize that the basic idea of a lease implies certain rights and powers of a landlord in the leased premises even *during* the term of the lease. The most important one is the reversionary right itself: the right to take possession at some point in the future. That's a right the tenant can't take away, even while the tenant has the right to possession. The landlord might be interested in selling (or mortgaging) this reversionary right, even before the lease ends. And if she does sell or mortgage her interest (which she may, subject to the tenant's interest), the thing sold is not "the property"; it is *the landlord's reversion*: a legal interest in real property *that exists in the present* but will not entitle its holder to *possession* of that real property until some point *in the future.*

When learning about estates and future interests, we will follow some conventions that will simplify our discussion as much as possible. Most of our problems will involve an owner of land transferring some interest in that land to one or more other parties. Following longstanding tradition in the study of Anglo-American property law, we will refer to the parcel of land in question as "Blackacre" (or "Whiteacre," "Greenacre," "Ochreacre," etc. if more than one parcel is at issue). We will refer to the original owner as O, and the other parties as A, B, C, etc.

In addition, there are a variety of technical terms that arise, a few of which you should be familiar with:

- A *grant* or *conveyance* is a transfer of an interest in property. The person making the grant is the *grantor* (or *transferor*); the person receiving the grant is the *grantee* (or *transferee*). If the grant is made during the life of the grantor, it is said to be an *inter vivos* conveyance (literally, "between the living"). If in a will, it is said to be a *testamentary* conveyance. A testamentary conveyance of real property is called a *devise.* A testamentary conveyance of personal property is called a *bequest* (or sometimes a *legacy*).
- When a person dies, they will either have left a valid will or not. A person who dies with a valid will dies *testate*; one who dies without a valid will dies *intestate.* Either way, the dead person can be referred to as a *decedent.* If the decedent did leave a valid will, they may also be referred to as a *testator* if male, or a *testatrix* if female.

- The assets that a decedent owned at her death are collectively referred to as the decedent's *estate*. An estate can sometimes take on the qualities of a legal person—it is not uncommon to say that a certain asset is owned by "the estate of O." The property rights of this fictional legal person are managed by an actual person whose title depends on whether the decedent left a will. The instructions in a will are carried out by an *executor* (if male) or *executrix* (if female), designated as such in the will itself. An intestate estate is disposed of by a court-appointed *administrator* (if male) or *administratrix* (if female).
- The authority of an administrator or executor to dispose of the estate's assets is conferred by a *probate court*. When a valid will is filed with the probate court and deemed valid, the court will *admit the will to probate* (or *probate the will*), and will issue *letters testamentary* to the executor authorizing him to take possession of the estate's assets and dispose of them according to the will's instructions. If the decedent died intestate, the court will issue *letters of administration* to an administrator authorizing him to take possession of the estate's assets and dispose of them according to the laws of intestate succession.
- If the decedent did leave a valid will, it will typically contain instructions for transferring assets to various identified people or entities. The parties receiving the bequests are referred to as the will's *beneficiaries*, *devisees* (for real property), or *legatees* (for personal property). When a decedent passes property by will he or she is said to have *devised* that property. A property interest that the decedent has the power to transfer by will is said to be *devisable*.
- Sometimes a will fails to provide instructions for all the assets owned by the testator at death; in this case the unallocated assets are said to create a *partial intestacy*. When this happens, assets designated in the will are distributed according to the will's terms, while the estate's remaining assets are distributed according to the laws of intestate succession. In order to avoid partial intestacy, it is good practice to include a *residuary clause* in a will, disposing of all the assets of the decedent not devised through specific bequests. Such unenumerated assets are referred to as the *residuary estate*.
- If the decedent did not leave a valid will, her property will pass to her *heirs* (sometimes referred to as *heirs at law*). Heirs are those who are designated by law as successors to property that passes by intestate succession rather than by will. When heirs take such property, they are said to *inherit* it. A property interest that can pass by intestate succession is said to be *descendible*.
- Note that until the decedent actually dies, we don't know who her heirs are; rights of inheritance are allocated only to relatives of the decedent who *survive* her—who are still alive when the decedent dies. Thus, until a property owner dies, her relatives have no legally enforceable rights in her property under the laws of intestate succession. It is

sometimes said that such relatives have a mere *expectancy*, and they are sometimes referred to as *heirs apparent*.

- Heirs under intestacy laws are drawn from various categories of relatives. In addition to spouses, there are *issue*: the direct descendants of the decedent (children, grandchildren, great-grandchildren, etc.); *ancestors* (parents, grandparents, great-grandparents, etc.); and *collaterals*: relatives who are not direct ancestors or descendants (siblings, aunts, uncles, nieces, nephews, cousins).
- If a person dies without a will and without any heirs at law, any property in their estate *escheats* to the state, which becomes its owner.

C. Basic Estates and Future Interests

We will begin by examining two possessory estates—the **fee simple absolute** and the **life estate**—and two future interests—the **reversion** and the **remainder**.

1. The Fee Simple Absolute

The *fee simple absolute* is the most complete interest in land that the law will recognize. When we say that "O owns Blackacre" without any further qualification, what we actually mean is that O owns a *presently possessory fee simple absolute* in Blackacre. The key distinguishing characteristic of the fee simple absolute is that it has no inherent end—it is an estate of *indefinite duration*. It is descendible, devisable, and alienable *inter vivos*; so it can be *transferred* to a new owner, but it cannot be destroyed. At most, it can be carved up into lesser estates and interests for a while, and we will spend most of the rest of this chapter understanding how that happens.

At common law, as previously noted, the fee simple absolute was created by the formula: "to A and his heirs." That formula still works, but in modern usage it is sufficient to simply say "to A," and the use of such language in a conveyance from the owner of a fee simple absolute will be presumed to create a fee simple absolute in A.

2. The Life Estate

The *life estate* is just what it sounds like: an estate that confers a right to possession for the life of its owner. The owner of a life estate is referred to as a *life tenant*. The life estate terminates by operation of law upon the owner's death (i.e., it ceases to exist). It is created by the formula: "to A for life." Because it must by definition end—we all have to die sometime—any land held by a life tenant must also be subject to a *future interest* in some other person. We'll explore what those future interests might be shortly.

Recall the legal principle of *nemo dat quod non habet* (or *nemo dat* for short), which we encountered in our discussion of good faith purchasers: a grantor cannot convey title to something she doesn't herself own. Following this principle, life estates are alienable *inter vivos* during the life of the life tenant, but obviously not devisable or descendible: they cease to exist upon the death of their owner, so the life tenant's estate has nothing to convey. *Nemo dat* also implies that the owner of an interest in real property cannot convey *more* than their interest; a life tenant cannot convey a fee simple absolute, for example. More to the point, if a life tenant A transfers her life estate to a grantee B, B cannot receive anything more than what A owns: a possessory estate that will terminate by operation of law *when A dies*. Because such an interest is measured by the life of someone other than its owner, it is called a *life estate pur autre vie* (literally, in Law French, "for another life"). A life estate *pur autre vie* can also be created explicitly, as by a grant "to A for the life of B."

We'll hold off on any further illustrative problems at this point, because we still need some exposition of what happens *after* a life tenant dies. The answer, as we've already noted, involves *future interests*.

3. The Reversion

We encountered the reversion once before, when discussing leases as an introduction to the concept of a future interest. But reversions often arise in non-leasehold contexts too. Consider what happens when A, owning a life estate in Blackacre, dies. A's life estate terminates by operation of law; it simply ceases to exist and disappears. Who has the right to possess Blackacre now? It seems obvious that *somebody* must have a right to possession of the land, but it seems equally obvious that whoever that somebody is, she had *no right to possession* before A died. Whoever she is, during the term of A's life estate she must have held an interest that would entitle her to take possession at *some point in the future* (that is, a *future interest*).

There are two candidates for such an interest. We will begin with the most basic: the **reversion**. Suppose that O, owning a fee simple absolute in Blackacre, conveys Blackacre "to A for life," and says nothing more? What is the legal effect of this grant?

Based on the formula we just learned, it should be clear that A receives a life estate in Blackacre. But what other effects does the grant have on the legal rights of the parties? Think about the interest O held prior to the conveyance: the fee simple absolute. Remember that a fee simple absolute is an interest of *infinite duration*—it never ends. So when O starts with a possessory interest of infinite duration, and then gives away a life estate—whose duration is limited by a human lifespan—to A, *something was left over*. Specifically, O never gave away the right to possession of Blackacre from the day of A's death to the end of time. Whether meaning to or not, O gave away less of an interest in Blackacre than what he owned, meaning *he still holds some interest.* We call this type of interest—the residual interest left over when a grantor gives away less than they have—a *retained* interest.

This retained interest can't entitle O to possession during A's life—A has the exclusive right to possession as the life tenant. So O's interest must be a *future interest* during the term of A's life estate: an interest that will entitle O to possession *after the natural termination of the life estate.* As we discussed in the example of the lease, we call this kind of future interest a **reversion**. It is a *retained interest in the grantor*—created when a grantor conveys less than his entire interest—that will become possessory by operation of law upon the *natural termination* of the preceding estate. Colloquially, we say that Blackacre "reverts" to O. In some opinions, you will see the holder of a reversion referred to as a "reversioner."

A reversion can of course also be created explicitly, for example, if O conveys Blackacre "to A for life, then to O." In this case, O has explicitly created a life estate in A followed by a reversion in O.

4. The Remainder

A **remainder** is a type of future interest created in someone *other than* the grantor. The distinguishing characteristic of the remainder is that—like a reversion—it *cannot cut short or divest any possessory estate.* (We will later encounter other future interests that can.) A remainder simply "remains," sitting around and waiting for the natural termination of the preceding possessory estate (be it a life estate or a lease), at which point the remainder will become possessory by operation of law. Suppose that O, owning a fee simple absolute in Blackacre, conveys Blackacre "to A for life, *and then to B.*" Again, A would have a life estate, but now O has also affirmatively created a future interest in B. Because the future interest is created in someone *other than* the grantor, it isn't a reversion. And because it cannot cut short A's life estate (note the "and then" language), it must therefore be a **remainder**. You will often see the holder of a remainder referred to as a "remainderman," regardless of that person's gender.

Future interests get a lot more complicated than this, but you now have enough to begin examining some problems that can arise from even this limited set of interests.

Questions

1. O, owner of a fee simple absolute in Blackacre, conveys Blackacre "to A for life, then to B for life." (Assume that both A and B are alive at the time of the grant.) What is the state of title in Blackacre?

    a. What will be the state of title if A dies, survived by B and O?

b. What will be the state of title if B dies, survived by A and O?
c. What will be the state of title if O dies, then A dies, then B dies?

2. What will be the state of title if, while O, A, and B are still alive, B conveys her interest to C?

   a. What will be the state of title if, after B conveys her interest to C, A dies, survived by B, C, and O?
   b. What will be the state of title if, after B conveys her interest to C, C dies, leaving D as his heir, and is survived by A, B, and O?
   c. What will be the state of title if, after B conveys her interest to C, B dies, survived by A, C, and O?

D. Construing Ambiguous Grants

We've recited a few formulas for creating the small number of common-law interests you've encountered. For example, "to A and his heirs" creates a fee simple absolute in A; "to B for life, then to C" creates a life estate in B and a remainder in C. But the actual language of documents conveying legal interests in real property don't always stick to the formula—especially (but unfortunately not exclusively) when they are drafted without the assistance of counsel. Consider the following case.

In the Estate of Dalton Edward Craigen
305 S.W.3d 825 (Ct. App. Tex. 2010)

HOLLIS HORTON, Justice.

We are asked to determine whether the trial court properly interpreted the dispository language in a holographic will. If the will is ambiguous, the applicable rules of will construction yield one result. If the will is unambiguous, the trial court was required to give effect to the express language of the will, and arguably should have reached a different result.

The trial court, in construing the testator's intentions under the will, found "[t]hat it was the intent of the [t]estator to leave his entire estate to his surviving wife in full." The trial court further found "[t]hat there was no intention to leave a life estate to her." In a single issue on appeal, the testator's adult children contend the testator intended to leave a life estate to his wife, and they argue that the remainder of the estate passed to them through the laws of descent and distribution. We find the will is ambiguous and hold that under the appropriate rules of will construction, the trial court properly construed the will. Accordingly, we affirm the judgment.

THE WILL

Dalton Edward Craigen left a holographic will that in its entirety stated:

Last Will & testament
Debbie gets everything till
she dies.
Being of sound mind & this
is my w. last will & testament.
I leave to my Wife Daphne
Craigen all p. real & personal property.
12–17–99 Dalton Craigen

CONTENTIONS OF THE PARTIES

The parties stipulated "[t]hat Debbie and Daphne named in Dalton Craigen's will are one and the same person." Brian Craigen and Sabrina Brumley, Craigen's adult children, argue that the testator's intent under the will is "crystal clear—the testator left everything (all of his real and personal property, his definition of 'everything') to his wife for as long as she lived." According to Brian and Sabrina, the dominant provision of the will (the first sentence) creates a life estate, and the will's third sentence can be harmonized with the will's first sentence by construing the third sentence to define the property that Craigen intended to include in his wife's life estate. Brian and Sabrina ask that we render a judgment in their favor by holding that Daphne received only a life estate under Craigen's will.

Daphne died on January 17, 2009. Yvonne Christian, the independent administratrix of Daphne's estate, argues we should affirm the trial court's judgment. According to Christian, the will is not ambiguous as it reflects Craigen's intent to leave his entire estate to Daphne.

RULES OF CONSTRUCTION

The rules involved in construing wills are well settled. "The primary object of inquiry in interpreting a will is determining the intent of the testator." *Gee v. Read*, 606 S.W.2d 677, 680 (Tex.1980). "The [testator's] intent must be drawn from the will, not the will from the intent." *Id.* We ascertain intent from the language found within the four corners of the will. "In construing the will, all its provisions should be looked to, for the purpose of ascertaining what the real intention of the [testator] was; and, if this can be ascertained from the language of the instrument, then any particular paragraph of the will which, considered alone, would indicate a contrary intent, must yield to the intention manifested by the whole instrument." *McMurray v. Stanley*, 69 Tex. 227, 6 S.W. 412, 413 (1887).

When a will has been drafted by a layperson who is not shown to be familiar with the technical meanings of certain words, courts do not place "'too great emphasis on the precise meaning of the language used where the will is the product of one not familiar with legal terms, or not trained in their use.'" *Gilkey v. Chambers*, 146 Tex. 355, 207 S.W.2d 70, 71 (1947) (quoting 69 C.J. Wills § 1120 (1934)). Instead, in arriving at the meaning intended by the layman-testator, courts refer to the popular meaning of the words the testator chose to use. In summary, the testator's intent, as gathered from the will as a whole, prevails against a technical meaning that might be given to certain words or phrases, unless the testator intended to use the word or phrase in the technical sense.

With respect to the creation of a life estate, no particular words are needed to create a life estate, but the words used must clearly express the testator's intent to create a life estate. A very strong presumption arises that when a person makes a will, the testator intended a complete disposition of his property. "[T]he very purpose of a will is to make such provisions that the testator will not die intestate." *Gilkey*, 207 S.W.2d at 73. When faced with ambiguity, and in applying that presumption, courts generally interpret wills to avoid creating an intestacy.

...In reconciling different parts of a will, the Texas Supreme Court has explained:

> Where, however, the language of one part of a will is not easily reconciled with that used in another, the principal and subordinate provisions should be construed in their due relation to each other, and the intent which is disclosed in the express clause ought to prevail over the language used in subsidiary provisions, unless modified or controlled by the latter. And a clearly expressed intention in one portion of the will will not yield to a doubtful construction in any other portion of the instrument.

Heller v. Heller, 114 Tex. 401, 269 S.W. 771, 774 (1925).

ANALYSIS

A will is ambiguous if it is capable of more than one meaning. Because Debbie and Daphne are in fact the same person, the ambiguity in Craigen's will becomes apparent. Why would Craigen in the first sentence grant his wife a life estate, but then in the concluding sentences bestow upon her all of his property? The resolution of that question by Craigen's children seems reasonable, as the last sentence could be construed to merely describe the property that Craigen intended to include in Daphne's life estate.

On the other hand, Craigen did not mention his children in his will and he made no provisions to expressly benefit them. Moreover, Brian and Sabrina's construction of Craigen's will would, if adopted, allow all of Craigen's property to pass under the laws of intestacy at Daphne's death. Brian and Sabrina's construction assumes that Craigen, when writing his will, did not intend to completely dispose of his estate. The rule that Craigen did not likely intend to create an intestacy favors the construction of the will that the trial court adopted.

Brian and Sabrina contend that the will gave Daphne a life estate, but Craigen did not utilize those exact words in his will. Although no particular words are needed to create a life estate, the words used must clearly express the testator's intent to create one. In the absence of a remainderman clause, we are skeptical that Craigen used the phrase "till she dies" in a technical sense to create a life estate. Instead, Craigen likely intended to limit Daphne's use of his property; nevertheless, the will manifests an intent that she have his property in fee simple absolute. Consequently, although the first sentence in the will is susceptible to the interpretation that Craigen created a life estate, the will becomes ambiguous when, in the will's third sentence, Craigen expressly names Daphne as the beneficiary of all of his property and he makes no further provision for his estate upon her death.

We conclude that the will is reasonably capable of more than one meaning; therefore, we resort to the rules of construction that apply to ambiguous wills.... Craigen's will can be interpreted to avoid the intestacy certain to result under Brian and Sabrina's construction of the will. The potential intestacy is avoided if the phrase "till she dies" is interpreted as a conditional bequest. The third sentence then functions as intended to give Daphne all of Craigen's property in fee simple. The immediate vesting construction favors Daphne, the sole beneficiary named in Craigen's will. It also affords the phrase "till she dies" a nontechnical meaning.

We decline to apply the presumption that Craigen did not intend to disinherit his children when the will expressly states that Craigen gave all of his real and personal property to Daphne and when Brian and Sabrina offered no evidence regarding Craigen's situation and the circumstances surrounding the execution of the will. Taking the will as a whole, the dominant gift is all of Craigen's real and personal property, and he made that gift to his wife. As this is the dominant clause, Craigen's expressed intention prevails.

We hold that under the appropriate rules of will construction, the trial court correctly construed the will. We overrule the issue and affirm the judgment.

AFFIRMED.

Notes and Questions

1. **Holographic Wills.** A holographic will—a will handwritten by the testator—often presents a particular challenge for courts attempting to interpret it. Indeed, they are thought to be so problematic that about half of American jurisdictions refuse to recognize them as valid wills at all. *See* Stephen Clowney, *In Their Own Hand: An Analysis*

of Holographic Wills and Homemade Willmaking, REAL PROPERTY, TRUST AND ESTATE LAW JOURNAL 27 (2008) (arguing that the defects of holographic wills, though real, are overstated). Lay testators attempting to settle their affairs without assistance of counsel often make legal or technical errors of various kinds, including errors of ambiguity such as the one that generated the litigation in *Craigen*.

2. **Presumptions and Rules of Construction.** The court reviews a number of rules of construction applied by courts in construing ambiguous grants. Most jurisdictions have similar rules of construction—sometimes promulgated by statute, other times judge-made. In *Craigen*, two rules in particular do considerable work: the presumption against intestacy and the clear-statement rule for creation of a life estate. The latter rule is sometimes expressed in other jurisdictions as a presumption in favor of the largest estate the grantor could convey. *See, e.g.*, *White v. Brown*, 559 S.W.2d 938, 939 (Tenn. 1977) (quoting Tenn. C. Ann. § 32-301) ("Every grant or devise of real estate, or any interest therein, shall pass all the estate or interest of the grantor or devisor, unless the intent to pass a less estate or interest shall appear by express terms, or be necessarily implied in the terms of the instrument.").

   What justification is there for presuming that an ambiguous grant conveys a fee simple absolute rather than a life estate? Is it any different for the justification underlying the presumption against intestacy? Was *Craigen* an appropriate case for the application of these presumptions?

3. **Finding Ambiguity.** Are you convinced by the court's arguments that the language "till she dies" does not "clearly express the testator's will to create a life estate"? What do you think Dalton Craigen meant by this phrase?

4. **Dueling Presumptions.** The court mentions another rule of construction—the presumption against disinheritance—but declines to apply it. Why? Is its reason for following the presumption against intestacy but declining to follow the presumption against disinheritance persuasive? How is a court to decide when a presumption or other rule of construction applies and when it doesn't?

White v. Brown

559 S.W.2d 938 (Tenn. 1977)

BROCK, Justice.

This is a suit for the construction of a will. The Chancellor held that the will passed a life estate, but not the remainder, in certain realty, leaving the remainder to pass by inheritance to the testatrix's heirs at law. The Court of Appeals affirmed.

Mrs. Jessie Lide died on February 15, 1973, leaving a holographic will which, in its entirety, reads as follows:

> "April 19, 1972
>
> "I, Jessie Lide, being in sound mind declare this to be my last will and testament. I appoint my niece Sandra White Perry to be the executrix of my estate. I wish Evelyn White to have my home to live in and not to be sold.
>
> "I also leave my personal property to Sandra White Perry. My house is <u>not</u> to be <u>sold</u>.
>
> Jessie Lide" (Underscoring by testatrix).

Mrs. Lide was a widow and had no children. Although she had nine brothers and sisters, only two sisters residing in Ohio survived her. These two sisters quitclaimed any interest they might have in the residence to Mrs. White. The nieces and nephews of the testatrix, her heirs at law, are defendants in this action.

Mrs. White, her husband, who was the testatrix's brother, and her daughter, Sandra White Perry, lived with Mrs. Lide as a family for some twenty-five years. After Sandra married in 1969 and Mrs. White's husband died in 1971, Evelyn White continued to live with Mrs. Lide until Mrs. Lide's death in 1973 at age 88.

Mrs. White, joined by her daughter as executrix, filed this action to obtain construction of the will, alleging that she is vested with a fee simple title to the home. The defendants contend that the will conveyed only a life estate to Mrs. White, leaving the remainder to go to them under our laws of intestate succession. The Chancellor held that the will unambiguously conveyed only a life interest in the home to Mrs. White and refused to consider extrinsic evidence concerning Mrs. Lide's relationship with her surviving relatives. Due to the debilitated condition of the property and in accordance with the desire of all parties, the Chancellor ordered the property sold with the proceeds distributed in designated shares among the beneficiaries.

I.

Our cases have repeatedly acknowledged that the intention of the testator is to be ascertained from the language of the entire instrument when read in the light of surrounding circumstances. See, e.g., Harris v. Bittikofer, 541 S.W.2d 372, 384 (Tenn. 1976); Martin v. Taylor, 521 S.W.2d 581, 584 (Tenn. 1975); Hoggatt v. Clopton, 142 Tenn. 184, 192, 217 S.W. 657, 659 (1919). But, the practical difficulty in this case, as in so many other cases involving wills drafted by lay persons, is that the words chosen by the testatrix are not specific enough to clearly state her intent. Thus, in our opinion, it is not clear whether Mrs. Lide intended to convey a life estate in the home to Mrs. White, leaving the remainder interest to descend by operation of law, or a fee interest with a restraint on alienation. Moreover, the will might even be read as conveying a fee interest subject to a condition subsequent (Mrs. White's failure to live in the home).

In such ambiguous cases it is obvious that rules of construction, always yielding to the cardinal rule of the testator's intent, must be employed as auxiliary aids in the courts' endeavor to ascertain the testator's intent.

In 1851 our General Assembly enacted two such statutes of construction, thereby creating a statutory presumption against partial intestacy.

Chapter 33 of the Public Acts of 1851 (now codified as T.C.A. §§ 64-101 and 64-501) reversed the common law presumption[1] that a life estate was intended unless the intent to pass a fee simple was clearly expressed in the instrument. T.C.A. § 64-501 provides:

"Every grant or devise of real estate, or any interest therein, shall pass all the estate or interest of the grantor or devisor, unless the intent to pass a less estate or interest shall appear by express terms, or be necessarily implied in the terms of the instrument."

Chapter 180, Section 2 of the Public Acts of 1851 (now codified as T.C.A. § 32-301) was specifically directed to the operation of a devise. In relevant part, T.C.A. § 32-301 provides:

> "A will ... shall convey all the real estate belonging to [the testator] or in which he had any interest at his decease, unless a contrary intention appear by its words and context."

Thus, under our law, unless the "words and context" of Mrs. Lide's will clearly evidence her intention to convey only a life estate to Mrs. White, the will should be construed as passing the home to Mrs. White in fee. "`If the expression in the will is doubtful, the doubt is resolved against the limitation and in favor of the absolute estate.'" Meacham v. Graham, 98 Tenn. 190, 206 (1897) (quoting Washbon v. Cope, 144 N.Y. 287); Weiss v. Broadway Nat'l Bank, 204 Tenn. 563 (1959); Cannon v. Cannon, 182 Tenn. 1 (1945).

Several of our cases demonstrate the effect of these statutory presumptions against intestacy by construing language which might seem to convey an estate for life, without provision for a gift over after the termination of such life estate, as passing a fee simple instead. In Green v. Young, 163 Tenn. 16 (1931), the testatrix's disposition of all of her property to her husband "to be used by him for his support and comfort during his life" was held to pass a fee estate. Similarly, in Williams v. Williams, 167 Tenn. 26 (1933), the testator's devise of real property to his children "for and during their natural lives" without provision for a gift over was held to convey a fee. And, in Webb v. Webb, 53 Tenn. App. 609 (1964), a devise of personal property to the testator's wife "for her maintenance, support and comfort, for the full period of her natural life" with complete powers of alienation but without provision for the remainder passed absolute title to the widow.

II.

Thus, if the sole question for our determination were whether the will's conveyance of the home to Mrs. White "to live in" gave her a life interest or a fee in the home, a conclusion favoring the absolute estate would be clearly required. The question, however, is complicated somewhat by the caveat contained in the will that the home is "not to be sold" — a restriction conflicting with the free alienation of property, one of the most significant incidents of fee ownership. We must determine, therefore, whether Mrs. Lide's will, when taken as a whole, clearly evidences her intent to convey only a life estate in her home to Mrs. White.

Under ordinary circumstances a person makes a will to dispose of his or her entire estate. If, therefore, a will is susceptible of two constructions, by one of which the testator disposes of the whole of his estate and by the other of which he disposes of only a part of his estate, dying intestate as to the remainder, this Court has always preferred that construction which disposes of the whole of the testator's estate if that construction is reasonable and consistent with the general scope and provisions of the will. See Ledbetter v. Ledbetter, 188 Tenn. 44 (1949); Cannon v. Cannon, supra; Williams v. Williams, supra; Jarnagin v. Conway, 21 Tenn. 50 (1840); 4 Page, Wills § 30.14 (3d ed. 1961). A construction which results in partial intestacy will not be adopted unless such intention clearly appears. Bedford v. Bedford, 38 Tenn. App. 370 (1954); Martin v. Hale, 167 Tenn. 438 (1934). It has been said that the courts will prefer any reasonable construction or any construction which does not do violence to a testator's language, to a construction which results in partial intestacy. Ledbetter, supra.

The intent to create a fee simple or other absolute interest and, at the same time to impose a restraint upon its alienation can be clearly expressed. If the testator specifically declares that he devises land to A "in fee simple" or to A "and his heirs" but that A shall not have the power to alienate the land, there is but one tenable construction, viz., the testator's intent is to impose a restraint upon a fee simple. To construe such language to create a life estate would conflict with the express specification of a fee simple as well as with the presumption of intent to make a complete testamentary disposition of all of a testator's property. By extension, as noted by Professor Casner in his treatise on the law of real property:

> "Since it is now generally presumed that a conveyor intends to transfer his whole interest in the property, it may be reasonable to adopt the same construction, [conveyance of a fee simple] even in the absence of words of inheritance, if there is no language that can be construed to create a remainder." 6 American Law of Property § 26.58 (A.J. Casner ed. 1952).

In our opinion, testatrix's apparent testamentary restraint on the alienation of the home devised to Mrs. White does not evidence such a clear intent to pass only a life estate as is sufficient to overcome the law's strong presumption that a fee simple interest was conveyed.

Accordingly, we conclude that Mrs. Lide's will passed a fee simple absolute in the home to Mrs. White. Her attempted restraint on alienation must be declared void as inconsistent with the incidents and nature of the estate devised and contrary to public policy. Nashville C & S.L. Ry. v. Bell, 162 Tenn. 661 (1931).

The decrees of the Court of Appeals and the trial court are reversed and the cause is remanded to the chancery court for such further proceedings as may be necessary, consistent with this opinion. Costs are taxed against appellees.

COOPER and FONES, JJ., concur.

HARBISON, J., dissents.

HENRY, C.J., joins in dissent.

HARBISON, Justice, dissenting.

With deference to the views of the majority, and recognizing the principles of law contained in the majority opinion, I am unable to agree that the language of the will of Mrs. Lide did or was intended to convey a fee simple interest in her residence to her sister-in-law, Mrs. Evelyn White.

The testatrix expressed the wish that Mrs. White was "to have my home to live in and not to be sold". The emphasis is that of the testatrix, and her desire that Mrs. White was not to have an unlimited estate in the property was reiterated in the last sentence of the will, to wit: "My house is *not* to be *sold*."

The testatrix appointed her niece, Mrs. Perry, executrix and made an outright bequest to her of all personal property.

The will does not seem to me to be particularly ambiguous, and like the Chancellor and the Court of Appeals, I am of the opinion that the testatrix gave Mrs. White a life estate only, and that upon the death of Mrs. White the remainder will pass to the heirs at law of the testatrix.

The cases cited by petitioners in support of their contention that a fee simple was conveyed are not persuasive, in my opinion. Possibly the strongest case cited by the appellants is Green v. Young, 163 Tenn. 16 (1931), in which the testatrix bequeathed all of her real and personal property to her husband "to be used by him for his support and comfort during his life." The will expressly stated that it included all of the property, real and personal, which the testatrix owned at the time of her death. There was no limitation whatever upon the power of the husband to use, consume, or dispose of the property, and the Court concluded that a fee simple was intended.

In the case of Williams v. Williams, 167 Tenn. 26 (1933), a father devised property to his children "for and during their natural lives" but the will contained other provisions not mentioned in the majority opinion which seem to me to distinguish the case. Unlike the provisions of the present will, other clauses in the Williams will contained provisions that these same children were to have "all the residue of my estate personal or mixed of which I shall die possessed or seized, or to which I shall be entitled at the time of my decease, to have and to hold the same to them and their executors and administrators and assigns forever."

Further, following some specific gifts to grandchildren, there was another bequest of the remainder of the testator's money to these same three children. The language used by the testator in that case was held to convey the fee simple interest in real estate to the children, but its provisions hardly seem analogous to the language employed by the testatrix in the instant case.

In the case of Webb v. Webb, 53 Tenn. App. 609 (1964), the testator gave his wife all the residue of his property with a clear, unqualified and unrestricted power of use, sale or disposition. Thereafter he attempted to limit her interest to a life estate, with a gift over to his heirs of any unconsumed property. Again, under settled rules of construction and interpretation, the wife was found to have a fee simple estate, but, unlike the present case, there was no limitation whatever upon the power of use or disposition of the property by the beneficiary.

On the other hand, in the case of Magevney v. Karsch, 167 Tenn. 32 (1933), a gift of the residue of the large estate of the testator to his daughter, with power "at her demise [to] dispose of it as she pleases... ." was held to create only a life estate with a power of appointment, and not an absolute gift of the residue. In other portions of the will the testator had given another beneficiary a power to use and dispose of property, and the Court concluded that he appreciated the distinction between a life estate and an absolute estate, recognizing that a life tenant could not dispose of property and use the proceeds as she pleased.

In the present case the testatrix knew how to make an outright gift, if desired. She left all of her personal property to her niece without restraint or limitation. As to her sister-in-law, however, she merely wished the latter have her house "to live in", and expressly withheld from her any power of sale.

The majority opinion holds that the testatrix violated a rule of law by attempting to restrict the power of the donee to dispose of the real estate. Only by thus striking a portion of the will, and holding it inoperative, is the conclusion reached that an unlimited estate resulted.

In my opinion, this interpretation conflicts more greatly with the apparent intention of the testatrix than did the conclusion of the courts below, limiting the gift to Mrs. White to a life estate. I have serious doubt that the testatrix intended to create any illegal restraint on alienation or to violate any other rules of law. It seems to me that she rather emphatically intended to provide that her sister-in-law was not to be able to sell the house during the lifetime of the latter — a result which is both legal and consistent with the creation of a life estate.

In my opinion the judgment of the courts below was correct and I would affirm.

I am authorized to state that Chief Justice HENRY joins in this opinion.

13. Complex Estates Problems: Method

We now turn to a more comprehensive review of the system of common law estates and future interests. We begin with a warning: estates and future interests problems do not generally reward creative thinking. They reward mechanical, tedious, careful application of logical rules according to a set procedure—an algorithmic approach. They require you to break a big problem up into lots of smaller problems, and solve each small problem one at a time, in order. Attempts to short-circuit the analysis will get you into trouble. In this chapter, we are going to adopt a routine process for breaking down future interest problems into a series of questions that will generate pieces of the answer we are trying to reach, then build the answer out of those pieces. The best way to really learn this material is with *practice*, and you should review the explanatory problems in the text several times before trying your hand at the questions at the end of this section.

In any problem involving estates and future interests, we must:

1. **Break the fact pattern down into chronological steps, or points in time.**
2. **For each point in time:**
   a. **If the point in time is the making of a conveyance, construe the language of any conveyance by**
      i. **Parsing the interests created by the conveyance**
      ii. **Identifying the nature and quantum of each interest**
      iii. **Determining whether there is any residual interest in the grantor, and if so its nature and quantum.**
   b. **If the point in time is any other event (e.g., a birth, a death, or the satisfaction or failure of a condition) construe the effect of the event on the interests of the parties.**
   c. **Based on the analysis of Steps 2.a or 2.b, describe the interests of every party at each point in time: this is the *state of title* as of that step.**
3. **Arrange the state of title for each point in time sequentially to compose a *chain of title*.**

Once you have a chain of title, you can answer any question you might be asked about the rights of any party at any point in time. We will talk about how to go about Step 2 in more detail as we dig in to the substance of the various estates and future interests. Throughout this chapter, important rules that we will apply in Step 2 of our method will be in bold, indented type, just like the description of the method above. At the end of the exposition, we will plug all these rules we have learned into the method above to arrive at a comprehensive approach to the subject.

Step 1: Building A Chronology

Let's revisit a problem we encountered earlier in introducing the life estate:

> **Problem 1**
>
> **O, owner of a fee simple absolute in Blackacre, conveys Blackacre "to A for life, then to B for life." (Assume that both A and B are alive at the time of the grant.) What is the state of title in Blackacre?**

Let's apply Step 1 of our method to this problem.

Note that, even though it isn't explicit on the face of the problem, we really have two points in time here that we need to distinguish:

1. O owns a fee simple absolute in Blackacre.
2. O conveys Blackacre "to A for life, then to B for life."

Again, the state of title at Point 1 is self-explanatory. Point 2 involves a conveyance, which we will have to parse in Step 2.a.i. of our method. We'll learn how to do that shortly. First, note that Step 1 generates longer chronologies as our problem becomes more complex. For example, we could add on the complications we encountered when first considering this problem:

> **Problem 1A**
>
> **O, owner of a fee simple absolute in Blackacre, conveys Blackacre "to A for life, then to B for life." (Assume that both A and B are alive at the time of the grant.) While O, A, and B are still alive, B conveys her interest to C. B then dies, survived by A, C, and O. What is the state of title in Blackacre?**

Although our chronology becomes a bit longer in this version of the problem, it begins exactly the same way:

1. O owns a fee simple absolute in Blackacre.
2. O conveys Blackacre "to A for life, then to B for life."

We can then simply add the additional points in time presented by the problem:

3. B conveys her interest to C.
4. B dies.

We will next learn how to analyze each point in this chronology using Step 2 of our method, and then put all our analyses together to build a chain of title using Step 3 of our method. Let's get started:

Step 2.a.i: Parsing a Conveyance

The conveyance at Point 2 of the chronology for Problem 1 reads "to A for life, then to B for life." This is a complex grant—it creates multiple interests in multiple parties. We are going to introduce a rule for breaking up such complex grants for analysis:

> **Reading from left to right, the <u>first</u> comma, semicolon, or period following *words of purchase* indicates the end of one interest, and the beginning of the next interest.**

"Words of purchase" is a technical term in conveyancing law. Despite the ordinary English meaning of the word "purchase," "words of purchase" do not necessarily mean that the grantee paid a valuable consideration in exchange for the grant. They merely identify *who the grantee is.* So, reading the conveyance in Problem 1 from left to right, we find that the first two words of the conveyance—"to A"—are our first words of purchase. To determine what interest this grant creates in A, we must take the entire clause beginning with those words of purchase and ending with the <u>first</u> comma, semicolon, or period we find. Thus, the first interest under this grant will be created by the words:

"to A for life"

Continuing to read the conveyance from left to right, we find our next words of purchase: "to B." Under our rule, the clause creating B's interest begins at the end of the previous clause and ends at the <u>first</u> comma, semicolon, or period following the words "to B." thus:

"then to B for life"

Taken together, we therefore have two clauses we will have to analyze in Step 2.a.ii of our method:

"to A for life"

"then to B for life"

You probably already have a decent idea of what interests are created by this language (or you may remember the answer from when we first encountered this problem), but let's approach the problem methodically so we can express our conclusion more precisely, and later extend our analysis to address novel problems.

Step 2.a.i: Identifying Legal Interests

In order to identify the legal interest created by a particular clause in a grant, we must identify both the nature of that interest and the quantum of the interest.

Identifying the Quantum of an Interest

The **quantum** of an estate is a measure of its "size" (if size is a meaningful concept with respect to intangible rights like estates). The common-law estates are, in decreasing order of quantum:

- **The Fee Simple**
- **The Fee Tail**
- **The Life Estate**
- **The Leasehold Estates**

Of these, we will concern ourselves here only with the fees simple and the life estate. The fee tail is relevant today only to those who wish to more fully appreciate certain works of 18th- and 19th-century English literature (and period dramas depicting the same era), in which the estate is a hackneyed plot device.[38] It was associated with hereditary aristocracy in the minds of

[38] The fee tail was created by a grant "to A and the heirs of his/her body," and land held in tail passed from the grantee to that grantee's direct descendants at the death of each successive owner. Thus no owner at any point in the family line had the power to dispose of the property upon their death. Land subject to this type of arrangement was said to be "entailed." The fee tail could be—and often was—limited even further to male heirs; hence the literary trope of the man with no sons nearing the end of his life and despairing for the future of his unwed daughters because he holds all his property in tail. *See,*

American legislators and jurists, and accordingly it been abolished, was never recognized, or is otherwise essentially moribund in all American jurisdictions.[39] The Leasehold Estates, in contrast, are quite important to modern real estate practice, but today they are governed by the law of Landlord and Tenant, which we cover in a separate unit. Based on the hierarchy of estates, then, the key fact for you to keep in mind during our study of the estates system is that *a life estate is a lesser estate than a fee simple*. This will be an important point when we begin our discussion of retained interests.

Let us illustrate the process of identifying the quantum of an interest with an example. Recall the first part of the grant we parsed in Problem 1. The language "to A for life," as we know, creates a life estate in A. But the **quantum** of A's interest—a life estate—is not indicated by the words of purchase ("to A"). Instead, it is indicated by the two words following the words of purchase: "for life." These two extra words are called *words of limitation*: they define or "limit" the nature or quantum of the estate that will be held by A. For example, the traditional words of limitation of a fee simple are "and his heirs."

But what if a grant includes no words of limitation? In this case, we require an additional rule to guide our analysis:

> **In the absence of clearly contrary words of limitation, a conveyance is presumed to convey the grantor's <u>entire</u> interest.**

This rule helps explain the modern formula by which the owner of a fee simple absolute can convey a fee simple absolute to another: "to A." Because words of purchase without any words of limitation convey the grantor's entire interest, the owner of a fee simple absolute who conveys an interest "to A" without any further qualification conveys his entire interest—i.e., a fee simple absolute—to A.

We will see that the fee simple may be further decomposed into the fee simple absolute (with which you are already familiar) and the defeasible fees (which you haven't seen yet). We will deal with the defeasible fees later, because identifying them is dependent on identifying the future interests that follow them. Let's turn to the identification of future interests now.

---

e.g., JANE AUSTEN, PRIDE & PREJUDICE ch.7 ("Mr. Bennett's property consisted almost entirely in an estate of two thousand a year, which, unfortunately for his daughters, was entailed, in default of heirs male, on a distant relation….").

[39] For a discussion of the abolition of the fee tail and a review of the vestiges of the estate in the few American jurisdictions that retain some form of it, see 2-14 Powell on Real Property (2015).

Identifying the Nature of an Interest

We are now going to learn a large number of rules for determining the *nature* (or *type*) of an interest created by a particular grant. Those rules can be applied methodically, according to a kind of algorithm. The flow chart on the next page presents that algorithm, which will make much more sense to you after you read the ensuing sections of the text. You will want to keep this flow chart handy as we continue our study of the estates system, and particularly when we start dealing with problems of the kind you might encounter on an exam.

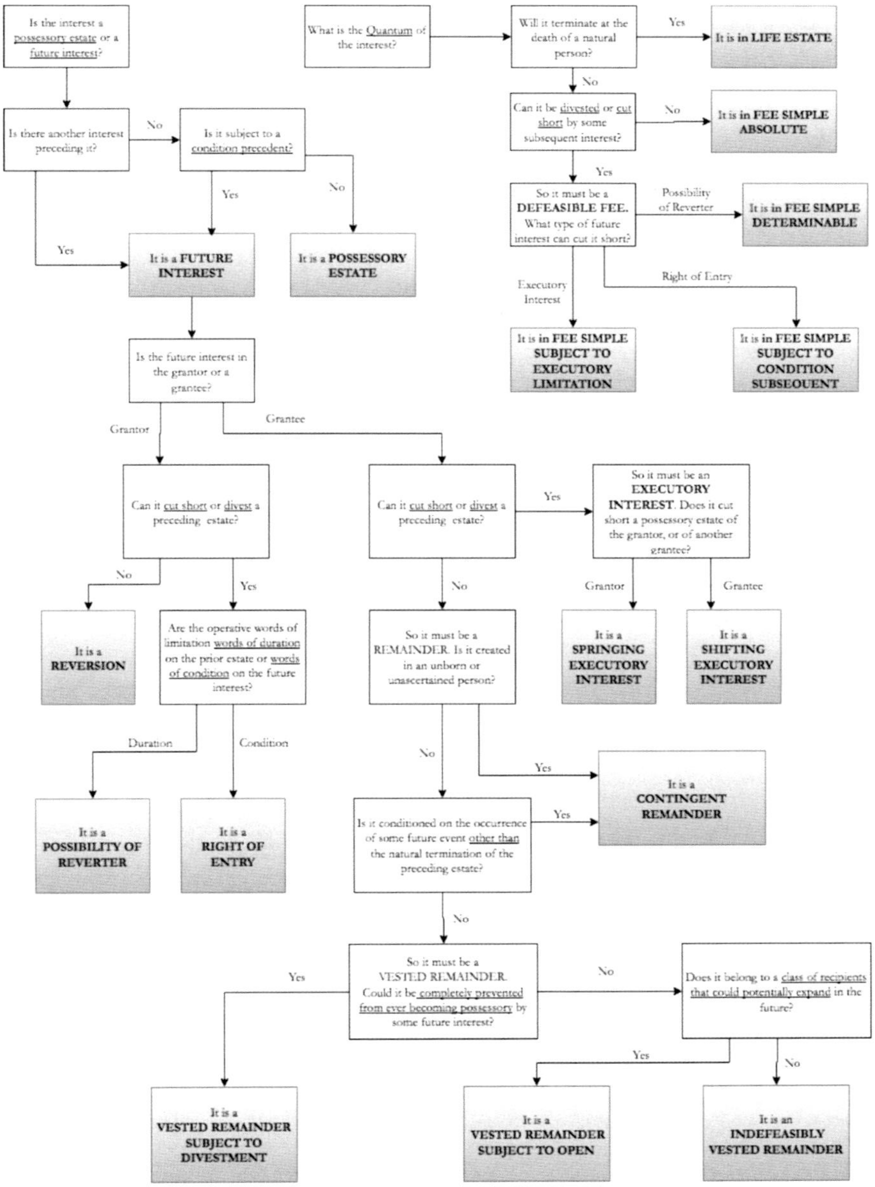

Possessory Estates vs. Future Interests

We now identify our rule for determining whether an interest is a possessory estate or a future interest:

An interest will be a *possessory estate* if:

1. **it is not preceded by any other interest; <u>and</u>**

2. it is not subject to any <u>condition precedent.</u>

An interest that is not a possessory estate is a *future interest.*

A **condition precedent** is just what it sounds like: a condition that *precedes* the possibility of an interest becoming possessory. That is, an interest is subject to a condition precedent if *something that has not yet happened* must happen in order for that interest to become possessory. For example, a conveyance "to A when A reaches her 21st birthday," made at a time when A is 10 years old, creates a *future interest* in A because A's interest is subject to a *condition precedent*: she must reach her 21st birthday in order to be entitled to possession, and she hasn't done that yet. (We will learn the name of this future interest shortly.)

The question whether an interest is a possessory estate or a future interest is different from the question of the *quantum* of that interest. One can hold a future interest in life estate, just as one can hold a possessory life estate. To illustrate this point, let's return to the conveyance from Problem 1. Recall that we determined that this conveyance had two operative clauses:

"to A for life"

"then to B for life"

The first clause, "to A for life" creates some interest in A. Is it a possessory estate or a future interest? First, we ask whether it is preceded by some other interest, and find that it isn't—it's the first interest created in the conveyance from O. Next, we ask whether it is subject to a <u>condition precedent</u>—does anything that hasn't yet happened have to happen in order for A to take possession? Again, the answer is no: the grant is "to A for life" with no other condition in the text of the relevant clause. Thus, A's interest is a *possessory estate.* And because the conveyance to A includes the *words of limitation* for a life estate ("for life"), we know that the *quantum* of A's possessory estate is a life estate. Thus, we conclude that under this language, A takes a *possessory life estate.*

What about B? The language "then to B" creates some interest in B—is it a possessory estate or a future interest? The word "then," following the grant to A, is a clue. When we ask the first question demanded by our rule—whether B's interest is preceded by any other interest—the answer is clearly <u>yes</u>: B's interest *follows* A's possessory life estate. Therefore B's interest must be a *future interest.* We also know, from the words of limitation "for life," that the *quantum* of that interest will be a life estate. So we know that B will take a future interest in life estate under this clause of the conveyance. But we do not yet know what *kind* of future interest B takes. To answer that question, we need to learn a few more rules.

Reviewing Familiar Interests

Recall that in our introduction to the basics of the estate system we encountered four interests: the **fee simple absolute**, the **life estate**, the **remainder**, and the **reversion**. You now understand that the fee simple absolute and the life estate are measures of the *quantum* of an interest—whether it be a possessory estate or future interest—while the remainder and the reversion are *types* of future interests. We can now formulate rules to identify the remainder and the reversion. Our rule for identifying the remainder is as follows:

If a future interest:

1. **is created in someone <u>other than</u> the grantor, <u>and</u>**
2. **cannot cut short or divest a preceding possessory or vested estate, but must instead wait until the preceding estate naturally terminates in order to become possessory,**

then the future interest is a <u>remainder</u>.

Remember: the distinguishing characteristic of the remainder is that it *cannot cut short or divest a prior estate*. It simply "remains," sitting around and waiting for the natural termination of the preceding possessory estate, at which point the remainder will become possessory by operation of law.

The reversion, like the remainder, cannot cut short or divest any possessory or vested estate. Our rule for identifying it is as follows:

If a future interest:

1. **is created in, or retained by, the <u>grantor</u> of the interest, <u>and</u>**
2. **cannot cut short or divest a preceding possessory or vested estate, but must instead wait until the preceding estate naturally terminates in order to become possessory,**

then the future interest is a <u>reversion</u>.

We now have the tools to complete our analysis of the conveyance at Point 2 of the chronology we developed for Problem 1. We identified two operative clauses in that conveyance:

"to A for life"

"then to B for life"

And we further concluded that the first of these clauses created a *possessory life estate in A*, while the second created some future interest in life estate in B. We can now determine what B's future interest is. B is not the grantor of this interest, and the interest cannot cut short A's life estate (the word "then" indicates that B's interest will become possessory only *after* A's life estate naturally terminates at A's death). Thus, B's interest must be a *remainder*. Moreover, because we know that the *quantum* of B's interest is a life estate, we can now precisely state exactly what interest B has at Point 2 of our chronology: B has a *remainder in life estate*. (Sometimes you will see this interest referred to as a *life estate in remainder*; the two formulations are equivalent.)

We have now analyzed all the language in the conveyance at Point 2 of our chronology in Problem 1. But if you refer back to our method, you will see that Step 2 of the method is not yet complete. We must undertake one more, crucially important, analysis: we must ascertain whether our grantor has *retained* any interest. This step is often overlooked, which can generate compounding errors at later points in the chronology of an estates problem.

Step 2.a.iii: Identifying Residual Interests

At Point 1 in our chronology O had a fee simple absolute, and at Point 2 O has conveyed two life estates—one possessory and one in remainder. The grant has not explicitly created any interest of the same quantum as O's interest—a fee simple absolute—and the express words of limitation on the grants to A and B mean that we cannot apply our presumption that O granted a fee simple absolute to either grantee. Therefore, *O must have something left over*. As we already know, that something is a reversion in fee simple absolute. Again, somebody must be in a position to legally take possession of Blackacre when the life estates have both terminated. Unless O identifies such a taker explicitly, O must have *retained* that right to take possession in the future. And because the *quantum* of O's original interest was a fee simple absolute, that will also be the quantum of O's reversion.

We can formalize our retained-interest analysis in the following rule:

> **If a conveyance does not create a <u>vested</u> interest of <u>equal quantum</u> to the grantor's interest, then there <u>must</u> be a reversion in the grantor of equal quantum to the grantor's original interest.**

You do not yet know what a vested interest is—we will turn to that shortly. For now, you should note the following rule:

> **All possessory estates, and all interests retained out of vested interests, are vested.**

Turning to Step 2.c of our method, we can now fully identify the state of title at Point 2 in our chronology for Problem 1:

2. A has a possessory life estate

   B has a remainder in life estate

   O has a reversion in fee simple absolute.

Before turning to the rest of the future interests, let us expand our analysis to include the additional Points in the chronology for Problem 1A. To do so, we need to apply Step 2.b of our method for solving estates problems.

Step 2.b: Construing the Effects of Events on Legal Interests

Recall the chronology we developed for Problem 1A:

1. O owns a fee simple absolute in Blackacre.
2. O conveys Blackacre "to A for life, then to B for life."
3. B conveys her interest to C.
4. B dies.

We have completed Step 2.c for Points 1 and 2 of this chronology:

1. O owns a fee simple absolute in Blackacre.
2. A has a possessory life estate

   B has a remainder in life estate

   O has a reversion in fee simple absolute

At Point 3, however, we have no conveyance language to parse or analyze. Instead, we must determine what the effect of B conveying "her interest" to C is. Whenever faced with this type of problem, it is best to be thorough. We must determine what the effect of this event is on *each and every interest* we identified in the previous Point of our chronology.

With respect to A's possessory life estate, B's conveyance has no effect. Remember the principle of *nemo dat quod non habet*: one cannot give away what one does not have. B's remainder in life estate is a *different interest* than A's possessory life estate; absent A's consent B cannot convey any part of A's interest. So at Point 3, A's interest remains unchanged.

What about B's interest? The problem tells us that B has conveyed "her interest" to C. Thus, B no longer has any interest in Blackacre. C, meanwhile, has acquired an interest in Blackacre—specifically, the remainder in life estate heretofore held by B. But let us take care: when will this interest terminate? *Nemo dat* again provides us with the answer: C can only take what B had. In this case, that is a life estate *measured by the life of B*. If you recall from our introduction to estates, we call this interest a *life estate pur autre vie*. That is, C now has a remainder in life estate *pur autre vie* for the life of B.

With respect to O's reversion, again, *nemo dat* tells us that B cannot convey that reversion without O's consent. So O's reversion remains unchanged.

Turning to Step 2.c of our method, we can now provide the state of title at Point 3 of our chronology:

3. A has a possessory life estate

   C has a remainder in life estate *pur autre vie* for the life of B

   O has a reversion in fee simple absolute

We can perform a similar analysis at Point 4 of our chronology, wherein B dies. Looking to A's interest, again, there is nothing that B can do to affect A's possessory life estate, which remains unchanged. The same is true for O's reversion: it too remains unchanged. But B's death terminates C's remainder in life estate *pur autre vie* by operation of law: the interest simply ceases to exist. (Note that this happens even though the interest never became possessory.) Turning to Step 2.c, we can provide the state of title at Point 4 of our chronology:

4. A has a possessory life estate

   O has a reversion in fee simple absolute

Step 3: Building a Chain of Title

We have now analyzed the state of title at each of the four Points in our chronology for Problem 1A; let's put them all together into a *chain of title*:

1. O owns a fee simple absolute in Blackacre.
2. A has a possessory life estate

   B has a remainder in life estate

   O has a reversion in fee simple absolute
3. A has a possessory life estate

C has a remainder in life estate *pur autre vie* for the life of B

O has a reversion in fee simple absolute

4. A has a possessory life estate

   O has a reversion in fee simple absolute

This chain of title provides all the information we could possibly need to answer any question about the interests of the parties in this problem at any point in time. As it turns out, the question asks for the state of title at the end of this chain of events. To answer that question, we simply look to the relevant Point in our chain of title (here, Point 4) and respond: A has a possessory life estate, O has a reversion in fee simple absolute.

Other Estates and Future Interests

We now have a complete method for solving estates problems, but have only scratched the surface of the types of estates and future interests we might encounter. We can now learn about the remaining estates and future interests, plugging them in to our method for additional practice.

Remainders, Part 2: Vested and Contingent Remainders

The first layer of complexity we will add to the mix is the distinction between *vested* and *contingent* remainders. "Contingent" here means something similar to what it means in ordinary usage: it refers to something that might or might not come to pass. There is a straightforward rule for distinguishing between vested and contingent remainders:

A remainder is *contingent* if:

1. **it is created in an *unascertained* or *unborn* person; <u>or</u>**
2. **it is subject to a <u>condition precedent</u> *other than the natural termination of the preceding possessory estate* (i.e., it requires the occurrence of some uncertain event or condition before it can become possessory).**

A remainder that is not contingent is *vested.*

Let's look at a problem involving one of these possibilities.

Problem 2

O, owning a fee simple absolute in Blackacre, conveys Blackacre "to A for life, then to A's first-born child," at a time when A has no children. Two years later, A's first child, B, is born. What is the state of title in Blackacre?

As always, we begin with Step 1 and break up this fact pattern to build a chronology:

1. O owns a fee simple absolute.
2. O conveys Blackacre "to A for life, then to A's first-born child." A has no children.
3. A's first child, B, is born.

Now we must go through each of these points in time to construe any grant or determine the legal effect of any event at each step. Point 1 is, as usual, self-explanatory. At Point 2, we have a conveyance that we have to parse under Step 2.a.i. Applying our rule, we break up the conveyance into two clauses:

"to A for life"

"then to A's first-born child."

Construing each of these clauses under Step 2.a.ii of our method, we see that the grant "to A for life" has no other interest preceding it, and is not subject to any other condition precedent, so it must be a presently possessory estate; the words of limitation "for life" indicate that it is a possessory life estate. The grant to A's first-born child follows A's life estate; it must therefore be a future interest. Because it is an interest in someone other than the grantor, and it cannot cut short A's life estate, it must be a remainder.

But who owns the remainder? Well … nobody we can identify yet, because the only person who could own the remainder—A's first-born child—hasn't yet been born (indeed, may never be born). *But the remainder still exists.* Whether or not it will become possessory depends on whether its owner—A's first-born child—ever comes into being. As you see, this is one of the criteria that will render a remainder *contingent* rather than *vested.* We will say that the remainder is a *contingent* remainder in the first-born child of A (even though there is, as yet, no such person). And what is the *quantum* of that remainder? Note that the grant to A's first-born child has no words of limitation in it. Thus we can apply our presumption to conclude that A's first-born child's contingent remainder is in fee simple absolute—the same estate O had prior to the grant.

Are we through with Point 2 of our chronology? Not quite. We still have to deal with Step 2.a.iii of our method—testing for a retained interest. To understand why this step is so tricky here, we have to imagine ourselves standing at Point 2, not knowing what the future holds, and contemplating every conceivable possibility, including the possibility that A will die without ever having children. (As you'll see, future interests problems require lawyers to dream up every manner of improbable tragedy.) If A were to die without having had any children, who would have the right to take possession of Blackacre at A's death?

You may have surmised that this is a situation similar to the situation in which a grantor conveys *vested* interests of a *lesser quantum* than his own. In Problem 1, for example, we *knew* that there would come a day when none of O's grantees had a right to possession—everybody dies someday, so A's and B's interests would eventually terminate. In our current problem, we don't know *for sure* that such a day will come, but we can see it as a very real *possibility*. O has conveyed a future interest in fee simple absolute (the remainder), but that interest is *contingent*: it is *possible* that this interest will never become possessory—that A will die without having had a first-born child. Therefore we need *someone* to be able to step in and take possession if this possibility materializes. And as before, the only person left to take possession is O. Therefore, O *must* have a future interest at Point 2, and because O's interest cannot cut short or divest either A's interest or the interest of A's first-born child, it *must be a reversion*. Moreover, because O's interest in Blackacre prior to the grant was a fee simple absolute, the reversion must also be in fee simple absolute.

Now you can better understand our rule for determining whether a grantor retains a reversion. Our rule identified the two circumstances in which the grantor will need to be in the position to retake possession in the future. In the first circumstance, the reversion was necessary because the grantor had conveyed *vested* interests of a *lesser quantum* than his own. In the second, the reversion was necessary because, although the grantor had conveyed an interest of the *same quantum* as his own, that interest was *contingent* and therefore not certain to become possessory. Both circumstances reflect the same underlying principle: if a conveyance creates some gap in rightful possession, that gap will be filled by the grantor's original (and hence retained) right to possession.

We are now prepared to move on to Step 2.c of our method and describe the state of title as of Point 2 in our chronology:

2. A has a life estate.

   A's (non-existent) first-born child has a contingent remainder in fee simple absolute.

   O has a reversion in fee simple absolute.

Note that because a reversion is *retained* from O's original possessory estate, it is always considered *vested*. However, that does not mean that it is certain to become possessory again. Analysis of Point 3 in our chronology will demonstrate why.

At Point 3, A has had a child, B. Under Step 2.b of our method, we need to ask: what effect does this event have on each of the interests we identified in Point 2? Let's again consider the interests one at a time.

- A's life estate would seem to be unaffected; neither the remainder nor the reversion identified at Point 2 in our chronology can cut short a preceding possessory estate such as A's.
- Circumstances have changed with respect to the remainder. We can now point to a living person who will have the right to possession of Blackacre under the remainder: B. And there is no future event (other than the natural termination of A's life estate) that must come to pass in order for the remainder to become possessory. As such, the remainder is no longer contingent at Point 3: it is in a known, living person and it is not subject to any condition precedent other than the termination of A's life estate—which we know will happen someday. We may therefore say that the remainder has *vested*, and that B is its owner. The quantum of the remainder remains the same: it is a vested remainder in fee simple absolute.
- What effect does the vesting of B's remainder have on O's reversion? Recall our test for determining whether there is a reversion: we need to know whether O's conveyance created a *vested* interest of *equal quantum* to the interest O held prior to the grant. The last interest created by O's grant is now a *vested remainder in fee simple absolute*. We therefore no longer need O to stand ready to take possession at A's death; B is *certain* to have a right to possession. Thus, we say that O's reversion is *divested* by the vesting of B's remainder: the reversion simply disappears. In this circumstance—where the occurrence of some condition both vests one future interest and destroys a different future interest—we say that the two interests are *alternative* future interests.

Based on this analysis, we are finally prepared to move on to Step 2.c of our method and give the state of title at Point 3 in our chronology, which is what we've been after all along:

3. A has a life estate.

   B has a vested remainder in fee simple absolute.

Problem 2 dealt with one circumstance that could render a remainder contingent: its creation in unborn or unascertained persons. We have yet to see an example of the other circumstance that can render a remainder contingent: being subject to a condition precedent. Let us consider such an example that also expands on the *alternative* nature of the future interests in Problem 2.

Remainders, Part 3: Alternative Contingent Remainders

Recall that in Problem 2, we identified two future interests as *alternatives*—a contingent remainder and a reversion. Either of them could become possessory, but not both. Multiple contingent remainders can also be alternatives *to one another*. Suppose that O, who owns Blackacre in fee simple, grants Blackacre "to A for life, and then to the first of B or C to have a child," at a time when neither B nor C has had any children. You should be able to recognize by now that this grant creates a life estate in A, and a future interest in both B and C. Because the future interests are in someone other than the grantor and cannot cut short A's life estate, they must be remainders. And because there are no words of limitation on the remainders, they are remainders in fee simple absolute (the same interest O had prior to the grant). Finally, because they are both subject to a condition precedent *other than the natural termination of A's life estate* before they can come possessory, they are both contingent remainders. But note that logically, *they can't both become possessory*. The satisfaction of the condition precedent to B's remainder is logically equivalent to the failure of the condition precedent to C's remainder, and vice versa. In this circumstance, we say that B and C have *alternative contingent remainders*. The vesting of one alternative contingent remainder necessarily means the destruction of the other.

There are some additional complications regarding vested remainders that we will have to discuss, but we will first need to build up some additional knowledge about other future interests. Before moving on, we should reinforce one final point about future interests raised by the alternative contingent remainders described in the previous paragraph. Even though neither B nor C has yet satisfied the condition precedent on her interest becoming possessory *and may never do so*, their contingent remainders *are still their property*. That property may not be worth very much, but it *exists* as soon as the conveyance from O is executed. In most American jurisdictions today, B or C could sell their interest, could mortgage it, or could give it away (though traditionally at common law the contingent remainder was merely descendible, not devisable or alienable *inter vivos*).

The Defeasible Fees

We mentioned earlier that the fee simple could be further decomposed into the **fee simple absolute** and the **defeasible fees**. The full taxonomy of the fee simple is as follows:

- **The Fee Simple**

- **The Fee Simple Absolute**
- **The Defeasible Fees**
    - **Fee Simple Determinable**
    - **Fee Simple Subject to Condition Subsequent**
    - **Fee Simple Subject to Executory Limitation**

You have already encountered the fee simple absolute—the most complete interest in land that the law will recognize. Recall that it is created by the modern formula "to A"; or the ancient formula "to A and his heirs."

Hopefully you have noticed that the reversion and the remainder share an important characteristic: they cannot cut short or divest a preceding possessory or vested estate. The reversion is typically a leftover: it sits and waits just in case it is needed. The remainder, as we've said, *remains:* it must wait until the natural termination of the preceding possessory estate before it can become possessory. But there are future interests that are not so polite. To the contrary, they can be rather pushy. These are future interests that *cut short* or *divest* an estate that precedes them upon the occurrence of some event or the satisfaction of some condition. Because the possessory estates preceding such "pushy" future interests can be taken away—the owner can lose their "fee"—we call them *defeasible* fees ("de-fee": get it?).[40]

Based on the principle that a defeasible fee is an estate that looks like a fee simple absolute, but can be *divested*—that is, cut short and destroyed—by some future interest upon the occurrence of some condition, we can now formulate a rule for identifying the *quantum* of an estate created by a conveyance:

> **If an estate can be divested or cut short by a future interest, it is a defeasible fee; if it will terminate at the death of a natural person it is a life estate; and if it has no inherent limitation it is a fee simple absolute.**

---

[40] Strictly speaking, the lesser common-law freehold estates—the fee tail and the life estate—can also be defeasible, but we will ignore that possibility in our study of the estates system because it is rare and of trivial importance. If you intend to experiment with such creatures of the common law, be aware that the future interest following a defeasible life estate is still called a remainder (if in a grantee) or a reversion (if in the grantor); the additional condition on the future interest following the life estate does not change it to a different future interest.

There are several different future interests that can cut short or divest a prior interest, and each of these "pushy" future interests generally goes hand-in-hand with a particular defeasible fee that precedes it; they are matched pairs. These pairings are set forth in the following table:

Table 1: The Defeasible Fees and Their Corresponding Future Interests

Defeasible Fee	Corresponding Future Interest
Fee Simple Determinable	Possibility of Reverter
Fee Simple Subject to Condition Subsequent	Right of Entry
Fee Simple Subject to Executory Limitation (in a grantor)	Springing Executory Interest
Fee Simple Subject to Executory Limitation (in a grantee)	Shifting Executory Interest

In order to determine which of the defeasible fees is created by a conveyance, we need to analyze its relationship to the future interest that follows it. There are a few rules to guide us here, having to do with the *identity of the holder of each interest* and the *words of limitation* creating the pair of interests. We begin with the first of these criteria:

> **If the future interest that cuts short or divests a prior interest is created in a grantee, it will be an *executory interest*, making the preceding estate a *fee simple subject to executory limitation.***

Executory interests are traditionally classified further depending on who holds the preceding defeasible estate:

> **An executory interest that divests or cuts short an estate held by the grantor of the executory interest is a *springing executory interest.* An executory interest that divests or cuts short an estate of a grantee is a *shifting executory interest.***

Let us explore the executory interest a bit further. As our rule indicates, if a defeasible fee is held by the grantor of the executory interest that could cut it short, the executory interest is called a "springing" executory interest. (It "springs up" to take away the grantor's retained possessory interest.) This typically happens when an owner conveys a conditional future interest in another while retaining the possessory estate. For example: if O, owning a fee simple absolute in Blackacre, conveys Blackacre "to A when A marries," A (assuming she is unmarried at the time) has no present right to possession. She has received only a future interest, meaning that

O must still have a possessory estate. It is tempting to think of A's interest as a contingent remainder—after all it is subject to the condition precedent that A marry before the interest can become possessory. But note that the natural termination of O's possessory estate is *irrelevant* to A's interest; O's right to possession could be cut short or *divested* by A if she satisfies the condition—if she marries. A remainder can't cut short or divest a preceding estate like that; it *remains*, waiting for the preceding estate to terminate naturally. The only future interest in a grantee that can cut short or divest a possessory estate is an *executory interest*, which is what A has. Thus, O's retained interest can no longer be a fee simple absolute—it must be a fee simple *subject to executory limitation*—because it can be cut short by A's executory interest. And because the person being divested (O) is the *grantor* of the future interest doing the divesting, A's future interest is a *springing executory interest.*

If, in contrast, the defeasible fee is held by a *grantee* under the conveyance that also created the executory interest, then the future interest is a *shifting executory interest* (it "shifts" the right to possession from one grantee to another). For example: if O, owning a fee simple absolute in Blackacre, conveys Blackacre "to A, but if B marries, then to B," A now has a possessory estate while B has a future interest. Because A's presently possessory estate can be cut short by a future interest held by another, it must be a *defeasible fee.* But which one? To answer that question we need to look at the future interest that could cut it short. Because that future interest is in a grantee (B) and can cut short the prior estate, it must be an *executory interest*, meaning that A's estate is a *fee simple subject to executory limitation.* And because the defeasible fee is held by a *grantee* of the executory interest (A), the satisfaction of the condition (B's marriage) will simply "shift" the right to possession from one of O's grantees to another (*i.e.*, from A to B). Therefore, B has a *shifting executory interest.*

An executory interest is <u>never</u> vested, because it is necessarily limited by a condition precedent: there must be some "trigger" that allows the executory interest to cut short or divest its predecessor. If that condition comes to pass, the executory interest vests and becomes possessory <u>at the same time</u>, cutting short and divesting whatever possessory estate is then in existence. The fact that executory interests are not vested is important primarily because it means they are subject to the Rule Against Perpetuities (discussed later).

We now turn to our rules concerning defeasible fees followed by future interests in a <u>grantor</u>:

> **If the future interest that cuts short the prior estate is created in (or retained by) the grantor, it will be <u>either</u> a *possibility of reverter* (which follows a *fee simple determinable*) or a *right of entry* (which follows a *fee simple subject to condition subsequent*).**

It is worth noting that at common law, neither the possibility of reverter nor the right of entry was transferrable *inter vivos* or devisable; they could only pass by inheritance to the grantor's heirs at law. Today, many states have by statute provided for the *inter vivos* transferrability and devisability of both future interests—though some have also put sharp limits on them. For example, in New York the holder of the equivalent of either a possibility of reverter or a right of entry must record in the title records a detailed formal declaration of their intent to preserve their interest "not less than twenty-seven years nor more than thirty years after the … [interest] was created," and follow up periodically with another formal declaration "after the expiration of nine years and before the expiration of ten years from the date when the [previous] declaration was recorded." N.Y. REAL PROP. L. § 345. Failure to do so results in extinguishment of the interest.

The precise identity of the defeasible fee/future interest in the grantor pair created by a conveyance depends on subtle distinctions in the language of the conveyance itself. We begin with the fee simple determinable and its paired future interest, the possibility of reverter:

> **If a defeasible fee interest is limited by <u>words of duration</u>, it is a *fee simple determinable*, and the grantor's retained future interest following the defeasible fee is a *possibility of reverter*.**

The *fee simple determinable* is created using *words of duration* as the words of limitation for the defeasible fee. This could include words such as "until," "so long as," "while," and so forth. The fee simple determinable is followed by a *possibility of reverter*.[41] The possibility of reverter is a future interest held by the grantor that will cut short the fee simple determinable and become possessory by operation of law if the condition on the continued existence of the fee simple determinable ever fails. It can be explicitly set forth in the grant, but it also may be a retained interest, created by implication where a grantor conveys a fee simple determinable and does not designate a future interest to follow it. So, for example, a conveyance "from O to A so long as Blackacre is used for residential purposes" creates a fee simple determinable in A, followed by

---

[41] There are some authorities that hold that a determinable (i.e., durationally limited) estate can be followed by an executory interest in a grantee, and indeed the Restatement (First) of Property calls such an estate a "fee simple <u>with an</u> executory limitation" (distinguishing it from the fee simple "subject to" executory limitation). We will not follow those authorities here; our rule is that any fee interest that can be cut short by a (valid) future interest in a grantee is a fee simple subject to executory limitation. The disagreement among courts on this issue is useful mainly for showing how confusing the estates system is *even to common law judges*, and how trivial some of its distinctions can be; the Restatement notes that this distinction "is applicable to such a restricted combination of circumstances that a set of facts permitting its application seldom exists." RESTATEMENT (FIRST) OF PROPERTY § 47, cmt. b (1936).

a (retained) possibility of reverter in fee simple absolute O. In this example, if A builds a factory or an office park on Blackacre, A's interest will terminate and O will have an immediate right to possession.

Note how important it is to be careful about terminology here: there is no such thing as a "reverter," or a "possibility of reversion." You should never use such terms. It is unfortunate that the common law settled on such similar names for these two different interests, but we are stuck with them and you must be clear which future interest you are referring to by using the correct name for it.

We can now turn to our final defeasible fee/future interest pairing:

> **If a future interest in the grantor that cuts short or divests a prior estate is limited by *words of condition*, it is a *right of entry*. The defeasible fee followed by a right of entry is a *fee simple subject to a condition subsequent.***

The *right of entry* (sometimes called a *power of termination*) is a future interest in the grantor that is limited by *words of condition*: phrases such as "but if," "provided that," "however if," "on condition that," and so forth. The key practical distinction between the possibility of reverter and the right of entry is that the right of entry *does not automatically become possessory by operation of law* upon the satisfaction or failure of the relevant condition. Rather, in order to be entitled to possession the owner of the right of entry must take some affirmative step to assert her rights (for example, by bringing an ejectment action). Until the owner of the power of entry exercises it, the state of title remains the same as it was before the condition triggering the right of entry was satisfied; the only change is that we would now say the right of entry "may be presently exercised."

The defeasible fee that can be cut short by a right of entry is called a *fee simple subject to condition subsequent*. Note here the difference here between a condition precedent—which is the type of condition that must be satisfied *before* a future interest such as a contingent remainder, executory interest, or right of entry can become possessory—and a *condition subsequent*—which is the type of condition that can arise *after* possessory estate begins and have the effect of divesting that estate. Put simply: a condition precedent must be satisfied *before* you can have your interest; a condition subsequent can arise *after* you get your interest and take it away. We will explore this distinction in more detail shortly.

Consider an example: O, an adherent of the Church of the Flying Spaghetti Monster owning a fee simple absolute in Blackacre, conveys Blackacre "to my son A, but if A ever marries a non-Pastafarian, to O." Under this conveyance, A has a possessory estate with no *inherent* limitation, but that estate is followed by a future interest that can cut short A's estate on the occurrence of an uncertain future condition (A's marriage outside the faith). Because this future interest is owned by the grantor (O), and because it can cut short the prior possessory estate, it must be either a possibility of reverter or a right of entry. And because there are no durational words of limitation on A's possessory interest, but there is a condition precedent on O's future interest, we know that O's interest is a right of entry. This, in turn, means that A's interest is the matching defeasible fee: the fee simple subject to condition subsequent. Now imagine that A falls in love with and marries B, an adherent of the Missionary Church of Kopimism. Upon their marriage, A's fee simple subject to condition subsequent *does not change*. Rather, all that happens is that O's right of entry—which has been there all along—becomes *presently exercisable*. In an ejectment or quiet title action between O and A, O would now prevail—but until such an action is brought there is nothing wrongful about A's continued possession of Blackacre.

If, in contrast, O's conveyance had been "to A so long as A does not marry a non-Pastafarian," A's interest would have been limited by words of duration, and thus would be a fee simple determinable followed by a possibility of reverter in fee simple absolute in O. Upon A's marriage to B, A's estate would immediately terminate by operation of law and O would have a presently possessory fee simple absolute. A's continued possession, in these circumstances, is wrongful against O.

Remainders, Part 4: Divestment of Future Interests; Types of Vested Remainders

Before finishing off our catalogue of future interests there is one last issue—and one more set of future interests—that we must examine. We already know that certain "pushy" future interests (the possibility of reverter, the right of entry, and the executory interest) can cut short a possessory interest. But it turns out that they can also divest a *vested future interest* even before it becomes possessory. This is particularly an issue for vested remainders (though it applies to the reversion as well). Consider the following example: O, owning a fee simple in Blackacre, conveys Blackacre "to A for life, and then to B, but if A ever remarries, then to C." Note that B's interest is a vested remainder in fee simple absolute: nothing other than the natural termination of A's life estate needs to happen in order for B to take possession. *However*, there is one thing that could happen that would *take away* B's otherwise certain right to possession: A's remarriage could trigger a *shifting executory interest in fee simple absolute* in C. And note that, if this happens, it will happen *before B's remainder becomes possessory*—A can't get remarried from the grave. So in this case, C's "pushy" future interest can *divest* B's future interest, but it could not cut short B's interest once that interest becomes possessory. We call B's interest a *vested remainder subject to divestment*, and we can encapsulate the rule for identifying such a future interest as follows:

Where a vested remainder could be prevented from *ever* becoming possessory by a different future interest, we say that it is a *vested remainder subject to divestment.* [42]

Note that there are potentially other ways that a vested remainder could be affected by events subsequent to its vesting. Consider an example: O, owning a fee simple absolute in Blackacre, conveys Blackacre "to A for life, then to A's children." At the time, A has no children. By now you can quickly conclude that A has a life estate and "A's children" have a future interest. Because the future interest is in a grantee and cannot cut short the preceding estate, it must be a remainder. There is no condition other than the natural termination of A's life estate on the remainder becoming possessory, but there is no one yet born who has a right to the remainder, so it must be a *contingent* remainder in fee simple absolute (O would also have a reversion in fee simple absolute—do you see why?).

So: what happens once A has her first child, B? Now we can identify *at least one* currently living individual who can take possession when the remainder becomes possessory. According to our rule for distinguishing vested from contingent remainders, B would seem to now have a *vested remainder* in fee simple absolute (destroying O's reversion). But something is still up in the air: what happens if A has more children before dying? Would those children have a right to share in the remainder? The answer is yes—they would clearly be within the definition of "A's children" in the words of purchase for the remainder. This is what we call a "class grant"—a conveyance to a group of people identified by their membership in some identified group, rather than as individuals. For such a grant, the "class" remains "open" until it logically could no longer add new members, at which point it "closes." In this case, once A dies, the class of "A's children" clearly can't get any new members. Note that this means that B's remainder, though vested, can be *diluted* by the addition of more members of the class entitled to take possession at the end of A's life estate. We call such a future interest a *vested remainder subject to open*, and can encapsulate the rule for identifying it as follows:

Where a vested remainder could be diluted by the addition of new members to the class of persons entitled to it, we say that it is a *vested remainder subject to open.*

---

[42] Different jurisdictions may have slightly different rules for differentiating between remainders that are "contingent" and those that are "vested subject to divestment," and the distinction has divided leading scholars over the centuries. We will confine ourselves to relatively straightforward examples in this course to avoid such disputations, but for an overview, see 3 Powell on Real Property §20.04.

Finally, we should note that it is sometimes good practice to make clear when identifying a vested remainder that it is neither subject to divestment nor subject to open. When this is the case, we say it is an *indefeasibly vested remainder.*

> **Where a vested remainder is neither subject to divestment nor subject to open, it is an *indefeasibly vested remainder.***

Future Interests Summary and Review

Congratulations! You've made your way through an introduction to all the common-law future interests. This is a lot of material to take in, and it can be difficult to keep it organized in your mind. You will likely want to refer to the following summary table, and back to the flow chart provided earlier in this chapter, to guide your thinking about how to identify a future interest when you come across it.

Table 2: The Common-Law Future Interests

<table>
<tr><th></th><th>Future Interests in the Grantor</th><th colspan="2">Future Interests in a Grantee</th></tr>
<tr><td rowspan="5"><u>Cannot</u> divest (cut short) a preceding vested or possessory estate</td><td rowspan="5">Reversion</td><td colspan="2">Remainders:</td></tr>
<tr><td rowspan="4"></td><td>Contingent Remainder</td></tr>
<tr><td>Indefeasibly Vested Remainder</td></tr>
<tr><td>Vested Remainder Subject to Open</td></tr>
<tr><td>Vested Remainder Subject to Divestment</td></tr>
<tr><td rowspan="3"><u>Can</u> divest (cut short) a preceding vested or possessory estate</td><td>Possibility of Reverter</td><td colspan="2">Executory Interests:</td></tr>
<tr><td rowspan="2">Right of Entry</td><td rowspan="2"></td><td>Springing Executory Interest</td></tr>
<tr><td>Shifting Executory Interest</td></tr>
</table>

Let's apply what we've learned with a review problem:

Problem 3

Do the following conveyances create the same legal interests?

1. **To A for life, then to B if B survives A, otherwise to A's heirs.**
2. **To A for life, then to B, but if B does not survive A, then to A's heirs.**

Solution: Let's return to our method. Step 1 is moot because we are analyzing the language of a grant rather than a sequence of events, so we move on to Step 2.a. Beginning with Step 2.a.i, and applying our punctuation rule, we can divide up each grant as follows:

1. To A for life, | then to B if B survives A, | otherwise to A's heirs.
2. To A for life, | then to B, but if B does not survive A, | to A's heirs.

or, rewriting each grant of an individual interest on a separate line:

1. (a) To A for life,
   (b) Then to B if B survives A,
   (c) Otherwise to A's heirs.
2. (a) To A for life,
   (b) Then to B,
   (c) But if B does not survive A, to A's heirs.

We can now move on to Step 2.a.ii and identify the interests created by each of these clauses. Let us begin with interest 1(a). It is a possessory estate, with words of limitation "for life," meaning it is a life estate. Interest 1(b) is a future interest (we know because of the existence of A's life estate and the introductory word "then"). Because it is an interest in a grantee (B), it must be either a remainder or an executory interest. The words of limitation "if B survives A" do not permit B's interest to cut short A's life estate, so it must be a remainder—it cannot become possessory until the natural termination of A's life estate. But note that it is also *subject to a condition precedent*: something else (besides A's death) must happen for B's interest to become possessory. That condition (that B survive—or live longer than—A) means that B's remainder must be *contingent*. And its quantum? It contains no inherent limitation, meaning we can apply our presumption that O conveyed a future interest in fee simple absolute—*unless* the next estate gives us reason to change this view. Looking at interest 1(c), we find a future interest in A's heirs. The word "otherwise" refers to the inverse of the condition on interest 1(b) (B surviving A), meaning that A's heirs will take if A survives B. This is yet another *condition precedent,* but does it allow interest 1(c) to cut short or divest any prior interest? Clearly not: it cannot become possessory during A's life estate, and the word "otherwise" indicates that 1(b) and 1(c) are *alternative* future interests: if B survives A, A will not have survived B (and vice versa). So interests 1(b) and 1(c) are *alternative contingent remainders*, and because neither can be cut short by any later interest (there being none), they are alternative contingent remainders in fee simple absolute. Finally, recall Step 2.a.iii of our method: we need to know whether O has retained any interest. Interest 1(a) is of a lesser quantum than O's fee simple absolute, and interests 1(b) and 1(c), while of the same quantum, are contingent, not vested. So O must have a reversion in fee simple absolute. Note that this is true even though the alternative nature of these interests would seem to guarantee that either B or A's heirs will take a fee simple absolute on A's death. Can you imagine any reason why we might nevertheless insist on O having a reversion?

Having completed Step 2.a of our method, we move on to Step 2.c. Given the analysis above, the state of title under Conveyance #1 is:

- Life estate in A
- Alternative contingent remainders in fee simple absolute in B and A's heirs
- Reversion in fee simple absolute in O.

Repeating this process for Conveyance #2, we again begin with a life estate in A. Interest 2(b), however, is somewhat different, in that it lacks the condition precedent that was present in interest 1(b)—indeed, it lacks any words of limitation at all. Thus, it is a *vested* rather than a contingent remainder. But what is its quantum? Since it has no words of limitation, we can apply our presumption to conclude that it conveys a vested remainder in fee simple absolute—*unless* the estate could be cut short or divested by some subsequent interest. And here we come to clause 2(c), which tells us that if B dies before A, A's heirs will take Blackacre *instead of* B. But this possibility does not mean that B's remainder is contingent: based on the language of the grant creating *this particular interest*, it is vested. However, there is a *condition subsequent* (i.e., a condition precedent to the vesting of a *subsequent* future interest) that could *divest* B. We therefore call B's interest a remainder *vested subject to divestment*. It is vested, but it could still be divested (i.e., taken away) if some *subsequent* condition is satisfied.

Interest 2(c), because it is a future interest in a grantee that can *divest* the interest of another grantee (B), is a *shifting executory interest*. Again, applying our presumption, the quantum of interest 2(c) is a fee simple absolute. Going back now to consider the effect of Interest 2(c) on the quantum of Interest 2(b), we should note that there is nothing Interest 2(c) could do to *cut short* interest 2(b) *after it becomes possessory:* either B will survive A and defeat the condition precedent to Interest 2(c), or B will predecease A and the vested remainder will be divested and disappear before it becomes possessory. We can therefore conclude that there is no future interest that could cut short B's possessory estate *once it becomes possessory*, meaning that under our presumption it is a vested remainder subject to divestment *in fee simple absolute*. Finally, we move to Step 2.a.iii, and note that unlike Conveyance #1, Conveyance #2 *has* created a vested interest of equal quantum to the grantor's interest: Interest 2(b). Therefore, there is *no reversion.*

Having completed Step 2.a of our method with respect to Conveyance #2, we move on to Step 2.c. The state of title is:

- Life estate in A
- Vested Remainder Subject to Divestment in Fee Simple Absolute in B
- Shifting Executory Interest in Fee Simple Absolute in A's Heirs.

As is apparent, these two conveyances, though appearing quite similar and turning on the same contingencies (the relative timing of the deaths of A and B), create quite different sets of legal interests.

Problems

1. O, who owns a fee simple absolute in Blackacre, conveys Blackacre "to A for life." A subsequently conveys "all my right, title, and interest in Blackacre to B." Several years later, B dies. A is still alive. What is the state of title in Blackacre? Support your conclusion with an analysis of the chain of title

2. O, who owns a fee simple absolute in Blackacre, conveys Blackacre "to A for life, then to B <u>or</u> her heirs." What interests are created by this grant? Who will own Blackacre if A survives B? If B survives A?

3. O, who owns a fee simple absolute in Blackacre, conveys Blackacre "to A, but if A ever divorces, then to the oldest of A's then-living children." At the time of the conveyance, A is married to B with one child, C. Five years later, A and B have a second child, D. Three years later, B is killed in a car accident. Three years after that, A remarries, to E. Two years later, A and E have a child, F. A and E then get a divorce. Who owns Blackacre? Support your answer with an analysis of the complete chain of title.

4. Imagine the same sequence of events as presented in Question 3, with the exception that the initial conveyance is "to A so long as A does not divorce," and that subsequent to A's divorce from E, A dies leaving a valid will devising all her property to her children in equal shares. Who owns Blackacre? Support your answer with an analysis of the complete chain of title.

5. O, who owns a fee simple absolute in Blackacre, conveys Blackacre "to A for life, then to A's children in equal shares," at a time when A has one child, B. A then has a second

child, C. B then marries D. B then dies, leaving a valid will devising all her property to her spouse, D. A then dies. What is the state of title in Blackacre? Support your answer with an analysis of the complete chain of title.

6. O, who owns a fee simple absolute in Blackacre, conveys Blackacre "to A for life, then to B if B graduates from law school, but if C graduates from law school, then to C." B and C are both living at the time of the conveyance. B then graduates from law school. A then dies. C then graduates from law school. Who owns Blackacre? Support your answer with an analysis of the complete chain of title.

7. O dies owning a fee simple absolute in Blackacre, and leaves a valid will devising Blackacre "to A for life, then to B and his heirs, unless B fails to graduate law school before his 25th birthday," and further devising O's residuary estate "to C and her heirs." B is 15 years old at the time of O's death. Five years after O's death, A dies. Seven years after O's death, C dies, leaving D as her sole heir. Nine years after O's death, D conveys "all my right, title and interest in Blackacre to E." Ten years after O's death, B turns 25 years old, not having graduated (or even enrolled in) law school.

   Assume that all future interests are freely devisable, descendible, and alienable. Provide a chain of title for Blackacre.

Property

14. Preserving Marketability

As we saw in our discussion of estates and future interests, the common law gave property owners a fairly diverse and subtle array of tools to effectuate their intent regarding the use and disposition of their property. But this level of control raises serious potential for conflicts between the plans and wishes of the property owners of yesterday and the needs and desires of (actual and aspiring) property owners of today.

Consider that about 80 years before the Empire State Building was constructed, the land on which it now stands was a farm situated a mile beyond the northern edge of the urban quarters of New York City. *See* JAMES REMINGTON MCCARTHY & JOHN RUTHERFORD, PEACOCK ALLEY: THE ROMANCE OF THE WALDORF-ASTORIA 4-10 (1931). What if the first private owner of that farm—John Thompson, who purchased it in 1799 out of the common lands held by the city government for $2,400 (*id.*)—had executed a conveyance of the land that included a future interest in "the eldest of my great-great-great-great-great grandchildren"? What if he had devised the land to his eldest child "on condition that the family farm may never be sold"? Or "on condition that the land may be used for farming purposes only"? Could the Empire State Building ever have been built? If not, is that a result we would be happy with?

The common law recognized that some property owners might try to dictate the disposition of property much farther into the future than could be justified by any legitimate interest or expertise they might have. As one commentator put it, writing in 1967: "[I]t would have been utterly impossible for any testator dying in 1866 to foresee the events that have taken place in the succeeding century, and ... any prediction as to what may occur in the century following 1966 would be even more unlikely to conform to reality." W. BARTON LEACH, PROPERTY LAW INDICTED! 71 (1967). As years pass, new generations undertake stewardship of resources, and the economic, social, and cultural demands on those resources change with the times. Allowing long-dead property owners to dictate the disposition of those resources to the fourth, fifth, or sixth generation after they're gone significantly limits the ability of the possessors of today to flexibly direct resources to uses appropriate to the age.

The common law developed various doctrines designed to balance respect for property owners' wishes to provide for their families as they see fit with vigilance against the dangers of dead-hand control. One powerful tool for striking this balance is the infamous Rule Against Perpetuities. Its classic formulation—that an interest in property is void unless it necessarily will vest within 21 years of the end of a life in being at the time the interest is created—essentially operates to limit a property owner's control to one generation beyond the end of his own life. For example, a grant to John Thompson's great-great-great-great-great grandchild would be clearly invalid under the Rule Against Perpetuities, but a grant by John Thompson to his living daughter's yet-unborn child would almost certainly be valid.[43]

Beyond limiting the *duration* of property owners' control, the common law developed additional rules regarding the *types* of restrictions grantors could place on otherwise valid interests in property that they conveyed. The following cases provide some examples. As you read them, consider how the principles they rely on relate to the aforementioned balance between respecting property owners' wishes and guarding against dead-hand control.

A. Restraints on Alienation

Ford v. Allen

526 S.W.2d 643 (Ct. Civ. App. Tex. 1975)

O'QUINN, Justice.

Chester Melvin Ford and Lola Mae Ford, the deceased persons whose wills are under review, were married in August of 1943, and Clyde M. Ford, appellant here and plaintiff below, was the only child born to their marriage. Mr. [Chester] Ford had been married twice prior to his marriage to Mrs. Ford, but had no children from those marriages. Mrs. Ford also had been married earlier, and from that marriage she had a son, Otis Martin Allen, who died in April of 1958, leaving three sons, resulting from two marriages. The three surviving sons were defendants below and are appellees in this appeal.

The undisputed evidence supports the finding of the trial court that Chester Melvin Ford and his wife, Lola Mae Ford, each executed a holographic will on the same day in April of 1960, and each of them devised 'all my property to my beloved' spouse, followed by certain additional identical language which is under dispute. Mr. Ford died November 25, 1972, and less than a month later Mrs. Ford died, on December 18, 1972.

---

[43] We say "almost" only because if Thompson for some reason made the future interest in his unborn grandchild subject to the condition precedent of that grandchild attaining an age of more than 21 years, the interest would be void under the common-law Rule Against Perpetuities.

It also appears undisputed that, as the court found, Mr. Ford at the time of his death owned approximately 450 acres of land in Bell County....

The language of the wills giving rise to this suit, as contained in the will of Mr. Ford, follows:

> 'After the Payments of my Just Debts I devise all my property to my beloved wife Lola Mae Ford to do with as she See fit except that she is not to Sell, Morage (sic), or Lease any of our real Estate for more than Three (3) years without the written agreement of our son Clyde Melvin Ford.'

Appellant contends that the language is ambiguous and requires construction, and that under a proper construction the language 'created a life estate in real property in Lola Mae Ford with remainder to Clyde M. Ford in fee simple, or alternatively created a testamentary trust expressly or by implication for the use and benefit of Clyde M. Ford.'

... The trial court concluded (1) that the language in the wills, providing that the devisee was not to sell, mortgage, or lease any of the realty for three years without written agreement of Clyde M. Ford, was 'void as being a restraint on alienation and repugnant to the devise in fee;' and (2) the language of the wills ... devised fee simple title to all property, since the wills contained no 'language clearly showing a lesser estate than the fee was intended to be devised.' We approve these conclusions as correct applications of the law to the language of the wills.

Appellant contends that by extrinsic evidence it may be demonstrated that the true intent of Mr. and Mrs. Ford was to devise their real property to their only son, Clyde M. Ford, and that because of the ambiguity of the language in the wills, such evidence should have been considered....

In brief, the evidence was that the real estate was the separate property of Mr. Ford, and that the three grandsons of Mrs. Ford were not kin to Mr. Ford; that Clyde M. Ford had helped to work the lands contained in the 450 acres, whereas the defendants had never worked any part of the land; that the grandsons were not close to their grandmother or to Mr. Ford, and none of them attended either the funeral of Mr. Ford or their grandmother; that Mrs. Ford set up a savings account for the grandsons and this alone was intended to take care of them; that Clyde M. Ford was close to his parents and was the natural object of the deceaseds' bounty, and the defendants were not; that during their life both Mr. and Mrs. Ford indicated orally that they wanted Clyde to have the land.

It is the established rule that an ambiguity arises only when the meaning which emanates from language used in the will admits of more than one interpretation. We find no ambiguity in the language of the Ford wills which in each writing clearly and plainly devises all property to the other spouse to do with as the other may see fit. The attempt, in language that follows, to place a restraint on alienation could not change or nullify the devise. It is not a function of the courts, nor is it a role the courts may assume, to revise or to make over the writing in a will to achieve results different from results which flow from the plain language used by the maker of the will. The courts may not speculate, from extrinsic evidence or otherwise, that some other result may have been intended.

… Appellant also urges that the trial court erred in refusing to make a determination of heirship, and under these points insists that if Mrs. Ford died intestate, appellant is entitled to one-half of her estate and defendants are entitled only to the remaining one-half. The trial court correctly declined to decide the matter of heirship since administration of the estates is still pending in Bell County, where the County Court has acquired jurisdiction to determine heirs of the deceased.

All of appellant's point of error have been carefully examined and considered, and all points are overruled.

The trial court in its judgment denied the request of Clyde M. Ford that attorney's fees, court costs, and other expenses incurred by this suit to construe the wills be paid out of the two estates as costs and expenses of administration, and ordered all such costs and expenses to be paid by Ford individually.

The judgment of the trial court is in all things affirmed. It is ordered that costs of this appeal be taxed against appellant, Clyde M. Ford, individually.

Notes and Questions

1. Do you think Clyde is right that his parents wanted him to have the farm after both of them died? Or at least that they would rather Clyde have it than Lola Mae's estranged grandchildren from another marriage? If so, why do you think both Chester and Lola Mae executed wills without any explicit devise to Clyde? If not, why do you think the Fords' wills included a restriction on alienating the farm without Clyde's consent? (Incidentally, what is a "holographic" will?)

2. Why is the court unwilling to consider Clyde's evidence that his parents wanted him to have the farm? What's wrong with looking outside the four corners of the will itself to understand what the testator *really* wanted? Would we take a similar view of extrinsic evidence if the document being interpreted were, say, a contract for the sale of goods?

3. Justice O'Quinn says that the language of the Fords' wills "clearly and plainly devises all property to the other spouse to do with as the other may see fit." But this is at best

disingenuous and at worst deliberately false: the wills also, *in the very next clause*, "clearly and plainly" purport to limit what the other spouse can do with the property in the absence of Clyde's consent. Why does the court enforce the former clause and render the latter clause void?

The reasoning of the trial court in this case may help explain things. Note that the trial court is said to have given two somewhat different reasons for invalidating Clyde's power to block any effort by his surviving parent to alienate the farm (and with it any future interest he might have claimed by implication from this right). We are told that an attempt to convey such a power to Clyde must be void, both "as a restraint on alienation," and as "repugnant to the … fee." These reasons invoke two long-standing common-law principles: a policy against restraints on alienation, and the doctrine of *numerus clausus.*

Courts have generally strongly disfavored overt restraints on a grantee's right to alienate their interest. Such restraints can make it quite difficult to move resources from lower-valued to higher-valued uses. A current owner of a resource might well be willing to sell it to a willing buyer who wants it more and can make more valuable use of it, but if we enforce a restraint on alienation imposed on the current owner by a past grantor, such a beneficial transaction cannot happen. The result would be serious misallocation of resources, and the rule that restraints on alienation are void demonstrates the common law's willingness to defeat even the clearly expressed intent of a grantor where necessary to avoid such misallocation.

Numerus clausus (literally, "the number is closed") is a legal principle derived from civil law systems but invoked in Anglo-American property law to refuse recognition of any interest in land other than the traditional common-law estates. Under this principle property owners may not create any new "bundle of rights" other than those that are already represented by the common-law estates themselves. So, because a possessory estate subject to a veto on the right of alienation by someone other than the possessory estate's owner is not a "bundle of rights" that we can identify among our common-law estates, it must be outside the power of the Fords to create it. Courts have similarly rejected efforts by testators to, for example, give their surviving spouses unfettered control over devised property while also giving any property left over at the surviving spouse's death to another beneficiary. Such hybrid bequests are, like the devise in *Ford,* typically treated as a fee simple (rendering the putative future interest void). *See, e.g.*, Sumner v. Borders, 98 S.W.2d 918 (Ky. 1936).

Is the rule of *numerus clausus* motivated by the same rationales that give rise to the rule against restraints on alienation? Imagine if, rather than selecting from the fixed menu of common-law estates, property owners were free to build their own tailored bundles of property interests for grantees, with their own ad hoc collections of limitations and restrictions on the rights of those grantees, and that these idiosyncratic collections of rights and limitations became commonplace across society. Suppose you now want to buy a parcel of land in that society. Can you be sure what you're buying? How? How well would we expect a real estate market built on a potentially infinite variety of interests in real property to function? *See generally* Thomas W. Merrill & Henry E. Smith, *Optimal Standardization in the Law of Property: The Numerus Clausus Principle*, 110 YALE L. J. 1 (2000).

4. Are there other principles underlying the rule against restraints on alienation or the *numerus clausus* principle other than ensuring a well-working market for property rights? Consider that the law of *intellectual property* has long included a so-called "first sale" doctrine, which provides that the first authorized purchaser of a good embodying an intellectual property right (for example, a book embodying a copyrighted work, or a machine embodying a patented invention) has the power to alienate *that particular article* free of any claim by the intellectual property right owner. *See, e.g.*, 17 U.S.C. § 109(a) (copyright); Adams v. Burke, 84 U.S. 453, 456 (1873) ("[W]hen the patentee, or the person having his rights, sells a machine or instrument whose sole value is in its use, he receives the consideration for its use and he parts with the right to restrict that use.") At least where the owners of the relevant intellectual property rights can be clearly identified, can this rule be justified by the same principle as the rule against restraints on alienation of *land?* If not, what is the rationale for the first-sale doctrine?

5. Consider the following excerpts from the September 6, 2012 Amazon Kindle Store Terms of Use Agreement (available at http://www.amazon.com/gp/help/customer/display.html?nodeId=201014950), which governs the downloading of electronic copies of copyrighted literary works from Amazon for viewing on electronic devices.

> "Kindle Content" means digitized electronic content obtained through the Kindle Store, such as books, newspapers, magazines, journals, blogs, RSS feeds, games, and other static and interactive electronic content.
>
> . . .
>
> **Use of Kindle Content.** Upon your download of Kindle Content and payment of any applicable fees (including applicable taxes), the Content Provider grants you a non-exclusive right to view, use, and display such Kindle Content an unlimited number of times, solely on the Kindle or a Reading Application or as otherwise permitted as part of the Service, solely on the number of Kindles or Supported Devices specified in the Kindle Store, and solely for your personal, non-commercial use. Kindle Content is licensed, not sold, to you by the Content Provider....

> **Limitations.** Unless specifically indicated otherwise, you may not sell, rent, lease, distribute, broadcast, sublicense, or otherwise assign any rights to the Kindle Content or any portion of it to any third party, and you may not remove or modify any proprietary notices or labels on the Kindle Content. In addition, you may not bypass, modify, defeat, or circumvent security features that protect the Kindle Content.
>
> …
>
> **Termination.** Your rights under this Agreement will automatically terminate if you fail to comply with any term of this Agreement. In case of such termination, you must cease all use of the Kindle Store and the Kindle Content, and Amazon may immediately revoke your access to the Kindle Store and the Kindle Content without refund of any fees. Amazon's failure to insist upon or enforce your strict compliance with this Agreement will not constitute a waiver of any of its rights.

Is this agreement consistent with the rules you've just learned? If not, is it enforceable? *See* Vernor v. Autodesk, Inc., 621 F.3d 1102, 1111 (9th Cir. 2010).

6. Might a grantor impose restrictions on a grantee *other than* explicit limitations on the power to alienate that would raise the same concerns as those that motivate the rule against restraints on alienation? Consider the following cases:

Wills v. Pierce
208 Ga. 417 (1951)

… Mrs. Walter Tilley Pierce and others filed in Terrell Superior Court, against Mrs. J. C. Wills and others, a petition, which alleged substantially the following: On December 1, 1923, J. W. Tilley by warranty deed conveyed described realty known as the Aven Home to J. C. Wills. The deed contained the clause: 'The above property is conveyed to J. C. Wills [the grantee] to be used as a home by himself, his family and his heirs, upon condition that the same be used by him or them as a home and a residence, and further that upon the failure of the said condition and the abandonment of said property as a residence by [the grantee], … his family or heirs, the same shall revert to [the grantor's] … estate and go as directed by [the grantor's] … will.' The grantor died testate in 1924, and under the terms of his will the petitioners are the owners of the reversionary interest in the realty. The grantee died intestate in 1945, leaving as his sole surviving heirs his widow, Mrs. J. C. Wills, and two named children, who are the defendants. The condition under which the realty was conveyed has been violated, in that the defendants have abandoned the property as a home and residence, and are now residing elsewhere. … The petitioners prayed … that the interest of the defendants in the realty be declared forfeited, and the fee-simple title thereof be decreed to be in the petitioners; and that the petitioners have general equitable relief.

The defendants demurred to the petition on the ground that it failed to set forth any cause of action against them. The trial court overruled the demurrer, and the defendants excepted....

ATKINSON, Presiding Justice (after stating the foregoing facts).

The granting clause in the deed under consideration was: 'In consideration of the sum of one dollar to me paid, I ... do hereby sell and convey to [the grantee and] ... his heirs, a tract or parcel of land and appurtenances in fee simple.' Then followed a description of the land, after which the grantor inserted the provision that the property was to be used as a home by the grantee, his family, and his heirs, and that upon the abandonment of the property as a residence by the grantee, his family, or his heirs, the same should revert to the grantor's estate and go as provided in his will.

Standing alone, the first clause in the deed would have conveyed an unconditional fee-simple estate, and the sole question for determination is whether or not the condition subsequent under which the forfeiture is claimed is valid and enforceable.

A provision in a deed or will that a fee-simple estate may not be sold is void as being repugnant to the estate granted.

While no express language is used in the present deed inhibiting alienation of the property, nevertheless—the condition being that the property was to be used as a home by the grantee, his family, and his heirs—the requirement to use as a home and the right to sell are mutually exclusive, and whether or not the case falls within the rule against perpetuities, the conclusion is inescapable that since the grantee and his heirs must use the premises as a home they cannot sell it.

...A different question would have been presented if the condition subsequent had been that the premises should be used 'as a home' or 'for residential purposes' generally. See, in this connection, City of Barnesville v. Stafford, 161 Ga. 588(1), 131 S.E. 487, 43 A.L.R. 1045; Taylor v. Bird, 150 Ga. 626, 104 S.E. 502; Rustin v. Butler, 195 Ga. 389, 24 S.E.2d 318; Williams v. Ramey, 201 Ga. 737(1), 41 S.E.2d 159; Tabor v. Gilmer County, 205 Ga. 439(1), 53 S.E.2d 915; and similar cases, where conditions subsequent requiring use of property generally for park, school, religious, and courthouse purposes were held valid and enforceable.

Accordingly, the present petition, seeking to enforce a forfeiture for breach of a void condition subsequent, failed to set forth a cause of action, and the trial court erred in overruling the defendants' general demurrer.

Judgment reversed.

All the Justices concur.

Notes and Questions

1. We learned in our unit on estates and future interests that grantors may use the defeasible fees to impose conditions subsequent on the continued enjoyment of a possessory estate. Are we still confident that grantors have such a power? If so, what are its limits?

2. Why does the court consider the enforcement of the condition that the property at issue "be used as a home by [the grantee], his family and his heirs" to present a "different question" than the enforcement of a condition "that the premises should be used 'as a home' or 'for residential purposes' generally"? What makes these questions different?

3. Is there any relationship between the holding of *Wills* and our previously discussed rule against restraints on alienation or the principle of *numerus clausus?* If so, what's the connection?

Davis v. Davis

791 SE 2d 714 (NC Ct. App., 2016)

Dillon, Judge.

This matter involves a family dispute over a beach property in Dare County (the "Property"). Defendant Dorothy C. Davis owns a life estate in the Property. The remainder interest is held by nominal Defendant MKR Development, LLC (the "LLC"), a limited liability company owned by and benefitting three of Mrs. Davis's children — Kaye Davis and Plaintiffs Melvin L. Davis, Jr., ("Mel") and J. Rex Davis ("Rex"). Plaintiffs commenced this suit to enjoin Mrs. Davis from renting the Property during her lifetime to vacationers, contending that certain language in the deed conveying Mrs. Davis her life estate interest (the "Deed") restricts her from renting out the Property.

This matter was designated a mandatory complex business case by Chief Justice of our Supreme Court Mark D. Martin and assigned to Judge Gregory P. McGuire, a Special Superior Court Judge for Complex Business Cases.

The parties filed cross motions for summary judgment. Judge McGuire granted Mrs. Davis summary judgment, holding that the restrictive language in the Deed — to the extent that it could be construed to restrict Mrs. Davis's ability to rent the Property — was void. We affirm Judge McGuire's order.

I. Background

Property

Sometime in the 1980s, Mrs. Davis and her husband ("Mr. Davis") purchased the Property. In order to help pay for Property expenses, Mr. and Mrs. Davis occasionally rented the Property to vacationers through a real estate agency.

In 2009, Mr. and Mrs. Davis decided to transfer a remainder interest in the Property to three of their children (including Plaintiffs). Accordingly, Mr. and Mrs. Davis executed the Deed and conveyed a remainder interest in the Property to the LLC, reserving for themselves (Mr. and Mrs. Davis) a life estate.

In July 2012, Mr. Davis died, leaving Mrs. Davis as the Property's sole life tenant. Less than two weeks later, Plaintiffs prepared a letter advising their mother that the Deed required that the Property "remain available for [her] personal use and [could] not be used to provide income to [her]."

Notwithstanding this letter, Mrs. Davis entered into an agreement with a real estate agency in 2013 to rent the Property to vacationers, just as she and her husband had done in years past.

In July 2013, Plaintiffs filed this declaratory judgment action to enjoin their mother from renting the Property without the express permission of the LLC.

In May 2015, both parties filed summary judgment motions. Judge McGuire granted Mrs. Davis's summary judgment motion. Plaintiffs timely appealed.

II. Analysis

On appeal, Plaintiffs argue that the Deed contains a restriction which prevents their mother from renting out the Property during her life tenancy. Specifically, they point to the following language in the Deed:

The Grantors [Mr. and Mrs. Davis] hereby reserve unto themselves, a life estate in the Property, said life estate to be personal to the use of the Grantors, or the survivor thereof, and may not be utilized by any other person, nor may it be reduced to a cash value for the benefit of the Grantors, or the survivor thereof, but must remain always during the lifetime of said Grantors, or the survivor thereof, available for their individual and personal use without interference from either the remaindermen or any other person.

We disagree. We hold that the Deed language creates an unreasonable restraint on the alienation of Mrs. Davis's life estate and is therefore void. Accordingly, we affirm Judge McGuire's summary judgment order.

Restraints on alienation are generally disfavored in North Carolina due to the "necessity of maintaining a society controlled primarily by its living members and the desirability of facilitating the utilization of wealth." Smith v. Mitchell, 301 N.C. 58 (1980). Nevertheless, it is fundamentally important that a property owner "should be able to convey [property] subject to whatever condition he or she may desire to impose on the conveyance."

To balance these competing policy interests, our Supreme Court has held that any unlimited restraint on alienation "is per se invalid." However, restrictions which "provide only that someone's estate may be forfeited or be terminated if he alienates, or that provides damages must be paid if he alienates, may be upheld if reasonable." (emphasis added). That is, our courts will generally uphold any reasonable restraints on alienation except unlimited restraints, which are per se unreasonable.

Our Supreme Court has applied this restraints doctrine to life estates. Lee v. Oates, 171 N.C. 717 (1916). ("[T]his Court has for many years consistently held that the doctrine as to restraints of alienation applies as well to estates for life as to estates in fee simple[.]"). See also Crockett v. First Fed. Sav. & Loan Assoc. of Charlotte, 289 N.C. 620 (1976) (reaffirming caselaw that applies restraints doctrine to life estates); Pilley v. Sullivan, 182 N.C. 493 (1921) ("The clause which purports to ingraft upon the devise an unlimited restraint on alienation is not only repugnant to the [life] estate devised, but is in contravention of public policy, and therefore void."); Wool v. Fleetwood, 136 N.C. 460 (1904) (voiding a will provision prohibiting the life tenant from selling the life estate).

In the present case, Plaintiffs concede that the Deed creates an unlimited restraint on Mrs. Davis's ability to alienate her life estate. Indeed, as noted in the summary judgment order, "[P]laintiffs contend that not only is [Mrs. Davis] prohibited from selling the life estate, she cannot rent or even permit others to use the Property." To justify this position, Plaintiffs aver that the caselaw prohibiting unlimited restraints does not apply as Mrs. Davis is both the grantor who created the restraint and the life tenant who is subject to the restraint. Plaintiffs contend that Lee is distinguishable as the restraint at issue attached to a conveyance between a grantor and a life tenant, whereas here, Mrs. Davis reserved a life estate for herself and therefore voluntarily restricted that interest.

We hold that whether the life estate was created by conveyance by a third party or by reservation by the life tenant herself is irrelevant. An unlimited restraint is against public policy; it makes no difference if the restraint is self-imposed. Plaintiffs have failed to cite precedent, either from North Carolina or from another jurisdiction, that would recognize this distinction. Indeed, the adverse party in Lee argued that the conveyance restraint should nonetheless be upheld as the life tenant herself signed the deed, "thereby agree[ing] ... not to alien her estate[.]" Our Supreme Court, however, rejected this argument, holding that an otherwise invalid restraint on alienation is not validated merely because the life tenant assented to the restraint by signing the instrument: "[To conclude otherwise] would enforce a restriction by estoppel[,] which the law declares void. The covenant was a `dead letter' when it was entered into, and we do not think it can be vitalized in this way." Based on our Supreme Court's reasoning in Lee, we conclude that the restraint on Mrs. Davis's ability to rent her Property is per se void even though Mrs. Davis was also the person who created the restraint. We therefore affirm Judge McGuire's order granting summary judgment to Mrs. Davis.

AFFIRMED.

Judges BRYANT and STEPHENS concur.

Smedley v. City of Waldron
739 F.2d 399 (8th Cir. 1984)

PER CURIAM.

In 1940, the City of Waldron, lacking funds to acquire a reservoir site, asked Hannah Smedley to donate land for that purpose. The governing agreement provided in part that:

> 5. The City of Waldron shall never sell, transfer, convey, lease, rent or otherwise dispose of the lands herein above described to other persons, firms, groups and/or corporations, except successors and/or assigns of itself, and if it attempts to do so, the lands immediately revert to Hannah Smedley and her heirs[.]

In 1977, Harry Smedley (Hannah Smedley's sole heir and devisee) sued unsuccessfully for reconveyance, arguing that the city had abandoned the land. In dismissing the complaint, the district court found that the city had not abandoned the reservoir; rather, it continuously maintained and used it as a reserve water supply.

In 1981, the city leased the oil and gas rights of the deeded land to Texas Oil and Gas Corporation. As a result, Harry Smedley brought this case, alleging that the city's lease of the mineral rights subjacent to the land violated paragraph 5 of the 1940 agreement. For relief, he demanded immediate reconveyance of the land and payment of all monies the city received under the lease. Both parties moved for summary judgment. The district court found that the agreement was an impermissible restraint on alienation and granted the city's motion for summary judgment. We reverse and remand for further proceedings.

Some Arkansas courts have disapproved restraints on alienation. *See, e.g., First National Bank of Fort Smith v. Graham,* 195 Ark. 586, 593, 113 S.W.2d 497 (1938); *Letzkus v. Nothwang,* 170 Ark. 403, 408, 279 S.W. 1006 (1926). … [But w]hen the grant is to a governmental unit for a public purpose, Arkansas courts have been reluctant to void the grant as impermissibly restraining alienation if doing so would flout the grantor's intent. One line of Arkansas cases, for example, approved disabling language in grants to localities where the land was to be used for school purposes. *McCrory School Dist. of Woodruff v. Brogden,* 231 Ark. 664, 333 S.W.2d 246, 249–50 (1960); *Vanndale Special School Dist. No. 6 v. Feltner,* 215 Ark. 252, 220 S.W.2d 131, 133 (1949); *Taylor v. School Dist. No. 45 of Searcy County,* 214 Ark. 434, 216 S.W.2d 789 (1949); *Coffelt v. Decatur School Dist. No. 17,* 212 Ark. 743, 208 S.W.2d 1, 2 (1948); *Milner v. New Edinburg School Dist.,* 211 Ark. 337, 200 S.W.2d 319, 322 (1947); *Williams v. Kirby School Dist.,* 207 Ark. 458, 181 S.W.2d 488, 490 (1944); *Steel v. Rural Special School Dist. No. 15,* 180 Ark. 36, 20 S.W.2d 316, 317 (1929). Because summary judgment in favor of the city ignores the public purpose of the grant and defeats the donor's intent, we reverse the district court's judgment.

Having decided that the restraint on alienation here is not impermissible, we remand the case to the district court to resolve the important remaining factual questions. The district court shall determine whether the mineral lease is a violation of the parties' agreement. Because Arkansas courts hold that if the restraint is valid the intent of the donor controls, *Gibson v. Pickett,* 256 Ark. 1035, 512 S.W.2d 532, 535 (1974), the district court shall determine whether the donor intended that the city would lose the land only if the land was not used for a reservoir. Finally, the district court should determine the best means of fulfilling the donor's intent: will her intentions be satisfied merely by awarding her heirs the revenues from the lease, or will the extreme remedy of forfeiture of the reservoir to the heirs be necessary?

Notes and Questions

1. **Wait…what?** How can Hannah Smedley's clearly expressed intent to absolutely forbid the City of Waldron from alienating the reservoir get around the common-law rule against restraints on alienation? And why can't Chester Ford's far more modest but no less clearly expressed intent to restrain Lola Mae's right to alienate do the same thing?

2. **Restraints on Alienation vs. Restrictions on Use.** In *Wills* the court seemed to be concerned that the condition subsequent restricting the grantee's use of the land conveyed was a sort of restraint on alienation in disguise. Could a naked restraint on alienation—such as the one in *Smedley*—really be a restriction on *use* in disguise? If so, would it be any less offensive to the principles underlying the rule against restraints on alienation?

3. Does *Smedley* reach the opposite result from *Ford* and *Wills* because the grantor's *motivation* is different in *Smedley* than in the other cases? (Is it?) Because the grantee is a public entity rather than a private individual? Because the restraint on the grantee is less onerous? (Is it?)

B. The Rule Against Perpetuities

City of Klamath Falls v. Bell
490 P.2d 515 (Oregon, 1971)

Before SCHWAB, C.J., and FOLEY and FORT, JJ.

SCHWAB, C., J.

In 1925, a corporation conveyed certain land to the city of Klamath Falls as a gift for use as the site for a city library. The deed provided, among other things, that the city should hold the land "so long as" it complied with that condition with regard to its use.

In 1969, the city terminated the use of the land for a library, and the question presented by this appeal is, "Does the title to the land remain in the city or did the termination of use as a library cause title to pass to the descendants of the shareholders of the donor-corporation (now dissolved)?"

The issue was presented to the trial court in the form of an agreed narrative statement, pertinent portions of which, in addition to the facts set forth above, are: the donor-corporation was known as the Daggett-Schallock Investment Company; the corporate deed provided that if at any time the city ceased to use the land for library purposes, title to the land should pass to Fred Schallock and Floy R. Daggett, their heirs and assigns; on September 19, 1927, the corporation was voluntarily dissolved, all creditors paid, and all assets (which we interpret as including the rights of the corporation, if any, in the land in question) were distributed in accordance with law to the sole shareholders Schallock and Daggett.

The city of Klamath Falls built a library on the land in 1926 in compliance with the conditions set out in the deed. The library continued in use from that date until July 1, 1969, when the books were moved to the County Library Building. Since that time, the city library services have been provided by Klamath County on a contract basis. The City Library building has not been used for any other purpose and now stands vacant.

After the library closure, the city of Klamath Falls filed a complaint against all the heirs of Schallock and Daggett for declaratory judgment pursuant to ORS ch. 28, asking the court to adjudicate the respective rights of the parties under the deed. The city joined Constance F. Bell, the sole heir of Fred Schallock, and Marijane Flitcraft and Caroline Crapo, the sole heirs of Floy R. Daggett, along with George C. Flitcraft, the husband of Marijane Flitcraft, and Paul Crapo, the husband of Caroline Crapo, as all the necessary parties to the suit.

The defendants Constance F. Bell, Caroline Crapo, and Paul Crapo conveyed their interests in the real property to the defendant Marijane Flitcraft in May and June 1970.

The trial court found that title to the real property was vested in the city of Klamath Falls. Its decision was based on a finding that the gift over to Fred Schallock and Floy R. Daggett was void under the rule against perpetuities.

The deed, in pertinent part, is as follows:

"KNOW ALL MEN BY THESE PRESENTS That Daggett-Schallock Investment Company a corporation organized and existing under the laws of the State of Oregon, for and as a gift and without any consideration, does hereby give, grant and convey unto the City of Klamath Falls, Oregon, so long as it complies with the conditions hereinafter set forth, and thereafter unto Fred Schallock and Floy R. Daggett, their heirs and assigns, the following described parcel of real estate, in Klamath County Oregon, to-wit

"* * *

"To have and to hold the same unto the said City of Klamath Falls, Oregon (and to any other municipal corporation which may lawfully succeed it) so long as it complies with the conditions above set forth, and thereafter unto Fred Schallock and Floy R. Daggett, their heirs and assigns forever.

"* * *."

I

We conclude that the estate that passed to the city under this deed was a fee simple on a special limitation, which is also known as a fee simple determinable, or a base or qualified fee.

The "magic" words "so long as" have generally been held to create such an estate. Simes and Smith, The Law of Future Interests 345, § 287 (2d ed. 1956), states:

"* * * The words of duration `so long as' will almost certainly be judicially recognized as the distinctive insignia of such an estate, and, if coupled with a provision which clearly calls for an automatic termination of the estate granted, there is little room for construction. * * *"

O'Connell, Estates on Condition Subsequent and Estates on Special Limitation in Oregon, 18 Or.L.Rev. 63, 73 (1939), stresses the use of words:

"* * * [T]he creation of an estate on a special limitation is characterized generally by the use of certain words. Typical words are `so long as,' `until,' or `during.' However, any language in the instrument indicating an intent that the estate shall automatically end upon the occurrence of a designated event will be sufficient."

See also, Magness v. Kerr et al., 121 Or. 373, 380 (1927).

One of the features of the fee simple on a special limitation thus created is that it terminates automatically upon breach of condition.[2] Fremont Lbr. Co. v. Starrell Pet. Co., 228 Or. 180 (1961), and cases cited therein; Clark v. Jones, 173 Or. 106, 107 (1943); see Wagner v. Wallowa County, 76 Or. 453, 461-466 (1915).

II

Upon breach of the condition, the deed provided for a gift over to Fred Schallock and Floy R. Daggett or their heirs and assigns. This gift over was an attempt to grant an executory interest since only an executory interest can follow an earlier grant in fee simple.
The rule against perpetuities applies to executory interests. Agan et al. v. United States National Bank, 227 Or. 619, 626 (1961); Closset et al. v. Burtchaell et al., 112 Or. 585 (1924).

Gray's classic statement of the rule is as follows:

"No interest is good unless it must vest, if at all, not later than twenty-one years after some life in being at the creation of the interest." GRAY, THE RULE AGAINST PERPETUITIES 191, § 201 (4th ed. 1942).

One of the main characteristics of a defeasible fee simple estate is that the first grantee might continue in possession in perpetuity. The city of Klamath Falls could have maintained a library on the site for an indefinite time in the future, or even forever. Therefore, the trial judge correctly found that the gift over to Fred Schallock and Floy R. Daggett, their heirs and assigns, was void ab initio under the rule against perpetuities.

III

---

[2] There would be a different result if the interests of the city of Klamath Falls were characterized as a fee simple on a condition subsequent, which is also known as a fee simple conditional. When such an estate is created, there is no forfeiture until the grantor exercises his right of re-entry. Wagner v. Wallowa County, 76 Or. 453 (1915); Raley v. Umatilla County, 15 Or. 172, 179-181 (1887).

The trial court's conclusion does not, however, dispose of the case at bar. Just because the gift over is invalid, it does not follow that the city of Klamath Falls now has an absolute interest in the property in question. There remains the question of whether under the deed a possibility of reverter remained in the grantor corporation.

When a deed reveals an unquestionable intent to limit the interest of the first grantee (here the city of Klamath Falls) to a fee simple on a special limitation, the courts of the United States do not create an indefeasible estate in the first grantee when a subsequent executory interest (here that of Schallock and Daggett) is void under the rule against perpetuities. Instead, the grantor (here the corporation) retains an interest known as a possibility of reverter.[3]

The general rule has been stated to be:

"* * * [W]hen an executory interest, following a fee simple interest in land * * * is void under the rule against perpetuities, the prior interest becomes absolute unless the language of the creating instrument makes it very clear that the prior interest is to terminate whether the executory interest takes effect or not. * * *" Simes and Smith, The Law of Future Interests 316, 318, § 827 (2d ed. 1956).

All the jurisdictions in the United States which have dealt with a determinable fee and an executory interest void under the rule against perpetuities have followed this rule. Fletcher v. Ferrill, 216 Ark. 583 (1950); Brown v. Independent Baptist Church of Woburn, 325 Mass. 645 (1950) (which followed the earlier Massachusetts cases); Institution for Savings in Roxbury and its Vicinity v. Roxbury Home for Aged Women, 244 Mass. 583 (1923); First Universalist Society

---

[3] It is well settled that the rule against perpetuities does not apply to possibilities of reverter. Gray, The Rule Against Perpetuities 46, 348, 349, §§ 41, 313, 314 (4th ed. 1942); Simes and Smith, The Law of Future Interests 311, § 825 (2d ed. 1956); Tiffany, Real Property 167, § 404 (3d ed. 1939). This historical anomaly has been criticized for allowing "dead hand rule" and creating "appalling practical results" when a possibility of reverter does fall in many years after the original grant. Leach, Perpetuities in Perspective: Ending the Rule's Reign of Terror, 65 Harv.L.Rev. 721, 739 (1952); Leach, Perpetuities: The Nutshell Revisited, 78 Harv.L.Rev. 973, 980 (1965).

However, as pointed out in 18 Or.L. Rev. supra, at 79:

"* * * [A] rule restricting the alienation of such interests will tend to avoid a long-outstanding 'contingent' interest and thereby effectuate the policy behind the rule against perpetuities * * * it would be far more desirable to expressly make rights of entry and possibilities of reverter subject to the rule against perpetuities rather than accomplish the same result by indirection."

Where the rule against perpetuities has been applied to possibilities of reverter, it has always been done by legislative action. See, 78 Harv.L.Rev. 973, supra, at 989; Sparks, A Decade of Transition in Future Interests, 45 Va.L.Rev. 339, 362 (1959).

of North Adams v. Boland, 155 Mass. 171 (1892); Leonard v. Burr, 18 N.Y. 96 (1858); Yarbrough v. Yarbrough, 151 Tenn. 221 (1924). This conclusion is favored by Restatement, 2 Property, app. 34-47, §§ 228, 229.

IV

However, before this conclusion can be reached, an unusual Oregon rule must be considered. Oregon is one of a small minority of states that holds that a possibility of reverter cannot be alienated, Magness v. Kerr, 121 Or. 373, 383 (1927); see, Annotation, 53 A.L.R.2d 224 (1957), but the Oregon Supreme Court has never held that an attempt to alienate a possibility of reverter destroys it. In the case at bar, the grantor-corporation did attempt to alienate the possibility of reverter with its abortive gift over to Schallock and Daggett. Thus, the question of whether an attempt to alienate a possibility of reverter destroys it is presented to an Oregon appellate court for the first time.

The Oregon Supreme Court has dealt with the consequences that follow a grantor's attempt to transfer the interest that remains in him when he grants a defeasible fee on two occasions.

Wagner v. Wallowa County, supra, involved a fee simple estate on a condition subsequent. The grantors gave land to the county for a high school. The county had taken possession of the land and had built and operated a high school on the property until the electorate voted to abolish the school. The election was held November 5, 1912. Prior to the election, during October 1912, the plaintiff and his wife had executed a deed to a Wallowa County school district. The court there applied a strict rule of construction and found that the grantors destroyed their right to re-enter when they attempted to convey it before the breach of the condition.

In Magness v. Kerr et al., supra, the Oregon Supreme Court dealt with a fee simple determinable:

"* * * [T]he rule applied in the Wallowa County cases that an attempted conveyance by the grantor of his possibility of reverter, operates to destroy his right and vest an indefeasible estate in his first grantee, ought not to be applied in this case. First, the rule is a harsh one and produces a result not contemplated by the parties to the transaction, and therefore ought not to be applied unless required by some positive rule of law; secondly, in this case under the admitted facts in the case, the estate granted to the Equity Queen Canning Company had been determined by its failure to use the property for co-operative purposes, which was the contingency by which the estate was to be divested, and since by the happening of such a contingency the estate had been determined and the property had reverted. * * *" 121 Or. at 383, 254 P. at 1016.

While Magness criticizes the holding in Wagner as harsh, that portion of Magness is dictum, for Magness turned on the fact that the event upon which the estate was to end had occurred before the transfer of the future interest.

Nothing in Wagner or Magness is conclusive in determining whether an attempt to alienate a possibility of reverter destroys it.

In Pure Oil Co. v. Miller-McFarland Drilling Co., 376 Ill. 486 (1941), the Illinois court held that a possibility of reverter is not destroyed when the grantor tries to transfer it, even though the possibility of reverter is not alienable under Illinois law. In Reichard v. Chicago, B. & Q.R. Co., 231 Iowa 563 (1942), which involved a conveyance after termination of a fee simple subject to a special limitation, the same facts as in Magness v. Kerr et al., supra, the court said:

"* * * It seems rather fantastic to us, that a conveyance which is ineffective to convey what it attempts to convey is nevertheless an effective means of destroying it. * * *" 231 Iowa at 576.

We hold that an attempt by a grantor to transfer his possibility of reverter does not destroy it.

V

The remaining issue is the city's contention that upon dissolution of the corporation in 1927, or at the latest, upon the post-dissolution, winding-up period, ORS 57.630(2), the corporation was civilly dead and without a successor to whom the possibility of reverter could descend. As is pointed out in Addy and Errett v. Short et al., 47 Del. 157, 162 (1952), the statutory provision for distribution of corporate assets upon dissolution,

"* * * is in effect a statutory expansion of the equitable doctrine that upon dissolution of a corporation its property, notwithstanding the technical rules of the early common law, does not escheat to the sovereign or revert to the original grantor, and will be administered * * * for the purpose of winding up the corporate affairs and distributing the assets to those equitably entitled to them. * * *"

In Addy, the corporation owning a possibility of reverter was dissolved and five years later the event (the abandonment of the use upon which the deed was conditioned) occurred. Delaware had only a three-year corporate dissolution winding-up period. The Delaware statutes did contain a provision that even after the three-year period, upon application of creditors or shareholders of a dissolved corporation, the court could appoint a receiver to take charge of the estate of the corporation and to collect debts and property due and belonging to the company. Addy held that neither the dissolution of the corporation nor the expiration of the three-year dissolution period worked an extinguishment of the possibility of reverter retained by the deed in question, and that upon the abandonment of the land by the grantee, the possibility of reverter was enlarged to a fee simple title. It further held that as statutory successors to the rights and powers of the corporation the receivers were entitled to the land.

Oregon has no such receivership statute, but the Oregon statutes make it clear that corporate assets no longer escheat or revert to the original grantor upon dissolution. In this case, the parties agree that the corporation was lawfully dissolved, all the creditors paid, and that Daggett and Schallock, the sole shareholders of the corporation, were statutorily entitled to and did receive all of the remaining assets of the corporation. One such asset was the possibility of reverter of the land in question.

The parties further agree that the defendants in this case were all of the heirs of Daggett and Schallock. As is pointed out in 18 Or.L.Rev. 63, supra, there is no Oregon decision on the issue of the descendability of the possibility of reverter. However, the weight of authority recognizes that such an interest is descendable. Restatement, 2 Property 606, Comment a, § 164, and 3 Simes 144-45, § 707 (1936). We discern no sound policy considerations which lead us to a contrary conclusion.

Marijane Flitcraft acquired all rights to the property when the other defendants conveyed their interests to her in 1970.

Reversed.

Notes and Questions

1. **The Rule Against Perpetuities.** The Rule Against Perpetuities is one of the most notoriously complicated doctrines in the legal world. In Lucas v. Hamm, 56 Cal.2d 583, 15 Cal.Rptr. 821, 364 P.2d 685 (1961), the California Supreme Court ruled that a lawyer who made a drafting error that rendered a gift invalid due to the Rule Against Perpetuities was not guilty of malpractice or negligence. The Court stated that "the rules relating to perpetuities and restraints on alienation ... have long perplexed the courts and the bar. ... Of the California law on perpetuities and restraints it has been said that few, if any, areas of the law have been fraught with more confusion or concealed more traps for the unwary draftsman; that members of the bar, probate courts, and title insurance companies make errors in these matters; that the code provisions adopted in 1872 created a situation worse than if the matter had been left to the common law, and that the legislation adopted in 1951 (under which the will involved here was drawn), despite the best of intentions, added further complexities." The Court quoted both W. Barton Leach "describing the rule as a 'technicality-ridden legal nightmare' and a 'dangerous

instrumentality in the hands of most members of the bar,'" and John Chipman Gray stating that the Rule "seems to facilitate error, perhaps [] because the mode of reasoning is unlike that with which lawyers are most familiar," resulting in a "long list [that] might be formed of the demonstrable blunders with regard to its questions made by eminent men."

2. **Evolution of the Rule.** The Rule Against Perpetuities originated in the Duke of Norfolk's Case, 22 Eng. Rep. 931 (Ch. 1681), and it took some time to reach its classic formulation. The classic formulation was given its final concise form by Gray: **"No interest is good unless it must vest, if at all, not later than twenty-one years after some life in being at the creation of the interest."** The rule was designed to limit the ability of testators and grantors to control the fate of property more than a generation beyond those that the grantor could know personally. The aim of the Rule was straightforward, but the mechanics proved difficult.

3. **Mechanics of the Rule**. One of the most difficult aspects of the rule is its application as a logical thought experiment, rather than an evaluation of facts. The Rule forbids grants that might vest remotely using only logic and the knowledge available at the time of the grant, irrespective of what happens later. That means that the grant in City of Klamath Falls v. Bell is invalid because the city "could have maintained a library on the site for an indefinite time in the future, or even forever." It is irrelevant that we now know that the land was used as a library only until 1969.

   The thought experiment demanded by the Rule Against Perpetuities is not an easy one. The Rule applies to "unvested" interests, which means that only certain kinds of future interests are vulnerable to the Rule---contingent remainders, executory interests, and class gifts (class gifts are vulnerable because part of the class is unvested even if another part is already vested). The Rule requires us to determine when that future interest will vest (using only the knowledge we have at the time of the grant), and to figure out whether that time lies within the bounds of a life in being plus 21 years. If there is a person for whom we can be sure that the interest will vest in time (life plus 21 years), that person is the validating life proving the gift is valid. If there is no such person, the possibility of a remote vesting, even if uncertain, renders the gift invalid.

4. **Vesting.** Obviously, the meaning of "vesting" is critical to applying the Rule Against Perpetuities. A vested interest is one whose legally entitlement is sufficiently certain. Where the subject of the interest is already possessed, the interest has "vested in possession." For that reason, all present interests are already vested. For future interests, vesting requires the satisfaction of conditions precedent and the identification of all

grantees. But there are some peculiar quirks to vesting of future interests. Future interests reserved for the grantors are considered vested from creation. Executory interests, by contrast, are not considered vested until vested in possession. And, as noted, interests to a class of persons are considered as a whole—none of the interests (even the "vested" ones) are considered vested for purposes of the Rule Against Perpetuities until all are vested.

5. **Alternate Realities.** While the Rule Against Perpetuities is a thought experiment and a logic game, it necessarily involves factual assumptions about the world. Over the years, Rule Against Perpetuities cases have adopted some peculiar factual assumptions. For instance, in Jee v. Audley, 1 Cox 324, 29 Eng. Rep. 1186 (1787), the Court of Chancery had to determine the validity of a gift whose vesting depended, in part, on whether John and Elizabeth Jee, who were already in their seventies, could have future children. The Court determined that the gift was invalid because all couples, of any age, should be presumed capable of bearing children. In time, this ruling came to be summarized as the presumption of the *fertile octogenarian*—the presumed fertility of even the extremely elderly. Other cases have given rise to other factual assumptions with pithy names. For instance, the scenario of the *unborn widow* is based upon the assumption that persons may remarry spouses of any age. Thus, a gift to the "widow of A," where A is married to B and both are in their eighties, is not necessarily a gift to a life in being at the time of the grant. A and B might divorce or B might predecease A, and then A might marry an infant not yet born at the time of the grant, before passing away himself.

   Yet other factual assumptions—such as the disregarding of periods of gestations, or the assumption that gestation is instantaneous—have not yet earned themselves clever names.

   Interestingly, courts have tended to ignore some factual scenarios that might obviously influence the application of the rule. Current technology for freezing eggs and sperm, together with the possibility of artificial insemination, make it possible for children to be born many years after a parent's death. For purposes of applying the Rule Against Perpetuties, a gift to the "children of B" has always been presumed to vest upon B's death—B cannot have any more children after she dies. But thanks to technological advances, B can. Should courts now presume that a gift to the children of B can vest at any time? To date, courts have stuck to the traditional factual assumptions of the past, and ignored the effects of modern technology.

6. **Saving doctrines and saving clauses.** There are a handful of doctrines that courts have created over the years to rescue gifts from invalidation under the Rule Against

Perpetuities. The Two Charities rule, for instance, exempts from the Rule Against Perpetuities a future interest to a charity following a present interest to a "charity." For instance, if a will were to grant Blackacre to the City of Klamath Falls for so long as the building were used as a library, and thereafter to the Klamath Falls Soup Kitchen, the gift to the Soup Kitchen would be valid even though it is vulnerable to remote vesting.

Even without an assist from the courts, clever drafters can protect their future interests from getting invalidated by the Rule of Perpetuities with well-drafted saving clauses. Consider this saving clause: "All interests created by this interest shall be null and void and of no further force or effect unless vested within the lives of those descendants of the late Joseph P. Kennedy, Sr. living on the date hereof, plus twenty-one (21) years, and in the event of such invalidation, the corporate donee (hereafter designated) shall appoint the assets which the invalid interest purports to dispose of in such manner as will most closely approximate, within clearly permissible limits, the intention of grantor, provided that such appointment shall be made within the lives of those descendants of the late Joseph P. Kennedy, Sr. living on the date hereof, plus twenty-one (21) years."

The Symphony Space, Inc. v. Pergola Properties, Inc.
88 N.Y.2d 466 (1996)

KAYE, C., J.

This case presents the novel question whether options to purchase commercial property are exempt from the prohibition against remote vesting embodied in New York's Rule against Perpetuities (EPTL 9-1.1 [b]). Because an exception for commercial options finds no support in our law, we decline to exempt all commercial option agreements from the statutory Rule against Perpetuities.

Here, we agree with the trial court and Appellate Division that the option defendants seek to enforce violates the statutory prohibition against remote vesting and is therefore unenforceable.

I Facts

The subject of this proceeding is a two-story building situated on the Broadway block between 94th and 95th Streets on Manhattan's Upper West Side. In 1978, Broadwest Realty Corporation owned this building, which housed a theater and commercial space. Broadwest had been unable to secure a permanent tenant for the theater — approximately 58% of the total square footage of the building's floor space ... Broadwest also owned two adjacent properties, Pomander Walk (a residential complex) and the Healy Building (a commercial building). Broadwest had been operating its properties at a net loss.

Plaintiff Symphony Space, Inc., a not-for-profit entity devoted to the arts, had previously rented the theater for several one night engagements. In 1978, Symphony and Broadwest engaged in a transaction whereby Broadwest sold the entire building to Symphony for the below-market price of $10,010 and leased back the income-producing commercial property, excluding the theater, for $1 per year. Broadwest maintained liability for the existing $243,000 mortgage on the property as well as certain maintenance obligations. As a condition of the sale, Symphony, for consideration of $10, also granted Broadwest an option to repurchase the entire building. Notably, the transaction did not involve Pomander Walk or the Healy Building.

The purpose of this arrangement was to enable Symphony, as a not-for-profit corporation, to seek a property tax exemption for the entire building — which constituted a single tax parcel — predicated on its use of the theater. The sale-and-leaseback would thereby reduce Broadwest's real estate taxes by $30,000 per year, while permitting Broadwest to retain the rental income from the leased commercial space in the building, which the trial court found produced $140,000 annually. The arrangement also furthered Broadwest's goal of selling all the properties, by allowing Broadwest to postpone any sale until property values in the area increased and until the commercial leases expired. Symphony, in turn, would have use of the theater at minimal cost, once it received a tax exemption.

Thus, on December 1, 1978, Symphony and Broadwest — both sides represented by counsel — executed a contract for sale of the property from Broadwest to Symphony for the purchase price of $10,010. The contract specified that $10 was to be paid at the closing and $10,000 was to be paid by means of a purchase-money mortgage.

The parties also signed several separate documents, each dated December 31, 1978: (1) a deed for the property from Broadwest to Symphony; (2) a lease from Symphony to Broadwest of the entire building except the theater for rent of $1 per year and for the term January 1, 1979 to May 31, 2003, unless terminated earlier; (3) a 25-year, $10,000 mortgage and mortgage note from Symphony as mortgagor to Broadwest as mortgagee, with full payment due on December 31, 2003; and (4) an option agreement by which Broadwest obtained from Symphony the exclusive right to repurchase all of the property, including the theater.

It is the option agreement that is at the heart of the present dispute. Section 3 of that agreement provides that Broadwest may exercise its option to purchase the property during any of the following "Exercise Periods":

"(a) at any time after July 1, 1979, so long as the Notice of Election specifies that the Closing is to occur during any of the calendar years 1987, 1993, 1998 and 2003;

"(b) at any time following the maturity of the indebtedness evidenced by the Note and secured by the Mortgage, whether by acceleration or otherwise;
"(c) during the ninety days immediately following any termination of the Lease by the lessor thereof other than for nonpayment of rent or any termination of the Lease by the lessee thereof * * *
"(d) during the ninety days immediately following the thirtieth day after Broadwest shall have sent Symphony a notice specifying a default by Symphony of any of its covenants or obligations under the Mortgage."

Section 1 states that "Broadwest may exercise its option at any time during any Exercise Period." That section further specifies that the notice of election must be sent at least 180 days prior to the closing date if the option is exercised pursuant to section 3 (a) and at least 90 days prior to the closing date if exercised pursuant to any other subdivision.

The following purchase prices of the property, contingent upon the closing date, are set forth in section 4: $15,000 if the closing date is on or before December 31, 1987; $20,000 if on or before December 31, 1993; $24,000 if on or before December 31, 1998; and $28,000 if on or before December 31, 2003.

Importantly, the option agreement specifies in section 5 that "Broadwest's right to exercise the option granted hereby is * * * unconditional and shall not be in any way affected or impaired by Broadwest's performance or nonperformance, actual or asserted, of any obligation to be performed under the Lease or any other agreement or instrument by or between Broadwest and Symphony," other than that Broadwest was required to pay Symphony any unpaid rent on the closing date. Finally, section 6 established that the option constituted "a covenant running with the land, inuring to the benefit of heirs, successors and assigns of Broadwest."

Symphony ultimately obtained a tax exemption for the theater. In the summer of 1981, Broadwest sold and assigned its interest under the lease, option agreement, mortgage and mortgage note, as well as its ownership interest in the contiguous Pomander Walk and Healy Building, to defendants' nominee for $4.8 million. The nominee contemporaneously transferred its rights under these agreements to defendants Pergola Properties, Inc., Bradford N. Swett, Casandium Limited and Darenth Consultants as tenants in common.

Subsequently, defendants initiated a cooperative conversion of Pomander Walk, which was designated a landmark in 1982, and the value of the properties increased substantially. An August 1988 appraisal of the entire blockfront, including the Healy Building and the unused air and other development rights available from Pomander Walk, valued the property at $27 million assuming the enforceability of the option. By contrast, the value of the leasehold interest plus the Healy Building without the option were appraised at $5.5 million.

Due to Symphony's alleged default on the mortgage note, defendant Swett served Symphony with notice in January 1985 that it was exercising the option on behalf of all defendants. The notice set a closing date of May 6, 1985. Symphony, however, disputed both that it was in default and Swett's authority to exercise the option for all of the defendants. According to Symphony, moreover, it then discovered that the option agreement was possibly invalid. Consequently, in March 1985, Symphony initiated this declaratory judgment action against defendants, arguing that the option agreement violated the New York statutory prohibition against remote vesting and clogged its equity of redemption under the mortgage.

Defendant Pergola subsequently served Symphony with separate notice of default dated April 4, 1985, informing Symphony that it was exercising the option on behalf of all defendants pursuant to sections 1, 3 (b) and 3 (d) of the option agreement and setting the closing date for July 10, 1985. Pergola further notified Symphony that it was alternatively exercising the option under section 3 (a) of the option agreement, which was not contingent upon Symphony's default, with the closing date scheduled for January 5, 1987. Symphony did not appear for any of the closing dates contained in Swett's or Pergola's notices.

A dispute among the defendants over Swett's authority to serve the initial notice developed into a separate litigation, culminating in the trial court authorizing Pergola to exercise the option on behalf of all defendants. In March 1987, Pergola thus served Symphony with another notice that it was exercising the option pursuant to section 3 (a), with the closing scheduled for September 11, 1987. The trial court's judgment was stayed, however, and Symphony did not appear at the March closing.

Thereafter, the parties cross-moved for summary judgment in the instant declaratory judgment proceeding. The trial court granted Symphony's motion while denying that of defendants. In particular, the court concluded that the Rule against Perpetuities applied to the commercial option contained in the parties' agreement, that the option violated the Rule and that Symphony was entitled to exercise its equitable right to redeem the mortgage. The trial court also dismissed defendants' counterclaim for rescission of the agreements underlying the transaction based on the parties' mutual mistake.

In a comprehensive writing by Justice Ellerin, the Appellate Division likewise determined that the commercial option was unenforceable under the Rule against Perpetuities and that rescission was inappropriate. The Appellate Division certified the following question to us: "Was the order of the Supreme Court, as affirmed by this Court, properly made?" We conclude that it was and now affirm.

II

The Rule against Perpetuities evolved from judicial efforts during the 17th century to limit control of title to real property by the dead hand of landowners reaching into future generations. Underlying both early and modern rules restricting future dispositions of property is the principle that it is socially undesirable for property to be inalienable for an unreasonable period of time. These rules thus seek "to ensure the productive use and development of property by its current beneficial owners by simplifying ownership, facilitating exchange and freeing property from unknown or embarrassing impediments to alienability" (Metropolitan Transp. Auth. v Bruken Realty Corp., 67 N.Y.2d 156, 161, citing De Peyster v Michael, 6 N.Y. 467, 494).

The traditional statement of the common-law Rule against Perpetuities was set forth by Professor John Chipman Gray: "No interest is good unless it must vest, if at all, not later than twenty-one years after some life in being at the creation of the interest" (Gray, The Rule Against Perpetuities § 201, at 191 [4th ed 1942]).

In New York, the rules regarding suspension of the power of alienation and remoteness in vesting — the Rule against Perpetuities — have been statutory since 1830. Prior to 1958, the perpetuities period was two lives in being plus actual periods of minority (see, Real Property Law former § 42). Widely criticized as unduly complex and restrictive, the statutory period was revised in 1958 and 1960, restoring the common-law period of lives in being plus 21 years (see, L 1958, ch 153; L 1960, ch 448).

Formerly, the rule against remote vesting in New York was narrower than the common-law rule, encompassing only particular interests (see, Real Property Law former §§ 46, 50; Buffalo Seminary v McCarthy, 86 AD2d 435, 440, affd 58 N.Y.2d 867). A further 1965 amendment enacted a broad prohibition against remote vesting (see, L 1965, ch 670, § 1). This amendment was intended to make clear that the American common-law rule of perpetuities was now fully in force in New York (see, 1965 NY Legis Ann, at 206-207).

New York's current statutory Rule against Perpetuities is found in EPTL 9-1.1. Subdivision (a) sets forth the suspension of alienation rule and deems void any estate in which the conveying instrument suspends the absolute power of alienation for longer than lives in being at the creation of the estate plus 21 years (see, EPTL 9-1.1 [a] [2]). The prohibition against remote vesting is contained in subdivision (b), which states that "[n]o estate in property shall be valid unless it must vest, if at all, not later than twenty-one years after one or more lives in being at the creation of the estate and any period of gestation involved" (EPTL 9-1.1 [b]). This Court has described subdivision (b) as "a rigid formula that invalidates any interest that may not vest within the prescribed time period" and has "capricious consequences" (Wildenstein & Co. v Wallis, 79 N.Y.2d 641, 647-648). Indeed, these rules are predicated upon the public policy of the State and constitute nonwaivable, legal prohibitions (see, Metropolitan Transp. Auth. v Bruken Realty Corp., 67 NY2d at 161).

In addition to these statutory formulas, New York also retains the more flexible common-law rule against unreasonable restraints on alienation. Unlike the statutory Rule against Perpetuities, which is measured exclusively by the passage of time, the common-law rule evaluates the reasonableness of the restraint based on its duration, purpose and designated method for fixing the purchase price. (See, Wildenstein & Co. v Wallis, 79 NY2d at 648; Metropolitan Transp. Auth. v Bruken Realty Corp., 67 NY2d at 161-162, supra.)

Against this background, we consider the option agreement at issue.

III Validity of the Option Agreement

Defendants proffer three grounds for upholding the option: that the statutory prohibition against remote vesting does not apply to commercial options; that the option here cannot be exercised beyond the statutory period; and that this Court should adopt the "wait and see" approach to the Rule against Perpetuities. We consider each in turn.

A. Applicability of the Rule to Commercial Options

Under the common law, options to purchase land are subject to the rule against remote vesting (see, Simes, Future Interests § 132 [2d ed 1966]; Simes and Smith, Future Interests § 1244 [2d ed]; Leach, Perpetuities in a Nutshell, 51 Harv L Rev 638, 660; see also, London & S. W. Ry. Co. v Gomm, 20 Ch D 562). Such options are specifically enforceable and give the option holder a contingent, equitable interest in the land (Dukeminier, A Modern Guide to Perpetuities, 74 Cal L Rev 1867, 1908; Leach, Perpetuities in Perspective: Ending the Rule's Reign of Terror, 65 Harv L Rev 721, 736-737). This creates a disincentive for the landowner to develop the property and hinders its alienability, thereby defeating the policy objectives underlying the Rule against Perpetuities (see, Dukeminier, A Modern Guide to Perpetuities, 74 Cal L Rev 1908; 5A Powell, Real Property ¶ 771 [1]).

Typically, however, options to purchase are part of a commercial transaction. For this reason, subjecting them to the Rule against Perpetuities has been deemed "a step of doubtful wisdom" (Leach, Perpetuities in Perspective: Ending the Rule's Reign of Terror, 65 Harv L Rev 737; see also, Dukeminier, A Modern Guide to Perpetuities, 74 Cal L Rev 1908; Note, Options and the Rule Against Perpetuities, 13 U Fla L Rev 214, 214-215). As one vocal critic, Professor W. Barton Leach, has explained, "[t]he Rule grew up as a limitation on family dispositions; and the period of lives in being plus twenty-one years is adapted to these gift transactions. The pressures which created the Rule do not exist with reference to arms-length contractual transactions, and neither lives in being nor twenty-one years are periods which are relevant to business men and their affairs" (Leach, Perpetuities: New Absurdity, Judicial and Statutory Correctives, 73 Harv L Rev 1318, 1321-1322).

Professor Leach, however, went on to acknowledge that, under common law, "due to an overemphasis on concepts derived from the nineteenth century, we are stuck with the application of the Rule to options to purchase," urging that "this should not be extended to other commercial transactions" (id., at 1322; see also, Simes and Smith, Future Interests § 1244).

It is now settled in New York that, generally, EPTL 9-1.1 (b) applies to options. In Buffalo Seminary v McCarthy (86 AD2d 435, supra), the court held that an unlimited option in gross to purchase real property was void under the statutory rule against remote vesting, and we affirmed the Appellate Division decision on the opinion of then-Justice Hancock (58 N.Y.2d 867). Since then, we have reiterated that options in real estate are subject to the statutory rule (see, e.g., Wildenstein & Co. v Wallis, 79 NY2d at 648, supra).

Although the particular option at issue in Buffalo Seminary was part of a private transaction between neighboring landowners, the reasoning employed in that case establishes that EPTL 9-1.1 (b) applies equally to commercial purchase options. In reaching its conclusion in Buffalo Seminary, the court explained that, prior to 1965, New York's narrow statutory rule against remote vesting did not encompass options (86 AD2d at 443). A review of the history of the broad provision enacted in 1965, however, established that the Legislature specifically intended to incorporate the American common-law rules governing perpetuities into the New York statute (id., at 441-442).

Because the common-law rule against remote vesting encompasses purchase options that might vest beyond the permissible period, the court concluded that EPTL 9-1.1 (b) necessarily encompasses such options (id., at 443). Inasmuch as the common-law prohibition against remote vesting applies to both commercial and noncommercial options, it likewise follows that the Legislature intended EPTL 9-1.1 (b) to apply to commercial purchase options as well.

Consequently, creation of a general exception to EPTL 9-1.1 (b) for all purchase options that are commercial in nature, as advocated by defendants, would remove an entire class of contingent future interests that the Legislature intended the statute to cover. While defendants offer compelling policy reasons — echoing those voiced by Professor Leach — for refusing to apply the traditional rule against remote vesting to these commercial option contracts, such statutory reformation would require legislative action similar to that undertaken by numerous other State lawmakers (see, e.g., Cal Prob Code § 21225; Fla Stat Annot ch 689.225; Ill Stat Annot ch 765, para 305/4).

Our decision in Metropolitan Transp. Auth. v Bruken Realty Corp. (67 N.Y.2d 156, supra) is not to the contrary. In Bruken, we held that EPTL 9-1.1 (b) did not apply to a preemptive right in a "commercial and governmental transaction" that lasted beyond the statutory perpetuities period. In doing so, we explained that, unlike options, preemptive rights (or rights of first refusal) only marginally affect transferability:

"An option grants to the holder the power to compel the owner of property to sell it whether the owner is willing to part with ownership or not. A preemptive right, or right of first refusal, does not give its holder the power to compel an unwilling owner to sell; it merely requires the owner, when and if he decides to sell, to offer the property first to the party holding the preemptive right so that he may meet a third-party offer or buy the property at some other price set by a previously stipulated method" (id., at 163).

Enforcement of the preemptive right in the context of the governmental and commercial transaction, moreover, actually encouraged the use and development of the land, outweighing any minor impediment to alienability (id., at 165-166).

Bruken merely recognized that the Legislature did not intend EPTL 9-1.1 (b) to apply to those contingent future interests in real property that encourage the holder to develop the property by insuring an opportunity to benefit from the improvements and to recapture any investment (see Metropolitan Transp. Auth. v Bruken Realty Corp., 67 NY2d at 165; Morrison v Piper, 77 N.Y.2d 165, 170). In these limited circumstances, enforcement would promote the purposes underlying the rule.

Bruken, then, did not create a sweeping exception to EPTL 9-1.1 (b) for commercial purchase options. Indeed, we have since emphasized that options to purchase are to be treated differently than preemptive rights, underscoring that preemptive rights impede alienability only minimally whereas purchase options vest substantial control over the transferability of property in the option holder (see, Wildenstein & Co. v Wallis, 79 NY2d at 648, supra; Morrison v Piper, 77 NY2d at 169-170, supra). We have also clarified that even preemptive rights are ordinarily subject to the statutory rule against remote vesting (see, Morrison v Piper, 77 N.Y.2d 165, supra). Only where the right arises in a governmental or commercial agreement is the minor restraint on transferability created by the preemptive right offset by the holder's incentive to improve the property.

Here, the option agreement creates precisely the sort of control over future disposition of the property that we have previously associated with purchase options and that the common-law rule against remote vesting — and thus EPTL 9-1.1 (b) — seeks to prevent. As the Appellate Division explained, the option grants its holder absolute power to purchase the property at the holder's whim and at a token price set far below market value. This Sword of Damocles necessarily discourages the property owner from investing in improvements to the property. Furthermore, the option's existence significantly impedes the owner's ability to sell the property to a third party, as a practical matter rendering it inalienable.

That defendants, the holder of this option, are also the lessees of a portion of the premises does not lead to a different conclusion here.

Generally, an option to purchase land that originates in one of the lease provisions, is not exercisable after lease expiration, and is incapable of separation from the lease is valid even though the holder's interest may vest beyond the perpetuities period (see, Berg, Long-Term Options and the Rule Against Perpetuities, 37 Cal L Rev 1, 21; Leach, Perpetuities: New Absurdity, Judicial and Statutory Correctives, 73 Harv L Rev 1320; Simes and Smith, Future Interests § 1244). Such options — known as options "appendant" or "appurtenant" to leases — encourage the possessory holder to invest in maintaining and developing the property by guaranteeing the option holder the ultimate benefit of any such investment. Options appurtenant thus further the policy objectives underlying the rule against remote vesting and are not contemplated by EPTL 9-1.1 (b) (see, Metropolitan Transp. Auth. v Bruken Realty Corp., 67 NY2d at 165, supra; see also, Buffalo Seminary v McCarthy, 86 AD2d at 441, n 5, supra).

To be sure, the option here arose within a larger transaction that included a lease. Nevertheless, not all of the property subject to the purchase option here is even occupied by defendants. The option encompasses the entire building — both the commercial space and the theater — yet defendants are leasing only the commercial space. With regard to the theater space, a disincentive exists for Symphony to improve the property, since it will eventually be claimed by the option holder at the predetermined purchase price.

Furthermore, the option is not contained in the lease itself, but in a separate agreement. Indeed, section 5 of the option agreement specifies that the right to exercise the option is wholly independent from the lease, stating that it "shall not be in any way affected or impaired by * * * performance or nonperformance, actual or asserted, of any obligation to be performed under the Lease or any other agreement." The duration of the option, moreover, exceeds the term of the lease. Consequently, defendants could compel Symphony to sell them the property even after they have ceased possession as lessee.

Put simply, the option here cannot qualify as an option appurtenant and significantly deters development of the property. If the option is exercisable beyond the statutory perpetuities period, refusing to enforce it would thus further the purpose and rationale underlying the statutory prohibition against remote vesting.

B. Duration of the Option Agreement

1. Duration Under Section 3 (a) of the Agreement

Defendants alternatively claim that section 3 (a) of the agreement does not permit exercise of the option after expiration of the statutory perpetuities period. According to defendants, only the possible closing dates fall outside the permissible time frame.

Where, as here, the parties to a transaction are corporations and no measuring lives are stated in the instruments, the perpetuities period is simply 21 years (see, Metropolitan Transp. Auth. v Bruken Realty Corp., 67 NY2d at 161, supra). Section 1 of the parties' agreement allows the option holder to exercise the option "at any time during any Exercise Period" set forth in section three. Section 3 (a), moreover, expressly provides that the option may be exercised "at any time after July 1, 1979," so long as the closing date is scheduled during 1987, 1993, 1998 or 2003.

Even factoring in the requisite notice, then, the option could potentially be exercised as late as July 2003 — more than 24 years after its creation in December 1978. Defendants' contention that section 3 (a) does not permit exercise of the option beyond the 21-year period is thus contradicted by the plain language of the instrument.

Nor can EPTL 9-1.3 — the "saving statute" — be invoked to shorten the duration of the exercise period under section 3 (a) of the agreement. That statute mandates that, "[u]nless a contrary intention appears," certain rules of construction govern with respect to any matter affecting the Rule against Perpetuities (EPTL 9-1.3 [a]). The specified canons of construction include that "[i]t shall be presumed that the creator intended the estate to be valid" (EPTL 9-1.3 [b]) and "[w]here the duration or vesting of an estate is contingent upon * * * the occurrence of any specified contingency, it shall be presumed that the creator of such estate intended such contingency to occur, if at all, within twenty-one years from the effective date of the instrument creating such estate" (EPTL 9-1.3 [d]).

By presuming that the creator intended the estate to be valid, the statute seeks to avoid annulling dispositions due to inadvertent violations of the Rule against Perpetuities. The provisions of EPTL 9-1.3, however, are merely rules of construction. While the statute obligates reviewing courts, where possible, to avoid constructions that frustrate the parties' intended purposes (see, Morrison v Piper, 77 N.Y.2d 165, 173-174, supra), it does not authorize courts to rewrite instruments that unequivocally allow interests to vest outside the perpetuities period (compare, EPTL 9-1.2 [reducing age contingency to 21 years, where interest is invalid because contingent on a person reaching an age in excess of 21 years]).

Indeed, by their terms, the rules of construction in EPTL 9-1.3 apply only if "a contrary intention" does not appear in the instrument. Thus, as the Practice Commentary explains, "[t]he court cannot validate an unambiguous disposition on the basis of the grantor's probable intent, but where construction is needed [subd (b)] will be useful in helping to establish the creator's intent" (Turano, Practice Commentaries, McKinney's Cons Laws of NY, Book 17B, EPTL 9-1.3, at 543).

For example, where a deed contains contradictory phrases, one of which is valid under the Rule (see, Morrison v Piper, 77 N.Y.2d 165, 173-174, supra), or where one of two possible interpretations of a term in an agreement would comply with the Rule (see, Payne v Palisades Interstate Park Commn., 204 AD2d 787), the court will adopt the construction validating the disposition (see also, Restatement of Property § 375 [1944]). By contrast, an option containing no limitation in duration demonstrates the parties' intent that it last indefinitely, and EPTL 9-1.3 does not permit "an extensive rewriting of the option agreement * * * so as to make it conform to the permissible period" (see, Buffalo Seminary v McCarthy, 86 AD2d at 446, supra).

The unambiguous language of the agreement here expresses the parties' intent that the option be exercisable "at any time" during a 24-year period pursuant to section 3 (a). The section thus does not permit a construction that the parties intended the option to last only 21 years.

Given the contrary intention manifested in the instrument itself, the saving statute is simply inapplicable.

2. Duration Under Sections 3 (b)-(d) of the Agreement

Section 3 (b), (c) and (d) of the agreement also allow the option to be exercised after the 21-year perpetuities period, which would expire in December 1999.

Section 3 (b) authorizes the option to be exercised "at any time" following the maturity of the mortgage note. The only limit on duration is found in section 4, which designates December 31, 2003, to be the latest possible closing date. The option could thus be exercised until October 2003 pursuant to section 3 (b).

Section 3 (c) and (d) each permits exercise of the option for a defined period following a specified contingency. Section 3 (c) is contingent upon termination of the lease; section 3 (d) is contingent upon Symphony's default on the mortgage. Neither the lease nor the mortgage, however, expires until a date in 2003. The lease could therefore be terminated, or Symphony could default on the mortgage, some time prior to 2003 but after the 21-year period lapses in December 1999. Defendants, in turn, could potentially exercise the option during this interval.

Defendants urge that, under EPTL 9-1.3 (b), (d), we must presume the parties expected these contingencies to occur, if at all, within the 21-year period. A contrary intention, however, appears in the agreement itself. By specifying in section 4 that the closing date could be scheduled as late as December 31, 2003, the parties manifested their expectation that the contingency might occur and the option might be exercised as late as October 2003, well beyond December 1999.

Again, EPTL 9-1.3 (b), (d) cannot "save" these provisions.

C. "Wait and See" Approach

Defendants next urge that we adopt the "wait and see" approach to the Rule against Perpetuities: an interest is valid if it actually vests during the perpetuities period, irrespective of what might have happened (see, Dukeminier, A Modern Guide to Perpetuities, 74 Cal L Rev 1867, 1880). The option here would survive under the "wait and see" approach since it was exercised by 1987, well within the 21-year limitation.

This Court, however, has long refused to "wait and see" whether a perpetuities violation in fact occurs. As explained in Matter of Fischer (307 N.Y. 149, 157), "[i]t is settled beyond dispute that in determining whether a will has illegally suspended the power of alienation, the courts will look to what might have happened under the terms of the will rather than to what has actually happened since the death of the testator" (see also, Matter of Roe, 281 N.Y. 541, 547-548).

The very language of EPTL 9-1.1, moreover, precludes us from determining the validity of an interest based upon what actually occurs during the perpetuities period. Under the statutory rule against remote vesting, an interest is invalid "unless it must vest, if at all, not later than twenty-one years after one or more lives in being" (EPTL 9-1.1 [b] [emphasis added]). That is, an interest is void from the outset if it may vest too remotely (see, Turano, Practice Commentaries, McKinney's Cons Laws of NY, Book 17B, EPTL 9-1.1, at 481; see also, Metropolitan Transp. Auth. v Bruken Realty Corp., 67 NY2d at 163, supra ["(t)he validity of the provision must be judged by the circumstances existing at the time of the grant"]). Because the option here could have vested after expiration of the 21-year perpetuities period, it offends the Rule.

We note that the desirability of the "wait and see" doctrine has been widely debated (see, 5A Powell, Real Property ¶ 827F [1], [3]; see also, Waggoner, Perpetuity Reform, 81 Mich L Rev 1718 [describing "wait and see" as "(t)he most controversial of the reform methods"]). Its incorporation into EPTL 9-1.1, in any event, must be accomplished by the Legislature, not the courts.

We therefore conclude that the option agreement is invalid under EPTL 9-1.1 (b). In light of this conclusion, we need not decide whether the option violated Symphony's equitable right to redeem the mortgage.

IV Remedy

As a final matter, defendants argue that, if the option fails, the contract of sale conveying the property from Broadwest to Symphony should be rescinded due to the mutual mistake of the parties. We conclude that rescission is inappropriate and therefore do not pass upon whether Broadwest's claim for rescission was properly assigned to defendant Pergola.

A contract entered into under mutual mistake of fact is generally subject to rescission (see, Matter of Gould v Board of Educ., 81 N.Y.2d 446, 453). CPLR 3005 provides that when relief against mistake is sought, it shall not be denied merely because the mistake is one of law rather than fact. Relying on this provision, defendants maintain that neither Symphony nor Broadwest realized that the option violated the Rule against Perpetuities at the time they entered into the agreement and that both parties intended the option to be enforceable.

CPLR 3005, however, does not equate all mistakes of law with mistakes of fact (see, Mercury Mach. Importing Corp. v City of New York, 3 N.Y.2d 418, 427). Rather, the provision "removes technical objections in instances where recoveries can otherwise be justified by analogy with mistakes of fact" (id.). Indeed, this Court has held that the predecessor statute, Civil Practice Act § 112-f, did not mandate the court to grant relief where taxes had been paid on the assumption that a taxing statute subsequently found to be unconstitutional was valid (id.). Likewise, CPLR 3005 "does not permit a mere misreading of the law by any party to cancel an agreement" (Siegel, Practice Commentaries, McKinney's Cons Laws of NY, Book 7B, CPLR 3005, at 621).

Here, the parties' mistake amounts to nothing more than a misunderstanding as to the applicable law, and CPLR 3005 does not direct undoing of the transaction (cf., Gimbel Bros. v Brook Shopping Ctrs., 118 AD2d 532 [lack of diligence in determining legal obligations under contract did not entitle party to restitution on the ground that it acted under a mistake of law]).

The remedy of rescission, moreover, lies in equity and is a matter of discretion (Rudman v Cowles Communications, 30 N.Y.2d 1, 13). Defendants' plea that the unenforceability of the option is contrary to the intent of the original parties ignores that the effect of the Rule against Perpetuities — which is a statutory prohibition, not a rule of construction — is always to defeat the intent of parties who create a remotely vesting interest. As explained by the Appellate Division, there is "an irreconcilable conflict in applying a remedy which is designed to void a transaction because it fails to carry out the parties' true intent to a transaction in which the mistake made by the parties was the application of the Rule against Perpetuities, the purpose of which is to defeat the intent of the parties" (214 AD2d 66, 80).

The Rule against Perpetuities reflects the public policy of the State. Granting the relief requested by defendants would thus be contrary to public policy, since it would lead to the same result as enforcing the option and tend to compel performance of contracts violative of the Rule. Similarly, damages are not recoverable where options to acquire real property violate the Rule against Perpetuities, since that would amount to giving effect to the option (see, 5A Powell, Real Property ¶ 771 [3]).

Accordingly, the order of the Appellate Division should be affirmed, with costs, and the certified question answered in the affirmative.

Order affirmed, etc.

Notes and Questions

1. **Modern Rule Against Perpetuities Litigation.** Modern cases litigating the Rule Against Perpetuities tend to involve commercial options like purchase rights or rights of refusal rather than the traditional future interests such as contingent remainders and executory interests. Like New York, many jurisdictions find the Rule applicable to such interests.

2. **Aftermath of Litigation.** The aftermath of the Symphony Space litigation proved just how costly the drafting error was. Symphony Space sold its air rights to a developer, Related Companies, in 1998 for $10 million. Related Companies then built a 22-story residential tower over the theater and the next-door Healy Building site, which had also been bought by the developer.

3. **Rule Against Perpetuities Reform.** As we shall shortly see, most states have adopted one or more reforms designed to reduce the harsh results of the traditional Rule Against Perpetuities. Some of these reforms are discussed by the Court of Appeal in *Symphony*

Space. Two of the most important reforms are: (a) "wait and see" — in some jurisdictions, the courts reject the traditional approach of applying the Rule Against Perpetuities as a thought experiment using only knowledge from the time of transaction. Instead, they wait and see whether the interest actually vests during the perpetuities period as it plays out. (b) cy pres — in many situations courts rewrite the language of a grant in order to reach the result "intended" by the grantor. Some states order courts to use their *cy pres* power to fix Rule Against Perpetuities problems. See, for example, Tex. Prop. Code Ann. §5.043(a) (2015), which provides that "[w]ithin the limits of the rule against perpetuities, a court shall reform or construe an interest in real or personal property that violates the rule to effect the ascertainable general intent of the creator of the interest. A court shall liberally construe and apply this provision to validate an interest to the fullest extent consistent with the creator's intent." As we shall see, these reforms and others are incorporated within the Uniform Statutory Rule Against Perpetuities.

Note on the Uniform Statutory Rule Against Perpetuities

The Uniform Statutory Rule Against Perpetuities was first proposed in 1986 and became a runaway success. Today, a majority of states have adopted the USRAP.

Uniform Statutory Rule Against Perpetuities (1986/1990)

Section 1. Statutory rule against perpetuities.
(a) [Validity of Nonvested Property Interest.] A nonvested property interest is invalid unless:

(1) when the interest is created, it is certain to vest or terminate no later than 21 years after the death of an individual then alive; or

(2) the interest either vests or terminates within 90 years after its creation.

(b) [Validity of General Power of Appointment Subject to a Condition Precedent.] A general power of appointment not presently exercisable because of a condition precedent is invalid unless:

(1) when the power is created, the condition precedent is certain to be satisfied or becomes impossible to satisfy no later than 21 years after the death of an individual then alive; or

(2) the condition precedent either is satisfied or becomes impossible to satisfy within 90 years after its creation.

(c) [Validity of Nongeneral or Testamentary Power of Appointment.] A nongeneral power of appointment or a general testamentary power of appointment is invalid unless:

(1) when the power is created, it is certain to be irrevocably exercised or otherwise to terminate no later than 21 years after the death of an individual then alive; or

(2) the power is irrevocably exercised or otherwise terminates within 90 years after its creation.

(d) [Possibility of Post-death Child Disregarded.] In determining whether a nonvested property interest or a power of appointment is valid under subsection (a)(1), (b)(1), or (c)(1), the possibility that a child will be born to an individual after the individual's death is disregarded.

(e) [Effect of Certain "Later-of" Type Language.] If, in measuring a period from the creation of a trust or other property arrangement, language in a governing instrument (i) seeks to disallow the vesting or termination of any interest or trust beyond, (ii) seeks to postpone the vesting or termination of any interest or trust until, or (iii) seeks to operate in effect in any similar fashion upon, the later of (A) the expiration of a period of time not exceeding 21 years after the death of the survivor of specified lives in being at the creation of the trust or other property arrangement or (B) the expiration of a period of time that exceeds or might exceed 21 years after the death of the survivor of lives in being at the creation of the trust or other property arrangement, that language is inoperative to the extent it produces a period of time that exceeds 21 years after the death of the survivor of the specified lives.

...

Section 2. When Nonvested Property Interest Or Power Of Appointment Created.

(a) Except as provided in subsections (b) and (c) and in Section 5(a), the time of creation of a nonvested property interest or a power of appointment is determined under general principles of property law.

(b) For purposes of this [act], if there is a person who alone can exercise a power created by a governing instrument to become the unqualified beneficial owner of (i) a nonvested property interest or (ii) a property interest subject to a power of appointment described in Section 1(b) or 1(c), the nonvested property interest or power of appointment is created when the power to become the unqualified beneficial owner terminates. [For purposes of this [act], a joint power with respect to community property or to marital property under the Uniform Marital Property Act held by individuals married to each other is a power exercisable by one person alone.]

(c) For purposes of this [act], a nonvested property interest or a power of appointment arising from a transfer of property to a previously funded trust or other existing property arrangement is created when the nonvested property interest or power of appointment in the original contribution was created.

Section 3. Reformation.

Upon the petition of an interested person, a court shall reform a disposition in the manner that most closely approximates the transferor's manifested plan of distribution and is within the 90 years allowed by Section 1(a)(2), 1(b)(2), or 1(c)(2) if:

(1) a nonvested property interest or a power of appointment becomes invalid under Section 1 (statutory rule against perpetuities);

(2) a class gift is not but might become invalid under Section 1 (statutory rule against perpetuities) and the time has arrived when the share of any class member is to take effect in possession or enjoyment; or

(3) a nonvested property interest that is not validated by Section 1(a)(1) can vest but not within 90 years after its creation.

Section 4. Exclusions From Statutory Rule Against Perpetuities.

Section 1 (statutory rule against perpetuities) does not apply to:

(1) a nonvested property interest or a power of appointment arising out of a nondonative transfer, except a nonvested property interest or a power of appointment arising out of

(A) a premarital or postmarital agreement,

(B) a separation or divorce settlement,

(C) a spouse's election,

(D) a similar arrangement arising out of a prospective, existing, or previous marital relationship between the parties,

(E) a contract to make or not to revoke a will or trust,

(F) a contract to exercise or not to exercise a power of appointment,

(G) a transfer in satisfaction of a duty of support, or

(H) a reciprocal transfer;

(2) a fiduciary's power relating to the administration or management of assets, including the power of a fiduciary to sell, lease, or mortgage property, and the power of a fiduciary to determine principal and income;

(3) a power to appoint a fiduciary;

(4) a discretionary power of a trustee to distribute principal before termination of a trust to a beneficiary having an indefeasibly vested interest in the income and principal;

(5) a nonvested property interest held by a charity, government, or governmental agency or subdivision, if the nonvested property interest is preceded by an interest held by another charity, government, or governmental agency or subdivision;

(6) a nonvested property interest in or a power of appointment with respect to a trust or other property arrangement forming part of a pension, profit-sharing, stock bonus, health, disability, death benefit, income deferral, or other current or deferred benefit plan for one or more employees, independent contractors, or their beneficiaries or spouses, to which contributions are made for the purpose of distributing to or for the benefit of the participants or their beneficiaries or spouses the property, income, or principal in the trust or other property arrangement, except a nonvested property interest or a power of appointment that is created by an election of a participant or a beneficiary or spouse; or

(7) a property interest, power of appointment, or arrangement that was not subject to the common-law rule against perpetuities or is excluded by another statute of this State.

Section 5. Prospective Application.
(a) Except as extended by subsection (b), this [act] applies to a nonvested property interest or a power of appointment that is created on or after the effective date of this [act]. For purposes of this section, a nonvested property interest or a power of appointment created by the exercise of a power of appointment is created when the power is irrevocably exercised or when a revocable exercise becomes irrevocable.
(b) If a nonvested property interest or a power of appointment was created before the effective date of this [act] and is determined in a judicial proceeding, commenced on or after the effective date of this [act], to violate this state's rule against perpetuities as that rule existed before the effective date of this [act], a court upon the petition of an interested person may reform the disposition in the manner that most closely approximates the transferor's manifested plan of distribution and is within the limits of the rule against perpetuities applicable when the nonvested property interest or power of appointment was created.

Section 6. Short Title.
This [act] may be cited as the Uniform Statutory Rule Against Perpetuities.

Section 7. Uniformity of Application and Construction.
This [act] shall be applied and construed to effectuate its general purpose to make uniform the law with respect to the subject of this [act] among states enacting it.

Section 8. Time of Taking Effect.
This [act] takes effect ________________________.

Section 9. [Supersession] [Repeal].
This [act] [supersedes the rule of the common law known as the rule against perpetuities] [repeals (list statutes to be repealed)].

Notes and Questions

1. **The Effect of USRAP.** As you can see, USRAP does not make the rules of perpetuities simple. Perhaps the most important part of USRAP is that it simultaneously adopts a wait-and-see approach while creating an alternative perpetuities period. Gifts that potentially create perpetuities trouble are given two chances to prove themselves valid. First, the gifts are examined under the traditional Rule Against Perpetuities. If found invalid at this stage due to the possibility of remote vesting, the gifts may still be validated if a wait-and-see approach finds the gifts to have actually been vested during perpetuities period. However, USRAP provides that perpetuities period while waiting and seeing is not the traditional life in being plus 21 years, but, rather, a fixed period of 90 years.

Additionally, under USRAP, courts have the power to reform granting instruments with perpetuities flaws. This cy pres power permits courts to avoid perpetuities problems without waiting the requisite 90 years.

2. **Other interests.** USRAP applies the Rule Against Perpetuities to many unvested future interests. However, USRAP excludes options. By excluding options from the act, the drafters of USRAP apparently intended to abolish the application of the Rule Against Perpetuities to options and other commercial transactions. But, ironically, several states have interpreted USRAP as *preserving* the application of the classic Rule Against Perpetuities to options and other commercial transactions, while *excluding* those options from the USRAP reforms. In other words, these states preserve intact the classic version of the Rule for options and other commercial transactions, even though they have adopted USRAP. Thus, in North Carolina and several other states that have adopted USRAP, options are not only subject to the Rule Against Perpetuities, they are also ineligible for the 90-year period of wait and see, and for cy pres.

C. Present vs. Future: The Doctrine of Waste

Even if we are very clear on the nature and allocation of possessory and future interests in a parcel of land, we soon run into a practical problem: it can be difficult to protect the value of a future interest while someone else is in possession of the land, acting for most purposes as its owner. What if a life tenant burns down the structures on the parcel? Or decides to undertake a remodeling project that would make the parcel less desirable to future renters? Or fails to do anything about a leaky pipe, leading to a costly mold infestation? What if the possessor uses the property in such a way as to maximize its current value at the expense of its future value—depleting natural resources, wearing out buildings and fixtures without repairing or maintaining them—in ways that can't be recovered? Can it be wrongful—as a matter of property law—for a lawful possessor to use the possessed premises however they wish, for good or for ill?

The common law recognized that it *could* be wrongful for a present lawful possessor to take (or fail to take) certain acts with respect to land in their possession—if those acts affected the ability of a *future* possessor to enjoy their interest when their turn came around. To vindicate the rights of these future interest holders, the common law gave them a private right of action to enjoin, and obtain damages for, the acts and omissions of possessors that permanently decrease the value of the future interest. This was the action for waste.

Jackson v. Brownson

7 Johns. 227 (N.Y. Sup. Ct. 1810)

… THIS was an action of ejectment for a farm in Whitestown. The cause was tried at the Oneida circuit, the 5th June, 1809, before Mr. Justice Yates.

At the trial, the plaintiff gave in evidence the counterpart of a lease, dated the 3d September, 1790, from Philip Schuyler,[1] of Albany, to the defendant, for the premises in question, for the lives of the defendant, his wife, and Samuel Shaw, respectively. The farm contained 133 acres and a half. The lease contained various covenants, reservations and conditions, among which was the following: …"And it is further conditioned on the part of the said lessee, that neither the said lessee, his executors, &c., … shall, at any time hereafter, commit any waste."

"And in case the said lessee, his, &c., shall not perform, fulfil, abide by, and keep all and every of the covenants and conditions herein covenanted and conditioned, &c., then in each of the said cases, it shall thenceforth be lawful for the lessor, his, &c., into the whole of the said premises, or into any part thereof, in the name of the whole, to reënter, and the same to have again, repossess and enjoy, as his or their former estate," &c.

The lessors were the heirs of Philip Schuyler; this action was brought to recover the possession of the south half of the premises, on the ground of forfeiture by a breach of the covenant; the lessee or his assigns having committed waste thereon by clearing and draining off the land more than a reasonable and due proportion of the wood. It was admitted that, at the date of the lease, the premises were wild and uncultivated, and covered throughout with a forest of heavy timber.

The plaintiff proved that the defendant occupied the south half of the premises, which were entirely cleared of wood, before the commencement of the suit; and that on the north half occupied by Shaw, the whole was cleared except about six or eight acres, on which more than half the wood and timber had been cut down and removed, before the commencement of the suit.

---

[1] Philip John Schuyler was a general in the Continental Army during the War of Independence. He subsequently served as a state senator in New York and then as United States Senator from New York. His son Philip Jeremiah Schuyler also entered politics, and served in Congress as Representative from New York's Fifth District. Philip John Schuyler is often referred to as Philip Schuyler while Philip Jeremiah Schuyler is referred to as Philip J. Schuyler.

It was also proved, that a permanent supply of fuel, timber for buildings, and wood for fences, for the use of the demised premises, would require that, at least, thirty acres should have been preserved in wood.

... It was also proved, that about 12 years since, there were 35 acres of land covered with wood and timber on the premises, and about 12 acres of woodland, on that part in the possession of the defendant, only half of which was good for timber, ... that the defendant had cut no wood or timber on the part in his possession, except for fuel, fences, and building for the use of the farm, and which had been gradually cut, ... [that] the defendant had built a house on the premises, which was completed about four years since; and had used the farm in a husbandlike manner, and had carried on more materials for fences than he had taken off; that ... cleared land was of much greater value than land covered with wood and timber; and that good farms in the vicinity of the premises had not reserved more than 12 acres of woodland out of 100 acres....

The judge was of opinion, ... that the gradual clearing of that part in possession of the defendant, ... did not, in law, amount to waste; and he directed the jury to find a verdict for the defendant; and the jury found accordingly.

A motion was made to set aside the verdict and for a new trial, for the misdirection of the judge....

VAN NESS, J.

... It is a general principle, that the law considers every thing to be waste which does a permanent injury to the inheritance. Now, to say that cutting down the wood on almost every acre of the demised premises is not waste, within the spirit and meaning of the covenant in the case, is to say that no waste, by the destruction of wood, can be committed at all. We are bound to give effect to this covenant if we can, but to decide that the facts stated in the case do not constitute waste, would be destroying it almost altogether. That the destruction of the timber is a lasting injury to the reversion cannot be disputed. For this injury the lessors of the plaintiff may, at their election, bring covenant, or enter as for condition broken.

... It is true, that what would in England be waste, is not always so here. The covenant must be construed with reference to the state of the property at the time of the demise. The lessee undoubtedly had a right to fell part of the timber, so as to fit the land for cultivation; but it does not follow that he may, with impunity, destroy all the timber, and thereby essentially and permanently diminish the value of the inheritance. Good sense and sound policy, as well as the rules of good husbandry, require that the lessee should preserve so much of the timber as is indispensably necessary to keep the fences and other erections upon the farm in proper repair. The counsel for the defendant is mistaken when he says that lessees in England are prohibited from cutting wood upon the demised premises altogether; the prohibition, in principle, extends no further, in this respect, there than it does here. In England, that species of wood which is denominated timber shall not be cut down, because felling it is considered as an injury done to the inheritance, and therefore waste. Here, from the different state of many parts of our country, timber may, and must be cut down to a certain extent, but not so as to cause an irreparable injury to the reversioner. To what extent wood may be cut before the tenant is guilty of waste, must be left to the sound discretion of a jury, under the direction of the court, as in other cases.... The principle upon which all these cases were decided is that which I have before stated, namely, that whenever wood has been cut in such a manner as materially to prejudice the inheritance, it is waste; and that is the principle upon which I place the decision of this cause.

...My opinion, therefore, is, that the motion for setting aside the nonsuit, and granting a new trial, ought to be granted.

KENT, Ch. J., and THOMPSON, J., were of the same opinion.

SPENCER, J.

... The land was covered with heavy timber; and, for the use of it, the lessee was to pay a rent. The parties must, therefore, have intended that the lessee should be at liberty to fell the timber to a certain extent, at least, for agricultural purposes.

If the restriction to commit waste would operate to restrain the lessee from the use of the premises, it would be void, as repugnant to the grant. I shall have no difficulty in maintaining that, according to the common law of England, the lessee could not enjoy the land, nor derive any benefit from it, without the commission of waste; and should that point be established, this covenant must be rejected. The general definition of waste is, that it is a destruction in houses, gardens, trees, or other corporeal hereditaments, to the disherison of him in remainder or reversion. It is not every injury to lands that the law considers as waste, nor every act which injures the remainder-man, or the reversioner. To test this supposed waste, by considering the reversioner injured by the acts done, is not warranted by law; and, in point of fact, when the premises were cleared of the timber, cleared land was more valuable than wood land.... I insist that, according to the common law of England, no tenant can cut down timber, &c., or clear land for agricultural purposes; and that the quantity of timber cut down never enters into the consideration whether waste has or has not been committed; but that it is always tested by the fact of cutting timber, without the justifiable excuse of having done it.... A single tree cut down, without such justifiable cause, is waste as effectually as if a thousand had been cut down; and the reason is this, that such trees belong to the owner of the inheritance, and the tenant has only a qualified property in them for shade and shelter.

The doctrine of waste, as understood in England, is inapplicable to a new, unsettled country. ...The rule furnished by the common law is fixed and certain; and the lessor knows what wood he may cut, and for what purposes; but if a covenant not to commit waste is hereafter to be considered as a covenant to leave a sufficient quantity of land in wood, no lessee is safe. If the act of cutting timber on the premises, without the justifiable excuse already stated, was not waste, cutting more or less was immaterial. Under the covenant not to commit waste, we have no right to say some waste might be committed, and other waste might not; the covenant is inapt to the case, and if any remedy exists, it must lie in covenant. I am, therefore, against granting a new trial.

YATES, J., was of the same opinion.

Rule granted.

Notes and Questions

1. What exactly is the dispute between the majority and the dissent? Do they agree on the existence of a remedy for waste under New York law? On the definition of waste? On the applicability of waste doctrine to the lease before the court? On the remedy for waste?

2. Although this case deals with a lease for life—a peculiar hybrid estate that is not recognized in many jurisdictions—the doctrine of waste applies between freehold possessory estate holders and future interest holders just as it applies between leasehold tenants and landlords. Thus, even in the absence of a lease contract, Brownson could have been held liable for damages, or enjoined from felling any further timber, in an action for waste by the reversioners (if the jury concluded that it would indeed be waste for a possessor in Brownson's position to fell such timber).

3. **Forms of Waste.** Waste can be either *voluntary* or *permissive*. Volutnary waste (sometimes called *affirmative* waste) refers to *acts* of the holder of the possessory estate, such as erecting or demolishing a structure, or extracting non-replenishing natural resources. Permissive waste refers to *omisssions* of the holder of the possessory estate, such as failing to pay property taxes, or failure to make needed repairs. Either can support a claim for waste by the owner of a future interest whose rights are permanently devalued as a result. Which form of waste was at issue in *Jackson*?

4. **Theories of Waste.** One commentator argues that *Jackson* was the starting point for a peculiarly American departure from the English doctrine of waste deplored by the dissenters. In this view, "courts created the American law of waste for several reasons: to promote efficient use of resources that the English rule would have inhibited; to advance an idea of American landholding as a republican enterprise, free of feudal

hierarchy; and perhaps to advance a belief that a natural duty to cultivate wild land underlay the Anglo-American claim to North America." Jedediah Purdy, *The American Transformation of Waste Doctrine: A Pluralist Interpretation*, 91 CORNELL L. REV. 653, 661 (2006). And indeed, the sensitivity of both opinions in *Jackson* to local conditions, the desirability of converting wild lands to agricultural use, and the sustainability of yeoman farming tend to support this pluralist view.

5. Law-and-economics theorists, in contrast, identify waste doctrine solely with the criterion of efficiency, and particularly the internalization of externalities and mitigation of holdout problems. As Judge Posner puts it: "The incentive of a life tenant is to maximize not the value of the property—that is, the present value of the entire stream of future earnings obtainable from it—but only the present value of the earnings stream obtainable during his expected lifetime. So he will, for example, want to cut timber before it has attained its mature growth even though the present value of the timber would be greater if the cutting of some or all of it were postponed; for the added value from waiting would inure to the remainderman.... [Moreover,] since tenant and remainderman would have only each other to contract with, the situation would be one of bilateral monopoly and transaction costs might be high." To avoid these problems, "[t]he law of waste forbids the tenant to reduce the value of the property as a whole by considering only his own interest in it." Richard A. Posner, *Comment on Merrill on the Law of Waste*, 94 MARQ. L. REV. 1095-96 (2011).

A Note on Ameliorative Waste

What if, instead of doing something that *decreases* the value of the future interest, the holder of the possessory estate does something that *increases* the market value of the land, but in doing so changes the premises in ways the future interest holder doesn't like? Such alterations—known as *ameliorative waste*—have generated two types of approaches in the courts.

The first approach, adopted in *Melms v. Pabst Brewing Co.*, 79 N.W. 738 (Wisc. 1899), looks to the effect of the life tenant's actions on the market value of the parcel and whether those actions were necessitated by a change in conditions surrounding the parcel. In *Melms*, the Pabst Brewing Company had torn down an old mansion abutting a brewery it owned, mistakenly believing it owned the lot in fee simple when in fact it owned only the life estate of the widow Melms (the remainder being owned by her children). At the time of the demolition, the neighborhood around the house had become heavily industrialized, and had been re-graded such that the house stood 20-30 feet above street level and was worthless as a residential property. In these circumstances, the court held, whether the act of destroying the mansion and re-grading the lot on which it stood to street level constitutes waste is a question of fact for the jury. The court suggested that such actions will not constitute waste "when it clearly appears that the change

will be, in effect, a meliorating change, which rather improves the inheritance than injures it." *Id.* at 739.

The second approach—more consistent with the common-law roots of waste doctrine—holds that *any* material change to real property caused by a lawful possessor without the consent of the holder of the future interest is waste, full stop. This approach informed the decision of the New York Supreme Court in *Brokaw v. Fairchild*, 237 N.Y.S. 6 (Sup. Ct. N.Y. Cty. 1929). In that case, the court refused to allow the life tenant of a stately mansion on New York's Fifth Avenue at 79th Street to tear the mansion down over the objections of the holders of future interests in the lot, even though living in the mansion had become cost-prohibitive and the neighborhood had become a prime location for luxury apartment buildings, which could be built and operated on the site for a substantial profit. The theory underlying this result is that a life tenant has merely the rights of use, not full rights of ownership, and that the holder of the future interest is entitled to take possession of the parcel in substantially the same condition as it existed at the time the future interest was created: "The act of the tenant in changing the estate, and whether or not such act is lawful or unlawful, i.e., whether the estate is so changed as to be an injury to the inheritance, is the sole question involved." *Id.* at 15.

The opinion in *Brokaw* generated a backlash in New York's reform-minded legislature, which enacted a statute redefining waste law along the lines set forth in *Melms*; that statute remains in force today. *See* N.Y. REAL PROP. ACTS. & PROCS. L. § 803. But interestingly, the opinion in *Melms* itself seems to have arisen from a number of questionable factual and legal pronouncements from the Wisconsin courts. The full, fascinating story is recounted in Thomas W. Merrill, Melms v. Pabst Brewing Co. *and the Doctrine of Waste in American Property Law*, 94 MARQ. L. REV. 1055 (2011). As of 2009, the rule of *Melms* was followed in most U.S. jurisdictions, while a small number continued to follow the rule of *Brokaw*. *Id.* at 1083 (citing Gina Cora, *Want Not, Waste Not: Contracting Around the Law of Ameliorative Waste* (Apr. 1, 2009) (Yale Law School Student Prize Papers: Paper 47), http://digitalcommons.law.yale.edu/ylsspps_papers/47).

Which of these two rules do you think is most consistent with the pluralist justifications for waste doctrine described by Professor Purdy? Which do you think is most consistent with the law-and-economics approach? Do either of the rules require some other form of justification, and if so, what might that justification be?

Made in the USA
Las Vegas, NV
17 January 2026

f7ec6b55-95cc-4392-b355-f64d4b31ade6R03